Principles of

FLUID MECHANICS
and
FLUID MACHINES

Principles of

FLUID MECHANICS

and

FLUID MACHINES

Third Edition

N Narayana Pillai

Formerly Director
and
Professor Emeritus
Amrita School of Engineering, Coimbatore

Universities Press

Universities Press (India) Private Limited

Registered Office
3-6-747/1/A & 3-6-754/1, Himayatnagar, Hyderabad 500 029 (A.P.), India
E-mail: *info@universitiespress.com*

Distributed by
Orient Blackswan Private Limited

Registered Office
3-6-752, Himayatnagar, Hyderabad 500 029 (A.P.), India

Other Offices
Bangalore / Bhopal / Bhubaneshwar / Chennai / Ernakulam / Guwahati
Hyderabad / Jaipur / Kolkata / Lucknow / Mumbai / New Delhi / Patna

First published 2003
Second Edition 2006
Third Edition 2009
Reprinted 2011, 2013

ISBN 978 81 7371 675 1

Set in Times New Roman 10/12 *by*
OSDATA, Hyderabad 500 049

Printed at
Graphica Printers and Binders
Hyderabad - 500 013.

Published by
Universities Press (India) Private Limited
3-6-747/1/A & 3-6-754/1, Himayatnagar, Hyderabad 500 029 (A.P.), India

To

Sadguru Mata Amritanandamayi Devi

Contents

Foreword

The authors should be congratulated for bringing out a textbook on *Principles of Fluid Mechanics and Fluid Machines*. The book is aimed at improving the knowledge level of the reader in the field. It does not merely emphasize on an examination-based approach. Concepts appear to dominate instead of a mere discussion of mathematical formulations. Wherever possible, the authors have provided alternate simplified equations. A few of the equations are those developed by one of the authors — Dr. N. Narayana Pillai, and they are not commonly available in other books. Chapters on potential flow, boundary layer, drag on immersed bodies and water hammer have been dealt with in detail to bring out their features and applications.

The worked out examples, though not numerous, give an insight into the practical aspects of applications. Sufficient number of review questions and problems have been provided with answers to numerical ones.

Essentially, the presentation of the subject matter by the authors is different from several other textbooks in the market.

I appreciate the painstaking efforts of Dr. N. Narayana Pillai and Dr. C.R. Ramakrishnan in bringing out a useful and worthy book on Fluid Mechanics and Fluid Machines.

Dr. S. Subramanyan,
Former Vice Chancellor, Bharathiar University, Coimbatore and
Former Principal, PSG College of Technology, Coimbatore.

August 28, 2002

Preface to the Third Edition

Principles of Fluid Mechanics and Fluid Machines was well-received by both teachers and students. The author is thankful to them for their suggestions. In some cases more explanations were suggested. It was also desired that some more advanced topics and examples be included.

Significant additions have been made to the text in the present edition. Propagation of errors has been added in Chapter 1. The variation of temperature and pressure in the earths atmosphere and stability of the atmosphere have been discussed in Chapter 3. A number of examples applying concept of control volume and pressure momentum transport rate equation have been added in Chapter 10. The force on a firemans nozzle has been discussed in detail; propulsion of turbojets and rockets has also been included in this chapter. In Chapter 13, the Reynolds equation for turbulent flow has been derived and Reynolds stresses have been explained in more detail. Temperature as an independent dimension, in addition to M, L and T is considered in Chapter 14 on dimensional analysis and important non-dimensional quantities for thermal engineering have been derived. The Blasius solution for boundary layer on a flat plate and Karmans integral equation has been added in Chapter 15. In Chapter 17, a standing wave flume for measurement of discharge in irrigation channels has been presented. The characteristics of centrifugal pumps and the various considerations for selection of pumps have been discussed in Chapter 19.

Considering the importance of compressible flow, a new chapter on elements of compressible flow has been added.

Every attempt has been made to make the concepts lucid and prepare student to solve any problem. Mathematical explanations to support logical formulations have been given, but only briefly. Importance has been given to units and dimensions of the physical quantities involved. Mostly SI units have been used. In many cases, the results have been expressed in non-dimensional form to extend the range of applicability. Simple procedures have been indicated for the solution of many problems.

The author is grateful to all those who have been helpful in the improvement of the book. He is thankful to his colleague Dr. C.R. Ramakrishnan for his unstinted support and for his valuable suggestions. The assistance of Mr. C. Lakshmikanthan and Mr. R. Rajasekar in making the drawings is gratefully acknowledged. The author is indebted to many of his friends for rendering timely help when needed, in the completion of the revision of the book.

N.Narayana Pillai

Preface to the First Edition

There are a large number of textbooks in the area of fluid mechanics. *Principles of Fluid Mechanics and Fluid Machines* differs from many other books because it lays stress on the basic principles underlying fluid mechanics and at the same time introduces some new methods in the analysis and solution of problems. Intended as an introductory course, many details and data have been purposely avoided. The new methods and simplified formulae used have been introduced by the senior author in his long years as a teacher and have been found to be useful to students.

The book introduces the Reynolds transport theorem without formal proof. Students will be able to apply the theorem to problems with confidence, especially in a later study of computational fluid dynamics. A proof is given for the Navier–Stokes equation to make the student understand the underlying assumptions. Topics in potential flow, boundary layer theory, drag and open channel hydraulics are dealt with in a concise manner. But the stress has always been to simplify the results so that the student can grasp the underlying principles with some sincere effort. As in all books on mathematical subjects, the students will do well to follow the steps in the derivation by working it out themselves. The importance of and the ease with which SI units can be used is illustrated. In every chapter a number of problems are given. They are designed to cover the various practical aspects. The student should have practice in the use of formulae, units and a calculator to acquire speed and accuracy.

Work on this book began while the senior author was teaching as a professor at the Regional Engineering College, Kurukshetra. He acknowledges the help of Dr. D.V.S. Verma and Dr. Subodh Ranjan, both in the faculty at R.E.C. Kurukshetra.

The book was given final shape at the Amrita Institute of Technology and Science, Coimbatore by the authors. They acknowledge the help of the institute and the staff in the college and the computer centre in completing the work. Special mention is made of the assistance rendered by Mr. C. Lakshmikanthan, Mr. K. Ramesh Kumar, Mr. P. Pradeep Kumar and Mrs. Sunitha K. Nair in preparing the drawings and typing the material.

Dr. N. Narayana Pillai
Dr. C.R. Ramakrishnan.

1 Introduction

Scope of fluid mechanics — Development — Units of measurement

1.1 Scope of Fluid Mechanics

Fluid mechanics is essentially a study of statics, kinematics and dynamics of fluids. It has important applications in diverse branches of engineering like mechanical, aeronautical, chemical, civil engineering and mining. The meteorological phenomena of air mass movement and rainfall, and hydrological elements like runoff and movement of water through soil involve the principles of fluid mechanics. A sound knowledge of fluid mechanics is essential in the design of dams and irrigation structures, canals, turbines and pumps, highway drainage and water supply. Research in fluid mechanics has helped in developing new and efficient methods of lubrication, and in reducing wear and tear. The flow of electricity in a conducting media is analogous to the potential flow of fluids.

The advent of fast computers has been a major factor in the development of computational fluid dynamics (CFD) during the last two decades. The great advances made in CFD help in solving many problems of heat and mass transfer and aerodynamics in modern technology. Fluid mechanics at present finds applications in new fields like bio-medical engineering and magneto-hydrodynamics.

Being a basic science, fluid mechanics helps to develop an insight into common problems dealing with the movement of air and water that surround us.

1.2 Development of Fluid Mechanics

Construction of dams, irrigation and navigation canals and efforts to train rivers have been made by man from antiquity. It is inferred that they were done by a process of trial and error as necessity arose. Archimedes is credited with the explanation of the principle of buoyancy. Newton, Leibnitz and Euler laid the firm foundation of mechanics in the beginning of the 18th century. John Bernoulli developed equations governing ideal fluid flow while D'Alembert made contributions in experimental hydrodynamics. Kirchoff, Rankine, Kelvin and others made great contributions to hydrodynamics in the 19th century. Classical hydrodynamics developed without taking into consideration the viscous resistance of fluid. But later, Newton, Navier, Stokes, Poiseuille and Reynolds conducted studies on viscous flows.

Engineers confronted with the problems involved in the design of irrigation and water supply works, which could not be solved by simple mathematical analyses, had to develop working equations for discharge through various structures and measuring devices; practically significant results were obtained by introducing coefficients in the formulae. The contributions of Chezy, Kutter and Manning were significant in channel flows. Darcy developed equations for flow through pipes and soil media. Dupuit is known for his formula in well hydraulics. Henry Pitot, Venturi and Borda developed measuring instruments. Froude introduced the towing tank technique of testing ship models. American engineers were introduced to the work done in Europe by Freeman and Bakhmeteff. The works of Raleigh and Buckingham in dimensional analysis and similitude extended the scope of model testing. The founder of modern fluid mechanics is considered to be Ludwig Prandtl who introduced the concept of boundary layer in 1901. Blasius, Nikuradse and Von-Karman continued his work. The development of the theory of turbulence and laws of surface resistance is significant to the modern understanding of fluid mechanics.

A significant development of fluid mechanics is in the area of compressible flow where thermodynamic effects and changes in density become appreciable. Some notable contributors in compressible flow were Bernoulli, Euler, Helmoholtz, Laval, Rankine, Prandtl, Buseman and Glauert. In the last century, rapid strides were made in the area due to the advent of airborne flights; increased war efforts and space programmes. The present day Boeing 777, the Concorde and turbojets are examples of the high degree of attainment in the field.

1.3 Units of Measurement

In fluid mechanics, measurement and solutions of problems require the use of compatible units for various quantities. Some units in the SI system are discussed below.
The SI and CGS system of units are absolute system of units and it is easy to solve problems using the formula directly.

SI system of units

Quantity	Dimensions	Symbol	Name
Mass	M	kg	kilogramme
Length	L	m	metre
Time	T	s	second
Force	MLT^{-2}	N	newton
Pressure	$ML^{-1}T^{-2}$	Pa	pascal
Work	ML^2T^{-2}	J	joule
Power	ML^2T^{-3}	W	watt
Frequency	T^{-1}	Hz	hertz
Temperature	θ	C	degree celsius
Thermodynamic temperature	θ	K	kelvin

In the CGS system, the unit of force is the dyne, which is equal to 1 g cm/s^2.

Sometimes the gravitational units kg_f and g_f are used as force units which need to be converted to SI units.

1.3.1 Some important conversions

1 kg_f	=	9.81 N
1 g_f	=	981 dynes
1 N	=	10^5 dynes
1 J	=	1 N m
1 W	=	1 J/s
1 Pa	=	1 N/m^2
1 kPa	=	10^3 Pa
1 MPa	=	10^6 Pa
1 GPa	=	10^9 Pa
1 metric HP	=	75 kg_f m/s = 736 watts

Conversion of temperature The units used for temperature measurement are K (kelvin), °C (degree Centigrade) and °F (degree Farenheit). The melting point of ice corresponds to 273 K, 0°C and 32°F respectively. The magnitude of the K unit is the same as that of the Centigrade unit. A Farenheit unit is 5/9 times a Centigrade unit.

Example 1.1 Convert 1 N s/m^2 to dyne s/cm^2.

$$\frac{1\text{ N s}}{\text{m}^2} = \frac{\text{N s}}{\text{m}^2} \times \frac{10^5\text{ dyne}}{\text{N}} \times \frac{1\text{m}^2}{100 \times 100 \times \text{cm}^2} = \frac{10\text{ dyne s}}{\text{cm}^2}.\ \text{(Ans.)}$$

Example 1.2 Convert $\frac{1\text{kg}_\text{f}}{\text{cm}^2}$ to Pa.

$$\frac{1\text{ kg}_\text{f}}{\text{cm}^2} = \frac{1\text{ kg}_\text{f}}{\text{cm}^2} \times \frac{9.81\text{ N}}{1\text{ kg}_\text{f}} \times \frac{100 \times 100\text{ cm}^2}{1\text{ m}^2} = \frac{9.81 \times 10^4\text{ N}}{\text{m}^2} = 98.1\text{ KPa. (Ans.)}$$

Example 1.3 Convert 10°C to K and °F.

$$10\,°\text{C} = (273 + 10)\text{K} = 283\text{ K. (Ans.)}$$

$$10\,°\text{C} = (10 \times 9/5 + 32)\ °\text{F} = 50\,°\text{F. (Ans.)}$$

Example 1.4 Convert −40 °F to °C and K.

$$-40\,°\text{F} = (-40 - 32) \times 5/9 = -40\,°\text{C. (Ans.)}$$

$$-40\,°\text{F} = -40\,°\text{C} = (-40 + 273)\text{ K} = 233\text{ K. (Ans.)}$$

Example 1.5 In a particular case, the shear stress at a distance x from the leading edge of a plate parallel to air flow is given by the equation $\tau = \frac{12}{x^{0.2}}$, where τ is in $\text{lb}_\text{f}/\text{ft}^2$ and x is in ft (feet). Convert the equation to SI units.

$$\tau \frac{\text{lb}_\text{f}}{\text{ft}^2} = \frac{k_1}{x^{0.2}},$$ where x is in feet. k_1 has the dimension $\frac{F}{L^{1.8}}$

$1\text{lb}_\text{f} = 0.4536\ \text{kg}_\text{f} = 4.45\ \text{Pa}$; 1 ft. = 0.3048 m.

$$k_2 = k_1 \times \frac{4.45}{0.3048^{1.8}} = 37.77k_1 = 453.24$$

Hence the formula in SI system is $\tau = \dfrac{453.24}{x^{0.2}}$ Pa, where x is in metres. (Ans)

1.4 Propagation of Random Errors in Measurement

Estimation of a physical quantity may involve the measurement of various parameters — there is a good chance that these values have some random errors which might have occurred during the measuring process. Knowledge of the errors in the measured quantity will help to reduce possible errors in the final estimation.

Let Y be calculated from the measured parameters $x_1, x_2, \ldots x_n$, and the measured values be $x_1 \pm \delta x_1$, $x_2 \pm \delta x_2, \ldots, x_n \pm \delta x_n$ respectively.

$$\delta Y_1 = \frac{\partial Y}{\partial x_1}, \delta Y_2 = \frac{\partial Y}{\partial x_2}\delta x_2 \text{ etc.}$$

Then it can be proved that $$\left\{\frac{\delta Y}{Y}\right\}^2 = \sum_{i=1 \text{ to } n} \left\{\frac{x_i}{Y} \times \frac{\partial Y}{\partial x_i} \times \frac{\delta x_i}{x_i}\right\}^2$$

Example 1.6 Flow in pipes A and B are measured as 18±0.3 l/s and 180±0.8 l/s respectively. Find the combined discharge.

The expected value of combined discharge $Q = 18 + 180 = 198$ l/s

Flow through pipe A = $x_1 = 18 \pm 0.3$ l/s: Hence

$$\frac{\delta x_1}{x_1} = \frac{\pm 0.3}{18} = \pm 0.0167$$

Flow through pipe B = $x_2 = 180 \pm 0.8$ l/s. Hence,

$$\frac{\delta x_2}{x_2} = \frac{\pm 0.8}{180} = \pm 0.00444, \qquad Q = x_1 + x_2$$

$$\frac{\partial Q}{\partial x_1} = 1 : \quad \frac{\partial Q}{\partial x_2} = 1;$$

$$\left\{\frac{\delta Q}{Q}\right\}^2 = \sum_{i=1 \text{ to } 2} \left\{\frac{x_i}{Q} \times \frac{\partial Q}{\partial x_i} \times \frac{\delta x_i}{x_i}\right\}^2$$

$$= \left\{\frac{18}{198} \times 1 \times 0.0167\right\}^2 + \left\{\frac{180}{198} \times 1 \times 0.00444\right\}^2 = 1.86 \times 10^{-5}$$

Hence, $\frac{\delta Q}{Q} = \pm 4.312 \times 10^{-3}; \delta Q = Q \times (\pm 4{:}312 \times 10^{-3}) = \pm 0.8538 \text{ l/s}$

$Q = 198 \pm 0.8538$ l/s. Ans.

Example 1.7 The coefficient of velocity C_v, for an orifice at the side of a water tank is experimentally determined by measuring the trajectory of a jet issuing from the orifice and the head of water H above the orifice.

$$C_v = \sqrt{\frac{X^2}{4HY}},$$

If $X = 1.35 \pm 0.005$ m: $Y = 0.4 \pm 0.005$ m; and $H = 1.21 \pm 0.002$ m, find the value of C_v.

Let $C_v^2 = \frac{X^2}{4HY} = A$: Expected value of $A = \frac{1.35^2}{4 \times 1.21 \times 0.4} = 0.9414$

Expected value of $C_v = \sqrt{A} = 0.970$

$x_1 = X$; $x_2 = Y$; and $x_3 = H$

$$\frac{\delta x_1}{x_1} = \pm\frac{0.005}{1.35} = \pm 3.704 \times 10^{-3}; \quad \frac{\delta x_2}{x_2} = \pm\frac{0.005}{0.4} = \pm 0.0125$$

$$\frac{\delta x_3}{x_3} = \frac{\pm 0.002}{1.21} = \pm 1.653 \times 10^{-3}$$

$$\frac{\partial A}{\partial x_1} = \frac{2A}{x_1}; \frac{\partial A}{\partial x_2} = -\frac{A}{x_2}; \frac{\partial A}{\partial x_3} = -\frac{A}{x_3}$$

$$\left\{\frac{\partial A}{A}\right\}^2 = \sum_{i=1 \text{ to } 3} \left\{\frac{x_i}{A} \times \frac{\partial A}{\partial x_i} \times \frac{\delta x_i}{x_i}\right\}^2 = \left\{\frac{x_i}{A} \times \frac{2A}{x_1} \times 3.704 \times 10^{-3}\right\}^2 +$$

$$\left\{\frac{x_2}{A} \times \frac{A}{x_2} \times 0.0125\right\}^2 + \left\{\frac{x_3}{A} \times \frac{A}{x_3} \times 1.653 \times 10^{-3}\right\}^2 = 2.139 \times 10^{-4}$$

$$\frac{\delta A}{A} = \sqrt{2.139 \times 10^{-4}} = \pm 0.0146;$$

$$A = C_v^2; \frac{dA}{A} = \frac{2C_v dC_v}{C_v^2}.$$

Hence $\dfrac{\delta C_v}{C_v} = \dfrac{1}{2} \times \dfrac{\delta A}{A} = \pm 0.0073$

$$\delta C_v = \pm 0.0073 \times C_v = \pm 0.0073 \times 0.970 = \pm 0.0071$$

Hence $C_v = 0.973 \pm 0.0071$. Ans.

REVIEW QUESTIONS AND PROBLEMS

1.1 Convert erg i.e., dyne cm to joules.

1.2 Convert 1 kg /kW hr to lbs /HP h, given that 1 kg = 2.206 lbs and 1HP = 746 watts.

1.3 Convert $R = 0.0596$ kcal /kg K to J/kg K given that 1 kcal = 4186 J.

1.4 Convert thermal conductivity λ in calorie per second centimetre degree Celsius to watt per metre kelvin, given that one kilocalorie per hour = 1.163 watt.

1.5 What are the dimensions of the following physical quantities?

(i) Speed in rpm

(ii) Angle in radians

(iii) Torque

(iv) Mass moment of inertia

(v) Area moment of inertia

(vi) Momentum

(vii) Discharge

ANSWERS

1.1. 10^{-7} J; **1.2.** 1.6456 lbs/HP h; **1.3.** 249.49 J/kg K; **1.4.** 418.68 W/m K; **1.5.** (i) T^{-1};(ii) dimensionless; (iii) $ML^2\ T^{-2}$; (iv) ML^2; (v) L^4; (vi) MLT^{-1}; (vii) L^3T^{-1}

2 Properties of Fluids

Introduction — Pressure in fluids — Specific mass — Specific volume — Specific weight — Specific gravity — Dynamic viscosity — Kinematic viscosity — Newtonian and Non-Newtonian fluids — Surface tension — Capillarity — Compressibility — Gas Laws — Vapour pressure — Cavitation — Real and ideal fluids.

2.1 Introduction

General laws governing fluid motion can be formulated if we include the various properties of the fluid in the analysis of the fluid flow. In fluid mechanics, the flow is studied at the macro-level and the fluid is assumed to be a continuum.

A fluid is a substance, which deforms continuously when a shear stress is applied, however small the shear stress may be. In case of solids,a finite deformation will result when a shear stress (within the yield stress) is applied.

Fluids do not have a definite shape and they can exist as liquids or gases. A mass of a fluid at a particular temperature and pressure possesses a definite volume. A liquid offers great resistance to change in volume (it is practically considered as incompressible), but assumes the shape of the containing vessel. If the vessel is of a bigger volume, it forms a free surface. Gases adopt the shape of the container and occupy the whole volume of the vessel without any free surface. Gases are highly compressible.

2.1.1 Pressure in fluids

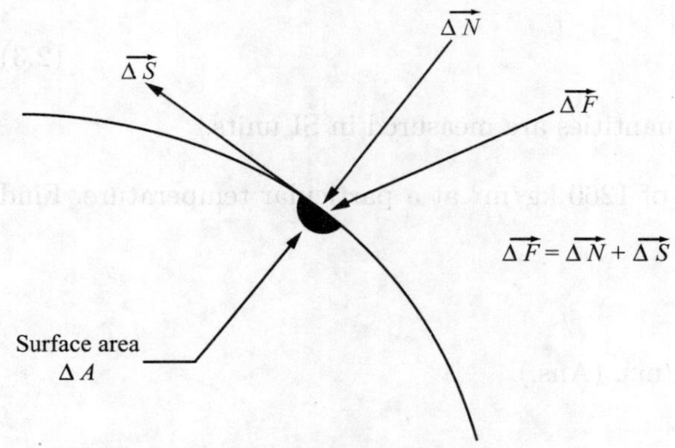

Fig. 2.1 *Normal and shear force*

Pressure is a general characteristic for all fluids. The force $\Delta\vec{F}$ acting on an elementary area ΔA can be resolved into two components—one normal and the other parallel to the boundary. In Fig. 2.1, the normal force is the pressure force $\Delta\vec{N}$ and the tangential force is the shear force $\Delta\vec{S}$.

Then intensity of pressure $p = \underset{\Delta A \to 0}{\text{lt}} \dfrac{\Delta\vec{N}}{\Delta A}$

and the shear stress $\tau = \underset{\Delta A \to 0}{\text{lt}} \dfrac{\Delta\vec{S}}{\Delta A}$.

When a fluid is at rest, and also when the shear force is negligible, the intensity of pressure will be equal in all directions and it becomes a condition of the fluid at the point under consideration. The equality of pressure in all directions at a point is known as Pascal's law. The pressure intensity is measured in N/m^2 (pascal).

2.2 Properties of Fluids

Fluids have some important engineering properties, which are discussed below.

2.2.1 Specific mass (ρ) and specific volume (v)

The specific mass or density of a fluid (ρ) is the mass of fluid per unit volume.

$$\rho = \frac{M}{\forall}, \tag{2.1}$$

where M is the mass and $\forall$ is the volume of the fluid. It varies with temperature and pressure. In many problems ρ_w (ρ of water) can be taken as 1000 kg/m^3 and ρ_{air} as 1.22 kg/m^3.

The specific volume (v) of a fluid is the volume of fluid per unit mass

$$v = \frac{1}{\rho}, \tag{2.2}$$

2.2.2 Specific weight (γ)

The specific weight of a fluid (γ) is the weight of the fluid per unit volume.

$$\gamma_w = 1000\,\text{kg}_f/\text{m}^3 = 9810\,\text{N/m}^3.$$

The formula

$$\gamma = \rho g. \tag{2.3}$$

can be applied without difficulty if all the quantities are measured in SI units.

Example 2.1 Glycerin has a specific mass of 1260 kg/m^3 at a particular temperature. Find its specific weight.

$$\rho = 1260\ \text{kg/m}^3;\ g = 9.81\ \text{m/s}^2.$$

$$\gamma = \rho g = 1260 \times 9.81 = 1.236 \times 10^4\ \text{N/m}^3.\ \text{(Ans.)}$$

2.2.3 Specific gravity (S)

Specific gravity of a fluid is the ratio of the weight of any volume of the fluid to the weight of an equal volume of water at 4°C and at standard atmospheric pressure. It will be equal to

$$S = \frac{\gamma_f}{\gamma_w} = \frac{\rho_f}{\rho_w}, \tag{2.4}$$

values of γ_w, ρ_w being found at standard conditions. Being a ratio of similar quantities, specific gravity is dimensionless. The specific gravity of mercury is nearly 13.6 and that of kerosene oil is 0.81.

2.2.4 Dynamic viscosity (μ)

Shear strain in case of solids is $d\phi = \delta x/y$ as shown in Fig. 2.2(a). Figure 2.2(b) shows a fluid element having a variation of velocity u only in the y direction. The fluid element is undergoing a shear, and the shear deformation after a time δt is equal to $\frac{\partial u}{\partial y}\delta y \delta t$. Hence the rate of shear strain is $\frac{\partial u}{\partial y}$.

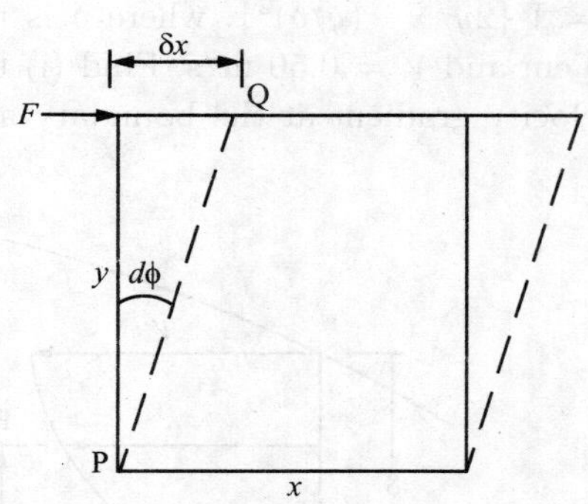

Fig. 2.2(a) Shear strain in solids

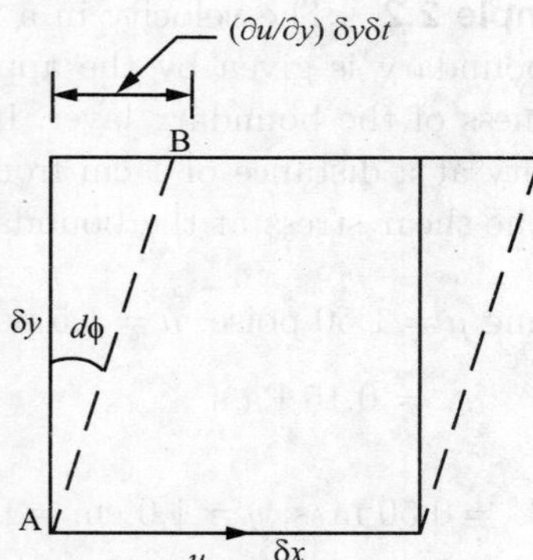

Fig. 2.2(b) Rate of shear strain in fluids

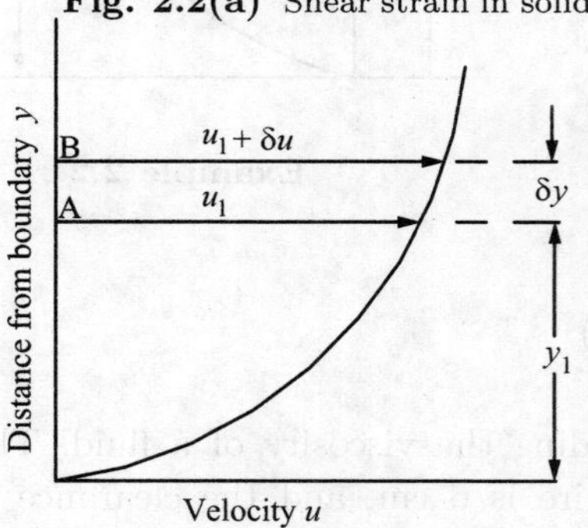

Fig. 2.3 Variation of velocity with y

Figure 2.3 shows a typical variation of the velocity of the fluid flow away from a rigid boundary. The velocities in the adjoining layers A and B are different which gives rise to a shear stress τ between the layers. τ = shear force/area under shear. The rate of shear strain (cross velocity gradient) is equal to $\frac{\partial u}{\partial y} = \frac{du}{dy}$, u being a function of y alone.

Newton formulated the law

$$\tau = \mu\, du/dy, \tag{2.5}$$

where μ is the dynamic viscosity of the fluid. This law known as the Newton's law of viscosity governs many fluids like air, water, oils etc. μ, the constant of proportionality is called the dynamic viscosity of the fluid.

The SI unit for dynamic viscosity (μ) is N s/m^2 or Pa s which is also equal to kg/m s. A much more common unit is poise.

1 poise = 1 dyne s/cm^2 = 1 g/cm s.

Also 1 poise = 1/10 SI unit.

For water at 20 °C, μ = 1 centipoise. μ for air at 20 °C is about 1.8×10^{-4} poise.

The dynamic viscosity of liquids decreases with increase in temperature, whereas for gases it increases with temperature. This can be explained by the fact that the property of viscosity is (i) due to inter-molecular forces of cohesion and (ii) because of the momentum transfer due to exchange of molecules between adjacent layers of fluid under shear. In gases, the momentum transfer due to exchange of molecules between adjacent layers becomes very important at higher temperatures.

The change in dynamic viscosity with pressure is not appreciable.

Example 2.2 The velocity in a laminar boundary layer at a point P, at a distance y from the boundary is given by the approximate equation $v = V\{2y/\delta - (y/\delta)^2\}$, where δ is the thickness of the boundary layer. If δ is found to be 2.50 cm and V = 0.50 m/s. Find (i) the velocity at a distance of 1 cm from the plate, (ii) the velocity gradient at the boundary and (iii) the shear stress at the boundary.

Assume μ = 1.50 poise. μ = 1.5 poise = 1.50/10

= 0.15 Pa s.

(i) $V = 0.50$ m/s; $y = 1.0$ cm $= 0.01$ m;

$\delta = 2.50$ cm $= 0.025$ m;

$y/\delta = 0.01/0.025 = 0.40.$

$$(v)_{y=0.01} = V\{2y/\delta - (y/\delta)^2\}_{y=0.01}$$
$$= 0.5(2 \times 0.40 - 0.40^2) = 0.32\text{m/s. (Ans.)}$$

(ii) $$(dv/dy)_{y=0} = V\{2/\delta - 2y/\delta^2\}_{y=0}$$
$$= 2V/\delta = 2 \times 0.50/0.025 = 40/\text{s. (Ans.)}$$

(iii) $\tau = (\mu dv/dy)_{y=0} = 0.15 \times 40 = 6$ N/m^2 = 6 Pa. (Ans.)

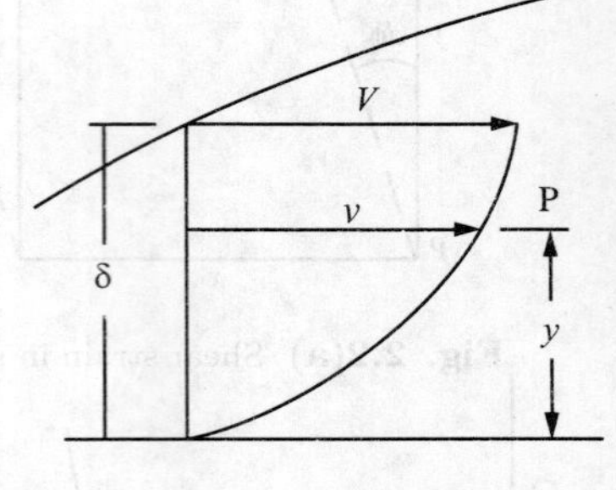

Example 2.2

Example 2.3 The figure shows an arrangement for finding the viscosity of a fluid. The diameter of the inner cylinder suspended by a torsion wire is 6 cm, and the clearance is 1mm. The bottom gap can be assumed to be so large that the shear at the bottom can be neglected. The length of the cylinder in contact with the liquid is 10 cm. If the torque measured using the torsion wire when the outer cylinder rotates at 60 rpm is 1.25×10^{-3} kg_f m, find the viscosity of the oil in the gap.

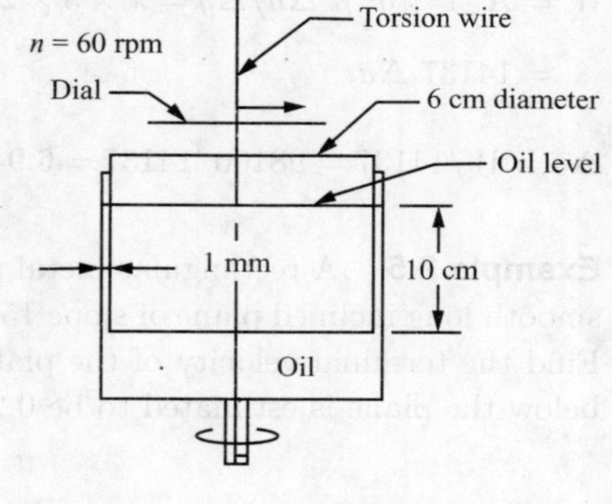

Example 2.3

$\Delta y = 1 \text{ mm} = 10^{-3}$ m; $T = 1.25\times10^{-3}\,\text{kg}_\text{f}$.m.

$= 0.01226$ N m.

$l = 10$ cm $= 0.10$ m; $d = 6$ cm $= 0.06$ m; $r = 0.03$ m;

$n = 60$ rpm.

$\Delta u = \pi d\, n/60 = \pi \times 0.06 \times 60/60 = 0.1885$ m/s.

$\Delta u/\Delta y = 0.1885/10^{-3} = 188.50$/s.

$A = \pi dl = \pi \times 0.06 \times 0.10 = 0.01885\ \text{m}^2$.

$T = 1.25 \times 10^{-3}\ \text{kg}_\text{f}$ m $= 0.01226$ N m.

$F = T/r = 0.01226/0.03 = 0.4087$ N. (1)

$F = A\tau = A\mu\, du/dy$

$= 0.0377 \times 188.5\, \mu = 3.553\, \mu$. (2)

From equations (1) and (2), $\mu = 0.4087/3.553 = 0.1150$ Pa s. (Ans.)

Note: Solving problems becomes easier by (a) writing the related equation and (b) converting all known data to consistent units, say SI units. The problem at hand involves viscosity, shear force, speed of rotation and torque.

Torque T = Total shear force F around the cylinder × Radius.

$T = F \times r$.

$F = \tau \times A$; $A = \pi dl$ (A is the area under shear).

$\tau = \mu \dfrac{\Delta u}{\Delta y}$; $\Delta u = \pi\, d\, n/60$.

In the problem r, d, l, n, Δy and T are given.
The above equations can be solved for μ.

Example 2.4 A sleeve 20 cm long encases a long vertical rod 3 cm in diameter with a radial clearance of 0.20 mm. The rod and sleeve are separated by an oil of viscosity 1.50 poise. If the effective weight of the sleeve is 100 g_f, what will be the terminal velocity of the fall of the sleeve?

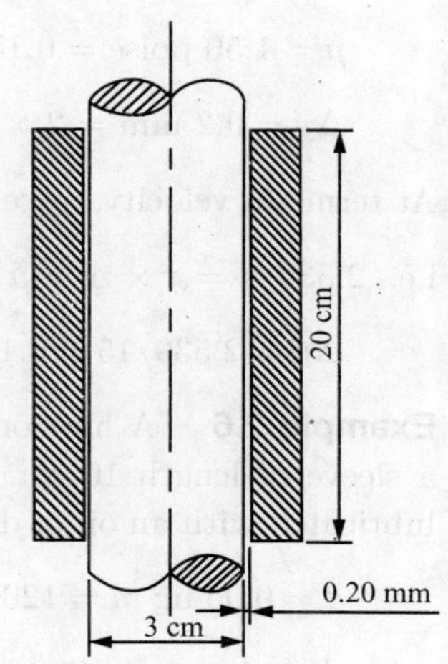

Example 2.4

The terminal velocity will be reached when the effective weight is equal to the resistance. Let us use CGS units.

$W = 100\text{g}_\text{f} = 98100$ dynes; $l = 20$ cm ; $d = 3$ cm.

Clearance $\Delta y = h = 0.2$ mm $= 0.02$ cm; $\mu = 1.50$ poise.

Area under shear $A = \pi dl$.

$W = A\tau = \pi dl\ \mu\ \Delta u/\Delta y = \pi \times 3 \times 20 \times 1.5 \times \Delta u/0.02$

$= 14137\ \Delta u$.

$\Delta u = W/14137 = 98100/14137 = 6.94$ cm/s. (Ans.)

Example 2.5 A rectangular metal plate of size 20 cm × 10 cm, weighing 1 kg_f slides over a smooth long inclined plane of slope 15°. The slope is covered with an oil of viscosity 1.50 poise. Find the terminal velocity of the plate over the inclined plane if the thickness of the oil film below the plane is estimated to be 0.2 mm.

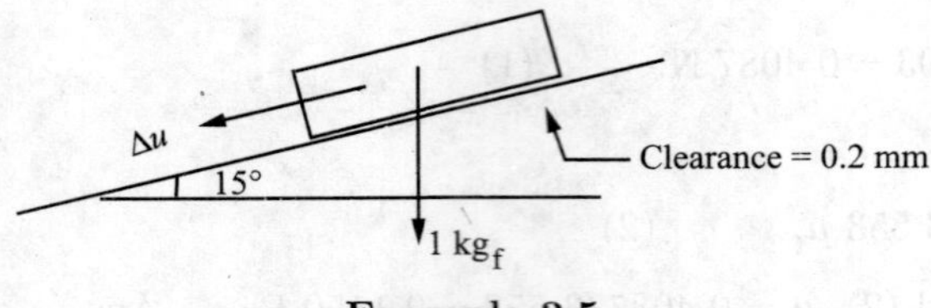

Example 2.5

$A = 0.20$ m $\times$ 0.10 m $= 0.02$ m^2.

$W = 1\text{kg}_f = 1\times 9.81$ N.

Force causing motion $= 1\times 9.81 \times \sin 15° = 2.539$ N.

$\mu = 1.50$ poise $= 0.15$ Pa s.

$\Delta y = 0.2$ mm $= 2 \times 10^{-4}$ m.

At terminal velocity, force causing motion = resistance force.

i.e., $2.539\text{ N} = \tau \times A = \mu \times (\Delta u/\Delta y) \times A = 0.15 \times \Delta u/(2 \times 10^{-4}) \times 0.02 = 15\Delta u$.

$\Delta u = 2.539/15 = 0.169$ m / s. (Ans.)

Example 2.6 A horizontal shaft of diameter 5 cm rotates at a speed of 1200 rpm, inside a sleeve of length 10 cm. The clearance between the shaft and the sleeve is 1 mm. If it is lubricated with an oil of dynamic viscosity 3.50 poise, find the HP lost in the bearing.

$d = 0.05$ m; $n = 1200$ rpm $l = 0.10$ m.

$dy = 1$ mm $= 10^{-3}$ m; $\mu = 3.50$ poise $= 0.35$ Pa s.

$du = v = \pi dn/60 = \pi \times 0.05 \times 1200/60 = 3.1416$ m/s.

$\tau = \mu \times du/dy = 0.35 \times 3.1416/10^{-3} = 1099.56 \text{ N/m}^2.$

$F_s = \tau \times A = \tau \times \pi dl = 1099.56 \times \pi \times 0.05 \times 0.1 = 17.27 \text{ N}.$

Power = Rate at which work is done = $F_s \times v = 17.27 \times 3.1416 \text{ W} = 54.3 \text{ W}$

$= 54.3/736 \text{ HP} = 0.074 \text{ HP}$. (Ans.)

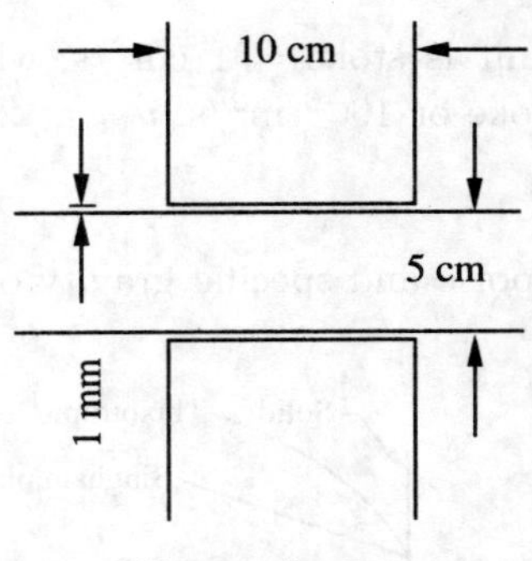

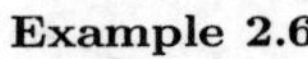
Example 2.6

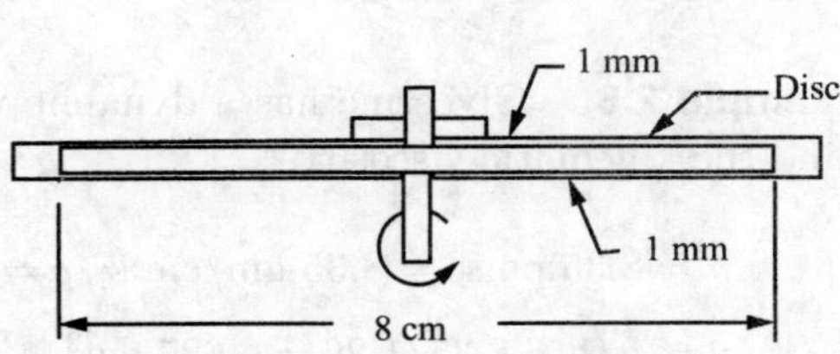

Example 2.7

Example 2.7 A disc of diameter 8 cm is rotated on a spindle and is enclosed in a small chamber filled with oil of viscosity 2 poise as shown in the diagram. If the clearance at the top and the bottom of the disc is 1mm, find the torque required to rotate the disc at 60 rpm.

Let us solve the problem in CGS units.

$R = 4$ cm.

$\mu = 2$ poise.

$\Delta y = 1 \text{ mm} = 0.10 \text{ cm};\ n = 60 \text{ rpm}.$

$\Delta u = v = 2\pi rn/60 = 6.28\ r.$

$\tau = \mu \Delta u/\Delta y = 2 \times 6.28\ r/0.1 = 125.66\ r.$

$dT = \tau \times$ elementary area (on both sides) $\times\ r$

$= 125.66\ r \times 2\pi r dr \times 2 \times r = 1579.1\ r^3\ dr.$

$$T = \int_0^R dT = \int_0^R 1579.14\ r^3 dr = \left[1579.14 \frac{r^4}{4}\right]_0^4 = 1579.1 \times \frac{256}{4}$$

$= 1.0106 \times 10^5$ dyne cm. (Ans.)

2.2.5 Kinematic viscosity (ν)

The dynamic viscosity of a fluid involves the dimensions of mass. The elimination of the mass dimension by dividing μ by ρ gives rise to a quantity called the kinematic viscosity,

$$\nu = \mu/\rho. \tag{2.6}$$

The SI unit for kinematic viscosity is m^2/s. A common unit is stoke $= 1\ cm^2/s$, which is 1/10,000th of the SI unit. Water at 20°C has $\nu = 1$ centistoke or $10^{-6}\ m^2/s$. ν_{air} at 20°C is nearly $14.80 \times 10^{-6}\ m^2\ /s$.

Example 2.8 Glycerine has a dynamic viscosity of 8.35 poise and specific gravity of 1.26. Find the kinematic viscosity.

$$\mu = 8.35 \text{ poise} = 8.35 \text{ gm/cm s};\ \rho = 1.26 \text{ gm/cm}^3.$$

$$\nu = \mu/\rho = 8.35/1.26 = 6.627 \text{ cm}^2/\text{s. (Ans.)}$$

2.2.6 Non-newtonian fluids

The deformation characteristics of a fluid under shear stress can be studied by means of a graph between the rate of shear strain du/dy and the shear stress τ. In a Newtonian fluid, when du/dy is equal to zero, τ should be zero. Also τ should vary linearly with du/dy as shown in Fig. 2.4.

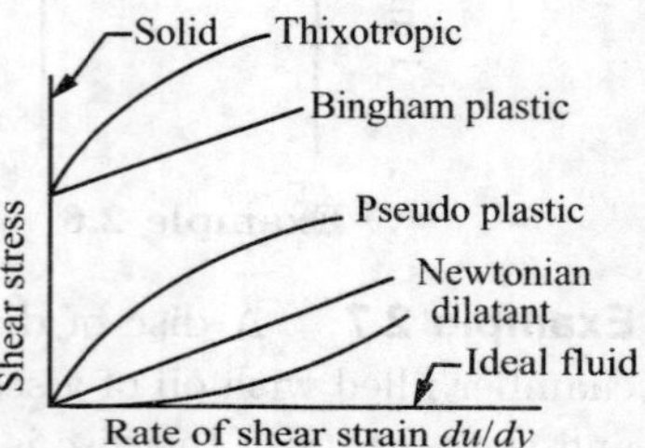

Fig. 2.4 Types of fluids

The figure shows the behaviour of dilatant fluids like printing ink, butter etc. and pseudo-plastic fluids like suspension of paints, paper pulp etc. There are also a wide range of substances which have properties between fluids and solids. For example, some liquids have time-dependent characteristics.

2.2.7 Surface tension (σ)

In a liquid, the intermolecular forces give rise to the property of cohesion. Work done against this force for the formation of a surface, appears as surface energy. Inside a fluid mass, the intermolecular forces acting on any molecule are balanced; but a molecule at the surface will experience an unbalanced force. On a curved surface, the analysis of such a force system will yield results which are in many cases equivalent to that of having an imaginary layer of liquid at the surface under tension.

Surface tension σ is measured as energy per unit area or force per unit length. Water at 20°C (for boundary with air) has $\sigma = 0.073$ N/m. For a mercury–air interface at 20°C, $\sigma = 0.48$ N/m. The phenomenon of surface tension is important in problems involving surfaces between liquids and gases like the formation of bubbles and drops, small waves on liquids surfaces and capillarity.

Example 2.9 In the bubble method of measuring surface tension of a liquid of specific gravity 0.80, a tube of diameter 3 mm is immersed in the liquid to a depth of 6 cm. The maximum pressure of air that could be applied through the tube was 510 Pa above atmosphere. Find the surface tension.

$$\gamma = 0.80 \times 1000 \times 9.81 = 7848 \text{ N/m}^3; \ d = 0.003 \text{ m}.$$

Neglecting small differences in depth due to bubble formation,

$h = 6$ cm $= 0.06$ m.

The net pressure acting on the film $= 510 - \gamma\, h$.

$$= 510 - 7848 \times 0.06 = 39.12 \text{ Pa}.$$

This pressure acts on the projected area of $\pi d^2/4$. The film does not rupture because of tension σ on the periphery πd.

$$\text{So,}\ \frac{\pi d^2}{4} \times 39.12 = \sigma \pi d.$$

$$\sigma = 39.12 \times (\pi d^2)/4\pi d = 39.12 \times 0.003/4 = 0.02934 \text{ N/m. (Ans.)}$$

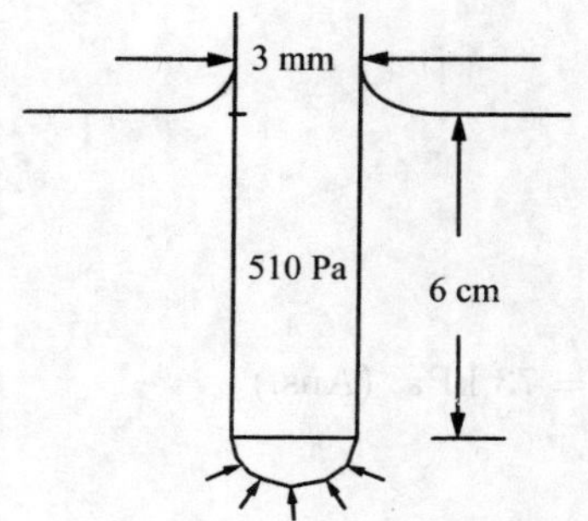

Example 2.9

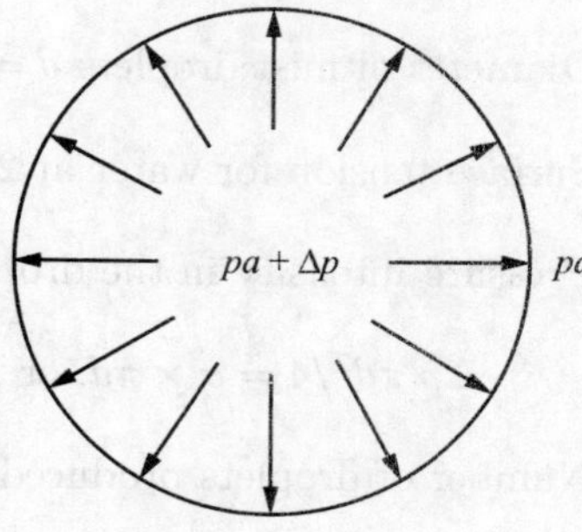

Example 2.10

Example 2.10 Find the pressure inside a rain drop of 2 mm diameter if $\sigma = 0.074$ N/m.

Consider a droplet having pressure Δp above the atmosphere. The film of liquid on the surface can be assumed to be in tension. The length to be ruptured is the circumference πd. The bursting force is equal to

$$\Delta p \times \text{projected area} = \Delta p\ \pi d^2/4.$$

Hence $\pi d\ \sigma = \Delta p\ \pi d^2/4$;

$$\Delta p = \frac{4\pi\ \sigma d}{\pi\ d^2} = \frac{4\sigma}{d} = \frac{4 \times 0.074}{2 \times 10^{-3}} = 148\ \text{N/m}^2.\ \text{(Ans.)}$$

Note: For a gas bubble inside a liquid there will be only one spherical surface and the formula for pressure will also be

$$\Delta p = 4\sigma/d. \tag{2.7}$$

Example 2.11 If the inside pressure of a soap bubble 4 cm in diameter is greater than the atmospheric pressure by 18 Pa. Find the value of surface tension.

In this case, there are two surfaces formed, one inside and another outside. The net pressure of 18 Pa acts on the projected area of $\pi d^2/4$ and is resisted by the tension σ on two circular arcs of length πd (one inside and another outside).

$$D = 4\ \text{cm} = 0.04\ \text{m};\ \Delta p = 18\ \text{Pa};\ \ 2\pi d\sigma = \pi d^2\ \Delta p/4.$$

$$\sigma = \Delta p \times d/8 = 18 \times 0.04/8 = 0.09\ \text{N/m. (Ans.)}$$

Example 2.12 Ignoring thermal effects, compute the power required to convert 1 litre of water per minute a+ a temperature of 20°C into a mist having an average drop size of $4{\times}10^{-3}$ mm. What will be the pressure intensity inside the mist droplets?

Diameter of mist droplets $d = 4 \times 10^{-3}$ mm $= 4 \times 10^{-6}$ m.

Surface tension for water at 20°C = 0.073 N/m.

Pressure intensity in the drop is given by the equation

$$\Delta p\ \pi d^2/4 = \sigma \times \pi d,\ \text{or}\ \Delta p = 4\sigma/d = 4 \times 0.073/(4 \times 10^{-6}) = 73\ \text{kPa. (Ans.)}$$

Number of droplets produced per second

$$= 1 \times 10^{-3}/60/[(\pi/6) \times (4 \times 10^{-6})^3]$$

$$= 10^{14}/(64\pi) = 4.974 \times 10^{11}.$$

Therefore power required $=\sigma \times$ rate of surface area production

$$= 0.073 \times 4.974 \times 10^{11} \times 4\pi \times (2 \times 10^{-6})^2$$

$$= 1.825\ \text{watts.(Ans.)}$$

Example 2.13 A jet of water issuing to the atmosphere from an orifice is 3 mm thick. Find the pressure inside the jet.

Taking a length of jet δl, the bursting is resisted by a length $2\delta l$.

Hence $2\delta l\sigma = \delta l d\Delta p$.

$$\Delta p = 2\sigma/d = 2 \times 0.074/(3 \times 10^{-3}) = 49.33 \text{ Pa. (Ans.)}$$

2.2.8 Capillarity

Very closely connected with surface tension, is the property of rise or fall of liquid in capillary tubes. The intermolecular forces of the liquid and that of the solid boundaries in contact with it, cause a force of adhesion. If θ is the angle of contact, the net force of cohesion $\vec{C}$ will be acting at an angle $\theta/2$ with the wall and the force of adhesion $\vec{A}$ will be normal to the wall as shown in Fig. 2.5(a). The resultant $\vec{R}$ will be normal to the surface formed, since the fluid under static condition cannot take a tangential force.

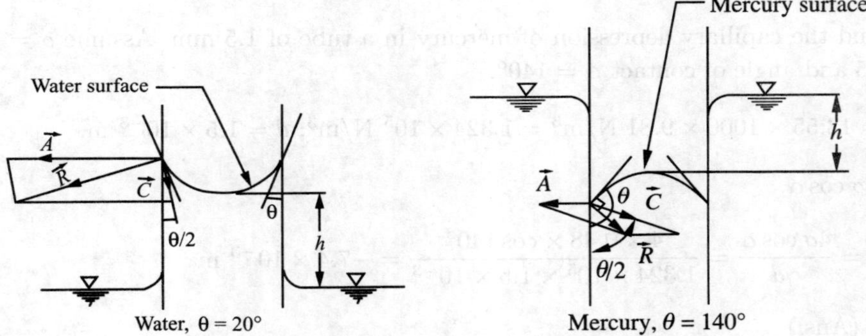

Fig. 2.5(a) Capillary rise of water **Fig. 2.5(b)** Capillary depression of mercury

In case of water in contact with a glass surface, since $\vec{A}$ is very high as compared to $\vec{C}$, angle θ will be very small, often assumed to be zero. In the case of mercury in contact with the glass surface as shown in Fig. 2.5(b), $\vec{C}$ is very large compared to $\vec{A}$ and angle θ is found to be of the order of 140°. The capillary rise of water in a glass tube is shown in Fig. 2.6. It can be estimated by assuming a surface film under tension, equal to σ per unit length, acting at the circumference πd. But this force being inclined to the vertical, the upward component $\vec{F}$ is equal to $\pi d\, \sigma \cos\theta$.

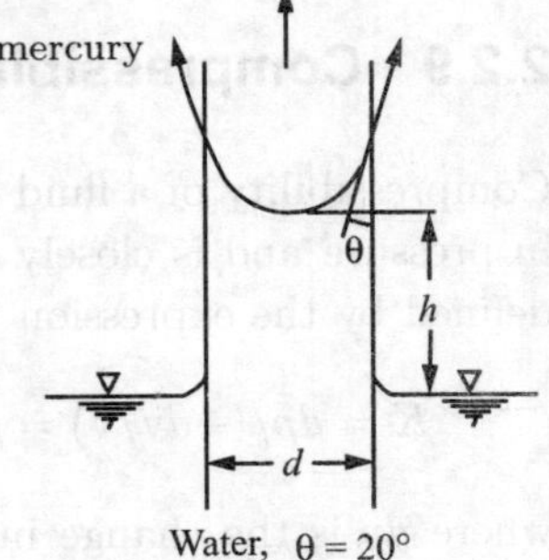

Fig. 2.6 Capillary rise in a tube

This force can be assumed to support the weight of the water column of height h, which will be equal to $W = (\pi d^2/4)h\gamma$.

Equating F and W we get,

$$h = 4\, \sigma \cos\theta/\gamma d. \quad (2.8)$$

The same formula can be used for finding the depression of mercury surface in a capillary tube, $\cos\theta$ being negative when $\theta = 140°$.

Example 2.14 How high will moisture rise in soil from its normal ground water level, if the distance between the soil grains is 0.60 mm. Assume $\sigma = 0.073$ N/m and $\theta = 0°$.

The condition may be assumed to be similar to that of a capillary tube of diameter 0.60 mm. Let h be the capillary rise; $\sigma = 0.073$ N/m; $\gamma = 9810$ N/m^3; $\theta = 0°$.

$$d = 0.60 \text{ mm} = 6 \times 10^{-4} \text{ m.}$$

$$h = 4\,\sigma\,\cos\theta/\gamma d = 4 \times 0.073 \times 1/(9810 \times 6 \times 10^{-4})$$

$$= 0.0496 \text{ m} = 4.96 \text{ cm. (Ans.)}$$

Example 2.15 Find the capillary depression of mercury in a tube of 1.5 mm. Assume $\sigma = 0.48$ N/m, $S = 13.55$ and angle of contact $\alpha = 140°$.

$$S = 13.55;\ \gamma = 13.55 \times 1000 \times 9.81 \text{ N/m}^3 = 1.324 \times 10^5 \text{ N/m}^3;\ d = 1.5 \times 10^{-3} \text{ m.}$$

$$\frac{\pi d^2}{4} \times \gamma h = \pi d\sigma \cos\alpha.$$

$$h = \frac{\pi d\sigma\cos\alpha}{\pi d^2\gamma} = \frac{4\sigma\cos\alpha}{\gamma d} = \frac{4 \times 0.48 \times \cos 140°}{1.324 \times 10^5 \times 1.5 \times 10^{-3}} = -7.4 \times 10^{-3} \text{ m}$$

$$= -7.4 \text{ mm. (Ans.)}$$

2.2.9 Compressibility

Compressibility of a fluid is a measure of volumetric strain of the fluid caused by unit change in pressure and is closely connected with the bulk modulus of elasticity K of the fluid. K is defined by the expression

$$K = dp/(-d\forall/\forall) = \rho\ dp/d\rho, \tag{2.9}$$

where dp is the change in the pressure, $d\rho$ is the change in density and $d\forall$ is the change in volume of fluid from the original volume $\forall$.

Gases are highly compressible. Generally, liquids can be assumed to be practically incompressible as compared with gases. Still in some phenomena like water hammer, compressibility of water plays a role.

K for water is nearly 2.20 GPa = 2.20×10^9 N/m^2.

Example 2.16 Find the pressure change required to cause 0.1% volume change in water.

$K = 2.20$ GPa.

$-d\forall/\forall = 1/1000 = 10^{-3}$; $K = 2.20 \times 10^9$ N/m^2.

$dp = K \times (-d\forall/\forall) = 2.20 \times 10^9 \times 10^{-3} = 2.20 \times 10^6$ N/m^2 = 2.20 MPa. (Ans.)

The velocity of propagation of an elastic wave through a fluid media is related to the bulk modulus of elasticity by the equation

$$c = \sqrt{\frac{dp}{d\rho}} = \sqrt{\frac{K}{\rho}}. \tag{2.10}$$

The above expression is the basis for the calculation of water hammer pressures in pipe lines carrying water.

Example 2.17 Find the velocity of propagation of an elastic wave through water (velocity of sound through water), given $K = 2.20$ GPa, $\rho = 1000$ kg/m^3.

$$c = \sqrt{\frac{K}{\rho}} = \sqrt{\frac{2.2 \times 10^9}{1000}} = 1483.2 \text{ m/s. (Ans.)}$$

2.2.10 Compressibility of gases—thermodynamic consideration

Most common gases obey the perfect gas law, the equation of state being

$$\frac{p}{\rho} = p\nu = RT, \tag{2.11}$$

where p is the absolute pressure, ρ is the specific mass, v is the specific volume, T is the absolute temperature in kelvin and R is the gas constant having the dimension of specific heat. By the application of Avogadro's law that gases at the same temperature and pressure contain equal number of molecules, a universal constant $R = m_1R_1 = m_2R_2$ is found to have a value of about 8312 J/kg K. Hence $R = 8312/m$ for any gas, where m is the molecular weight of gas. For air, R is found to be 287 J/kg K.

Example 2.18 Find the gas constant for oxygen.

Molecular weight of oxygen $= 2 \times 16 = 32$.

$R = 8312/32 = 259.75$ J/kg K. (Ans.)

The volume changes in gases are governed by thermodynamic effects which in turn depend on the process of volume change.

In the isothermal process, the temperature is kept constant by transfer of heat across the boundary when volumes and pressures vary. Since T is constant and $pv = RT$, $p = RT/v$.

$$\frac{dp}{dv} = -\frac{RT}{v^2}; \qquad K = -\frac{dp}{dV/V} = -\frac{dp}{dv/v} = \frac{RT}{v^2} \times v = \frac{RT}{v} = p.$$

i.e., $K = p$ (2.12)

for an isothermal process.

In the adiabatic process, the volume and pressure change take place without any exchange of heat across the boundary of the fluid. For an adiabatic process pv^k is a constant, where k is the ratio c_p/c_v = specific heat at constant pressure/specific heat at constant volume.

For air, $k \approx 1.4$. It may also be seen that $R = c_p - c_v$.

Starting from the equation $pv^k = c$ or $p = c/v^k$,

$$\frac{dp}{dv} = -\frac{ck}{v^{k+1}}; \quad K = -\frac{dp}{dV/V} = -\frac{dp}{dv/v} = -\frac{ck}{v^{k+1}}v = \frac{ck}{v^k} = kp.$$

i.e., $K = kp$ (2.13)

for an adiabatic process.

When the pressure changes occur very fast as in transmission of sound through air, the process is adiabatic and

$$c = \sqrt{\frac{kp}{\rho}} = \sqrt{kRT}, \tag{2.14}$$

where $k = \dfrac{c_p}{c_v} = 1.4$, $R = 287$ J/kg K and T is the absolute temperature.

Example 2.19 Find the velocity of sound in air at 20 °C.

$T = 20 + 273 = 293$ K.

$c = \sqrt{kRT} = \sqrt{1.4 \times 287 \times 293} = 343$ m/s. (Ans.)

The ratio of velocity of motion of the gas or that of a body in the gas, to the velocity of sound through the gas is denoted by M, the Mach number, and is of much importance in the study of compressible flows.

2.2.11 Vapour pressure

There is always an escape of molecules from the free surface of a liquid to the space above by evaporation. Some molecules from the space above also re-enter the liquid. The vapour formed above, can exert a pressure on the surface. If it is a closed space above the liquid surface, the space may get saturated with vapour and a condition of equilibrium may be reached. The pressure exerted in such a case is called saturation vapour pressure. It is greatly dependent on temperature. For example, water at 0°C has a saturation vapour pressure of 0.615 kPa, whereas it changes to 2.34 kPa and 7.4 kPa at 20°C and 40°C respectively. The saturated vapour pressure of water at 100°C will be equal to the normal atmospheric pressure of 101.3 kPa. When the pressure is equal to the saturation vapour pressure, the liquid starts to boil.

2.3 Cavitation

In a flowing liquid, the reduction of pressure below vapour pressure may cause the liquid to vaporize and form small cavities. These cavities when transported to regions of higher pressure may collapse creating very high pressure variations, which are destructive. The alternate high and low pressure occurring near boundaries due to collapse of cavities may cause pitting of the boundaries due to fatigue. The phenomenon is known as cavitation and is accompanied by loss of efficiency, noise and vibration. Efforts are made to avoid such a phenomenon of cavitation in turbines, pumps and hydraulic structures.

2.4 Real and Ideal Fluids

All real fluids have the property of viscosity and compressibility. But in order to effect considerable simplification of mathematical analysis, a fluid having no viscosity and which is incompressible is conceived of as an ideal fluid. The formulation of the energy equation, the Bernoulli's theorem, is based on the assumption of an ideal fluid. Potential flow problems are a class of problems based on ideal flow theory. When viscous effects are important, corrections/modifications are made in the results obtained from the ideal fluid theory. A term for energy loss is introduced in the Bernoulli's equation and the pattern of flow around bodies are re-defined taking into consideration the viscous shear on the boundaries and separation from the boundaries.

REVIEW QUESTIONS AND PROBLEMS

Choose the correct answer (Q. 2.1 to 2.7)

2.1 A Newtonian fluid is a fluid (i) which is highly viscous (ii) which obeys Newton's law of viscosity.

2.2 Surface tension has the units of (i) force per unit area (ii) force per unit length.

2.3 Vapour pressure of a liquid ________ with temperature. (i) increases (ii) decreases

2.4 The pressure intensity inside a droplet is given by (i) $p = \dfrac{4\sigma}{r}$ (ii) $p = \dfrac{2\sigma}{r}$.

2.5 An ideal fluid is (i) compressive and gaseous (ii) incompressible and frictionless.

2.6 At a liquid–air–solid surface, the contact angle θ measured in the liquid is less than 90°. The liquid is (i) wetting (ii) non-wetting.

2.7 Capillarity is due to (i) both adhesion and cohesion (ii) adhesion only.

2.8 Define capillarity and surface tension and discuss the factors affecting them.

2.9 Distinguish between a Newtonian and a non-Newtonian fluid.

2.10 What is the unit for rate of shear strain?

2.11 What is a thixotropic substance? Explain.

2.12 Write down the unit of viscosity.

2.13 What do you understand by the term, 'perfect gas'?

2.14 Explain why in liquids, the viscosity decreases when the temperature is increased whereas it increases in the case of gases.

2.15 Write down the expression for the capillary rise of water in a tube.

2.16 What is Pascal' law?

2.17 Define bulk modulus.

2.18 When does capillary fall take place? Explain.

2.19 Differentiate between specific weight and mass density.

2.20 Define compressibility.

2.21 Discuss factors which affect the viscosity of a liquid.

2.22 What is the bulk modulus for a gas undergoing adiabatic change?

2.23 Explain vapour pressure of a liquid.

2.24 Define kinematic viscosity and state its unit.

2.25 Express a poise in SI units.

2.26 Distinguish between dynamic viscosity and kinematic viscosity.

2.27 Explain the importance of vapour pressure in fluid mechanics problems.

2.28 The specific .weight of alcohol is given as 6900 N/m^3. Determine its density, specific volume and specific gravity.

2.29 A mass of liquid weighs 500 N when exposed to standard earth's gravity g = 9.806 m/s^2. (i) What is its mass? (ii) What will be its weight in a planet with the acceleration due to gravity as 3.5 m/s^2.

2.30 Air has a specific mass of 1.22 kg/m^3. Find the specific volume and specific weight.

2.31 For a flow of a viscous fluid with viscosity 1 N s/m^2 and with $u = 0.9y - y^2$, find the shear stress at $y = 0.45$ m and at $y = 0.3$ m.

2.32 A cylindrical shaft 90 mm in diameter rotates about a vertical axis inside a cylindrical tube of length 50 cm and 95 mm internal diameter. If the space between them is filled with oil of viscosity 2 poise, find the power lost in friction for a shaft speed of 240 rpm.

2.33 The space between two parallel horizontal plates kept 3 mm apart is filled with an oil of dynamic viscosity 0.2 Pa s. What is the shear stress on the lower fixed plate if the upper one is moved with a velocity of 1.5 m/s.

2.34 A flat plate 30 cm × 50 cm slides on oil ($\mu = 0.75$ Pa s) over a large plane surface. What force is required to drag the plate at a uniform velocity of 1.6 m/s, if the separating oil film is 0.4 mm thick?

2.35 A square plate 50 cm × 50 cm weighing 200 N slides down an inclined plane of slope, 1vertical:2.5 horizontal with a uniform velocity of 0.4 m/s. If a thin layer of oil of thickness 0.5 cm fills the space between the plate and the inclined plane, determine the coefficient of viscosity of oil.

2.36 Find the kinematic viscosity of a fluid whose specific gravity is 0.95 and viscosity is 0.0011 N s/m^2.

2.37 Two large plane surfaces are 20 mm apart and the gap contains oil of dynamic viscosity

0.6 Pa s. A thin plate of 0.50 m^2 is to be pulled through the gap at a constant velocity of 0.6 m/s. It is 8 mm from one of the surfaces. Neglecting edge effects, calculate the force required to pull the plate.

2.38 Castor oil of viscosity 0.9 N s/m^2 fills the space between two concentric cylinders of 25 cm height, and 15 and 15.5 cm diameters respectively. What torque is required to rotate the inner cylinder at 20 rpm, the outer one remaining stationary?

2.39 Lateral stability of a long shaft with a 15 cm diameter is obtained by means of a 25 cm stationary bearing having an internal diameter of 15.3 cm. If the space between the bearing and the shaft is filled with a lubricant of dynamic viscosity 0.25 N s/m^2, what power will be required to overcome viscous resistance when the shaft is rotated at a constant speed of 180 rpm?

2.40 The equation of velocity profile for a flow is given by $V = 4y^{2/3}$, where V is the velocity in m/s and y is the distance in metres from the boundary. Compute the velocity gradient at $y = 0.3$ m and 0.6 m.

2.41 A liquid drop of diameter 2.5 mm has an internal pressure of 120 N/m^2 in excess of atmospheric pressure (76 cm of mercury). Find the surface tension of the liquid film.

2.42 A capillary tube of 3 mm bore is introduced in a liquid. The rise of fluid in the tube is found to be 5 mm. If the surface tension of the liquid is 0.048 N/m and if the specific weight is 12000 N/m^3, find the angle of contact.

2.43 Obtain an expression for the height of capillary rise for a liquid of surface tension σ and contact angle 0° between two parallel vertical plates with a gap b between them.

2.44 Estimate the pressure inside a water droplet of size 0.3 mm. Assume $\sigma = 0.0728$ N/m.

2.45 Find the capillary depression in a 2 mm diameter tube when dipped in mercury. Assume $\sigma = 0.51$ N/m.

2.46 A bubble 2 cm in diameter is formed by a soap film. If $\sigma = 0.09$ N/m, find the pressure inside the bubble.

2.47 The bulk modulus of elasticity of water is 2.07×10^6 kN/m^2 at standard atmospheric conditions. Determine the increase of pressure necessary to produce 1% reduction in volume at the same temperature.

2.48 Calculate the percentage change in the volume of water, if the pressure is increased by 500 N/cm^2. Assume bulk modulus of water as 2.0×10^5 N/cm^2.

2.49 Find the velocity of sound through air at 0°C.

ANSWERS

2.1. (ii); **2.2.** (ii); **2.3.** (i); **2.4.** (ii); **2.5.** (ii); **2.6.** (i); **2.7.** (i); **2.10.** 1/s; **2.12.** Ns/m^2 or kg/(m.s); **2.22.** $K = kp$; **2.24.** m^2/s; **2.25.** 1 poise = 0.1 SI unit; **2.28.** 703.34 kg/m^3; 1.42×10^{-3} m^3/kg; 0.703; **2.29.** 50.99 kg; 178.46 N; **2.30.** 0.82 m^3/kg; 11.97 N/m^3; **2.31.** zero; 0.3 N/m^2; **2.32.** 14.47 watts; **2.33.** 100 N/m^2; **2.34.** 450 N; **2.35** 3.71 Pa s; **2.36.** 1.158×10^{-6} m^2/s; **2.37.** 37.5 N; **2.38.** 0.5 Nm; **2.39.** 39.26 watts; **2.40.** 3.983/s; 3.161/s; **2.41.** 0.075 N/m; **2.42.** 20.36°; **2.43.** $2\sigma/\gamma b$; **2.44.** 0.97 kPa; **2.45.** 5.86 mm; **2.46.** 36 Pa; **2.47.** 2.07×10^7 Pa; **2.48.** 0.25 %; **2.49.** 331.2 m/s.

3 Fluid Pressure and its Measurement

Fluid pressure — Pressure at a point — Pascal's law — Hydrostatic law — Measurement of fluid pressure — Piezometer — Manometer — Differential manometers — U-tube and inverted U-tube manometers — Two liquid manometers — Variation of pressure and temperature in atmosphere — Stability of atmosphere.

3.1 Fluid Pressure

Let us consider an elementary area ΔA inside the fluid mass as shown in Fig. 3.1. Let the normal force acting on the area be ΔF.

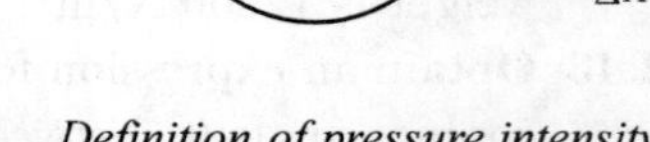

Fig. 3.1 *Definition of pressure intensity*

The pressure intensity $p = \underset{\Delta A \to 0}{\text{lt}} \dfrac{\Delta F}{\Delta A} = \dfrac{dF}{dA}$.

3.1.1 Pascal's law

Pascal's law states that the pressure intensity at a point, in a static fluid, is equal in all directions. It can be proved in the following way.

Consider a tetrahedron of sides Δx, Δy and Δz inside a fluid as shown in Fig. 3.2. Let 'O', a point inside the fluid be the origin. Let area ABC = ΔA and pressure on ΔA be equal to p_n. The weight of a fluid element in the tetrahedron = $(\gamma \cdot \Delta x \cdot \Delta y \cdot \Delta z)/6$.

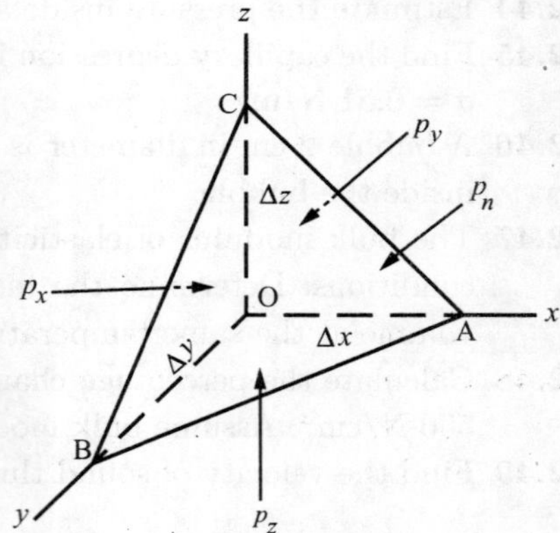

Fig. 3.2 *Analysis of forces on a small fluid element*

The weight is proportional to the third order of magnitude of very small quantities like Δx, Δy and Δz, whereas the pressure forces are proportional to the second order of magnitude. Hence, weight can be neglected in comparison to the pressures when Δx, Δy, Δz tend to zero. Since the element is in a static condition, the net forces in the x, y and z directions are zero.

The component of $p_n\ dA$ in the x direction = $p_n . dA. \cos(n, x)$, where $\cos(n, x)$ is the cosine of the angle between the normal to the surface and the x direction. Resolving forces in the x direction and equating the net force to zero, for static equilibrium conditions,

$$p_n \, dA \cos(n, x) = p_x \frac{1}{2} dzdy.$$

But geometrically,

$$dA \cos(n, x) = \text{area OBC} = \frac{1}{2} dzdy.$$

So $p_n = p_x$.

Similarly, resolving forces in the y and z directions and equating the net forces to zero for the static condition, it can be proved that $p_n = p_y$ and $p_n = p_z$.

Thus, $p_n = p_x = p_y = p_z$, which proves Pascal's law. Pascal's law does not hold good in flows having shearing layers. In such cases, pressure p is defined as $p = \dfrac{p_x + p_y + p_z}{3}$, where p_x, p_y, p_z are pressure intensities in three mutually perpendicular directions.

3.2 Free Surface of Liquids

The weight W of a liquid element in Fig. 3.3 has a component tangential to the surface $= W \sin\theta$, where θ is the angle of the water surface to the horizontal. This will cause motion of the liquid due to shear. In a static liquid, $W \sin\theta = 0$ or the surface is horizontal.

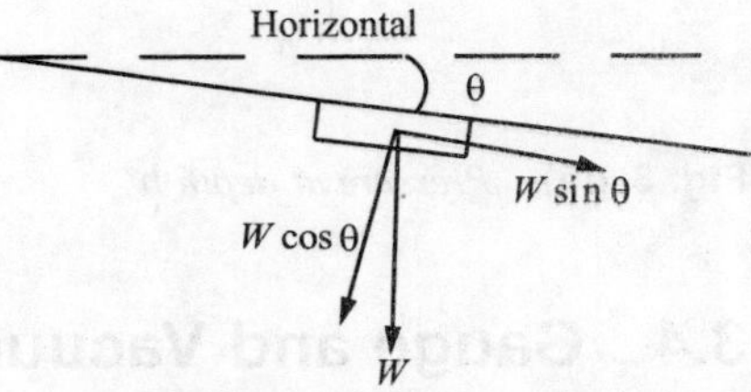

Fig. 3.3 *Fluid element on the surface*

3.3 Change of Pressure with Depth

Take a vertical cylinder of fluid having an area of cross-section A below the surface as shown in Fig. 3.4(a). Pressures act normal to the surface of the cylinder. At the top, force due to atmospheric pressure $= p_a A$. At the bottom, force due to liquid pressure $= pA$. Being symmetrical, the pressures acting on the sides will cancel out. The weight of liquid $= \gamma \, h \, A$, where $\gamma = \rho$ g. Since the cylinder is in equilibrium

$$pA = p_a \, A + \gamma \, h \, A \;\text{ or }\; p = p_a + \gamma \, h.$$

If pressures are measured above atmosphere,

$$p = \gamma \, h. \tag{3.1a}$$

or in the differential form

$$dp = -\gamma dh, \tag{3.1b}$$

where h is positive upwards.

This is known as the hydrostatic law.

The law of transmissibility of pressure states that in static conditions, the pressures at connected points at the same level are the same. (Fig. 3.4(b))

Pressure at P = Pressure at Q

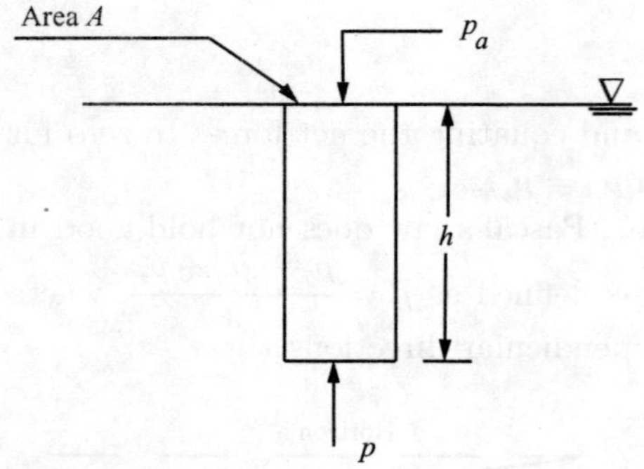

Fig. 3.4(a) *Pressure at depth h*

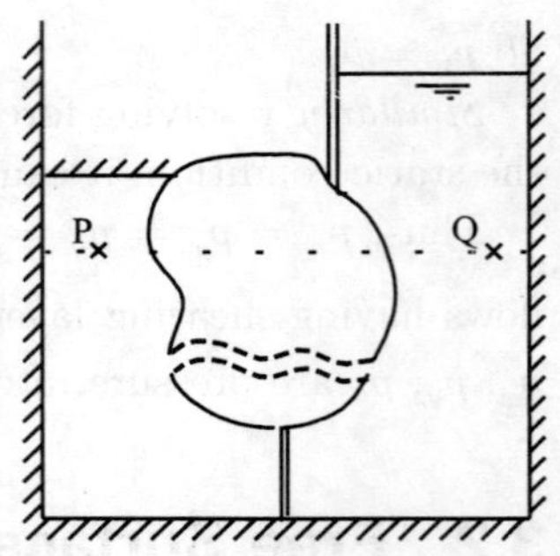

Fig. 3.4(b) *Transmissibility of pressure*

3.4 Gauge and Vacuum Pressures

Absolute zero pressure corresponds to a perfect vacuum. The pressure measured above the local atmospheric pressure is gauge pressure and the pressure measured below the local atmospheric pressure is vacuum pressure.

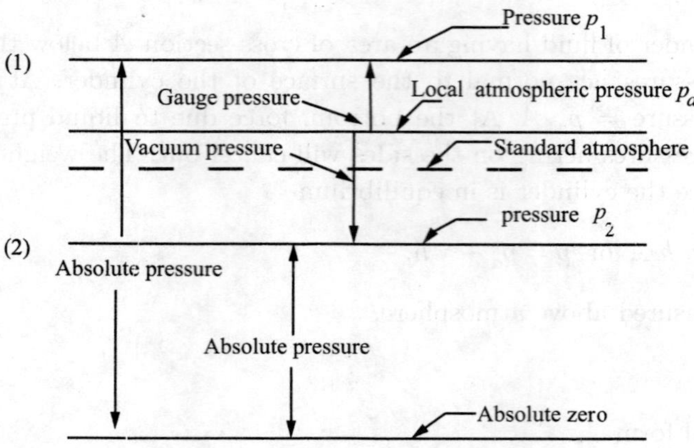

Fig. 3.5 *Gauge and vacuum pressure*

Example 3.1 Convert the standard atmospheric pressure of 760 mm of mercury to (i) kN/m^2, (ii) kg_f/cm^2, (iii) millibars and (iv) m of water. Assume density of mercury as 13.59 g/cm^3.

(i) Standard atmospheric pressure $= \gamma h = \rho gh$

$$= (13.59 \times 1000) \times 9.81 \times 0.76 = 101.32 \text{ kN/m}^2$$

$$= 101.32 \text{ kPa. (Ans.)}$$

(ii) Standard atmospheric pressure $= \dfrac{101.32 \times 1000 \text{ N}}{m^2 \times 9.81} = 1.033 \text{ kg}_f/\text{cm}^2$. (Ans.)

(iii) Since 1 bar $= 10^5$ N/m^2,

Standard atmospheric pressure $= \dfrac{101.32 \times 10^3}{10^5} = 1.0132$ bars

$$= 1013.2 \text{ millibars. (Ans.)}$$

(iv) Standard atmospheric pressure $h_w = \rho_m \times h_m = 13.59 \times 0.76 = 10.33$ m. (Ans.)

Note: 1 kg_f /cm^2 is equal to 10 m of water.

Example 3.2 The local atmospheric pressure is measured to be 750 mm of mercury. Express the following absolute pressures as gauge pressures.

(i) 2 kg_f/cm^2 (ii) 80 kPa

Local atmospheric pressure $= \rho gh = (13.59 \times 1000)\ 9.81 \times 0.75 \text{ N/m}^2 = 99.99 \times 10^3 \text{ N/m}^2$

$$= \frac{99.99 \times 10^3}{9.81} \times 100 \times 100 \text{ kg}_f/\text{cm}^2 = 1.019 \text{ kg}_f/\text{cm}^2.$$

(i) 2 kg_f/cm^2 (absolute) $= 2 - 1.019 = 0.981$ kg_f/cm^2 (gauge). (Ans.)

(ii) 80 kPa (absolute) $= 80 - 99.99 = -19.99$ kPa (gauge) $= 19.99$ kPa (vacuum). (Ans.)

Example 3.3 The bottom opening of a diving bell as shown in the figure is at a depth of 9.5 m below the water surface. If the pressure of air inside is 0.8 kg_f/cm^2 (gauge), to what depth will the water rise in the diving bell?

$p = 0.8 \text{ kg}_f/\text{cm}^2 = 8$ m of water.

$8 = 9.5 - h.$

Therefore, $h = 1.5$ m. (Ans.)

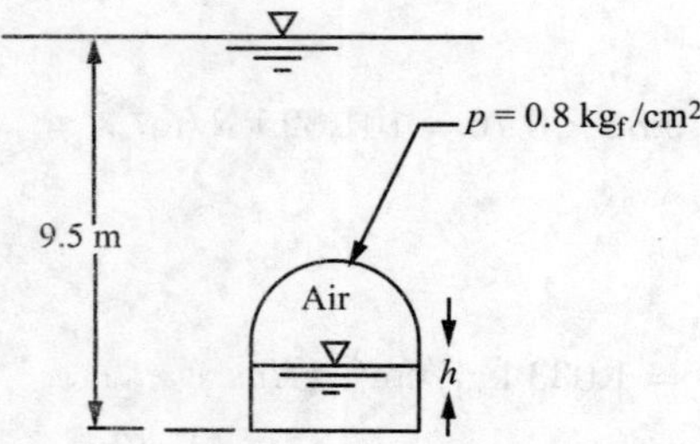

Example 3.3

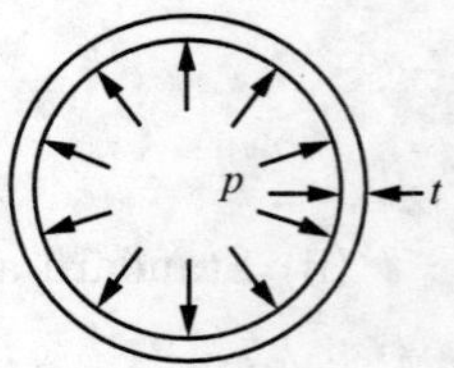

Example 3.4

Example 3.4 A steel penstock 2 m in diameter conveys water at a pressure of 15 kg_f/cm^2. If the working tensile stress in the material of the pipe is 80 MPa, find the required thickness of the wall of the pipe.

The hoop tension $f_t = 80$ MPa.

$$p = 15 \text{ kg}_f/\text{cm}^2 = 15 \times 9.81 \times 10^4 \text{ N/m}^2$$

$$= 1.4715 \text{ MPa}.$$

Total bursting force per metre length of pipe

$$= \text{pressure on projected area}$$

$$= p \times 1 \times d = 2 \times p = 2 \times 1.4715 \text{ MPa} = 2.943 \times 10^6 \text{ N}.$$

Let t be the thickness of the wall of the penstock.

Resisting force per metre length $= 2t \times f_t$.

$$2 \times t \times 80 \times 10^6 = 2.943 \times 10^6 \text{ or } t = 0.0184 \text{ m or } 1.84 \text{ cm. (Ans.)}$$

3.5 Measurement of Pressure

Pressure in fluids is usually measured by means of liquid piezometers and manometers. The Bourdon gauge, shown in Fig. 3.6, is a mechanical gauge commonly used for measuring high pressures. It consists of a flattened tube in the form of an arc.

When it is connected with a high pressure source, the tube deflects outward under pressure and moves the pointer through a linkage mechanism as shown in the figure. It is calibrated to read gauge pressures directly. When open to atmosphere, it reads zero.

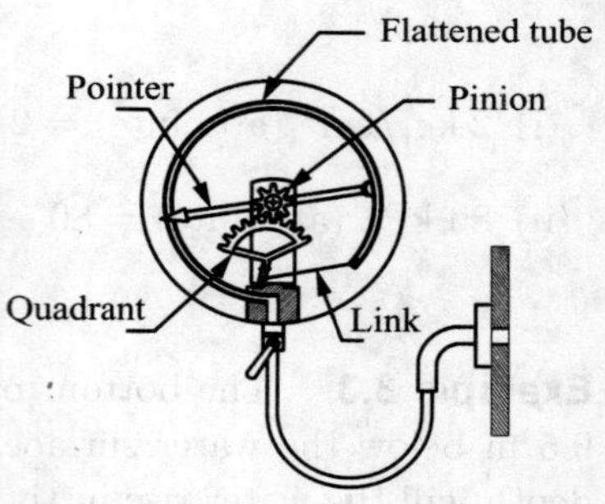

Fig. 3.6 *The Bourdon gauge*

There are piezoelectric transducers using quartz crystals which have diaphragms installed flush with the wall to respond rapidly to change in pressures. They can be used to obtain a continuous record of rapid pressure fluctuations as in turbulent flows.

The local atmospheric pressure can be measured using a mercury barometer. For the measurement of high and low pressures in fluid systems, varied types of liquid manometers are used.

3.6 Liquid Piezometers and Simple Manometers

Piezometers are essentially single column manometers. The usual types of single column manometers are shown in Fig. 3.7. The pressure is calculated by the equation $p = \gamma h$.

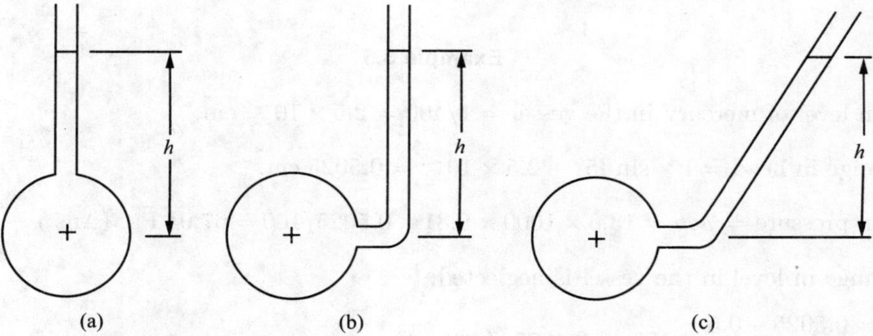

Fig. 3.7 *Manometers for measurement of positive pressures in liquids*

A simple U-tube is shown in Fig. 3.8. It contains a manometric liquid heavier than the fluid flowing in the pipe. In determining the pressure at A in the pipe, the locations of the surfaces of manometric liquid are important. In the figure, N and M are surfaces of manometric liquid in the left and right limb respectively. The liquid has continuous connections between N and N′ (on the other limb) at the same horizontal. This is not the case with M. So pressures at N and N′ are to be equated. p_{N} and $p_{\mathrm{N'}}$ can be expressed in terms of p_{A} and p_{atm} and thus p_{A} can be determined.

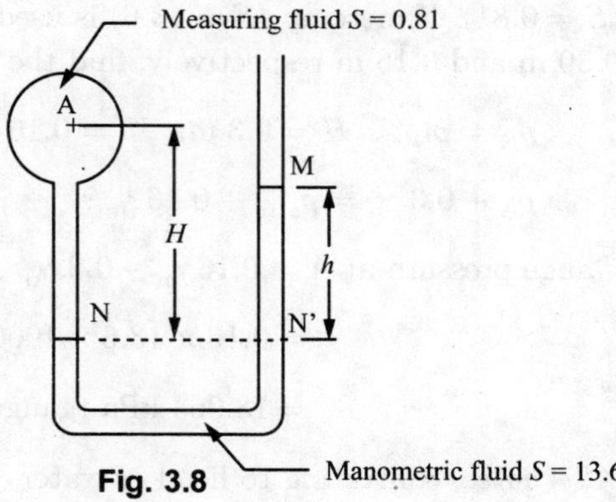

Fig. 3.8

Example 3.5 The figure shows a single column inclined manometer to measure pressure. If the length of the mercury column in the tube changes by 1 cm, what is the change in pressure? What is the percentage error in neglecting the change in level in the vessel?

$$\text{Ratio of areas} = \frac{\pi \times 6^2}{4} \times \frac{4}{\pi \times 0.3^2} = 400.$$

Change in length of column = 1 cm.

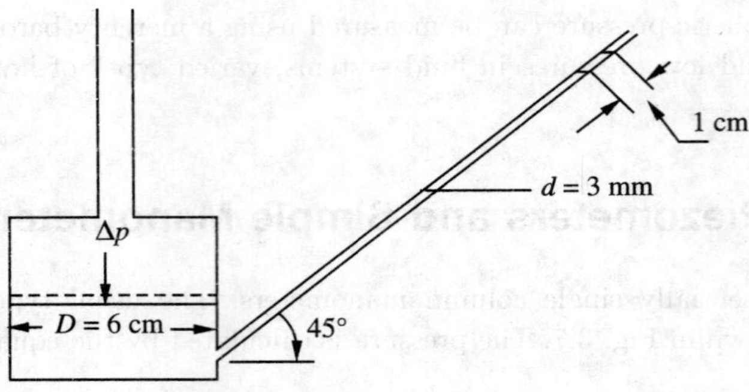

Example 3.5

Change in level of mercury in the vessel $= 1/400 = 2.5 \times 10^{-3}$ cm.

Total change in head $= 1 \times \sin 45° + 2.5 \times 10^{-3} = 0.5025$ cm.

Change in pressure $= \rho g h = 13.6 \times 1000 \times 9.81 \times 0.5025/100 = 67.04$ Pa. (Ans.)

If the change in level in the vessel is neglected,

$$\% \text{ error} = \frac{0.5025 - 0.5}{0.5025} \times 100 = 0.4975\ \%. \text{ (Ans.)}$$

Example 3.6 Figure 3.8 shows a U-tube manometer connected with a pipe carrying an oil ($S = 0.81$). If mercury ($S = 13.6$) is used as the manometric liquid and H and h are noted as 0.30 m and 0.16 m respectively, find the pressure in the pipe A.

$$p_N = p_{N'}; \quad H = 0.3 \text{ m}; \quad h = 0.16 \text{ m}.$$

$$p_A + 0.3\,\gamma_o = p_{atm} + 0.16\,\gamma_m.$$

Gauge pressure at A $= 0.16\gamma_m - 0.3\,\gamma_o$

$$= 0.16 \times 13.6 \times 1000 \times 9.81 - 0.3 \times 0.81 \times 1000 \times 9.81 \text{ Pa}$$

$$= 18.963 \text{ kPa (gauge). (Ans.)}$$

Alternately converting to head of water

$$\frac{p_A}{\gamma_w} = \frac{p_{atm}}{\gamma_w} + 0.16 \times 13.6 - 0.3 \times 0.81 = \frac{p_{atm}}{\gamma_w} + 1.933 \text{ metres of water.}$$

gauge pressure $p_A = 1.933\,\gamma_w = 1.933 \times 1000 \times 9.81 = 18.963$ kPa (gauge). (Ans.)

Example 3.7 The figure shows a U-tube with an enlarged vessel on one side containing a liquid up to level A such that the water level in the other limb is at level B. If the liquid in A is drained to level B′, (in the plane of B), the water level changes by 10 cm to C, find the specific gravity of the liquid.

Let the initial difference in water surface level in the two limbs be y. Equating pressure heads of water (in cm) in both the limbs at level P and P′

$$(15 + y)\ S = y. \qquad \text{(i)}$$

After the liquid is drained to B, the water in the left limb goes up by 10 cm to Q and in the right limb, it falls by 10 cm to C. The difference in water surface reduces to $(y - 2 \times 10)$ cm. Equating the pressure heads of water (in cm) in both limbs, at the new level Q – Q′,

$$(y - 10)\ S = y - 20. \qquad \text{(ii)}$$

Solving (i) and (ii) simultaneously,

$$y = 60 \text{ cm}; \quad \text{and } S = 0.8. \text{ (Ans.)}$$

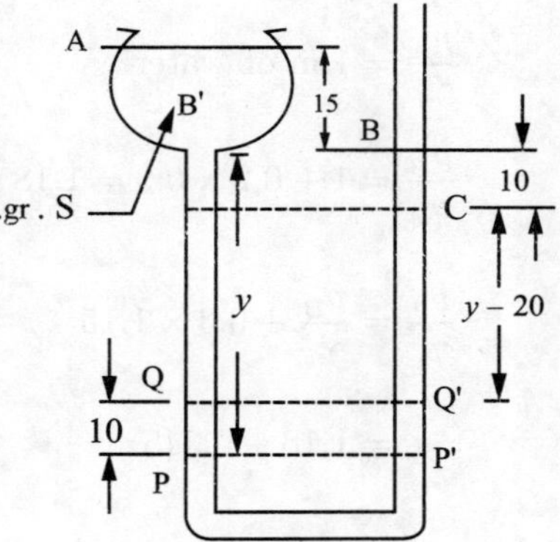

Example 3.7

3.7 Pressure Head and Piezometric Head

At any point inside a static liquid, the pressure head refers to the height of liquid above the point to the free surface. If p_A is the pressure at point A, the pressure head $h_A = p_A/\gamma$.

In Fig. 3.9, points A and A_1 have the same pressure head h_A, whereas at point B the pressure head is h_B. The pressures at A and B are different. The piezometric head at any point, however, refers to the pressure head plus the elevation of the point with reference to an arbitrary datum. In the figure, points A and B have the same piezometric heads because $Z_A + h_A = Z_B + h_B$.

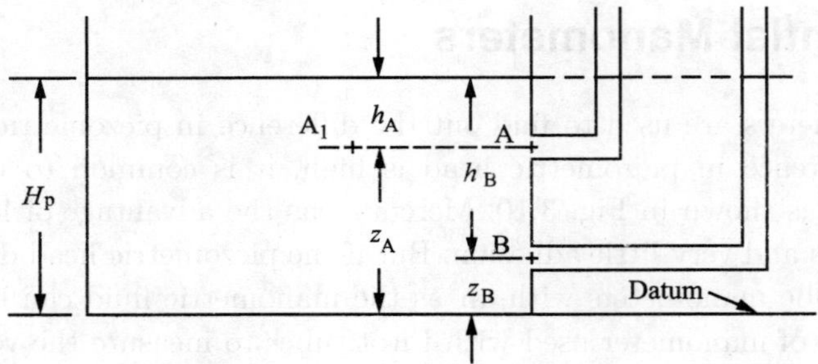

Fig. 3.9 *Pressure head and piezometric head*

Example 3.8 The figure shows a vessel containing different fluids. Find (a) elevations of piezometric surfaces in the piezometers (above the XX′ plane) at P and Q.

Let us have XX′ as the datum.

$p_A = 0.1$ kg /cm^2.

$\frac{p_A}{\gamma_w} = 1$ m of water.

$\frac{p_B}{\gamma_w} = 1 + 0.2 \times 0.9 = 1.18$ m of water.

$\frac{p_P}{\gamma_w} = \frac{p_B}{\gamma_w} + 0.3 \times 1.15$

$= 1.18 + 0.345$

$= 1.525$ m of water.

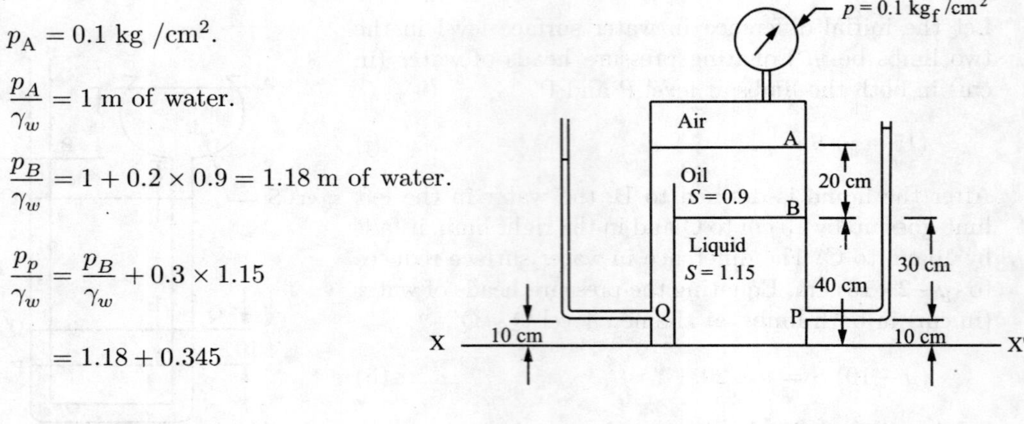

Example 3.8

$\frac{p_P}{\gamma_l} = \frac{p_P}{\gamma_w} \times \frac{\gamma_w}{\gamma_l}$

$= \frac{p_P}{\gamma_w} \times \frac{1}{S_l} = \frac{1.525}{1.15} = 1.326$ m of liquid.

Piezometric head at P above XX′ = 1.326 + 0.1 = 1.426 m. (Ans.)

$\frac{p_Q}{\gamma_w} = \frac{p_A}{\gamma_w} + 0.5 \times 0.9 = 1 + 0.45 = 1.45$ m of water $= \frac{1}{.45} 0.9 = 1.611$ m of oil.

Piezometric head at Q above XX′ = 1.611 + 0.1 = 1.711 m of oil. (Ans.)

3.8 Differential Manometers

Differential manometers are used to find out the difference in piezometric head between two points. If the difference in piezometric head is high, it is common to use mercury as the manometric liquid as shown in Fig. 3.10. Mercury has the advantage of having high density, low vapour pressure and very little adhesion. But if the piezometric head difference is not very high, inverted U-tube manometers with air as the manometric fluid can be used. This is the most common type of manometer used with Pitot tubes to measure the velocity in liquids.

In situations where the piezometric head difference is very low, a magnified difference in head can be obtained by using an inverted U-tube manometer with the manometric liquid having a little lower density than the measuring liquid. In all differential manometers, the manometric liquid has to be immiscible with the measuring liquid and should give a clear common surface.

3.8.1 Measurement of head difference in a venturimeter (U-tube manometer)

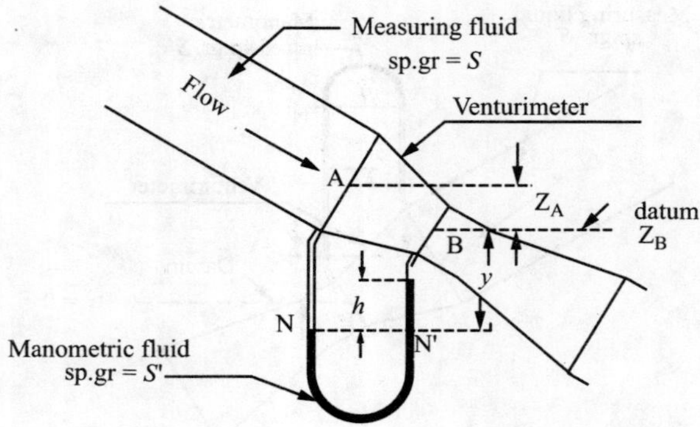

Fig. 3.10 *U-tube manometer connected to venturimeter*

Let γ be the specific weight of the measuring fluid and γ' the specific weight of the manometric liquid. Equating pressure at N and N′,

$$p_A + \gamma(z_A + y) = p_B + (z_B + y - h)\gamma + \gamma' h.$$

Dividing by γ and rearranging,

$$\left(\frac{p_A}{\gamma} + z_A\right) - \left(\frac{p_B}{\gamma} + z_B\right) = h\left(\frac{\gamma'}{\gamma} - 1\right),$$

$$\text{i.e., } p_h = h\left(\frac{\gamma'}{\gamma} - 1\right) = h\left(\frac{S'}{S} - 1\right), \tag{3.2}$$

where p_h is the difference in piezometric head.

Example 3.9 A differential manometer is connected to the inlet and throat of a venturimeter conveying water as shown in Fig. 3.10. Point A is 0.2 m above B. The manometric liquid used is mercury. If the head difference is 30 cm, find (a) the piezometric head difference between points A and B, (b) the pressure difference between points A and B.

$S = 1$; $S' = 13.6$; $\mathrm{Z_A} - \mathrm{Z_B} = 0.2$ m; $h = 0.2$ m.

Piezometric head difference $= p_h = h(S'/S - 1) = 0.3\ (13.6/1 - 1) = 3.78$ m. (Ans.)

$$\left(\frac{p_A}{\gamma} + z_A\right) - \left(\frac{p_B}{\gamma} + z_B\right) = 3.78.$$

Hence, $\dfrac{p_A}{\gamma} - \dfrac{p_B}{\gamma} = 3.78 - (z_A - z_B) = 3.58$ m of water $= 35.12$ kPa. (Ans.)

3.8.2 Measurement of head difference in venturimeter (inverted U-tube manometer)

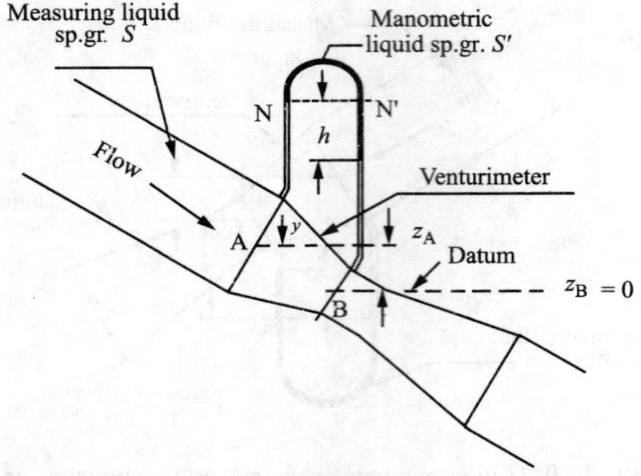

Fig. 3.11 *Inverted U-tube manometer connected to venturimeter*

Equating pressure at N and N′,

$$p_A - (y+h)\gamma = p_B + z_B - (z_A + y)\gamma - h\gamma',$$

$$p_h = \left(\frac{p_A}{\gamma} + z_A\right) - \left(\frac{p_B}{\gamma} + z_B\right) = -h\left(\frac{\gamma'}{\gamma} - 1\right). \tag{3.3}$$

Example 3.10 The differential manometer with an inverted U-tube is connected to the inlet and throat of a venturimeter conveying water. A is 0.3 m above B. The manometric fluid has a specific gravity of 0.95. If the differential head indicated is 30 cm. Find the piezometric head difference between A and B.

Piezometric head difference,

$$p_h = -h(S'/S - 1) = 0.30\ (0.95/1 - 1) = 0.015 \text{ m. (Ans.)}$$

Example 3.11 The figure shows a differential manometer connected to pipes A and B carrying liquids of specific gravity 0.9 and 0.8 respectively. Point B is 0.8 m below A. If the mercury level in the left limb is 0.2 m below A and the difference in levels of mercury surfaces in the two limbs is 0.95 m, find the pressure difference between A and B.

$$\text{BN} = 0.2 + 0.95 - 0.8 = 0.35 \text{ m.}$$

Equating the pressures at N′ and N in terms of head of water,

$$\frac{p_A}{\gamma_w} + S_1 \times 0.2 + S_m \times 0.95 = \frac{p_B}{\gamma_w} + S_2 \times 0.35.$$

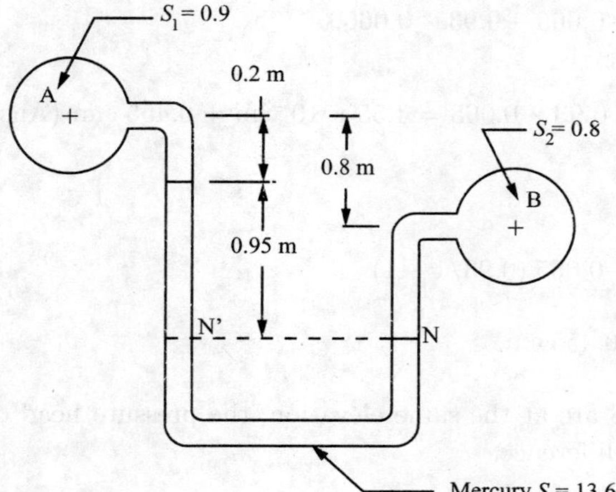

Example 3.11

$$\frac{p_A}{\gamma_w} + 0.9 \times 0.2 + 13.6 \times 0.95 = \frac{p_B}{\gamma_w} + 0.8 \times 0.35.$$

or, $$\frac{p_A - p_B}{\gamma_w} = 0.8 \times 0.35 - 0.9 \times 0.2 - 13.6 \times 0.95 = -12.82 \text{ m of water.}$$

or, $$\frac{p_B - p_A}{\gamma_w} = 12.82 \text{ m.}$$

or, $p_B - p_A = 12.82 \times 9810 \text{ N/m}^2.$

$(p_B - p_A) = 125.76$ kPa. (Ans.)

Example 3.12 The dynamic and static openings of a Prandtl's Pitot static tube in water are connected to an inverted U-tube manometer using a liquid of relative density 0.93 as the manometric fluid. When the difference in level of the separating surface in the two limbs is 6.5 cm, find the difference in head in terms of water.

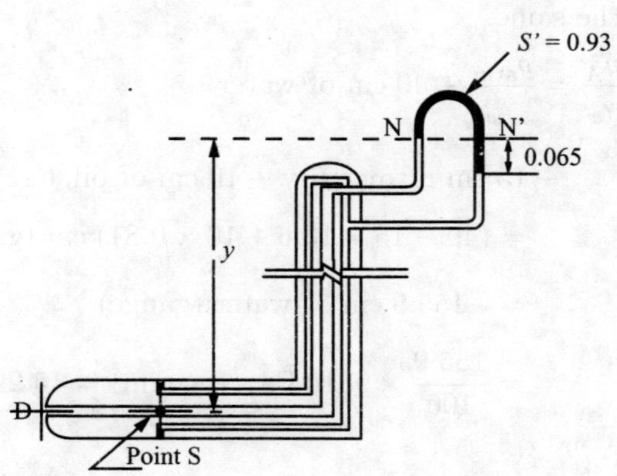

Example 3.12

Measuring pressures in terms of head of water,

$$\frac{p_N}{\gamma_w} = \frac{p_D}{\gamma_w} - y. \qquad \text{(i)}$$

$$\frac{p_{N'}}{\gamma_w} = \frac{p_S}{\gamma_w} - (y - 0.065) - 0.93 \times 0.065. \qquad \text{(ii)}$$

Equating the pressure heads at N and N′ and neglecting the thickness of the Pitot tube,

$$\frac{p_D}{\gamma_w} - y = \frac{p_S}{\gamma_w} - y + 0.065 - 0.93 \times 0.065,$$

or, $$\frac{p_D - p_S}{\gamma_w} = 0.065 - 0.93 \times 0.065 = 4.55 \times 10^{-3}\text{m} = 0.455 \text{ cm. (Ans.)}$$

Alternate solution

$$\Delta h_p = -h(S'/S - 1) = -0.065\ (0.93/1 - 1)$$

$$= 4.55 \times 10^{-3} \text{ m} = 0.455 \text{ cm.}$$

Since the points D and S are at the same elevation, the pressure head difference is the same as the piezometric head difference.

Example 3.13 Find the gauge pressure at point A for the system of manometers shown in the figure.

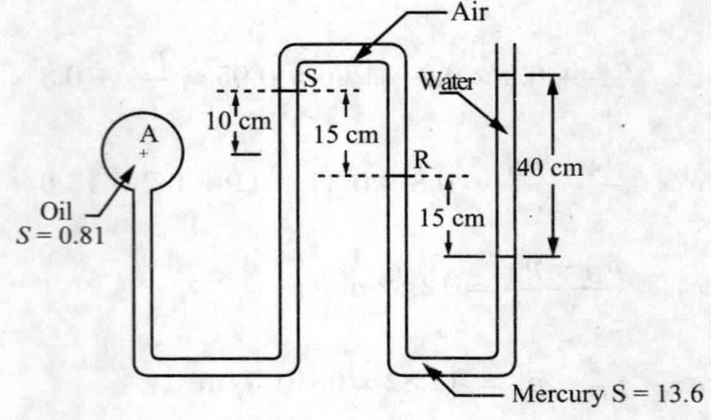

Example 3.13

Since air is very light compared to liquids, the pressure at R and S can be assumed to be the same.

$$\frac{p_A}{\gamma_w} = \frac{p_{atm}}{\gamma_w} + 40 \text{ cm of water}$$

$$- 15 \text{ cm of mercury} + 10 \text{ cm of oil.}$$

$$= (40 - 15 \times 13.6 + 10 \times 0.81) \text{ cm (gauge)}$$

$$= -155.9 \text{ cm of water (gauge).}$$

$$= \frac{155.9}{100} \times 9810 \text{ Pa (vacuum)} = 15.294 \text{ kPa (vacuum). (Ans.)}$$

3.9 Accuracy and Sensitivity of Manometers

In the usual type of differential manometers, the differential head is limited to low pressure differences. By using a mercury manometer, high differential heads can be conveniently measured. Inverted U-tube manometers can be used for measurement of low differential heads.

Inclined manometers allow measurements with greater accuracy. The sensitivity of a manometer refers to the rapidity at which it will respond to pressure changes. Liquid manometers usually have low sensitivity and hence for dynamic measurements, pressure transducers are used.

3.10 Micro-manometer

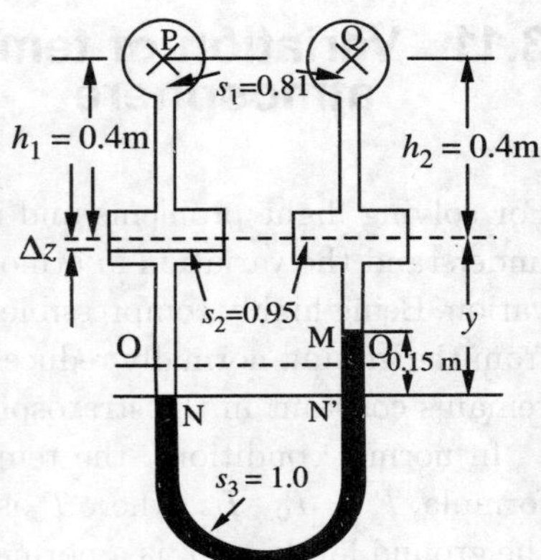

Fig. 3.12 *Micro-manometer*

The micro-manometer consists of a U-tube with enlarged ends at the top. A liquid of high relative density will be at the bottom and that of a slightly lower density will be poured on top, the top surface being within the enlarged ends. Due to pressure difference on the surfaces, the common surface between the liquids in the two limbs will be displaced as shown in Fig. 3.12. The pressures at N and N′ can be expressed in terms of pressures at P and Q and the columns of liquid above. Equating p_{N} and $p_{\mathrm{N'}}$ the difference in pressure can be found.

Example 3.14 In a micro-manometer, the specific gravity of the liquids used at the bottom and top portions of the U-tube are 1.0 and 0.95 respectively. The ratio of areas at the enlarged end to that of the tube is 20. If the displacement of the common surface is 15 cm, when connected to two pipes P and Q conveying oil of specific gravity 0.81 as shown in Fig. 3.12, find the difference in pressure between P and Q.

Equating the volumes displaced,

$$a \times L/2 = A \times \Delta z,$$

or, $$\Delta z = \frac{L.a}{2A} = \frac{0.15}{2} \times \frac{1}{20} = 0.00375.$$

Equating the pressure heads at N′ and N,

$$\frac{p_Q}{\gamma_w} + (h_2 - \Delta z) \times s_1 + (y + \Delta z - L/2) \times s_2 + L \times s_3 = \frac{p_P}{\gamma_w} + (h_1 + \Delta z) \times s_1 + (y + L/2 - \Delta z) \times s_2.$$

$$\frac{p_P}{\gamma_w} = \frac{p_Q}{\gamma_w} + (h_2 - \Delta z) \times s_1 + (y + \Delta z - L/2) \times s_2 + L \times s_3 - (y + L/2 - \Delta z) \times s_2 - (h_1 + \Delta z) \times s_1.$$

$\Delta z = 0.00375$; $h_2 = 0.4$ m; $h_1 = 0.4$ m; $L = 0.15$; $s_1 = 0.81$; $s_2 = 0.95$; $s_3 = 1.0$.

$$\frac{p_P}{\gamma_w} - \frac{p_Q}{\gamma_w} = (0.4 - 0.00375) \times 0.81 + (0.00375 - 0.075) \times 0.95 + 0.15 \times 1.0 - (0.075 - 0.00375) \times 0.95 - (0.4 + 0.00375) \times 0.81$$

$$= 0.32 - 0.0677 + 0.15 - 0.0677 - 0.327 = 0.0086 \text{ m of water},$$

or $p_P - p_Q = 0.0086 \times 1000 \times 9.81 = 87.37$ Pa. (Ans.)

Note: It may be noted in the above problem that for a small change of pressure head, of about 0.0086 m of water between P and Q, the change in the common level in the narrow tube is 0.15 m. This is the advantage of a micro-manometer.

3.11 Variation of temperature and pressure in the atmosphere

For solving flight problems and studying the stability of the atmosphere, it is important to understand the variation in atmospheric temperature and pressure. Pressure reduces with elevation. Being highly compressible, the density of air also varies with elevation. The temperature from the ground normally reduces linearly up to an elevation of 11 km (troposphere) and then remains constant in the stratosphere.

In normal conditions, the temperature has a linear reduction with elevation given by the formula, $T_z = T_0 - Lz$, where T_z is the temperature at an elevation of z, T_0 is the temperature at the ground level and L is a normal adiabatic lapse rate equal to 0.0065 K/m. The temperature is measured in kelvin. The dry adiabatic lapse rate can be 0.0098 K/m.

3.11.1 Determination of dry adiabatic lapse rate

The basic equations are the perfect gas law, $pv = RT$ and the adiabatic process law, $pv^k =$ constant. k is the ratio of $c_p/c_v =$ the ratio of specific heat at constant pressure and specific heat at constant volume respectively. $c_p - c_v = R$ from which c_p can be found to be $Rk/(k-1)$ for dry air, $R = 287$ J/kg K and $k = 1.4$. Hence,

$$c_p = 287 \times \frac{1.4}{(1.4-1)} = 1005 \text{ J/kg K.}$$

Consider a parcel of air rising under adiabatic conditions. The total heat exchange is zero, the air will expand doing work, and the internal energy will reduce.

$$dq = 0 = dU + W = c_v dT + pdv$$

$$= (c_p dT - RdT) + pdv$$

$$= c_p dT - d(pv) + pdv = c_p dT - vdp.$$

Substituting the relationship $dp = \rho g dz$ and $\rho v = 1$,

$$L = -dT/dz = g/c_p. \tag{3.4}$$

In dry adiabatic conditions, the temperature lapse rate

$$L = -dT/dz = g/c_p = 9.81/1005 = 0.0098 \text{ K/m.}$$

But under normal conditions of humid atmosphere, the value of lapse rate can be taken as 0.0065 K/ m. This is mainly because of the humidity in the atmosphere. An equivalent k value can be assumed as 1.235; the corresponding value of c_p is 1509 J/kg K.

3.11.2 Calculation of pressure and specific mass of air at any elevation

The pressure at any elevation can be calculated by assuming a lapse rate. The variation of acceleration due to gravity g and the gas constant R can be neglected.

$$\frac{dp}{dz} = -\rho g = -\frac{pg}{RT};$$

Separating the variables and integrating between limits 0 to z,

$$\int \frac{dp}{p} = \int \frac{g}{RT} dz$$

Assuming variation in temperature at a lapse rate L

$$T = T_0 - Lz$$

$$\int \frac{dp}{p} = -\int \frac{gdz}{R(T_0 - Lz)};$$

Integrating for p from limits p_0 to p_z and for z, from 0 to z,

$$\ln \frac{p_z}{p_0} = \frac{g}{RL} \ln \frac{T_0 - Lz}{T_0}$$

and hence,

$$p_z = p_0 \left(1 - \frac{Lz}{T_0}\right)^{\frac{g}{RL}} \tag{3.5}$$

3.11.3 Stability of atmosphere

In stable atmospheric conditions, pollutants like chimney exhausts, carbon dust and automobile exhausts, once trapped, cannot be dispersed upwards. A parcel of air containing them, if taken upwards will be of higher density than the surrounding air and sink down again. This is the case when the atmospheric lapse rate is less than the normal lapse rate and also when there is an inversion of temperature (the temperature increases with elevation). When the lapse rate is greater than the normal lapse rate, it is called the super-adiabatic lapse rate and the atmosphere is unstable. The pollutants if any will be dispersed upwards leaving the area safe.

Example 3.15 Calculate the pressure, temperature and density of air at a height of 7 km for the normal atmospheric conditions, given the ground temperature as 293 K and pressure as 1.013 k Pa.

$p_0 = 101.3$ kPa; $z = 7000$ m.; $T_0 = 293$ K ; $R = 287$ J/kg K.

ii) Taking into account the temperature variation

$$T_z = T_0 - Lz = 293 - 0.0065 \times 7000 = 247.5 \text{ K (Ans.)}$$

$$p_z = p_0\left(1 - \frac{Lz}{T_0}\right)^{\frac{g}{RL}} = 101.3\left(1 - \frac{0.0065 \times 7000}{293}\right)^{\frac{9.81}{287\times0.0065}} = 41.17 \text{ kPa (Ans.)}$$

$$\rho_z = \frac{p_z}{RT_z} = \frac{41.17 \times 10^3}{287 \times 247.5} = 0.587 \text{ kg/m}^3. \text{ (Ans.)}$$

Example 3.16 Assuming the polytropic law $pv^{1.3}$ = constant for the humid atmosphere, find the lapse rate. $R = 287$ J/kg K

$$c_p = Rk/(k-1) = 1243.67 \text{ J/kg K};$$

$$\text{Lapse rate} = -\frac{dT}{dz} = g/C_p$$

$$= 9.81/1243.67 = 0.0079 \text{ K/m (Ans)}$$

Example 3.17 Discuss the stability of the atmosphere when the temperature on the ground is 30°C and that at an elevation of 500 m is 28°C. Assume a normal lapse rate of 0.0065 K/m.

$$L_n = 0.0065 \text{ K/m};$$

$$L_a = (30 - 28)/500 = 0.004 \text{ K/m}$$

$$L_a < L_n;$$

Hence it is stable. This implies that air pollutants, once trapped will not be able to escape to upper layers.

3.11.4 Standard atmosphere

In order to compare the performance of aircrafts tested under varying conditions of pressure and temperature, the International Civil Aviation Organization (ICAO) has specified the values for standard atmosphere at sea level as follows.

$P_0 = 101.36$ k Pa:

$T_0 = 288$ K;

$\rho_0 = 1.226$ kg/m^3;

$R = 287$ J/kg K.

REVIEW QUESTIONS AND PROBLEMS

3.1 Define Pascal's law.

3.2 What do you mean by a single column manometer?

3.3 Distinguish between a simple manometer and a differential manometer.

3.4 Explain with sketches how (i) an inverted U-tube manometer and (ii) an inclined U-tube manometer is used to measure small pressure differences.

3.5 The pressure at a point P in a pipe is 150 kPa gauge. If the atmospheric pressure is 75.7 cm of mercury, what is the absolute pressure?

3.6 Convert a pressure head of 250 kN/m^2 of an oil of mass density 900 kg/m^3 into metres.

3.7 Determine the pressure at a depth of 4 m below the free surface of an oil of specific gravity 0.75.

3.8 Express 10.2 m of water in N/m^2.

3.9 The two limbs of a U-tube differential mercury manometer are connected to horizontal pipes A and B conveying water. A is 1m above B. If the level of mercury in the limb connected to A is higher than that connected to B by 10 cm, find (i) the difference in piezometric head and (ii) the difference in pressure head between water in the pipes A and B.

3.10 The left limb of a single U-tube manometer containing mercury is connected to a pipe in which a fluid of specific gravity 0.8 is flowing at a pressure below atmospheric pressure. The other end of the manometer is open to the atmosphere. Find the vacuum pressure in the pipe, if the level of mercury in the left limb of the manometer is 5 cm above the level in the right limb and 30 cm below the centre of the pipe.

3.11 An inverted U-tube manometer with an inclination of 30 degree and a manometric liquid with $S = 0.93$ in a pitot tube is used to measure velocity in water. If the distance between the separating surfaces in the two limbs is 7.5 cm, find the velocity. Assume that the coefficient of the Pitot tube is 0.97.

3.12 A plane is flying at an elevation of 11 km. If the lapse rate is 0.0065 K/m and the temperature and pressure at sea level are 288 K and 101.36 k Pa respectively, find the temperature, pressure and density of air at the level of the plane.

ANSWERS

3.5. 251 kPa; **3.6.** 28.316 m; **3.7.** 29.43 kN/m^2; **3.8.** 100.062 kPa; **3.9.** −1.26 m; −2.26 m; **3.10.** 9,025.2 Pa; **3.11.** 0.2201 m/s; **3.12.** 216.5 K, 22.64 kPa, 0.364 kg/m^3

4 Pressure on Immersed Surfaces

Geometrical properties of plane areas—Pressure head and piezometric head—Pressure on surfaces—Total pressure on immersed bodies and centre of pressure

4.1 Some Geometrical Properties

4.1.1 First and second moments of area

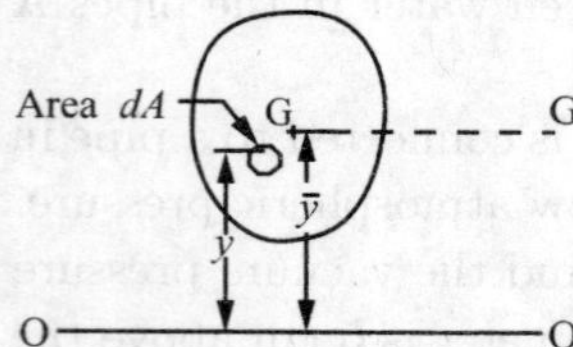

Fig. 4.1 *First and second moments of an area*

Consider the area A and the moments of the area about the line OO (Refer to Fig. 4.1). The first moment of area about OO is $\int y dA$, which will be equal to $A\overline{y}$, where A is the area and $\overline{y}$ is the distance of the centre of gravity of area from OO.

The second moment of area (area moment of inertia) $I_{OO} = \int y^2 dA$, but by the parallel axis theorem, $I_{OO} = I_{GG} + A\overline{y}^2$, where I_{GG} is the moment of inertia about an axis GG parallel to OO through the centre of gravity G.

4.1.2 Areas, position of centroid and I_{GG} of some common geometrical figures

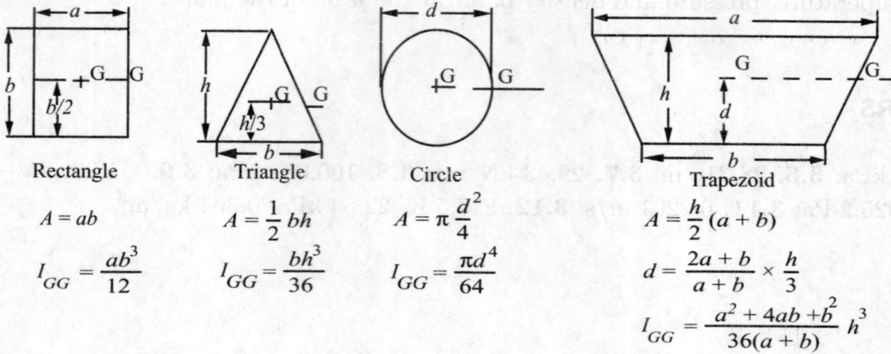

Fig. 4.2 *Geometrical parameters of common figures*

4.2 Pressure on Surfaces

4.2.1 Definition

In a static fluid, the force on an immersed surface can only be normal to the surface. Any tangential component of force on the surface will set the fluid in motion. If p is the pressure acting at point P (mid-point of CD in Fig. 4.3) on an elemental area dA, the total pressure will be the resultant sum of quantities pdA for the whole area.

For any imaginary surface within a fluid, the total pressure on either side, $P = \int pdA$ should be the same as shown in Fig. 4.3, because there cannot be any net force on it to set this surface in motion.

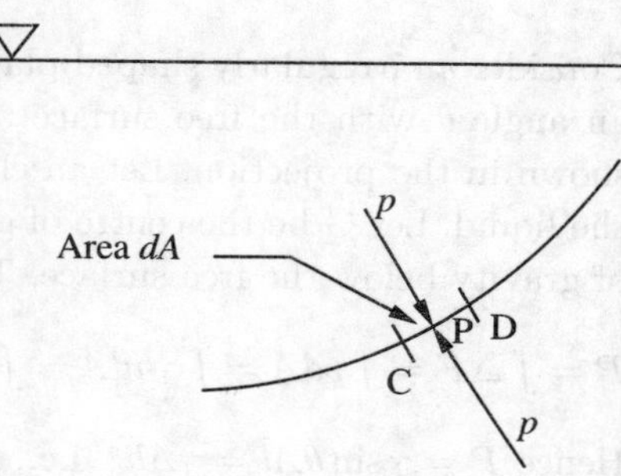

Fig. 4.3 *Pressure on an immersed surface*

4.2.2 Total pressure on an immersed surface (general case)

Figure 4.4 shows the upper surface AB and the lower surface A′B′ of an imaginary lamina inside a tank of water 1 m wide. The water is up to the level DE. PQ is another surface exactly similar to A′B′. Since the prism DEABCD is in equilibrium, the horizontal forces and vertical forces on it must balance. The force P_1 on DC is balanced by an equal and opposite force on AE. The force P_2 on CB should be balanced by the force exerted by surface AB. Hence the horizontal component of the force on AB, $P_h = P_2$.

The weight of the water in prism DEABCD, W should be balanced by the upward force exerted by the surface of AB on the water. Hence $P_v = W$. The resultant force of water on AB is R as shown in the figure. The force F on lamina AB is equal and opposite to that on A'B' equal to R.

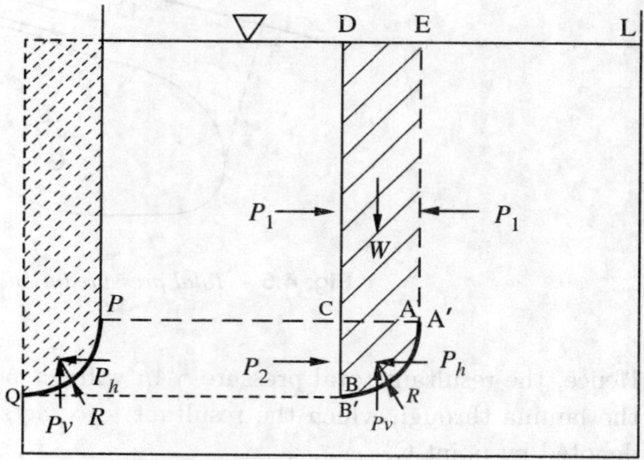

Fig. 4.4 *Forces acting on an immersed surface*

The surface PQ is exactly similar to surface A′B′ and it has the same pressure as on A′B′; the force on it is R. The piezometric level on any point on PQ will also be up to the level of DEL. Hence the pressure on PQ can be found by imagining water on PQ to a level of DEL.

4.3 Total Pressure Acting on an Immersed Inclined Plane Lamina

Consider an irregularly shaped plane lamina AB kept immersed in a liquid. Let its plane make an angle θ with the free surface and cut it on a line OO′. The true shape of the lamina is shown in the projection. Let an elemental area dA be at a depth h below the free surface of the liquid. Let G be the centre of gravity of the lamina. Let $\bar{h} = h_G$ be the depth of the centre of gravity below the free surface. Then the elementary force on the area dA will be

$$P = \int \Delta F = \int p dA = \int \gamma h dA = \int \gamma l \sin\theta dA = \gamma \sin\theta \times \text{ First moment of area } A \text{ about OO}'$$

$$\text{Hence } P = \gamma \sin\theta A\bar{l} = \gamma A\bar{h} \quad \text{i.e., } P = \gamma A\bar{h} \tag{4.1}$$

The lamina will have higher pressures at lower regions compared to the upper part.

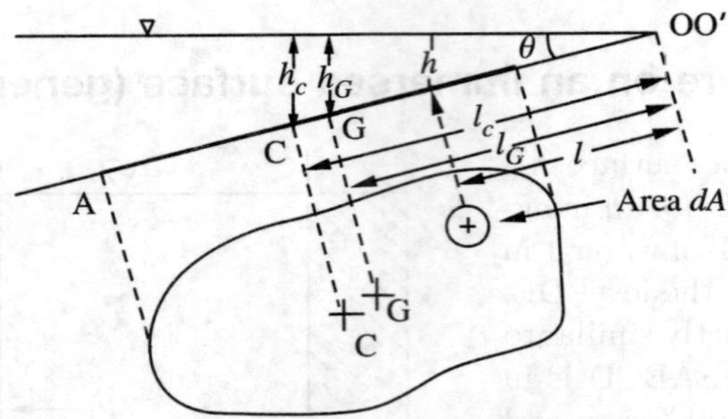

Fig. 4.5 *Total pressure on an immersed plane lamina*

Hence, the resultant total pressure $\gamma A\bar{h}$ will act below the centre of gravity G. The point on the lamina through which the resultant force acts is called the centre of pressure. Let it be denoted by point C.

Taking moments of forces about OO′,

$$F \times l_c = \int \Delta F \times l = \int \gamma \, l \sin\theta \; dA \times l = \gamma \int l^2 \sin\theta \; dA$$

$$= \gamma \sin\theta \times \text{2nd moment of area about OO}'$$

$$l_c = \frac{\gamma \sin\theta \times \text{2nd moment of area about OO}'}{F}$$

$$= \frac{\gamma \sin\theta I'_{\text{OO}}}{\gamma A\bar{h}} = \frac{\gamma \sin\theta I_{\text{OO}'}}{\gamma \sin\theta \; A\bar{l}} = \frac{I_{\text{OO}'}}{A\bar{l}} = \frac{I_{\text{GG}} + A\bar{l}^2}{A\bar{l}} \text{ (parallel axis theorem).}$$

Hence, $l_c = \bar{l} + \dfrac{I_{GG}}{A\bar{l}}$.

or, multiplying throughout by $\sin\theta$,

$$l_c \sin\theta = \bar{l}\sin\theta + \frac{I_{GG}\sin\theta}{A\bar{l}}.$$

Since $h_c = l_c \sin\theta$ and $\bar{h} = \bar{l}\sin\theta$,

$$h_c = \bar{h} + \frac{I_{GG}\sin^2\theta}{A\bar{h}}.$$

Example 4.1 A dam with a vertical upstream face 20 m high retains water to a depth of 18 m. Find the total pressure per m run of the dam and the location of the centre of pressure.

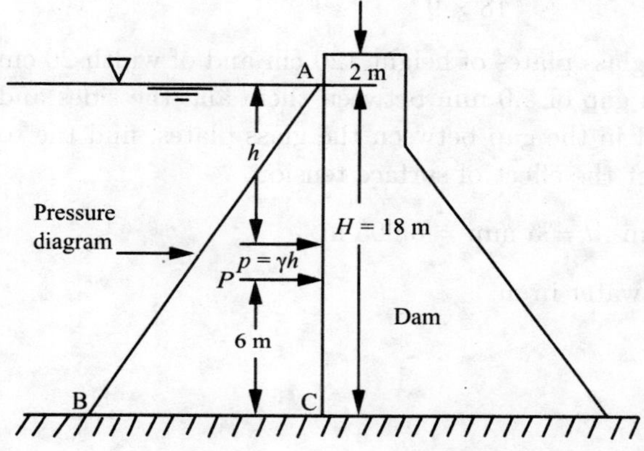

Example 4.1

The pressure intensity at any depth h below the water surface is equal to γh. Consider one metre width of the dam. Since the pressure varies linearly with h, the variation can be depicted by a triangle (hydrostatic pressure distribution).

Total pressure P = area of the pressure diagram ABC × width

$$= \frac{1}{2}(\gamma_w H)H \times 1 = \gamma_w \frac{H^2}{2} = 1000 \times 9.81 \times \frac{18^2}{2} = 1.589 \times 10^6 \text{ N. (Ans.)}$$

The point of application of the hydrostatic force can be obtained by finding the depth of the centroid of the pressure distribution diagram. Being a triangle, the centroid will be at $H/3$ i.e., $18/3 = 6.0$ m above the base.

Hence, depth of the centre of pressure = 18 − 6

= 12 m below the water surface. (Ans.)

Alternately,

$$\gamma = 1000 \times 9.81 = 9810 \frac{\text{N}}{\text{m}^3}.$$

$$A = 1 \times H = 18 \text{ m}^2. \text{ (1 m width is considered).}$$

$$\bar{h} = \frac{H}{2} = \frac{18}{2} = 9.0 \text{ m}.$$

$$P = \gamma A\bar{h} = 9810 \times 18 \times 9 = 1.589 \times 10^6 \text{ N. (Ans.)}$$

$$\theta = 90°. \text{ Therefore, } \sin\theta = 1; \bar{h} = 9 \text{ m}, \quad I_{GG} = \frac{bd^3}{12} = \frac{1 \times 18^3}{12} = 486 \text{ m}^4.$$

$$h_c = \bar{h} + \frac{I_{GG}\sin^2\theta}{A\bar{h}} = 9 + \frac{486 \times 1}{18 \times 9} = 12 \text{ m. (Ans.)}$$

Example 4.2 Two glass plates of height 120 cm and of width 20 cm are held vertically so that there is a uniform gap of 5.0 mm between them and the sides and bottom are sealed. If 1 kg of water is poured in the gap between the glass plates, find the total pressure on one of the glass plates. Neglect the effect of surface tension.

$$b = 20 \text{ cm} = 0.2 \text{ m}, \ t = 5 \text{ mm} = 0.005 \text{ m}.$$

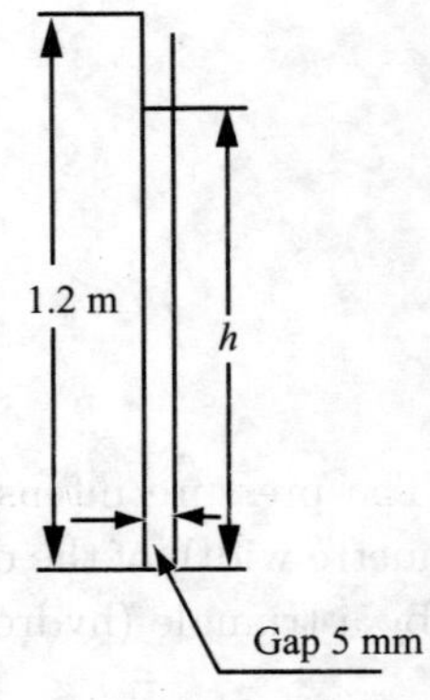

Example 4.2

Let h be the height of water in m.

Mass of water = 1 kg.

$$\rho = 1000 \text{ kg/m}^3.$$

Volume $\forall$ of water = 1/1000 m^3 = bth.

$$h = \frac{\forall}{bt} = \frac{1}{1000 \times 0.2 \times 0.005} = 1 \text{ m}.$$

$$\gamma_w = 1000 \times 9.81 \text{ N/m}^3.$$

$$A = 0.2 \times 1 = 0.2 \text{ m}^2.$$

$$\bar{h} = \frac{1}{2} = 0.5 \text{ m}.$$

Total pressure on the glass plate = $\gamma A\bar{h} = 9810 \times 0.2 \times 0.5 = 981$ N. (Ans.)

Example 4.3 A rectangular gate 5 m × 3 m is placed under water such that the 3 m edges are parallel to the free surface. The top and bottom edges are 4.0 m and 8.0 m below the water surface respectively. Determine the total pressure and the position of the centre of pressure on the gate.

$\gamma = 1000 \times 9.81\ \text{N/m}^3$; $A = 5 \times 3 = 15\ \text{m}^2$.

$\overline{h} = 4 + 2 = 6$ m.

$P = \gamma A\overline{h} = 1000 \times 9.81 \times 15 \times 6 = 8.829 \times 10^5$ N. (Ans.)

$\sin\theta = 4/5 = 0.8$.

$I_{GG} = bd^3/12 = 3 \times 5^3/12 = 31.25\ \text{m}^4$.

$$h_c = \overline{h} + \frac{I_{GG}\sin^2\theta}{A\overline{h}} = 6 + \frac{31.25 \times 0.8^2}{15 \times 6} = 6.22\ \text{m. (Ans.)}$$

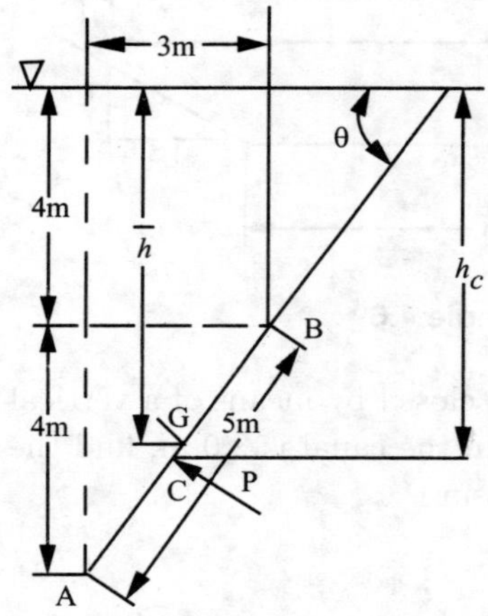

Example 4.3

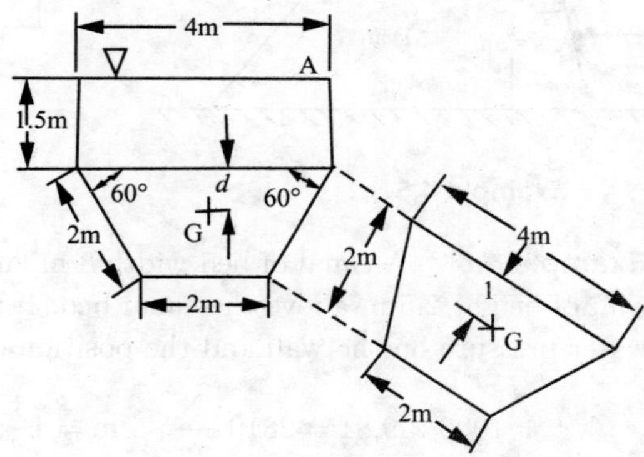

Example 4.4

Example 4.4 A hopper is to be filled up with a liquid of relative density 1.2 to a level A as shown in the figure. Find the total pressure and the centre of pressure on one of the sloping sides.

$\gamma = 1.2 \times 1000 \times 9.81\ \text{N/m}^3$.

$$A = \frac{1}{2} \times h(a + b) = \frac{1}{2} \times 2 \times (4 + 2) = 6\ \text{m}^2; \quad l = \frac{2 \times 2 + 4}{4 + 2} \times \frac{2}{3} = \frac{8}{9}.$$

$d = l \sin 60° = 0.77$ m.

$\overline{h} = 1.5 + d = 1.5 + 0.77 = 2.27$ m.

Therefore, total pressure $P = \gamma A\overline{h} = 11772 \times 6 \times 2.27 = 1.603 \times 10^5$ N. (Ans.)

Example 4.5 A gate closes a circular opening of 2 m diameter in a dam. If the centre line of the opening is 12 m below the water surface and the inclination of the gate to the vertical is 10°, find the total pressure on the gate and the position of the centre of pressure.

$$\gamma_w = 1000 \times 9.81 = 9810 \text{ N/m}^3; \; A = \pi\, d^2/4 = \pi 2^2/4 = \pi/4.$$

$$I_{GG} = \frac{\pi(2)^4}{64} = \frac{\pi}{4} \text{ m}^4.$$

$$\text{Therefore, } h_c = \bar{h} + \frac{I_{GG}\sin^2\theta}{A\bar{h}} = 12 + \frac{(\pi/4)\sin^2 80}{\pi \times 12} = 12.02 \text{ m. (Ans.)}$$

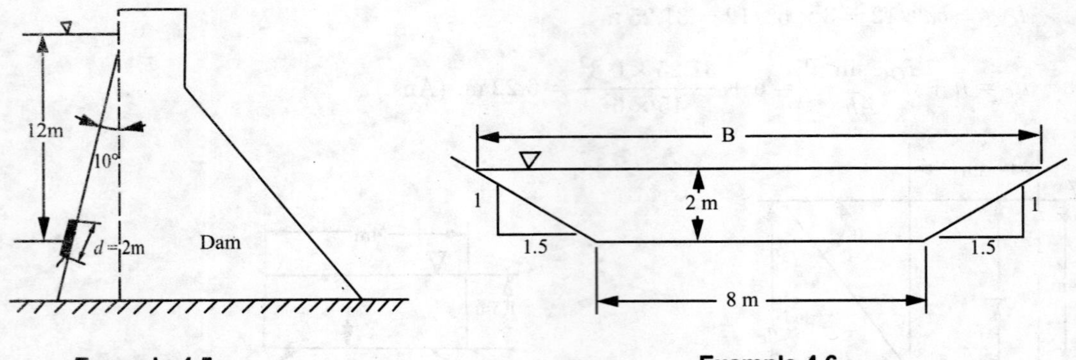

Example 4.5 **Example 4.6**

Example 4.6 A canal of bed width 8 m and side slope 1.5:1 is closed by means of a vertical wall of height 2.5 m above the canal bed. If the depth of water in the canal is 2.0 m, find the water pressure on the wall and the position of the centre of pressure.

$$\gamma = 1000 \times 9.81 = 9810 \frac{\text{N}}{\text{m}^3}; \quad \text{m} = 1\frac{1}{2};$$

$$B = b + 2md = 8 + 2 \times 1\frac{1}{2} \times 2 = 14 \text{ m}.$$

$$A = \frac{14+8}{2} \times 2 = 22 \text{ m}^2.$$

$$\bar{h} = \frac{14 + 2\times 8}{14+8} \times \frac{2}{3} = \frac{10}{11} = 0.909 \text{ m}.$$

Therefore, total water pressure on the wall, $P = \gamma A\bar{h}$

$$= 9810 \times 22 \times 0.909 = 1.962 \times 10^5 \text{ N. (Ans.)}$$

$$I_{GG} = \frac{14^2 + 4\times 14 \times 8 + 8^2}{36(14+8)} \times 2^3 = 7.15 \text{ m}^4.$$

Since $\theta = 90°, \sin\theta = 1.$

$$\text{Therefore, } h_c = \bar{h} + \frac{I_{GG}\sin^2\theta}{A\bar{h}} = 0.909 + \frac{7.15 \times 1}{22 \times 0.909}$$

$$= 1.267 \text{ m below the water surface. (Ans.)}$$

Example 4.7 An opening to an oil pipe of 1m diameter is closed by a butterfly valve as shown in the figure. Find the force F at the bottom so that it will not open until the head is 4 m above the centre line of the pipe. Specific gravity of oil = 0.9.

$$\gamma_{oil} = 0.9 \times 1000 \times 9.81 \text{ N/m}^3 = 8829 \text{ N/m}^3.$$

$$A = \frac{\pi}{4} \times 1^2 = 0.785 \text{ m}^2; \bar{h} = 4 \text{ m};$$

Therefore, total pressure acting on the gate, $P = \gamma A\bar{h} = 8829 \times 0.785 \times 4$

$$= 27.72 \times 10^3 \text{ N} = 27.72 \text{ kN}.$$

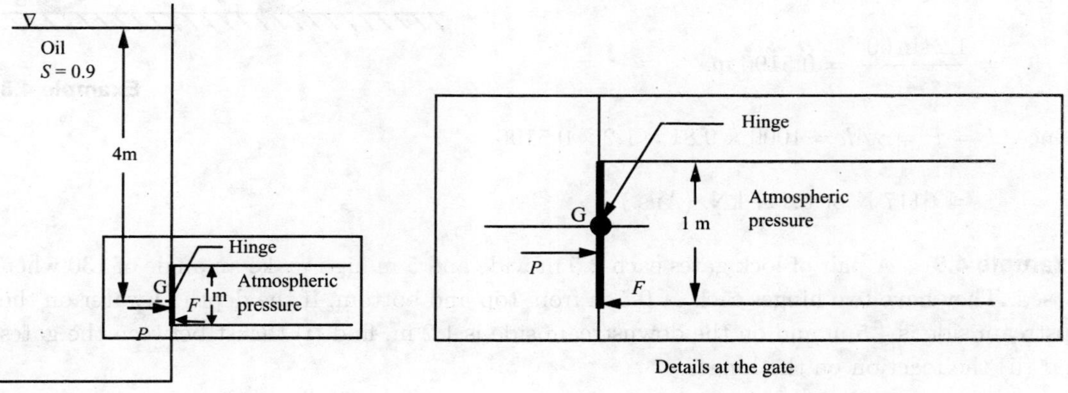

Example 4.7

Therefore, $h_c = \bar{h} + \dfrac{I_{GG} \sin^2\theta}{A\bar{h}} = 4 + \dfrac{0.049 \times 1}{0.785 \times 4} = 4.0156$ m.

The moments of force P and F about G should balance each other.

$$F \times 0.5 = P \times 0.0156 \quad \text{or,} \quad F = \frac{27.72 \times 10^3 \times 0.0156}{0.5} = 864.86 \text{ N. (Ans.)}$$

Example 4.8 The figure shows an arrangement to store water up to a particular level in a tank above which the flash board will collapse allowing overflow. What is the maximum load the strut has to take? Neglect the weight of the flashboard. Assume the width of board to be 1 m.

If the resultant pressure acts above C, the arrangement will collapse. Hence the maximum height of the centre of pressure is up to C.

The distribution of pressure on the board is triangular and hence the centre of pressure can be at C only if the length of the flash board, AD = 3 × AC = 3 × 0.4 = 1.2 m.

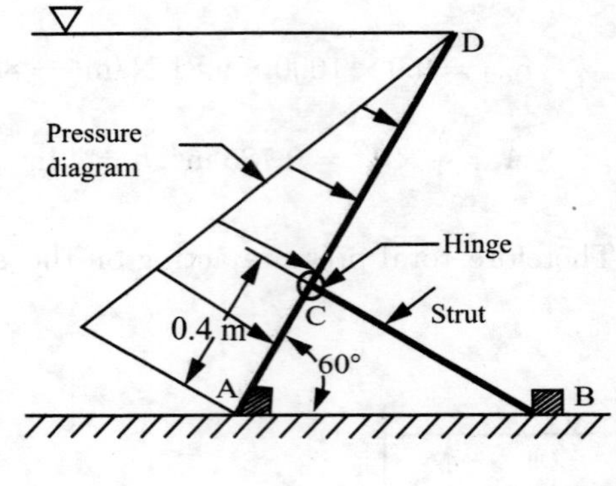

Example 4.8

Now, $A = 1.2 \times 1 = 1.2\ \text{m}^2$.

$$\gamma = 1000 \times 9.81\ \text{N/m}^3.$$

$$\bar{h} = \frac{h}{2}$$

$$= \frac{1.2 \sin\theta}{2}$$

$$= \frac{1.2 \sin 60^\circ}{2} = 0.5196\ \text{m}.$$

Hence, $T = P = \gamma A\bar{h} = 1000 \times 9.81 \times 1.2 \times 0.5196$

$= 6117$ N or 6.117 kN. (Ans.)

Example 4.9 A pair of lock gates each 2.5 m wide and 5 m high make an angle of 130 when closed. They have two hinges each at 0.5 m from top and bottom. If the depth of water on the upstream side is 4.5 m and on the downstream side is 1.2 m, find (i) thrust between the gates and (ii) the reaction on the hinges.

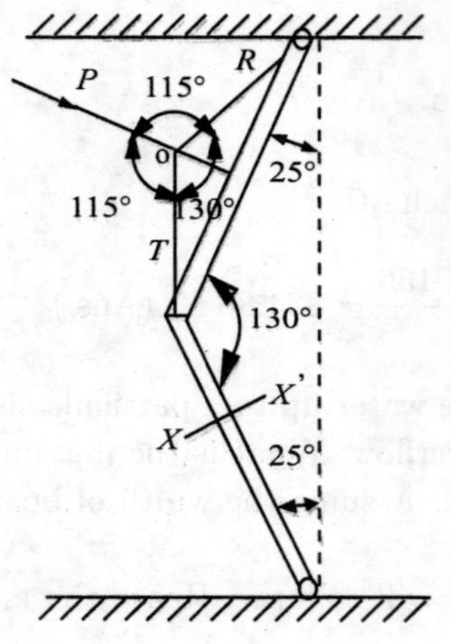

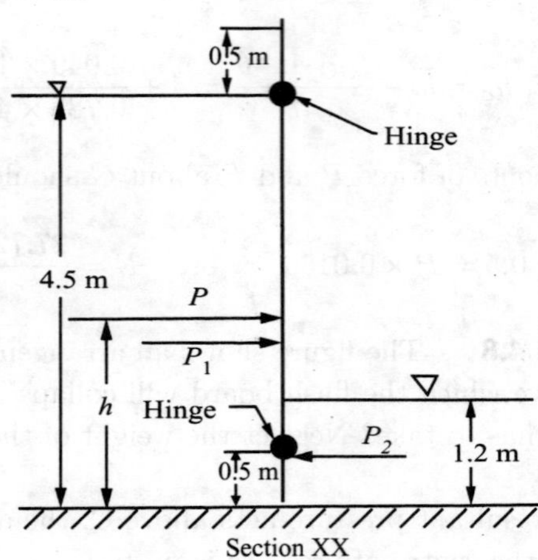

Example 4.9

Net pressure P acting on each gate.

$$P_1 = \gamma \frac{h_1^2}{2}; w = \frac{9.81 \times 4.5^2}{2} \times 2.5 = 248.32 \text{ kN acting at 1.5 m from the bottom.}$$

$$P_2 = \gamma \frac{h_2{}^2}{2}, w = \frac{9.81 \times 1.2^2}{2} \times 2.5 = 17.66 \text{ kN acting at 0.4 from the bottom.}$$

So, net pressure $= P = P_1 - P_2 = 248.32 - 17.66 = 230.66$ kN.

Taking moments about the bottom of the gate,

$$P_1 \times 1.5 - P_2 \times 0.4 = P \times h,$$

$$\text{Hence, } h = \frac{248.32 \times 1.5 - 17.66 \times 0.4}{230.66} = 1.584 \text{ m.}$$

Applying Lami's theorem at point O,

$$\frac{T}{\sin 115°} = \frac{R}{\sin 115°} = \frac{P}{\sin 130°},$$

which gives $T = 272.89$ kN and $R = 272.89$ kN.

The reaction R is assumed to act at a height of 1.584 m from the bottom. Let R_b and R_t be the reactions at hinges on the bottom and top respectively.

Taking moments about R_b,

$$272.89 \times (1.584 - 0.5) = R_t \times (4.5 - 0.5),$$

$$R_t = \frac{272.89 \times 1.084}{4} = 73.95 \text{ kN}; \; R_b = R - R_t = 272.89 - 72.95 = 198.94 \text{ kN. (Ans.)}$$

4.4 Forces on Curved Surfaces

As explained in Section 4.2.2, the forces on a curved surface like AB, A′B′ and PQ can be found out (see Fig. 4.4). The components of the force are:

(a) The horizontal force on the horizontally projected area $= P_h$.

(b) The vertical force equal to the weight of the fluid above the surface (real or imaginary, as in case of PQ) equal to $R = \sqrt{P_h^2 + P_v^2}$.

Example 4.10 Find the resultant water pressure per m length of the drum shown in the figure.

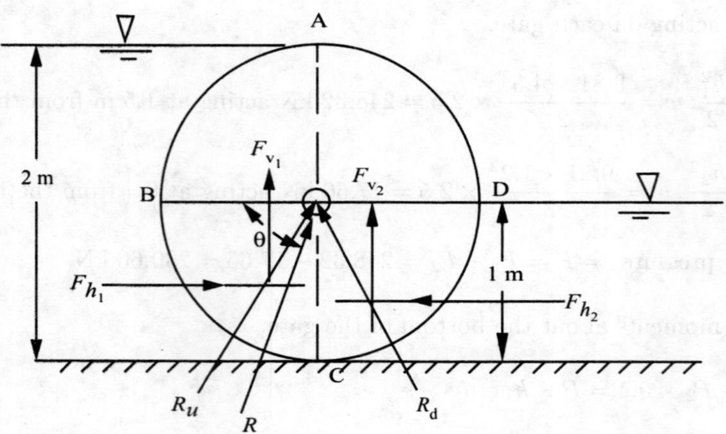

Example 4.10

Let us consider 1 m length of drum.

(i) Upstream portion.

Net vertical pressure = Weight of volume of water that can be retained in ABCA.

$$F_{v_1} = \gamma \times \frac{1}{2} \times \frac{\pi d^2}{4} = 9.81 \times \frac{1}{2} \times \frac{\pi \times 2^2}{4} = 15.41 \text{ kN upwards.}$$

Horizontal pressure on the projected area,

$$F_{h_1} = \gamma A\bar{h} = \gamma(2 \times 1) \times 1 = 19.62 \text{ kN.}$$

Therefore, resultant force upstream $= \sqrt{(15.41)^2 + (19.62)^2} = 24.947$ kN.

(ii) Downstream portion

Vertical pressure on CD is the weight of water that can be contained in volume OCD,

i.e. $F_{v_2} = \gamma \times \frac{1}{4} \times \frac{\pi d^2}{4} = 7.7$ kN upwards.

Horizontal pressure on the projected area,

$$F_{h_2} = \gamma A\bar{h} = \gamma(1 \times 1) \times 0.5 = 4.905 \text{ kN.}$$

Therefore, resultant force downstream $= \sqrt{(07.7)^2 + (4.905)^2} = 9.13$ kN.

(iii) Resultant total force

Total vertical component $= 15.41 + 7.7 = 23.11$ kN upwards.

Total horizontal component $= 19.62 - 4.905 = 14.715$ kN downstream.

Therefore, resultant total pressure $= \sqrt{(23.11)^2 + (14.715)^2} = 27.39$ kN. (Ans.)

angle $\theta = \tan^{-1}(23.11/14.715) = 57.505°$. (Ans.)

Example 4.11 A tainter gate having a length of 3 m is mounted on a spillway in the position shown in the figure. When water stands up to the top of the gate, what are the magnitude and direction of the resultant pressure on the gate?

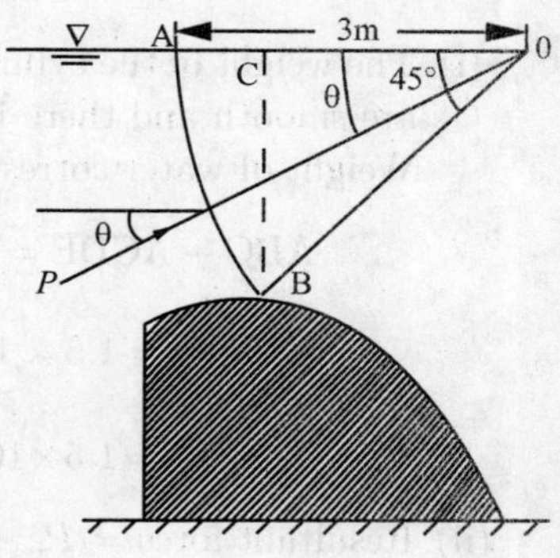

Example 4.11

$\gamma = 9.81$ kN/m^3.

Projected area $= 3 \times 3/\sqrt{2} = 6.364$ m.

$$P_h = \gamma A\bar{h} = 9.81 \times 6.364 \times \frac{3}{2\sqrt{2}} = 66.22 \text{ kN}.$$

$P_v =$ Weight of water of volume ABC

$$= \gamma \times 3\left[\pi \times 3^2\left(\frac{45}{360}\right) - \frac{1}{2} \times \frac{3}{\sqrt{2}} \times \frac{3}{\sqrt{2}}\right]$$

$$= 9.81 \times 3\,[3.534 - 2.25] = 37.79 \text{ kN}.$$

$$P = \sqrt{P_h^2 + P_v^2} = \sqrt{66.22^2 + 37.79^2} = 76.24 \text{ KN at an angle } \theta = \tan^{-1}\frac{37.79}{66.22} = 29.71°$$

with the horizontal and passing through O.

Example 4.12 A cylinder of radius 0.3 m is placed in water as shown in the figure. The cylinder and wall are smooth. For a 1.5 m length of cylinder, find

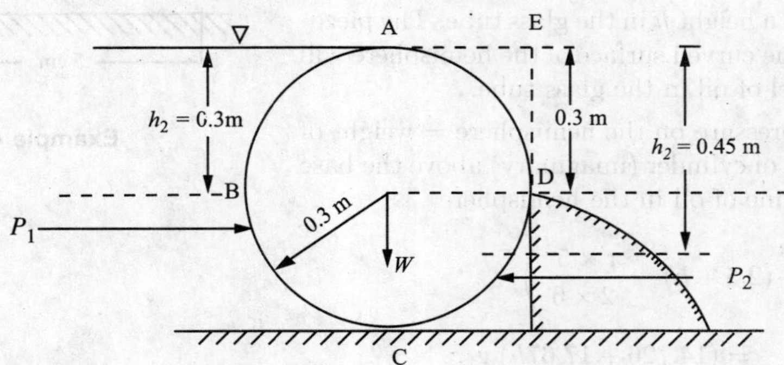

Example 4.12

(i) its weight,

(ii) the resultant force exerted by the wall on the cylinder and

(iii) the resultant moment about the centre of the cylinder due to water forces on the cylinder.

(i) The weight of the cylinder is equal to the total upward force. (the wall and the cylinder are smooth and there is no net vertical force)
Weight of water corresponding to volume

$$\text{ABC} + \text{ACDE} = L\gamma A$$

$$= 1.5 \times 1000 \times 9.81 \left(\frac{1}{2}\pi \times 0.3^2 + \frac{1}{4}\pi \times 0.3^2 + 0.3^2\right)$$

$$= 1.5\times1000\times9.81 \times (0.1414 + 0.0707 + 0.09) = 4445 \text{ N. (Ans.)}$$

(ii) Resultant force $= P_1 - P_2 = \gamma \times (1.5 \times 0.6) \times 0.3 - \gamma \times (1.5 \times 0.3 \times 0.45)$

$$= 662.175 \text{ N.}$$

Hence, $P = 662.175$ N. (Ans.)

(iii) Since all the forces on the cylinder are radial there is no net moment acting.

Example 4.13 A hollow hemispherical shell of internal diameter 5 cm and weighing 30 g_f has a small glass tube filled at the top as shown in the figure. An oil ($S = 0.9$) is poured through the glass tube until the hemisphere is lifted up. Find the height of the oil column above the hemisphere.

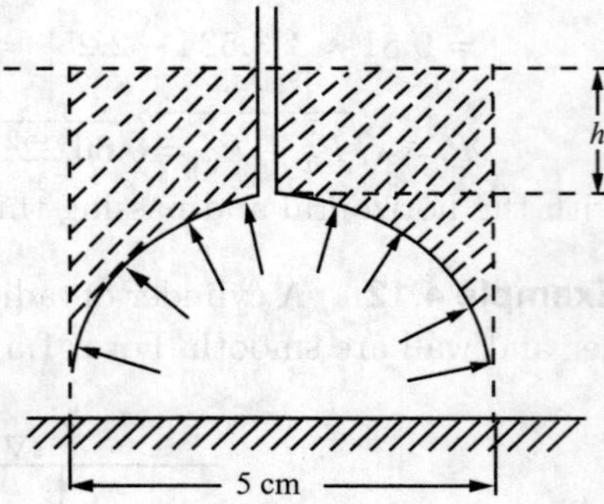

Example 4.13

S for oil $= 0.9$. Hence, $\gamma = 0.9\ g_f/\text{cm}^3$.

Let the oil rise to a height h in the glass tube. The piezometric head on the curved surface of the hemisphere will be up to the level of oil in the glass tube.

Hence, upward pressure on the hemisphere = weight of oil in the volume of cylinder (imaginary) above the base – weight of volume of oil in the hemisphere.

$$0.9\left(\frac{\pi \times 5^2}{4}(2.5 + h) - \frac{\pi \times 5^3}{2 \times 6}\right)$$

$$= (14.726 + 17.67h)\ g_f.$$

Hence, $14.726 + 17.67h = 30$ or $h = 0.864$ cm. (Ans.)

REVIEW QUESTIONS AND PROBLEMS

4.1 Derive an expression for the total pressure and the position of the centre of pressure of a rectangular lamina of breadth b and depth d immersed (i) vertically in a fluid of specific gravity S; (ii) at an angle θ with the horizontal.

4.2 Show that the centre of pressure is always below the centre of gravity.

4.3 A rectangular lamina 5 m × 3 m is immersed vertically in a liquid of specific gravity 0.8, with 3m side horizontal and touching the surface. Find the total pressure on one side and the position of the centre of the pressure.

4.4 A rectangular lamina 5 m × 3 m is immersed in water as shown in the figure. Find the resultant pressure and the position of the centre of pressure.

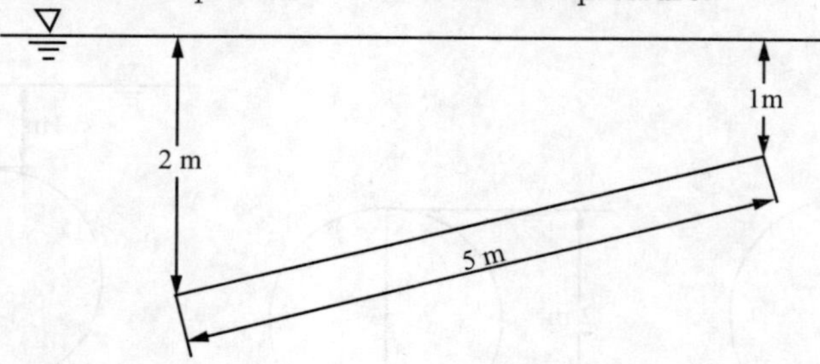

Problem 4.4

4.5 A circular lamina 2.5 m diameter is immersed in water as shown in the figure. Find the total pressure and locate the centre of pressure.

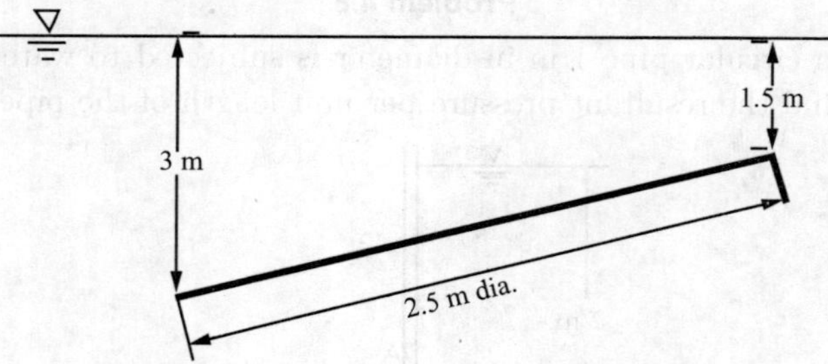

Problem 4.5

4.6 A gate hinged at one end closes an opening in the wall of a dam as shown in the figure. Find the total pressure on the gate and its point of application. Find the normal force which should be applied at the bottom of the gate to prevent the gate from opening.

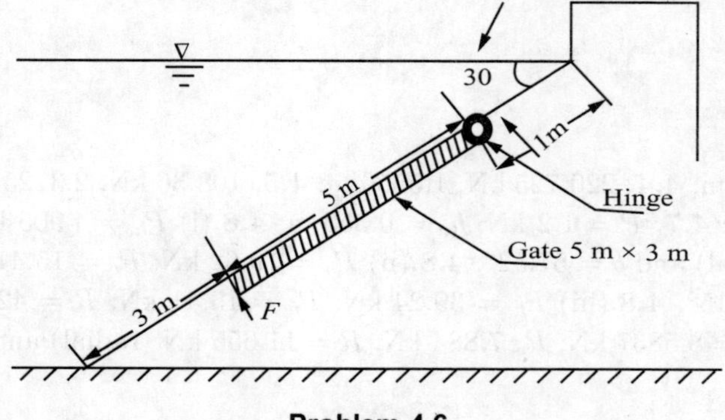

Problem 4.6

4.7 A channel to convey liquid ($S = 0.85$) has a semicircular cross-section of diameter 1.2 m. The channel is closed by a semicircular gate. Find the total pressure and the position of the center pressure on the gate. [Hint: Centre of gravity of semicircle is $4r/3\pi$ distance from the base.]

4.8 A cylindrical drum of 2 m diameter is subjected to different conditions of water pressure as shown in the figure. Find the resultant pressure and their direction, per unit length in each case.

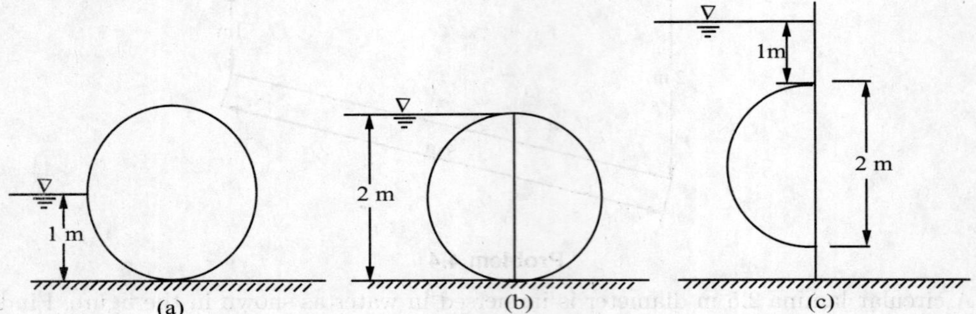

Problem 4.8

4.9 A quadrant of a circular pipe 1 m in diameter is subjected to water pressure as shown in the figure. Find the resultant pressure per unit length of the pipe.

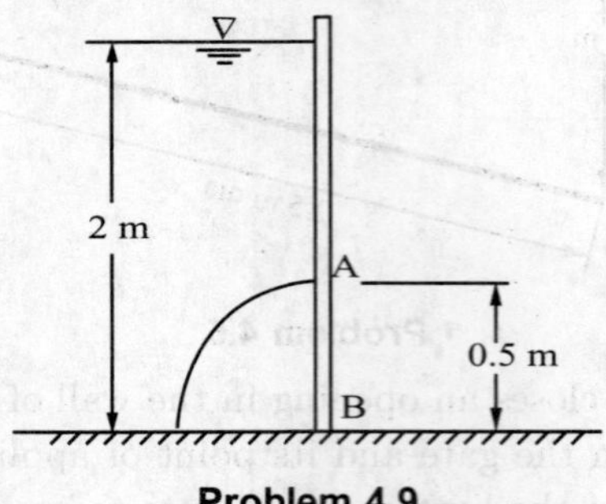

Problem 4.9

ANSWERS

4.3. 294.3 kN, 3.333 m; **4.4.** 220.725 kN, 1.5556 m; **4.5.** 108.36 kN, 2.3125 m; **4.6.** 257.52 kN, 2.0476 m, 159.42 kN; **4.7.** $P = 1.2$ kN; $h_c = 0.353$ m; **4.8.**(i) $P_h = 4.905$ kN; $P_v = 7.706$ kN; $R = 9.1346$ kN (radial) and $\theta = 57.52°$; **4.8.**(ii) $P_h = 19.62$ kN; $P_v = 15.41$ kN; $R = 24.95$ kN (radial) and $\theta = 38.15°$; **4.8.**(iii) $P_h = 39.24$ kN; $P_v = 15.41$ kN; $R = 42.16$ kN(radial) and $\theta = 21.44°$; **4.9.** $P_h = 8.5837$ kN; P_v 7.884 kN; $R = 11.655$ kN (radial) and $\theta = 42.57°$

5 Buoyancy and Floatation

Buoyancy and floatation — Stability of floating bodies — Determination of meta-centric height

5.1 The Principle of Buoyancy

The forces acting on a body can be classified as surface and body forces. The total weight of the body is a body force and is the sum of weights of each and every part of the body acting throughout its volume. The pressure forces are surface forces.

Imagine a closed surface inside a liquid (may or may not include the free surface). How is the fluid in equilibrium? The horizontal components of pressure on the surfaces cancel with each other. The net vertical pressures on the surface will be upwards since the pressure at the bottom will be higher, but when it is filled by the liquid it is balanced by the weight of the liquid and is in equilibrium.

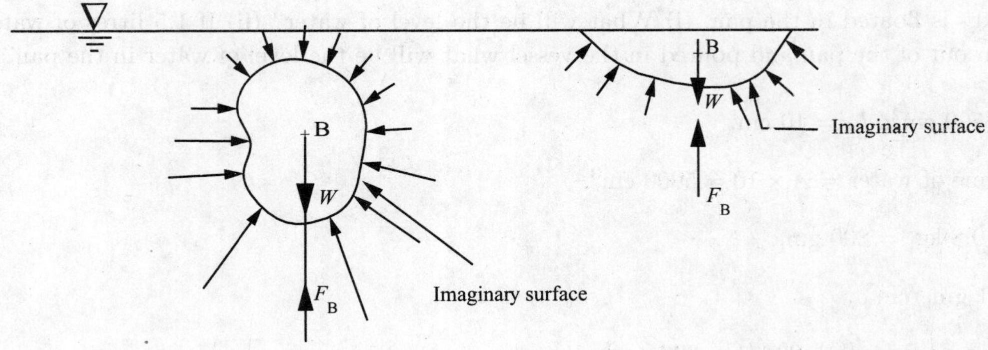

Fig. 5.1 *Centre of buoyancy and buoyant force*

The upward force is called the buoyant force and it acts at the centre of gravity of the fluid mass which can be contained in the closed surface. This point is known as the centre of buoyancy.

The above arguments regarding buoyant forces are valid even when the imaginary closed surface contains any other body. The body will sink, stay at the same level or go up in the liquid depending on whether the weight of the body is greater, equal to or less than the buoyant force respectively.

The centre of gravity of the body depends on the distribution of mass within it and hence, can be different from the centre of buoyancy. If the centre of buoyancy and the centre of gravity are not in the same vertical line, the body will be subjected to a tilting moment.

5.2 Archimedes Principle

Archimedes is credited with the discovery of the principle that the apparent loss of weight of a body when immersed in a liquid is equal to the weight of the liquid displaced by the body. It is clear that the apparent loss of weight is due to the force of buoyancy, which is a net result of the pressure forces acting on the surface of the body.

Example 5.1 A body of weight 3.8 kg_f in air has an apparent weight of 3 kg_f in water. What is its specific gravity?

Let $\forall$ be the volume of the body. The loss of weight in air is neglected.

Apparent loss of weight when submerged in water $= 3.8 - 3.0 = 0.8$ kg_f

$= 0.8 \times 9.81$ N,

which should be equal to the weight of water of volume $\forall$.

Specific gravity = Weight of the body of volume $\forall$/Weight of equal volume of water

$= (3.8 \times 9.81)/(0.8 \times 9.81) = 4.75$. (Ans.)

Example 5.2 A pan of area 500 cm^2 contains water to a depth of 10 cm. A vessel weighing 0.8 kg_f is floated in the pan. (i) What will be the level of water? (ii) If 1.5 litres of water is taken out of the pan and poured in the vessel what will be the level of water in the pan?

$A = 500$ cm^2; $h_1 = 10$ cm.

Volume of water $= A \times 10 = 5000$ cm^3.

$w = 0.8$ $kg_f = 800$ gm_f.

$\gamma = 1$ gm_f/cm^3.

Displaced volume $= 800/1 = 800$ cm^3.

(i) Let the depth be h_2.
$\forall = 5000 = A\,h_2 - 800$. Hence, $h_2 = 11.6$ cm. (Ans.)

(ii) The water in the pan will reduce by 1.5 litres, but the displacement will increase by 1.5 litres. Hence, $h_3 = 11.6$ cm. (Ans.)

5.3 Conditions of Equilibrium

A body is said to be in stable equilibrium if a small force applied to disturb it from the equilibrium position will induce forces and moments which will try to restore the body to the earlier position. The concept of stability is illustrated by the conditions of stability of equilibrium of a cone.

Figure 5.2 (a), (b) and (c) show the stable, unstable and neutral conditions of equilibrium of the cone respectively. When the forces and moments induced after a slight displacement are not able to restore the body to the earlier position as in Fig. 5.2(b), the body is in an unstable condition. In case of the cone in Fig. 5.2(c), the forces and moments induced, will not restore the body to the original position, but will make the body assume a similar position as before. It is said to have neutral equilibrium.

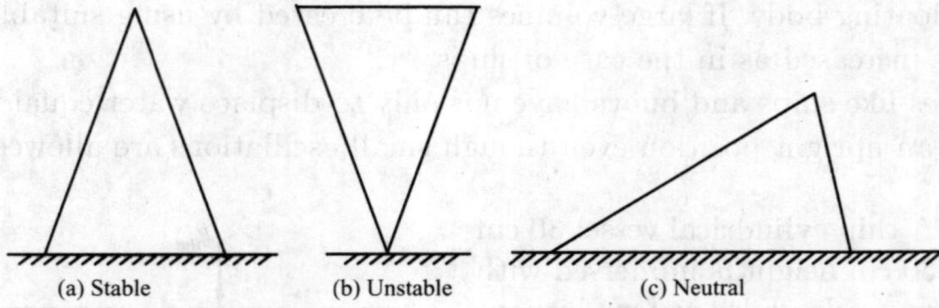

Fig. 5.2 *Conditions of equilibrium*

5.4 Discussions on Stability

5.4.1 Stability of equilibrium of a fully immersed body

For a fully immersed body to be in equilibrium at a particular position

(i) The weight of the body should be equal to the weight of the displaced fluid.
(ii) The centre of gravity of the body should be below the centre of buoyancy.

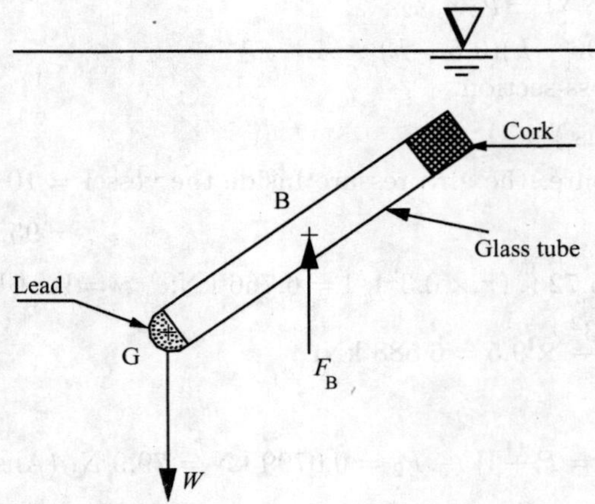

Fig. 5.3 *Stability of a submerged tube*

Figure 5.3 shows a body immersed in a fluid. The weight W of the body and buoyant force F_B will be the same. The position of G should be below the centre of buoyancy B, for stable equilibrium.

5.4.2 Floating bodies (partially immersed bodies)

A body will float in a liquid if the weight of the body is equal to the weight of the displaced liquid. Since the buoyant force is a surface force, it does not get affected by the contents or material of the floating body. If large volumes can be created by using suitable materials, the buoyancy can be increased as in the case of ships.

Floating bodies like ships and buoys have not only to displace water equal to their weights but also float in an upright position even though small oscillations are allowed.

Example 5.3 A thin cylindrical vessel 30 cm in diameter and 50 cm height is immersed with the open end downwards under water (without the air escaping) so that the open end is at a depth of 10 m. Find out how high the water will rise inside the vessel. Assume isothermal conditions and that p_{atm} =101 kPa. If the vessel weighs 10 kg$_f$, what is the force required to keep the vessel in position. Neglect thickness of vessel.

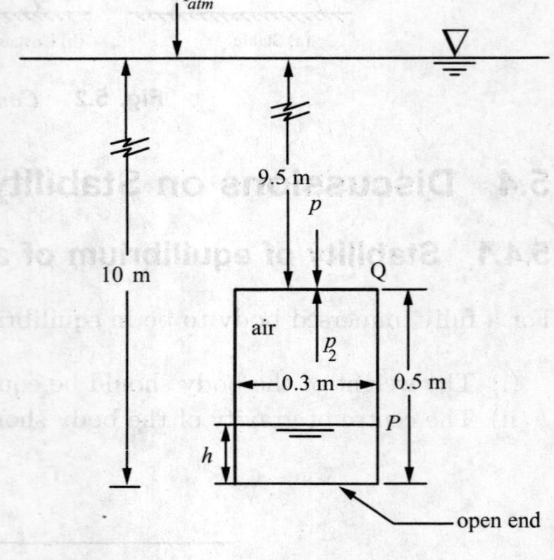

Example 5.3

p_{atm} = 101 kPa = 10.296 m of water; we have to work with absolute pressure.

Pressure head inside the vessel = (10.296 + 10 – h) = (20.296 – h)m of water.

As per Boyle's law, $p_{atm} \times \forall_1 = p_2 \times \forall_2$.

$10.296 \times 0.5 \times A = (20.296 - h)(0.5 - h) \times A$, where A is the area of cross-section.

Solving, $h = 0.243$ m. (Ans.)

Working with gauge pressure, the air pressure inside the vessel = 10 – 0.243 m of water

= 95.72 kPa.

P_2 = pressure × area = $95.72 \times (\pi \times 0.3^2)/4 = 6.766$ kN; $\gamma = 9.81$ kN/m^3.

$$P = \gamma A\bar{h} = 9.81 \times \frac{\pi \times 0.3^2}{4} \times 9.5 = 6.588 \text{ kN.}$$

W = 10 kg$_f$ = 0.0981 kN.

Downward force required = $P + W - P_2$ = 0.0799 kN = 79.9 N. (Ans.)

Example 5.4 An iceberg (S = 0.9) floats in sea water (S = 1.023). If the volume of ice above the water surface is 15 m^3, find the weight of the iceberg.

γ for sea water $= 1.023 \times 9.81$ kN/m^3

$= 10.036$ kN/m^3.

γ for ice $= 0.9 \times 9.81 = 8.829$ kN/m^3.

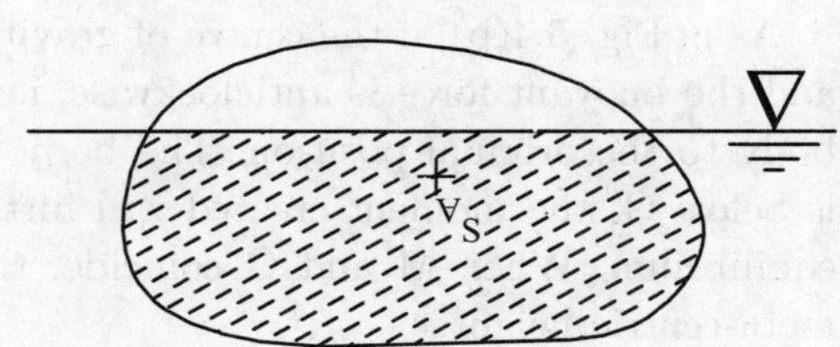

Example 5.4

Let $\forall$ be the volume of ice and $\forall_s$,
the volume of ice below the water surface.

Weight of iceberg $= 8.829 \times \forall = \forall_s \times 10.036$.

or, $\forall_s = 0.88\ \forall$.

or, $\forall_a = \forall - \forall_s = 0.12 \quad \forall = 15$ m^3.

or, $\forall = 15/0.12 = 125$ m^3.

Weight of iceberg $= \gamma$ for ice $\times \forall = 8.829 \times 125 = 1103.6$ kN. (Ans.)

5.5 Meta-centre

5.5.1 Meta-centre and conditions of equilibrium

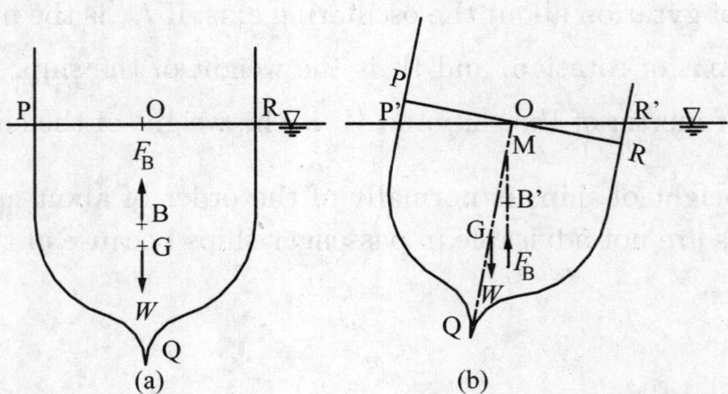

Fig. 5.4 *Floating of ship model*

Figure 5.4(a) shows a ship model floating in water. The weight of the model W acts at G. It displaces the volume of liquid PQROP of weight W. The buoyant force $F_B = W$ will act upwards through B, the centre of buoyancy.

If the body is tilted slightly as in Fig. 5.4(b), the new volume displaced will be P$'$QR$'$OP$'$. Due to the modified displacement, the centre of buoyancy will change to B$'$, even though the buoyant force will again be W. The vertical through B$'$ will cut line BG at point M, which is called a meta-centre.

When a body is tilted from its upright floating position, the point of intersection of the vertical through the new centre of buoyancy, and the vertical line through the centre of gravity in the initial upright position is called the meta-centre.

As in Fig. 5.4(b), if the centre of gravity is below M, the couple of forces due to the weight and the buoyant force is anticlockwise, i.e., a righting moment will be produced to bring the body to the original position. The body will, therefore, be stable. If, however, the point M is below G, the moment created will further tilt the body and the body will be in unstable equilibrium. When M and G coincide, there will be neutral equilibrium. GM is called the meta-centric height.

If GM is positive	stable equilibrium.
If GM is negative	unstable equilibrium.
If GM is zero	neutral equilibrium.

5.5.2 Meta-centric height and period of oscillation

The meta-centric height is related to the period of oscillation of the floating body by the relationship

$$T = 2\pi\sqrt{\frac{k^2}{g.GM}}, \tag{5.1}$$

where k is the radius of gyration about the oscillating axis. If I_m is the mass moment of inertia of the ship about its axis of rotation, and W is the weight of the ship, $I_m = \frac{W}{g}k^2$, where I_m is the mass moment of inertia of the ship and W is the weight of the ship.

The meta-centric height of ships is normally of the order of about a metre. Higher values of meta-centric heights are not advisable in passenger ships because of the higher frequency of oscillations caused.

5.5.3 Analytical determination of meta-centric height

Consider a small length of ship dL, the cross-section of which is shown in Fig. 5.5. Let the centre of buoyancy be B which is the centre of gravity of displaced volume PQROP.dL. When the ship gets tilted by a small angle θ, the displaced volume will be P′QR′OP′.dL.

Let B′ be the new centre of buoyancy, the centre of gravity of the modified displaced volume. The centre of gravity of displaced volume is shifted because a volume of water, PP′O $\times$ dL rose from the water and RR′O $\times$ dL got submerged in the water due to tilting.

Additional moment about O due to removal of volume PP′O $\times$ dL

$= \gamma \times$ volume $\times$ distance CO of the centre of gravity from O

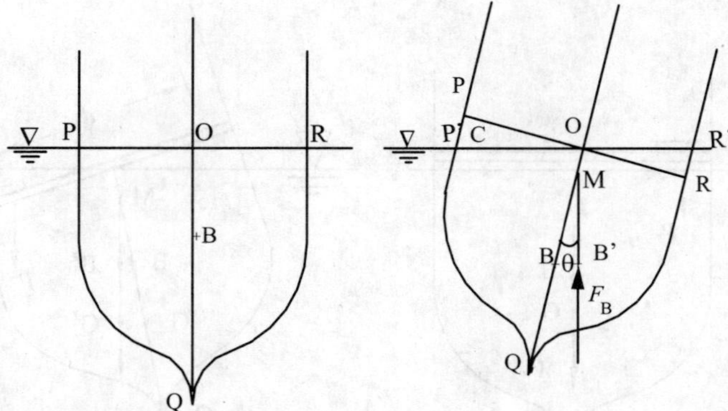

Fig. 5.5 *Analytical determination of meta-centric height*

$$= \gamma \left[\frac{1}{2}(b/2)^2 \times \theta \times dL \right] \times (2/3) \times (b/2)$$

$$= \gamma \times dL \times \frac{b^3}{24} \times \theta. \text{ (θ being very small)}$$

Similarly additional moment about O due to addition of volume RR′O × dL

$$= \gamma \times dL \times \frac{b^3}{24} \times \theta.$$

The above two moments will have the same sense of moments for tilting the ship.

Sum of moments $= \gamma \times (dL \times \frac{b^3}{12}) \times \theta = \gamma \times dI \times \theta.$

So the total moment for the whole ship $= \gamma \times \theta \int dI = \gamma \theta I.$

Because of the above moment, the centre of buoyancy will shift from B to B′.

BB′ = change in moment / buoyant force,

or, $BB' = \frac{\gamma \times \theta \times I}{\gamma \times \forall} = I \times \theta / \forall$, where $\forall$ is the total displacement of the ship.

But, $BB' = BM \times \theta$. (θ being small)

So, $\quad BM = BB'/\theta = \frac{\gamma \times I}{\gamma \times \forall} = \frac{I}{\forall}.$

5.5.4 Experimental determination of the meta-centric height

In the experimental determination of the meta-centric height, the displaced volume of the ship $\forall$ should be known or calculated. In laboratory models, the volume can be determined by floating the model in a measuring tank containing water and finding the rise in the water level.

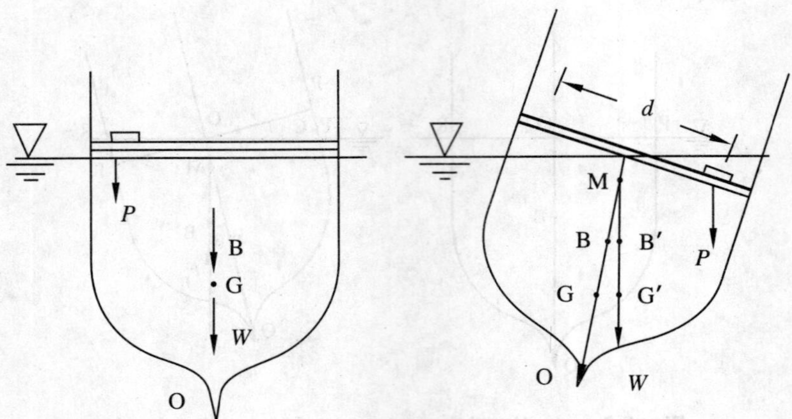

Fig. 5.6 *Experimental determination of the meta-centric height*

Let A be the area of the tank and h be the rise in water level, the displaced volume $\forall = A \times h$ and the weight of the ship $= \gamma \times \forall$.

Let G and B be the centre of gravity and the centre of buoyancy in the upright position. A known weight P is moved laterally by a distance d causing a moment $P \times d$. The ship will be tilted and a new position of equilibrium condition will be reached.

Let the new centre of buoyancy in the tilted position of the ship be B′. Since there was lateral movement of the weight, the centre of gravity will be shifted to G′. As the ship is now in static equilibrium, the centre of gravity G′ should be in the same vertical line through B′. Let B′G′ and BG intersect at M, the meta-centre. GM is the meta-centric height.

Equating the moments,

$$W \times \text{GG}' = P \times d \qquad \text{or,} \qquad W \times \text{GM} \times \tan\theta = P \times d.$$

$$\text{i.e.,}\ \text{GM} = \frac{P \times d}{W \times \tan\theta}. \tag{5.1}$$

In the above equation, the angle of tilt can be measured by the angle of deflection of a plumb line and GM can be calculated.

Example 5.5 A cylinder 9 cm long is in equilibrium as shown in the figure. Find the specific gravity of the solid. If more oil is poured, will the solid submerge more in water?

Let A be the area of cross-section of the cylinder and S be the specific gravity.

Pressure head at P = 7 cm of oil.

Pressure head at Q = 10 cm of oil + 6 cm of water.

So, difference of pressure at P and Q = 3 cm of oil + 6 cm of water

$$= 0.03 \times 0.8 \times 9.81 + 0.06 \times 9.81 = 0.824 \text{ kPa}.$$

So the buoyant force = pressure difference between upper and lower surfaces = $0.824 \times A$ kN.

Since the cylinder is in equilibrium, the buoyant force should be equal to the weight of the solid.

Weight of the cylinder $= \gamma_s Ah = S\gamma_w Ah$.

$$S \times 9.81 \times A \times 0.09 = 0.824 \times A.$$

or, $\quad S = 0.933$. (Ans.)

Since the pressure difference between P and Q is independent of the depth of the oil, no difference will be caused by pouring more oil. (Ans.)

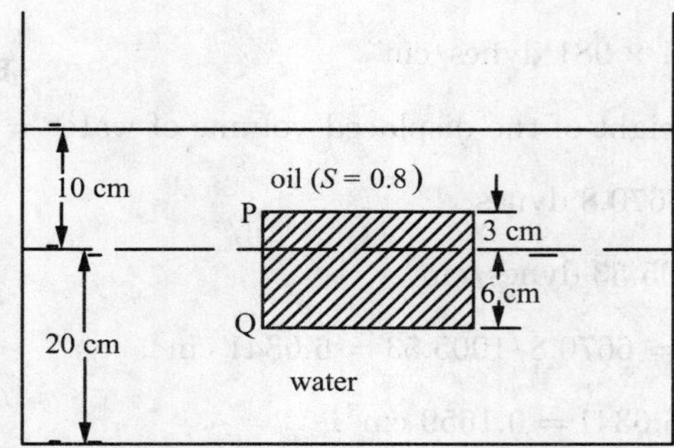

Example 5.5

Example 5.6 A ship having a displacement of 8000 tonnes has a draft of 4 m in the ocean. If the water plane area is 800 m^2, how much will the draft be when it enters fresh water. Assume that ρ for sea water is 1020 kg/m^3.

γ for sea water = 1020×9.81 N/m^3.

Weight of ship = 8000 tonnes = $8000 \times 1000 \times 9.81$ N $= 7.848 \times 10^7$ N.

$$\text{Displaced volume in sea water} = \text{weight}/\gamma \text{ for sea water} = \frac{7.848 \times 10^7}{1020 \times 9.81} = 7843.14 \text{ m}^3.$$

$$\text{Displaced volume in fresh water} = \text{weight}/\gamma \text{ for water} = \frac{7.848 \times 10^7}{9.81 \times 10^3} = 8000 \text{ m}^3.$$

Increase in displaced volume $= 8000 - 7843.14 = 156.86$ m^3.

Level rise $= 156.86/800 = 0.196$ m.

New draft $= 4 + 0.196 = 4.196$ m. (Ans.)

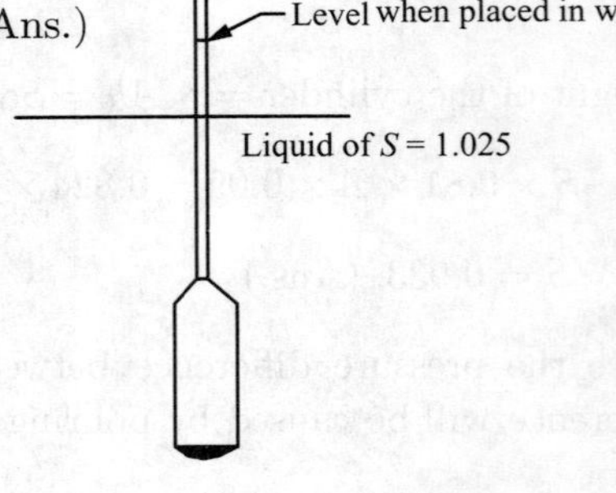

Example 5.7

Example 5.7 A hydrometer when placed in water displaces a volume of 6.8 cm^3. If the stem of the hydrometer is of diameter 3 mm, find out how much the hydrometer will go up when placed in a liquid of specific gravity 1.025.

γ for water $= 1\text{gm}_f/\text{cm}^3$. (981 dynes/cm^3)

Adopting CGS units, $\gamma_w = \rho_w \times g$

$$= 1 \times 981 \text{ dynes/cm}^3$$

Weight of hydrometer $=$ Weight of the displaced volume of water $= \forall \times \gamma_w = 6.8 \times 981$

$$= 6670.8 \text{ dynes.}$$

$$\gamma_l = 1.025 \times 981 = 1005.53 \text{ dynes/cm}^3.$$

Volume displaced in liquid $= 6670.8/1005.53 = 6.6341$ cm^3.

Change in volume $= 6.8 - 6.6341 = 0.1659$ cm^3.

Cross-section area of stem $= \dfrac{\pi}{4}(0.3)^2 = 0.07069$ cm^2.

Change in depth $= 0.1659/0.07069 = 2.347$ cm. (Ans.)

Example 5.8 A rectangular barge 15 m long has a width of 4 m. It weighs 150 tonnes and its centre of gravity is 1.5 m above the bottom. Find the meta-centric height, when it floats in fresh water.

Weight of the barge $= 150$ tonnes $= 150 \times 9.81$ kN.

γ for fresh water $= 9.81$ kN/m^3.

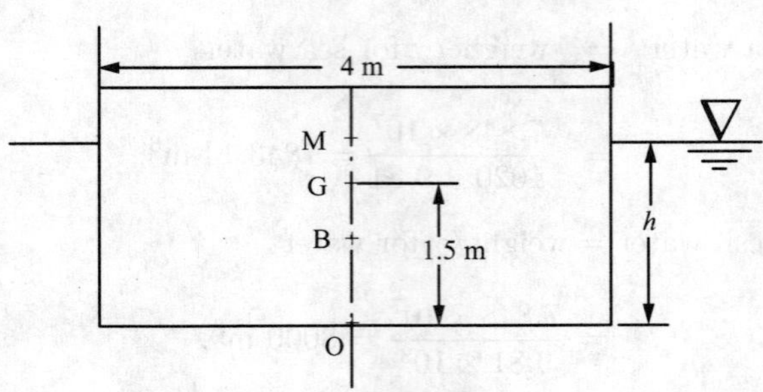

Example 5.8

Volume displaced, $\forall = \dfrac{150 \times 9.81}{9.81} = 150 \text{ m}^3$.

Let h be the depth of immersion. $4 \times 15 \times h = 150$.

or, $h = 2.5$ m.

$$I = \frac{bd^3}{12} = \frac{15 \times 4^3}{12} = 80 \text{ m}^4.$$

$$\text{BM} = \frac{I}{\forall} = \frac{80}{150} = 0.533 \text{ m}.$$

$$\text{t OM} = \text{OB} + \text{BM} = 1.25 + 0.533 = 1.783 \text{ m}.$$

$$\text{GM} = \text{OM} - \text{OG} = 1.783 - 1.5 = 0.283 \text{ m. (Ans.)}$$

Example 5.9 A wooden cylinder has a diameter of 3 cm. If relative density of wood is 0.8, find the maximum height of the cylinder, which will float in water in the upright position, and be in stable equilibrium?

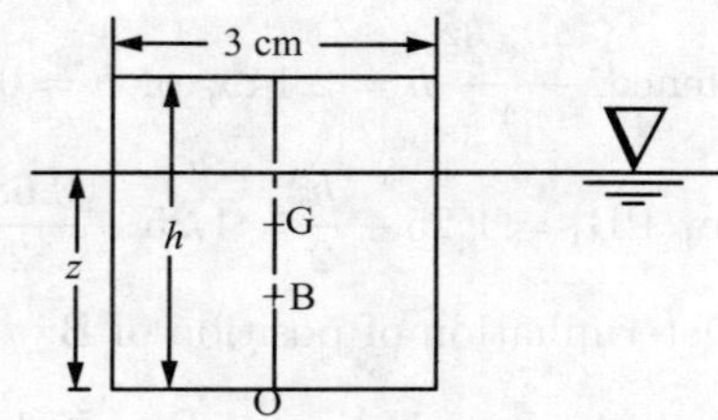

Example 5.9

Let the height of the cylinder be h and the depth of immersion be z.

Area of cross-section $A = \dfrac{\pi \times 3^2}{4} = 7.0686 \text{ cm}^2$.

Equating weight of the cylinder with weight of displaced water,

$A \times h \times 0.8\,\gamma = A \times z \times \gamma$ or, $z = 0.8\,h$.

$I = \pi \times d^4/64 = \pi \times 3^4/64 = 3.976 \text{ cm}^4$.

Volume of water displaced $\forall = A \times z = 7.0686 \times 0.8 \times h$

$$= 5.655\,h \text{ cm}^3.$$

$$\text{BM} = \frac{I}{\forall} = \frac{3.976}{5.655\,h} = \frac{0.7031}{h} \text{ cm}.$$

At the maximum height, M and G coincide. i.e., OM = OG.

$$\text{OM} = \text{OB} + \text{BM} = \frac{z}{2} + \frac{0.7031}{h} = 0.4\,h + \frac{0.7031}{h} \text{ cm}.$$

$$\text{OG} = 0.5\,h; \text{ Now, } 0.4\,h + \frac{0.7031}{h} = 0.5\,h; \text{ or } h = 2.654 \text{ cm. (Ans.)}$$

Example 5.10 A buoy carrying a beacon light has the upper portion cylindrical with a 2 m diameter and a depth of 1.25 m. The lower portion which is curved, displaces a volume of 400 litres and its centre of buoyancy is situated 1.3 m below the top of the cylinder. The centre of gravity of the whole buoy and beacon is situated 0.95 m below the top of the cylinder and total displacement is 2.6 tonnes. Find the meta-centric height. Take the specific mass of sea water as 1020 kg/m^3.

Let h be the submerged depth of cylinder, B_1 the centre of buoyancy of the portion of the cylinder which is submerged, B_2 the centre of buoyancy of the curved portion submerged and B the combined centre of buoyancy. $\gamma_s = \gamma_w \times S = 1020 \times 9.81$ N/m^3.

The total displaced volume $= \dfrac{2.6 \times 1000 \times 9.81}{1020 \times 9.81} = 2.549$ m^3.

Portion of cylinder submerged $= 2.549 - (400 \times 10^{-3}) = 2.149$ m^3.

Volume of cylinder submerged $= \dfrac{\pi \times 2^2}{4} h$.

Hence, $\dfrac{\pi \times 2^2}{4} h = 2.149$; or $h = 0.684$ m.

so, $PB_1 = 1.25 - \dfrac{h}{2} = 1.25 - \dfrac{0.684}{2} = 0.908$ m.

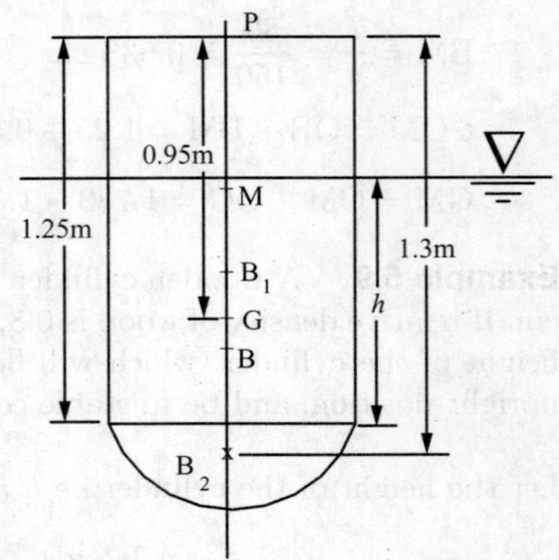

Example 5.10

Determination of position of B:

Buoyant force acting at $B_1 = 2.149 \times \gamma_s$.

Buoyant force acting at $B_2 = 0.4 \times \gamma_s$.

Total buoyant force through B $= 2.549\ \gamma_s$.

Taking moment about P,

$$2.149 \times \gamma_s \times PB_1 + 0.4 \times \gamma_s \times PB_2 = 2.549\ \gamma_s \times PB,$$

or, $$PB = \frac{2.149 \times 0.908 + 0.4 \times 1.3}{2.549} = 0.9695 \text{ m.}$$

Moment of inertia of waterline area about axis,

$$I = \frac{\pi d^4}{64} = \frac{\pi \times 2^4}{64} = 0.785 \text{ m}^4; \quad BM = \frac{I}{\forall} = \frac{0.785}{2.549} = 0.308 \text{ m.}$$

$$PM = PB - BM = 0.9695 - 0.308 = 0.6615 \text{ m.}$$

$$PG = 0.95 \text{ m.}$$

Hence $GM = PG - PM = 0.95 - 0.6615 = 0.2885$ m. (Ans.)

Example 5.11 A hollow conical buoy of diameter 2 m and height 4 m is floating in the sea ($S = 1.02$) in the upright position with vertex downwards. Its weight is 3.8 tonnes and the centre of gravity is 1.2 m below the top surface. Find the meta-centric height of the buoy.

Let the cone get submerged to a depth h as shown in the figure.

Example 5.11

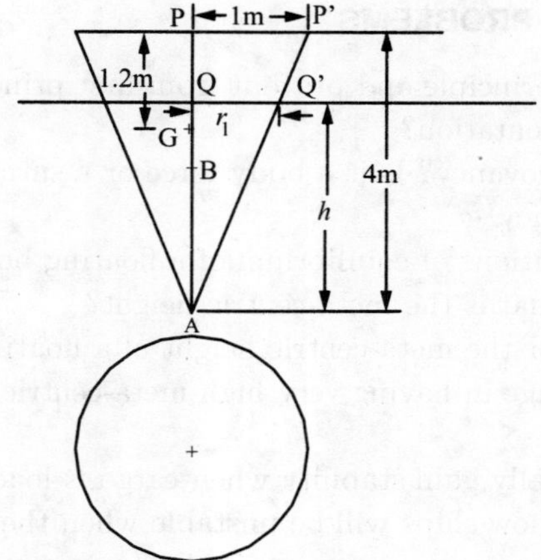

By the property of similar triangles,

$$\frac{QQ'}{PP'} = \frac{h}{AP}$$

or $\quad r_1 = QQ' = \frac{PP'}{AP}h = \frac{1}{4}h.$

Volume submerged $= \frac{1}{3} \times$ (base area) $\times$ height $= \frac{\pi}{3} \times \left(\frac{h}{4}\right)^2 \times h = \frac{\pi}{48}h^3.$

Weight of buoy = 3.8 tonnes = 3.8×9.81 kN; $\gamma = 1.02 \times 9.81$ kN.

Displacement $= \frac{3.8 \times 9.81}{1.02 \times 9.81} = 3.725 \text{ m}^3.$

$$\frac{\pi}{48}h^3 = 3.725; \text{ or, } h = 3.847 \text{ m.}$$

$$QB = \frac{h}{4} = 0.9618 \text{ m. (C.G of submerged conical portion)}$$

Hence, AB = AQ – QB = 3.847 – 0.9618 = 2.8852.

Diameter of waterline $= d_1 = \frac{h}{2} = 1.9235$ m.

Moment of inertia of waterline area $= \frac{\pi}{64} \times 1.9235^4 = 0.6711 \text{ m}^4.$

Volume submerged = 3.725 m^3; BM $= \frac{I}{\forall} = \frac{0.6711}{3.725} = 0.1802$ m.

AM = AB + BM = 2.8852 + 0.1802 = 3.0654 m.

PG = 1.2 m, AG = 4.0 – 1.2 = 2.8 m.

Hence, GM = AM – AG = 3.0654 – 2.8 = 0.2654 m.

REVIEW QUESTIONS AND PROBLEMS

5.1 State the Archimedes principle and prove it from first principles.

5.2 What are the laws of floatation?

5.3 What is the force of buoyancy? Is it a body force or a surface force?

5.4 Define centre of buoyancy.

5.5 Explain the three conditions of equilibrium of a floating body?

5.6 Define meta-centre. What is the meta-centric height?

5.7 Derive an expression for the meta-centric height of a floating body.

5.8 What is the disadvantage in having very high meta-centric heights for passenger ships? Explain.

5.9 Why does a ship generally gain stability when cargo is loaded?

5.10 Explain with sketches how ships will be unstable when the meta-centric height is negative.

5.11 Explain how the meta-centric height of a floating body can be determined experimentally?

5.12 A stone weighs 2.5 kg_f in air and 1.75 kg_f in an oil of specific gravity 0.8. Find the specific gravity of the stone.

5.13 A ball weighing 2 kg_f is floating in water with a fourth of its diameter submerged in water. What is the diameter of the ball?

5.14 A log of wood 1 m in diameter and 3 m in length floats in fresh water. If the log has a specific gravity of 0.6, find the depth of immersion.

5.15 A hydrometer has a mass of 10 g. It has a bulb at the bottom and a long stem of diameter 3 mm. Graduations in mm are made in increasing order upwards on the stem. If it indicated a reading of 65 mm when put in pure water, what will be the specific gravity of brine in which the reading is 30 mm.

5.16 A rectangular pontoon is 4 m long, 2.5 m wide and 1 m high. It weighs 8000 kgf. (i) Find the meta-centric height and examine its stability when floating in water. A weight of 1500 kgf having its centre of gravity 1 m above its base is placed above the pontoon. (ii) Find the new meta-centric height and examine whether it can be in stable equilibrium.

5.17 A cylindrical block of wood of specific gravity 0.8 and of diameter 6 cm is floating in water with the axis vertical. Find the maximum height of the block to ensure stability when floating in an upright position.

5.18 A glass tube 3 cm in diameter and 20 cm long contains lead at its bottom. It has its centre of gravity 8 cm from the bottom. If the tube weighs 100 gm_f, find out whether the tube is stable when floating in the upright position.

5.19 A wooden disc with 20 cm diameter and specific gravity 0.5 is floating in oil of sp. gravity 0.8 with the axis horizontal. Find the minimum length of the disc so that it can float in a stable position with the axis horizontal. (The centre of gravity of a circular disc is $4r/3\pi$ from the centre).

5.20 Show that a cylindrical buoy of diameter d, height h and density ρ, floating in a liquid of density ρ_1, will be in stable equilibrium, only if, $\dfrac{h}{d} < \dfrac{1}{\sqrt{8S(1-S)}}$, where $S = \rho/\rho_l$.

5.21 A conical buoy 1 m diameter and 3 m high is floating in water with its vertex downwards. It displaces 0.6 m^3 of sea water of specific gravity 1.025. (i) If the centre of gravity of the buoy is 2.5 m from the vertex, find the meta-centric height. (ii) The buoy is now anchored and a chain pulls the buoy downwards at the vertex with a force of 100 kg_f. Examine the stability. [Hint. Find the resultant point of action of the weight of the cone and the pull by the chain. Also find the new depth of immersion.]

ANSWERS

5.12. 2.667; **5.13.** 0.2518 m; **5.14.** 0.579 m; **5.15.** 1.0254; **5.16.** (i) 0.551 m, stable; (ii) 0.251 m, stable; **5.17.** 5.303 cm; **5.18.** – 0.8872 cm, unstable; **5.19.** 0.20 cm; **5.20.**(i). –0.388 m, unstable; **5.21** (ii). 0.0717, stable

6 Relative Equilibrium of Moving Fluids

Fluids moving at constant velocity—Fluids moving at constant acceleration—Vortex motion

6.1 Fluids Moving at Constant Velocity

Fluids moving at constant velocity can be brought to a relative equilibrium condition by considering it relative to a coordinate system moving at same constant velocity in the same direction. Alternatively, an equal and opposite velocity can be added to the fluid to bring it to relative rest. All laws of mechanics remain unaltered in uniformly moving systems.

6.2 Fluids Moving at Constant Acceleration

Fluid elements are acted upon by gravity and its weight acts vertically downwards. If in addition, a uniform acceleration $\vec{a}$ is imparted to the fluid, the total acceleration $\vec{f}$ will be $\vec{f} = \vec{g} + \vec{a}$.

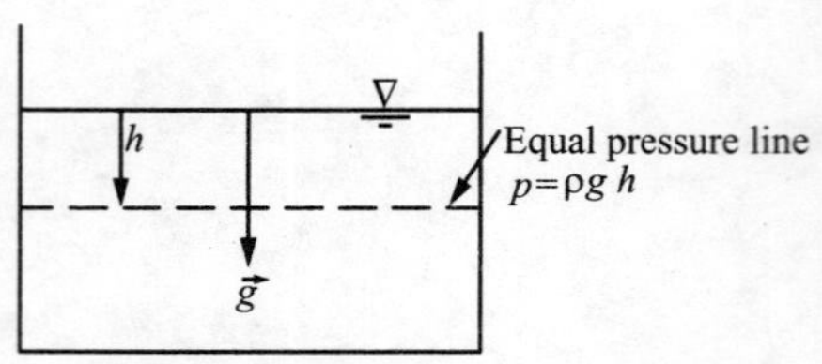

Fig. 6.1(a) *Fluid at rest*

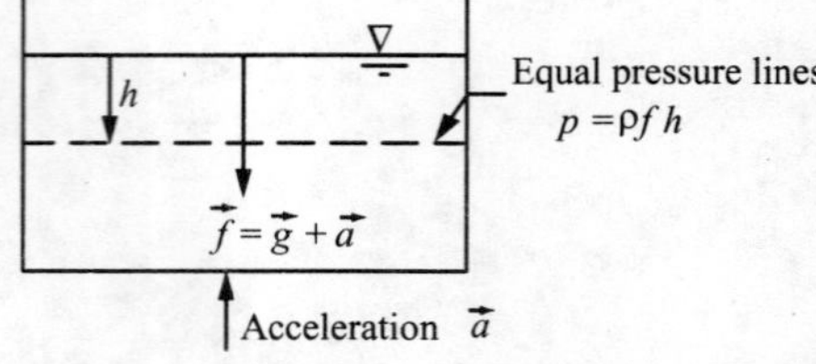

Fig. 6.1(b) *Fluid subjected to upward acceleration*

In Fig. 6.1(a), acceleration $\vec{g}$ is acting on a fluid element and the water surface is horizontal. The equal pressure lines will be parallel to the surface and $dp/dh = \rho g$ and $p = \rho g h$, where h is measured downwards from the surface.

Figure 6.1(b) shows the condition when a uniform acceleration $\vec{a}$ upwards to the vessel is added. The surface will be perpendicular to the vector $\vec{f} = \vec{g} + \vec{a}$, i.e., horizontal. The equal pressure lines will be parallel to the water surface and $p = \rho f h$, where h is the depth below the surface.

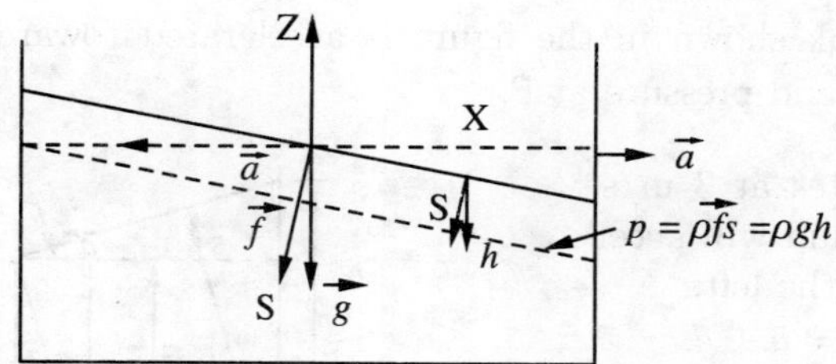

Fig. 6.2 *Fluid with acceleration towards the right*

Figure 6.2 shows a condition where the vessel is having an acceleration $\vec{a}$ towards the right. With respect to the ground, the water will have an acceleration $\vec{a}$ towards the left. Let $\vec{f} = \vec{g} + \vec{a}$ have a direction s. Then the water surface will be perpendicular to s. Equal pressure lines will be parallel to the surface and $p = \rho f s$.

Example 6.1 A tank of water as shown in the figure moves at a constant velocity of 2 m/s towards the right. Find the depth of water and pressure at P.

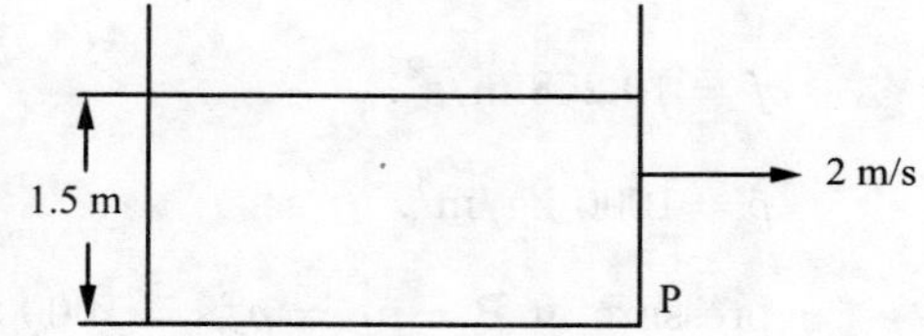

Example 6.1

Since the tank is moving at a constant velocity, the surface will remain horizontal and the laws of mechanics are the same.
Depth of water at P = 1.5 m. (Ans.)
Pressure at P $= \rho gh = 1000 \times 9.81 \times$ 1.5 Pa or 14.715 kPa. (Ans.)

Example 6.2 A tank 3 m long, 2 m high and 2 m wide as shown in figure has half its volume filled with water. If it is moving at a constant velocity of 3 m/s up a slope of 20°, find the maximum pressure of water at the bottom of the tank.

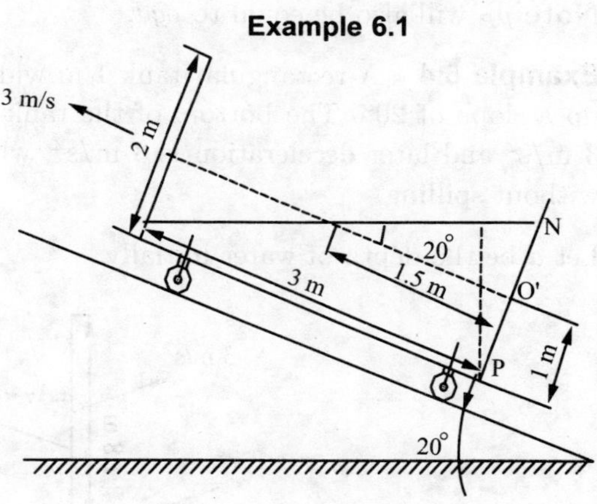

Example 6.2

Since the tank and the contents are moving at a constant velocity, the conditions are the same as in static conditions. The water surface will be horizontal.

Let d be the maximum depth of water. From the figure,

$$\text{NO}' = 1.5 \tan 20° = 0.546 \text{ m.}$$

$$\text{PN} = \text{NO}' + \text{O}'\text{P} = 0.546 + 1 = 1.546 \text{ m.}$$

$$\text{So } d = \text{PN} \cos 20° = 1.546 \cos 20° = 1.453 \text{ m.}$$

Pressure at P $= \rho g d = 1000 \times 9.81 \times 1.453 = 14.25$ KPa. (Ans.)

Example 6.3 The tank shown in the figure is accelerated towards the right at 3 m/s^2. Find the depth of water and pressure at P.

When the tank accelerates at 3 m/s^2 towards the right, the fluid will accelerate at 3 m/s^2 towards the left.
The total acceleration $\vec{f} = \vec{a} + \vec{g}$.

$$f = \sqrt{3^2 + 9.81^2} = 10.258 \text{ m/s}^2$$

$$\tan\theta = \frac{3}{9.81} = 0.3058; \text{ or } \theta = 17°; d_0 = 2 \text{ m.}$$

$$d = d_0 + 2\tan\theta = 2.61 \text{ m. (Ans.)}$$

Example 6.3

$$s = d\cos\theta = 2.496 \text{ m.}$$

$$f = 10.258 \text{ m/s}^2.$$

$$\rho = 1000 \text{ kg/m}^3.$$

$$\text{pressure at P} = p_P = \rho f s = 1000 \times 10.258 \times 2.496 \text{ Pa} = 25.6 \text{ kPa. (Ans.)}$$

Note p_P will also be equal to $\rho g d$.

Example 6.4 A rectangular tank 1 m wide, 2 m long and 1.8 m deep is used to haul water up a slope of 20°. The bottom of the tank was kept horizontal. If the initial acceleration is 3 m/s^2 and later deceleration is 3 m/s^2, what is the maximum amount of water it can haul without spilling?

Let d be the depth of water initially.

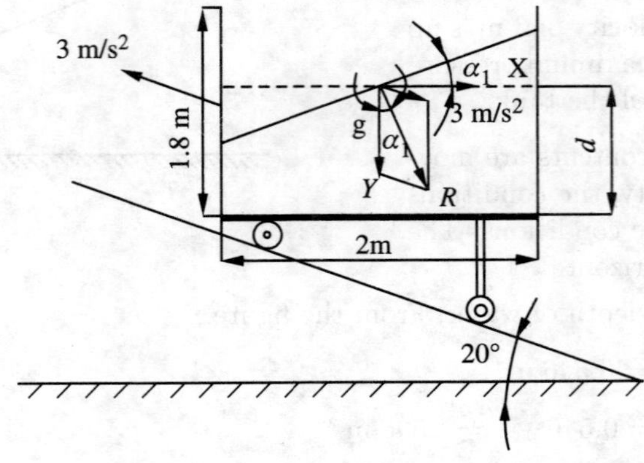

Example 6.4(a)

(a) initial accelerating condition:

$$a_x = 3\cos 20^\circ = 2.819 \text{ m/s}^2;$$

$$a_y = 9.81 + 3\sin 20^\circ$$

$$= 10.836 \text{ m/s}^2$$

$$\tan\alpha_1 = a_x/a_y = 0.26$$

Maximum depth of water

$= d + 1 \times \tan\alpha_1 = d + 0.26$

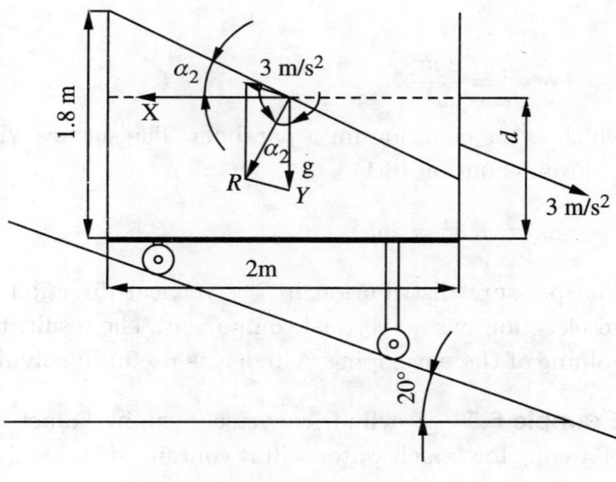

Example 6.4(b)

(b) final decelerating condition:

$$a_x = 3\cos 20^\circ = 2.819 \text{ m/s}^2;$$

$$a_y = 9.81 - 3\sin 20^\circ = 8.784$$

$$\tan\alpha_2 = a_x/a_y = 0.321$$

Maximum depth of water $= d + 1 \times \tan\alpha_2 = d + 0.321$

For the critical condition, $d + 0.321 = 1.8$.

Hence $d = 1.479$ m. Volume of water $= 2 \times 1 \times 1.479 = 2.958 \text{ m}^3$. (Ans.)

6.3 Vortex Motion

6.3.1 Forced vortex motion

When a cylindrical vessel containing a liquid is rotated at a constant speed, the liquid assumes a parabolic shape as shown in Fig. 6.3. The motion is called a forced vortex motion.

Let ω be the constant angular velocity.

Centrifugal acceleration on a particle at a radius $r = v^2/r = \omega^2 r$.

The resultant acceleration on the particle will be due to $\omega^2\vec{r}$ and $\vec{g}$.

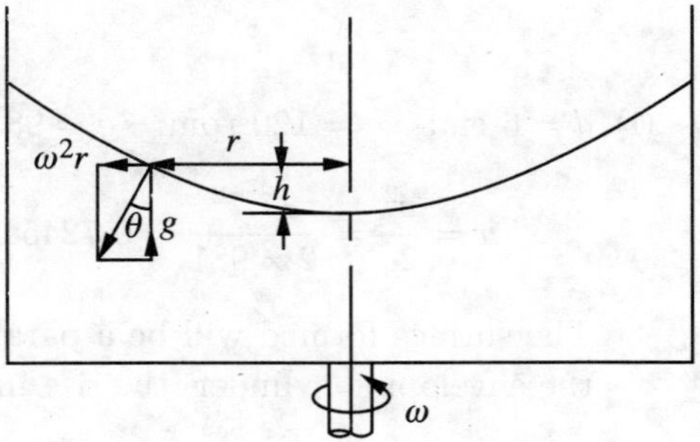

Fig. 6.3 *Forced vortex*

$$\frac{dh}{dr} = \tan\theta = \frac{\omega^2 r}{g}; \quad r\,dr = \frac{g\,dh}{\omega^2}.$$

Integrating, $\dfrac{r^2}{2} = \dfrac{gh}{\omega^2} + C$. When $r = 0,\ h = 0$, hence $C = 0$,

$$\text{or } r^2 = \frac{2gh}{\omega^2}, \tag{6.1}$$

which is the equation for a parabola. The surface will be a paraboloid of revolution.

From equation (6.1),

$$\omega^2 r^2 = v^2 = 2gh.$$

The pressure distribution in the vertical direction will be hydrostatic since the centrifugal acceleration has no vertical component. The result, that the volume of a paraboloid is half the volume of the enveloping cylinder, is useful in solving many problems.

Example 6.5 A cylindrical vessel 6 cm in diameter and 6 cm high contains water to a depth of 4 cm. How much water will it contain, if rotated at a uniform speed of (i) 120 rpm (ii) 390 rpm.

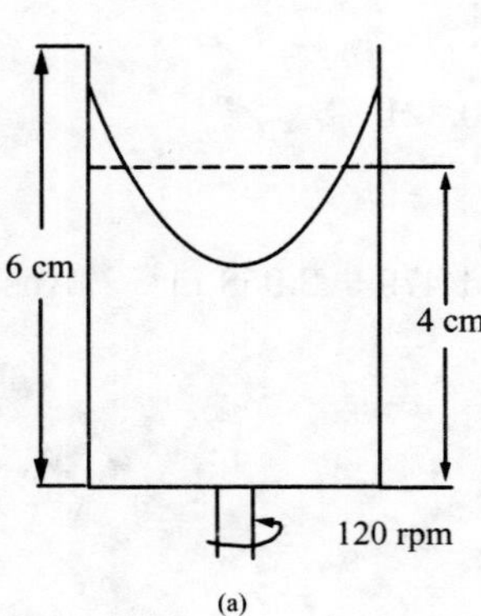

(a)

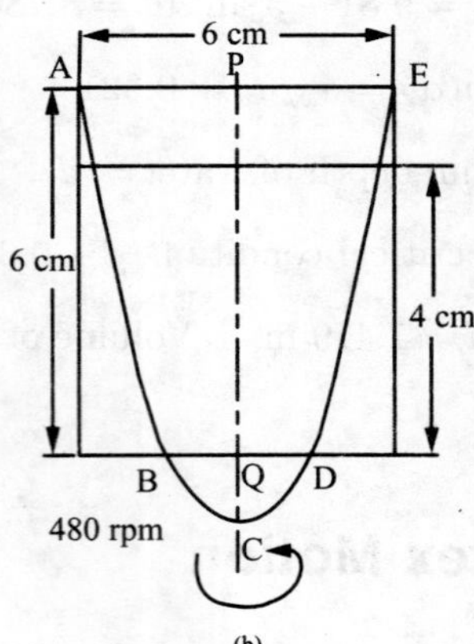

(b)

Example 6.5

(i) $d = 6$ cm; $n = 120$ rpm; $g = 981$ cm/s^2; $v = \pi dn/60 = 37.7$ cm/s.

$$h = \frac{v^2}{2g} = \frac{37.7^2}{2 \times 981} = 0.7245 \text{ cm.}$$

The surface formed will be a paraboloid and since the volume of the paraboloid is half the enveloping cylinder, the rise in level $= 0.7245/2 = 0.3623$ cm.

Total height $= 4 + 0.3623 = 4.3623$ cm.

So no water will be spilled and the volume remains equal to the original volume of $\dfrac{\pi d^2 h}{4} = \dfrac{\pi \times 6^2 \times 4}{4} = 113.1 \text{ cm}^3$. (Ans.)

(ii) $v = \frac{\pi d n}{60} = \frac{\pi \times 6 \times 390}{60} = 122.52$ cm/s.

$h = \frac{v^2}{2g} = \frac{122.52^2}{2 \times 981} = 7.651$ cm.

The height of the calculated paraboloid is more than the height of the vessel. Let the height be PC. The surface being paraboloid,

$$\frac{BQ^2}{AP^2} = \frac{CQ}{CP} = \frac{7.651 - 6}{7.651} = 0.216$$

or, $BQ = \sqrt{0.216} \times AP = 0.465 \times 3 = 1.359$ cm.

Volume of water remaining in the vessel

= volume of cylinder − volume of frustum of the paraboloid ABDE

= volume of cylinder − volume of paraboloid ABCDE + volume of paraboloid BCD

$$= \pi \times 3^2 \times 6 - \frac{1}{2}(\pi \times 3^2 \times 7.651) + \frac{1}{2}(\pi \times 1.359^2 \times 1.59)$$

$= 169.656 - 108.15 + 5.047$

$= 66.553$ cm^3. (Ans.)

Example 6.6 A U-tube containing mercury is rotated about an axis as shown in the figure. If the head difference is 0.5 cm, find the speed of rotation.

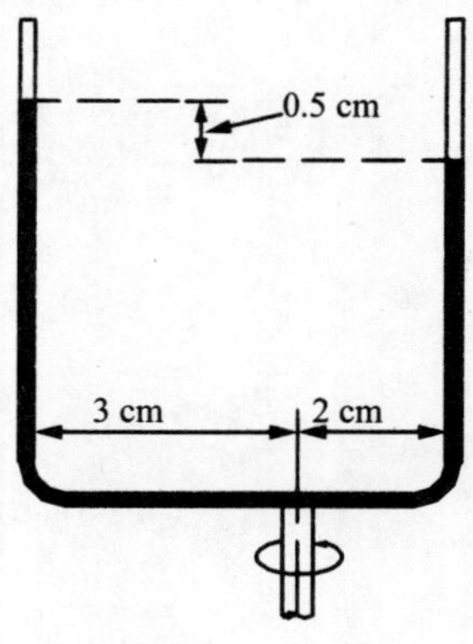

Example 6.5

Let n be the speed in rpm.

$r_1 = 3$ cm ; $r_2 = 2$ cm.

$$v_1 = \frac{2\pi r_1 n}{60} = 0.31416n \text{ cm/s;}$$

$$v_2 = \frac{2\pi r_2 n}{60} = 0.2094n \text{ cm/s.}$$

$$\frac{v_1^2}{2g} - \frac{v_2^2}{2g} = 0.5;$$

i.e., $$\frac{(0.31416^2 - 0.2094^2)n^2}{2 \times 981} = 0.5,$$

or $n = 133.8$ rpm. (Ans.)

6.3.2 Free vortex motion

As the name implies, irrotational or free vortex is produced without any external power input. There is no rotation of the fluid element about its own mass centre and the flow is irrotational.*

Such a vortex can be formed when there is an orifice or opening at the bottom of the container discharging water. Since the flow is irrotational, the line integral $\oint \vec{v}.\vec{dl}$ (circulation) around any element ABCD should be zero. (More detailed discussion about circulation will be done in Chapter 7.)

Let us consider a small element of fluid ABCD. A is at a radius of r_1 and has angular velocity ω_1. B is at radius r_2 and has angular velocity ω_2.

Taking the circulation along ABCD and equating to zero,

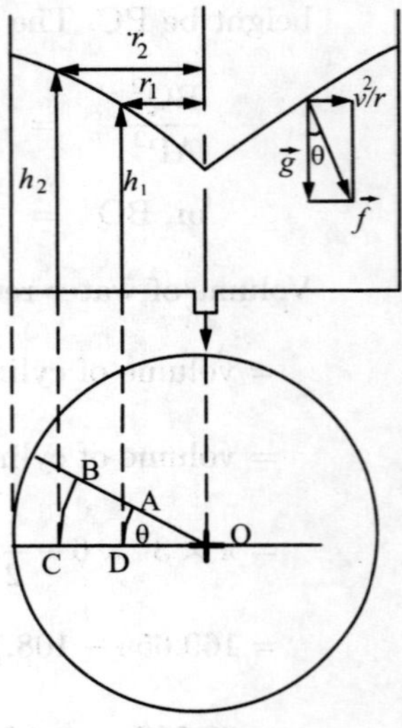

Fig. 6.4 *Free vortex*

$$\oint vdl = 0$$

$$\text{i.e., } 0 \times (r_2 - r_1) + \omega_2 r_2 \times r_2\theta$$

$$+0 \times (r_2 - r_1) - \omega_1 r_1 \times r_1\theta = 0.$$

So, $\omega_2 r_2^2 = \omega_1 r_1^2$, i.e., $v_1 r_1 = v_2 r_2$,

or, $v = \dfrac{C}{r}$, where C is a constant.

At radius r, tangential velocity $v = C/r$, and hence

normal acceleration $= v^2/r = (C/r)^2/r = C^2/r^3$.

$$\frac{dh}{dr} = \tan\theta = \frac{C^2}{r^3 g} \text{ or } \frac{C^2}{r^3 g}dr = dh.$$

Integrating, $-\dfrac{C^2}{2gr^2} = h + k_1$ or $-\dfrac{v^2}{2g} = h + k_1$.

If we assume $h = h_1$ when $r = r_1$,

$$-\frac{v^2}{2g} = h_1 + k_1 \text{ or } k_1 = -(h_1 + \frac{v_1^2}{2g}).$$

Hence, $-\dfrac{v_2^2}{2g} = h_2 - \left(h_1 + \dfrac{v_1^2}{2g}\right)$.

*The concept of irrotational motion can be understood by the following example. A person going around an object in the normal way, will have a rotational motion about his own mass centre. But if he keeps on facing the same direction, say north, as he goes around the object, he will not have a rotational motion.

i.e, $h_1 + \frac{v_1^2}{2g} = h_2 + \frac{v_2^2}{2g}$, where $v = \frac{C}{r}$.

The surface will form in such a way that the total energy will be same (except near the centre).

REVIEW QUESTIONS AND PROBLEMS

6.1 Explain forced vortex motion with a sketch.

6.2 Differentiate between forced vortex and free vortex flow.

6.3 Show that a free vortex is an example of an irrotational motion.

6.4 Derive an expression for the difference of pressure between two points in a free vortex flow.

6.5 A tank containing water to a depth of 1 m is freely falling under gravity. What is the difference of pressure at the surface of water and at the bottom of the tank?

6.6 A tank 5.0 m long, 2.5 m wide and 2 m deep is completely filled with a liquid. If it is accelerated along its length at an acceleration of 2 m/s^2, what will be the volume of the liquid that gets spilled out of the tank?

6.7 A cylindrical tank of diameter 1 m and depth 0.2 m contains water to half its depth. At what horizontal acceleration will the tank start spilling water? What will be the maximum pressure at the bottom of the tank when the water starts spilling?

6.8 A rectangular tank 1 m wide, 2 m long and 1.8 m deep is used to haul water up along a slope of 20°. The bottom of the tank was kept horizontal. The initial acceleration was 3 m/s^2. What is the maximum depth of water so that there will not be any spilling. What is the maximum deceleration at the end so that spilling can be avoided?

6.9 An open circular cylinder of 25 cm diameter and 100 cm length contains water up to a height of 50 cm. It is rotated about its vertical axis. Find the speed of rotation when the axial depth is 30 cm?

6.9 A glass tube of 50 mm diameter, open at the top and containing liquid, rotates about its axis at 700 rpm. What is the lowest level of the surface formed with respect to the initial surface of the liquid?

6.11 A circular tank 1 m high and 0.3 m in diameter is filled up to 0.8 m with water. If the cylinder is to rotate about its axis, what is the minimum angular velocity at which the water starts spilling?

6.12 A hollow cylinder 1 m in diameter, open at the top, spins about its axis which is vertical, thus producing a forced vortex motion of the liquid contained in it. Calculate the height of the vessel if the liquid just reaches the top when rotating at 60 rpm and the minimum depth of water is 15 cm.

6.13 A free vortex is formed in a circular vessel 1 m in diameter. If the depth at $r = 0.2$ m and $r = 0.5$ m are 0.25 m and 0.4 m respectively, find the velocity when $r = 0.2$ m.

ANSWERS

6.5. 0; **6.6.** 6.372 m^3; **6.7.** 1.962 m/s^2, 1.962 kPa; **6.8.** 1.54 m, 2.479 m/s^2; **6.9.** 213.9 rpm; **6.10.** 0.0856 m; **6.11.** 18.676 rad/s; **6.12.** 0.653 m; **6.13.** 1.872 m/s;

7 Fluids Kinematics

Basic principles—Lagrangian and Euler's methods of approach—Concept of flow field—Control volume—Reynolds transport theorem —Equation of continuity in three dimensions—One-dimensional approach—Stream lines—Streak lines—Path lines—Stream function in two-dimensional incompressible steady flows

7.1 Introduction

Fluid kinematics deals with the description and analysis of motion of fluids. Kinematic quantities involving only length and time like velocity, acceleration, discharge, deformation, translation and rotation of fluid elements are considered without taking into account the associated forces. The analysis is, however, helpful in understanding fluid dynamics.

A fluid element of mass dm may move a distance dr in time dt, $d\vec{r} = \vec{i}dx + \vec{j}dy + \vec{k}dz$.

The velocity of the elements in the x, y, and z directions are $u = \dfrac{dx}{dt}; v = \dfrac{dy}{dt}$ and $w = \dfrac{dz}{dt}$.

The accelerations will have components defined by $a_x = \dfrac{d^2x}{dt^2}$; $a_y = \dfrac{d^2y}{dt^2}$; and $a_z = \dfrac{d^2z}{dt^2}$.

7.2 Lagrangian Description of Motion

The motion of a particular element of fluid of mass dm can be studied in the same manner as the kinematics of a solid particle by the Lagrangian system. An infinitesimal element of fluid can be given an identification by the coordinates $\vec{r}_0(x_0, y_0, z_0)$ it occupies at time t_0. At subsequent time t, let it occupy $r(x, y, z)$, x, y and z are functions of x_0, y_0, z_0 and t.
The velocity of the element in the three coordinate directions are

$$u = \frac{dx}{dt} = \left(\frac{\partial x}{\partial t}\right)_{r_0\, =\, \text{constant}} ;v = \frac{dy}{dt} = \left(\frac{\partial y}{\partial t}\right)_{r_0\, =\, \text{constant}} ;w = \frac{dz}{dt} = \left(\frac{\partial z}{\partial t}\right)_{r_0\, =\, \text{constant}}.$$

In the above expression, since the motion of a particular element is analysed, r_o is kept constant.
The accelerations are

$$a_x = \left(\frac{\partial^2 x}{\partial t^2}\right)_{r_0\, =\, \text{constant}} ; a_y = \left(\frac{\partial^2 y}{\partial t^2}\right)_{r_0\, =\, \text{constant}} ; a_z = \left(\frac{\partial^2 z}{\partial t^2}\right)_{r_0\, =\, \text{constant}}.$$

The equation of the path line or the path that an element of fluid follows in its motion can be obtained as follows

$$\frac{dx}{dt} = u(x, y, z, t); \frac{dy}{dt} = v(x, y, z, t); \frac{dz}{dt} = w(x, y, z, t),$$

subject to the initial condition $x(t_0) = x_0$; $y(t_0) = y_0$ and $z(t_0) = z_0$.

The Lagrangian method thus follows the history of movement of an element in question. It can also be used to analyse the movement of a system of elements. A system will consist of the same elements of the fluids and may move due to the action of various forces.

7.3 Concept of the Flow Field

For every point in a region of flow, the properties of the flow or fluid are assumed to be same as that of a very small element of fluid surrounding it. The properties defined may be indicated by $e(x, y, z, t)$. Depending on whether e is scalar, vector or tensor, we may designate the region as a scalar, vector or tensor field.

7.4 Eulerian Description of Motion

In most cases, it becomes too complicated to study the motion of various individual elements of fluids in a flow field by the Lagrangian method. In the Eulerian method, one does not follow an individual element, but rather describes what happens at various points in the flow field as a function of time. Even then, the concept of velocity at particular point and time can only be related to an element that occupies the point at that instant.

The property e of the fluid at a point P is a function of the coordinates of the point and time. i.e., $e(x, y, z, t)$. Hence, components of velocity of point P can be written as $u = f_1(x, y, z, t); v = f_2(x, y, z, t); w = f_3(x, y, z, t)$.

Change in the property e,

$$de = \frac{\partial e}{\partial x}dx + \frac{\partial e}{\partial y}dy + \frac{\partial e}{\partial z}dz + \frac{\partial e}{\partial t}dt.$$

Substituting $dx = udt$, $dy = vdt$, and $dz = wdt$, which is true for any element of fluid passing through the point, the total or substantial derivative

$$\frac{de}{dt} = u\frac{\partial e}{\partial x} + v\frac{\partial e}{\partial y} + w\frac{\partial e}{\partial z} + \frac{\partial e}{\partial t}.$$

7.4.1 Fluid acceleration at a point

If the property concerned is the velocity in the x, y and z directions,

$$a_x = \frac{du}{dt} = \frac{\partial u}{\partial t} + u\frac{\partial u}{\partial x} + v\frac{\partial u}{\partial y} + w\frac{\partial u}{\partial z}, \tag{7.1}$$

$$a_y = \frac{dv}{dt} = \frac{\partial v}{\partial t} + u\frac{\partial v}{\partial x} + v\frac{\partial v}{\partial y} + w\frac{\partial v}{\partial z} \text{ and} \tag{7.2}$$

$$a_z = \frac{dw}{dt} = \frac{\partial w}{\partial t} + u\frac{\partial w}{\partial x} + v\frac{\partial w}{\partial y} + w\frac{\partial w}{\partial z}. \tag{7.3}$$

The partial derivatives with respect to t is due to the temporal variation of velocity at the same location and are called local accelerations. The last three terms on the right-hand side of the above equations represent the acceleration caused by the spatial changes in the velocity field and are called convective acceleration terms.

The total acceleration is the vector sum of a_x, a_y and a_z.

7.4.2 Acceleration of a fluid in a curvilinear flow

Consider a steady flow when the motion is in a straight line. There can be acceleration $\vec{a}_r$ along the direction of motion. But in case of a curved path, there will also be an acceleration in a direction normal to flow.

Let P and Q be two points on the curved path and ds be the distance. From Fig. 7.1, $ds = rd\theta$ or $\frac{d\theta}{ds} = \frac{1}{r}$. Let the velocity in the s direction be increased by δv_s as it moves from P to Q. Let δv_n be the normal component such that the tangential velocity at Q is $v_{s'}$.

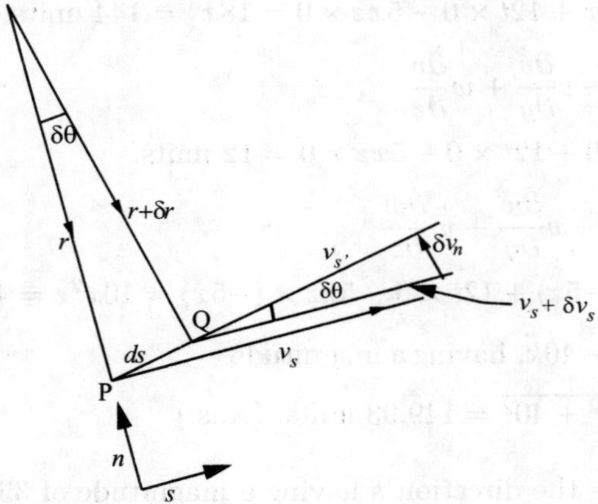

Fig. 7.1 *Change in velocity of a fluid in curvilinear flow*

$$\delta\, v_n = (v_s + \delta\, v_s)\delta\theta \approx v_s\delta\theta,$$

or $$\frac{dv_n}{d\theta} = v_s.$$

Acceleration along the tangential direction,

$$a_s = \frac{dv_s}{dt} = \frac{dv_s}{ds} \times \frac{dv_s}{dt} = \frac{dv_s}{ds} \times v_s. \tag{7.4}$$

Acceleration along the radial (towards centre),

$$a_n = \frac{dv_n}{dt} = \frac{dv_n}{d\theta} \cdot \frac{d\theta}{ds}\frac{ds}{dt} = v_s \frac{1}{r} v_s = \frac{v_s^2}{r} \tag{7.5}$$

If $\vec{s}$ and $\vec{n}$ are unit vectors in the tangential and the radial (towards centre) direction,

$$\text{total acceleration} = \vec{s} v_s \frac{dv_s}{ds} + \vec{n} \frac{v_s^2}{r}. \tag{7.6}$$

Examples 7.1 The velocity field in a flow is given by $\vec{V} = 3x^2\vec{i} + 12t\vec{j} - 5xz\vec{k}$. Find the velocity and acceleration at (2, 1, 1) when $t = 3$.

$u = 3x^2; v = 12t$ and $w = -5xz$.

At $(2, 1, 1)$, $u = 12$; $v = 36$; $w = -10$.

$\vec{V} = 12\vec{i} + 36\vec{j} - 10\vec{k}$, having a magnitude of $\sqrt{12^2 + 36^2 + 10^2} = 39.24$ units.

$$\begin{aligned}
a_x &= \frac{\partial u}{\partial t} + u\frac{\partial u}{\partial x} + v\frac{\partial u}{\partial y} + w\frac{\partial u}{\partial z} \\
&= 0 + 3x^2 \times 6x + 12t \times 0 - 5xz \times 0 = 18x^3 = 144 \text{ units.} \\
a_y &= \frac{\partial v}{\partial t} + u\frac{\partial v}{\partial x} + v\frac{\partial v}{\partial y} + w\frac{\partial v}{\partial z} \\
&= 12 + 3x^2 \times 0 + 12t \times 0 - 5xz \times 0 = 12 \text{ units.} \\
a_z &= \frac{\partial w}{\partial t} + u\frac{\partial w}{\partial x} + v\frac{\partial w}{\partial y} + w\frac{\partial w}{\partial z} \\
&= 0 + 3x^2 \times (-5z) + 12t \times 0 - 5xz \times (-5x) = 10x^2z = 40 \text{ units.} \\
\vec{a} &= 144\vec{i} + 12\vec{j} + 40\vec{k}, \text{ having a magnitude} \\
&= \sqrt{144^2 + 12^2 + 40^2} = 149.93 \text{ units. (Ans.)}
\end{aligned}$$

$\vec{V} = 12\vec{i} + 36\vec{j} - 10\vec{k}$ along the direction s having a magnitude of 39.24.

$$\text{unit vector } \vec{s} = \frac{1}{39.24}(12\vec{i} + 36\vec{j} - 10\vec{k}) = 0.3058\vec{i} + 0.9174\vec{j} - 0.2548\vec{k}.$$

$$\vec{a}.\vec{s} = (144\vec{i} + 12\vec{j} + 40\vec{k})\ (0.3058\vec{i} + 0.9174\vec{j} - 0.2548\vec{k}) = 44.04 + 11 - 10.19$$

$$= 44.81 \text{ units.}$$

Hence, $\vec{a}_n = \sqrt{149.93^2 - 44.81^2} = 143.08$ units. (Ans.)

7.5 Steady and Unsteady Flows

In general, the parameters of flow at a point in space vary with time. Such flows are called unsteady flows for which, quantities like $\frac{\partial v}{\partial t}, \frac{\partial \rho}{\partial t}$ etc., will not be zero.

In steady flows, there is no change of the flow parameters at a point with time. In such cases, $\frac{\partial v}{\partial t}, \frac{\partial \rho}{\partial t}$ etc., will be zero.

7.6 Stream Lines, Path Lines and Streak Lines

The concept of stream lines, path lines and streak lines helps in understanding the patterns of flow. *Stream lines are imaginary lines, the tangent at any point of which will indicate the direction of velocity at that point.* The velocity vector being tangential to stream lines, the equation to stream lines can be written as

$$\frac{dx}{u} = \frac{dy}{v} = \frac{dz}{w} \tag{7.7}$$

The instantaneous velocities of water around a body can be visualized in a laboratory by taking a photograph (with very small time exposure) of the pattern of streaks formed by the dust of aluminum put in water. Continuous lines can be drawn tangential to the streaks to get the stream lines.

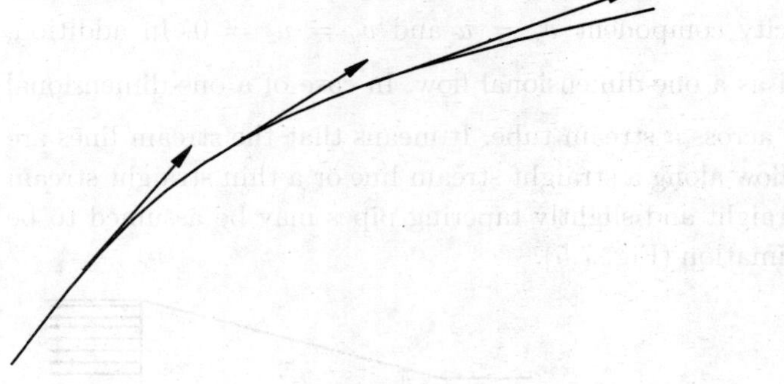

Fig. 7.2(a) *Stream line*

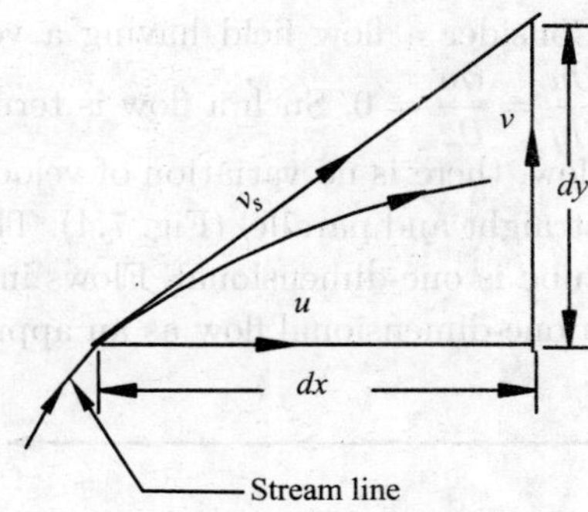

Fig. 7.2(b) *Stream line and the velocity components*

If all the stream lines passing through a closed curve be drawn, they will form a tube, known as the stream tube. Since the velocity at the stream lines are tangential, there is no flow possible across the stream tube.

A *path line is the path traced by a particular particle during a time interval.* It can be traced in the laboratory by introducing a coloured particle (of density close to that of the fluid) and studying its movement.

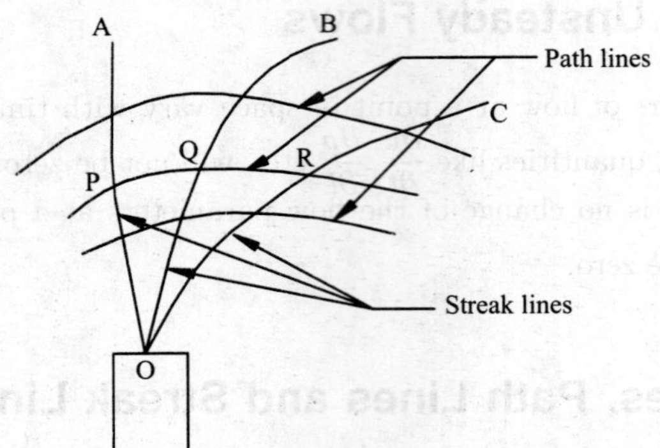

Fig. 7.3 *Path lines and streak lines*

If one introduces a series of particles at a particular point at small intervals and observe the pattern formed by the released particles after some time, one can get a streak line. The smoke coming out of a incense stick illustrates streak lines.

In Fig. 7.3, OA is a streak line and if a wind swayed it to positions OB and OC, the particle at P may traverse to positions Q and later to R. Then, line PQR will be the path line. In steady flows, the stream lines, path lines and streak lines will coincide and in an unsteady flow the stream lines, path lines and streak lines can be different.

7.7 One-, Two- and Three- Dimensional Flows

Consider a flow field having a velocity component $v_x = u$ and $v_y = v_z = 0$. In addition, $\dfrac{\partial u}{\partial y} = \dfrac{\partial u}{\partial z} = 0$. Such a flow is termed as a one-dimensional flow. In case of a one-dimensional flow, there is no variation of velocity across a stream tube. It means that the stream lines are straight and parallel (Fig. 7.4). The flow along a straight stream line or a thin straight stream tube is one-dimensional. Flows in straight and slightly tapering pipes may be assumed to be a one-dimensional flow as an approximation (Fig. 7.5).

Fig. 7.4 *One-dimensional flow* **Fig. 7.5** *Approximation of a one-dimensional flow*

In two-dimensional flows, there can be velocity components and variation of velocity in two perpendicular directions, say x and y. But, $w = 0$ and $\dfrac{\partial u}{\partial z} = \dfrac{\partial v}{\partial z} = 0$, which means that the components of velocity and the variation of velocity in the z direction must be zero. Flow in a wide rectangular channel has velocity component only in the direction of flow but the velocity varies with the depth and, hence such a flow is treated as a two-dimensional flow. Flow over a long weir is also considered as a two-dimensional flow, as the flow velocities has components in two directions. Flow between parallel plates also falls in this category.

In three-dimensional flows, velocity components and variation of velocities can be in three directions x, y and z. In general, flows are three-dimensional and three coordinates are essential to describe the velocity field. In many practical problems, for simplifying the analysis, it is common to neglect the variation of velocity components in one or two directions. Asymmetrical flows are special cases of three-dimensional flows.

7.8 Trajectory of Liquid Jets

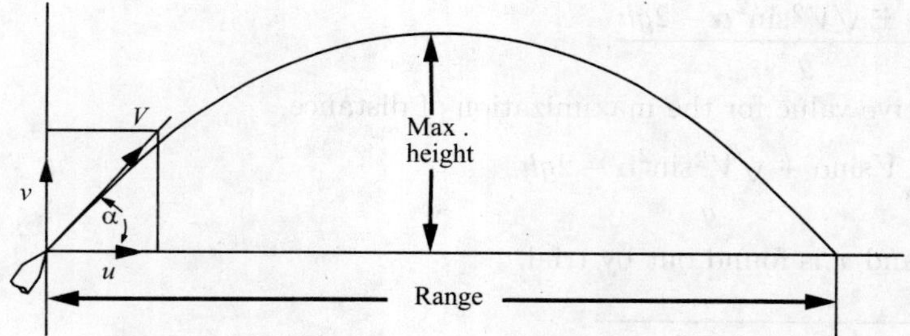

Fig. 7.6 *Trajectory of a liquid jet*

Let a jet of a liquid issue forth from a nozzle at a velocity V making an angle α with the horizontal as in Fig. 7.6. At time $t = 0$, the velocity components are $u = V\cos\alpha$ and $v = V$ $\sin\alpha$.

Since the friction due to air is neglected, total energy will be conserved. At time t,

$$u = V\cos\alpha. \tag{7.8}$$

$$v = V\sin\alpha t - gt. \tag{7.9}$$

i) Maximum height reached:

When $h = h_{\max}$, $V = 0$ and hence $t = V\sin\alpha/g$.

$h_{\max} = V\sin\alpha t - 0.5gt^2$.

Substituting value of t,

$$h_{\max} = \frac{V^2\sin^2\alpha}{2\text{g}}. \tag{7.10}$$

ii) Range (for the same elevation),

$$R = 2\cos\alpha t = 2V\cos\alpha \frac{V\sin\alpha}{g} = \frac{V^2\sin 2\alpha}{2g}. \tag{7.11}$$

Example 7.2 A fireman must reach a window 28 m above the ground with a free stream from a nozzle issuing a jet at 30 m/s. Neglecting air resistance and assuming that the height of the nozzle is 1.5 m, find the greatest distance from the building at which the fireman can stand and still play the jet on the window.

$V = 30$ m/s; $h = 28 - 1.5 = 26.5$ m.

$h = V\sin\alpha t - 0.5\, gt^2$;

dividing by 0.5 g and simplifying,

$$t^2 - \left(\frac{2V\sin\alpha}{g}\right)t + \frac{2h}{g} = 0.$$

So, $$t = \frac{V\sin\alpha \pm \sqrt{V^2\sin^2\alpha - 2gh}}{g}.$$

Taking the positive value for the maximization of distance,

$$x = V\cos\alpha \frac{V\sin\alpha + \sqrt{V^2\sin^2\alpha - 2gh}}{g}.$$

The value of α and x is found out by trial.

α	t	x
60°	3.918	58.77
62°	4.074	57.38
58°	3.744	59.52
57°	3.649	59.62
56.5°	3.599	59.595

From the table, it is seen that the maximum distance is 59.62 m and $\alpha = 57$.

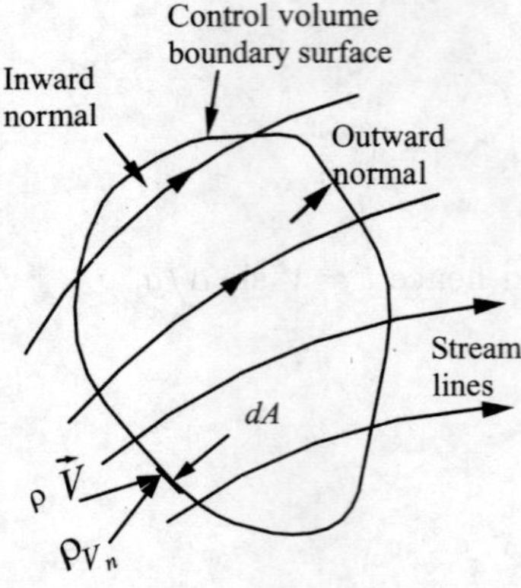

Fig. 7.7 *Control volume*

7.9 Concept of Control Volume

A definite volume with control boundary surfaces in space is a control volume (Fig. 7.7). The concept is useful to solve problems without the need of studying the motion of a single fluid element or a group of fluid elements[34,42]. Many elements of fluids will enter, occupy and leave the control volume as time progresses, but at any time t, the elements inside the control volume should obey the basic laws of mechanics.

7.10 System of Elements in a Control Volume at Time *t* — Reynolds' Transport Theorem

In the system approach, we are concerned with a definite set of elements of mass dm. But in the control volume approach, we are only concerned with a definite volume which may be occupied by different elements at different times. A very useful result known as Reynold's transport equation connecting the two approaches can be developed as follows.

Imagine a system of elements occupying a control volume at time t. Let η be a scalar intensive property. For example, η can be the momentum transport rate/unit mass of the fluid. i.e., η can be $\dfrac{\rho V}{\rho}$ i.e., equal to V. Let us consider an extensive property, $N = \iiint\limits_{v} \eta\rho \, d\forall$, ($N$ is a property like mass, momentum, energy etc., depending on the mass), where $\forall$ is the volume. After a small interval of time t, the system will move to a new position as shown in Fig. 7.8. It requires inflow into the control volume and an outflow from the control volume. The following result can be obtained neglecting second order infinitesimal quantities,

$$\frac{\partial}{\partial t} \iiint\limits_{cv} \eta(\rho \, d\forall) = \frac{DN}{Dt} - \oiint\limits_{cs} \eta\left(\rho \vec{V} d\vec{A}\right),$$

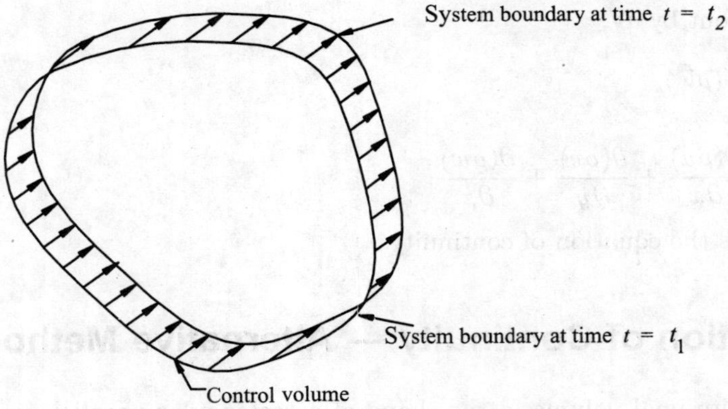

System boundary at time $t = t_2$

System boundary at time $t = t_1$

Control volume

Fig. 7.8 *System of elements*

where cv – control volume, cs – control surface, d∀ – elementary volume, $\vec{V}$ – velocity and dA – elementary area.

The quantity on the left indicates the rate of change of $\eta\rho$ in the control volume due to inflow and outflow across the boundaries. For steady flows it will be zero. $\frac{DN}{Dt}$ indicates the change of quantity N in the system. When N is the mass, $\frac{DN}{Dt}$ will be zero. The second quantity on the right indicates the algebraic sum of the outward and inward transport of the quantity across the control surface $\eta\rho.\vec{V}.d\vec{A}$ will be $\eta\rho V_n \times dA$, where V_n will be the normal component. $\eta\rho\ V_n$ is taken positive for the outward normal and negative for the inward normal.

The equation can be written as

$$\frac{DN}{Dt} = \frac{\partial}{\partial t}\iiint_{cv} \eta\ \rho\ d\forall + \oint\!\!\oint_{cs} \eta\left(\rho\vec{V}.d\vec{A}\right). \tag{7.12}$$

7.11 Application to the Law of Conservation of Mass

The above equation can be applied to an infinitesimally small system of mass M and having a control volume $d\forall$ same as its boundaries. When we consider fluid property $\rho, \eta = \rho/\rho = 1$ and applying the condition that $\frac{DN}{Dt} = \frac{DM}{Dt} = 0$ for the system (law of conservation of mass),

$$0 = \frac{\partial}{\partial t}\iiint_{dV} \rho d\forall + \oint\!\!\oint_{cs}\left(\rho\vec{V}d\vec{A}\right).$$

By applying Gauss theorem,

$$0 = \frac{\partial}{\partial t}\iiint_{dV} \rho d\forall + \iiint_{dV} \bar{\nabla}\left(\rho\bar{V}\right) d\forall.$$

Dividing throughout by $d\forall$,

$$0 = \frac{\partial\rho}{\partial t} + \nabla(\rho\vec{V}).$$

$$0 = \frac{\partial\rho}{\partial t} + \frac{\partial(\rho u)}{\partial x} + \frac{\partial(\rho v)}{\partial y} + \frac{\partial(\rho w)}{\partial z}, \tag{7.13}$$

which is known as the equation of continuity.

7.12 Equation of Continuity — Alternative Method

Consider an infinitesimal volume in the shape of a rectangular parallelopiped of dimensions dx, dy and dz along the x, y and z axes respectively as in Fig. 7.9. Let the velocity components of flow at the central point C (x, y, z) be u, v and w and the density be ρ.

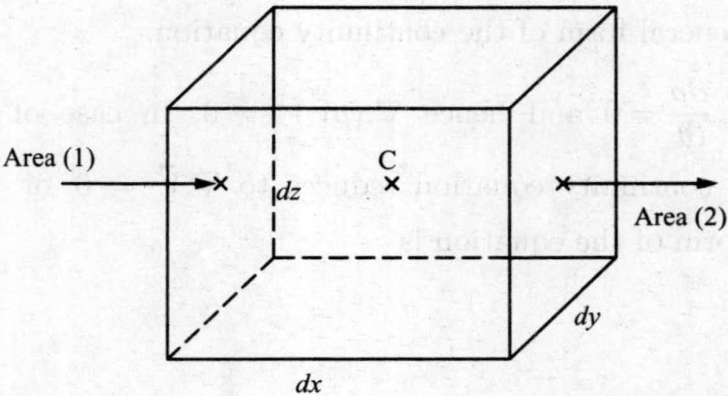

Fig. 7.9 *Control volume dx dy dz*

The mass influx rate into the volume along the X direction across area (1).

$$I_1 = \left(\rho u - \frac{\partial(\rho u)}{\partial x}\frac{dx}{2}\right) dydz.$$

The mass efflux rate across area (2),

$$E_2 = \left(\rho u + \frac{\partial(\rho u)}{\partial x}\frac{dx}{2}\right) dydz.$$

The net influx rate in the X direction $= I_1 - E_2 = -\dfrac{\partial(\rho u)}{\partial x} dxdydz.$

Similarly, the net mass influx in the Y and Z directions are

$$-\frac{\partial(\rho v)}{\partial y} dxdydz \text{ and } -\frac{\partial(\rho w)}{\partial z} dxdydz.$$

Therefore, total mass influx rate $= -\left(\dfrac{\partial(\rho u)}{\partial x} + \dfrac{\partial(\rho v)}{\partial y} + \dfrac{\partial(\rho w)}{\partial z}\right) dx\,dy\,dz.$

Let the change in density of fluid inside the volume due to the above mass influx be $d\rho$. The rate of change in mass within the control volume $= \dfrac{\partial \rho}{\partial t} dx\,dy\,dz$. By the principle of conservation of mass,

$$\frac{\partial \rho}{\partial t} dx\,dy\,dz = -\left(\frac{\partial(\rho u)}{\partial x} + \frac{\partial(\rho v)}{\partial y} + \frac{\partial(\rho w)}{\partial z}\right) dx\,dy\,dz,$$

$$\text{or, } \frac{\partial \rho}{\partial t} + \frac{\partial(\rho u)}{\partial x} + \frac{\partial(\rho v)}{\partial y} + \frac{\partial(\rho w)}{\partial z} = 0.$$

In the vector notation it can be written as

$$\frac{\partial \rho}{\partial t} + \nabla.\left(\rho \vec{V}\right) = 0. \tag{7.14}$$

Expression (1) is the general form of the continuity equation.

If the flow is steady, $\dfrac{\partial \rho}{\partial t} = 0$ and hence $\nabla.(\rho\vec{V}) = 0$. In case of incompressible fluids, ρ is constant and the continuity equation reduces to $\nabla.\vec{V} = 0$ or $\dfrac{\partial u}{\partial x} + \dfrac{\partial v}{\partial y} + \dfrac{\partial w}{\partial z} = 0$. The two-dimensional form of the equation is

$$\frac{\partial u}{\partial x} + \frac{\partial v}{\partial y} = 0. \tag{7.15}$$

7.13 One-dimensional Approximation

For a steady flow problem through a stream tube, when the flow is assumed to be one-dimensional,

$$\oiint_{cs} (\rho\vec{V}.d\vec{A}) = 0.$$

Flow can enter in surface (1) and go out only from surface (2) for the stream tube shown in Fig. 7.9. So, $\rho_1 A_1 V_1 = \rho_2 A_2 V_2$. For an incompressible flow, the continuity equation reduces to $A_1 V_1 = A_2 V_2$ (cross-sections are taken normal to the direction velocities).

Example 7.3 A velocity field of an incompressible fluid is described by the equation $\vec{V} = (x^2 z - y^2 + 2xyz)\,\vec{i} + (x^2 - 2y^2 - y^2 z)\,\vec{j} + w\,\vec{k}$. Find the velocity component w.

Here,

$$u = x^2 z - y^2 + 2xyz; v = x^2 - 2y^2 - y^2 z.$$

$$\frac{\partial u}{\partial x} = 2xz + 2yz\ ; \frac{\partial v}{\partial y} = -4y - 2yz.$$

Applying continuity equation,

$$\frac{\partial u}{\partial x} + \frac{\partial v}{\partial y} + \frac{\partial w}{\partial z} = 0.$$

$$2xz + 2yz - 4y - 2yz + \frac{\partial w}{\partial z} = 0.$$

$$\text{or, } \frac{\partial w}{\partial z} = -2xz + 4y;$$

Integrating, $w = -xz^2 + 4yz + c$. (Ans.)

7.14 Circulation and Vorticity

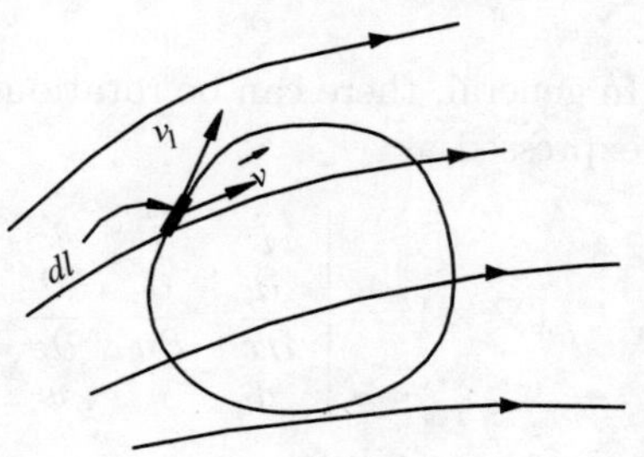

Fig. 7.10 *Circulation*

Circulation Γ around a closed path is defined as

$$\Gamma = \oint_0 \vec{v}.d\vec{l} = \oint_0 v_l dl, \tag{7.16}$$

where v_l is the velocity component tangent to the line element dl as shown in Fig. 7.10. The circulation is closely connected with the angular velocity of rotation of the fluid element.

For example, taking a small circular two-dimensional element of fluid of radius r rotating at an angular velocity of ω, the circulation will be $2\pi r\omega$. The vorticity will be Γ/area=2ω. The circulation in anticlockwise direction is usually taken as positive.

7.15 Angular Velocity for an Element of Fluid

Imagine a fluid element in the XY plane of sides dx and dy as in Fig. 7.11.

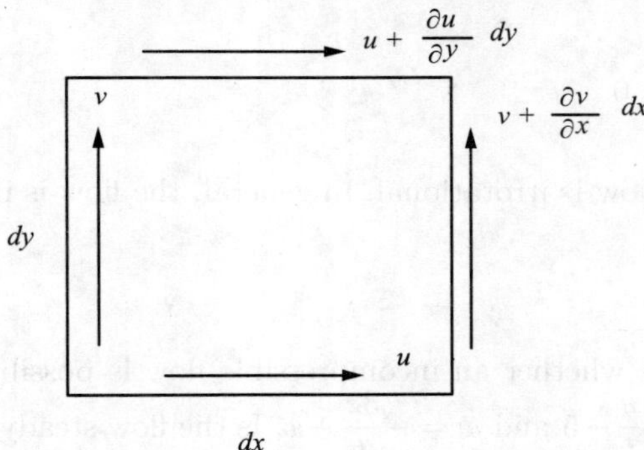

Fig. 7.11 *Element of fluid subjected to rotation*

$$\begin{aligned}\text{Circulation} \quad &= udx + \left(v + \frac{\partial v}{\partial x}dx\right)dy - \left(u + \frac{\partial u}{\partial y}dy\right)dx - vdy \\ &= \frac{\partial v}{\partial x}dxdy - \frac{\partial u}{\partial y}dxdy = \left(\frac{\partial v}{\partial x} - \frac{\partial u}{\partial y}\right)dxdy. \qquad (\text{area } = dxdy)\end{aligned}$$

$$\text{Vorticity} = \frac{\text{circulation}}{\text{area}} = \left(\frac{\partial v}{\partial x} - \frac{\partial u}{\partial y}\right). \tag{7.17}$$

Angular velocity about the z axis,

$$\omega_z = \frac{1}{2}\text{ vorticity } = \frac{1}{2}\left(\frac{\partial v}{\partial x} - \frac{\partial u}{\partial y}\right). \tag{7.18}$$

In general, there can be rotations about all the three axes. The general vorticity vector can be expressed as

$$\nabla \times \vec{V} = \begin{vmatrix} \vec{i} & \vec{j} & \vec{k} \\ \dfrac{\partial}{\partial x} & \dfrac{\partial}{\partial y} & \dfrac{\partial}{\partial z} \\ u & v & w \end{vmatrix} = \vec{i}\left(\frac{\partial w}{\partial y} - \frac{\partial v}{\partial z}\right) + \vec{j}\left(\frac{\partial u}{\partial z} - \frac{\partial w}{\partial x}\right) + \vec{k}\left(\frac{\partial v}{\partial x} - \frac{\partial u}{\partial y}\right) \tag{7.19}$$

and it can be recognised that

$$2\,\omega_x = \left(\frac{\partial w}{\partial y} - \frac{\partial v}{\partial z}\right);\ 2\,\omega_y = \left(\frac{\partial u}{\partial z} - \frac{\partial w}{\partial x}\right);\ 2\,\omega_z = \left(\frac{\partial v}{\partial x} - \frac{\partial u}{\partial y}\right).$$

7.16 Irrotational and Rotational Flows

The angular velocity of rotation of a fluid element about its own centre can be studied by means of the above equations. When $\omega = 0$, the fluid flow is irrotational, i.e., there is no rotation of the fluid element about its own centre.
In a two-dimensional flow in the XY plane.

$$\omega_z = \left(\frac{\partial v}{\partial x} - \frac{\partial u}{\partial y}\right) = 0 \tag{7.20}$$

i.e., when $\dfrac{\partial v}{\partial x} = \dfrac{\partial u}{\partial y}$, the flow is irrotational. In general, the flow is irrotational when

$$\nabla \times \vec{V} = 0. \tag{7.21}$$

Example 7.4 Examine whether an incompressible flow is possible with the velocity component $u = \dfrac{2x}{t} + z;\quad v = \dfrac{y}{t} - 5$ and $w = -\dfrac{3z}{t} + x$. Is the flow steady? Is the flow irrotational?

$$\frac{\partial u}{\partial x} + \frac{\partial v}{\partial y} + \frac{\partial w}{\partial z} = \frac{2}{t} + \frac{1}{t} - \frac{3}{t} = 0.$$

Hence it satisfies continuity equation.

The velocity changes with time, so the flow is unsteady.

$$2\omega_x = \left(\frac{\partial w}{\partial y} - \frac{\partial v}{\partial z}\right) = 0.$$

$$2\omega_y = \left(\frac{\partial u}{\partial z} - \frac{\partial w}{\partial x}\right) = 1 - 1 = 0.$$

$$2\omega_z = \left(\frac{\partial v}{\partial x} - \frac{\partial u}{\partial y}\right) = 0.$$

Hence the flow is irrotational.

REVIEW QUESTIONS AND PROBLEMS

7.1. Differentiate between Lagrangian and Eulerian descriptions of flow. Which description is useful to study path lines?

7.2. Distinguish between stream lines, streak lines and path lines.

7.3. What are steady and unsteady flows?

7.4. A steady flow can be non-uniform. Discuss.

7.5. Derive an equation for a trajectory of a jet of velocity V making an angle α with the horizontal.

7.6. Derive equations for maximum height and conditions for maximum range at the same elevation of projection of a jet.

7.7. State and explain the Reynold's transport theorem.

7.8. Derive the general equation of continuity for compressible fluids.

7.9. State the continuity equation for one-dimensional steady flow.

7.10. What are irrotational flows?

7.11. State the conditions for a three-dimensional flow to be irrotational.

7.12. A jet issuing from a nozzle at an angle 30 gains a height of 3 m when it moves 8 m horizontally. Find the velocity at the nozzle and the maximum elevation reached by the jet.

7.13 A jet issues from an orifice at the side of a tank at a velocity of 4.34 m/s. At what distance from the tank will the jet area be reduced to half?

7.14. The x component of velocity $u = x^2 + y^2 - 5$ and the y component $v = y^2 + z^2$. Find the simplest z component of velocity, which satisfies the continuity equation.

7.15. The x component of velocity in a two-dimensional incompressible flow is given by $u = ax^3 + by^2$. Find the y component v if at $y = 0, v = 0$ for all values of x.

7.16. The x component of velocity in a two-dimensional incompressible flow is described by $u = Ax^2 + By^2$. Use the continuity equation to find the y component of velocity V. Assume for all values of $x; v = 0$ at $y = 0$.

7.17. Determine which of the velocity component sets given below satisfy the equation of continuity, (i) $u = cx; v = -\, cy$. (ii) $u = A\sin(xy); v = -A\sin(xy)$.

7.18. Determine the magnitude of velocity and acceleration at A ($x = 2; y = -3; z = 1; t = 1$) for the velocity vector $V = (10t + xy)\,\vec{i} + (-yz - 10t)\,\vec{j} + (-yz + z^2/2)\,\vec{k}$.

7.19. In a two-dimensional flow, the x component is $u = x^2 - 4xy - 3y$, find the component of velocity in the y direction.

7.20. A 30 cm diameter pipe conveying water, branches into two pipes of diameter 20 cm and 15 cm respectively. If the average velocity in the 30 cm diameter pipe is 2.5 m/s, find the total discharge in this pipe. Also determine the velocity in the 15 cm pipe if the average velocity in the 20 cm diameter pipe is 2 m/s.

ANSWERS

7.12. 16.08 m/s; 3.295 m; **7.13.** 3.324 m; **7.14.** $w = -2xz - 2yz + f(x,y)$; **7.15.** $v = -3ax^2y$; **7.16.** $-2Axy$; **7.17.**(i) Satisfied; **7.17.** (ii) Not satisfied; **7.18.** 8.789 m/s; 27.445 m/s^2; **7.19.** $v = 2y^2 - 2xy + f(x)$; **7.20.** $Q = 0.1767$ m^3/s; $V_2 = 6.44$ m/s.

8 Principles of Ideal Fluid Flow

Stream function — Velocity potential — Stream function in two-dimensional incompressible steady flows — Vorticity — Circulation — Flow net — Flow net construction — Different methods

8.1 Stream Function in Two-dimensional Steady Incompressible Flow

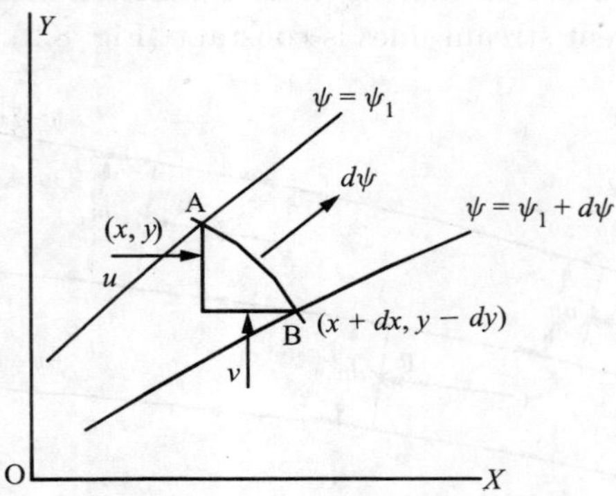

Fig. 8.1 *Stream function*

In a two-dimensional incompressible flow, consider a stream tube of unit width and having a very small interval between them. The stream lines are shown in Fig. 8.1. Since there cannot be any velocity across the stream line, the discharge between them will be constant, say $d\psi$ per unit width. The same discharge has to flow across AC and BC and also across AB. By the equation of continuity,

$$vdx + u(-dy) = d\psi = \frac{\partial \psi}{\partial x}dx + \frac{\partial \psi}{\partial y}dy$$

$$\text{or } u = -\frac{\partial \psi}{\partial y}{}^{\dagger}.$$

† The description, $u = -\dfrac{\partial \psi}{\partial y}$ and $v = \dfrac{\partial \psi}{\partial x}$ is followed by many authors like Milne-Thomson[15], V.L.Streeter[35], James A. Liggett[14], R.J.Garde[7] and Modi & Seth.[16] Many others follow the opposite signs for u and v. The student is advised to consistently follow one description.

$$\text{and } v = \frac{\partial \psi}{\partial x}. \tag{8.2}$$

When $d\psi = 0$, i.e., when we are concerned with only one stream line ψ = constant or $\psi = \psi_1$. Each stream line can be designated by a function called stream function ψ and the difference in ψ between two stream lines, $d\psi$, indicates the discharge per unit width passing between them. It may be seen that (8.1) and (8.2) satisfy the continuity equation for incompressible flow,

$$\frac{du}{dx} + \frac{dv}{dy} = 0$$

8.2 System of Stream Lines and Velocity at any Point

A system of stream lines is drawn so that the stream function increases progressively and the discharge between the adjacent stream lines is constant (Fig. 8.2).

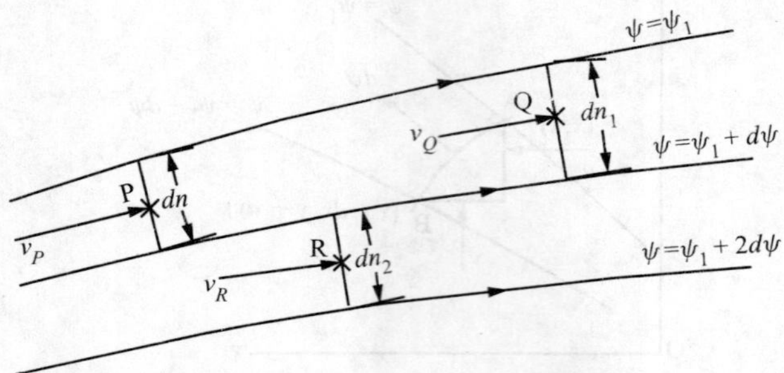

Fig. 8.2 *System of stream lines*

Let the velocity of flow at any point P be v and the normal distance between the stream lines at the point be *dn*.

$d\psi = v_P\, dn = v_Q dn_1 = v_R dn_2$.

The velocity at any point Q and R in the flow field can be obtained as

$$v_Q = \frac{v_P dn}{dn_1} \quad \text{and} \quad v_R = \frac{v_P dn}{dn_2}. \tag{8.3}$$

8.3 Resultant of Two Flow Patterns

Let $\psi = \psi_1, \psi = \psi_1 + d\psi$ and $\psi = \psi_1 + 2d\psi$ etc., represent a set of stream lines in a two-dimensional flow, the discharge between them being $d\psi$ per unit width. Let another set of stream lines $\psi = \psi_2, \psi = \psi_2 + d\psi$ and $\psi = \psi_2 + 2d\psi$ etc., corresponding to another two-dimensional flow pattern is superimposed on it as in Fig. 8.3. $d\psi$ being small, ABDC can be assumed to be a parallelogram. The resultant velocity at A can be found as follows

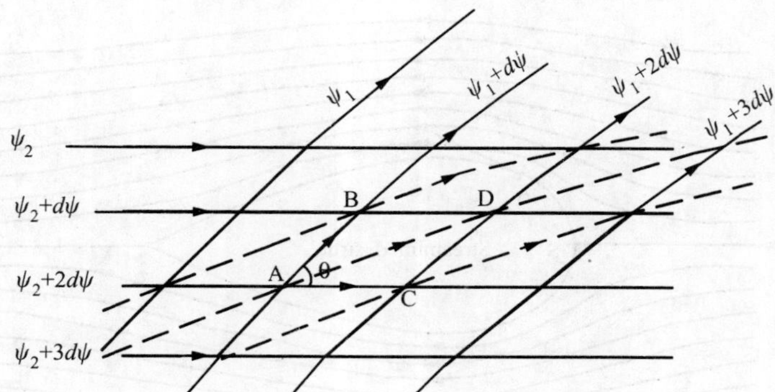

Fig. 8.3 *Combination of two stream functions*

Velocity at A due to flow (1) $= \dfrac{d\psi}{\text{AC}\sin\theta}$ along AB.

Velocity at A due to flow (2) $= \dfrac{d\psi}{\text{AB}\sin\theta}$ along AC.

The ratios of velocities are

$$\frac{d\psi}{\text{AC}\sin\theta} : \frac{d\psi}{\text{AB}\sin\theta} = \text{AB} : \text{AC}.$$

The direction for velocity in the case of a combined flow will be the direction of resultant AD of AB and AC. The flow between the combined stream lines will be flow (1) across AC + Flow (2) across AB = 2 dψ across BC.

8.4 Patterns of Stream Lines for Unsteady Flow Around an Object

Unsteady flows can be transformed to a steady flow by a Galilean transformation (by moving the coordinate system). When a body moves at constant velocity through an otherwise stationary large expanse of liquid like a lake, the flow around the body appears unsteady to an observer at rest on the banks.

But if the frame of reference is changed by adding a velocity equal to that of the body to the observer, the flow will become steady. This principle of transformation can be used to get the pattern of stream lines for an unsteady flow.

Figure 8.4(a) shows the pattern of stream lines for steady flow around a streamlined body (as viewed from the body). Another set of stream lines is drawn depicting a parallel flow with velocity equal to that of the body. The vectorial addition of velocities will result in the stream line pattern as in Fig. 8.4(b). These stream lines are only instantaneous patterns and change rapidly in space as the body moves through the liquid.

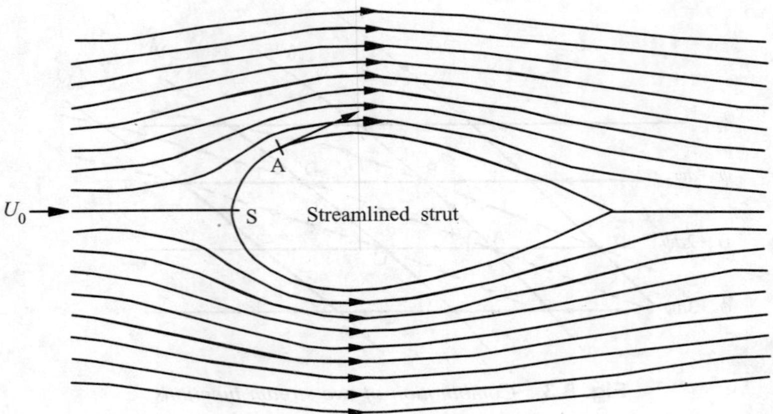

Fig. 8.4(a) *Pattern of stream lines for a steady flow*

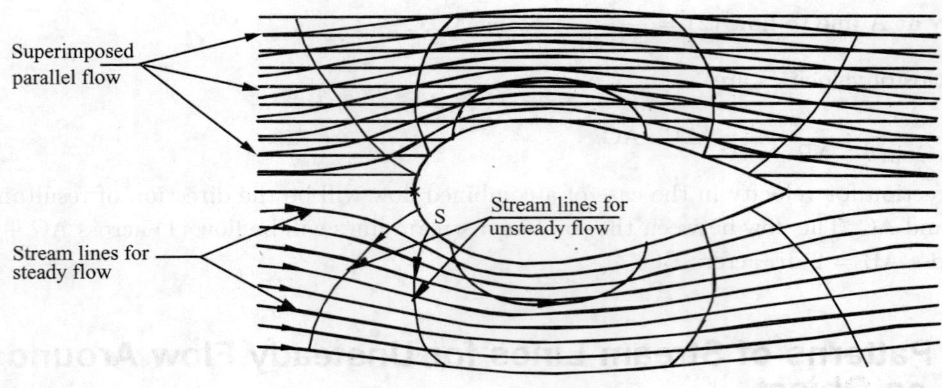

Fig. 8.4(b) *Unsteady flow pattern*

From the above discussion it is clear that in unsteady flow, the pattern of stream line changes in space with the movement of the body. A particle may follow the path of a stream line only for an infinitely small duration and then may be moving in the direction of another stream line and so on. Hence, the path line can be different from the stream line.

Example 8.1 A person on the bank sees a boat crossing a river 80 m wide at right angles to the bank. If the velocity of the boat is 2 m/s and the river flow velocity is 1 m/s, what is the time required to cross the river?

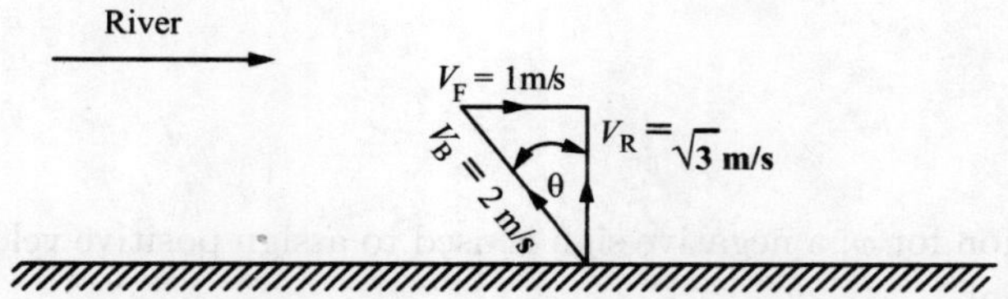

Example 8.1

In the diagram shown, $V_F = 1$ m/s and $V_B = 2$ m/s.

$\theta = \sin^{-1}(1/2) = 30°$.

$V_R = 2\cos 30° = \sqrt{3}$ m/s.

Time $= 80/\sqrt{3} = 46.2$ s. (Ans.)

8.5 Potential Function

In an irrotational flow, if we consider any closed curve, the circulation

$$\oint \vec{v}.d\vec{l} = \oint v_1.dl = 0.$$

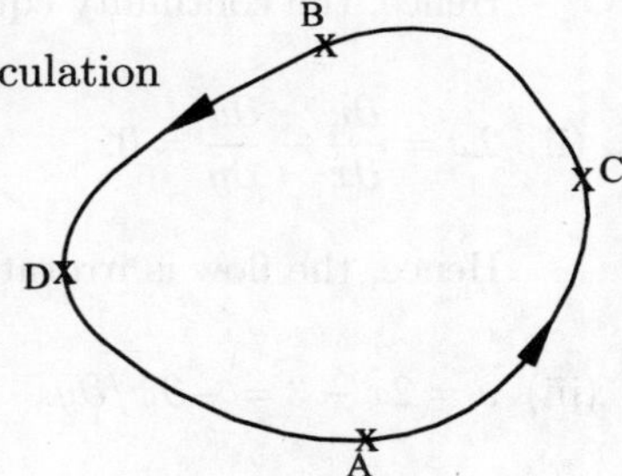

Fig. 8.5 *Flow along a closed curve*

If we take a closed curve as in Fig. 8.5,

$$\oint \vec{v}.d\vec{l} = \int_{ACB} v_l dl + \int_{BDA} v_l dl = 0.$$

Therefore, $\int_{ACB} v_l dl = \int_{ADB} v_l dl$

i.e., the value of integral depends only on the position of A and B. A function of position ϕ is assumed such that $\phi = -\int_A^B v_l dl$; ϕ is called the velocity potential of B with respect to A.

Hence, $v_l = -\dfrac{\partial \phi}{\partial l}$, the direction being arbitrary.

$$u = -\frac{\partial \phi}{\partial x}; \tag{8.4}$$

$$v = -\frac{\partial \phi}{\partial y}; \tag{8.5}$$

and

$$w = -\frac{\partial \phi}{\partial z}. \tag{8.6}$$

Hence in the expression for ϕ, a negative sign is used to assign positive velocity in the direction of decreasing potential.

Example 8.2 In a two-dimensional flow, the velocity is given by $u = 2x - 3$ and $v = -2y$. (i) Show that the continuity equation is satisfied. (ii) Show that the flow is irrotational. (iii) Find the stream function. (iv) Find the potential function. (v) Find the equation to the stream line passing through the point (2, –4).

(i) $u = 2x - 3; \quad v = -2y$

$$\frac{\partial u}{\partial x} + \frac{\partial v}{\partial y} = 0.$$

Hence, the continuity equation is satisfied. (Ans.)

(ii) $2\omega = \dfrac{\partial v}{\partial x} - \dfrac{\partial u}{\partial y} = 0.$

Hence, the flow is irrotational. (Ans.)

(iii) $u = 2x - 3 = -\partial\psi/\partial y.$

Hence, $\psi = -2xy + 3y + f_1(x).$ (1)

$v = -2y = \partial\psi/\partial x.$

Hence, $\psi = -2xy + f_2(y).$ (2)

Considering both (1) and (2),

$\psi = -2xy + 3y + c_1.$ (Ans.)

A solution is $\psi = -2xy + 3y.$ (Ans.)

(iv) $u = 2x - 3 = -\partial\phi/\partial x.$

Hence, $\phi = -x^2 + 3x + f_3(y).$ (3)

$$v = -2y = -\,\partial\phi/\partial y.$$

Hence, $\phi = y^2 + f_4(x)$. (4)

Considering (3) and (4),

$$\phi = y^2 - x^2 + 3x + c_2.$$

A solution is $\phi = y^2 - x^2 + 3x$. (Ans.)

(v) The equation of the stream line is $\psi = -2xy + 3y$

Since it passes through the point (2, –4), $\psi = -2xy + 3y = -2 \times 2 \times -4 + 3 \times -4 = 4$

Hence the equation of the stream line is $2xy - 3y + 4 = 0$ (Ans.)

This is the equation of the stream line passing through (2, −4) (Ans)

Example 8.3 Show that $\phi = A\ \tan^{-1} y/x$ represent a potential flow. Find ψ.

$$u = -\frac{\partial\phi}{\partial x} = +\frac{1}{(1+y/x)^2} \times y \times \frac{1}{x^2} = \frac{Ay}{(x^2+y^2)}.$$

$$v = -\frac{\partial\phi}{\partial y} = -\frac{A}{(1+y/x)^2} \times \frac{1}{x} = -\frac{Ax}{(x^2+y^2)}.$$

$$\frac{\partial v}{\partial x} - \frac{\partial u}{\partial y} = \frac{(x^2+y^2) \times -A + Ax \times 2x}{(x^2+y^2)^2} - \frac{(x^2+y^2) \times A - Ay \times 2y}{(x^2+y^2)^2}$$

$$= \frac{A(x^2-y^2)}{(x^2+y^2)^2} - \frac{A(x^2-y^2)}{(x^2+y^2)^2} = 0.$$

Hence, the flow is irrotational and represents a potential flow.

$$u = -\frac{\partial\psi}{\partial y} = \frac{Ay}{(x^2+y^2)} \rightarrow \psi = -\int\left(\frac{Ay}{x^2+y^2}\right)dy = -\frac{1}{2} \times A \ln\,(x^2+y^2) + f(x).$$

$$v = \frac{\partial\psi}{\partial x} = \frac{-Ax}{(x^2+y^2)} \rightarrow \psi = \int -\left(\frac{Ax}{x^2+y^2}\right)dx = -\frac{1}{2} \times A \ln\,(x^2+y^2) + f(y).$$

$$\psi = \frac{1}{2}\ln\,(x^2+y^2).$$

8.6 Equipotential Lines

Equipotential lines are lines along which there is no variation of ϕ, i.e., ϕ remains constant. At any point P, let the tangent to the equipotential $\phi = \phi_1$ be $\vec{dn}$ (Fig. 8.6). Since $\delta\phi = 0$, velocity along $dn = -\dfrac{\partial \phi}{\partial n} = 0$, i.e., the component of velocity in the direction of $dn = 0$. Hence, the equipotential lines should be normal to the stream lines.

Alternately, the orthogonality of the equipotentials and stream lines can be proved as follows:

$$\mathrm{d}\psi = \frac{\partial \psi}{\partial x}\,\mathrm{d}x + \frac{\partial \psi}{\partial y}\,\mathrm{d}y.$$

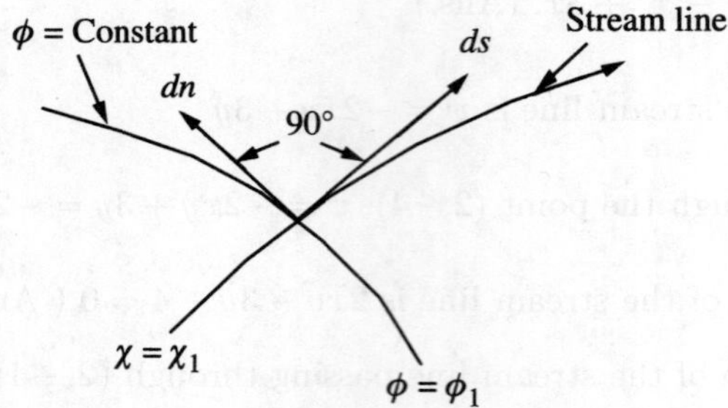

Fig. 8.6 *Stream function and velocity potential function*

When ψ is a constant $\mathrm{d}\psi = 0$ or

$$\left[\frac{dy}{dx}\right]_{\psi=\psi_1} = \frac{-\partial\psi/\partial x}{\partial\psi/\partial y} = \frac{v}{u}, \text{ say equal to } m.$$

$$d\phi = \frac{\partial \phi}{\partial x}dx + \frac{\delta \phi}{\delta y}dy.$$

When ϕ is constant $d\phi = 0$ or

$$\left[\frac{dy}{dx}\right]_{\phi=\phi_1} = -\frac{\partial\phi/\partial x}{\partial\phi/\partial y} = -\frac{u}{v}, \text{ say equal to } m_2.$$

$$m_1 \times m_2 = -1.$$

Hence, $\psi = \psi_1$ and $\phi = \phi_1$ are orthogonal to each other.

8.7 Laplace Equation Governing Potential Flow

The stream function ψ and the potential function ϕ satisfy the Laplace's equation in case of two-dimensional, incompressible and irrotational flow.

8.7.1 Stream function ψ

By virtue of the equation of continuity, the stream function ψ exists when the flow is incompressible and two-dimensional.

$$u = -\frac{\partial\psi}{\partial y} \text{ and } v = \frac{\partial\psi}{\partial x}.$$

In addition, if the flow is irrotational, $\dfrac{\partial v}{\partial x} - \dfrac{\partial u}{\partial y} = 0$. Substituting the values of u and v,

$$\frac{\partial^2\psi}{\partial x^2} + \frac{\partial^2\psi}{\partial y^2} = 0 \text{ or } \nabla^2\psi = 0. \tag{8.7}$$

8.7.2 Potential function ϕ

A potential function exists when the flow is irrotational.

$$u = -\frac{\partial\phi}{\partial x};\ v = \frac{\partial\phi}{\partial y} \text{ and } w = -\frac{\partial\phi}{\partial z}.$$

In addition, if the flow is incompressible and two-dimensional by the equation of continuity, $\dfrac{\partial u}{\partial x} + \dfrac{\partial v}{\partial y} = 0$. Substituting the values of u and v,

$$\frac{\partial^2\phi}{\partial x^2} + \frac{\partial^2\phi}{\partial y^2} = 0 \quad \text{or} \quad \nabla^2\phi = 0. \tag{8.8}$$

8.8 The Flow Net

The quantities ϕ and ψ have units m^2/s. It is convenient to draw a system of stream lines and equipotential lines with the same increments of $\delta\psi$ and $\delta\phi$ so that they intersect to form a net (Fig. 8.7).

$$|v_s| = \left|-\frac{\partial\phi}{\partial s}\right| = \left|-\frac{\partial\psi}{\partial n}\right|,$$

Since at any point when $\delta\phi$ and $\delta\psi$ are kept equal, δs and δn will be equal. Since the stream lines and equipotential lines intersect orthogonally and are very small, the flow net consists of curvilinear squares.

8.9 Examples of Potential Flow

The flow of an ideal fluid with given boundary conditions are examples of potential flow. It is also satisfied in most cases by the slow motion of viscous liquids through porous media.

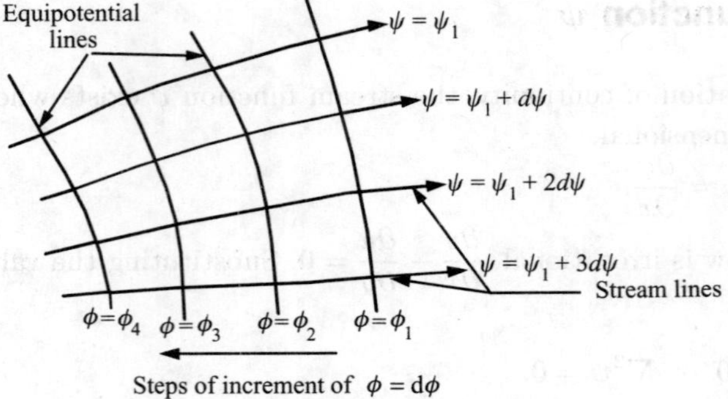

Fig. 8.7 *The flow net*

The condition is that the flow should be irrotational. Another case, as we will find later, is creeping motion where the potential flow pattern becomes a solution of the equation governing flow. Since a sufficient condition for potential flow to exist is the Laplace equation $\nabla^2\psi = 0$ or $\nabla^2\phi = 0$, solutions of Laplace equation give examples of potential flow. Even though, in general, potential flow can be three-dimensional, only two-dimensional flows or plane potential flows are discussed below.

8.10 Solution of the Laplace Equation

Even though real fluids are viscous, many cases of flow like that over a sharp crested weir, flow around streamlined bodies and flow in transitions can be studied by assuming potential flow.

In laminar flow through homogeneous porous media, the superficial velocity across the section is proportional to the gradient of the piezometric head h. i,e.,

$$v_1 = -k\frac{\partial h}{\partial l}, \tag{8.9}$$

where k is the permeability of the porous medium. In addition, the flow satisfies the continuity equation,

$$\frac{\partial u}{\partial x} + \frac{\partial v}{\partial y} = 0. \tag{8.10}$$

Hence it satisfies,

$$\nabla^2 h = 0. \tag{8.11}$$

On a gross scale, the flow pattern becomes a potential flow solution.

8.11 Solution of Potential Flows—Methods

There are many methods of solution to potential flows. It is common to discuss the graphical trial and error procedure, the method of analytic complex functions and transformations, the electrical analogy and the creeping flow analogy as in the Hele Shaw model.

Since the Laplace equation is linear, combinations of solutions can provide other examples. For instance, $\psi = \psi_1$ and $\psi = \psi_2$ satisfy the Laplace equation. i.e., $\nabla^2\psi_1 = 0$ and $\nabla^2\psi_2 = 0$. Then $\nabla^2\psi = 0$, where $\psi = \psi_1 + \psi_2$.

8.12 Graphical Trial and Error Procedure

With the given boundaries consisting of equipotential and stream lines, only one pattern of flow net (subdivision of flow net is possible) can be constructed graphically. The procedure is to draw a set of stream lines with equal increments by judgment and draw the equipotentials so that they are orthogonal and the net forms approximately curvilinear squares. The net formed can be refined by trial and error adjustments so that the end result is satisfactory. The curvilinear squares can be judged for their accuracy by trying to enclose circles touching the sides.

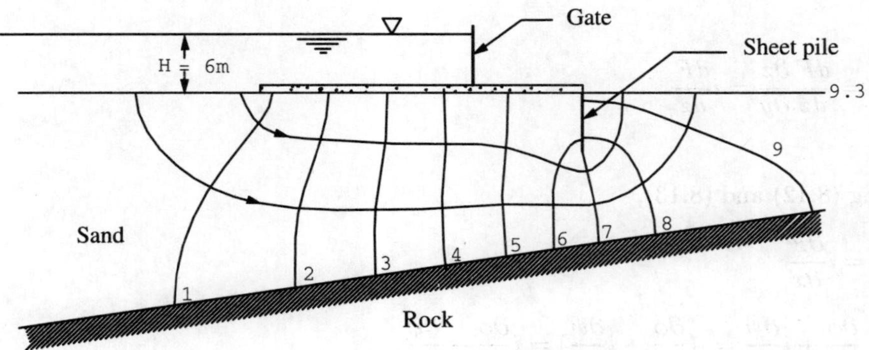

Fig. 8.8 *Flow net for seepage flow under a barrage*

Figure 8.8 shows a flow net sketched for seepage under a barrage. The potential head of 6 m is dissipated in nearly 9.3 steps as the seepage takes place. There are 3 flow paths. If the permeability $k = 5 \times 10^{-6}$ m/s for sand,

$$\text{the seepage} = \frac{n_f}{n_d} \times kH = \frac{3}{9.3} \times 5 \times 10^{-6} \times 6$$

$$= 9.68 \times 10^{-6}\ \text{m}^3/\text{s/m} = 0.836\ \text{m}^3/\text{day/m. (Ans.)}$$

8.13 Analytic Complex Functions

The real and imaginary parts of an analytical function of complex arguments are solutions of the Laplace equation.

A function of z which is single-valued and which possesses a unique derivative with respect to z (neither zero or infinite) at every point of some region R is said to be analytic in that region.

They can always be split into real and imaginary parts.

If $z = x + iy$ and $F(z) = f(x + iy) = \phi\ (x, y) + i\psi\ (x, y)$; where ϕ and ψ are real functions of x and y and $\dfrac{\partial z}{\partial x} = 1;\ \dfrac{\partial z}{\partial y} = i,$

$$\frac{\partial F}{\partial x} = \frac{dF}{dz}\frac{\partial z}{\partial x} = \frac{dF}{dz}. \tag{8.12}$$

$$\frac{\partial^2 F}{\partial x^2} = \frac{\partial}{\partial x}\left(\frac{dF}{dz}\right) = \frac{d}{dz}\left(\frac{dF}{dz}\right)\frac{\partial z}{\partial x} = \frac{d^2F}{dz^2}.$$

$$\frac{\partial F}{\partial y} = \frac{dF}{dz}\frac{\partial z}{\partial y} = i\frac{dF}{dz}. \tag{8.13}$$

Comparing (8.12) and (8.13),

$$\frac{\partial F}{\partial y} = i\frac{\partial F}{\partial x}$$

$$\text{i.e.,}\quad \frac{\partial \phi}{\partial y} + i\frac{\partial \psi}{\partial y} = i\left(\frac{\partial \phi}{\partial x} + i\frac{\partial \psi}{\partial x}\right) = i\frac{\partial \phi}{\partial x} - \frac{\partial \psi}{\partial x}.$$

Equating the real and imaginary parts,

$$\frac{\partial \phi}{\partial x} = \frac{\partial \psi}{\partial y} \text{ and } \frac{\partial \phi}{\partial y} = -\frac{\partial \psi}{\partial x},$$

which are known as the Cauchy–Reimann conditions. Further,

$$\frac{\partial^2 F}{\partial y^2} = \frac{\partial}{\partial y}\left(i\frac{dF}{dz}\right) = \frac{d}{dz}\left(i\frac{dF}{dz}\right)\frac{\partial z}{\partial y} = -\frac{d^2F}{dz^2}.$$

$$\frac{\partial^2 F}{\partial x^2} + \frac{\partial^2 F}{\partial y^2} = \frac{d^2F}{dz^2} - \frac{d^2F}{dz^2} = 0,\ i.e., \nabla^2 F = 0,$$

where φ and ψ can represent the potential and stream functions.

$$\begin{aligned} dF &= \frac{\partial F}{\partial x}dx + \frac{\partial F}{\partial y}dy = \left(\frac{\partial \phi}{\partial x} + i\frac{\partial \psi}{\partial x}\right)dx + \left(\frac{\partial \phi}{\partial y} + i\frac{\partial \psi}{\partial y}\right)dy \\ &= (-u + iv)\ dx + (-v - iu)\ dy \\ &= -\{(u - iv)\ dx + i(u - iv)\ dy\} \\ &= -(u - iv)\ dz. \end{aligned}$$

$$\text{So, } \frac{dF}{dz} = -(u - iv) = -\overline{w}, \tag{8.14}$$

where $\overline{w}$ is the complex quantity conjugate to $w = u + iv$.

Therefore, by finding dF/dz the velocity can be calculated.

Example 8.4 Sketch the flow pattern depicted by the transformation $F(z) = z^2$ and show the velocity at the point (20, 10).

$F(z) = z^2$.

i.e., $\phi + i\psi = (x + iy)^2 = x^2 - y^2 + 2xyi$; So, $\phi = x^2 - y^2$ and $\psi = 2xy$.

A set of stream lines and equipotentials are drawn in the figure.

$$\frac{dF}{dz} = 2z = 2(x + iy) = -(u - iv).$$

At the point (20, 10), $2(x + iy) = 2(20 + 10i) = -(u - iv)$.

Hence, $u = -40$; $u = 20$; $V = \sqrt{(40^2 + 20^2)} = 44.72$ units.

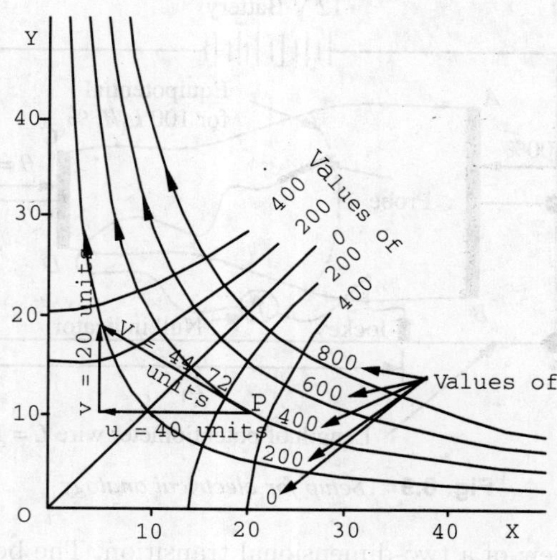

Example 8.4

8.14 Electrical Analogy

An analogy exists between two phenomena when the mathematical equations governing them and the boundary conditions (mathematically expressed) are the same. A physical solution of the problem in one phenomenon can then be of use in the solution of the problem in the other phenomenon.

The two-dimensional flow of electricity in a conducting media between two equipotentials having a difference in electromotive force is analogical to the two-dimensional irrotational flow of fluids between similar boundaries.

The analogical quantities in electrical and fluid flow are given below.

Two-dimensional electrical flow field	Two-dimensional fluid flow field
E: electromotive force	ϕ: velocity potential
I: current; J: Current intensity = I/unit area	V: velocity
Kirchoff's law: $\dfrac{\partial J_x}{\partial x} + \dfrac{\partial J_y}{\partial y} = 0$	Equation of continuity: $\dfrac{\partial u}{\partial x} + \dfrac{\partial v}{\partial y} = 0$
Ohms law: $J_x = -c\dfrac{\partial E}{\partial x}$	$u = V_x = -\dfrac{\partial \phi}{\partial x}$
$\nabla^2 E = 0$	$\nabla^2 \phi = 0$

The application of electrical analogy to solve fluid flow problems can be illustrated by an example of flow in a transition.

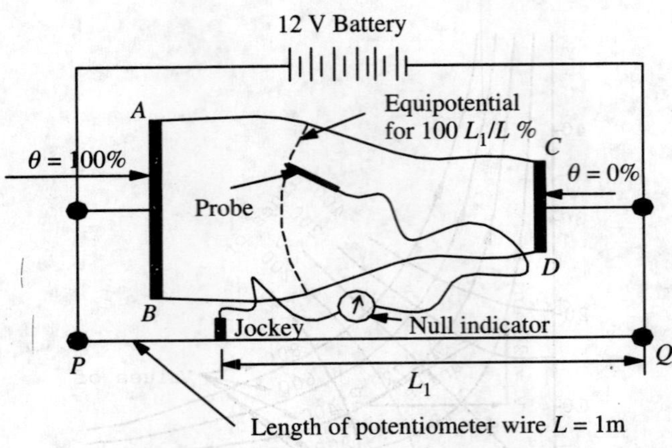

Fig. 8.9 *Setup for electrical analogy*

Figure 8.9 shows a top view of a two-dimensional transition. The bottom and side sheets AC and BD are made of nonconducting sheets. AB and CD are copper plates and the space in between is filled with water to a depth of about 2 cm. In order to make water more conducting, a little salt or acid is added. The copper plates are connected to a 12 V battery and also to a 1 m potentiometer. A null indicator is connected on one end to a jockey which can be moved along the potentiometer wire, and the other end to a probe which is to be dipped in the water.

Assuming AB to be at 100% and CD at 0% potential, a point on the equipotential 60% can be located by fixing the jockey on the potentiometer wire 60 cm away from Q and finding the positions of the probe in the tank for which the null indicator shows zero reading. Joining such points, 60% potential can be obtained. Similarly, other potentials can be drawn. A system of stream lines can be drawn normal to the equipotentials to form a flow net. The construction of the model is simplified if electrically conducting papers (Teledectos paper) is available. Equipotentials AB and CD can be obtained by applying silver paint.

8.15 The Hele Shaw Flow

The Hele Shaw apparatus consists of a creeping flow between parallel plates spaced very close to each other with the cross-sectional model interspaced between them. The flow is allowed at very low velocities. Neglecting the inertial forces for steady flow, the governing equation becomes the bi-harmonic equation[14,33],

$$\nabla^4\psi = \nabla^2\left(\nabla^2\psi\right) = \frac{\partial^4\psi}{\partial x^4} + 2\frac{\partial^4\psi}{\partial x^2\partial y^2} + \frac{\partial^4\psi}{\partial y^4} = 0, \tag{8.15}$$

for which $\nabla^2\psi = 0$ becomes a solution[14,33]. The model can be used obtain a stream line pattern and the potential flow. Patterns of flow around an aerofoil and a Rankine body are shown in Photographs 1 and 2.

8.16 Rectangular and Polar Coordinates

The relationship between the stream functions and potential functions can be expressed as follows.

Rectangular coordinates

$$u = -\frac{\partial\psi}{\partial y}; \quad (8.1) \qquad v = \frac{\partial\psi}{\partial x}. \quad (8.2)$$

$$u = -\frac{\partial\phi}{\partial x}; \quad (8.4) \qquad v = -\frac{\partial\phi}{\partial y}. \quad (8.5)$$

Polar coordinates

$$v_r = -\frac{1}{r}\frac{\partial\psi}{\partial\theta}; \quad (8.16) \qquad v_\theta = \frac{\partial\psi}{\partial r}. \quad (8.17)$$

$$v_r = -\frac{\partial\phi}{\partial r}; \quad (8.18) \qquad v_\theta = -\frac{1}{r}\frac{\partial\phi}{\partial\theta}. \quad (8.19)$$

1. Flow past an airfoil

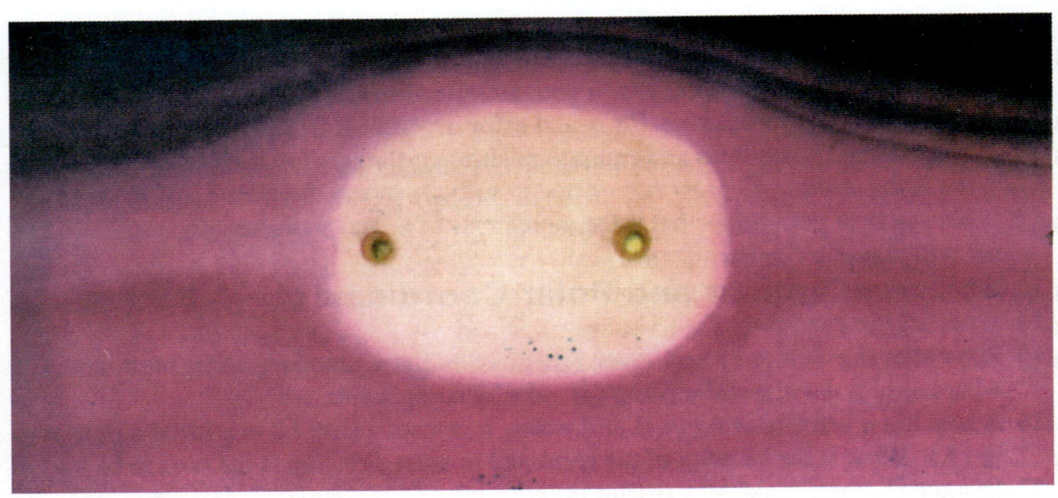

2. Formation of a Rankine body (combination of source and sink)

REVIEW QUESTIONS AND PROBLEMS

8.1 Define stream function. How is it derived? What conditions are assumed for the fluid and for the flow?

8.2 What is the unit for ψ? How is it related to stream lines?

8.3 Show how combinations of stream line flows can be studied?

8.4 Show with an illustration how a steady flow may appear as unsteady for another observer.

8.5 What is an irrotational flow?

8.6 Show that $v = C/r$ represents an irrotational vortex?

8.7 Explain the significance of a potential function.

8.8 What conditions are necessary for a potential function to exist?

8.9 Derive the Laplace's equation for ψ and ϕ for irrotational incompressible flows.

8.10 Show that the stream lines and equipotentials are orthogonal to each other.

8.11 What is the unit for ϕ? How is it related to velocity in any direction?

8.12 What is a flow net? Show that if the increments of ψ and ϕ are kept the same, the flow net will have curvilinear squares.

8.13 What are the Cauchy–Reiman conditions connecting ψ and ϕ?

8.14 What are the conditions for a function to be analytic?

8.15 Show that if $z = x + iy$ and $F = F(z)$ is an analytic function, dF/dz represents $-\overline{w}$, where $w = u + iv$, u and v being the velocity components.

8.16 A boat has a velocity of 6 m/s in still water. It crosses a river 60 m wide at a right angle in 15 s. What is the velocity of the river, and in what direction is the boat to be rowed?

8.17 In a two-dimensional flow, $u = 2x$ and $v = -2y$. Find the stream function.

8.18 Find the equation for the stream line passing through (1, 3) for the incompressible flow $v = y^2 - 6x$.

8.19 In a two-dimensional flow, the velocity potential is given by $\phi = 4x\ (3y - 4)$. Determine the velocity and stream function at point (2, 3).

8.20 For a uniform flow 8 m/s parallel to the X axis, find the stream function.

8.21 $u = x^2 - 4x - 2xy$ and $v = y^2 - 2xy + 4y$, find the stream function.

8.22 In a two-dimensional incompressible flow, the velocity components are $u = x - 4y$ and $v = -y - 4x$. Show that the velocity potential exist and determine its form. Find also the stream function.

8.23 Show that the velocity potential Ax, where A is a constant represents a possible case of fluid flow. Determine the stream function and draw a set of stream lines and equipotentials.

8.24 Find whether the function $\phi = -4xy$ describes a case of incompressible flow.

8.25 Which of the following functions represents a irrotational flow (i) $\psi = 2\ kxy$ (ii) $\psi = ax + by$?

8.26 If for a two-dimensional potential flow, the velocity potential is given by $\phi = 2xy - x$, determine the velocity at the point P (4, 5). What is the value of ψ at the point?

8.27 If $\phi = 3xy$, find the x, y components of velocity at (1, 3) and (3, 3). Determine the discharge between stream lines passing through these points.

8.28 The velocity components of a possible incompressible fluid flow field are $u = 2cxy$ and $v = c(a^2 + x^2 - y^2)$. (i) Do they satisfy the continuity equation? (ii) Is the flow irrotational? (iii) Find the stream function and the potential function if any.

8.29 In a two-dimensional flow, $u = \dfrac{-x}{x^2 + y^2}$ and $v = \dfrac{-y}{x^2 + y^2}$. Show that the velocity components satisfy the continuity equation and find the stream function.

8.30 If $\psi = x^2 - y^2$, find the potential function.

8.31 If $\phi = \dfrac{Ax}{x^2 + y^2}$, find the stream function.

8.32 If $\psi = \dfrac{1}{2}\ln(x^2 + y^2)$, find the potential function.

8.33 The velocity components of a two dimensional flow field is given by $u = x^2y - 2x - \dfrac{y^3}{3}$ and $v = \dfrac{x^3}{3} - xy^2 + 2y$. (i) Show that it satisfies the condition for incompressible flow. (ii) Show that it is an irrotational flow. (iii) Find the stream function. (iv) Find the potential function.

ANSWERS

8.16. 4.472 m/s; 41.8° with the bank **8.17.** $\psi = -2xy$; **8.18.** $xy^2 - 3x^2 - 6 = 0$; **8.19.** $v = 31.24$ units at an angle of 309.81°, $6y^2 - 16y - 6x^2 + 18 = 0$; **8.20.** $\psi = -8y$; **8.21.** $\psi = xy^2 - x^2y + 4xy$; **8.22.** $\phi = y^2/2 - x^2/2 + 4xy$, $\psi = -xy + 2y^2 - 2x^2$; **8.23.** $\psi = Ay$; **8.24.** ϕ exists; **8.25.** (i) irrotational (ii) irrotational; **8.26.** 12.04 m/s @ angle 221.63°; $\psi = 4$; **8.27.** $-9, -3$; $9, -9$; $q = 12$ units; **8.28.** (i) yes (ii) irrotational (iii) $\psi = 1/3\ cx^3 + ca^2x - cxy^2$ and $\phi = 1/3\ cy^3 - cx^2y - ca^2y$; **8.29.** $\psi = \tan^{-1}(y/x)$; **8.30.** $-2xy$; **8.31.** $\psi = -Ay/(x^2 + y^2)$; **8.32.** $\phi = \tan^{-1}(y/x)$. **8.33**(iii) $\psi = \dfrac{x^4}{12} - \dfrac{x^2y^2}{2} + 2xy + \dfrac{y^4}{12}$

8.33(iv) $\phi = \dfrac{xy^3}{3} - \dfrac{x^3y}{3} + x^2 - y^2$

9 Analysis of Flow Patterns

Uniform parallel flow—Source—Sink and vortex combinations—Rankine half-body—Rankine body—Doublet—Flow past a cylinder— circulation — Magnus effect, lift —Method of images.

In the previous chapter, stream functions and potential functions were defined and their interrelationships discussed in rectangular and polar coordinates. In this chapter, some flow patterns will be analyzed.

9.1 Uniform Parallel Flow

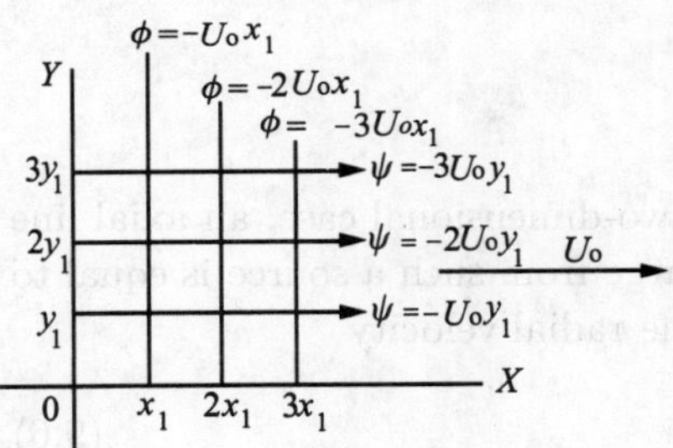

Fig. 9.1 *Parallel uniform flow*

Transformation $F(z) = -U_0 z$. (9.1)

$F(z) = \phi + i\psi = -U_0(x + iy)$.

Hence, $\phi = -U_0 x$. (9.2)

and

$\psi = -U_0 y$. (9.3)

$$u = -\frac{\partial \phi}{\partial x} = U_0; \quad \nu = -\frac{\partial \phi}{\partial y} = 0.$$

The pattern of stream lines and equipotentials are given in Fig. 9.1

9.2 Uniform Flow Inclined at an Angle α with the X Axis

Transformation $F(z) = -U_0 z e^{-i\alpha}$ (9.4)

$$\begin{aligned} F(z) &= \phi + i\psi = -U_0\ (x + iy)(\cos\alpha - i\sin\alpha) \\ &= -U_0(x\cos\alpha + y\sin\alpha) - U_0 i(-x\sin\alpha + y\cos\alpha). \end{aligned}$$

$$u = -\frac{\partial \psi}{\partial y} = U_0\ \cos\alpha;\ \nu = \frac{\partial \psi}{\partial x} = U_0 \sin\alpha.$$

Hence, $\psi = -U_0\ (-x\ \sin\alpha + y\ \cos\alpha)$. (9.5)

For a value of $U_0 = 5$m/s and $\alpha = 30°$ and letting $\psi = 0$ pass through the origin, the stream lines are shown in Fig. 9.2.

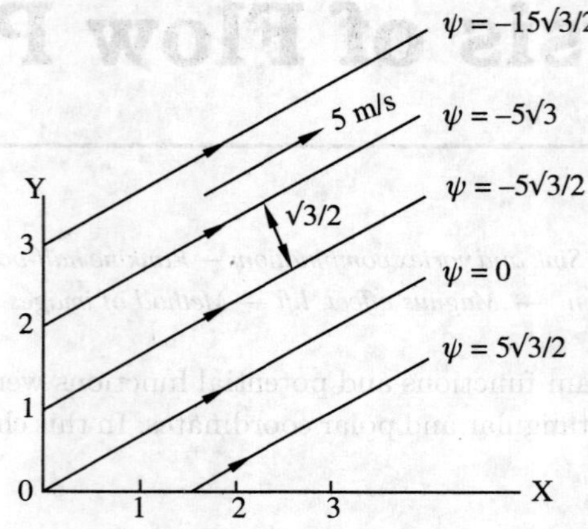

Fig. 9.2 *Uniform inclined flow*

9.3 Flow from a Line Source

A source is a point from which flow occurs outwards. In a two-dimensional case, an axial line from which radial flow emanates is a line source. The discharge from such a source is equal to q per metre length, known as the strength of the source. The radial velocity

$$v_r = \frac{q}{2\pi r}. \tag{9.6}$$

and

$$v_\theta = 0. \tag{9.7}$$

$$\nu_r = -\frac{\partial\psi}{r\partial\theta} \text{ and } v_\theta = \frac{\partial\psi}{\partial r} \text{ from which}$$

$$\psi = -\frac{q}{2\pi}\theta. \tag{9.8}$$

$$\nu_r = -\frac{\partial\phi}{\partial r} \text{ and } v_\theta = -\frac{\partial\phi}{r\partial\theta} \text{ from which}$$

$$\phi = -\frac{q}{2\pi}\ln r. \tag{9.9}$$

$$F(z) = \phi + i\psi = -\frac{q}{2\pi}\ln r - \frac{q}{2\pi}i\theta = -\frac{q}{2\pi}\ln z. \tag{9.10}$$

The above transformation represents a line source of strength q.
Figure 9.3 shows the flow pattern for a line source.

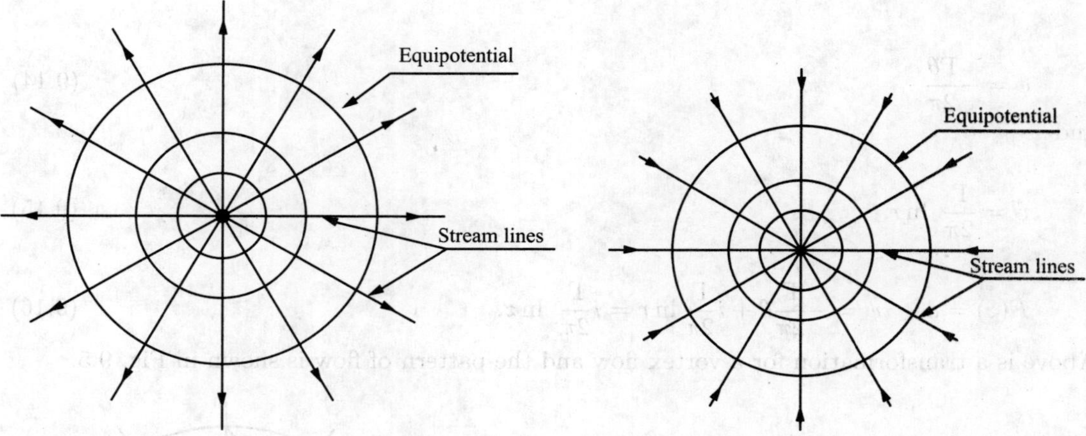

Fig. 9.3 *A line source*

Fig. 9.4 *A line sink*

9.4 Flow towards a Line Sink

Line sink is a reversal of a line source and the transformation for line sink is

$$F(z) = \frac{q}{2\pi} \ln z \tag{9.11}$$

from which

$$\phi = \frac{q}{2\pi} \ln r \tag{9.12}$$

and

$$\psi = \frac{q}{2\pi}\, \theta. \tag{9.13}$$

The flow pattern is shown in Fig. 9.4.

9.5 Free Vortex Flow

Let there be a circulation Γ around a point.

$$v_\theta = \frac{\Gamma}{2\pi r} \text{ and } v_r = 0.$$

$$v_\theta = \frac{-\partial\phi}{r\partial\theta} = \frac{\partial\psi}{\partial r} \text{ and } v_{\mathrm{r}} = -\frac{\partial\phi}{\partial r} = -\frac{\partial\psi}{r\partial\theta}.$$

It can be shown that

$$\phi = -\frac{\Gamma\theta}{2\pi} \tag{9.14}$$

and

$$\psi = \frac{\Gamma}{2\pi} \ln r. \tag{9.15}$$

$$F(z) = \phi + i\psi = -\frac{\Gamma}{2\pi}\theta + i\frac{\Gamma}{2\pi}\ln r = i\frac{\Gamma}{2\pi}\ln z. \tag{9.16}$$

Above is a transformation for a vortex flow and the pattern of flow is shown in Fig. 9.5.

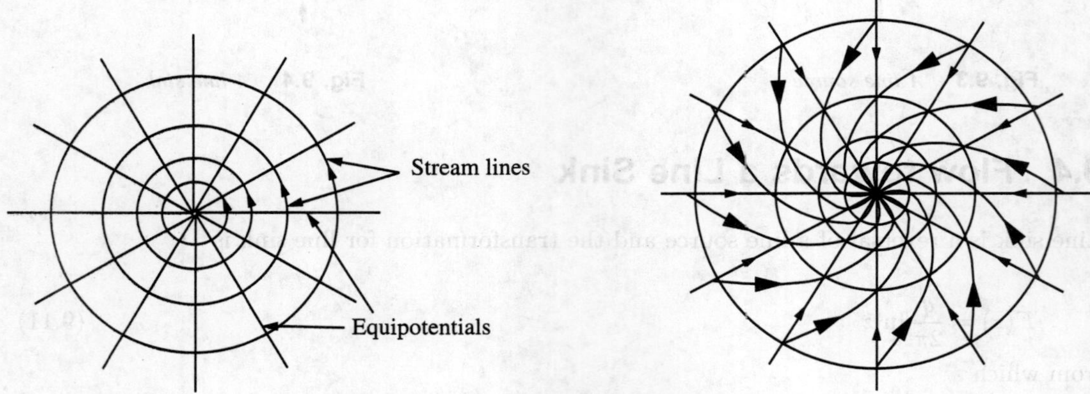

Fig. 9.5 *A free vortex*

Fig. 9.6 *A whirlpool*

9.6 Combination of Sink and Vortex (Whirlpool)

The combined stream function is

$$\psi = \frac{q}{2\pi}\theta + \frac{\Gamma}{2\pi}\ln r. \tag{9.17}$$

The resulting pattern of flow is shown in Fig. 9.6.

9.7 Combination of Source and Uniform Parallel Flow (Flow Past a Half-body)

The stream function for a combination of a source and a uniform parallel flow can be written as

$$\psi = -U_0 y - \frac{q}{2\pi}\theta = -U_0\, r\, \sin\theta - m\theta,$$

$$\text{where } m = \frac{q}{2\pi}, \tag{9.18}$$

$$v_r = -\frac{\partial \psi}{r\partial \theta} = U_0 \cos\theta + \frac{m}{r}.$$

$$v_\theta = \frac{\partial \psi}{\partial r} = -U_0 \sin\theta.$$

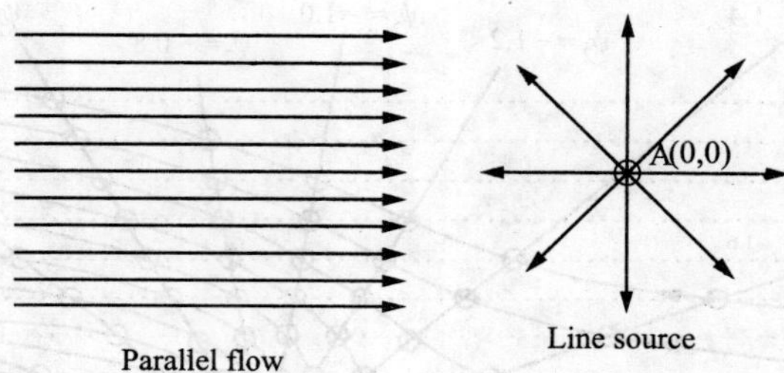

Fig. 9.7 *Source with parallel flow*

Let the source be located at (0, 0) and the uniform parallel flow from left to right be as shown in Fig. 9.7.

When $\theta = 0, v_r = U_o \cos\theta + \dfrac{q}{2\pi r} \neq 0$. But when $\theta = \pi$ and $r = \dfrac{q}{2\pi U_0}, v_r = 0$. Also, when $\theta = \pi, v_\theta = 0$; i.e., when $\theta = \pi$, there is a stagnation point

$$S\left[\frac{-q}{(2\pi U_0)}, 0\right]. \tag{9.19}$$

The limiting stream line can be obtained through the stagnation point when $\theta = \pi$

$$\psi = -U_0 r \sin\theta - \frac{q\theta}{2\pi} = \frac{-q}{2}. \tag{9.20}$$

Hence,

$$U_0 r \sin\theta + \frac{q\theta}{2\pi} = \frac{q}{2}$$

is the equation of a body of liquid enclosed by the limiting stream line. It is called a Rankine half-body or bluff-body. The equation of the body can be written as

$$y = r\sin\theta = \frac{m(\pi - \theta)}{U_0}, \tag{9.21}$$

where $m = \dfrac{q}{2\pi}$. The maximum thickness of the body can be found when $\theta \to 0$ and is equal to

$$2 \times y_{\text{max}} = \frac{q}{U_0}. \tag{9.22}$$

The thickness of the body at the source can be found when $\theta = \pi/2$ and is equal to

$$q/2U_0. \tag{9.23}$$

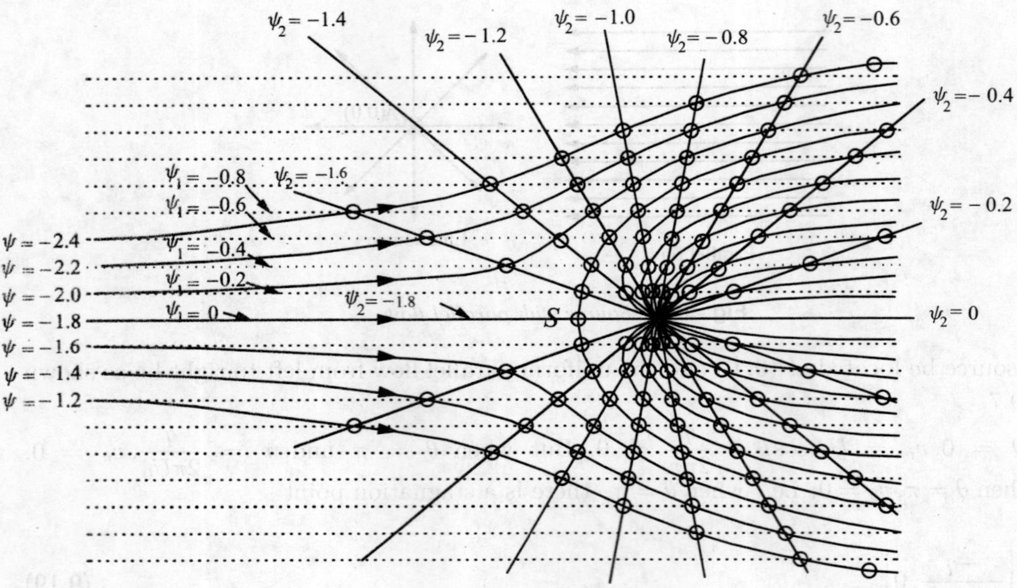

Fig. 9.8 *Parallel flow combined with a source*

The flow pattern is shown in Fig. 9.8.

Example 9.1 A line source of strength $q = 3.6 \ \text{m}^2/\text{s}$ is placed in a parallel flow with $U_0 = 2$ m/s. Find (i) the distance of the stagnation point from the source, (ii) the thickness of the half-body at the source and (iii) the maximum thickness of the half-body. (iv) Plot the pattern of flow.

$q = 3.6 \ \text{m}^2/s$; $U_0 = 2$ m/s.

(i) $r_s = \dfrac{q}{2\pi U_0} = \dfrac{3.6}{4\pi} = 0.2685$ m.

(ii) Thickness of body at the source $= \dfrac{q}{2U_0} = \dfrac{3.6}{2 \times 2} = 0.9$ m.

(iii) Maximum thickness $= \dfrac{3.6}{2} = 1.8$ m.

(iv) Assuming there are 18 stream tubes from the source, flow from each tube $= \dfrac{3.6}{18}$ $= 0.2$ m^2/s.

The spacing required for parallel flow stream lines to have the same discharge $= 0.2/2 = 0.1$ m. The resulting flow pattern formed by combining the parallel flow and the flow from the source is shown in Fig. 9.8.

9.8 Combination of Source and Sink of Equal Strength

Let the source be located at $(a, 0)$ and the sink at $(a,0)$ as in Fig. 9.9.

The combined stream function is

$$\psi = -m\,\theta_1 + m\,\theta_2 = m \times (\theta_2 - \theta_1'). \tag{9.24}$$

When ψ is a constant, $(\theta_2 - \theta_1) = \alpha =$ a constant. Hence, the points on the stream line ψ is a circle passing through P. In Fig. 9.9, the line S_0S_i subtends a constant angle α at the points on the stream line. So the stream lines are circles passing through S_0 and S_i.

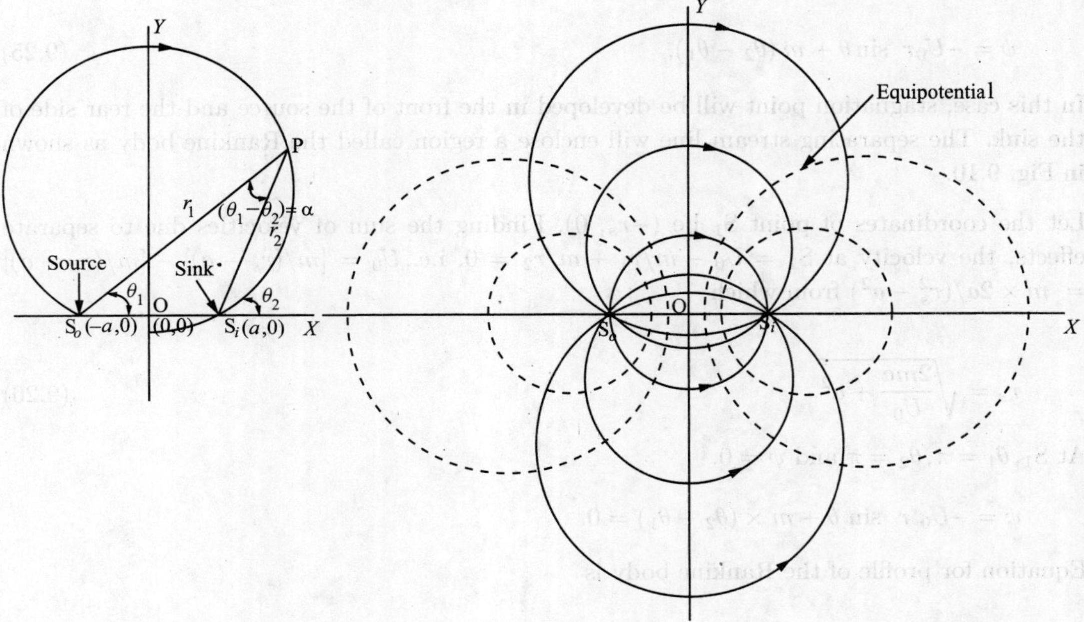

Fig. 9.9 *Combination of source and sink*

The combined potential function is $\phi = -m \times \ln r_1 + m \times \ln r_2 = m \times \ln(r_2/r_1)$.

Substituting ${r_2}^2 = (x-a)^2 + y^2$ and ${r_1}^2 = (x+a)^2 + y^2$,

$$\phi = m \ln\left(\frac{r_2}{r_1}\right) = \frac{m}{2}\ln\left(\frac{{r_2}^2}{{r_1}^2}\right) = \frac{m}{2}\ln\frac{(x-a)^2+y^2}{(x+a)^2+y^2}.$$

When ϕ is a constant, the above equation can be reduced to

$$(x-a)^2 + y^2 = k_1[(x+a)^2 + y^2].$$

$\dfrac{(x-a)^2+y^2}{(x+a)^2+y^2}$ is a constant, say $= k_1$ which can be reduced to

$x^2 + y^2 + 2 \times \dfrac{k_1+1}{k_1-1}ax + a^2 = 0$ which is an equation of a circle

The pattern of stream lines and equipotential lines are shown in Fig. 9.9.

9.9 Combination of Source and Sink with Parallel Flow[40]

The combined stream function can be written as

$$\psi = -U_0 r \ \sin\theta + m\,(\theta_2 - \theta_1). \tag{9.25}$$

In this case, stagnation point will be developed in the front of the source and the rear side of the sink. The separating stream line will enclose a region called the Rankine body as shown in Fig. 9.10.

Let the coordinates of point S_1 be $(-r_s, 0)$. Finding the sum of velocities due to separate effects, the velocity at $S_1 = U_0 - m/r_1 + m/r_2 = 0$. i.e., $U_0 = [m/(r_s - a)] - [m/(r_s + a)] = m \times 2a/(r_s^2 - a^2)$ from which

$$r_s = \sqrt{\frac{2ma}{U_0} + a^2}. \tag{9.26}$$

At $S_1, \theta_1 = \pi, \theta_2 = \pi$ and $\psi = 0$.

$$\psi = -U_0 \ r \ \sin\theta + m \times (\theta_2 - \theta_1) = 0.$$

Equation for profile of the Rankine body is

$$r = m \times \frac{\theta_2 - \theta_1}{U_0 \sin\theta}. \tag{9.27}$$

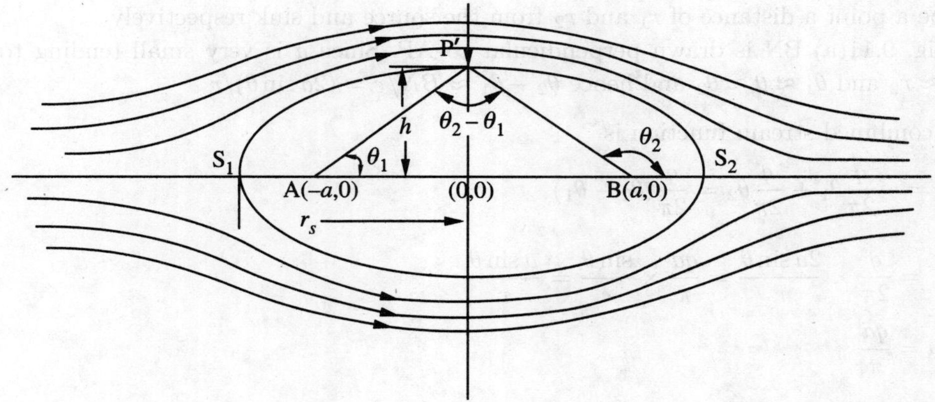

Fig. 9.10 *Flow around a Rankine body*

At point P′ in Fig. 9.10, $\sin\theta = 1$ and $r = h$. Substituting in (9.27),

$$\theta_2 - \theta_1 = \frac{hU_0}{m}.$$

Also from the Fig. 9.10, at point P', $r = h = a\cot(\theta_2 - \theta_1)$,

$$\text{or } h = a\cot\left(\frac{U_0 h}{2m}\right) \tag{9.28}$$

from which h can be found by trial.

9.10 The Doublet

Let there be a source and sink of equal strength $m = q/2\pi$ separated by a distance of $2a$. The source and sink as shown in Fig. 9.11 are brought very close to each other so that the value of qa/π is held a constant equal to μ.

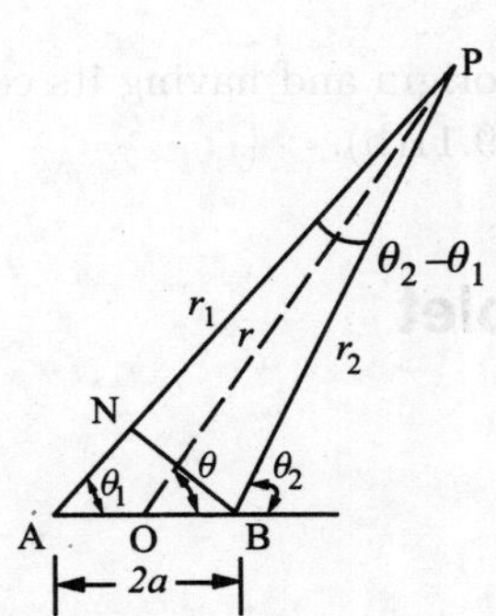

Fig. 9.11(a) *Source and sink close to each other*

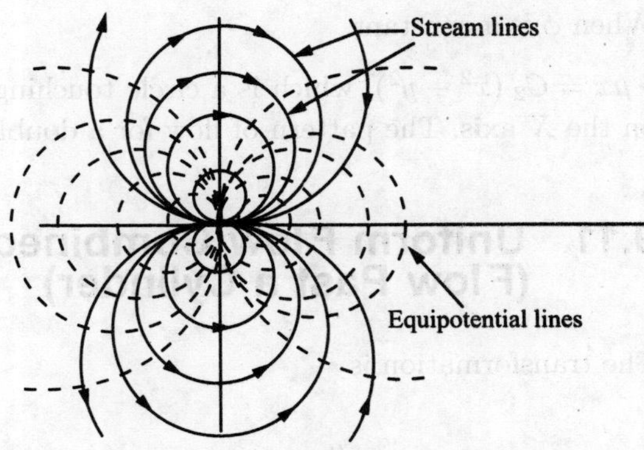

Fig. 9.11(b) *A doublet*

Let P be a point a distance of r_1 and r_2 from the source and sink respectively

In Fig, 9.11(a) BN is drawn perpendicular to AP. Since a is very small tending to zero, $r_1 \approx r \approx r_2$ and $\theta_1 \approx \theta \approx \theta_2$ and hence $\theta_2 - \theta_1 \approx BN/r = (2a\sin\theta)/r$

The combined stream function is

$$\psi = -\frac{q}{2\pi}\theta_1 + \frac{q}{2\pi}\theta_2 = \frac{q}{2\pi}(\theta_2 - \theta_1) \tag{9.29}$$

$$= \frac{q}{2\pi} \times \frac{2a\sin\theta}{r} = \frac{qa}{\pi} \times \frac{\sin\theta}{r} = \frac{\mu\sin\theta}{r} \tag{9.30}$$

where $\mu = \dfrac{qa}{\pi}$

$$v_r = -\frac{1}{r}\frac{\partial\psi}{\partial\theta} = \frac{-\mu\cos\theta}{r^2} = -\frac{\partial\phi}{\partial r} \tag{9.31}$$

Integrating

$$\phi = -\frac{\mu\cos\theta}{r} \tag{9.32}$$

$$F(z) = \phi + i\psi = -\frac{\mu}{r}(\cos\theta - i\sin\theta) = -\frac{\mu}{re^{i\theta}} = -\frac{\mu}{z}. \tag{9.33}$$

The stream function $\psi = \dfrac{\mu\sin\theta}{r} = \dfrac{\mu y}{x^2 + y^2}$.

When $\psi =$ constant,

$$\mu y = C_1(x^2 + y^2),$$

which is a circle touching the X axis at the origin and having its centre on the Y axis.

The potential function $\phi = -\dfrac{\mu\cos\theta}{r} = \dfrac{-\mu x}{x^2 + y^2}$.

When ϕ is a constant,

$-\mu x = C_2\,(x^2 + y^2)$, which is a circle touching the Y axis at the origin and having its centre on the X axis. The pattern of flow for a doublet is shown in Fig. 9.11(b).

9.11 Uniform Flow Combined with a Doublet (Flow Past a Cylinder)

The transformation is

$$F(z) = -U_0 z - \frac{\mu}{z} \tag{9.34}$$

$$\phi + i\psi = -U_0 re^{i\theta} - \frac{\mu e^{-i\theta}}{r} = -U_0 r(\cos\theta + i\sin\theta) - \frac{\mu(\cos\theta - i\sin\theta)}{r}.$$

Hence, $\phi = -U_0 r\cos\theta - \dfrac{\mu\cos\theta}{r}$ (9.35)

and

$$\psi = -U_0 r\sin\theta + \frac{\mu\sin\theta}{r}. \tag{9.36}$$

When, $\psi = 0, \mu = U_0 r^2$ or $r = \sqrt{\dfrac{\mu}{U_0}}$.

i.e. the boundary is a circle of radius $r_0 = \sqrt{\dfrac{\mu}{U_0}}$, (9.37)

ψ can be written as

$$\psi = -U_0 r\ \sin\theta + U_0\frac{{r_0}^2}{r}\sin\theta = -U_0 r(1 - \frac{{r_0}^2}{r^2})\sin\theta. \tag{9.38}$$

On the periphery of the circle when $\theta = \pi$ and when $\theta = 0$ it can be shown that v_r and v_θ are equal to zero. They are the stagnation points S_1 and S_2 in Fig. 9.12.

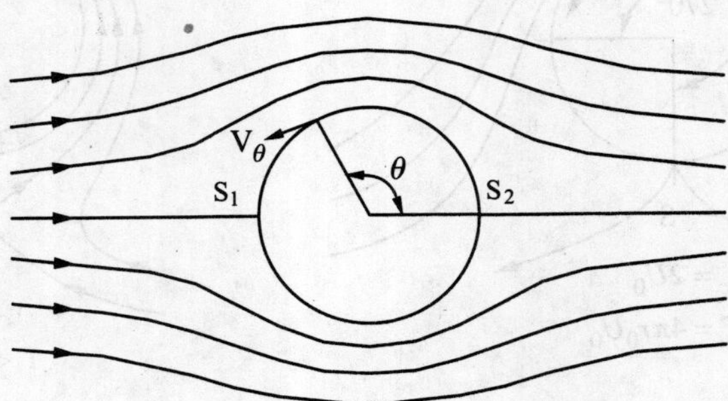

Fig. 9.12 *Flow around a cylinder*

On the surface of the cylinder,

$$\nu_\theta = \frac{\partial\phi}{\partial r} = -U_0\sin\theta - \frac{\mu}{r^2}\sin\theta = -2U_0\sin\theta. \tag{9.39}$$

The maximum magnitude of velocity will occur when — sin θ — is maximum. i.e., when $\theta = \pi/2$ or $\theta = 3\pi/2$ i.e., $V_{\max} = 2U_0$ in the X direction. The pattern of flow is shown in Fig. 9.12.

9.12 Flow Around a Cylinder with Circulation

Let the circulation be Γ, which will be equal to $2\pi r_0 v_c$ where the circumferential velocity of the cylinder is v_c.

$$\text{The stream function } \psi = -U_0 r \sin\theta + \frac{U_0 {r_0}^2}{r}\sin\theta + \frac{\Gamma}{2\pi}\ln r. \tag{9.40}$$

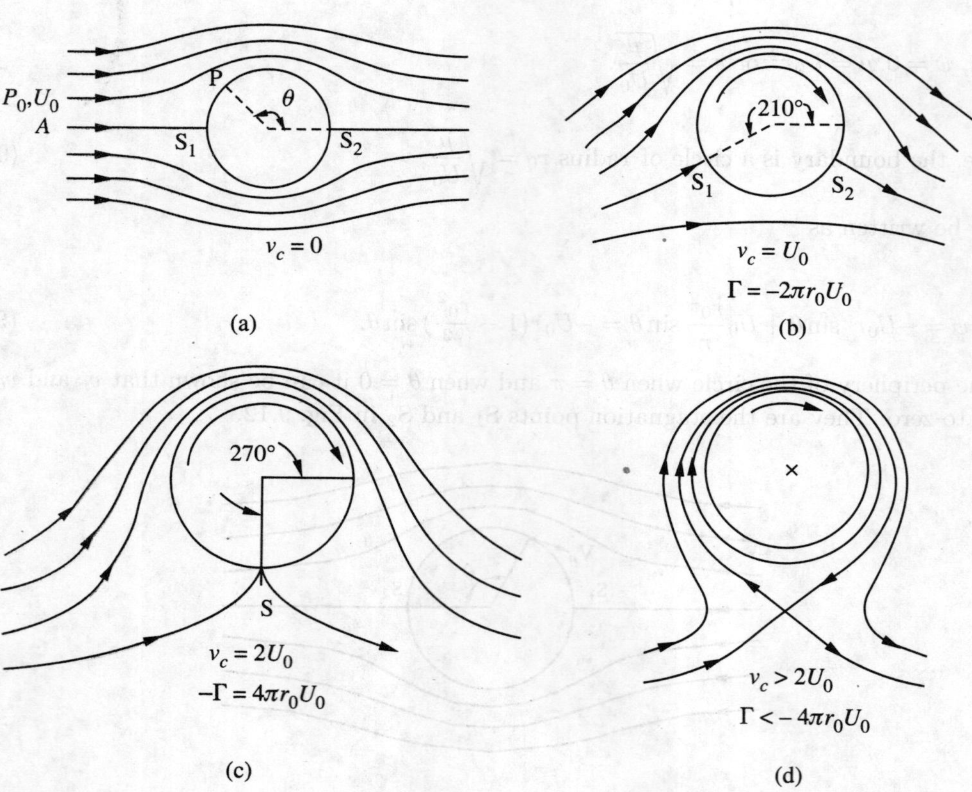

Fig. 9.13 *Effect of rotation on flow pattern around a cylinder*

From (9.40)

$$v_\theta = \frac{\partial \psi}{\partial r} = -U_0\left(1 + \frac{r_0^2}{r^2}\right)\sin\theta + \frac{\Gamma}{2\pi r}$$

$$\text{At radius } r = r_0.\ v_\theta = -2U_0\sin\theta + \frac{\Gamma}{2\pi r_0} \tag{9.41}$$

At stagnation point

$$v_\theta = 0; \sin\theta = +\frac{\Gamma}{4\pi r_0 U_0} = \pm\frac{v_c}{2U_0} \tag{9.42}$$

depending on Γ is positive or negative

$$\text{When } \Gamma = 0, \quad \theta = 0 \text{ (Fig. 9.13(a))} \tag{9.43}$$

Let us assume that the circulation is negative due to clockwise rotation of cylinder as in Figs. 9.13(b)–(d).

$$\text{In Fig. 9.13(b)}, v_c = U_0, \Gamma = -2\pi r_0 U_0; \sin\theta = -\frac{v_c}{2U_0} = -\frac{1}{2} \text{ and } \theta = 210° \text{ or } 330° \tag{9.44}$$

$$\text{In Fig. 9.13(c)}, v_c = 2U_0, \Gamma = -4\pi r_0 U_0; \sin\theta = -\frac{v_c}{2U_0} = 1 \text{ and } \theta = 270° \tag{9.45}$$

In Fig. 9.13(d), $v_c > 2U_0, \tau < -4\pi r_0 U_0$, the stagnation point will be away from the boundary. Equation (9.40) can be modified by subtracting a constant $(\Gamma/2\pi)\ln r_0$ and changing it to a non-dimensional form by dividing by $U_0 r_0$

$$\psi' = \frac{\psi}{U_0 r_0} = -\frac{r}{r_0}\sin\theta + \frac{r_0}{r}\sin\theta + \frac{\Gamma}{2\pi U_0 r_0}\ln\frac{r}{r_0}$$

For any value of r/r_0 and Γ, ψ can be calculated for various values of θ.

The stream lines for different cases are schematically shown in Fig 9.13(a), 9.13(b), 9.13(c) and 9.13(d).

9.12.1 Application of the energy equation (Bernoulli's equation)

Application of Bernoulli's theorem between points A and P on the cylinder gives

$$\frac{p_0}{\gamma} + \frac{U_0^2}{2g} = \frac{p}{\gamma} + \frac{1}{2g} \times \left[-2U_0\sin\theta + \frac{\Gamma}{2\pi r_0}\right]^2$$

$$\Delta p = p - p_0 = \frac{1}{2}\rho U_0^2\left[1 - \left(-2\sin\theta + \frac{\Gamma}{2\pi r_0 U_0}\right)^2\right]. \tag{9.46}$$

Net drag (force in the X direction) = 0, since there is symmetry about the Y axis.

If L is the length of the cylinder,

$$\text{Lift force } F_L = -\int_0^{2\pi} L\Delta p r_0 \sin\theta d\theta.$$

This can be shown to be equal to $L\rho U_0\Gamma$. The phenomenon of development of such a force is known as the Magnus effect. In the case as illustrated in Fig. 9.13 (b), (c) and (d), the force will be acting upwards. The Magnus effect can explain the forces acting on spinning balls swinging them from the normal trajectory.

Introducing the lift equation, $F_L = C_L \frac{1}{2}\rho U_0^2 A$, where C_L is the coefficient of lift,

$$F_L = C_L \frac{1}{2} \rho U_0^2 A = L\rho U_0 \Gamma, \tag{9.47}$$

where $A = 2r_0 L$

$$\text{Theoretically, } C_L = \frac{F_L}{\frac{1}{2}\rho U_0^2 \times 2r_0 L} = \frac{\Gamma}{r_0 U_0} = \frac{2\pi r_0 v_c}{U_0} = 2\pi \frac{v_c}{U_0}. \tag{9.48}$$

In practice, the value of C_L is only nearly half the theoretical value.

Example 9.2 A circular cylinder lies in an air stream having a velocity of 60 m/s. In addition, there is a flow around the cylinder with a circulation of 400 m^2/s (clockwise). Neglecting all viscous and compressibility effects, determine the following: (i) Maximum velocity due to air stream alone (ii) Velocity at the cylinder surface due to circulation alone (iii) Location of stagnation point (iv) Lift force per unit length of the cylinder.
The density of air is 1.22 kg/m^3 and the cylinder diameter is 1.2m.

$U = 60$ m/s; $D = 1.2$ m; $\Gamma = 400$ m^2/s; $\rho = 1.22$ kg/m^3.

(i) Velocity due to air stream alone: $u = 2U \sin\theta$.

This is maximum when $\sin\theta$ is maximum. i.e., when $\theta = 90°$.

Therefore, $u_{\max} = 2 \times 60 = 120$ m/s. (Ans.)

(ii) Velocity at the cylinder due to circulation:

$\Gamma = 2\pi r v_c$.

$$v_c = \frac{\Gamma}{2\pi r} = \frac{400}{(2\pi \times 0.6)} = 106.1 \text{ m/s. (Ans.)}$$

(iii) At the stagnation point:

$$\sin\theta = -\frac{v_c}{2U} = -\frac{106.1}{2 \times 60} = -0.884; \text{ therefore, } \theta = 242.13° \text{ or } 297.87. \text{ (Ans.)}$$

(iv) $F_L = \rho U \Gamma L = 1.22 \times 60 \times 400 \times 1 = 29280 \text{ N} = 29.28 \text{ kN}$. (Ans.)

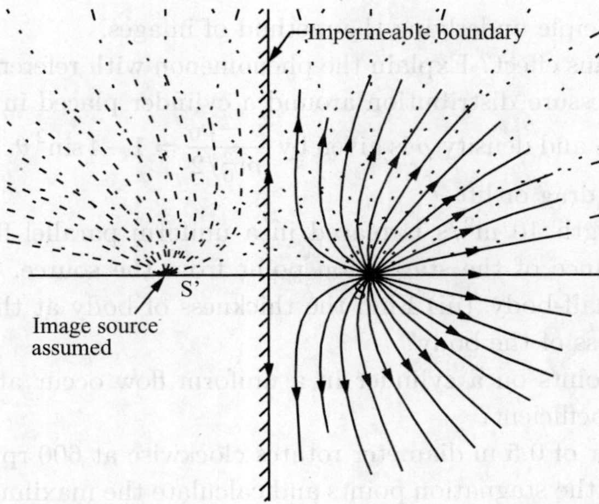

Fig. 9.14 *Flow from a source near a wall*

9.13 The Method of Images

When a line source is located very near to an impermeable boundary, the condition of flow can be simulated by assuming a mirror image of the source reflected at the impermeable boundary and combining the flows of the source and the image. This will ensure a flow parallel to the impermeable boundary as shown in the Fig. 9.14. The combined flow pattern of the two sources are drawn.

REVIEW QUESTIONS AND PROBLEMS

9.1 Give the stream function and the potential for a uniform flow parallel to the X axis.
9.2 What is a source? What are the stream and potential functions for a source?
9.3 Give the stream and potential functions for a sink of strength q.
9.4 Express the stream function and potential function in a free vortex flow.
9.5 Express the stream function and potential function for a whirlpool.
9.6 What is a Rankine half-body? Explain what combinations will give the flow pattern.
9.7 What is the thickness of the Rankine half-body and the distance of the stagnation point from the source?
9.8 Explain the combination of flow that result in a Rankine oval.
9.9 What is a doublet? What combination of stream function and potential function give a doublet?
9.10 Show that in a doublet the stream lines and equipotentials are circles.
9.11 Show that the transformation $-\mu/z$ gives the stream function and potential function for a doublet.
9.12 What combination of flow will result in flow around a cylinder?

9.13 Illustrate the principle underlying the method of images.

9.14 What is the Magnus effect? Explain the phenomenon with reference to the flow pattern.

9.15 Show that the pressure distribution around a cylinder placed in an uniform ideal fluid flow of pressure p_0 and density ρ is given by $\frac{p - p_0}{\rho v_0^2/2} = 1 - 4\sin^2\theta$. Show that the cylinder will not have any drag or lift.

9.16 A source of strength 10 m^2/s is placed in a uniform parallel flow of velocity 4 m/s. (i) Find the distance of the stagnation point from the source. (ii) Find the equation for the Rankine half-body. (iii) Find the thickness of body at the source. (iv) What is maximum thickness of the body?

9.17 The stagnation points on a cylinder in a uniform flow occur at angles 20° and 160°. What is the lift coefficient?

9.18 A circular cylinder of 0.5 m diameter rotates clockwise at 600 rpm in a uniform stream of 15 m/s. Locate the stagnation points and calculate the maximum rotational speed for an attached stagnation point. Assuming air of density 1.22 kg/m^3

9.19 A source and sink equal strength 1.0 $m^2/s/m$ are placed along the X axis 0.5m apart. A uniform parallel flow of velocity 2 m/s is superimposed on it. Find (i) the length of Rankine oval and (ii) the thickness of the Rankine oval formed.

9.20 A cylinder of 0.3 m diameter and 1m long is rotating in a clockwise direction 500 rpm in a parallel uniform air flow of 12 m/s. Find the position of stagnation points and lift produced. $\rho = 1.22$ kg/m^3.

ANSWERS

9.16 (i) 0.398 m; (ii) r $\sin\theta + 0.398\,\theta = 1.25$; (iii) 1.25 m; (iv) 2.5 m; **9.17** $C_L = -4.3$; **9.18** (i) 211.57 and 328.43; (ii) 1145.92 rpm; **9.19** (i) 0.64 m; (ii) 0.319 m; **9.20** 108.4 N.

10 Fluid Dynamics

Euler's equations of motion — Bernoulli's theorem — Conservation of energy — Loss of energy in flow — Momentum transport equation — Impact of jets on vanes — Loss of head in a sudden pipe expansion — Flow through orifices — Determination of hydraulic coefficients — Time of emptying tank — Discharge from one tank to another — Loss of head at sudden contraction — Mouthpieces

10.1 Introduction

In fluid dynamics, the forces acting on the fluid mass and the resultant motion of the fluid are studied. The basic principle involved is Newton's second law of motion. This law can be stated, as *the rate of change of momentum is equal to the impressed force in the same direction.* i.e., $F = \frac{d}{dt}(mv)$. It can also be expressed as $F = ma$.

The forces acting on the fluid element are generally due to pressure, gravity, viscosity, surface tension and elastic forces. The net result can be acceleration produced on the mass. In its simpler analysis, the force due to pressure and weight of the fluid element is studied for an incompressible, non-viscous fluid and the resultant acceleration is found.

10.2 Euler's Equation

Taking a parallelopiped element of sides dx, dy and dz as in Fig. 10.1 and considering only pressure and gravity forces, let us assume the pressure at the centre of face ABCD to be p. The net pressure force acting on the surfaces ABCD and EFGH is $-\frac{\partial p}{\partial x} dxdydz$ and will be acting in the X direction

The component of weight $= \rho\ dx\ dy\ dz\ g_x$, where g_x is the component of acceleration in the X direction. The acceleration produced will be

$$\frac{du}{dt} = \frac{\partial u}{\partial t} + \frac{\partial u}{\partial x}\frac{dx}{dt} + \frac{\partial u}{\partial y}\frac{dy}{dt} + \frac{\partial u}{\partial z}\frac{dz}{dt}$$

$$= \frac{\partial u}{\partial t} + u\frac{\partial u}{\partial x} + v\frac{\partial u}{\partial y} + w\frac{\partial u}{\partial z}.$$

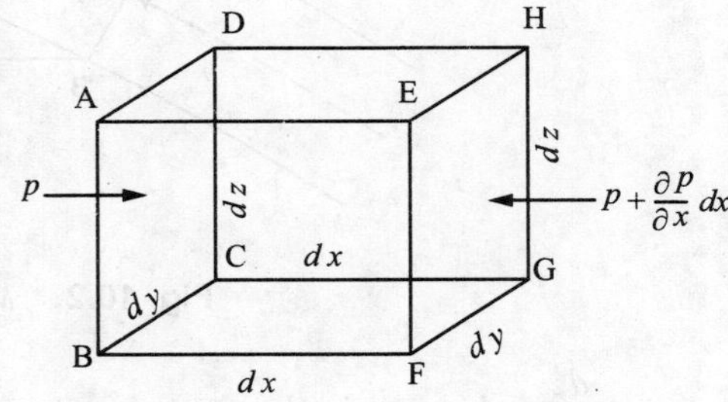

Fig. 10.1 *Pressure variation on the control volume*

Equating force with mass × acceleration in the X direction,

$$\rho\, dxdydz\frac{du}{dt} = -\frac{\partial p}{\partial x}dxdydz + g_x\rho\, dxdydz.$$

i.e., $$\frac{du}{dt} = -\frac{1}{\rho}\frac{\partial p}{\partial x} + g_x,$$

or, $$\frac{\partial u}{\partial t} + u\frac{\partial u}{\partial x} + v\frac{\partial u}{\partial y} + w\frac{\partial u}{\partial z} = -\frac{1}{\rho}\frac{\partial p}{\partial x} + g_x. \tag{10.1}$$

Similarly in the Y and Z directions,

$$\frac{\partial v}{\partial t} + u\frac{\partial v}{\partial x} + v\frac{\partial v}{\partial y} + w\frac{\partial v}{\partial z} = -\frac{1}{\rho}\frac{\partial p}{\partial y} + g_y. \tag{10.2}$$

$$\frac{\partial w}{\partial t} + u\frac{\partial w}{\partial x} + v\frac{\partial w}{\partial y} + w\frac{\partial w}{\partial z} = -\frac{1}{\rho}\frac{\partial p}{\partial z} + g_z. \tag{10.3}$$

The above equations are Euler's equations of motion in the three directions.

10.3 Euler's Equation of Motion along a Stream Line and Bernoulli's Equation

If one takes a thin stream tube through which the flow is steady (Fig. 10.2), it can be assumed to be one-dimensional along s and the streamlines are assumed to be nearly parallel.

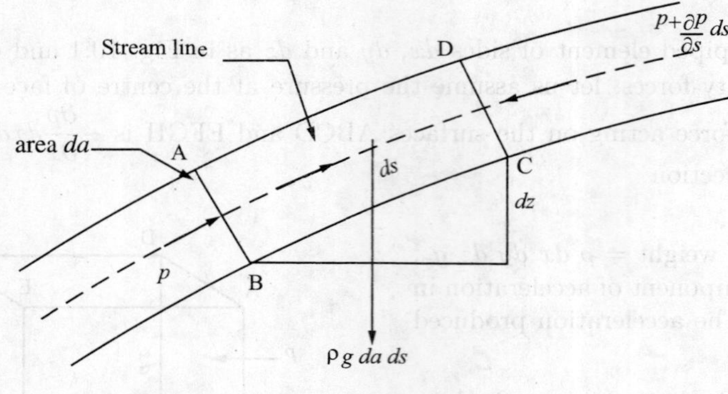

Fig. 10.2 *Motion along a stream line*

$g_s = -g\dfrac{dz}{ds}$, where g_s is the component of g along s.

Considering acceleration and forces along the direction of flow, mass × acceleration of element ABCD $= \rho\, da\, ds \times v_s\dfrac{\partial v_s}{\partial s}$.

$$\text{Net external force acting} = pda - \left(p + \frac{\partial p}{\partial s}ds\right)da - \rho\, g\, da\, ds \times \frac{dz}{ds}.$$

Neglecting higher order of small terms and dividing throughout by $\rho\, da\, ds$,

$$\frac{\text{Net force}}{\text{Unit mass}} = -\frac{1}{\rho}\frac{\partial p}{\partial s} - g\frac{dz}{ds},$$

which is equal to the acceleration along s. Hence,

$$\frac{dv_s}{dt} = v_s\frac{dv_s}{ds} = -\frac{1}{\rho}\frac{\partial p}{\partial s} - g\frac{dz}{ds}.$$

Because the variation is only in the s direction, partial derivatives can be replaced by total derivatives. Multiplying by ds, we get,

$$v_s dv_s = -\frac{dp}{\rho} - gdz. \tag{10.4}$$

The above equation is called the Euler's equation for steady, incompressible, non-viscous flow along a stream line. Integrating along a stream line,

$$\frac{{v_s}^2}{2} = -\frac{p}{\rho} - gz + c.$$

Since $\gamma = \rho g$, the above equation can be written as

$$\frac{p}{\gamma} + z + \frac{v^2}{2g} = \text{a constant}. \tag{10.5}$$

The above statement is known as the Bernoulli's theorem. It states that *in a steady flow of an incompressible, non-viscous fluid, the total energy per unit weight of the fluid, given by the expression* $\frac{p}{\gamma} + z + \frac{v^2}{2g}$, *is constant along a stream line.*

10.4 Applicability of Bernoulli's Equation Normal to Stream Lines

The acceleration normal to the stream lines can be written as

$$\frac{dv_n}{dt} = v_s\frac{\partial v_n}{\partial s} + v_n\frac{\partial v_n}{\partial n} = v_s\frac{\partial v_n}{\partial s}.$$

Since $v_n = 0$, the Euler's equation normal to the stream line is

$$v_s \frac{\partial v_n}{\partial s} = -\frac{1}{\rho}\frac{\partial p}{\partial n} - g\frac{\partial z}{\partial n}$$

Hence force-acceleration equation in the direction n will be

$$-\frac{1}{\rho}\frac{\partial p}{\partial n} - g\frac{\partial z}{\partial n} - v_s\frac{\partial v_s}{\partial n} = v_s\left(\frac{\partial v_n}{\partial s} - \frac{\partial v_s}{\partial n}\right).$$

When the flow is irrotational, the expression on the right-hand side is zero and the equation can be integrated. After multiplying by dn, we get $\frac{p}{\rho} + gz + \frac{v_s^2}{2} =$ constant or $\frac{p}{\gamma} + z + \frac{v^2}{2g}$ is constant.

Thus the Bernoulli's theorem will be applicable to the whole flow field only if the flow is irrotational.

10.5 Bernoulli's Equation as a Principle of Conservation of Energy

The Bernoulli's principle illustrates the conservation of energy. Let a system with boundary ABCD have a slight displacement to assume a boundary A′ B′ C′ D′ (Fig. 10.3). $a_1\delta s_1 = a_2\delta s_2 = \Delta\forall$ (fluid is assumed incompressible and the same volume is displaced).

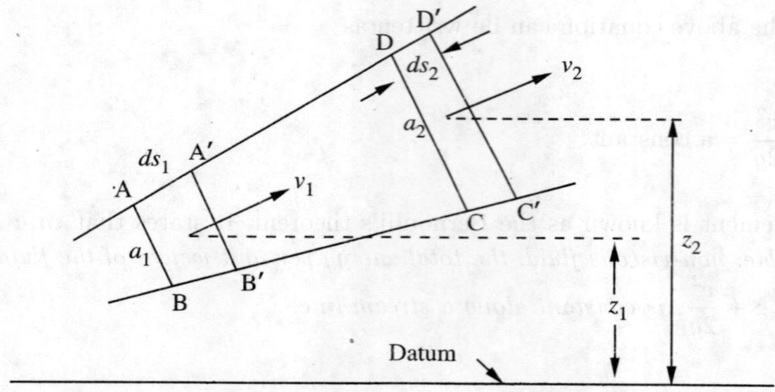

Fig. 10.3 *Energy balance of a displaced volume*

Considering the energy balance of the displaced volume,

Work done by pressure $= p_1a_1\delta s_1 - p_2a_2\delta s_2 = (p_1 - p_2)\,\Delta\forall$.

Work done by weight of fluid of volume $\Delta\forall = \gamma\Delta\forall\,(z_2 - z_1)$.

Gain in kinetic energy $= \rho\Delta\forall\frac{(v_2^2 - v_1^2)}{2}$.

By the law of conservation of energy,

$$(p_1 - p_2)\Delta\forall = \gamma\Delta\forall(z_2 - z_1) + \rho\Delta\forall\frac{{v_2}^2 - {v_1}^2}{2}$$

or, $$p_1 + \gamma z_1 + \frac{\rho {v_1}^2}{2} = p_2 + \gamma z_2 + \frac{\rho {v_2}^2}{2}$$

or,

$$\frac{p_1}{\gamma} + z_1 + \frac{{v_1}^2}{2g} = \frac{p_2}{\gamma} + z_2 + \frac{{v_2}^2}{2g}. \tag{10.6}$$

This is the energy equation applied to unit weight of fluid. The terms in the equation have the dimensions of length and are known as pressure head, elevation head and velocity head (or kinetic energy head) respectively. The elevation head can be measured above any convenient datum.

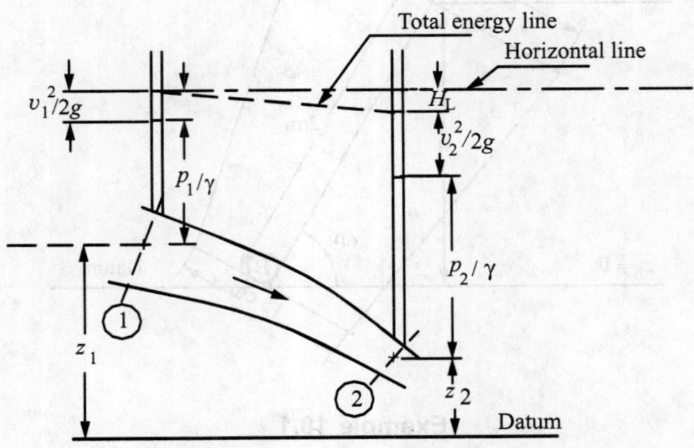

Fig. 10.4 *Flow with energy loss*

Figure 10.4 shows the total energy line and the head due to elevation, pressure and velocity above the datum line. The energy loss between Sections (1) and (2), H_L is shown in the figure. The energy loss can be accounted for by modifying the equation as

$$\frac{p_1}{\gamma} + z_1 + \frac{v_1^2}{2g} = \frac{p_2}{\gamma} + z_2 + \frac{v_2^2}{2g} + H_L, \tag{10.7}$$

where H_L is the energy head loss or loss of energy per unit weight of fluid.

Example 10.1 A discharge of 30 l/s of oil ($S = 0.81$) occurs downwards through a converging pipe line held inclined at 60° to the horizontal. The inlet diameter is 20 cm and the outlet diameter 15 cm and the length of the pipe is 2 m. If the pressure at the top of the inlet is 0.8 $\text{kg}_\text{f}/\text{cm}^2$, find the pressure at the outlet. Neglect the energy loss.

Applying Bernoulli's theorem between Sections (A) and (B),

$$\frac{p_A}{\gamma_o} + z_A + \frac{v_A^2}{2g} = \frac{p_B}{\gamma_o} + z_B + \frac{v_B^2}{2g}; S = 0.81 = \frac{\gamma_o}{\gamma_w}; p_A = 0.8 \text{ kg/cm}^2 = 8 \text{ m of water.}$$

$$z_B = 0; \frac{p_A}{\gamma_o} = \frac{p_A}{S\gamma_w} = \frac{0.8}{0.81} = 9.877 \text{ m of oil.}$$

$$z_A = h = 2\sin 60° = 1.732 \text{ m}; \ a_A = \frac{\pi \times 0.2^2}{4} = 0.0314 \text{ m}^2; Q = 30 \text{ l/s} = 0.03 \text{ m}^3/\text{s}.$$

$$v_A = \frac{Q}{a_A} = \frac{0.03}{0.0314} = 0.955 \text{ m/s}; \frac{v_A^2}{2g} = 0.0465 \text{ m.}$$

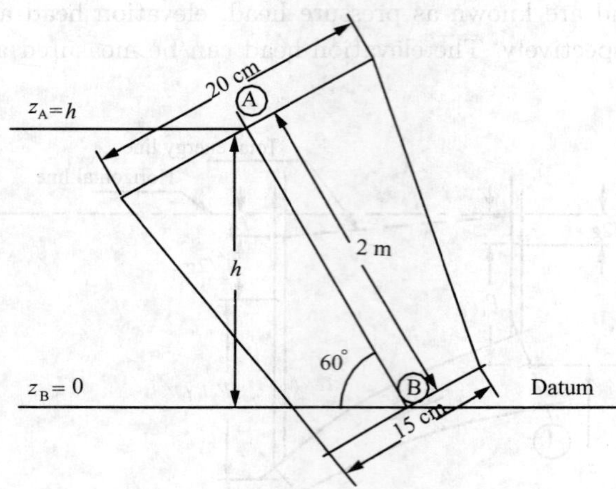

Example 10.1

$$z_B = 0; a_B = \frac{\pi \times 0.15^2}{4} = 0.0177 \text{ m}^2; v_B = \frac{0.03}{0.0177} = 1.695 \text{ m/s}; \frac{v_B^2}{2g} = 0.146 \text{ m.}$$

Therefore, $\frac{p_B}{\gamma_o} = \frac{p_A}{\gamma_o} + z_A + \frac{v_A^2}{2g} - z_B - \frac{v_B^2}{2g} = 9.877 + 1.732 + 0.0465 - 0 - 0.146 = 11.528$ m of oil.

$p_B = 11.528 \times 0.81$ m of water $= 9.338$ m of water $= 0.9338 \text{ kg}_f/\text{cm}^2$.

10.6 Flow Around a Cylinder

The stream function for the two-dimensional flow of an ideal fluid around a cylinder can be obtained by considering the stream functions given by (9.2),

$$\psi = -U_0 r \left(1 - \frac{{r_0}^2}{r^2}\right) \sin\theta,$$

where r is the radial distance and r_0 is the radius of the cylinder. The velocity at any point on the surface of cylinder is $v_\theta = -2U_0 \sin\theta$.

Figure 10.5 shows the pattern of irrotational flow around a cylinder with the axis vertical. S and S′ are the stagnation points of zero velocity. Applying Bernoulli's equation for points A and S along stream line AS,

$$\frac{p_0}{\gamma} + \frac{{U_0}^2}{2g} = \frac{p_S}{\gamma} + 0.$$

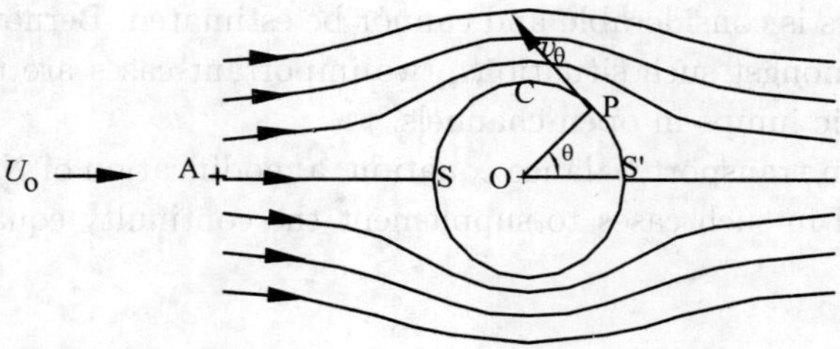

Fig. 10.5 *Flow around a cylinder*

Hence, $\frac{p_S}{\gamma} = \frac{p_0}{\gamma} + \frac{U_0^2}{2g}$.

At point S, the kinetic energy head will be transformed into a pressure head. At point C i.e., at $\theta = \pi/2, v_\theta = -2U_0 \sin \pi/2 = -2U_0$. So velocity at C in the X direction $= 2U_0$. By the application of Bernoulli's theorem between A and C along the stream line AC,

$$\frac{p_0}{\gamma} + z + \frac{{U_0}^2}{2g} = \frac{p_c}{\gamma} + z + \frac{(2U_0)^2}{2g}.$$

$$\frac{p_c}{\gamma} = \frac{p_0}{\gamma} - 3\frac{{U_0}^2}{2g}.$$

Hence, the highest velocity and the lowest pressure in the flow field will be at point C.

Example 10.2 A cylinder of diameter 3 cm is placed in a parallel flow of water normal to the axis. The ambient velocity of flow is 0.8 m/s and the stagnation pressure is 18 kPa. Find the minimum pressure around the cylinder.

$$v_0 = 0.8 \text{ m/s}; \frac{{v_0}^2}{2g} = 0.0326 \text{ m}; h_s = \frac{p_s}{\gamma_w} = \frac{18}{9.81} = 1.835 \text{ m}.$$

$$\frac{p_s}{\gamma_w} = \frac{p_0}{\gamma_w} + \frac{{v_0}^2}{2g}.$$

Minimum pressure will occur at C,

$$\frac{p_c}{\gamma_w} = \frac{p_0}{\gamma_w} - 3\frac{v_0^2}{2g} = \frac{p_s}{\gamma_w} - 4\frac{v_0^2}{2g} = 1.835 - 4 \times 0.0326 = 1.7046 \text{ m}; \gamma = 9.81 \text{ kPa}.$$

Minimum $p_c = 1.7046 \times 9.81 = 16.722$ kPa. (Ans.)

10.7 Loss of Energy in Flow

The loss of energy in flow of fluids occurs due to the action of viscosity but this energy manifests as addition of heat to the system. In laminar flow, it is quite evident that viscous shear causes energy loss. But in turbulent flow, in addition to viscous shear due to mean velocity gradients, the loss of energy takes place because of intense shear between eddies and within the eddies.

When the energy loss is considerable and cannot be estimated, Bernoulli's equation cannot be directly applied. Amongst such situations, two important cases are that of a sudden pipe expansion and hydraulic jumps in open channels.

The force momentum transport balance equation, a modification of Newton's second law of motion, can be applied in such cases to supplement the continuity equation, and the energy loss can be calculated.

10.8 The Force–Rate of Momentum Transport Balance Equation

10.8.1 General case

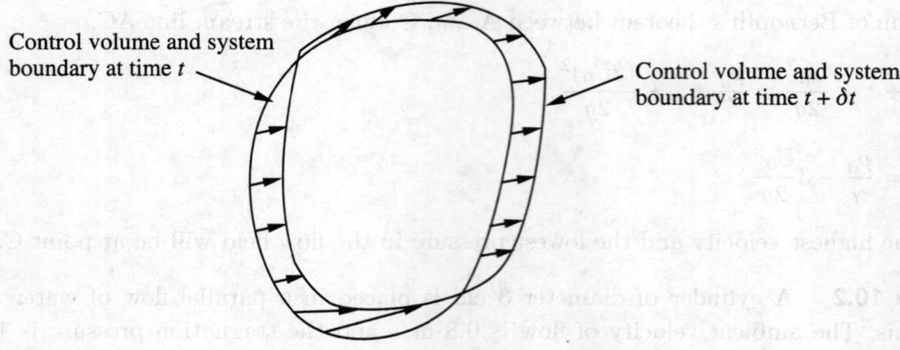

Fig. 10.6 *Control volume*

Consider a system of fluid elements occupying a control volume $\forall$ in Fig. 10.6. By Reynold's transport equation (see Section 7.10),

$$\left(\frac{dN}{dt}\right)_{\text{system}} = \frac{\partial}{\partial t}\iiint_{\forall}(\eta\rho)d\forall + \oint\!\!\!\oint_{cs}(\eta\rho)\vec{V}.d\vec{A},$$

where $N = \iiint_{\forall}(\eta\rho)d\forall$.

If η is the velocity $\vec{V}$, $\eta\rho$ will be $\rho\vec{V}$, $\vec{N} = \iiint_{\forall} \rho\vec{V}\, d\forall$ and $\dfrac{d\vec{N}}{dt}$ = rate of change of momentum.

For steady flow, $\dfrac{\partial}{\partial t}\iiint_{\forall} (\rho\vec{V})d\forall = 0$ and hence $\left(\dfrac{d\vec{N}}{dt}\right) = \oiint_{cs} .(\rho\vec{V})\vec{V}.d\vec{A}$. Applying Newton's second law of motion,

Rate of change of momentum = impressed force in the same direction (direction being taken care of by using vector notation) i.e.,

$$\left(\frac{d\vec{N}}{dt}\right) = \oiint_{CS} .(\rho\vec{V})\vec{V}.d\vec{A} = \text{Total force } \vec{F}_r \tag{10.8}$$

10.8.2 One-dimensional case in the X direction

In a direction i, the equation will be $\vec{F}_{Ti} = \oiint_{cs} .\rho\vec{V}_i(\vec{V}.d\vec{A})$, applied in the X direction. Identifying $\vec{V}.d\vec{A}$ as dQ, the equation for total force in the X direction F_{TX} will lead to

$$F_X = (\rho QV_X)_{\text{outflow}} - (\rho QV_X)_{\text{inflow}} = \rho Qu_2 - \rho Qu_1, \tag{10.9}$$

where $u = V_X$

Similar equations can be obtained in the Y and Z directions.

10.9 Force on a bend of pipe conveying fluid

The pressures at the inlet of the bend and its outlet are to be considered in analyzing the forces on the bend. The shear force on the boundary is often neglected. Let the components of force of fluid on the bend be F_X and F_Y. The forces of bend on the fluid will be $R_X = -F_X$ and $R_Y = -F_Y$.

Figure 10.7 shows a bend in a pipe, the inlet area being a_1 and outlet area a_2. Let the velocity at inlet be V_1 and at outlet V_2. Let the inlet pressure be p_1 and outlet pressure p_2. Let W be the weight of fluid in the bend (if the bend is not in horizontal plane)

$$R_X + p_1a_1 - p_2a_2\cos\theta = \rho a_2V_2^2\cos\theta - \rho a_1V_1^2 \tag{10.10}$$

$$\text{and} \quad R_Y - p_2a_2\sin\theta - W = \rho a_2V_2^2\sin\theta \tag{10.11}$$

NOTE For the momentum analysis, first list the forces acting in any direction i. The total force $F_{Ti.}$ = Momentum transport outflow rate from the control volume in the i direction − Momentum transport inflow rate to the control volume in the i direction. Proper components and signs are to be used while writing the momentum transport outflow and inflow rates.

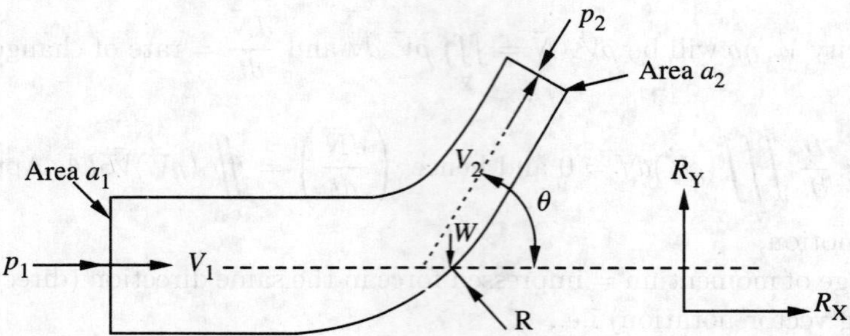

Fig. 10.7 *Forces of a bend of pipe on water.*

Example 10.3 Water is flowing through a horizontal pipe of diameter 30 cm. The direction of the pipe is changed by an angle of 135° by a bend. Find the magnitude and direction on the resultant force on the bend if the discharge is 0.25 m^3/s and pressure 4 kg/cm^2.

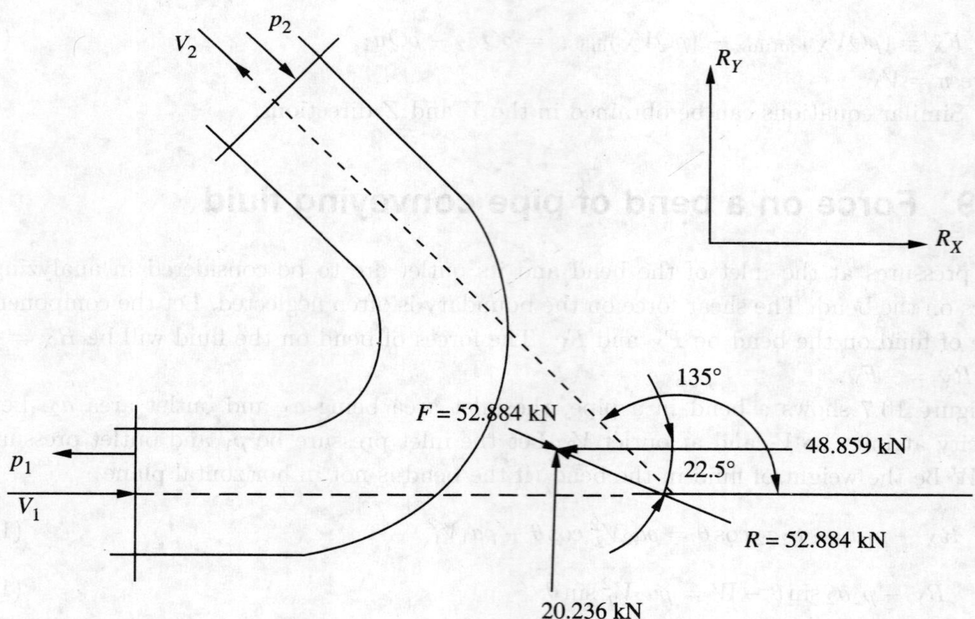

Example 10.3

$d = 30$ cm $= 0.3$ m; $a_1 = a_2 = 7.069$ m^2; $Q = 0.25$ m^3/s.

$V_1 = V_2 = Q/A = 3.5366$ m/s; $p_1 = p_2 = 4$ kg/ cm^2 $= 3.924 \times 10^5$ Pa.

Assume components of force of bend on water as R_X and R_Y as shown in the figure. Applying momentum equation,

(i) In the X direction: $p_1a_1 + R_X + p_2a_2 \cos 45° = \rho Q(-V_2 \cos 45° - V_1)$

$$3.924 \times 10^5 \times 7.069 \times 10^{-2} + R_X + 3.924 \times 10^5 \times 7.069 \times 10^{-2} \times 0.707$$

$$= 1000 \times 0.25 \times (-2.50 - 3.5366)$$

$$27738.8 + R_X + 19611.3 = -1509.15; R_X = -48.859 \text{ kN}.$$

Hence R_X is from right to left.

(ii) In the Y direction: $= \rho Q(V_2 \sin 45°)$

$$-p^2a_2 \sin 45° + R_Y = 1000 \times 0.25 \times 2.50$$

$$-3.924 \times 10^5 \times 7.069 \times 10^{-2} \times 0.707 + R_Y = 625$$

$$R_Y = 19611.3 + 625 = 20.236 \text{ kN}$$

Hence the resultant $R = \sqrt{48859.3^2 + 20236.3^2} = 52.884$ kN

$\theta = \tan^{-1}\dfrac{R_y}{R_x} = 22.5°$. The force F of water on the pipe will be equal and opposite to R.

Example 10.4 A horizontal steel pipe 30 cm diameter conveys a discharge of 120 l/s. The pipe reduces its diameter to 15 cm after a bend of 60°. The pressure in the pipe before the bend is 60 kPa. Find the forces acting on the bend.

Let the component of force acting on the water at the bends be F_X and F_Y. The force of the bend on the water is $R_X = -F_X$ and $R_Y = -F_Y$; R_X and R_Y are shown in the figure.

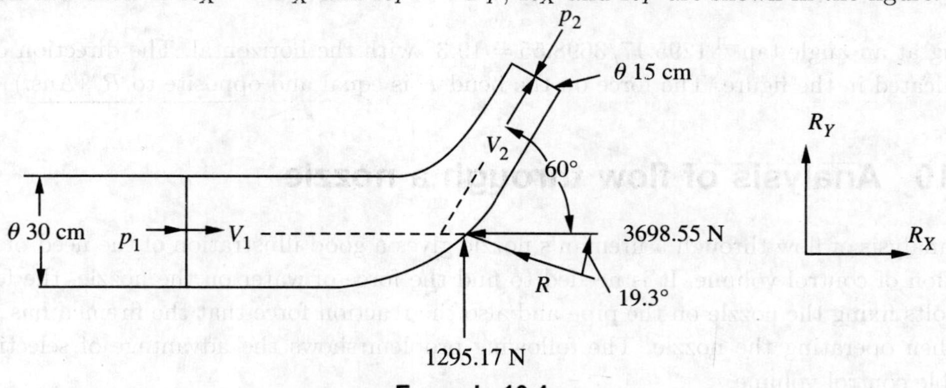

Example 10.4

Solution

$Q = 0.12\ \text{m}^3/\text{s}; \quad a_1 = 0.0707; \quad a_2 = 0.0177; V_1 = 1.697\ \text{m/s}; \quad V_2 = 6.791\ \text{m/s}$

Applying Bernoulli's theorem,

$$\frac{p_1}{\gamma} + \frac{V_1^2}{2g} = \frac{p_2}{\gamma} + \frac{V^2}{2g}$$

$$\frac{60 \times 1000}{9810} + \frac{1.697^2}{2g} = \frac{p_2}{\gamma} + \frac{6.791^2}{2g}$$

$$\frac{p_2}{\gamma} = 3.912\ \text{m}, \quad p_2 = 38376.7\ \text{N/m}^2$$

In the direction X,

$$R_X + p_1 a_1 - p_2 a_2 \cos\theta = \rho a_2 V_2^2 \cos\theta - \rho a_1 V_1^2$$

or $$R_X = \rho a_2 V_2^2 \cos\theta - \rho a_1 V_1^2 - p_1 a_1 + p_2 a_2 \cos\theta$$

$$= 1000 \times 0.0177 \times 6.791^2 \cos 60° - 1000 \times 0.0707 \times 1.697^2 - 60 \times 10^3 \times 0.0707$$
$$+38.376 \times 10^3 \times 0.0177 \cos 60° = -3698.55\ \text{N}$$

which is negative. Hence actual R_x is in the direction opposite to that one assumed.

In the direction Y,

$$-p_2 a_2 \sin\theta + R_Y = \rho a_2 V_2^2 \sin\theta$$

or $$R_Y = \rho a_2 V_2^2 \sin\theta + p_2 a_2 \sin\theta$$

$$= 1000 \times 0.0177 \times 6.791^2 \times \sin 60° + 38.376 \times 10^3 \times 0.0177 \times \sin 60° = 1295.17\ \text{N}$$

Resultant $R = \sqrt{3698.85^2 + 1295.17^2} = 3919.\text{N}$

Acting at an angle $\tan^{-1} 1295.17/3698.55 = 19.3°$ with the horizontal. The direction of force is indicated in the figure. The force on the bend F is equal and opposite to R. (Ans.)

10.10 Analysis of flow through a nozzle

The analysis of flow through a fireman's nozzle gives a good illustration of the need of proper selection of control volume. It is needed to find the force of water on the nozzle, the force on the bolts fixing the nozzle on the pipe and also the reaction force that the firemen has to take up when operating the nozzle. The following problem shows the advantage of selecting the suitable control volume.

Example 10.5 A fireman's fire hose nozzle is shown in the diagram. The pipe has a diameter of 3 cm and the nozzle 1.5 cm. The discharge is 6 l/s. If the atmospheric pressure is 101 kPa find (i) the force of water on the nozzle (ii) the force on the bolts that fix the nozzle to the pipe (iii) The force that the fireman has to exert to hold the nozzle horizontally while the jet is being played.

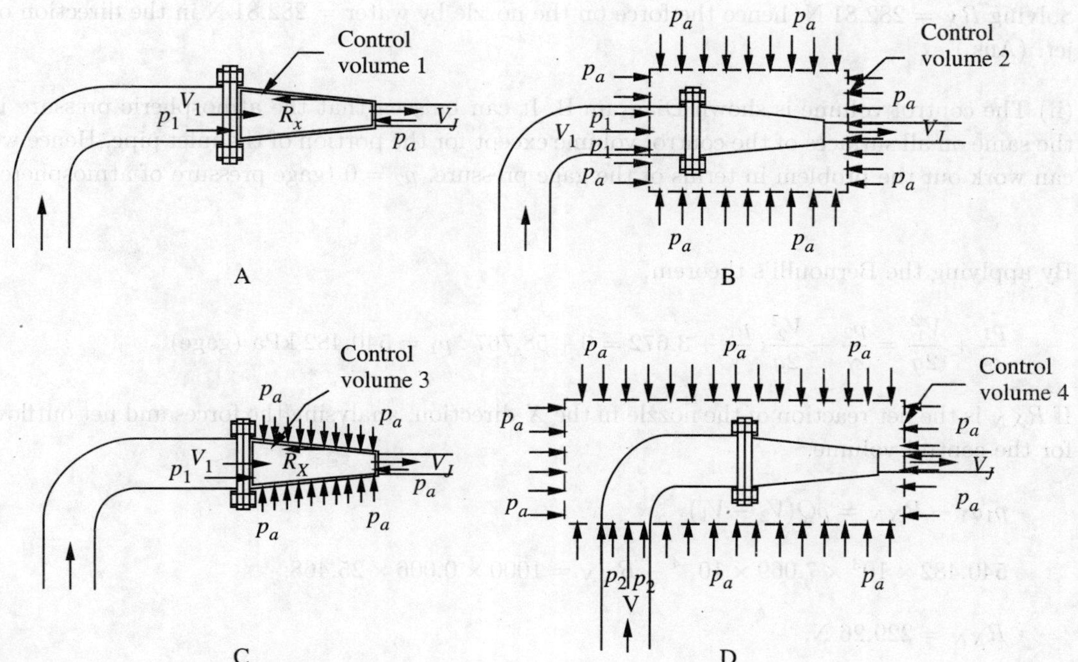

Example 10.5

$Q = 0.006$ m^3/s; $d_1 = 0.03$ m; $d_2 = 0.015$ m; $p_2 = 101$ kPa.

$a_1 = 7.069 \times 10^{-4}$ m^2; $a_2 = 1.7678 \times 10^4$ m^2.

$V_1 = Q/a_1 = 8.48$ m/s; $V_2 = Q/a_2 = 33.956$ m/s.

(i) Consider the control volume shown in diagram A. Let R_X be the force of the nozzle on water.

Appling Bernoulli's theorem,

$$\frac{p_1}{\gamma} + \frac{V_1^2}{2g} = \frac{p_2}{\gamma} + \frac{V_2^2}{2g}; \quad \frac{p_1}{\gamma} + 3.672 = \frac{101 \times 10^3}{9810} + 58.767 = 10.296 + 58.767$$

$$\frac{p_1}{\gamma} = 65.39 \text{ m}; \ p_1 = 641.486 \text{ kPa}.$$

By applying momentum theorem,

$$p_1 a_1 - R_X - p_2 a_2 = \rho Q(V_2 - V_1)$$

$$641.486 \times 10^3 \times 7.069 \times 10^{-4} - R_X - 101 \times 10^3 \times 1.767 \times 10^{-4} = 1000 \times 0.006 \times 25.468$$

Solving $R_X = 282.81$ N; hence the force on the nozzle by water $= 282.81$ N in the direction of jet. (Ans.)

(ii) The control volume is shown Diagram B. It can be seen that the atmospheric pressure is the same on all surfaces of the control volume except for the portion of the inlet pipe. Hence we can work out the problem in terms of the gage pressure. $p_2 = 0$ (gage pressure of atmosphere)

By applying the Bernoulli's theorem,

$$\frac{p_1}{\gamma} + \frac{V_1^2}{2g} = \frac{p_2}{\gamma} + \frac{V_2^2}{2g};\ \frac{p_1}{\gamma} + 3.672 = 0 + 58.767 : p_1 = 540.482 \text{ kPa (gage)}$$

If R_{XN} is the net reaction of the nozzle in the X direction, analysing the forces and net outflow for the control volume,

$$p_1 a_1 - R_{XN} = \rho Q(V_2 - V_1)$$

$$540.482 \times 10^3 \times 7.069 \times 10^{-4} - R_{XN} = 1000 \times 0.006 \times 25.468;$$

$$R_{XN} = 229.26 \text{ N.}$$

Hence the force on the bolts is a pull in the direction of the jet equal to 229.26 N. (Ans.)

Discussion The difference in the force on the nozzle in the above two cases is due to the fact that in the later case, the component of pressure of air on the inclined exterior surface of the nozzle is also included. See diagram C.

Component of force due to pressure on the inclined exterior surface of the nozzle

$$= p_2 \times (a_1 - a_2) = 101 \times 10^3\ (7.069 \times 10^{-4} - 1.767 \times 10^{-4}) = 53.55 \text{ N.}$$

The net force $= 282.81 - 53.55 = 229.26$ N. (Ans.)

(iii) Using the control volume in diagram D, $F = \rho Q V_2 = 1000 \times 0.006 \times 33.956 = 203.736$ N.

Discussion There is no contribution of p_1 and V_1 in the reaction force.

10.11 Impact of Jets on Vanes

Consider a jet of fluid impinging on a vane. If the vane is stationary, the mass flow striking the vane, $\rho Q = \rho a\text{V}$, where ρ is the specific mass, a is the cross-sectional area of the jet and V is the velocity of the jet. If the vane is moving, the effective velocity will depend on the relative velocity involved.

The principle involved in (10.10), $F_x = \rho Q u_2 - \rho Q u_1$ is used in finding the change in the momentum transport rate and hence force.

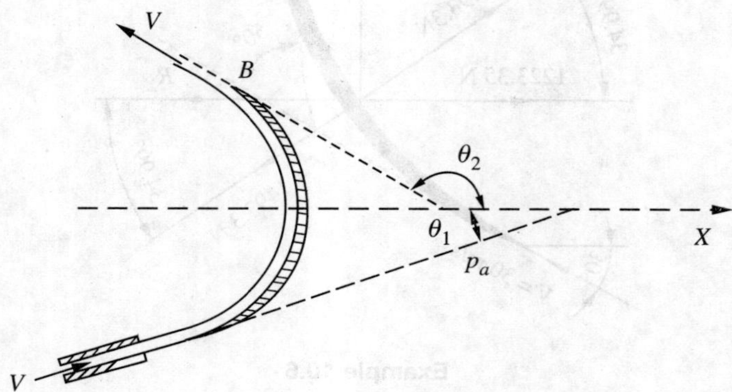

Fig. 10.8 *Jet impinging on a curved vane*

10.11.1 Force of jet on a vane

A jet of area a and velocity V is entering the vane tangentially at A and leaves the vane at B as shown in Fig 10.8. Angles at inlet and outlet with direction X are θ_1 and θ_2 respectively. Since the vane is smooth, the velocity at the outlet can be assumed as V.

$Q = \rho a V$

Change of momentum transport rate $= \rho a V^2(\cos\theta_2 - \cos\theta_1)$

Hence force in the X direction of the vane on the fluid $= \rho a V^2(\cos\theta_2 - \cos\theta_1)$

Force of fluid on vane $F_x = \rho a V^2(\cos\theta_1 - \cos\theta_2)$ (10.12)

Force of fluid on vane $F_y = \rho a V^2(\sin\theta_1 - \sin\theta_2)$ (10.13)

Resultant force $= \sqrt{F_x^2 + F_y^2}$ acting at an angle $\alpha = \tan^{-1}(F_y/F_x)$ (10.14)

with the direction of the jet.

Example 10.6 A jet of water of diameter 5 cm having a velocity of 30 m/s impinges on a fixed curved vane tangentially at one end at an angle of 30° with the horizontal. Calculate the resultant force of the jet on the vane, if the jet is deflected through an angle of 50°.

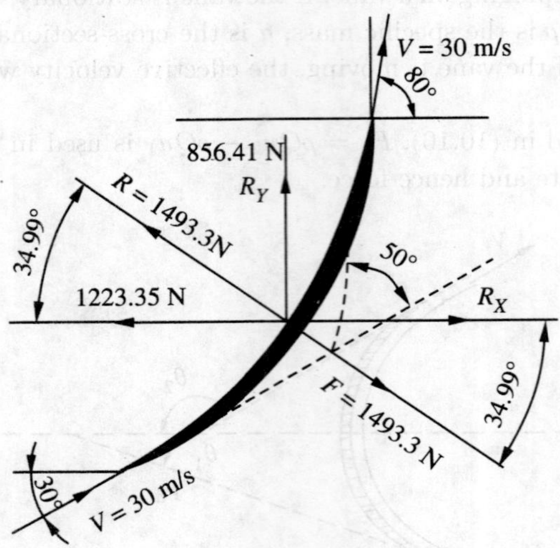

Example 10.6

$d = 0.05$ m; $a = 1.9635$ m^2; $V = 30$ m/s; $Q = a \times V = 0.0589$ m^3/s; $\rho Q = 58.9$ kg/s.

$R_X = \rho Q \times 30 \times \cos 80° - \rho Q \times 30 \times \cos 30° = 58.9 \times 20.77 = -1223.35$ N.

R_X is negative indicating that the force is from right to left.

$R_Y = \rho Q \times 30 \sin 80° - \rho Q \times 30 \sin 30° = 14.54 \times 58.9 = 856.41$ N.
$R = \sqrt{1223.35^2 + 856.41^2} = 1493.3$ N at an angle of $\tan^{-1}(856.41/1223.35) = 34.99°$ with the X axis. F is shown equal and opposite to R in the figure.

Example 10.7 A stationary vane as shown in the figure is acted upon by a jet of discharge 2 l/s having a velocity of 50 m/s . (i) Find the force on the vane. (ii) If the vane is moving in the X direction at a velocity of 15 m/s, find the force on the vane. Find the power developed.

The effective discharge of water impinging on the vane will depend on the movement of the vane.

(i) $Q_1 = 2$ l/s $= 2 \times 10^{-3}$m^3/s ; $\rho Q_1 = 1000 \times 2 \times 10^{-3} = 2$kg/s

$R_X = -(\rho Q_1) \times 50 \cos 40° (\rho Q_1) \times 50 = -2 \times 38.30 \times 2 \times 50 = -176.6$ N.

The negative sign indicates that the force is from right to left.

$R_Y = (\rho Q_1) \times 50 \sin 40° = 2 \times 32.14 = 64.28$ N.

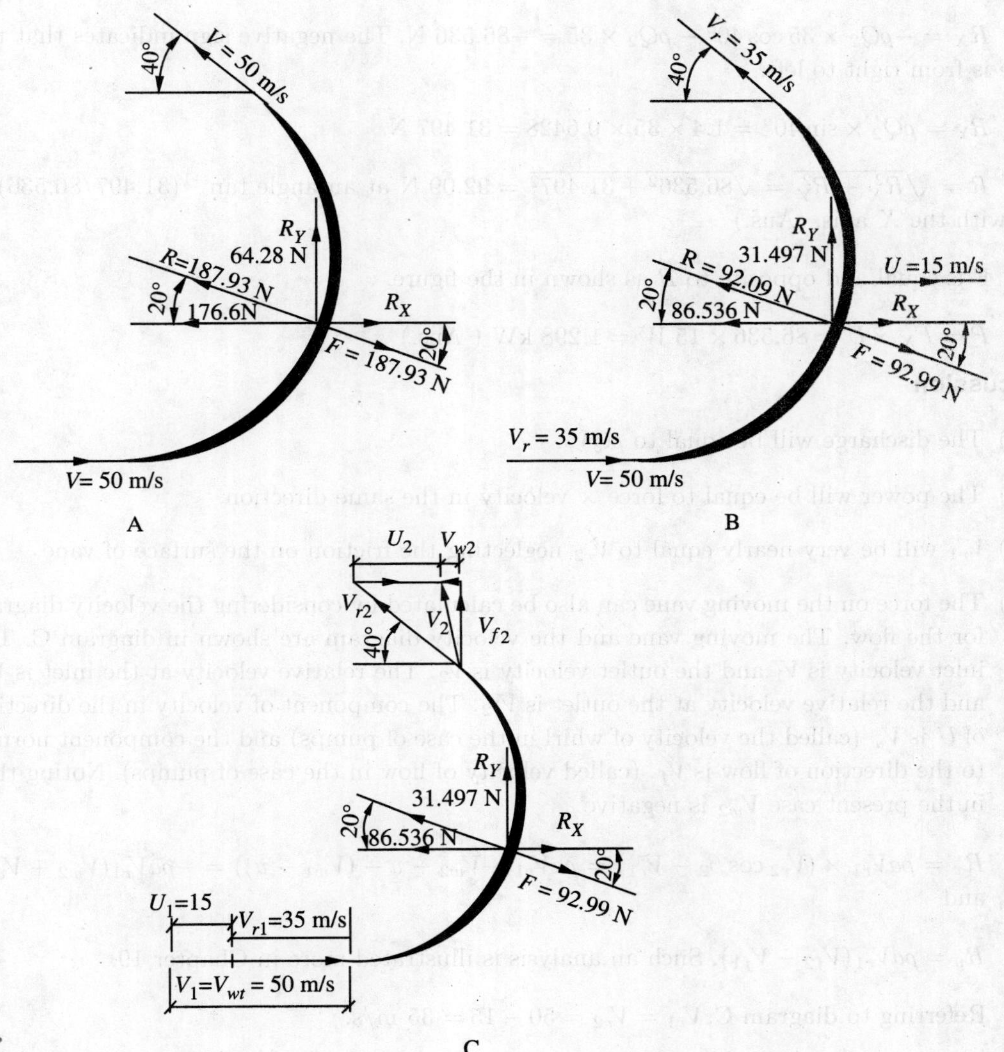

Example 10.7

$R = \sqrt{176.6^2 + 64.28^2} = 187.93$ N making an angle of $\tan^{-1}(64.28/176.6) = 20°$ with the X axis. The force F is shown in the figure as equal and opposite to R. (Ans)

(ii) It is a moving vane and hence the relative velocity $V_r = V - U = 50 - 15 = 35$ m/s.

$$Q_2 = Q_1 \times (V - U)/V = 0.7 \times Q_1$$

$$\rho\, Q_2 = 0.7 \times Q_1 = 0.7 \times 2 = 1.4 \text{ kg/s}$$

$R_X = -\rho Q_2 \times 35 \cos 40° - \rho Q_2 \times 35 = -86.536$ N. The negative sign indicates that the force is from right to left.

$R_Y = \rho Q_2 \times \sin 40° = 1.4 \times 35 \times 0.6428 = 31.497$ N.

$R = \sqrt{R_X^2 + R_Y^2} = \sqrt{86.536^2 + 31.497^2} = 92.09$ N at an angle $\tan^{-1}(31.497/86.536) = 20°$ with the X axis. (Ans.)

F is equal and opposite to R as shown in the figure.

$P = F_X \times U = 86.536 \times 15\ W = 1.298$ kW (Ans.)

Discussion

(i) The discharge will be equal to $\rho Q V_r$.

(ii) The power will be equal to force × velocity in the same direction.

(iii) V_{r1} will be very nearly equal to V_{r2} neglecting the friction on the surface of vane.

(iv) The force on the moving vane can also be calculated by considering the velocity diagram for the flow. The moving vane and the velocity diagram are shown in diagram C. The inlet velocity is V_1 and the outlet velocity is V_2. The relative velocity at the inlet is V_{r1} and the relative velocity at the outlet is V_{r2}. The component of velocity in the direction of U is V_w (called the velocity of whirl in the case of pumps) and the component normal to the direction of flow is V_f. (called velocity of flow in the case of pumps). Noting that in the present case V_{w2} is negative

$R_x = \rho a V_{r1} \times (V_{r2} \cos \beta_2 - V_{r1}) = \rho a V_{r1}(-V_{w2} - u - (V_{w1} - u)) = -\rho a V_{r1}(V_{w2} + V_{w1})$ and

$R_y = \rho a V_{r1}(V_{f2} - V_{f1})$. Such an analysis is illustrated more in Chapter 19.

Referring to diagram C, $V_{r1} = V_{r2} = 50 - 15 = 35$ m/s.

$\rho a V_r = 2 \times 35/50 = 1.4$ kg/s

$V_{w1} = V_1 \cos \alpha_1 = 50 \times \cos 0° = 50$ m/s

$V_{w2} = V_2 \cos \alpha_2 = \vec{V}_{r2} \cos \beta_2 + \vec{U} = -35 \cos 40° + 15 = -26.81 + 15 = -11.81$ m/s

$V_{f1} = 0$; and $V_{f2} = V_r \sin \beta_2 = 22.498$ m/s.

$R_x = \rho a V_r \times (V_{w2} - V_{w1}) = 1.4 \times (-11.81 - 50) = -1.4 \times 61.81 = -86.354$ N

$R_y = 1.4 \times (V_{f2} - V_{f1}) = 1.4 \times 22.498 = 31.497$ N

It may be noted that the value of R_x and R_y are the same as calculated previously.

10.11.2 Force on a moving curved vane deflecting the jet by 180°

It is an unsteady case as shown in Fig. 10.9(a). It is made steady by the addition of u to the velocities.
The equivalent problem is shown in Fig. 10.9(b)

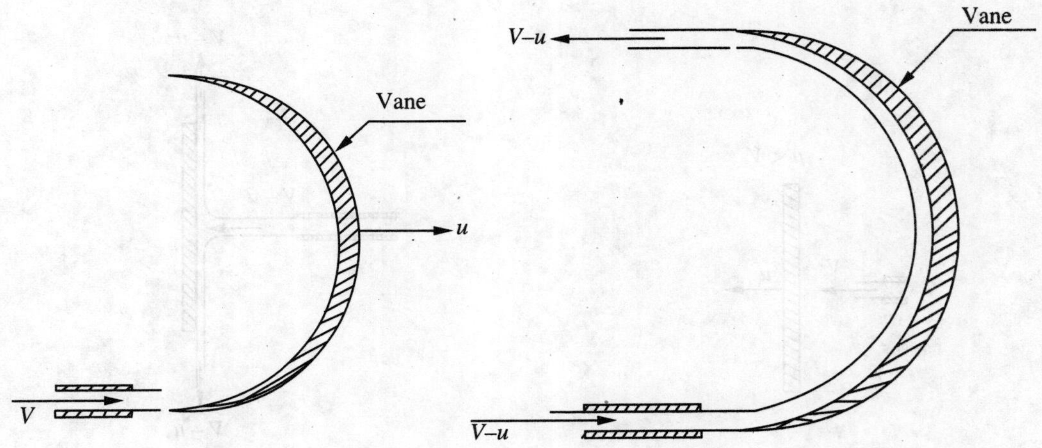

Fig. 10.9(a) *Moving curved vane, deflecting jet by* 180°

Fig. 9(b) *Moving curved vane, deflecting jet by 180°: steady case*

$$Q' = \rho a(V - u)$$

$$F_x = \rho a(V - u)\{(V - u) + (V - u)\}$$

$$= 2\rho a(V - u)^2 \qquad (10.15)$$

10.11.3 Force on a flat plate (Jet normal to plate)

In this case in direction X there is no discharge and hence momentum after impact is zero. Finding the change in momentum transport rate

$$F_x = \rho QV = \rho a V^2 \qquad (10.16)$$

Fig. 10.10 *Jet impinging on flat plate*

10.11.4 Force on flat plate moving at velocity u (jet normal to plate)

Let the plate be moving with a velocity u in the direction of the jet. The unsteady case may be made steady by adding a velocity $-u$.

And $F_x = \rho a(v - u)^2$ (10.17)

Fig. 10.11(a) *Jet impinging on moving flat plate*

Fig. 10.11(b) *Jet impinging on moving flat plate—steady case*

10.11.5 Force on inclined flat plate (jet making an angle α with the plate)

Due to asymmetry Q_1 and Q_2 will be different. Also there will not be any momentum transport in the N direction.

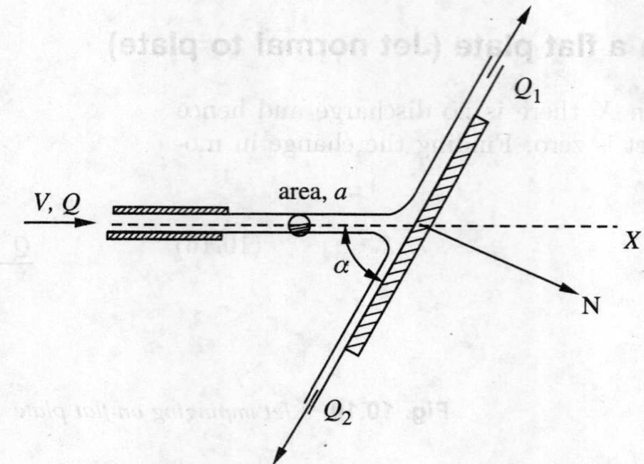

Fig. 10.12 *Jet impinging on inclined flat plate*

Comparing momentum transport rate along the direction N before and after impact

$$F_N = \rho QV \sin\alpha = \rho aV^2 \sin\alpha \quad (10.18) \text{ and}$$

$$F_x = \rho aV^2 \sin^2\alpha \quad (10.19)$$

Comparing momentum transport rate along the plate before and after impact

$$\rho QV \cos\alpha = \rho Q_1 V - \rho Q_2 V$$

Dividing by ρQv, $\cos\alpha = \dfrac{Q_1}{Q} - \dfrac{Q_2}{Q}$

By continuity $Q = Q_1 + Q_2$ or $1 = \dfrac{Q_1}{Q} + \dfrac{Q_2}{Q}$

Solving $Q_1 = \dfrac{1}{2}Q(1+\cos\alpha) \quad (10.20)$

$$Q_2 = \frac{1}{2}Q(1-\cos\alpha) \quad (10.21)$$

10.11.6 Force on moving inclined plate

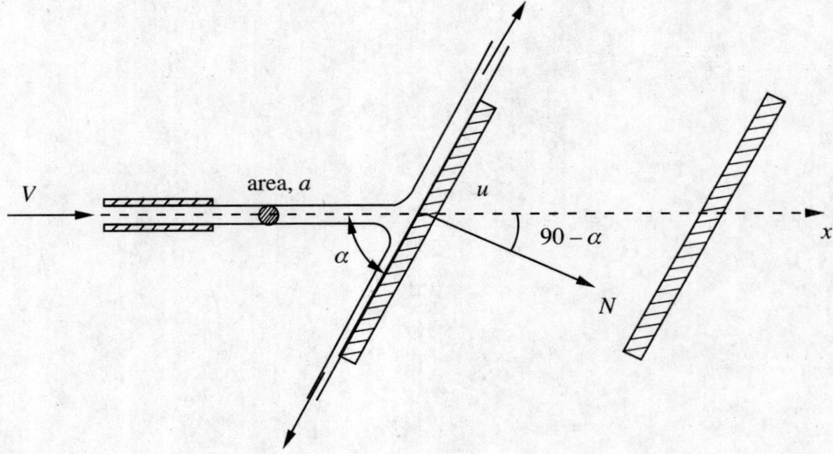

Fig. 10.13 *Jet impinging on an inclined moving flat plate*

Let the plate move in the direction of jet at a velocity of u
Comparing moment transport rate in the N direction before and after impact,

$$F_N = \rho a(V-u)^2 \sin\alpha \quad (10.22)$$

pressure and specific mass of air at the elevation are 22.65 kPa and 0.364 kg/m^3 respectively. The area of inlet of the turbojet is 2 m^2 and the outlet area is 1 m^2. The exhaust gases have a velocity of 500 m/s and a pressure of 20 kPa. The air fuel ratio is 20. Find the thrust of the engine.

The mass inflow rate of air $= \dot{m}_i = \rho_i A_i V_i = 0.364 \times 2 \times 280 = 203.84$ kg/s

mass rate of fuel $=203.84/20 = 10.192$ kg/s

Total exhaust mass flow $= 203.84 + 10.192 = 214.032$ kg/s. i.e $\dot{m}_e = 214.032$ kg/s

$$p_e = 20 \text{ kPa};\ V_e = 500 \text{ m/s}$$

Thrust $T = (p_e - p_0)A_e + \dot{m}_e V_e - (20 - 22.65) \times 10^3 \times 1 + 214.032 \times 500 - 203.84 \times 280 =$ $49,941$ N $= 49.941$ kN. (Ans)

Example 10.11 A rocket uses liquid hydrogen as fuel and liquid oxygen as oxidizer in the ratio of 1:8. The mass of hydrogen used per second is 10 kg. The exhaust vapour has a velocity of 3600 m/s, pressure of 1.2 kPa and area at the exit is 1.2 m^2. If moving at an altitude of 32 km the pressure is 0.889 kPa, find the thrust developed.

Mass flow rate $\rho_e Q_e = 10 + 10 \times 8 = 90$ kg/s.

$p_e = 1.2$ kPa; $\quad p_0 = 0.889$ kPa

$$T = (p_e - p_0 \times A_e + A_e = \rho_e Q_e V_e (1.2 - 0.889) \times 103 + 90 \times 3600$$

$$= 324311N = 324.311 \text{ kN (Ans)}$$

10.13 Momentum and Energy Correction Factors

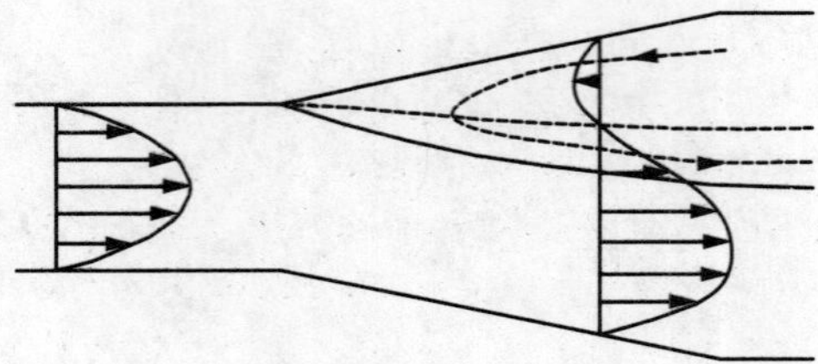

Fig. 10.14 *Non-uniform velocity distribution*

The velocity across a section may be non-uniform as in Fig. 10.14. The discharge across the section can be worked out by formula

$$\frac{d\forall}{dt} = \int_A v dA = AV,$$

where $V = \dfrac{Q}{A} = \dfrac{\int v dA}{\int dA}$. In finding the integral, the proper sign of v should be taken.

The momentum transport rate across the section is found out by the formula $\dfrac{dM}{dt} = \rho \int_A v|v| dA$, which can be written as $\beta \rho A V^2$, where

$$\beta = \frac{\int_A v|v| dA}{AV^2}. \tag{10.24}$$

β is known as the momentum correction factor.

The energy transport rate across the section is found out by the formula $\dfrac{dE}{dt} = \rho \int_A v^3 dA$, which can be written as $\alpha \rho A V^3$, where

$$\alpha = \frac{\int v^3 dA}{AV^3}. \tag{10.25}$$

α is known as the energy correction factor.

The values of α and β will be greater than one. When there is reverse flow, it may have very high values.

10.14 The Loss of Head in a Sudden Pipe Expansion

Consider a sudden pipe expansion in a horizontal pipe as in Fig. 10.15, having the pressure, velocity and area as indicated. At the expansion, the flow will separate at the corners and eddies will be formed on both sides. The region of separation will have low pressures. The discontinuity between the main flow and the eddies will be regions of high shear causing intense turbulence, and consequently there will be very high energy loss.
Assume v_2 as the average velocity in the X direction at Section (2).

Momentum transport rate at Section (2) $= \rho Q v_2$.

Momentum transport rate at Section (1) $= \rho Q v_1$.

$$F_x = p_1 A_1 + p_0 (A_2 - A_1) - p_2 A_2.$$

p_0 is experimentally found to be nearly equal to p_1. The component of weight in the X direction is zero.

area of cross-section of the jet here, a_c will be less than the area of the orifice, a. This section is called vena contracta and the ratio

$$\frac{a_c}{a} = C_c. \tag{10.28}$$

is defined as the coefficient of contraction.

There are small losses in energy due to friction between the tank boundary and the fluid flow elements themselves so that the velocity at C will be less than the theoretical velocity $\sqrt{2gh}$.

Coefficient of velocity C_v is defined as the ratio of the actual velocity at C to the theoretical velocity i.e.,

$$C_v = \frac{v_c}{\sqrt{2gh}}. \tag{10.29}$$

The coefficient of discharge C_d is defined as the ratio of the actual discharge through the orifice to the theoretical discharge through the orifice.

Fig. 10.17 *Flow through a sharp-edged orifice*

$$C_d = \frac{\text{Actual discharge}}{\text{Theoretical discharge}} = \frac{\text{Actual area} \times \text{Actual velocity}}{\text{Theoretical area} \times \text{Theoretical velocity}} \tag{10.30}$$

i.e., $$\frac{a_c v_a}{a\sqrt{2gh}} = C_c C_v \text{ or, } C_d = C_c C_v. \tag{10.31}$$

The usual values of C_v, C_c and C_d are about 0.97, 0.65 and 0.62 respectively.

10.17 Determination of Hydraulic Coefficients of an Orifice

The discharge through an orifice at the side of a tank when discharging at a constant head h can be measured by collecting the volume of liquid $\forall$ in a measuring tank for a known time t.

$$\text{Coefficient of discharge} \quad C_d = \frac{\text{Actual discharge}}{\text{Theoretical discharge}}$$

$$= \frac{\forall/t}{a\sqrt{2gh}}, \text{ where } a \text{ is the area of orifice.}$$

Coefficient of contraction The mean diameter d_m of jet at the vena contracta can be measured by a special equipment to measure the diameter of the jet, called a contraction gauge, consisting of a circular ring on which four screw gauges are mounted radially.

$$\text{Coefficient of contraction} = \frac{\pi d_m^2/4}{\pi d_m^2/4} = \left(\frac{dm}{d}\right)^2$$

Coefficient of velocity The trajectory of a jet after the vena contracta is parabolic. The velocity at the vena contracta will be in a horizontal direction. Assume coordinate axes with C as the origin, X axis as horizontal and Y axis as vertically downwards. After a time t, the fluid particle which was at C reaches C′. (See Fig. 10.17)

$$x = C_v\sqrt{2gh}\,t \text{ (the jet is falling under gravity).}$$

$$y = \frac{1}{2}gt^2.$$

Eliminating t,

$$\frac{x^2}{{C_v}^2 2gh} = \frac{2y}{g} \text{ or, } C_v = \sqrt{\frac{x^2}{4yh}}. \tag{10.32}$$

Example 10.13 A tank has water to a depth of 6 m and a small circular orifice on the side, 1.5 m from the water surface. Another orifice below issues a jet at the base level of the tank at the same point as the jet from above. Assuming $C_v = 1$, find the head of the second orifice and the point where the two will meet.

Since $C_v = 1, x^2 = 4hy$ (A)

For the orifice given and the jet meeting at the base, $h_1 = 1.5$ m and $y_1 = 6 - y_1 = 4.5$ m. $h_2 = 4.5$ and $y_2 = 1.5$ will also be another solution to satisfy equation (A). Hence the position of the other orifice is 4.5 m from the water surface. (Ans).

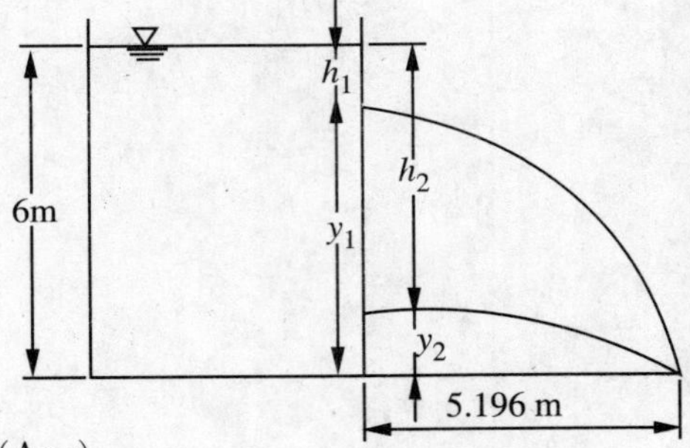

Example 10.13

$$x = \sqrt{4h_1y_1} = \sqrt{4h_2y_2} = \sqrt{4 \times 1.5 \times 4.5} = 5.196 \text{ m. (Ans).}$$

10.18 Time taken to Empty a Tank through an Orifice

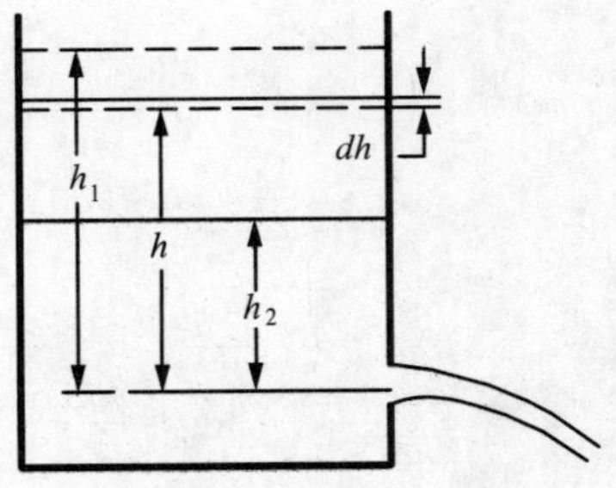

Fig. 10.18 *Emptying a tank through an orifice*

Referring to Fig. 10.18, the discharge in time dt through the orifice will lower the level of water by dh in a tank of area A. Equating the above volumes,

$Qdt = -A\,dh$ (−ve sign indicates the lowering of the level with increase in time).

$$C_d a\sqrt{2gh}\,dt = -Adh.$$

$$dt = \frac{-Adh}{C_d a\sqrt{2g}h^{1/2}} = \frac{-A}{C_d a\sqrt{2g}}h^{-1/2}dh.$$

10.24 Loss of Head at a Sudden Contraction

Fig. 10.24 Loss of head at a sudden contraction

10.21 Loss of Head at a Sudden Contraction

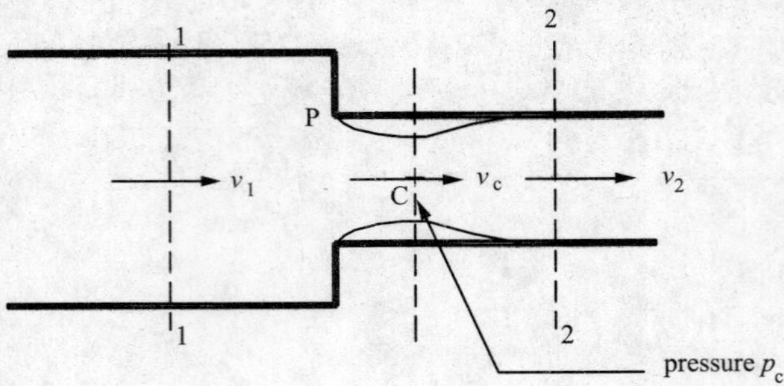

Fig. 10.21 *Loss of head at a sudden contraction*

Consider a pipe of diameter d_1 at Section (1) suddenly contracting to a diameter d_2 at Section (2) as in Fig. 10.21. Let the velocity and pressure be as indicated in the figure. The stream lines will separate from the boundary at P and the jet will contract up to a section (C), (vena contracta) where the area will be reduced to $C_c\, a_2$. The jet will then expand and fill the pipe. The loss of head from section (1) to section (C) can be neglected. In the stretch section (C) to section (2) the loss is due to a sudden expansion of the jet of area $C_c\, a_2$ to a_2.

Using the relation $v_c a_c = v_2 a_2$, head loss,

$$H_L = \frac{(v_c - v_2)^2}{2g} = \left(\frac{1}{C_c} - 1\right)^2 \frac{v_2^2}{2g}.$$

Usually C_c is assumed to be nearly 0.62 and

$$H_L = 0.375\frac{v_2^2}{2g}. \tag{10.36}$$

But C_c has been found to depend on the ratio d_2/d_1.

An approximate formula for the head loss in a sudden contraction is

$$H_L = 0.42\left[1 - \left(\frac{d_2}{d_1}\right)^2\right]\frac{v_2^2}{2g}.$$

The contraction loss is usually assumed as equal to $0.5\,\dfrac{v_2^2}{2g}$.

10.22 Flow through Mouthpieces

10.22.1 Cylindrical mouthpieces

Mouthpieces are short pipes attached internally or externally at an opening. The simplest case is of a cylindrical mouthpiece in which a circular pipe of about $4d$ in length is attached externally. After the contraction at the entry, the jet reattaches on the pipe wall and the pipe flows full at the exit.

Consider the flow situation in Fig. 10.22. Since the jet at E issues to the atmosphere, the pressure at E is atmospheric. Due to contraction at C, the velocity at C will be equal to $\dfrac{v_E}{C_c} \approx \dfrac{v_E}{0.62} = 1.612 v_E$. The loss of head between E and C due to the sudden expansion will be

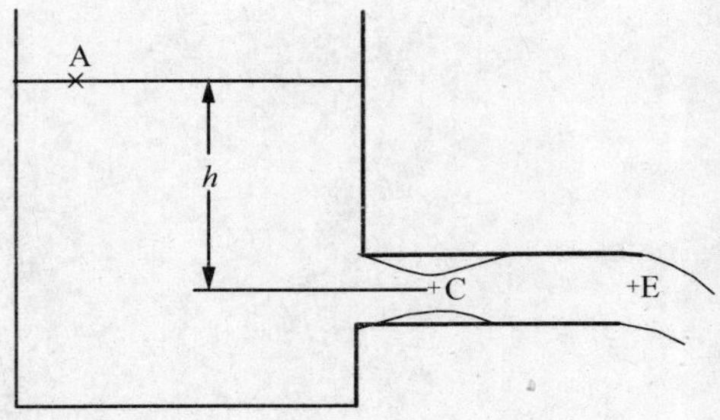

Fig. 10.22 *Flow through mouth piece*

$$\frac{(1.612 v_E - v_E)^2}{2g} \approx 0.375 \frac{v_E^2}{2g}.$$

Applying Bernoulli's theorem between A (at atmospheric pressure p_{atm}) and E,

$$\frac{p_{\text{atm}}}{\gamma} + h + \frac{v_A^2}{2g} = \frac{p_E}{\gamma} + 0 + \frac{v_E^2}{2g} + H_L = \frac{p_{\text{atm}}}{\gamma} + \frac{v_E^2}{2g} + 0.375 \frac{v_E^2}{2g}.$$

Hence $h = 1.375 \dfrac{v_E^2}{2g}$ or, $v_E = 0.85\sqrt{2gh}$. (10.37)

At point E, area of flow is a. Hence discharge $= v_E a = 0.85 a\sqrt{2gh}$. So, the coefficient of discharge $= 0.85$. But experimentally, the coefficient has been found to be of the order of 0.81.

Applying Bernoulli's theorem between A and C,

$$\frac{p_{\text{atm}}}{\gamma} + h + \frac{v_A^2}{2g} = \frac{p_c}{\gamma} + 0 + \frac{v_c^2}{2g} = \frac{p_c}{\gamma} + \frac{(1.612 v_E)^2}{2g} = \frac{p_c}{\gamma} + \frac{2.6 v_E^2}{2g} = \frac{p_c}{\gamma} + 1.39h.$$

$$\frac{p_c}{\gamma} = \frac{p_{\text{atm}}}{\gamma} - 0.89h. \quad \left(h = 1.375 \frac{v_E^2}{2g}\right) \tag{10.38}$$

When the pressure reduces to the vapour pressure of the liquid, cavities may form leading to cavitation.

It may be noted that the coefficient of discharge for a cylindrical mouthpiece is greater than that of an orifice. This may be explained by the fact that in the case of a mouthpiece, the pressure at the vena contracta is reduced below atmosphere by $0.89h$ and the effective head causing the discharge from the tank to C will be $1.89\ h$.

10.5 Explain the Reynolds transport equation and apply it to the transport rate–force balance for flow of fluids.

10.6 Derive the expression for the force on a moving curved vane when a jet of diameter d and velocity V is deflected by an angle of 180°

10.7 What is the need for momentum and energy correction factors? Derive the expression for the factors.

10.8 Derive the expression for the energy head loss in a pipe expansion.

10.9 Explain the terms (i) coefficient of contraction (ii) coefficient of discharge as applied to an orifice.

10.10 Determine an expression for the time of emptying of a tank of area A by an orifice of area a from a head h_1 to h_2.

10.11 Explain how the coefficient of velocity for an orifice can be determined by study of the jet geometry.

10.12 Two tanks of area A_1 and A_2 are connected by an orifice of area a. What time will be required for the differential head to fall from H_1 to H_2.

10.13 Determine an expression for the head loss in a sudden contraction.

10.14 Explain how the coefficient of discharge for a cylindrical mouth-piece is greater than that of an orifice.

10.15 What is a Borda's mouth-piece. Derive a formula for the discharge when the jet is flowing free.

10.16 Show the shape of flow conditions from a Bordas mouth-piece and give the value of coefficient of discharge in those cases.

10.17 Water is flowing through a short horizontal tapering pipe from A to B. The diameter of pipe at A is 30 cm and at B15 cm. If the pressure at A is 80 kPa and discharge is 100 l/s find the pressure at B.

10.18 Oil of specific gravity 0.85 flows down a tapering vertical pipe 1m long from A to B. if the diameters of pipe at A is 0.2 m and at B is 0.15 m, find the required pressure at A so that the pressure at B is 50 kPa when the flow is 80 l/s.

10.19 A horizontal pipe AB reduces from a diameter of 20 cm to 10 cm in a length of 1m. If the water pressure head at A and B are 18 kPa and 16 kPa what is the flow rate? Neglect the losses.

10.20 A pipe has a diameter of 0.3 m at section A and 0.2 m at section B. It is 10m long and laid at a slope of 20°, A being at the top. Oil of sp.gravity 0.8 flows from A to B. If the discharge is 60 l/s and the pressure at A is 60 kPa, find the pressure at B.

10.21 Water flows upwards in a vertical tapering pipe 2 m long. The inlet diameter is 30 cm and the outlet diameter is 20 cm. find the pressure at outlet if the pressure at inlet is 40 kPa and discharge is 60 l/s.

10.22 Oil of sp.gravity 0.85 in a pipeline 20 cm diameter passes through a reduced section of 15 cm diameter. If the discharge is 40 l/s and the minimum pressure at the reduced section is 55 kPa (absolute) what should be the pressure in 20 cm pipe before the reduced section.

10.23 At a section in a pipeline, the diameter is 15 cm and pressure is 65 kPa. At another section B, 3 m below A , the diameter is 30 cm and the pressure 105 kPa. Determine the direction of flow when the pipe is carrying oil of specific gravity 0.9 at the rate of 70 l/s What is the energy loss?

10.24 A reducing elbow changes the direction of the flow in a horizontal pipe by 60°. The inlet diameter is 30 cm and outlet diameter 25 cm. The inlet pressure is120 kPa and outlet pressure 80 kPa. Find the discharge and force on the bend.

10.25 The discharge through a pipe line 20 cm diameter is 0.1 m^3/s. The pipe turns by 180° and terminates in a nozzle of diameter 8 cm discharging to the atmosphere. Find (i) the pressure in the 20 cm diameter pipe before the bend. (ii) Find the force on the bend.

10.26 A pipe line 30 cm in diameter is gradually reduced to 20 cm diameter in a length of 30 cm and connects to a 20 cm diameter pipe line. If the discharge is 0.15 m^3/s and the pressure before the contraction is 180 kPa, (i) find the pressure after the contraction, (ii) calculate the force exerted by the flow on the contraction.

10.27 A pressure vessel 1 m 1 m 1 m is mounted on rollers on a horizontal smooth floor. It has water to a depth of 20 cm and air is kept under pressure in the rest of the space. The mass of the tank with contents is 400 kg. A horizontal jet 1 cm in diameter, issues from the bottom of the tank. If the coefficient of friction is 0.04, find the minimum pressure of air in the tank needed to make the tank move. If the tank attains a constant velocity of 1.5 m/s find what change will be there in the velocity of the jet. Neglect the change in the mass of tank.(Hint. Mechanical laws remain the same in uniformly moving systems.- A Einstein)

10.28 A jet of water 5 cm in diameter and having a velocity of 25 m/s flows tangentially to a stationary vane and gets deflected by an angel of 120o. Find (i) the resultant force on the vane. (ii) If the vane is moving in the direction of jet at 12 m/s find the force on the vane in the direction of jet and the power developed. .

10.29 A stationary vane having an inlet angle of zero degree and an outlet angle of 25° receives water at a velocity of 50 m/s. (i) Determine the components of force acting on it in the direction of jet velocity and normal to it, also find the resultant force in magnitude and direction (per unit mass flow rate) (ii) If the above vane is moving with a velocity of 20 m/s in the direction of the jet, calculate the force components in the direction of the jet and normal to it also find the magnitude and direction of the resultant force. Calculate the work done and horse power developed per unit mass flow rate..

10.30 A water jet of 5 cm diameter and having a velocity of 30 m/s impinges on an inclined flat plate making an angle of 60° with the axis of the jet. (i) What is the force on the plate when the plate is stationary? (ii) What is the force on the jet when the plate is moving at a velocity of 8 m/s parallel to itself? (iii) What is the power developed in case (ii) ? (iv) What is the efficiency of the jet in case (ii)?

10.31 A series of flat plates mounted on a wheel intercepts a jet of diameter 6 cm. and velocity 25 m/s normal to plate successively. If the plates move at a velocity of 10 m/s what is the power developed?

10.32 A plate of length 60 cm. and weighing 10 kg is hung from the hinge at top. It is hit by a jet of diameter 1.2 cm having a velocity of 20 m/s, the jet axis being 35 cm, below the hinge. Find the angle that the plate will make with the vertical when the jet (at the same level) plays on the plate?

10.33 In a pipe carrying oil, there is a sudden expansion from a diameter of 20 cm to 30 cm. The energy head loss is found to be 0.3 m (i) find the discharge. (ii) Find the change in piezometric head.

10.34 In a pipeline carrying a liquid the diameter of the pipe suddenly increases from 15 cm to 30 cm. The piezometric head increased by 0.5m. find the discharge.

10.35 A penstock 1.2 m diameter carries water at a rate of 2 m^3/s. If there is a 30° bend in the penstock and the pressure is 600 kPa find the forces on the bend.

10.36 Oil of sp.gravity 0.85 flows from a 4.25 cm diameter orifice under a pressure of 9 N/cm^2. The diameter of the jet at the vena-contracta is 3.32 cm and the discharge is 12.25 l/s. (i) What is the coefficient of contraction (ii) What is the coefficient of velocity and (c) Find the Coefficient of discharge.

10.37 A tank has an orifice of diameter 2 cm at the side. The head of water above the orifice is 37.2 cm. The jet issuing from the orifice falls down by 3 cm in a distance of 20.5 cm (i) Find the coefficient of velocity (ii) If C_c is 0.62 find the coefficient of discharge.

10.38 A square tank 0.75 m × 0.75 m has a 1cm diameter orifice on the side. Find the time for emptying the tank by the orifice from a head of 0.8 m to 0.4 m. Assume $C_d = 0.62$.

10.39 A large rectangular orifice at the side of a 2 m × 2 m diameter tank is of width 4cm and depth 3 cm. Find the discharge when the head of water above the centre of orifice is 20 cm. Assume $C_d = 0.62$.

10.40 A tank 2 m × 2 m and another 1m × 1m are connected at the bottom by a circular orifice of diameter 2 cm. If initially the larger tank has water 0.5 m above the smaller tank calculate the time required to reduce the level difference to 0.2 m. Assume $C_d = 0.62$.

10.41 A tank 1m × 1m has a 1.2 cm diameter mouthpiece at the side. When the head of water over the mouth-piece is 0.8 m, it is discharging freely to the atmosphere. Find the pressure at the vena-contracta formed inside the mouthpiece.

ANSWERS

10.17 64.98 kPa; **10.18** 47.6 kPa; **10.19** 0.0162 m^3/s; **10.20** 85.67 kPa; **10.21** 18.92 kPa; **10.22** 56.48 kPa; **10.23** Flow is upwards; Energy loss is 0.784 m; **10.24** $Q = 0.615$ m^3/s; $F = 11657$ N outwards making 58.85° with the direction of main pipe flow; **10.25** 192.8 kPa (gauge); 4386 N opposite to the direction of jet; **10.26** 170.855 kPa; 6956.85 N; **10.27** 249.78 kPa; No change in the velocity; **10.28** (i) 2135 N at angle 30° with jet; (ii) 957 N; 11.48 kW; **10.29** (i) 95.31 N/kg; 21.09 N/kg; 97.63 N/kg at an angle of 12.5° with the direction of jet. (ii) 57.18 N/kg; 12.67 N/kg; 58.57 N/kg at an angle of 12.5° with the direction of jet; **10.30** (i) 1530 N; (ii) 732.81 N; (iii) 5862 W (iv) 22.12%; **10.31** 10.601 kW; **10.32** 32.55°; **10.33** (i) 0.1371 m^3/s (ii) 0.48 m; **10.34** 0.0904 m^3/s; **10.35** $P_x = 91.388$ kN; $P_y = 341.068$ kN; $R = 353.1$ kN making 75° with X axis; **10.36** (i) 0.61 (ii) 0.9725 (iii) 0.593; **10.37** 0.601; **10.38** 1366.4 s; **10.39** 1.463×10^{-3} m^3 / s ; **10.40** 482.42 s; **10.41** 6.985 kPa (vacuum).

11 Flow Measurements

Pitot tube—Prandtl tube—Orificemeter—Venturimeter—Current meter— Rotameter — Velocity and discharge measurements in open channels—Flow under sluice gate—Weirs—Sharp and broad crested weirs—Suppressed weirs—Submerged weirs—Notches—Rectangular notch —Triangular notch —Cippolletti notch

11.1 Introduction

In fluid systems, the accurate measurement of flow is vital. Various situations arise where parameters such as area of flow, velocity, pressure, depth of flow and rate of flow are inter-related. Measurement of flow may include the determination of velocity at some points in the flow field. Discharge can be calculated if velocities are known by the equation

$$Q = \int \vec{v}.d\vec{A}. \tag{11.1}$$

Direct measurement of velocity can be done by determining the distance through which a small particle in the flow moves in a short time. Indirectly, some parameters like pressure head or rate of rotation (which are functions of velocity) are observed in instruments introduced in the flow and velocities are calculated.

Direct determination of discharge is done by collecting the fluid in a measuring tank for a known time. The discharge is equal to the volume collected in unit time. Indirect measurement of discharge is done by using some equipment or devices in the flow. In case of pipes, devices like venturimeter and orifice meter are commonly used. In channels, notches and weirs are installed for measurement of discharge.

11.2 Pitot Tube and Prandtl Tube

The Pitot tube in its simplest form is an L-shaped tube, one opening of which is placed in the flowing fluid facing the flow direction as shown in Fig. 11.1. A point of stagnation will develop at the front of the opening where the kinetic energy will get transformed into a pressure head and be added to the ambient pressure head. The liquid rising in the vertical limb above the piezometric head will be Δh, equal to the kinetic energy head. So, $v = \sqrt{2g\Delta h}$. In practice, $v = C\sqrt{2g\Delta h}$, where C is a coefficient which is slightly less than unity.

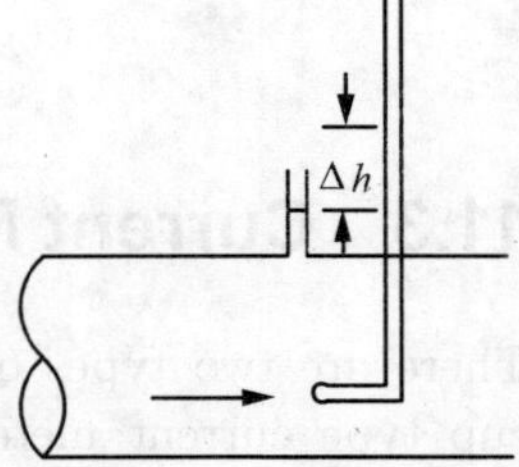

Fig. 11.1 *Pitot tube*

The measurement of Δh, the difference between the total head and the piezometric head, is done more conveniently using a Prandtl tube (shown in Fig. 11.2), which is connected to a differential manometer.

The Prandtl tube consists of two annular tubes, the inner one being connected to the front opening giving the total head and the outer one connected to the holes perpendicular to the flow direction on the periphery of the tube giving the piezometric head. The manometer reads the difference in heads between the openings equal to the kinetic energy head Δh and the velocity can be obtained as

$$v = C\sqrt{2g\Delta h}, \tag{11.2}$$

where C is the coefficient of the Pitot tube which is nearly equal to one.

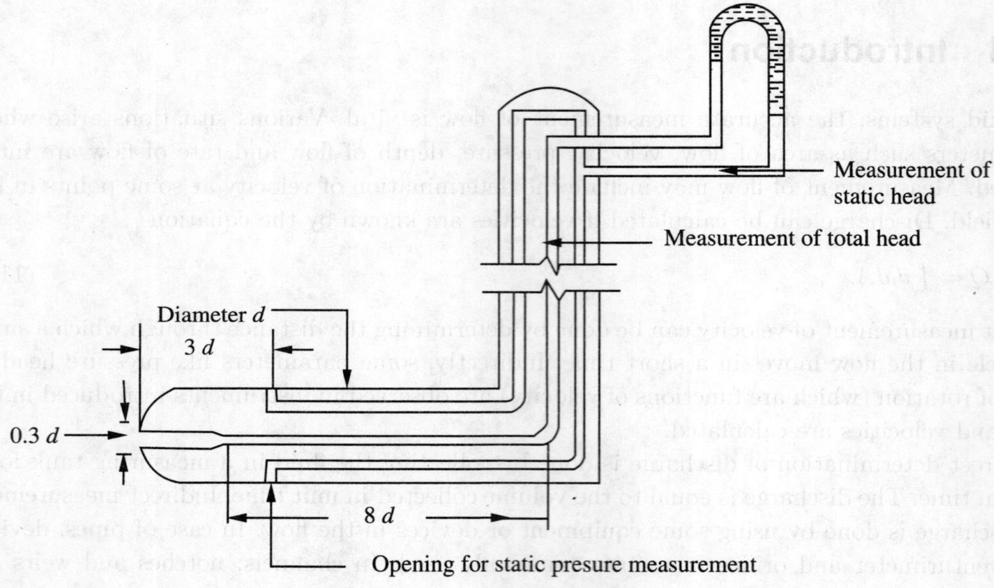

Fig. 11.2 *Prandtl tube*

11.3 Current Meter

There are two types of current meters, namely, the cup type and the propeller type. In a cup type current meter, cups are mounted on a horizontal ring, which rotates about the vertical axis. The propeller type current meter consists of fins or vanes with a small movable weight which is provided to keep the current meter in proper orientation in the flowing fluid. In case of higher velocities, a streamlined dead weight is attached to keep the instrument in position. The rate of rotation of the spindle is a function of the velocity and is measured by using a counter, actuated by an electrical make-and-break arrangement connected with the rotating spindle. The instrument needs calibration between revolutions/minute and velocity. Calibration is conducted in a towing tank using a trolley with a variable speed motor.

Current meters are available in various sizes. The big sizes find use in river gauging and the small ones in laboratories.

11.4 Discharge through a Circular Pipe by Velocity Measurement

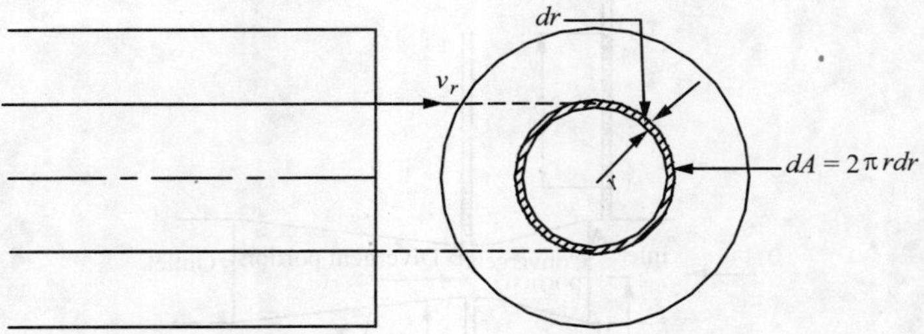

Fig. 11.3 *Discharge by velocity measurement*

Velocity measurements at points along the radii starting from the centre of the pipe can be made using a Pitot tube and the discharge can be found by the formula

$$Q = \int v_r dA = \int_0^r v_r 2\pi r dr, \tag{11.3}$$

the integration being done numerically.

Example 11.1 A Prandtl tube was used to get the velocity head at various points along the radius of a pipe 100 cm in diameter. If the velocity head measured at radius 30 cm is 12 cm, find the discharge through the annular space between a 25 cm and a 35 cm diameter.

$$h = 12 \text{ cm} = 0.12 \text{ m}.$$

$$v_r = \sqrt{2gh} = \sqrt{2 \times 9.81 \times 0.12} = 1.5344 \text{ m/s}.$$

$$r_{av} = 0.3 \text{ m}; dr = 10 \text{ cm} = 0.1 \text{ m}.$$

Annular area $= 2\pi r dr = 2\pi \times 0.3 \times 0.1 = 0.1885 \text{ m}^2$.

$$dQ = v_r \times 2\pi r dr = 1.5344 \times 0.1885 = 0.289 \text{ m}^3/\text{s}. \text{ (Ans.)}$$

11.5 Venturimeter

The discharge through a pipe can be conveniently measured using a venturimeter. The venturimeter consists of a converging cone, a throat and a diverging cone (see Fig. 11.4). The inlet and outlet diameters are d, equal to that of the pipe. The throat diameter can be about $d/2$. The converging cone has an angle of 20°, whereas the diverging cone is longer having an angle of about 6° to 8°. Gradual expansion is provided to avoid separation of the jet of fluid after the throat and consequent high energy losses.

The difference in piezometric head between the inlet and the throat is a function of the discharge through the venturimeter and is measured using a differential manometer.

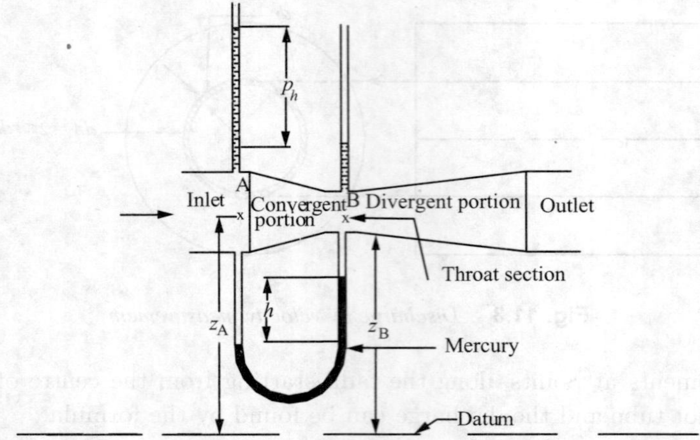

Fig. 11.4 *Venturimeter in a horizontal position*

Consider the flow through a venturimeter of inlet area a_1 and throat area a_2. Let the elevation of the inlet be z_A and that of the throat be z_B above a datum. The loss of energy between A and B is very small. Applying Bernoulli's theorem between these two sections,

$$\frac{p_A}{\gamma} + z_A + \frac{v_A{}^2}{2g} = \frac{p_B}{\gamma} + z_B + \frac{v_B{}^2}{2g}.$$

$$p_h = \left(\frac{p_A}{\gamma} + z_A\right) - \left(\frac{p_B}{\gamma} + z_B\right) = \frac{v_B{}^2}{2g} - \frac{v_A{}^2}{2g} = \frac{v_B{}^2}{2g}\left(1 - \left(\frac{a_2}{a_1}\right)^2\right)$$

$$= \frac{v_B{}^2}{2g}\left(\frac{a_1{}^2 - a_2{}^2}{a_1{}^2}\right),$$

where Δp_h is the piezometric head difference.

$$v_B = \frac{a_1\sqrt{2g\Delta p_h}}{\sqrt{a_1{}^2 - a_2{}^2}}.$$

$$\text{Hence, discharge } = a_2 v_B = \frac{a_1 a_2\sqrt{2g\Delta p_h}}{\sqrt{a_1{}^2 - a_2{}^2}}.$$

The actual discharge will be slightly different from the theoretical discharge due to friction in the convergent portion.

$$\text{Actual discharge} = C_d \times \text{theoretical discharge} = C_d \frac{a_1 a_2}{\sqrt{a_1^2 - a_2^2}} \sqrt{2g\Delta p_h}, \tag{11.4}$$

where C_d is the coefficient of discharge which is a function of a_2/a_1 and the Reynold's number. Its value is of the order of 0.91 to 0.98.

p_h can be determined by taking the difference in level h as indicated by the differential manometer,

$$\Delta p_h = \pm h \left(\frac{S'}{S} - 1 \right), \tag{11.5}$$

where S is the specific gravity of the measuring liquid and S' is the specific gravity of the manometric fluid. The negative sign will apply when the measurement is done using an inverted U-tube manometer. Since the discharge is a function of the difference in piezometric heads (and not pressure heads), the same formula is applicable in any inclined position of the venturimeter (Fig. 11.5).

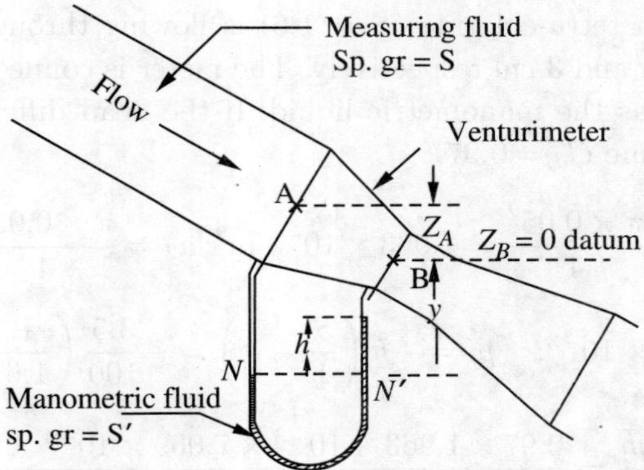

Fig. 11.5 *Venturimeter – inclined*

Example 11.2 A venturimeter has inlet and throat diameters of 20 cm and 10 cm respectively. The flow of water is downwards and the inclination of the meter with the horizontal is 60°. The mercury manometer connected to the inlet and throat indicates a differential head of 7.5 cm. Find the discharge if C_d for the venturimeter is 0.97.

Since the discharge is a function of piezometric head difference, the inclination and direction of flow does not affect the discharge.

$$C_d = 0.97; \quad a_1 = \frac{\pi \times 0.2^2}{4} = 0.0314 \text{ m}^2; \quad a_2 = \frac{\pi \times 0.1^2}{4} = 7.85 \times 10^{-3} \text{ m}^2.$$

$$\Delta p_h = h\left(\frac{S'}{S} - 1\right) = \frac{1.5}{100}\left(\frac{13.6}{1} - 1\right) = 0.189 \text{ m}; \sqrt{a_1^2 - a_2^2} = 0.0304 \text{ m}^2.$$

$$Q = \frac{C_d a_1 a_2 \sqrt{2g\Delta p_h}}{\sqrt{a_1^2 - a_2^2}} = \frac{0.97 \times 0.0314 \times 7.85 \times 10^{-3} \times \sqrt{2 \times 9.81 \times 0.189}}{0.0304}$$

$$= 0.0339 \text{ m}^3/\text{s. (Ans.)}$$

Example 11.3 The inlet and throat of a venturimeter conveying water is connected to a differential mercury manometer. It indicates a level difference of 1.8 cm of mercury. If the head loss in the converging cone is estimated to be 1.5 cm of water, find the C_d for the venturimeter.

$$\Delta p_h = \frac{1.8}{100}\left(\frac{13.6}{1} - 1\right) = 0.2268 \text{ m}.$$

$$\text{Theoretical head difference} = 0.2268 - \frac{1.5}{100} = 0.2118.$$

$$C_d = \frac{\sqrt{2g \times 0.2118}}{\sqrt{2g \times 0.2268}} = 0.966. \text{ (Ans.)}$$

Example 11.4 Carbon tetra-chloride ($S = 1.6$) is flowing through a venturimeter, having throat diameters of 5 cm and 3 cm respectively. The meter is connected to an inverted U-tube manometer with water as the manometric liquid. If the head difference indicated is 3.5 cm, find the discharge. Assume $C_d = 0.97$.

$$C_d = 0.97; \quad a_1 = \frac{\pi \times 0.05^2}{4} = 1.963 \times 10^{-3} \text{ m}^2; a_2 = \frac{\pi \times 0.03^2}{4} = 7.069 \times 10^{-4} \text{ m}^2.$$

$$\sqrt{a_1^2 - a_2^2} = 1.831 \times 10^{-3}; \quad p_h = -h\left(\frac{S'}{S} - 1\right) = -\frac{3.5}{100}\left(\frac{1}{1.6} - 1\right) = 0.013125 \text{ m}.$$

$$Q = \frac{C_d a_1 a_2 \sqrt{2gh}}{\sqrt{a_1^2 - a_2^2}} = \frac{0.97 \times 1.963 \times 10^{-3} \times 7.069 \times 10^{-4} \times \sqrt{2g \times 0.013125}}{1.831 \times 10^{-3}}$$

$$= 3.73 \times 10^{-4} \text{ m}^3/\text{s. (Ans.)}$$

11.6 Orifice Meter

The orifice meter consists of a circular sharp-edged orifice fitted between two flanges in a pipe. The diameter of the orifice d_2 can be about half the diameter of the pipe.

Let the area of the pipe be a_1 and that of the orifice be a_2. The jet will contract after B (Fig. 11.6) up to point C, where the area will be $C_c \times a_2$ (C_c is the coefficient of the contraction). The jet will then expand and fill up the pipe. The pressure in the separated regions will nearly be the same as that at C. Among the points A, B, C the energy losses are very small.

Let the theoretical velocity at the contraction be v_{ct}. Applying Bernoulli's theorem between A and C,

$$\frac{p_A}{\gamma} + z_A + \frac{{v_A}^2}{2g} = \frac{p_C}{\gamma} + z_C + \frac{{v_{ct}}^2}{2g}.$$

$$\Delta p_h = \left(\frac{p_A}{\gamma} + z_A\right) - \left(\frac{p_C}{\gamma} + z_C\right) = \frac{{v_{ct}}^2}{2g} - \frac{{v_A}^2}{2g},$$

or, $$\Delta p_h = \frac{{v_{ct}}^2}{2g}\left[1 - \left(\frac{a_2 C_c}{a_1}\right)^2\right],$$

or, $$v_{ct} = \frac{a_1\sqrt{2g\Delta p_h}}{\sqrt{a_1^2 - a_2^2 C_c^2}}.$$

Since actual velocity $v_{ca} = C_v \times V_{ct}$, and $Q = a_2 C_c v_{ca}$.

Hence, $$Q = \frac{C_v C_C a_1 a_2\sqrt{2g\Delta p_h}}{\sqrt{a_1^2 - a_2^2 C_c^2}} = \frac{C_d a_1 a_2 \sqrt{2g\Delta p_h}}{\sqrt{a_1^2 - (a_2 C_c)^2}}, \tag{11.6}$$

which can be written as

$$Q = C a_2 \sqrt{2g\Delta p_h}, \tag{11.7}$$

where C is an overall coefficient.

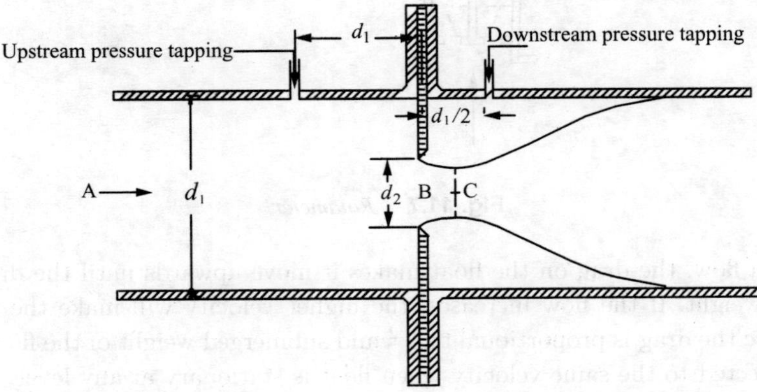

Fig. 11.6 *Orifice meter*

C_d in the above expression is dependent on the area ratio a_2/a_1 in addition to the flow conditions. When $a_2/a_1 = 0.25$, C_d is of the order of 0.6 for a turbulent flow in the pipe.

The orifice meter is less costly and occupies less space as compared to a venturimeter. But it has a higher loss of energy due to the sudden expansion from the contracted area to the pipe area downstream of the orifice. Hence, when the energy loss in the pipe is to be kept minimum, the venturimeter is preferred for the measurement of discharge.

11.7 Rotameter

A rotameter is a simple instrument used to measure the discharge of a fluid in a pipe line. It has a slightly tapering vertical tube with the larger portion at the top. (See Fig. 11.7.) An active element denser than the fluid (called the float) having an outer diameter of D_f closes the inlet of the tube when there is no flow through the meter. The tube increases its diameter from D_f at the bottom to $D_f + \alpha h$ upwards, where h is the height from the bottom and α is a small fraction.

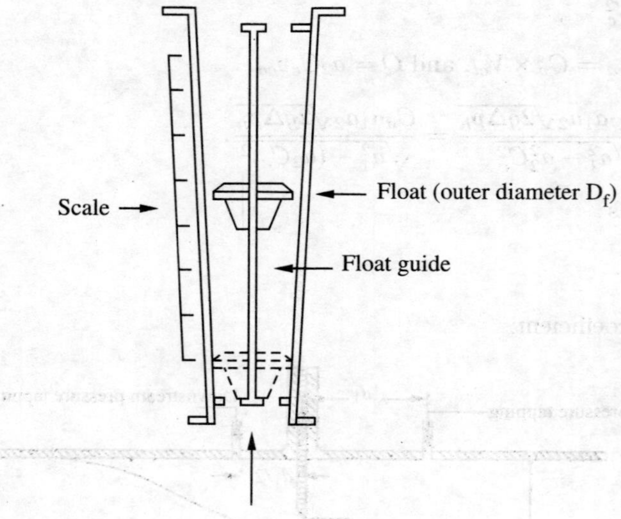

Fig. 11.7 *Rotameter*

When there is a flow, the drag on the float makes it move upwards until the drag is equal to its submerged weight. If the flow increases, the higher velocity will make the float to move further up. Since the drag is proportional to V^2 and submerged weight of the float is the same, it must be subjected to the same velocity when float is stationary at any level

The flow past the float is through the annular area $\pi[(D_f + \alpha h)^2 - D_f^2]$ which is nearly equal to $2D_f \propto h$. Since the velocity is nearly constant, the discharge Q is nearly proportional to h. Hence when the rotameter is calibrated for use, the scale along h for Q can be nearly linear. The tendency of the float to move to the side of the tube can be prevented by giving helical slots on the periphery of the float to make it rotate slightly. Alternatively, in some rotameters a thin rod is given in the centre of the tube for guiding it.

11.8 Discharge through Open Channels by Velocity Measurements

Open channels have their free surface open to the same intensity of pressure at all sections along its length and most commonly to atmospheric pressure. Flow in rivers, canals, open sewers and overland flow are examples of open channel flows. Sometimes, closed conduits or sewers flowing partly with free surface are treated as open channels.

The cross-sections, geometrical characteristics, bed configurations and plan forms of open channels are much varied. The discharge can best be measured in a straight reach of the channel with a flat bed so that the stream lines are nearly straight. The cross-section is divided into a number of segments and the average velocities for each segment is determined.

$$Q = \sum_{1}^{n} a_n v_n, \tag{11.8}$$

where a_n is the area of cross-section of any segment and v_n is the average velocity for that segment (Fig. 11.8).

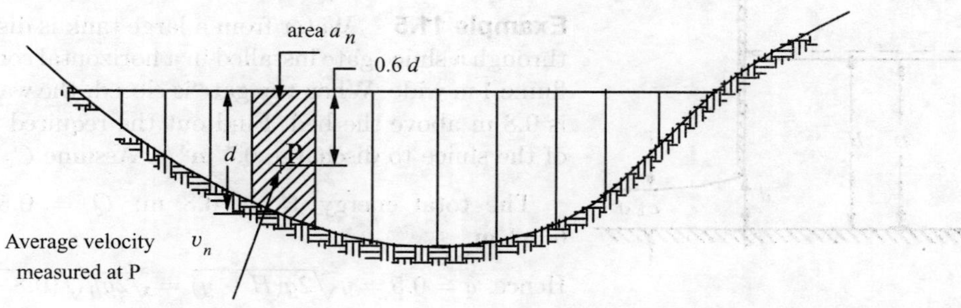

Fig. 11.8 *Discharge by velocity measurement*

The average velocity in a segment can be obtained by measuring the velocities at different depths using a current meter or a Pitot tube along the centre line of a segment and drawing the velocity profile. It is found that the average velocity in the vertical direction can be obtained approximately by determining the velocity at 0.6 times depth below the free surface. A better estimate can be the average of velocities observed at 0.2 and 0.8 depths below the free surface.

11.9 Flow Under a Sluice Gate

A sluice gate (Fig. 11.9) can be used to control and measure the discharge through a channel. When the sluice is kept open, the jet issuing will contract until the flow becomes parallel to the floor. The coefficient of contraction is nearly 0.61. The sheet of flow on the floor at Section (1) will have a hydrostatic pressure distribution.

As the water discharges under the sluice, the velocity in the channel will be $v_a = q/D$, where q is the discharge per m width and D the depth of water upstream. The energy loss in the region of contraction can be neglected. The water approaching the sluice gate has some velocity v_a, which is equal to q/D. When v_a is negligible, H, the total energy above the bed is D. When v_a is appreciable H, should include the effect of velocity of approach, $H = D + \frac{v_a^2}{2g}$.

Neglecting the velocity of approach,

$$H = C_c d + \frac{{v_1}^2}{2g},$$

or $\quad v_1 = \sqrt{2g(H - C_c d)}$.

The discharge per unit width, $q = C_c d\sqrt{2g(H - C_c d)}$,

or $\quad q = y\sqrt{2g(H - y)}, \qquad (11.9)$

where $y = C_c d$.

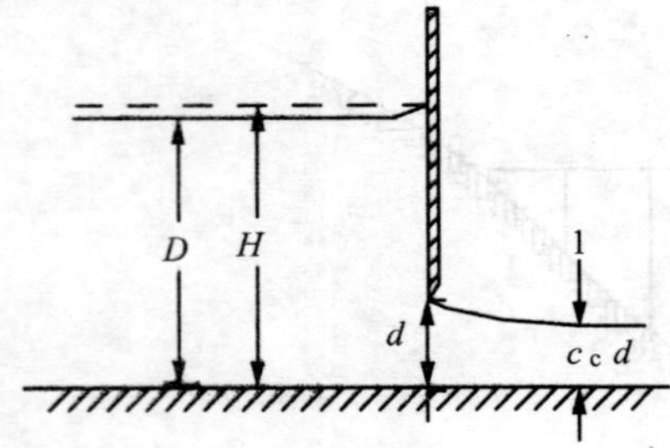

Fig. 11.9 *Flow under a sluice gate*

Example 11.5 Water from a large tank is discharged through a sluice gate installed in a horizontal connecting flume 1 m wide. When the gate is closed, the water level is 0.8 m above the bed. Find out the required opening of the sluice to discharge 0.5 m^3/s. Assume $C_c = 0.6$.

The total energy $H = 0.8$ m; $Q = 0.5$ m$^3/s$.; $b = 1$ m.

Hence, $q = 0.5 = y\sqrt{2g(H - y)} = \sqrt{2g}y\sqrt{(0.8 - y)}$.

$$f(y) = y\sqrt{0.8 - y} = \frac{0.5}{\sqrt{2g}} = 0.1129.$$

The above equation can be solved by trial and error.

y	$f(y)$
0.2	0.155
0.1	0.086
0.15	0.121
0.14	0.114
0.139	0.113

Hence $y = 0.139$ and the sluice opening $= \frac{0.139}{C_c} = \frac{0.139}{0.6} = 0.231$ m.

11.10 Flow Over Weirs

Weirs are structures built across channels and rivers for raising the water level upstream. In small channels, they can be made of metal plates whereas in rivers they are of concrete or masonry. When there is no overflow, the elevation of water can be up to the maximum level of the crest of the weir. In case of overflow, the water level will be continuously dropping (draw down) while approaching the weir as shown in Fig. 11.10.

The head over the weir H is the difference between the crest level and the water surface level at a point before the draw down. The head can be measured at a distance of about $6H$ upstream of the crest. The crest length of the weir is L.

Figure 11.10 shows a free flowing weir. When the downstream water level is above the crest level, the weir is considered submerged.

11.10.1 Sharp crested weirs

A sharp crested weir is a rectangular metal plate with a sharp beveled edge at the top, fitted across a rectangular channel. The sheet of flow over the weir or the nappe will be of the shape shown in Fig. 11.10.

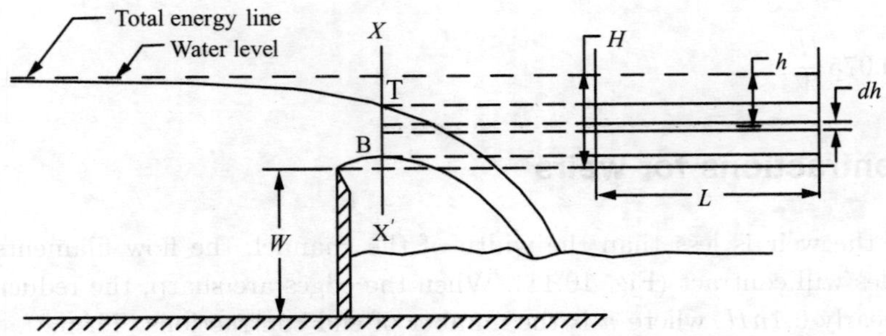

Fig. 11.10 *Flow over sharp crested weir*

At a section XX′, the pressure in the nappe will be atmospheric. When the head H over the weir is small compared to the height W of the weir, the velocity of approach in the channel will be negligible. The velocity at any point P will be equal to $\sqrt{2gh}$. The thickness of the nappe at XX′ will be BT and the flow is curvilinear. But for theoretical calculations, flow thickness of H with parallel flow is assumed and correction is made by the introduction of a coefficient of discharge C_d.

Discharge through an elementary strip of area $L\,dh = L\,dh\,\sqrt{2gh}$.

$$\text{(Total) theoretical discharge} = \int_0^H L dh \sqrt{2gh} = \frac{2}{3}\sqrt{2g}LH^{3/2}.$$

$$\text{Actual discharge } Q = \frac{2}{3} C_d \sqrt{2g} L H^{3/2}. \tag{11.10}$$

The coefficient C_d has been found to be nearly 0.61.

Consideration of velocity of approach When the head H is not small as compared to the weir height W, the velocity of approach $v_a = \dfrac{Q}{L(H+W)}$ cannot be neglected and the integration for obtaining the discharge should be done from limits $\dfrac{{v_a}^2}{2g}$ to $\left(H + \dfrac{{v_a}^2}{2g}\right)$.

$$\text{Discharge } Q = \frac{2}{3} C_d \sqrt{2g} \left[\left(H + \frac{{v_a}^2}{2g} \right)^{3/2} - \left(\frac{{v_a}^2}{2g} \right)^{3/2} \right]. \tag{11.11}$$

Q can be calculated by initially assuming $v_a = 0$ and v_a can be estimated using the equation $v_a = \dfrac{Q}{L(H+W)}$. A better estimate of Q can then be made by using the value of v_a in the expression of discharge considering the velocity of approach. An iterative method is adopted to get better estimates.

A direct estimate of Q can be made by using Bazin's formula (empirical) to correct C_d in the formula $Q = \frac{2}{3} C_d \sqrt{2g} L H^{3/2}$,

$$C_d = 0.611 + 0.075 \frac{H}{W}. \tag{11.12}$$

11.10.2 End contractions for weirs

When the length of the weir is less than the width of the channel, the flow filaments after separation at the sides will contract (Fig. 10.11). When the edges are sharp, the reduction of flow length will be nearly $0.1nH$, where n is the number of end contractions. Then,

$$Q = \frac{2}{3} C_d \sqrt{2g} (L - 0.1nH) H^{3/2}. \tag{11.13}$$

The coefficients for reduction of length can be much less than 0.1 if the contraction is made gradual.

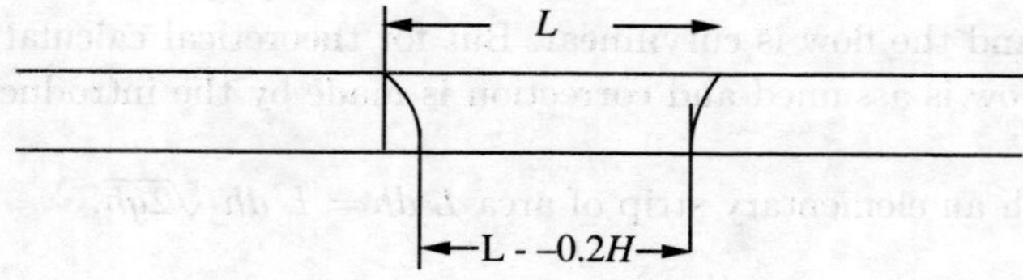

Fig. 11.11 *Weir with end contractions*

11.10.3 Suppressed weirs

There is no effect of end contraction for weirs which have the same length as the width of the channel. Such weirs are called suppressed weirs.

Aeration of nappe Unless the suppressed weir is located at the end of the channel, the air pressure under the nappe will get reduced below the atmospheric pressure. This is because the air from underneath the nappe is entrained by the flowing sheet of water, but cannot get replenished from the sides. When the head is low, the nappe may cling to the downstream surface of the weir (Fig.11.12(a)). For the given discharge conditions, the head required will also be lowered because the nappe will be discharging to regions of low pressure.

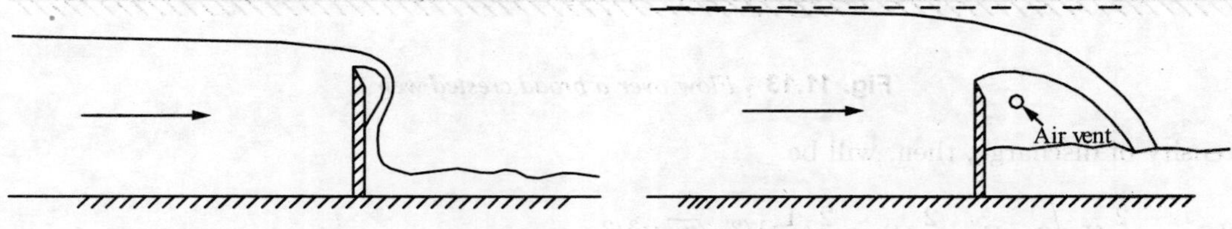

Fig. 11.12(a) *Clinging nappe* **Fig. 11.12(b)** *Aerated nappe*

In the case of measuring weirs, the underside of the nappe is to be well ventilated by providing holes in the side wall (to facilitate free circulation of air at the underside of the nappe) (Fig. 11.12(b)). In case of unventilated suppressed weirs, as the pressure reduces underneath the nappe, the discharge versus head relationship goes on changing. This will introduce error in the measurement of flow.

11.10.4 Broad crested weirs

The bigger weirs across rivers and channels are invariably made of masonry or concrete having broad crests. A simple type is shown in Fig. 11.13.

A parallel stream of flow occurs on the top of the weir and hydrostatic conditions prevail when the head is not too high compared to the breadth of the weir crest. For values of $H > 2.5B$, it will act nearly like a sharp crested weir. The upstream corner of the weir is usually given a smooth curvature to avoid separation.

Let us assume a sluice gate is placed over the weir extending to the point A. Let the depth of flow be y at a section where the sheet of flow of water flowing is parallel to the crest. The intensity of discharge $q = y\sqrt{2g(H - y)}$.

As the gate is opened, the discharge increases and attains a maximum value. When the gate is completely raised, the water flows freely over the weir. The condition for q to be maximum is when $y\sqrt{2g(H - y)}$ is maximum i.e., when $y = 2/3H$.

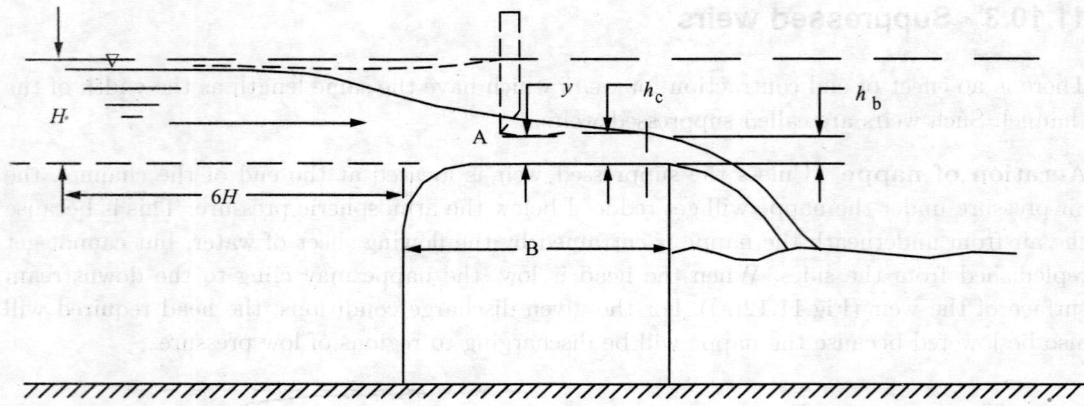

Fig. 11.13 *Flow over a broad crested weir*

Intensity of discharge, then, will be

$$q = \frac{2}{3}H\sqrt{2g(H - \frac{2}{3}H)} = \frac{2}{3}(\frac{1}{3})^{1/2}\sqrt{2g}H^{3/2},$$

or, $\quad q = KH^{3/2}, \qquad (11.14)$

where K is nearly 1.705.

The coefficient K varies depending upon the velocity of approach, entry conditions and friction on the weir floor etc.,

11.10.5 Submerged weirs

When the downstream water level is above the crest of the weir, it is said to be submerged (Fig. 11.14). The degree of submergence is defined by a parameter $\frac{h_2}{h_1 + h_2}$. There is a critical degree of submergence above which the upstream water level gets affected for the same discharge. For sharp crested and broad crested weirs, the critical values of submergence are nearly 0.6 and 0.8 respectively.

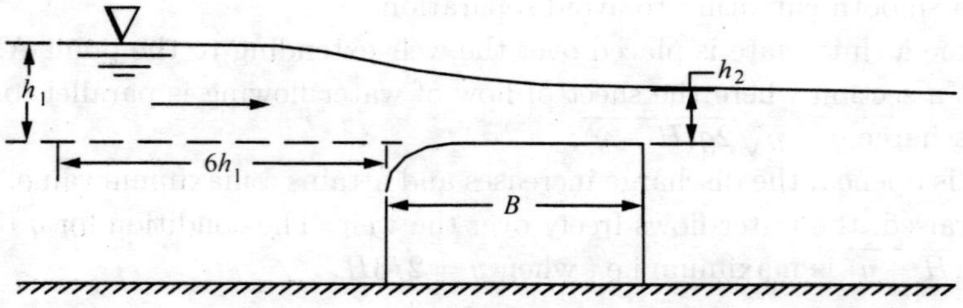

Fig. 11.14 *Submerged weir*

If the submergence exceeds the critical value, the discharge can be estimated by treating part of the flow as free flow and part as an orifice flow. The formula is

$$Q = \frac{2}{3} C_{d_1} L \sqrt{2g} (h_1 - h_2)^{3/2} + C_{d_2} L h_2 \sqrt{2g(h_1 - h_2)}. \tag{11.15}$$

11.11 Flow Over Notches

Notches are cuts made in a plate on the side of a tank or the end of a channel so that water can flow over them. The flow is similar to that of a sharp crested weir. It differs from an orifice since there will be a free surface at the notch. The notches can have rectangular, triangular, trapezoidal or other shapes.

11.11.1 Rectangular notch

A rectangular notch is a rectangular weir with a reduced width compared to the channel or tank and so there are end contractions. The equation governing the flow will be

$$Q = \frac{2}{3} C_d \sqrt{2g} (L - 0.2H) H^{3/2}, \tag{11.16}$$

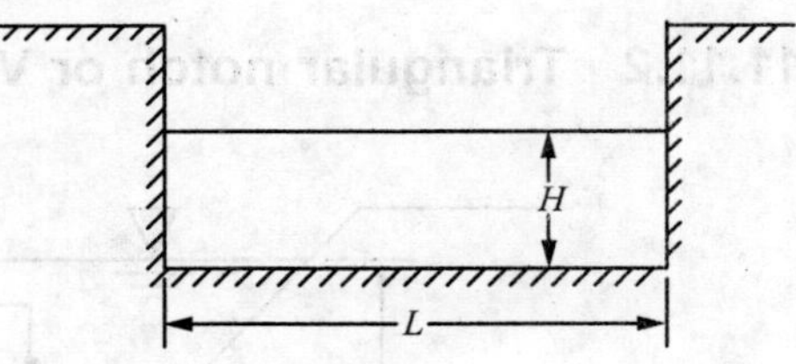

Fig. 11.15 *Rectangular notch*

where L is the width of the notch and H is the head over the notch.

Example 11.6 A sharp crested suppressed weir 1.5 m wide on the side of a rectangular water tank 12 m × 8 m is discharging with a head of 0.2 m. How long will it take to lower the water level in the tank by 0.1 m. Take $C_d = 0.62$.

Discharge from the tank in time dt = reduction of quantity of water in the tank.

$$\frac{2}{3} C_d \sqrt{2g} h^{3/2} dt = -A\, dh,$$

where A is the area of the tank and dh is the falling head in the tank in time dt.

Hence, $dt = \dfrac{-3A\, dh}{2C_d \sqrt{2g} h^{3/2}}$.

Integrating from head with limits 0.2 m to 0.1 m,

$$\int_0^T dt = \frac{-3A}{2C_d\sqrt{2g}} \int_{0.2}^{0.1} h^{-3/2} dh = \frac{-3 \times 12 \times 8}{2 \times 0.62 \times 4.43} \left[\frac{h^{-1/2}}{-1/2} \right]_{0.2}^{0.1}$$

$$= 52.43 \times 2\left(\frac{1}{0.1^{1/2}} - \frac{1}{0.2^{1/2}}\right) = 104.86\,(3.16 - 2.236)$$

$$= 96.86 \text{ s. (Ans.)}$$

Example 11.7 Find the discharge over a rectangular notch 80 cm wide when the head over the notch is 15 cm. Assume $C_d = 0.62$.

$L = 0.8$ m; $n = 2$; $H = 0.15$ m.

$$Q = \frac{2}{3}C_d\sqrt{2g}(L - 0.1nH)H^{3/2} = \frac{2}{3} \times 0.62 \times 4.43 \times (0.8 - 0.1 \times 2 \times 0.15) \times 0.15^{3/2}$$

$$= 0.0819 \text{ m}^3/\text{s. (Ans.)}$$

11.11.2 Triangular notch or V notch

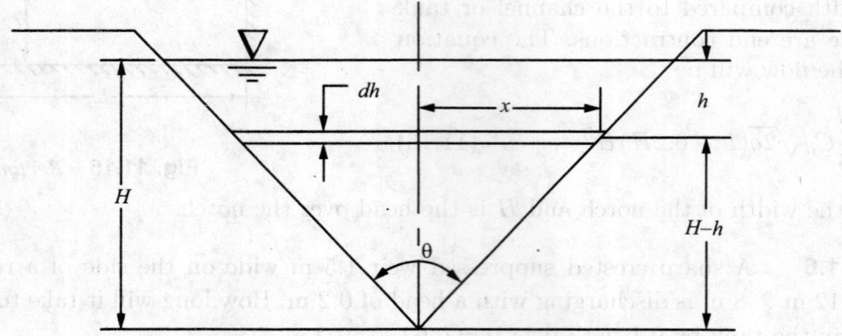

Fig. 11.16 *Triangular notch*

In the case of a triangular notch, the cut made in the plate will be triangular, in the shape of a V. The angle θ of the notch can be any convenient angle like 90° or 60°.

Let H be the head over the V notch (Fig. 11.6). Considering the flow filaments above the notch, the width of flow at a depth h below the water surface in the channel will be $2(H - h)\tan\theta/2$ and the velocity will nearly be $\sqrt{2gh}$. The discharge through an elementary strip of height dh will be $2(H - h)\tan\theta/2\sqrt{2gh}$. The depth of flow over the notch will be less than H due to draw down effects and the flow will be curvilinear. However, for a theoretical development, the integration is done for the limits of head 0 to H and a correction is applied by introducing a coefficient C_d which can be determined experimentally. Total discharge

$$Q = C_d \int_0^H 2(H-h)\tan\frac{\theta}{2}\sqrt{2gh}dh$$

$$= C_d 2\sqrt{2gh}\tan\frac{\theta}{2}\int_0^H \left(Hh^{3/2} - h^{3/2}\right)dh.$$

$$Q = \frac{8}{15}C_d\sqrt{2g}\tan\frac{\theta}{2}H^{5/2}. \tag{11.17}$$

When small discharges are to be measured, a rectangular notch will only give a very small head and the measurements of head will involve high error. But in the case of a triangular notch, the head can be much higher. For higher discharges, wide rectangular notches have the advantage of head within reasonable limits.

The error in measurement of head will affect discharge calculations. An error of 1% in the measurement of head will cause an error of 1.5% in discharge for rectangular notches and 2.5% for triangular notches. The value of C_d for a triangular notch is of the order of 0.6.

Example 11.8 The head over a 60° V notch is measured as 8.3 cm. The head measurement is likely to have an error of 0.6%. Find the probable percentage of error in the measurement of discharge.

$$Q = \frac{8}{15}C_d\sqrt{2g}\tan\frac{\theta}{2}H^{5/2} = KH^{5/2}.$$

$$dQ = \frac{5}{2}KH^{3/2}dH.$$

Dividing by Q,

$$\frac{dQ}{Q} = \frac{(5/2)KH^{3/2}dH}{KH^{5/2}} = \frac{5}{2}\frac{dH}{H}.$$

$$\frac{dH}{H} = 0.6\% = \frac{0.6}{100}.$$

Hence, $\dfrac{dQ}{Q} = \dfrac{5}{2}\dfrac{dH}{H} = \dfrac{5}{2} \times \dfrac{0.6}{100} = 1.5\%$. (Ans.)

11.11.3 Cippolletti notch

Notches can also be trapezoidal with a base L and a side slope m:1. A special type of notch known as the Cippolletti notch, can be made with a side slope so adjusted that the reduction of discharge due to the two end contractions from length L will be compensated by the increased discharge through the triangular elements.

Assuming C_d to be the same for all the elements,

$$Q = \frac{2}{3}C_d\sqrt{2g}LH^{3/2} = \frac{2}{3}C_d\sqrt{2g}(L - 0.2H)H^{3/2} + \frac{8}{15}C_d\sqrt{2g}\ \tan\ \theta/2H^{5/2}.$$

The above equation will yield the result $\tan\theta/2 = 1/4$ or $m = 1/4$. Hence, in a Cippolletti notch which is of a trapezoidal shape with a side slope $m = 1/4$, the discharge is given by

$$Q = \frac{2}{3}C_d\sqrt{2g}LH^{3/2}. \tag{11.18}$$

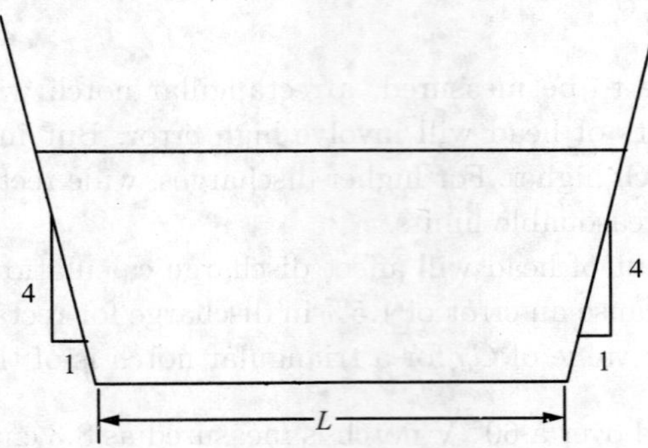

Fig. 11.17 *Cippolletti notch*

Example 11.9 Find the head over a Cippolletti notch having a width of 0.6 m to discharge 120 l/s. Assume $C_d = 0.61$

$$Q = 120\ \text{l/s} = 0.12\ \text{m}^3/\text{s}.$$

$$Q = \frac{2}{3}C_d\sqrt{2g} \times LH^{3/2}.$$

$$H^{3/2} = \frac{3Q}{2C_d\sqrt{2g}L} = \frac{3 \times 0.12}{2 \times 0.61 \times 4.43 \times 0.6} = 0.111.$$

$$H = 0.111^{2/3} = 0.231\ \text{m} = 23.1\ \text{cm}.$$

11.11.4 Measurement of flow in channels using standing wave flumes

The measurement of discharge through small open channels can be done by using standing wave flumes in which the flow passes through critical depth. The topic is explained in detail in Section 17.24.

REVIEW QUESTIONS AND PROBLEMS

11.1 Explain the principle of a Pitot tube.

11.2 Using a sketch, show how an inverted U-tube manometer is connected to a Prandtl tube and explain how the velocity at a point is measured.

11.3 What is the principle of operation of a current meter?

11.4 Explain how the discharge of air flow can be measured in a pipe line using a Pitot tube?

11.5 Sketch a venturimeter. Derive an equation for discharge in a venturimeter. Why is the converging cone of the venturimeter made short, while the diverging cone is made long?

11.6 Sketch an orifice meter and show how it is connected to the differential manometer. Derive an equation for finding the discharge of the orifice meter.

11.7 Make a comparison of a venturimeter and an orifice meter in the measurement of discharge through a pipe.

11.8 Explain the scheme of measurement of discharge in a channel by velocity measurements using a current meter.

11.9 Derive a formula for discharge for flow over a sharp crested weir.

11.10 What is the velocity of approach to a weir? How is the discharge calculated taking into account the velocity of approach?

11.11 What is Bazin's formula for coefficient of discharge for flow over sharp crested weirs?

11.12 What is end contraction for a weir? How is a correction applied for the discharge formula?

11.13 Explain the importance of aeration of a nappe for sharp crested weirs used for measuring discharge.

11.14 Show how discharge can be calculated for a flow under a sluice gate. Show that the flow over a broad crested weir is a limiting case of the above.

11.15 Derive a formula for discharge over a broad crested weir.

11.16 What is the critical submergence for a weir. Suggest a formula for discharge over a weir under submerged conditions.

11.17 What are notches? When are rectangular notches preferred to triangular notches.

11.18 Derive the formula for discharge over a V notch. What is the advantage of a V notch over a rectangular notch.

11.19 What are Cippolletti notches. Show how the effects of end contractions are accounted for in the formula of a Cippolletti notch.

11.20 The velocity of oil at a point in a pipe is measured by a Pitot tube connected to an inverted U-tube manometer with air at the top. If the difference in level in the manometer is 5 cm, find the velocity. Assume $K = 0.97$.

11.21 A Prandtl tube is used to measure the velocity of water at a point in a stream. Connections are made to an inverted U-tube manometer using a manometric liquid of specific mass 920 kg/m^3. If the differential head indicated is 8.2 cm, find the velocity.

11.22 A Pitot tube is used to measure the velocity of an air plane. A U-tube manometer connected to the Pitot tube registers a head of 90 mm of mercury. Find the speed of the plane. Assume $K = 0.98$ and $\rho_{\text{air}} = 1.02$ kg/m^3.

11.23 A venturimeter of diameter 200 mm at the inlet and 100 mm at the throat is laid with the axis horizontal and is used for measuring the velocity of an oil of specific gravity 0.8. The difference of levels of the mercury manometer reads 180 mm. Direct measurement was made by collecting 11520 kg of oil in 4 minutes. Calculate the discharge coefficient for the meter.

11.24 A venturimeter having a throat diameter of 5 cm is introduced in a horizontal pipe line of diameter 7.5 cm conveying water. The venturimeter is connected to an inverted U-tube manometer having a liquid of specific gravity 0.9 as the manometric liquid. If the difference in level of the separating surfaces is 6 cm, find the discharge. Assume $C_d = 0.98$.

11.25 A venturimeter is introduced in a pipe of 10 cm diameter inclined 60 to the horizontal for measuring the flow of oil. The throat diameter is 5 cm. The mercury differential manometer gives a reading of 10 cm. Find the discharge in the pipe if the specific gravity of oil is 0.85 and $C_d = 0.97$.

11.26 A venturimeter is used to measure the flow of water through a 25 cm diameter pipe. The pressure at the inlet is 6 m of water when the flow rate is 140 lps. Find the smallest diameter of the throat to ensure that the pressure head does not fall below the atmospheric pressure. Assume $C_d = 0.98$.

11.27 The inlet and throat diameters of a horizontal venturimeter conveying water are 30 cm and 10 cm respectively. The pressure intensity at the inlet is 140 kN/m^2. While the vacuum pressure at the throat is 37 cm of mercury, assume that 4% of differential head is lost between the inlet and the throat. Find C_d for the venturimeter.

11.28 An orifice meter conveying water is fitted to a pipe line of 10 cm diameter. The diameter of the orifice is 5 cm. If a mercury differential manometer indicates a reading of 12 cm, calculate the flow rate through the pipe line. Assume $C_c = 0.62$ and $C_v = 0.97$.

11.29 An orifice meter with orifice diameter 15 cm is inserted in a pipe of 25 cm diameter. The pressure gauges fitted upstream and downstream of the orifice gave readings of 19.82 N/cm^2 and 9.86 N/cm^2 respectively. The overall coefficient for the meter is given as 0.6. Find the discharge of water through the pipe.

11.30 An open channel has depths of flow measured at various distances from the bank. Velocities are measured at 0.6 times the depth of flow using a current meter. Readings are given in the table below. Find the discharge.

Distance from the bank (m)	0	1	3	5	6
Depth of flow (m)	0	0.2	0.5	0.3	0
Velocity (m/s)		0.25	0.4	0.25	

11.31 A sharp crested weir 2 m wide is installed in a wide rectangular flume for the measurement of discharge. The weir is 0.4 m high and is aerated downstream. If the head of the weir is 0.15 m. Find the discharge (i) taking into account the velocity of approach assuming $C_d = 0.62$ and (ii) by application of Bazin's formula for C_d. [Neglect end contractions]

11.32 A rectangular sharp crested weir 1 m wide on the side of a tank 15 m × 12 m is emptying the tank. What time is required by the head to fall from 0.15 m to 0.1 m. Assume $C_d = 0.62$.[Neglect end contractions]

11.33 Find the width of a broad crested weir to discharge 0.8 m^3/s when the head is 0.15 m.

11.34 A broad crested weir 3 m wide is discharging with 0.3 m head upstream. If the downstream level is 0.23 m above the crest, calculate the discharge. $C_d = 0.62$.

11.35 A triangular notch of 60 vertex angle is used for measuring discharge in a channel. If the head is 0.2 m, find the discharge. Assume $C_d = 0.62$.

11.36 A rectangular notch 0.2 m wide and a 90 V notch are on the side of a tank and have the same level of the crest. At what head of water will the V notch start to have more discharge than the V notch. Neglect the end contractions and use the same value for C_d.

11.37 Find the time required to empty a tank 10 m × 8 m by a 90 V notch from a level 0.2 m above the crest to 0.1 m above the crest. Assume $C_d = 0.62$.

11.38 A Cippolletti notch has a width of 0.8 m. Find the discharge when the head is 0.2 m.

ANSWERS

11.20. 0.961 m/s; **11.21.** 0.359 m/s; **11.22.** 153.44 m/s; **11.23.** 0.979; **11.24.** 7.368 × 10^{-4} m^3/s; **11.25.** 0.0107 m^3/s; **11.26.** 0.127 m; **11.27.** 0.98; **11.28.** 6.505 × 10^{-3} m^3/s; **11.29.** 0.15 m^3/s; **11.30.** 0.65 m^3/s; **11.31.** (*i*)0.2164 m^3/s; **11.31** (i) 0.2164 m^3/s; (ii) 0.219 m^3/s; **11.32.** 114.24 s; **11.33** 8.077 m; **11.34.** 0.6029 m^3/s; **11.35.** 0.01513 m^3/s; **11.36.** 0.25 m; **11.37.** 744.31 s; **11.38.** 0.1309 m^3/s.

12 Flow through Pipes

Frictional losses through pipes — Darcy–Weisbach equation — Smooth and rough pipes — Moody's diagram — Minor losses in pipes — Loss due to expansion — Contraction — Exit losses — losses at valves, bends etc., — Pipes in series — Parallel pipes — Three reservoir problem — Flow through syphons — Flow through nozzles — Power transmission through pipes — Pipe network

12.1 Introduction

Fluids are conveyed through pipes, mostly circular in shape. Water supply schemes and chemical industries use pipes made of various materials and of different sizes. The flow through the pipes could be laminar or turbulent. In case of laminar flow which is not very common in practical cases, the head loss in the flow, the velocity distribution and the shear at the boundary are found as discussed in detail in Chapter 13. In the present chapter, the discussion is mainly on the turbulent flow through pipes. A general formula for pipe resistance can be developed from dimensional considerations.

12.2 Darcy–Weisbach Equation

The loss of pressure head per unit length $\Delta p/l$ due to flow through a pipe of diameter d and having a roughness element of height k at the boundary, depends on the velocity of flow v. The fluid properties μ and ρ may also be included.

$$\frac{\Delta p}{l} = f(\mu, k, \rho, v, d).$$

Introducing a term $(\frac{\rho v^2}{2})$ to represent kinetic energy of flow and from dimensional considerations,

$$\frac{\Delta p}{\rho v^2/2} \times \frac{d}{l} = f(\frac{\rho v d}{\mu}, \frac{k}{d}),$$

where f is a function of $\frac{\rho v d}{\mu}$ and $\frac{k}{d}$. Rearranging $\frac{\Delta p}{\rho} = \frac{f l v^2}{2d}$ or head loss due to friction,

$$H_f = \frac{\Delta p}{\rho g} = \frac{f l v^2}{2gd}, \tag{12.1}$$

which can also be written in SI units as

$$\frac{flQ^2}{12.1d^5}. \tag{12.2}$$

This is known as the Darcy–Weisbach equation. f is known as the Darcy–Weisbach coefficient of friction and is a function of the Reynolds number, $\text{Re} = \dfrac{\rho v d}{\mu}$ and the relative roughness $\dfrac{k}{d}$.

12.3 Moody's Diagram

Moody developed a chart plotting f vs Re for various values of relative roughness, as shown in Fig. 12.1. Nikuradse investigated friction of smooth pipes and pipes with artificial uniform sand roughness. It was found that in the laminar range,

$$f = \frac{64}{\text{Re}}. \tag{12.3}$$

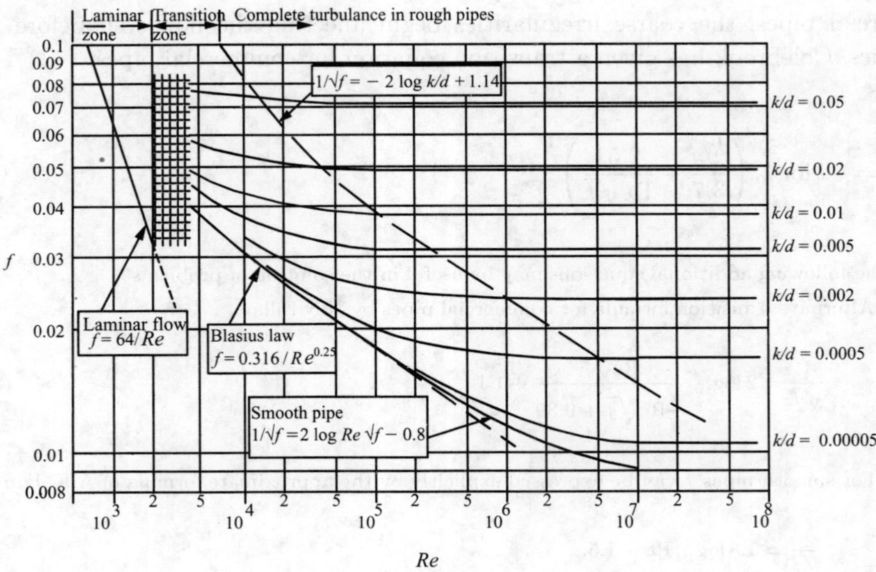

Fig. 12.1 *Moody's diagram*

A transition region is found before turbulence sets in. In smooth pipes, the value of f for rough turbulent flow is given by the formula

$$\frac{1}{\sqrt{f}} = 2\log_{10}(\text{Re}\sqrt{\text{f}}) - 0.8, \tag{12.4}$$

for a large range of Reynolds numbers. Up to a Reynolds number of 10^5, it can be approximated by the Blasius formula

$$f = \frac{0.316}{\text{Re}^{1/4}}. \tag{12.5}$$

At high Reynolds numbers, the roughnesses are more dominant in governing the flow. The value of f becomes independent of the Reynolds number and is given by the equation

$$\frac{1}{\sqrt{f}} = -2\log_{10}\left(\frac{k}{d}\right) + 1.14. \tag{12.6}$$

Since a pipe of any given roughness will function as a smooth pipe at low Reynolds numbers, a transition zone exists between the smooth and rough pipe diagram.
Colebrook and White found that for commercial pipes, the transition curve between the smooth and rough pipes deviated from that given by Nikuradse. Because of the non-uniform roughness in commercial pipes, the coarse irregularities begin affecting the flow well before the fine irregularities. Colebrook has given a transition equation for commercial pipes.

$$\frac{1}{\sqrt{f}} = -2\log_{10}\left(\frac{k/d}{3.7} + \frac{2.51}{\text{Re}\sqrt{f}}\right). \tag{12.7}$$

Note: The following additional equations may be useful in the solution of problems

i) Alternate transition formula for commercial pipes by N.N.Pillai

$$\frac{1}{\sqrt{f}} = 2\log_{10}\frac{\text{Re}\sqrt{f}}{\frac{k}{d}\text{Re}\sqrt{f} + 9.30} + 1.14. \tag{12.8}$$

ii) For smooth pipes f can be expressed explicitly by the approximate formula of A.K Jain[13] as

$$\frac{1}{\sqrt{f}} = 1.8\log_{10}\text{Re} - 1.5. \tag{12.9}$$

iii) In case of rough pipes, the following explicit formula by N.N.Pillai can be used,

$$\frac{1}{\sqrt{f}} = 1.8\log_{10}\frac{\text{Re}}{\left(\frac{k}{d}\right)^{1.11}\text{Re} + 30} + 1.14. \tag{12.10}$$

iv) When d, s [i.e., (H_f/l)], ν and k are given, Q can be found as follows[39]

$$\mathrm{Re}\sqrt{f} = \frac{(2gd^3 s)^{1/2}}{\nu} \tag{12.11}$$

$$\text{and } \mathrm{Re} = \mathrm{Re}\,\sqrt{f}\,(2\log_{10}\frac{\mathrm{Re}\sqrt{f}}{\frac{k}{d}\mathrm{Re}\sqrt{f}+9.30} + 1.14). \tag{12.12}$$

Knowing Re, the velocity and hence the discharge can be found.

v) If Q, s and ν are given, d can be found as follows. (SI unit only)

$$\mathrm{Re} \approx [0.633\mathrm{Q}^3 \frac{\mathrm{s}}{\nu^5}] \tag{12.13}$$

for laminar flow in smooth pipes.

$$\mathrm{Re} \approx [226\mathrm{Q}^3 \frac{\mathrm{s}}{\nu^5}]^{0.208} \tag{12.14}$$

for turbulent flow in smooth pipes.
Knowing Re, d can be found out. $d \approx 4Q/(\pi\nu\mathrm{Re})$

Following are the usual values of k for commercial pipes.

Material	Value of k in metres
Steel or wrought iron	4.6×10^{-8}
Galvanized iron	1.5×10^{-4}
Cast iron	2.6×10^{-4}
Concrete	3×10^{-4} to 3×10^{-3}
Riveted steel	9×10^{-4} to 9×10^{-3}

12.4 Discharge through Non-circular Pipes

Ducts of various shapes are commonly used in industries. When the flow is turbulent, the head loss can be found out by using Darcy's formula, $H_L = \dfrac{flv^2}{2gd_e}$, where d_e is the equivalent diameter of the duct. The equivalent diameter is

$$d_e = 4R, \tag{12.15}$$

where R is the hydraulic mean radius.

$$R = \frac{A}{P}, \tag{12.16}$$

where A is the area of cross-section of the duct and P is the perimeter of the section. The Reynold's number $\text{Re} = \frac{vd_e}{\nu} = \frac{4vR}{\nu}$, and the relative roughness using the Moody's diagram for finding out f can be $k/4R$.

When the flow is laminar, the use of the above method entails much error.

12.5 Loss of Head in Pipe Connections and Fittings

There are losses of head at pipe fittings. In addition to the small minor loss due to friction on the boundary in these fittings, the main part of loss is due to the separation of flow from the boundary and loss in eddies.

It is usual to express the head loss by the formula $H_l = k\frac{v^2}{2g}$, where k is a factor determined by experiments. The following expressions are used in estimating the head loss in pipe fittings.

Fig. 12.2(a) Fig. 12.2(b)

(i) **Sudden expansion of pipe** (Fig. 12.2(a))

$$H_l = \frac{(v_1 - v_2)^2}{2g} = \frac{kv_1{}^2}{2g}. \tag{12.17}$$

$$k = \left(1 - \frac{a_1}{a_2}\right)^2.$$

When $a_2 >> a_1$, $k = 1$.

(ii) **Sudden contraction of pipe** (Fig. 12.2(b))

$$H_l = \frac{(v_c - v_2)^2}{2g} \tag{12.18}$$

$$= \frac{kv_2{}^2}{2g}.$$

$$k = \left(\frac{1}{C_c} - 1\right)^2. \text{ If } C_c \text{ is assumed to be } 0.62,\ k = 0.375.$$

It is usual to assume the sudden contraction loss as

$$H_l = 0.5\frac{{v_2}^2}{2g}. \tag{12.19}$$

(iii) **Loss in bends** The loss depends on the ratio of the radius of the bend to the diameter of the pipe and also the total length and roughness of the bent pipe.

$$H_l = k\frac{v^2}{2g}, \text{ where } k \text{ can vary usually from 0.1 to 1.0.} \tag{12.20}$$

(iv) **Loss of head in elbows** The losses are generally greater than that in smooth bends.

(v) **Loss of head in valves** Open globe valves can usually have a factor for head loss of 5 to 10. Gate valves usually have factors ranging from 0.05 to 0.5. When the valves are partially closed, the factor increases manifold.

(vi) **Loss at exit** When the pipe discharges to the atmosphere or to a large reservoir, the velocity head at the exit is to be accounted for in the total head.

Example 12.1 Water at 20°C is pumped at the rate of 5 l/s through a G.I pipe of 5 cm diameter from a lower reservoir to a higher one, the difference in level being 30 m. The valves, bends, etc., are shown in the figure. The total length of the pipe is 80 m. If the height of roughness is 0.15 mm, find the HP required for the pump. Assume the efficiency of pump to be 70%.

$Q = 5$ l/s $= 0.005$ m^3/s; $\quad d = 0.05$ m; $\quad \nu = 10^{-6}$ m^2/s.

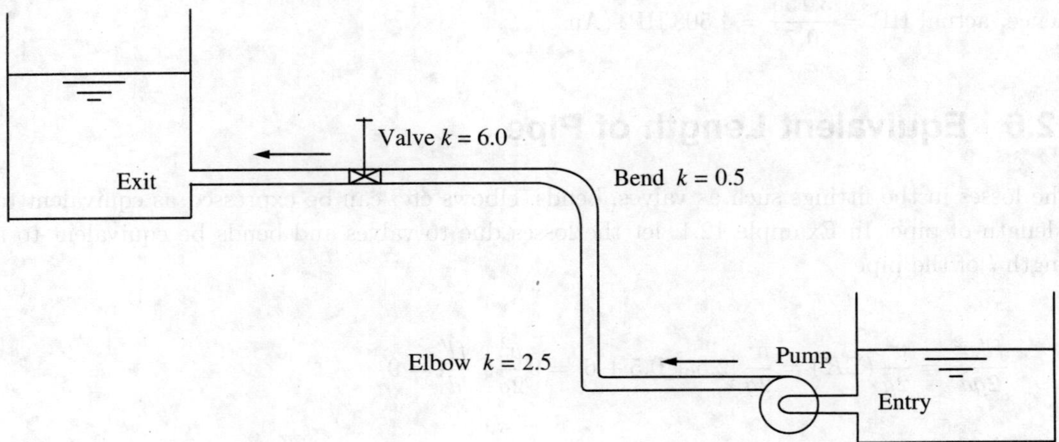

Example 12.1

$$v = \frac{Q}{A} = \frac{0.005 \times 4}{\pi \times 0.05^2} = 2.546 \text{ m/s.}$$

$$\text{Re} = \frac{vd}{\nu} = \frac{2.546 \times 0.05}{10^{-6}} = 127300.$$

$$k = 0.15 \text{ mm} = 1.5 \times 10^{-4} \text{ m}; \frac{k}{d} = 3 \times 10^{-3}.$$

Using the explicit equation,

$$\frac{1}{\sqrt{f}} = 1.8 \log \frac{\text{Re}}{(k/d)^{1.11}\,\text{Re} + 30} + 1.14, \qquad f = 0.02748.$$

Total head required = Static head + Head loss

$$= 30 + \frac{v^2}{2g}\left[\frac{fl}{d} + \sum k\right]$$

$$= 30 + \frac{2.546^2}{2 \times 9.81}\left[\frac{0.02748 \times 80}{0.05} + 0.5 + 2.5 + 0.5 + 6 + 1\right] = 47.995 \text{ m.}$$

Theoretical power $= \gamma QH = 1000 \times 9.81 \times 0.005 \times 47.995$ W $= 2.354$ KW

$$= \frac{2.354}{0.746} \text{ HP} = 3.155 \text{ HP. (Ans.)}$$

Hence, actual HP $= \dfrac{3.155}{0.7} = 4.508$ HP. (Ans.)

12.6 Equivalent Length of Pipe

The losses in the fittings such as valves, bends, elbows etc. can be expressed as equivalent to a length of pipe. In Example 12.1, let the losses due to valves and bends be equivalent to a length l of the pipe.

$$\frac{fl'v^2}{2gd} = \frac{v^2}{2g}(\Sigma K) = \frac{v^2}{2g}[2.5 + 0.5 + 6] = 9\frac{v^2}{2g}; \quad \frac{fl'}{d} = 9.$$

Hence $l' = \dfrac{9d}{f} = \dfrac{9 \times 0.05}{0.02748} = 16.38$ m. (Ans.)

12.7 Hydraulic Gradient and Total Energy Line

In many practical problems with pipe lines, it is necessary to find the piezometric (potential) head at any point on the pipe line. Only if the potential head is higher than a supply point, can water be drawn directly by gravity. The line joining the potential surfaces along the pipe is called the hydraulic gradient line. It represents the potential head $\left(\frac{p}{\gamma} + Z\right)$. If the kinetic energy head $\frac{v^2}{2g}$ is also added, the line joining the potential surfaces represents the energy gradient line. The hydraulic and the energy gradient line are plotted in Fig. 12.3.

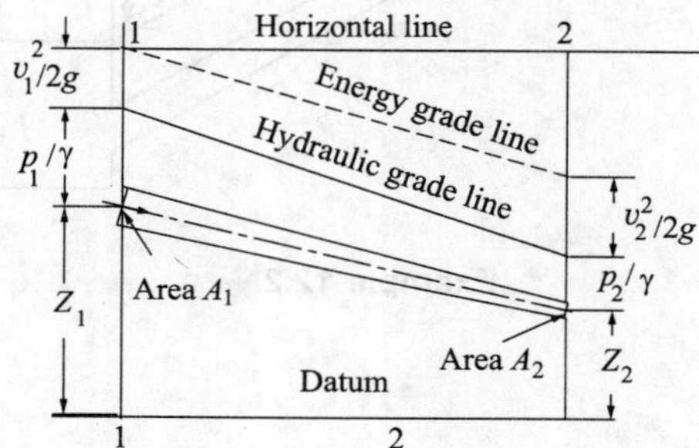

Fig. 12.3 *Hydraulic and energy gradient lines.*

When plotting the hydraulic gradient and the energy gradient lines, the variation at the fitting is assumed to occur abruptly for all practical purposes.

12.8 Flow through Pipes in Series

When pipes of different diameters are in series, the discharge through them is the same and the total head loss in the pipe line will be the sum of the head losses in the different pipes. It is similar to the addition of resistances in a series electrical connection whereas the current passing will be the same.

Example 12.2 Two reservoirs are connected by a pipe line consisting of a 400 m long pipe of 20 cm diameter in series with a 600 m long pipe of 30 cm diameter. The difference in water level between the reservoirs is 8 m. If f for the bigger pipe is 0.01 and for the smaller pipe is 0.016, find the discharge. Account for all the losses. Sketch the hydraulic grade line.

$$d_1 = 0.2 \text{ m};\ l_1 = 400 \text{ m};\ f_1 = 0.016;\ d_2 = 0.3 \text{ m};\ l_2 = 600 \text{ m};\ f_2 = 0.01.$$

$$A_1 v_1 = A_2 v_2 = Q; \qquad v_2 = \frac{A_1 v_1}{A_2} = \frac{0.2^2}{0.3^2} \times v_1 = 0.4444 v_1.$$

Equating the head causing flow,

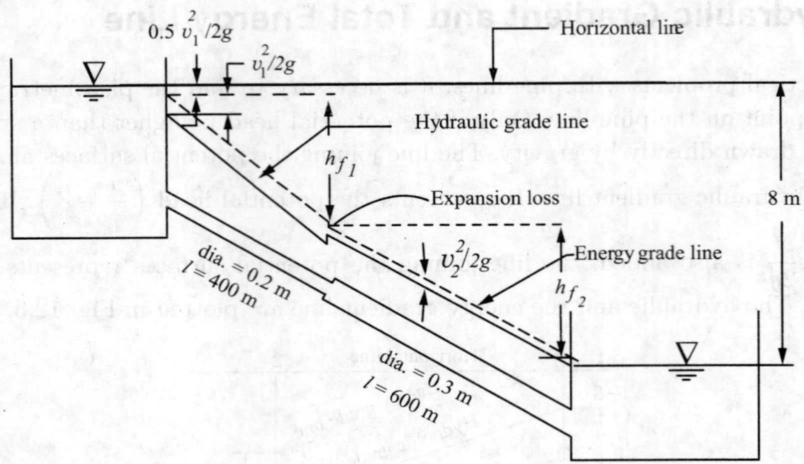

Example 12.2

$$
\begin{aligned}
8 &= 0.5\frac{{v_1}^2}{2g} + \frac{f_1 l_1 {v_1}^2}{2gd_1} + \frac{(v_1 - v_2)^2}{2g} + \frac{f_2 l_2 {v_2}^2}{2gd_2} + \frac{{v_2}^2}{2g} \\
&= \frac{{v_1}^2}{2g}\left[0.5 + \frac{0.016 \times 400}{0.2} + (1 - 0.4444)^2\right] + \frac{{v_2}^2}{2g}\left[\frac{0.01 \times 600}{0.3} + 1\right] \\
&= 32.809\frac{{v_1}^2}{2g} + 21\frac{{v_2}^2}{2g} \\
&= (32.809 + 21 \times 0.4444^2)\frac{{v_1}^2}{2g} = 36.95\frac{{v_1}^2}{2g}.
\end{aligned}
$$

$$
\text{i.e.,} \quad v_1 = \sqrt{\frac{2g \times 8}{36.957}} = 2.0608 \text{ m/s.}
$$

$$
Q = A_1 v_1 = \frac{\pi \times {d_1}^2}{4} \times 2.0608 = 0.0647 \text{ m}^3/\text{s. (Ans.)}
$$

12.9 Flow through Parallel Pipes

Let ACB and ADB be parallel pipes conveying water (Fig.12.4). Let h_a and h_b be the peizometric heads at A and B. The loss of head $= h_a - h_b$. Hence, loss of head in pipe ACB = Loss of head in ADB $= h_a - h_b$.

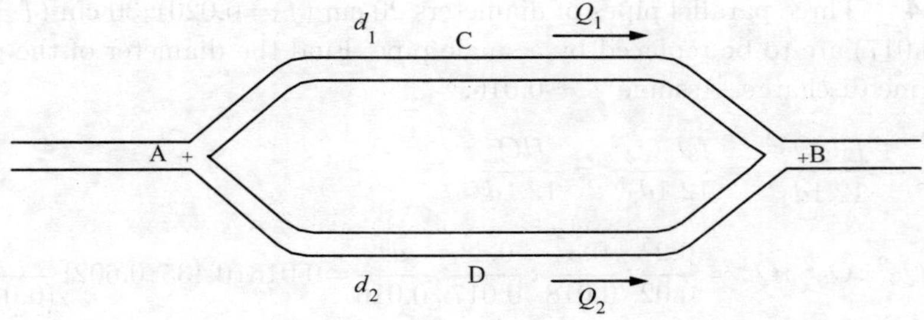

Fig. 12.4 *Flow through parallel pipe*

But by principle of continuity, $Q = Q_1 + Q_2$. The minor losses are usually neglected in the analysis. The problem of parallel pipes is analogous to the flow of current through parallel resistances.

$$h_A - h_B = \frac{f_1 l_1 Q_1^2}{12.1 d_1^5} = \frac{f_2 l_2 Q_2^5}{12.1 d_2^5}.$$

Example 12.3 Two parallel pipes 200 m long, one of 20 cm diameter ($f = 0.020$) and another of 30 cm diameter ($f = 0.018$) form part of a long pipe line. If the discharge is 0.15 m^3/s, find the discharge in each pipe. Find also the head loss.

dia. = 0.2 m, 1 = 200 m

dia. = 0.3 m, 1 = 200 m

Example 12.3

$$\frac{f_1 l_1 {Q_1}^2}{12.1 {d_1}^5} = \frac{f_2 l_2 {Q_2}^2}{12.1 {d_2}^5}.$$

$$\text{Hence, } \frac{Q_1}{Q_2} = \left(\frac{{d_1}^5}{{d_2}^5} \times \frac{f_2}{f_1}\right)^{1/2} = \left(\frac{0.2^5}{0.3^5} \times \frac{0.018}{0.02}\right)^{1/2} = 0.3443.$$

$$\frac{Q_1}{Q} = \frac{Q_1}{Q_1 + Q_2} = \frac{0.3443}{1.3443} = 0.2561.$$

Solving,

$$Q_1 = 0.2561 Q = 0.2561 \times 0.15 = 0.0384 \text{ m}^3/\text{s}.$$

$$Q_2 = Q - Q_1 = 0.15 - 0.0384 = 0.1116 \text{ m}^3/\text{s}.$$

$$\text{Head loss} = \frac{f_1 l {Q_1}^2}{12.1 d^5} = \frac{0.020 \times 200 \times 0.0384^2}{12.1 \times 0.2^5} = 1.5233 \text{ m. (Ans.)}$$

Example 12.4 Three parallel pipes of diameters 20 cm ($f = 0.020$), 30 cm ($f = 0.018$), and 40 cm ($f = 0.017$) are to be replaced by a single pipe. Find the diameter of the pipe required to give the same discharge. Assume $f = 0.016$.

$$\frac{f_1 l_1 {Q_1}^2}{12.1 {d_1}^5} = \frac{f_2 l_2 {Q_2}^2}{12.1 {d_2}^5} = \frac{f_3 l_3 {Q_3}^2}{12.1 {d_3}^5} = \frac{f l Q^2}{12.1 d^5}.$$

Hence, $${Q_1}^2 : {Q_2}^2 : {Q_3}^2 : Q^2 = \frac{0.2^5}{0.02} : \frac{0.3^5}{0.018} : \frac{0.4^5}{0.017} : \frac{d^5}{0.016} = 0.016 : 0.135 : 0.602 : \frac{d^5}{(0.016)}.$$

Therefore,

$$Q_1 : Q_2 : Q_3 : Q = 0.1265 : 0.3674 : 0.7759 : 1.2698. \ (Q = Q_1 + Q_2 + Q_3).$$

$$1.2698 = \frac{d^{5/2}}{(0.016)^{1/2}} \text{ or } d = 0.4812 \text{ m. (Ans.)}$$

Example 12.5 A large pipe of diameter 1 m has a looping line (a parallel smaller pipe) of diameter 5 cm connected between points 6 m away. f for the large and small pipes are 0.014 and 0.02 respectively. Taking into account the loss at entry and exit and bends ($k = 0.3$) in the loop, find the discharge in the main pipe when the discharge in the loop is 2 l/s.

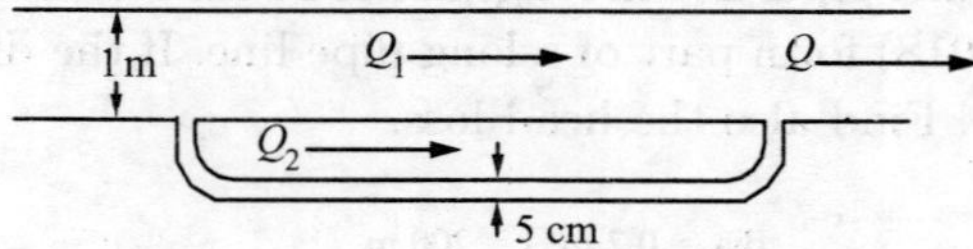

Example 12.5

Let Q_1 be the discharge in the main pipe.

$$v_2 = \frac{Q_2}{a_2} = 0.002 \times \frac{4}{\pi \times 0.5^2} = 1.0186 \text{ m/s}.$$

Considering there are two bends,

$$H_l = \frac{f_1 l_1 {Q_1}^2}{2 g d_1} = 0.5\frac{{v_2}^2}{2g} + 0.3\frac{{v_2}^2}{2g} + \frac{f_2 l_2 {v_2}^2}{2 g d_2} + 0.3\frac{{v_2}^2}{2g} + \frac{{v_2}^2}{2g}$$

$$= \frac{0.02 \times 6 \times 1.0186^2}{2 \times 9.81 \times 0.05} + 2.1 \times \frac{1.0186^2}{2 \times 9.81} = 0.23797 \text{ m}.$$

$$\frac{f_1 l_1 {Q_1}^2}{12.1 {d_1}^5} = 0.23797.$$

Hence, $$Q_1 = \sqrt{\frac{12.1 \times 1^5 \times 0.23797}{0.014 \times 6}} = 5.855 \text{ m}^3\text{/s}.$$

Total discharge $= Q_1 + Q_2 = 5.855 + 0.002 = 5.857$ m^3/s. (Ans.)

Example 12.6 Two reservoirs are connected by a pipe 3 km long and 30 cm in diameter ($f = 0.03$). The difference in water level is 12 m. Find the discharge in the pipe. A second pipe 30 cm in diameter ($f = 0.025$) is laid alongside the first for the last 1 km and connected with the first pipe and the reservoir. Neglecting all losses except the friction head, find the increase in discharge.

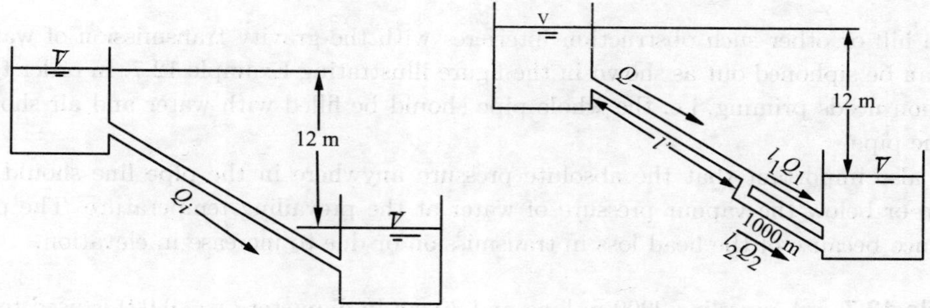

Example 12.6

$f_1 = 0.03$; $l = 3000$ m;

Let Q_i be the discharge initially.

$$H_{f1} = 12 = \frac{f_1 l Q_i{}^2}{12.1 d_1{}^5} = \frac{0.03 \times 3000 \times Q_i{}^2}{12.1 \times 0.3^5}.$$

Hence, $Q_i = 0.0626$ m³/s. (Ans.)

$l_1 = 2000$ m; $l_2 = 1000$ m. (lengths of parallel pipes)

Head loss in parallel pipes is the same.

$$\text{Therefore, } \frac{f_1 l_1 Q_1{}^2}{12.1 d_1{}^5} = \frac{f_2 l_2 Q_2{}^2}{12.1 d_2{}^5}; \text{ But, } d_1 = d_2.$$

$$Q_1{}^2 : Q_2{}^2 = \frac{1}{f_1} : \frac{1}{f_2} = 0.025 : 0.03 = 1 : 1.2.$$

$$Q_1 : Q_2 = 1 : \sqrt{1.12} = 1 : 1.095.$$

Hence, Q_1: Q_2: Q $= 1 : 1.095 : 2.095$. and hence $Q_1 = \dfrac{1}{2.2095} Q$

$$12 = \frac{f_1 l_1 Q^2}{12.1 d^5} + \frac{f_1 l_2 Q_1^2}{12.1 d^5} = \frac{f_1 l_1 Q^2}{12.1 d^5} + \frac{f_1 l_2 \left(\frac{1}{2.095} Q\right)^2}{12.1 d^5}$$

$$= \frac{Q^2}{12.1 \times 0.3^5} (0.03 \times 2000 + 0.03 \times 1000 \times 0.2278)$$

$$= Q^2 \times 2273.0; \quad Q = 0.0727 \text{ m}^3/\text{s}.$$

So increase in discharge $= 0.0727 - 0.0626 = 0.0101 \text{ m}^3/\text{s}$. (Ans.)

12.10 Siphons

When a hill or other such obstruction interferes with the gravity transmission of water, the water can be siphoned out as shown in the figure illustrating Example 12.7. In order to work, the siphon needs priming, i.e. the whole pipe should be filled with water and air should not enter the pipe.

It is also important that the absolute pressure anywhere in the pipe line should not be equal to or below the vapour pressure of water at the prevailing temperature. The pressure can reduce because of the head loss in transmission or due to increase in elevation.

Example 12.7 A pipe line 2200 m long and 30 cm in diameter ($f = 0.02$) is used to siphon water from a reservoir to another reservoir having a water level difference of 15 m. It has to be laid over a hill point B, 500 m away and 5 m above the upper reservoir. How deep should the excavation on the hill top be so that when the siphon works, the pressure at B will not be below 3 m of water (absolute)? Assume the atmospheric pressure to be 10.3 m of water.

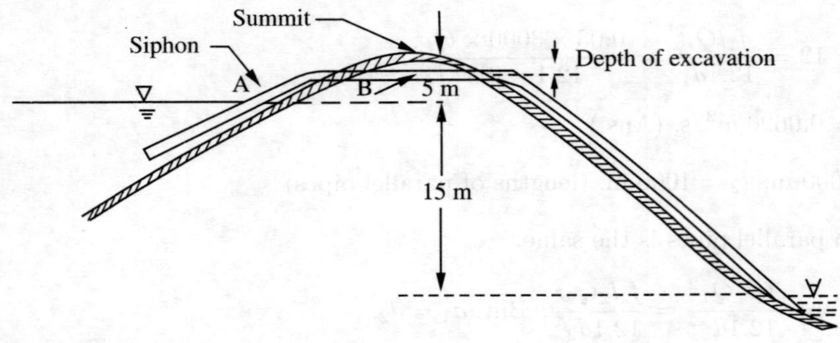

Example 12.7

$$15 = \frac{flQ^2}{12.1d^5} = \frac{0.02 \times 2200 \times Q^2}{12.1 \times 0.3^5}.$$

$$\text{Hence, } Q = 0.1\text{m}^3/\text{s}; \; v = \frac{0.1}{\pi \times \frac{0.3^2}{4}} = 1.415 \text{ m/s}.$$

Let h be the needed excavation. Pressure head at B is limited to 3 m. Applying Bernoulli's theorem between A and B (Datum at A),

$$10.3 = \text{losses up to B} + \frac{p}{\gamma} + z + \frac{v^2}{2g}.$$

$$10.3 = \left(0.5\frac{v^2}{2g} + \frac{0.02 \times 500 \times 0.1^2}{12.1 \times 0.3^5}\right) + 3 + (5 - h) + \frac{v^2}{2g},$$

where $v = 1.415$ m/s.

$h = 1.254$ m. (Ans.)

12.11 Maximum Transmission of Fluid Power through a Given Pipe

12.11.1 Pipe leading to a turbine

Let a pipe line of length l and diameter d be connected to a reservoir having a head H, above the outlet of the turbine. The power transmitted through the pipe will be equal to $\gamma Q(H - H_f)$, where Q is the discharge and H_f is head loss in the pipe.

Writing $H_f = \dfrac{flQ^2}{12.1d^5}$, where f is the Darcy–Weisbach coefficient.

$$P = \gamma Q\left(H - \frac{flQ^2}{12.1d^5}\right) = \gamma\left(QH - \frac{flQ^3}{12.1d^5}\right).$$

For P to be maximum,

$$\frac{\mathrm{d}P}{dQ} = 0; \text{ i.e., } H = \frac{3flQ^2}{12.1d^5} = 3H_f; \text{ so,}$$

$$H_f = \frac{1}{3}H. \tag{12.21}$$

12.11.2 Nozzle diameter for maximum power of a jet

In case of an impulse turbine, a nozzle of diameter d_n is required to be fitted to the end of the pipe of diameter d to give the maximum power out of the jet. The jet will be discharging to the atmosphere and head H will be above the level of the nozzle. Neglecting loss of energy in the nozzle, the total head available just before the nozzle is $H - H_f$ and power transmitted will be equal to $\gamma Q\,(H - H_f)$.‡

Hence as in the previous case, $H_f = 1/3\ H$ for P to be maximum.

Applying Bernoulli's equation between a point in the reservoir and on the jet,

‡ $\gamma Q\,(H - H_f)$ will be same as $\dfrac{\rho Q {v_j}^2}{2}$.

$$H = H_f + \frac{v_n{}^2}{2g} = \frac{1}{3}H + \frac{v_n^2}{2g}, \text{ where } v_n \text{ is the velocity of the jet.}$$

$$\frac{v_n{}^2}{2g} = \frac{2}{3}H = 2H_f.$$

$$\text{i.e. } \left(\frac{d}{d_n}\right)^4 \times \frac{v^2}{2g} = \frac{2flv^2}{2gd} \text{ or } \left(\frac{d_n}{d}\right)^4 = \frac{d}{2fl}; \quad \text{hence } \left(\frac{d_n}{d}\right) = \left(\frac{d}{2fl}\right)^{0.25}. \qquad (12.22)$$

The nozzle diameter for the maximum power of the jet can be worked out using the above equation.

Example 12.8 Power is to be transmitted from a reservoir to a distance of 400 m using a pipe of 20 cm diameter. If a nozzle is fitted to the end and the total head over the nozzle level is 45 m, find (i) the maximum power that can be transmitted through the pipe, (ii) the discharge required and (iii) the diameter of the nozzle. Assume $f = 0.02$.

$$H = 45 \text{ m}; \quad d = 0.2 \text{ m}.$$

By the condition for the maximum transmission of power by a given pipe,

$$H_f = 1/3\ H = 15 \text{ m}; \quad \frac{flQ^2}{12.1d^5} = 15;$$

$$Q = \left[\frac{15 \times 12.1 \times d^5}{fl}\right]^{\frac{1}{2}} = 0.0852 \text{ m}^3/\text{s. (Ans.)}$$

$$\text{P} = \gamma Q\,(H - H_f) = \rho g Q\left(\frac{2}{3}H\right)$$

$$= 1000 \times 9.81 \times 0.0852 \times (2/3) \times 45 \text{ W} = 25.074 \text{ kW. (Ans.)}$$

Let the diameter of the nozzle required be d_n.

$$\frac{d_n}{d} = \left(\frac{d}{2fl}\right)^{\frac{1}{4}} = \left(\frac{0.2}{2 \times 0.02 \times 400}\right)^{\frac{1}{4}} = 0.3344.$$

Hence $d_n = 0.3344 \times 0.2 = 0.0669 \text{ m} = 6.69 \text{ cm}$. (Ans.)

12.12 Efficiency of Power Transmission and the Selection of Diameter of the Pipe

In the analysis made in the previous section, the pipe is assumed to be selected and no limitation of discharge is considered. For the condition of maximum power transmitted, the efficiency of power transmission is

$$\frac{H - H_f}{H}, \tag{12.23}$$

which is $\dfrac{2/3\,H}{H} = 66.7\%$.

In actual cases, the discharge available is limited and normally too uneconomical to allow a loss of 33.3% of energy due to friction through pipe. A larger diameter of pipe can be used for higher efficiency.

The discharge and head available for power generation is normally known. For the design of a pipe, an initial diameter is assumed and the power transmitted is worked out. The diameter can be increased in small steps and the consequence studied. The diameter can be increased further if the additional expenditure and maintenance cost in having a bigger pipe is less than the annual additional income due to power saved.

Example 12.9 A hydro-electric power plant has a gross head of 30 m. The diameter and length of the pipe are 20 cm and 200 m respectively. Find the maximum power that can be transmitted. Find also the maximum discharge. $f = 0.02$.

For maximum power transmission, $H_f = (1/3)$ H $= (1/3)$ 30 $= 10$ m.

$$H_f = \frac{flQ^2}{12.1d^5} = \frac{0.02 \times 200 \times Q^2}{12.1 \times 0.2^5} = 10.$$

$$1033Q^2 = 10 \text{ or } Q = 98.38 \text{ l/s. (Ans.)}$$

$$P = \gamma Q H_e = 9810 \times 0.09838 \times 20 \text{ kW} = 19.3 \text{ kW. (Ans.)}$$

Example 12.10 In the above example, if the diameter of the pipe is increased to 30 cm and the discharge is the same, find the power transmitted and the efficiency.

$$H_f = \frac{flQ^2}{12.1d^5} = \frac{0.02 \times 200 \times 0.09838^2}{12.1 \times 0.3^5} = 5.267 \text{ m.}$$

$$H_e = 30 - 5.267 = 24.733 \text{ m.}$$

$$P = \gamma Q H_e = 9810 \times 0.09838 \times 24.733\text{W} = 23.87 \text{ kW. (Ans.)}$$

Efficiency $= 24.733/30 = 0.824$. (Ans.)

12.13 The Three Reservoir Problem

Three reservoirs A, B, and C are interconnected by a pipe meeting at junction J. Let us assume that the reservoir C is the lowest one and A and B have water levels a and b respectively above that of C. Let the piezometric head at junction J be h above the water level at C (Fig. 12.5).

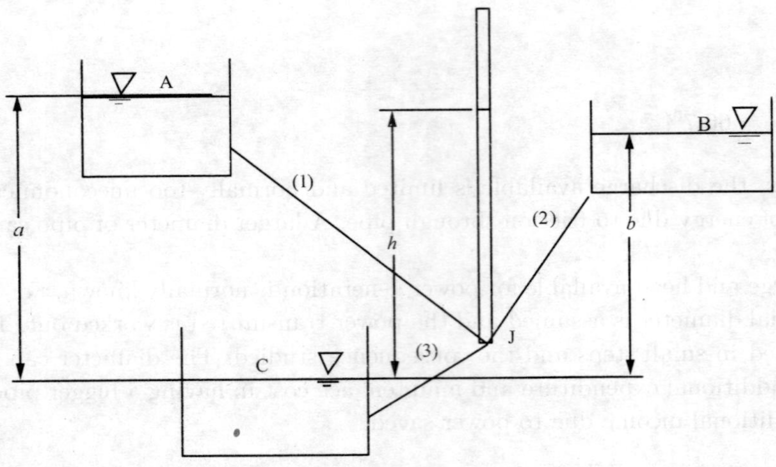

Fig. 12.5 *Three reservoir problem*

Let Q_1, Q_2 and Q_3 be the discharge in the three pipes.

The head loss in one pipe is given by equation $H_f = kQ^2$, where $k = \dfrac{fl}{12.1d^5}$.

Let k_1, k_2, and k_3 , be the constants for pipes (1), (2) and (3).

Assume the pipe (2) to be closed by a valve. Then the discharge will pass through pipes (1) and (3). Head loss at junction J,

$$h' = \frac{a \times k_3}{k_1 + k_3}. \tag{12.24}$$

If now the valve in pipe (2) is assumed to be opened, the direction of the flow can be determined.

If $h' < b$, flow is in the BJ direction (−ve).

If $h' > b$, flow is in the JB direction (+ve).

The equation of continuity can now be written as

$Q_1 = \pm\, Q_2 + Q_3$ (taking the proper sign of Q_2) or

$$+\sqrt{\frac{a-h}{k_1}} = \pm\sqrt{\frac{\pm\,(b-h)}{k_2}} + \sqrt{\frac{h}{k_3}}. \tag{12.25}$$

The value of h is found by trial and error and then the discharges in the pipes can be found.

Example 12.11 Given below are data regarding the elevations of three tanks and the connecting pipes (see Fig. 12.5). Find Q_1, Q_2 and Q_3.

$a = 45$ m; $b = 25$ m;

$$\begin{aligned} d_1 &= 0.7 \text{ m}; & l_1 &= 300 \text{ m}; & f_1 &= 0.016; \\ d_2 &= 0.45 \text{ m}; & l_2 &= 600 \text{ m}; & f_2 &= 0.024; \\ d_3 &= 0.6 \text{ m}; & l_3 &= 1200 \text{ m}; & f_3 &= 0.024; \end{aligned}$$

$$k_1 = \frac{f_1 l_1}{12.1 {d_1}^5} = 2.36; \; k_2 = \frac{f_2 l_2}{12.1 {d_2}^5} = 64.5; \; k_3 = \frac{f_3 l_3}{12.1 {d_3}^5} = 30.61.$$

h' for condition of no flow in pipe (2),

$$h' = \frac{a k_3}{k_1 + k_3} = \frac{45 \times 30.61}{2.36 + 30.61} = 41.78 \text{ but } b = 25 \text{ m},$$

hence flow is from J to B. i.e., Q_2 is + ve.

$$Q_1 = Q_2 + Q_3 \text{ or } \sqrt{\frac{a-h}{k_1}} = \sqrt{\frac{h-b}{k_2}} + \sqrt{\frac{h}{k_3}}.$$

$$\text{i.e., } \sqrt{\frac{45-h}{2.36}} = \sqrt{\frac{h-25}{64.4}} + \sqrt{\frac{h}{30.61}}.$$

Using the trial and error method,

let LHS – RHS = F where F should be nearly zero.

$h = 40, \text{F} = -0.1626.$

$h = 39, \text{F} = -0.001.$

Hence $h = 39.0$ m. (by interpolation)

$$Q_1 = \sqrt{\frac{45-h}{2.36}} = 1.594 \text{ m}^3/\text{s}.$$

$$Q_2 = \sqrt{\frac{h-25}{64.5}} = 0.466 \text{ m}^3/\text{s}.$$

$$Q_3 = \sqrt{\frac{h}{30.61}} = 1.129 \text{ m}^3/\text{s. (Ans.)}$$

Example 12.12 A horizontal pipe 20 cm in diameter and 700 m long is connected to a reservoir having a head of 16 m. If $f = 0.015$, find the discharge through the pipe. If an orifice 7.5 cm in diameter and of $C_d = 0.6$ at a distance of 200 m from the tank is kept open, find the decrease in discharge at the end of the pipe.

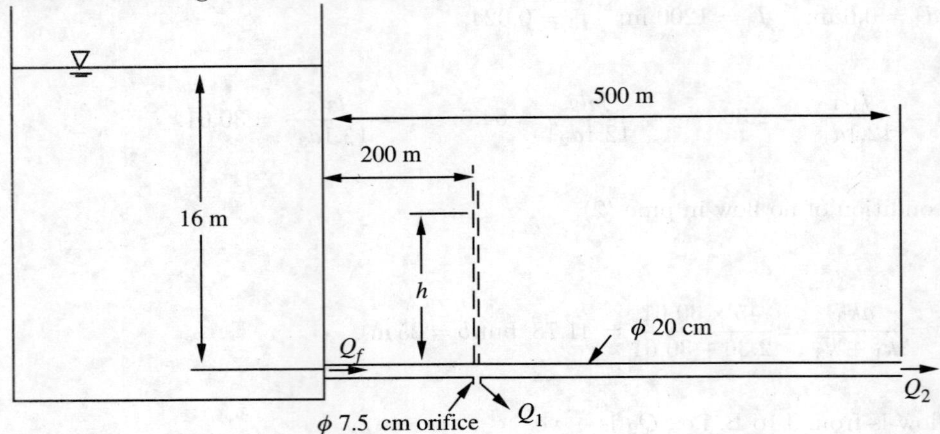

Example 12.12

Let Q_i be the discharge initially.

$$16 = \frac{flQ_1^2}{12.1d^5} = \frac{0.015 \times 700 Q_i^2}{12.1 \times 0.2^5} = 2711.8 Q_i^2 \quad \text{or} \quad Q_i = 0.0768 \text{ m}^3/\text{s (Ans)}$$

Let h be the head at the orifice, Q_1 be the discharge through the orifice, Q_2 be the discharge at the end of pipe and Q_f be the total discharge from the tank in the second case. The discharge through the orifice is

$$Q_1 = C_d A\sqrt{2gh} = 0.6 \times \frac{\pi \times 0.075^2}{4} \times \sqrt{2 \times 9.81 h} = 0.01174\sqrt{h} \tag{1}$$

$$\text{At the end of the pipe, } h = \frac{fl_2 Q_2^2}{12.1d^5} = \frac{0.015 \times 500 \times Q_2^2}{12.1 \times 0.2^5} = 1937 Q_2^2 \quad \text{or} \quad Q_2 = 0.0227\sqrt{h}$$

$$Q_f = Q_1 + Q_2 = (0.01174 + 0.0227)\sqrt{h} = 0.03444\sqrt{h}$$

$$\text{or} \quad h = 843.1 Q_f^2 \tag{2}$$

Considering the first 200 m of pipe with discharge Q_f

$$(16 - h) = \frac{flQ_1^2}{12.1d^5} = \frac{0.015 \times 200 \times Q_f^2}{12.1 \times 0.2^5} = 774.8 Q_f^2 \tag{3}$$

Adding (2) and (3), $16 = (843.1 + 774.8)Q_f^2 = 1617.9Q_f^2$ or $Q_f = 0.0994\ \text{m}^3/\text{s}$

From (2), $h = 843.1, Q_f^2 = 8.33$ m; hence from (1), $Q_1 = 0.01174\sqrt{h} = 0.03388\ \text{m}^3/\text{s}$

$$Q_2 = Q_f - Q_1 = 0.0994 - 0.03388 = 0.06552\ \text{m}^3/\text{s}$$

Hence, decrease in discharge $= Q_i - Q_f = 0.0768 - 0.06552 = 0.01128\ \text{m}^3/\text{s}$ (Ans)

12.14 Analysis of Flow in Pipe Networks

In a municipal water distribution system, analysis of flow rates in pipes and the pressures at junction of pipes form a basic problem. A simple network is shown in Fig. 12.6(a). The details of the pipe and values of k in the equation $H_f = kQ^2$ are also given for each pipe.

Pipe	Dia.	Length	f	$k = fl/12.1\ d^5$
1	0.3	1000	0.024	816.2
2	0.5	1200	0.02	63.47
3	0.3	800	0.024	653.0
4	0.4	1000	0.02	161.4
5	0.4	1200	0.02	193.7

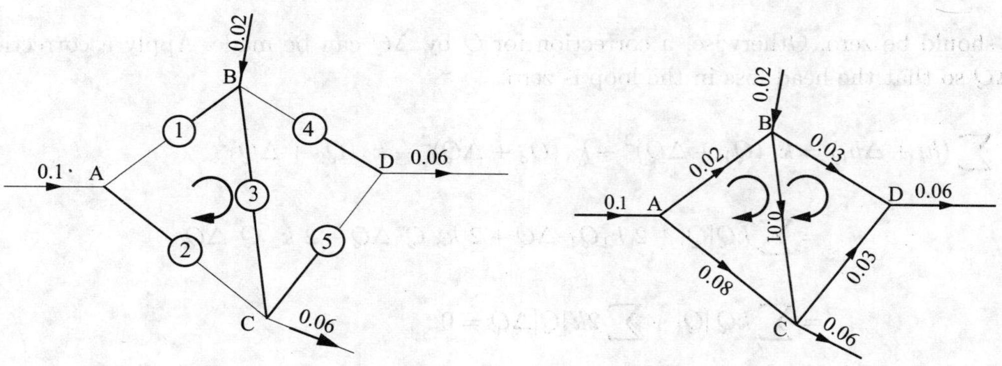

Fig. 12.6 (a) Fig. 12.6 (b)

It is assumed in the problem that f is constant, whereas it is actually a function of the Reynolds number and the roughness of the pipe. The direction of flow in the pipes are not known initially. The following conditions are satisfied for the flow,

(i) The algebraic sum of the flow towards the junctions A, B, C & D should be zero, i.e., the equation of continuity should hold good.

(ii) If one takes any loop say ABC, the algebraic sum of the head losses in AB, BC and CA should be equal to zero.

(iii) The head losses in the pipes conform to the Darcy–Weisbach formula.

A method of systematically solving the network by trial and correction procedure is by the Hardy Cross method. In this method, an initial assumption is made regarding the discharge and the flow in the pipes so that the equation of continuity is satisfied. The assumed discharges in the pipe are shown in Fig. 12.6(b). Let the initial assumption of flow in pipe 1 be from A to B, in pipe 2 be from A to C and in pipe 3 be from B to C respectively.

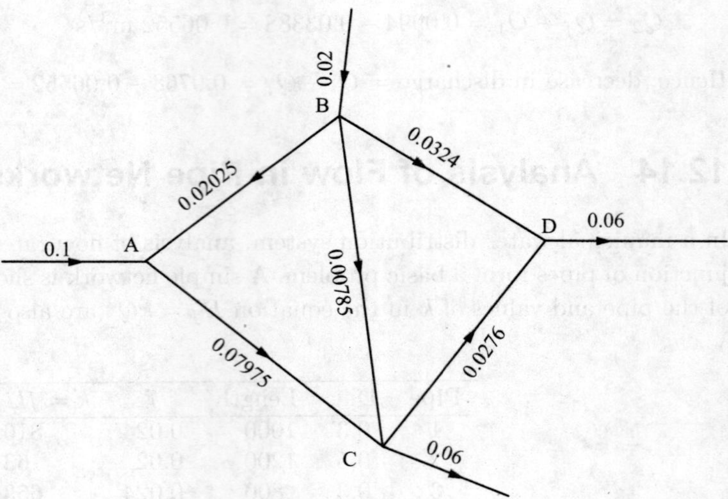

Fig. 12.6(c)

Considering the loop ABC,

$$\sum h_l = k_1 {Q_1}^2 + k_3 {Q_3}^2 - k_2 {Q_2}^2 = \sum kQ\,|Q|.$$

This should be zero. Otherwise, a correction for Q by ΔQ can be made. Apply a correction for ΔQ so that the head loss in the loop is zero.

$$\sum (h_l + \Delta h_l) = k_1\,(Q_1 + \Delta Q)^2 + k_3\,(Q_3 + \Delta Q)^2 - k_2\,(Q_2 + \Delta Q)^2$$

$$= \sum kQ|Q| + 2\,k_1 Q_1\,\Delta Q + 2\,k_3\,Q_3 \Delta Q - 2\,k_2\,Q_2 \Delta Q$$

$$= \sum kQ\,|Q| + \sum 2k\,|Q| \Delta Q = 0.$$

$$\text{Hence the correction to be applied} = -\frac{\sum kQ\,|Q|}{\sum 2k\,|Q|}. \qquad (12.26)$$

Correction is made in this way for all the loops taken repeatedly. It will give a new basis for the assumption of discharge in the pipes. The procedure is repeated until the error is small.

Reverting to our example:

For loop ABC

Pipe	k	Q	$kQ\|Q\|$	$2k\|Q\|$
AB	816.24	0.02	0.3265	32.65
BC	653	0.01	0.0653	13.06
CA	63.47	−0.08	−0.406	10.16
		Total	= −0.0142	55.87

$$\Delta Q_1 = -\frac{\sum kQ|Q|}{2\sum k|Q|} \cong 0.00025.$$

For loop BDC

Pipe	k	Q	$kQ\|Q\|$	$2k\|Q\|$
BD	169.4	0.03	0.1521	10.16
DC	193.7	−0.03	−0.1743	−11.62
CB	653	−0.01	−0.0653	13.06
		$\Sigma kQ\|Q\|$	−0.0835	34.84

$$\Delta Q_2 = -\frac{\sum kQ|Q|}{\sum 2k|Q|} = 0.0024.$$

The corrections are incorporated in the loop. For pipe BC common to loops, both corrections are applied taking into account the signs. Then the process is repeated.

Loop ABC

Pipe	k	Q	$kQ\|Q\|$	$2k\|Q\|$
AB	816.24	0.02025	0.3347	33.06
BC	653	0.00785	0.0402	10.25
CA	63.47	−0.07975	−0.403	10.12
		Total	−0.028	53.43

$\Delta Q_1 = 0.0005.$

For loop BDC

Pipe	k	Q	$kQ\|Q\|$	$2k\|Q\|$
BD	169.4	0.0324	0.1778	10.98
DC	193.7	−0.0276	−0.1476	10.69
CB	653	−0.00785	−0.040	10.25
			0.0098	31.92

$$\Delta Q_2 = -0.003.$$

Since the errors are negligible, the discharges in Fig. 12.6 (c) are assumed correct.

Example 12.13 A pipe of diameter 0.3 m has a height of roughness $k = 0.3$ mm. The head loss in a 1000 m length of pipe is limited to 10 m. If $\nu = 8.5 \times 10^{-7}$ m^2/s, find the maximum discharge through the pipe.

$$k = 0.3 \text{ mm} = 3 \times 10^{-4} \text{ m}; \quad d = 0.3 \text{ m}$$

$$\text{Re} = \text{Re}\sqrt{f}\left(2\log_{10}\frac{\text{Re}\sqrt{f}}{\frac{k}{d}.\text{Re}\sqrt{f} + 9.30} + 1.14\right) = 6.037 \times 10^5$$

$$\frac{vd}{v} = 6.037 \times 10^5; v = \frac{6.037 \times 10^5 \times v}{d} = 1.710 \text{ m/s}$$

$$Q = \frac{\pi d^2}{4} \times 1.710 = 0.1209 \text{ m}^3\text{/s. (Ans.)}$$

Example 12.14 In the previous example, if $Q = 0.121$ m^3/s; $s = 0.01$; $\nu = 8.5 \times 10^{-7}$ m^2/s, find the approximate diameter assuming that the pipe is smooth.

Assuming turbulent flow and using approximations,

$$\text{Re} = \left(\frac{226Q^3 s}{\nu^5}\right)^{0.208} = \left(\frac{226 \times 0.121^3 \times 0.01}{(8.5 \times 10^{-7})^5}\right)^{0.208} = 652700.$$

$$d = \frac{4Q}{\pi\nu\text{Re}} = \frac{4 \times 0.121}{\pi \times 8.5 \times 10^{-7} \times 6.527 \times 10^5} = 0.278 \text{ m. (Ans.)}$$

REVIEW QUESTIONS AND PROBLEMS

12.1 What is Darcy–Weisbach formula for friction through pipes? On what factors does the coefficient of friction depend?

12.2 Sketch Moody's diagram and show the variation of f with Reynold's number (i) in laminar range, (ii) for a turbulent flow in smooth pipes and (iii) for a fully established rough pipe flow.

12.3 What is the formula for the coefficient of friction in smooth pipes?

12.4 Give the transition formula for calculating f for pipes.

12.5 Express Darcy's formula for pipe friction in terms of discharge in SI units.

12.6 How is the friction loss estimated for flow through non-circular pipes?

12.7 What are the minor losses in pipes? Give the appropriate formulae to calculate the losses.

12.8 What is meant by an equivalent length of pipe?

12.9 Explain what is meant by a hydraulic gradient line?

12.10 What is a siphon? Explain its working.

12.11 Derive a condition for transmission of maximum power through a pipe line. What is the efficiency under such conditions?

12.12 How do you find the economic diameter of a pipe for power transmission?

12.13 Explain what is meant by a smooth pipe?

12.14 Explain briefly the procedure for analysing the flow through pipe networks.

12.15 The height of roughness elements in a concrete pipe of 30 cm diameter is 2 mm. What will be the value of f when discharging water at a rate of 0.3 m^3/s. Assume $\nu = 10^{-6}$ m^2/s [Hint: fully rough pipe, use the formula 12.12.]

12.16 A smooth pipe 10 cm in diameter and 30 m long is connected to a reservoir. If the head is 1.5 m, find the discharge. Assume $\nu = 10^{-6}\text{m}^2/\text{s}$. [Hint: Use equation [12.11] to find Re $\sqrt{f}$].

12.17 A rough pipe 10 cm in diameter and 30 m long is connected to a reservoir. If the head is 1.5 m and $k = 0.2$ mm, find the discharge. Assume $\nu = 10^{-6}\text{m}^2/\text{s}$.

12.18 A pipe 20 cm in diameter and 200 m long is connected to a tank. If the difference in the level between the water surface in the tank and outlet of the pipe is 8 m, find the discharge. Neglect the entry loss and assume $f = 0.02$.

12.19 A 30 m long pipe 20 cm in diameter has an orifice of 5 cm diameter fitted at the end. The pipe is connected to a tank and the outlet of the pipe is 6 m below the water level in the tank. Find the discharge taking into account all the losses. Assume $f = 0.02$.

12.20 A pipe 25 mm in diameter and 10 m long is connected to a tank. If the head is 2 m, find (i) the discharge and velocity through the pipe. (ii) If an orifice of diameter 10 mm is fixed at the end of the pipe, what will be the discharge and the velocity from the orifice? Assume $f = 0.02$.Consider all losses

12.21 Water is to be pumped up a hill through a pipe 30 cm in diameter and 300 m in length $f = 0.018$. If the level difference between the lower reservoir and the upper tank is 65 m, find the horse power required when the discharge is 0.05 m^3/s. Assume efficiency of 60%.

12.22 A tank is connected to a compound pipe, the initial 500 m of which is 40 cm in diameter and the rest 500 m is of 30 cm diameter. If the outlet of the pipe is 15 m below the water level in the tank, (i) find the discharge taking into account all the losses, assume f for the 40 cm diameter pipe as 0.018 and 0.02 for the 30 cm diameter pipe. (ii) Draw a sketch showing the hydraulic gradient. (iii) To what level will the water rise above the outlet at a distance of 400 m from the tank? Consider all losses.

12.23 Water is to be supplied to a town with a population of 2 00 000. If the consumption of water is 200 litres per head per day, find the suitable diameter of the pipe. The length of the pipe is 7.5 km and the discharge end is 40 m below the water level in a reservoir. $f = 0.02$. Assume half of the daily requirement to be delivered in 8 hours. Neglect minor losses.

12.24 A pipe 10 cm in diameter and 40 m long conveys water at a velocity of 2.4 m per second. If the central 20 m length of pipe is replaced by a 20 cm diameter pipe, find the saving in head lost for passing the same discharge. Take the changes of section as sudden and $f = 0.025$ for the 10 cm pipe and $f = 0.02$ for the 20 cm pipe. Consider all losses.

12.25 Water is taken from a tank which is at a height of 30 m from the discharge point by means of a long G.I. pipe. The total length of the pipe is 1200 m. The diameter of the pipe for the first 600 m is 40 cm and it is suddenly reduced to 20 cm for the rest of the pipe line. Water discharges freely at the end of the pipe. Find the discharge through the pipe in litres per second. Assume $f = 0.02$. Draw the hydraulic gradient line. Consider all losses.

12.26 A pipe 5 cm in diameter is 12 m long and the velocity in the pipe is 3 m/s. What loss of head will be saved if the central 4 m length of the pipe is replaced by a 7.5 cm diameter pipe, the change of sections being sudden. Assume discharge to remain the same and $f = 0.035$ for both the pipes.

12.27 Two reservoirs are connected by a compound pipe line consisting of 300 m of a 30 cm diameter pipe and 200 m of a 25 cm diameter pipe in series. If the difference in elevation between the water surfaces in the two reservoirs is 9 m, calculate the rate of flow through the pipes, taking into account all losses. $f = 0.02$ for all pipes.

12.28 Two pipes of diameter D and $2D$ are connected between two reservoirs in parallel. If the combined discharge is 5 m^3/s, and, if the friction factors are the same for both, find the discharge in each pipe.

12.29 A pipe is 0.6 m in diameter and 1.5 km long. In order to augment the discharge, another line of the same diameter is introduced parallel to the first in the second half of the length. Neglecting minor losses, find the increase in discharge if $f = 0.04$. The head at the inlet is 30 m.

12.30 A pipe of diameter 20 cm and length 2000 m connects two reservoirs having the difference of water levels as 20 m. If an additional pipe of diameter 20 cm and length 1200 m is attached parallel to the last 1200 m length of the existing pipe, find the increase in discharge. Take the friction factor as 0.04. Neglect minor losses.

12.31 For the distribution main of a town water supply, a 25 cm main is required. As pipes above 20 cm diameter are not available, it is decided to lay two parallel mains of the same diameter. Find the diameter of the parallel main.

12.32 Two reservoirs A and B are connected through a piping system consisting of one 60 cm pipe 500 m long branching into two pipes of 30 cm in diameter and 40 cm in diameter, each 700 m long. A pump situated at reservoir A pumps 0.40 m^3/s of water through the pipe system to the reservoir B, whose water surface elevation is 40 m above that of A. Assuming $f = 0.02$, determine the input power for the pump. Assume pump efficiency as 50%.

12.33 A pipe 10 cm in diameter and 400 m long has a nozzle fixed at the discharge end. The nozzle discharges at atmospheric pressure. If the pipe is horizontal and the head at the pipe inlet is 45 m, determine the maximum power that could be transmitted. What would be the corresponding size of the nozzle? Friction factor = 0.02.

12.34 A 50 cm diameter pipe conveys water for purposes of power generation. The pipe is 1 km long and has a head of 100 m at the outlet before the nozzle. Estimate the diameter of the nozzle for maximum transmission of power. What is the magnitude of maximum power? (assume $f = 0.019$)

12.35 Two reservoirs A and B whose surface level difference is 30 m (A is higher than B) are connected by a 60 cm diameter siphon pipe 3000 m long. The pipe line crosses a ridge whose summit is 9 m above level A and 300 m distance from it. Find the minimum depth below the ridge at which the pipe must be laid, if the absolute pressure in the pipe does not to fall below 2.5 metres of water and also calculate the discharge. $f = 0.08$. Consider all losses. Assume atmospheric pressure of 10.33 m of water.

12.36 Two reservoirs A and B have water levels 30 m and 18 m above the water level in tank C. Pipes AJ, BJ and JC interconnect them. The details of the pipes are as follows.

Pipe	Diameter	Length	f
AJ	30cm	600m	0.02
BJ	25cm	800m	0.024
CJ	30cm	500m	0.02

Find the discharge in each of the pipes.

12.37 A pipe network is given below. Estimate the flow in each of the pipes. Details of the pipes are given.

Pipe	Dia. (m)	Length (m)	f
AB	0.3	800	0.02
AC	0.25	550	0.024
BC	0.25	600	0.024
CD	0.3	800	0.02
BD	0.3	950	0.02

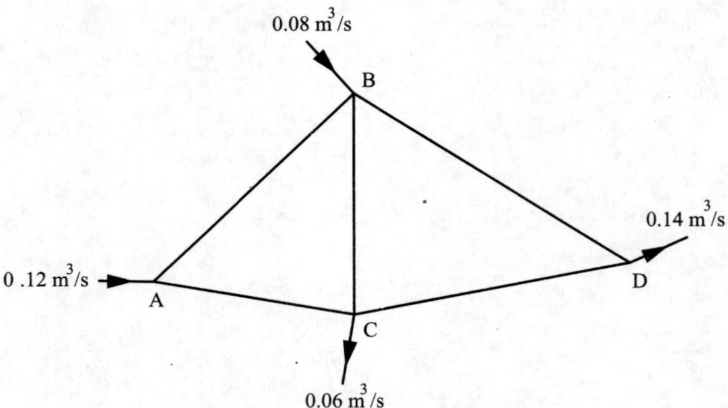

Problem 12.37

ANSWERS

12.15. f = 0.033; **12.16**. 0.0202 m^3/s; **12.17**. 0.0158 m^3/s; **12.18**. 0.088 m^3/s; **12.19**. 0.0213 m^3/s; **12.20**.(i) 9.98 $\times 10^{-4} m^3/s$; 2.032 m/s **12.20**.(ii) 4.46 $\times 10^{-4}$ m^3/s; **12.21**. 65.15 kW; **12.22**.(i) 0.1869 m^3/s; **12.22**.(ii) The drop in the heads are 0.0564, 2.536, 0.178, 11.873 and 0.356; **12.22**.(iii) 12.915 m; **12.23**. d = 0.684 m, so use a 70 cm dia. pipe; **12.24**. 1.108 m; **12.25**. 104.5 l/s; **12.26**. 0.745 m; **12.27**. 0.1246 m^3/s; **12.28**. Q_1 = 0.7510 m^3/s; Q_2 = 4.249 m^3/s; **12.29**. 0.1817 m^3/s; **12.30**. 0.01085 m^3/s; **12.31**. 0.1895 m; **12.32**. 391.4 kW; **12.33**. 0.281 m; **12.34**. 0.1693 m; 978.55 kW; **12.35**. 4.37 m; **12.36**. h_j = 16.15 m; Q_1 = 0.1862 m^3/s; Q_2 = 0.0337 m^3/s; Q_3 = 0.2179 m^3/s; **12.37**. The discharge in pipes AB, AC, BC, CD and BD are 0.055, 0.065, 0.050, 0.055 and 0.085 m^3/s respectively.

13 Viscous Flow—Laminar and Turbulent Flows

Laminar flow — Turbulent flow — Characteristics — Navier–Stokes equations — Flow between parallel plates — Poiseuille flow — Couette flow — Flow through circular pipes — Hagen–Poiseuille equation — Turbulence — Reynolds equations — Reynolds stresses, — Mixing length theory.

13.1 Introduction

All fluids are viscous and the flow of most common fluids like water, air and oils is governed by Newton's law of viscosity, $\tau = \mu \dfrac{du}{dy}$. Only in some flow problems can practical results be obtained by neglecting the effect of viscosity. The role of viscosity in fluid flow was investigated by Osborne Reynolds in 1883. He distinguished two types of flow—laminar and turbulent.

13.2 Reynolds Experiments

Osborne Reynolds conducted experiments on an apparatus similar to that shown in Fig. 13.1. It consisted of a tank, a long bell-mouthed transparent uniform pipe with a valve and a collecting tank to measure the discharge. A small vessel held above the tank contained a dye of density nearly equal to that of water. It is connected to a thin tube with a small nozzle to discharge the dye at the inlet of the tube. A valve controlled the flow of dye.

The large tank was first filled with water and the air was removed by opening the outlet valve. Then, water was allowed to rest for a long time without disturbance.

The experiment was done by slightly opening the outlet valve and letting the dye in. A straight thin streak of dye was seen along the centre line of the tube. This indicated laminar flow. The discharge from the pipe was measured by the collection of water for a known time. The velocity of flow in the tube v could be calculated by the formula

$$v = \frac{Q}{\pi d^2/4}, \text{ where } d \text{ is the diameter of the tube.}$$

The experiment is repeated for higher velocities of flow by opening the valve slowly and in each case allowing sufficient time to attain steady flow. It is found that at some particular velocity of flow through the pipe, the streak of dye begans to waver at the end and then the dye gets mixed with water. This indicated instability in the flow, the cessation of laminar flow and the establishment of turbulent flow.

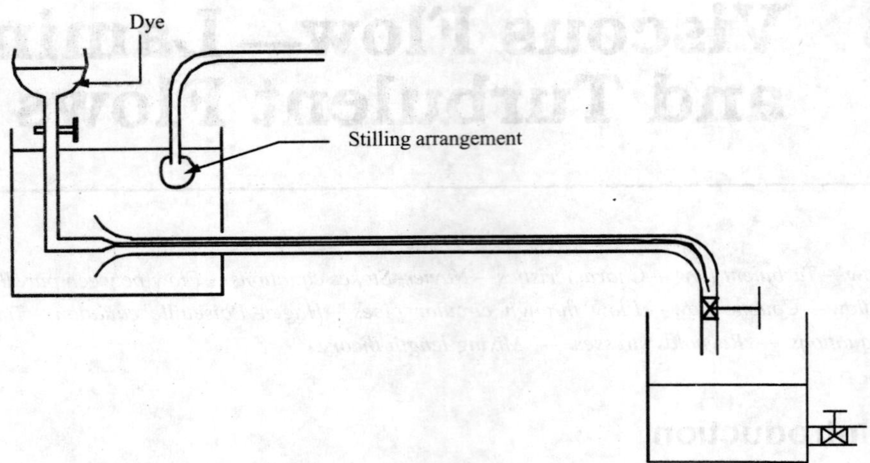

Fig. 13.1 *Reynold's experiment*

The magnitude of the non-dimensional parameter $\frac{\rho v d}{\mu}$, when turbulence sets in, has been found to depend on the conditions in which the experiment is conducted. This is called upper critical Reynolds number and could vary from about 2700 to 40000 or even more. When disturbances are less, a higher value of the Reynolds number can be obtained without the flow becoming turbulent.

When the discharge is reduced, it is found that the flow remains turbulent even below a Reynolds number of 2700. The laminar flow can be established, as indicated by the unbroken streak line of dye, only when the Reynolds number is below a value of nearly 2000. This value of Reynolds number, called the lower critical Reynolds number or generally critical Reynolds number, is of high practical value.

The critical Reynolds number is the Reynolds number of flow below which turbulent flow cannot be sustained. This is because at low Reynolds numbers, the viscous forces become very high and are able to dampen the disturbances, if any.

13.3 Description of Laminar and Turbulent Flows

Laminar flow can be defined as an orderly flow of fluid in layers. In case the velocities between adjacent layers are different, the momentum transfer between these layers occurs only due to the action of viscosity.

is a disorderly motion with the parameters of flow like velocity and pressure varying in a random manner in time and space, but for which statistical averages can be obtained (see Fig. 13.2). The average of velocity components at a point in three directions X, Y, Z may be $\overline{u}, \overline{v}$ and $\overline{w}$, whereas the actual components of velocity at any time can be $u = \overline{u} + u'$, $v = \overline{v} + v'$, $w = \overline{w} + w'$, where u', v' and w' are fluctuations of velocity.

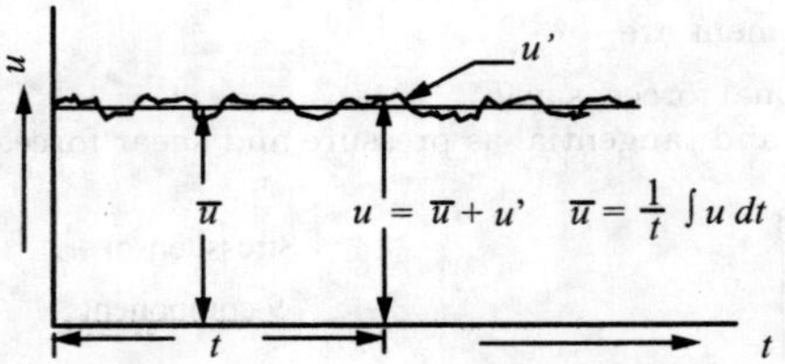

Fig. 13.2 *Turbulent flow*

The measure of the level of turbulence can be the quantities $\sqrt{u'^2}$, $\sqrt{v'^2}$ and $\sqrt{w'^2}$. When $\overline{u'} = \overline{v'} = \overline{w'} = 0$, the intensity of turbulence is defined as $\frac{1}{U}\sqrt{\left(\overline{u'^2} + \overline{v'^2} + \overline{w'^2}\right)}$, where U is the average velocity.

Turbulent flow can be envisaged as a superposition of eddies of different sizes on a main flow. In turbulent flow, apart from viscosity, there is an additional mechanism of momentum transfer between adjacent layers due to lumps of fluid transported across by the eddies. This causes more equalisation of velocity of flow in the cross-section. Also, since in eddies especially in small ones, the shearing action is more, there is the additional role of viscosity in energy transformation to heat.

13.4 The Navier–Stokes Equations§

The Navier–Stokes equations can be derived in a concise manner using Cartesian tensor notation.[9] Equations are obtained in all the three coordinate directions, $i = 1$, 2 and 3. By Einstein's summation convention, a repetition of an index indicates the sum of such terms in the three directions. Accordingly, $U_{ii} = U_{11} + U_{22} + U_{33}$.

The convectional acceleration term $u_j \dfrac{\partial u_i}{\partial x_j}$ has three components in the three directions:

In direction $X_1 : u_1 \dfrac{\partial u_1}{\partial x_1} + u_2 \dfrac{\partial u_1}{\partial x_2} + u_3 \dfrac{\partial u_1}{\partial x_3}$,

In direction $X_2 : u_1 \dfrac{\partial u_2}{\partial x_1} + u_2 \dfrac{\partial u_2}{\partial x_2} + u_3 \dfrac{\partial u_2}{\partial x_3}$ and

In direction $X_3 : u_1 \dfrac{\partial u_3}{\partial x_1} + u_2 \dfrac{\partial u_3}{\partial x_2} + u_3 \dfrac{\partial u_3}{\partial x_3}$.

The equations governing real fluids will include the viscous effects. The equations are known as the Navier–Stokes equations. The components of the equations can be acceleration terms. It can also be expressed as a balance between the rate of change of momentum transport and the force acting on a fluid element.

The acceleration components

$$a_i = \frac{\partial u_i}{\partial t} + u_j \frac{\partial u_i}{\partial x_j}. \tag{13.1}$$

§For advanced study

The forces acting on a fluid element are

(1) body forces—gravitational forces, say F_i
(2) surface forces—normal and tangential as pressure and shear forces.

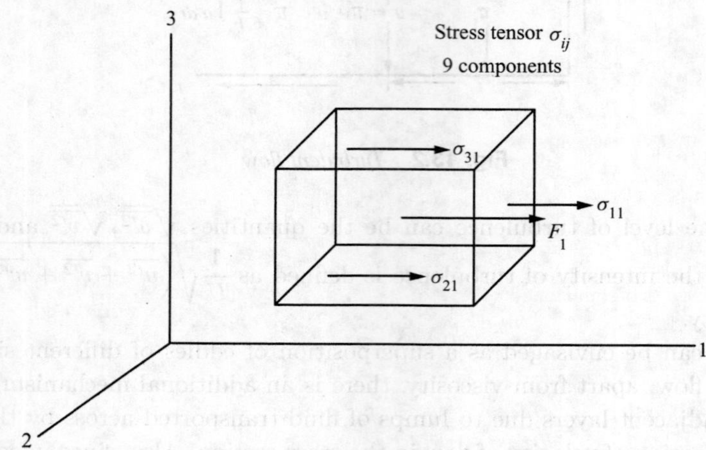

Fig. 13.3 *Meanings of stress components*

σ_{ij} is the stress acting on the surface element perpendicular to i in the direction j. The following net surface forces act in the direction 1,

$$\frac{\partial}{\partial x_1}\sigma_{11}dx_1.dx_2.dx_3;\ \frac{\partial}{\partial x_2}\sigma_{21}dx_2.dx_1.dx_3;\ \frac{\partial}{\partial x_3}\sigma_{31}dx_3.dx_1.dx_2.$$

By Newton's law,

$$\rho\frac{du_1}{dt} = \frac{\partial}{\partial x_1}\sigma_{11} + \frac{\partial}{\partial x_2}\sigma_{21} + \frac{\partial}{\partial x_3}\sigma_{31} + F_1$$

or

$$\rho\frac{du_i}{dt} = \frac{\partial}{\partial x_j}\sigma_{ji} + F_i. \tag{13.2}$$

σ_{ij} is a second order tensor with 9 components (Fig. 13.3). This stress can be divided into two parts: (1) average value of stress for all directions (hydrostatic pressure p); (2) a part in which the stresses are determined by other effects.

The average pressure $= -\frac{1}{3}\sigma_{ii}$. (Stoke's hypothesis)

$$\sigma_{ji} = -p\delta_{ji} + (\sigma_{ji} + p\delta_{ji}),$$

δ_{ji} is the Kronecker delta or unit second order tensor with the property $\delta_{ij} = 1$, when $i = j$ and $\delta_{ij} = 0$, when $i \neq j$.

The stresses σ_{ji} will cause deformation of the fluid elements. Since these deformations are determined by the spatial variations $\frac{\partial u_i}{\partial x_j}$, they also form a second order tensor, which can be divided into a symmetrical and an anti- symmetrical part.

$$\begin{aligned}\frac{\partial}{\partial x_j}u_i &= \frac{1}{2}\left(\frac{\partial u_i}{\partial x_j} + \frac{\partial u_j}{\partial x_i}\right) + \frac{1}{2}\left(\frac{\partial u_i}{\partial x_j} - \frac{\partial u_j}{\partial x_i}\right)\\ &= \frac{1}{2}D_{ij} + \frac{1}{2}\Omega_k\varepsilon_{ijk},\end{aligned}$$

where ε_{ijk} is the alternating, third order tensor with the property $\varepsilon_{123} = \varepsilon_{231} = \varepsilon_{312} = 1$, $\varepsilon_{321} = \varepsilon_{213} = \varepsilon_{132} = -1$ and all other values equal to zero.

D_{ij} is the deformation tensor,

Ω_k is the vector of the anti-symmetric tensor,

$\Omega_k \varepsilon_{ijk}$ is the tensor giving rotation and

$\Omega_k = \dfrac{\partial u_i}{\partial x_j}\varepsilon_{ijk}$ represents the vorticity.

For a Newtonian fluid,

$\sigma_{ji} = \mu D_{ji}$ for $j \neq i$ and $\sigma_{ji} + p\delta_{ji} = \mu D_{ji} + \lambda\Theta$ for $j = i$.

Combining the above two equations,

$$\sigma_{ji} + p\delta_{ji} = \mu D_{ji} + \lambda\Theta\delta_{ji},$$

where Θ is dilatation $= \dfrac{1}{2}D_{kk} = \dfrac{\partial u_k}{\partial x_k} = \dfrac{\partial u_1}{\partial x_1} + \dfrac{\partial u_2}{\partial x_2} + \dfrac{\partial u_3}{\partial x_3}$.

λ is the coefficient of bulk viscosity or second coefficient of viscosity.

When $i = j$,

$$\sigma_{ii} + p\delta_{ii} = \mu D_{ii} + \lambda\Theta\delta_{ii}.$$

i.e., $\sigma_{ii} + 3p = \mu D_{ii} + 3\lambda\Theta$.

Since $D_{ii} = 2\Theta$; and $\sigma_{ii} = -\dfrac{1}{3}p; 0 = (2\mu + 3\lambda)\Theta$.

Therefore, $\lambda = -\dfrac{2}{3}\mu$.

$$\sigma_{ji} = -p\delta_{ji} + \mu\left(D_{ji} - \frac{2}{3}\Theta\delta_{ji}\right).$$

Substituting in (13.2),

$$\rho\frac{du_i}{dt} = \frac{\partial}{\partial x_j}\left(-p\delta_{ji} + \mu D_{ji} - \frac{2}{3}\mu\Theta\delta_{ji}\right) + F_i \text{ or}$$

$$\rho\frac{du_i}{dt} = -\frac{\partial p}{\partial x_i} + \frac{\partial}{\partial x_j}\mu D_{ji} - \frac{2}{3}\frac{\partial}{\partial x_i}\mu\Theta + F_i.$$

$$\text{But } \frac{\partial}{\partial x_j}D_{ji} = \frac{\partial}{\partial x_j}\left(\frac{\partial u_j}{\partial x_i} + \frac{\partial u_i}{\partial x_j}\right) = \frac{\partial^2 u_i}{\partial x_j \partial x_j} + \frac{\partial^2 u_j}{\partial x_j \partial x_i}$$

$$= \frac{\partial^2 u_i}{\partial x_j \partial x_j} + \frac{\partial}{\partial x_i}\left(\frac{\partial u_j}{\partial x_j}\right) = \frac{\partial^2 u_i}{\partial x_j \partial x_j}\cdot\left(\frac{\partial u_j}{\partial x_j} = 0 \text{ for incompressible fluids}\right)$$

When μ is constant and the fluid is incompressible, $\Theta = 0$ and

$$\rho\frac{du_i}{dt} = -\frac{\partial p}{\partial x_i} + \mu\frac{\partial^2 u_i}{\partial x_j \partial x_j} + F_i.$$

13.5 The Navier–Stokes Equations in the Three Coordinate Directions

The Navier–Stokes equations for incompressible fluids in rectangular coordinates can be written as

$$\frac{\partial u}{\partial t}+u\frac{\partial u}{\partial x}+v\frac{\partial u}{\partial y}+w\frac{\partial u}{\partial z}$$

$$=-\frac{1}{\rho}\frac{\partial p}{\partial x}+\frac{\mu}{\rho}\left(\frac{\partial^2 u}{\partial x^2}+\frac{\partial^2 u}{\partial y^2}+\frac{\partial^2 u}{\partial z^2}\right)+g_x \text{ in the } X \text{ direction.} \tag{13.4}$$

Similarly, one can write the equations in the Y and Z directions as

$$\frac{\partial u}{\partial t}+u\frac{\partial v}{\partial x}+v\frac{\partial v}{\partial y}+w\frac{\partial v}{\partial z}=-\frac{1}{\rho}\frac{\partial p}{\partial y}+\frac{\mu}{\rho}\left(\frac{\partial^2 v}{\partial x^2}+\frac{\partial^2 v}{\partial y^2}+\frac{\partial^2 v}{\partial z^2}\right)+g_y \tag{13.5}$$

and

$$\frac{\partial w}{\partial t}+u\frac{\partial w}{\partial x}+v\frac{\partial w}{\partial y}+w\frac{\partial w}{\partial z}=-\frac{1}{\rho}\frac{\partial p}{\partial z}+\frac{\mu}{\rho}\left(\frac{\partial^2 w}{\partial x^2}+\frac{\partial^2 w}{\partial y^2}+\frac{\partial^2 w}{\partial z^2}\right)+g_z. \tag{13.6}$$

In addition, the continuity equation

$$\frac{\partial u}{\partial x}+\frac{\partial v}{\partial y}+\frac{\partial w}{\partial z}=0, \tag{13.7}$$

is also applicable.

In many practical cases, only a few of the components of the above equations are important and solutions are obtained by solving them along with the continuity equation for the given boundary conditions of the problem.

13.6 Laminar Flow Between Parallel Plates

This type of laminar flow occurs through narrow ducts of machine parts. When the parallel plates are fixed, the flow through the gap between them is termed as plane Poiseuille flow . When the plates move parallel to each other, with a small gap of fluid between them, it is termed as plane Couette flow.

In such flows, the inertial forces and consequent accelerations $u\frac{du}{dx}+v\frac{du}{dy}+w\frac{du}{dz}$ are negligible and for a steady uniform flow

$$\frac{1}{\rho}\frac{\partial p}{\partial x}=\frac{\mu}{\rho}\frac{\partial^2 u}{\partial y^2} \quad or \quad \frac{dp}{dx}=\mu\frac{d^2 u}{dy^2}. \tag{13.8}$$

The above result can also be obtained from the first principle as follows:

Consider a flow of fluid from left to right between two parallel plates as in Fig. 13.4. Considering an element of length Δx, thickness Δy and width Δz, the net shear force

$$= (\tau + \frac{d\tau}{dy}\Delta y)\Delta x\Delta z - \tau\Delta x\Delta z = \frac{d\tau}{dy}\Delta x\Delta y\Delta z. \tag{A}$$

In an uniform flow, it is balanced by the net pressure force

$$= (p + \frac{dp}{dx}\Delta x)\Delta y\Delta z - p\Delta y\Delta z = \frac{dp}{dx}\Delta x\Delta y\Delta z. \tag{B}$$

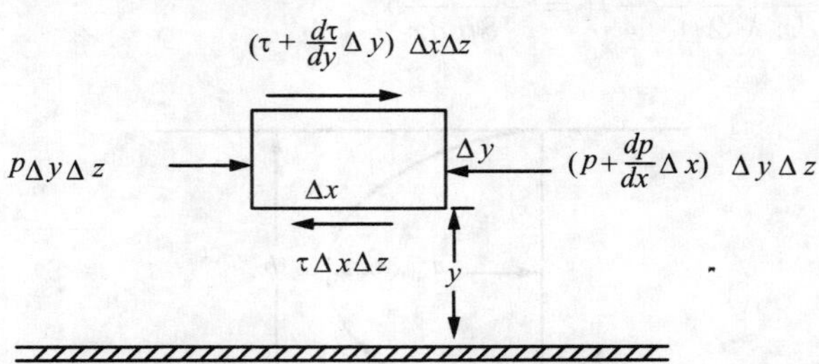

Fig. 13.4 *Laminar flow between two parallel plates*

Equating (A) and (B),

$$\frac{dp}{dx} = \frac{d\tau}{dy} = \mu\frac{d^2u}{dy^2}. \tag{13.9}$$

Since $\frac{dp}{dx}$ is constant, τ varies linearly with y.

13.6.1 Plane Poiseuille flow

In a plane Poiseuille flow, the equation $\frac{dp}{dx} = \mu\frac{d^2u}{dy^2}$, has the boundary condition $y = 0$, $u = 0$; and $y = b$, $u = 0$.

Rewriting equation (13.8) as $\frac{d^2u}{dy^2} = \frac{1}{\mu}\frac{dp}{dx}$ and integrating twice,

$$u = \frac{1}{\mu}\frac{dp}{dx}\frac{y^2}{2} + C_1y + C_2.$$

$u = 0$ when $y = 0$. Hence $C_2 = 0$. Therefore $u = \frac{1}{\mu}\frac{dp}{dx}\frac{y^2}{2} + C_1y.$

$u = 0$ when $y = b; 0 = \frac{1}{\mu}\frac{dp}{dx}\frac{b^2}{2} + C_1 b$ or, $C_1 = -\frac{1}{\mu}\frac{dp}{dx}\frac{b}{2}$, hence

$$u = \frac{1}{\mu}\frac{dp}{dx}\left(\frac{y^2}{2} - \frac{b}{2}y\right) \text{ or } u = -\frac{1}{2\mu}\frac{dp}{dx}\left(by - y^2\right), \tag{13.10}$$

which is a parabolic distribution (Fig. 13.5).

u is maximum when $(by - y^2)$ is maximum. i.e., $\frac{d}{dy}(by - y^2)$ is zero. Or,

$b - 2y = 0$ or $y = b/2$.

$$\text{So, } u_{\max} = -\frac{1}{2\mu}\frac{dp}{dx}\left(\frac{b^2}{2} - \frac{b^2}{4}\right) = -\frac{1}{8\mu}\frac{dp}{dx}b^2. \tag{13.11}$$

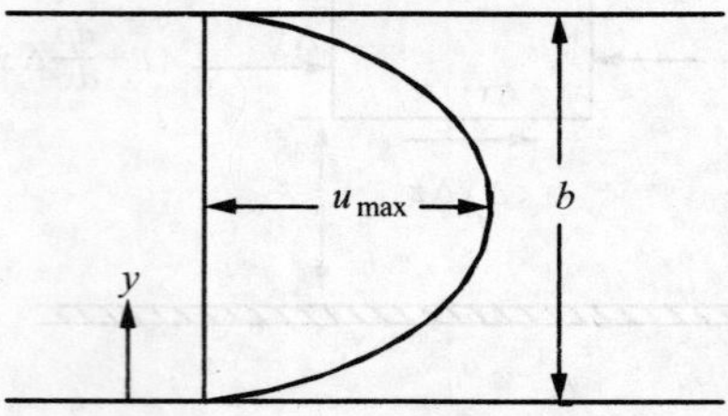

Fig. 13.5 *Plane Poiseuille flow*

Since the velocity distribution is parabolic, the average velocity is 2/3 rd of the maximum velocity.

$$V = \frac{2}{3}\left(\frac{1}{8\mu}\frac{dp}{dx}b^2\right) = -\frac{1}{12\mu}\frac{dp}{dx}b^2.$$

Hence

$$-\frac{dp}{dx} = \frac{p_1 - p_2}{L} = \frac{12\mu V}{b^2};\, H_L \text{ or } \frac{p_1 - p_2}{\gamma} = \frac{12\mu V L}{\gamma b^2}. \tag{13.12}$$

The shear stress, $\tau = \mu\frac{du}{dy} = \mu\frac{1}{-2\mu}\frac{dp}{dx}(b - 2y)$

or

$$\tau = -\frac{1}{2}\frac{dp}{dx}(b - 2y). \tag{13.13}$$

It is maximum when $y = 0$. So,

$$\tau_{\max} = -\frac{1}{2}\frac{dp}{dx}b. \tag{13.14}$$

Special case In case of laminar flow of a liquid on a uniform slope, the equation governing the flow is the same but the boundary conditions will be $u = 0$, $y = 0$; $u = u_{\max}$. When $y = Y$, the depth of flow, the solution can be obtained by substituting $b/2$ by Y.

So, $H_L = \dfrac{3\mu VL}{\gamma y^2}$. Since $V = \dfrac{q}{Y}$,

$$S = \frac{H_L}{L} = \frac{3\mu q}{\gamma Y^3} \text{ or, } q = \frac{\gamma Y^3 S}{3\mu}. \tag{13.15}$$

13.6.2 The plane Couette fow

When one of the parallel plates is moving with respect to the other, it affects the condition of fluid between them. The fluid at the boundary of the plates will have the same velocity as that of the plates.

Let the upper plate move with a velocity U (Fig. 13.6). The equation

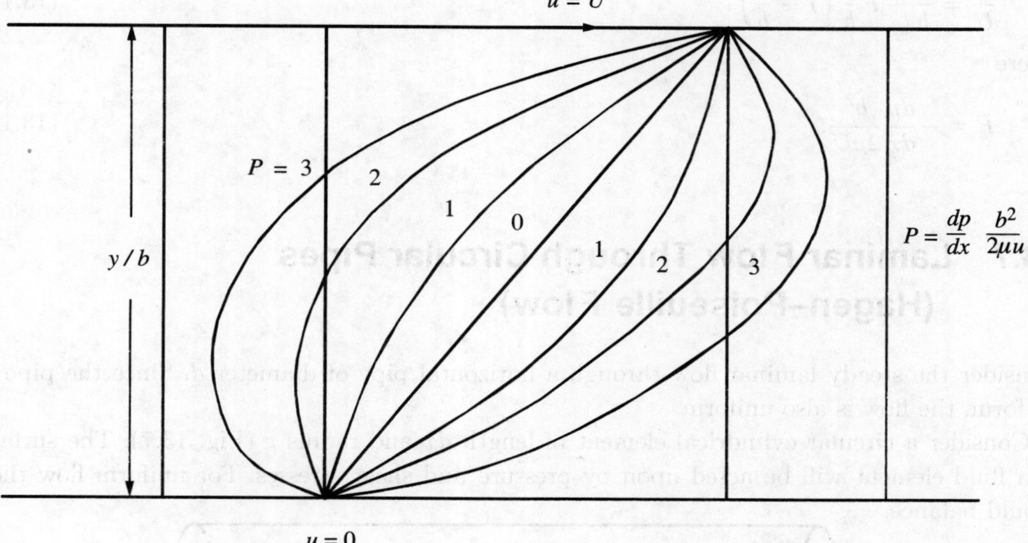

Fig. 13.6 *Velocity distribution in a Couette flow*

$$\frac{d^2u}{dy^2} = \frac{1}{\mu}\frac{dp}{dx}$$

has to be solved with the boundary conditions $y = 0$, $u = 0$; $y = b$, $u = U$.

Integrating the above equation twice,

$$u = \frac{1}{\mu}\frac{dp}{dx}\frac{y^2}{2} + C_1 y + C_2.$$

When $y = 0$, $u = 0$ and hence $C_2 = 0$; therefore,

$$u = \frac{1}{\mu}\frac{dp}{dx}\frac{y^2}{2} + C_1 y.$$

When $y = b$, $u = U$.

$$U = \frac{1}{\mu}\frac{dp}{dx}\frac{b^2}{2} + C_1 b, \text{ so, } C_1 = \frac{U}{b} - \frac{1}{2\mu}\frac{dp}{dx}b.$$

Hence the solution is

$$u = \frac{U}{b}y - \frac{1}{2\mu}\frac{dp}{dx}\left(by - y^2\right) \text{ or, } \frac{u}{U} = \frac{y}{b} - \frac{b^2}{2\mu U}\frac{dp}{dx}\left(\frac{y}{b} - \frac{y^2}{b^2}\right) \text{ or}$$

$$\frac{u}{U} = \frac{y}{b} + P\frac{y}{b}\left(1 - \frac{y}{b}\right), \tag{13.16}$$

where

$$P = -\frac{dp}{dx}\frac{b^2}{2\mu U}. \tag{13.17}$$

13.7 Laminar Flow Through Circular Pipes (Hagen–Poiseuille Flow)

Consider the steady laminar flow through a horizontal pipe of diameter d. Since the pipe is uniform, the flow is also uniform.

Consider a circular cylindrical element of length dx and radius r (Fig. 13.7). The surface of a fluid element will be acted upon by pressure and shear stresses. For uniform flow they should balance.

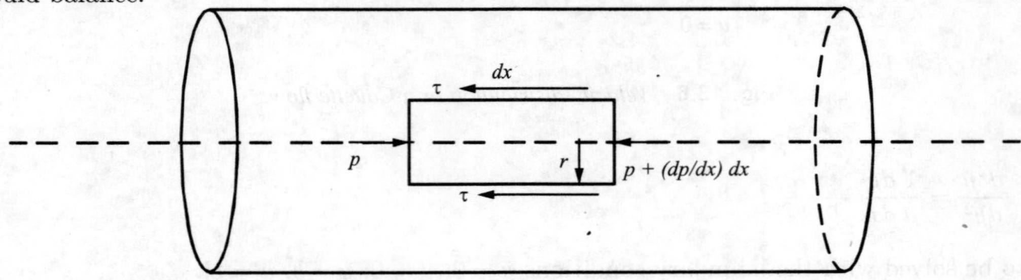

Fig. 13.7 *Laminar flow through pipes*

$$\pi r^2 p - \pi r^2 \left(p + \frac{\partial p}{\partial x} dx\right) = \tau 2\pi r dx,$$

hence $\tau = -\frac{dp}{dx}\frac{r}{2}$, which shows that the shear stress varies linearly with maximum value at the boundary and zero at the centre.

$$\tau = -\frac{dp}{dx}\frac{r}{2} = -\mu\frac{du}{dr},$$

hence $\frac{du}{dr} = \frac{1}{\mu}\frac{dp}{dx}\frac{r}{2}$, which gives the solution

$$u = \frac{1}{4\mu}\left(\frac{dp}{dx}\right) r^2 + c.$$

Substituting the boundary condition $u = 0$ when $r = R$,

$$u = -\frac{1}{4\mu}\left(\frac{dp}{dx}\right)(R^2 - r^2).$$

The maximum velocity will be obtained when $r = 0$, $u_{\max} = -\frac{1}{4\mu}\left(\frac{dp}{dx}\right) R^2$.

The discharge $Q = \int U 2\pi r dr = \int_0^R -\frac{1}{4\mu}\left(\frac{dp}{dx}\right)(R^2 - r^2) 2\pi r dr = \frac{\pi}{8\mu}\left(-\frac{dp}{dx}\right) R^4$.

The average velocity

$$U = \frac{Q}{\pi R^2} = \frac{1}{8\mu}\left(-\frac{dp}{dx}\right) R^2,$$

which can be seen to be $(1/2)\ u_{\max}$.

From the above equation

$$\frac{dp}{dx} = -\frac{8\mu U}{R^2} = -\frac{32\mu U}{D^2}.$$

Integrating between any two sections (1) and (2) at a distance L apart, where pressures are p_1 and p_2,

$$\int_{p_1}^{p_2} dp = -\frac{32\mu U}{D^2}\int_0^L dx \text{ or } p_1 - p_2 = \frac{32\mu U L}{D^2}. \tag{13.18}$$

Since the pipe is horizontal, $z_1 = z_2$ and the piezometric head loss due to friction H_f is given by

$$H_f = \left(\frac{p_1}{\gamma} + z_1\right) - \left(\frac{p_2}{\gamma} + z_2\right) = \frac{p_1 - p_2}{\gamma} = \frac{32\mu UL}{\gamma D^2}, \tag{13.19}$$

where U is the average velocity of flow. The expression is known as the Hagen–Poiseuille formula.

In case of a pipe inclined at an angle θ, when we analyze the forces on the cylindrical fluid element, the weight of the fluid element $(\pi r^2 dx)\gamma \sin\theta$, will be balanced by the increased pressure at the bottom face, namely, $\pi r^2 \gamma dz$, since $dz = dx \sin\theta$. Hence the loss in head in case of an inclined pipe will also be $H_f = \dfrac{32\mu UL}{\gamma D^2}$.

13.8 Laminar Flow Through Pipes of Non-circular Sections

The assumption of an equivalent diameter equal to four times the hydraulic mean radius for calculating resistance to flow through non-circular cross-sections can give acceptably good results for turbulent flow. But in case of laminar flow the error can be considerable.

13.8.1 Laminar flow through rectangular ducts

The equation governing laminar flow through rectangular ducts of width b and height c is given[39] as

$$Q = \frac{4}{-3\mu}\frac{dp}{dx} bc^3 \left[1 - \frac{6c}{b}\sum_{k=1}^{\infty} \frac{\tanh(\alpha_k b/c)}{\alpha_k^5}\right], \tag{13.20}$$

where

$$\alpha_k = (2k-1)\frac{\pi}{2}, k = 1, 2 \ldots \text{ etc.} \tag{13.21}$$

A simplified working formula is given by N.N. Pillai as

$$H_f = \frac{\beta\mu QL}{\gamma A^2}, \tag{13.22}$$

$$\text{where } \beta = 3.12\frac{P^2}{A} - 21.25, \tag{13.23}$$

P is the wetted perimeter and A is the area of cross-section. The above equation is found to give results very close to theoretical values.

13.8.2 Laminar flow through annular space between circular pipes

For a fully developed flow in the annular space between a concentric pipe of radius R and a cylinder inside of radius $r = kR$, the expression for discharge is given as[39].

$$Q = \frac{-\pi}{8\mu}\frac{dp}{dz}R^4\phi(k), \tag{13.24}$$

$$\text{where } \phi(k) = \left[(1-k^4) - \frac{\left(1-k^2\right)^2}{\ln(1/k)}\right]. \tag{13.25}$$

The head loss can be obtained by the formula as

$$H_f = \frac{8\mu QL}{\pi\gamma R^4\phi(k)}. \tag{13.26}$$

13.9 Eddy Viscosity

In turbulent flows there is a large amount of momentum transfer between adjacent layers due to lumps of fluid moving across with the help of eddies. This is in addition to the momentum change due to viscous shear.

The rate of change of momentum transferred is equivalent to the shear force being applied between the layers. The apparent shear force may be many times greater than the viscous shear in turbulent flow.

In analogy with the viscous shear, Boussinesq assumed an additional shear of

$$\eta\frac{du}{dy}, \text{ where } \eta = \rho\varepsilon, \tag{13.27}$$

is termed as the coefficient of eddy viscosity. Thus, total shear stress

$$\tau = \mu\frac{du}{dy} + \eta\frac{du}{dy}. \tag{13.28}$$

In turbulent flow η may be many times μ. It may be noted that ε is a property of the local characteristics of flow.

13.10 Reynolds Equation and Reynolds Stresses¶

The Reynolds equation is obtained when considering the force momentum balance for a turbulent flow. The Navier–Stokes equation for steady incompressible flow in the X direction is written as

¶for advanced study

$$\rho\left[u\frac{\partial u}{\partial x}+v\frac{\partial u}{\partial y}+w\frac{\partial u}{\partial z}\right]=-\frac{\partial p}{\partial x}+\mu\left[\frac{\partial^2 u}{\partial x^2}+\frac{\partial^2 u}{\partial y^2}+\frac{\partial^2 u}{\partial z^2}\right]+\rho g_x \tag{13.29}$$

In tensor notation, for the three directions,

$$\rho u_j\frac{\partial u_i}{\partial x_j}=-\frac{\partial p}{\partial x_i}+\mu\frac{\partial^2}{\partial x_j}\frac{u_i}{\partial x_j}+\rho g_i \quad i=1,2,3 \text{ and } j=1,2,3 \tag{13.30}$$

and the continuity equation is given by $\dfrac{\partial u_j}{\partial x_j}=0$

Using the continuity equations,

$$\rho u_j\frac{\partial u_i}{\partial x_j}=\rho u_j\frac{\partial u_i}{\partial x_j}+\rho u_i\frac{\partial u_j}{\partial x_j}=\rho\frac{\partial u_i u_j}{\partial x} \tag{13.31}$$

where u is the instantaneous velocity, p is the instantaneous pressure and g_i is the component of gravitational acceleration in the i direction. The equation gives the force–momentum balance equation for a unit volume of fluid.

Since $\dfrac{\partial u_j}{\partial x_j}=0$, $\rho u_j\dfrac{\partial u_i}{\partial x_j}$ can be written as $\rho u_j\dfrac{\partial u_i}{\partial x_j}+\rho\dfrac{\partial u_j}{\partial x_j}=\rho\dfrac{\partial(u_i u_j)}{\partial x_j}$

In turbulent flow,

$$u_i=\bar{u}_i+u_i',\, i=1.2.3,\ldots \tag{13.32}$$

where u is the instantaneous velocity, $\bar{u}_i$ is the average velocity in a time period T and u_i' is the turbulent fluctuation of velocity at the instant. Also

$$p=\bar{p}+p' \tag{13.33}$$

The continuity equations can be written as $\dfrac{\partial \bar{u}_j}{\partial x_j}=0$ and $\dfrac{\partial u_j'}{\partial x_j}=0$

The values of $\bar{u}_i'$ and $\bar{p}'$ and of terms like $\bar{u}_i\bar{u}_i'$ are zero.

Using (13.31), (13.32) and (13.33), equation (13.30) and after averaging for a time T

$$\rho\frac{\partial \bar{u}_i\bar{u}_j}{\partial x_j}+\rho\frac{\partial \overline{u_i'u'}}{\partial x_j}=-\frac{\partial \bar{p}}{\partial x_i}+\mu\frac{\partial^2 \bar{u}_i}{\partial x_j\partial x_j}+\rho g_i \tag{13.34}$$

$$\rho\frac{\partial \bar{u}_i\bar{u}_j}{\partial x_j}=\frac{\partial \bar{\sigma}_{ij}}{\partial x_j}+\rho g_i \tag{13.35}$$

where

$$\sigma_{ij}=-\bar{p}\delta_{ij}+\mu\frac{\partial \bar{u}_i}{\partial x_j}-\rho\overline{u_i'u_j'},\, i=1,2,3 \text{ and } j=1,2,3 \tag{13.36}$$

The terms $-\rho\overline{u_i'u_j'}$ are called Reynolds stresses. It is a symmetrical tensor with the diagonals giving the normal components and the others the tangential components. Since a positive value of u is normally associated with a negative value of v and vice versa, the terms $-\rho\overline{\mu_i' u_j'}$ are positive for $i \neq j$. In turbulent flow, the term can be many times the shear stress due to the mean velocity gradient and is the cause of high energy dissipation

The components of $-\rho\overline{u_i' u_j'}$ are $\begin{bmatrix} -\rho\overline{(u')^2} & -\rho\overline{u'v'} & -\rho\overline{u'w'} \\ -\rho\overline{u'v'} & -\rho\overline{(v')^2} & -\rho\overline{v'w'} \\ -\rho\overline{u'w'} & -\rho\overline{v'w'} & -\rho\overline{(w')^2} \end{bmatrix}$ (13.37)

where u', v', and w' are the turbulent velocity components in the three directions X, Y and Z.

13.11 Reynolds Stresses—Prandtl's Mixing Length Theory

In a one-dimensional turbulent flow, consider a fluid layer at a height y_1, having an area $dA = dxdz$.

Let the velocity be u (Fig. 13.8). $u = \overline{u} + u'$ so that $\overline{u}' = 0$; and $v = v'$ and $\overline{v} = 0$. Since there is fluctuation of velocity in the y direction, v' lumps of fluid of mass $\rho v' dA$ will cross the area at time t. But since $\overline{v'} = 0$ for a sufficiently long time T, the flux of fluid crossing

$$dA = \frac{1}{T}\int_0^T \rho v' dA dt = 0.$$

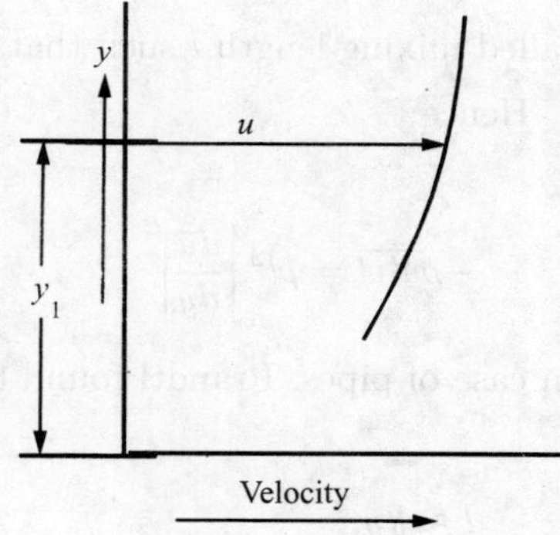

Fig. 13.8 *Vertical turbulent velocity profile*

But fluctuation of the normal velocity v', which is positive will cause a slowly moving lump of fluid to reach the upper layers across the area dA causing the momentum transport rate in the upper layers to decrease. If the fluctuation of the normal velocity v' is negative, the lump of fluids moving faster will cross the area downwards and increase the momentum transport rate in the lower layers.

$$\text{The net rate of transfer of momentum} = \frac{1}{T}\int_0^T \rho v' u dA dt = \frac{1}{T}\int_0^T \rho v'(\bar{u} + u') dA dt$$

$$= \rho\overline{u'v'} dA, \text{ because } \int_0^T \overline{u} v' dt = 0.$$

Hence for both cases, $v'(+\text{ ve})$ and $v'(-\text{ ve})$, tend to reduce the difference in momentum transport rate in layers below and above dA.

In analogy with the laminar flow where exchange of momentum between layers of fluid occurs due to dynamic viscosity and gives rise to shear force τ in turbulent flow, additional shear force is produced due to the rate of exchange of momentum $\rho\overline{u'v'}dA$. A positive value of u' is usually associated with a negative value of v' and hence

$$\tau = \frac{-\rho\overline{u'v'}dA}{dA} = -\rho\overline{u'v'}. \tag{13.38}$$

This is termed as Reynolds stress. Total shear stress on area AB $= \mu\dfrac{du}{dy} - \rho\overline{u'v'}$. In a turbulent flow, the turbulent shear stress is normally many times greater than that due to dynamic viscosity.

Measurement of the term $-\rho\overline{u'v'}$ requires instruments like hot wire anemometers with specially calibrated probes.

Prandtl hypothesized that u' is proportional to $\dfrac{d\bar{u}}{dy}$ and there is some characteristic length called mixing length l such that $u' \propto l\dfrac{d\bar{u}}{dy}$. v' is proportional to $\dfrac{d\bar{u}}{dy}$.

Hence

$$-\rho\overline{u'v'} = \rho l^2 \left|\frac{d\bar{u}}{dy}\right|^2. \tag{13.39}$$

In case of pipes, Prandtl found that

$$l \approx ky, \tag{13.40}$$

where k is a constant nearly equal to 0.4 and y is the distance from the boundary.

Prandtl's mixing length theory is an attempt to relate turbulent characteristics to mean flow characteristics. Even though they are based on rough assumptions on the structure of turbulence, they have been useful due to their simplicity in solving very complex problems.

Example 13.1 An oil is made to flow through the space between two parallel plates having a gap of 3 mm between them. If the width and the length of the plates are 10 cm and 40 cm, and the pressure head difference at the inlet and outlet is 1.8 m. Find the discharge. Assume $\mu = 3$ poise and $\rho = 810\ \text{kg/m}^3$.

Given: $h_L = 1.8$ m; $\mu = 3$ poise $= 0.3$ Pa s; $\rho = 810\ \text{kg/m}^3$.

$L = 40$ cm $= 0.4$ m.

$\gamma = 810 \times 9.81\ \text{N/m}^3$.

$b = 3$ mm $= 3 \times 10^{-3}$ m.

$$h_L = \frac{12\mu VL}{\gamma b^2}.$$

$$V = \frac{h_L \gamma b^2}{12\mu L} = \frac{18 \times 810 \times 9.81 \times 3 \times 10^{-3} \times 3 \times 10^{-3}}{12 \times 0.3 \times 0.4} = 8.94 \times 10^{-3} \text{ m/s.}$$

$$\begin{aligned} \text{Hence, } q = V \times a &= 8.94 \times 10^{-2} \times 0.1 \times 3 \times 10^{-3} \\ &= 2.68 \times 10^{-5} \text{ m}^3\text{/s. (Ans.)} \end{aligned}$$

Example. 13.2 Oil of specific gravity 0.90 and dynamic viscosity 1.2 poise has to be pumped through a smooth tube of length 15 m. If the head loss should not exceed 1.4 m and the discharge is 10 cm^3/s, what should the diameter of the tube be?

$$h_L = \frac{32\mu VL}{\gamma d^2} = \frac{32\mu L}{\gamma d^2} \times \frac{Q}{\frac{\pi d^2}{4}} = \frac{128\mu LQ}{\pi\gamma d^4}.$$

$$Q = 10 \text{ cm}^3\text{/s} = 10 \times 10^{-6} \text{ m}^3\text{/s}; S = 0.9$$

$\gamma = 0.9 \times 1000 \times 9.81 \text{ N/m}^3 = 8828 \text{ N/m}^3$; $\mu = 1.2 \text{ poise} = 0.12$ Pa s; $L = 15$ m; $h_L =$ 1.4 m.

$$d^4 = \frac{128\mu LQ}{h_L \pi \gamma} = \frac{128 \times 0.120 \times 15 \times 10 \times 10^{-6}}{1.4 \times \pi \times 8829} = 5.934 \times 10^{-8} \text{ m}^4.$$

$$d = 0.0156 \text{ m} = 1.56 \text{ cm (Ans.)}$$

Example 13.3 A rectangular duct 20 cm × 4 cm and 3 m long conveys fuel oil of specific gravity 0.94 and viscosity 10.2 poise. If the head loss is limited to 0.8 m, (i) find the discharge using the equivalent diameter, (ii) find the discharge assuming a two-dimensional flow and (iii) find the discharge taking into account the shape of the duct.

$$H_f = 0.8 \text{ m}; \ L = 3 \text{ m}; \ \mu = 10.2 \text{ Poise} = 1.02 \text{ Pa s};$$

$$h = 20 \text{ cm} = 0.2 \text{ m}; \ b = 4 \text{ cm} = 0.04 \text{ m}.$$

$$P = 2(0.2 + 0.04) = 0.48 \text{ m}; \ A = 0.2 \times 0.04 = 0.008 \text{ m}^2.$$

Assume laminar flow.

$$\text{(i) } R = \frac{A}{P} = \frac{0.008}{0.48} = 0.0167 \text{ m}.$$

$$d_e = 4R = 4 \times 0.0167 = 0.0668 \text{ m}.$$

$$H_f = \frac{32\mu VL}{\gamma d_e^2}; V = \frac{H_f \gamma d_e^2}{32\mu L}.$$

$$V = \frac{0.8 \times 0.94 \times 9810 \times 0.0668^2}{32 \times 1.02 \times 3} = 0.336 \text{ m/s.}$$

$$Q = 0.336 \times 0.008 = 0.00269 \text{ m}^3/\text{s}$$

(ii) $H_f = \dfrac{12\mu VL}{\gamma b^2}; V = \dfrac{H_f \gamma b^2}{12\mu L} = \dfrac{0.8 \times 0.94 \times 9810 \times 0.04^2}{12 \times 1.02 \times 3} = 0.321 \text{ m/s.}$

$$Q = 0.321 \times 0.008 = 0.00257 \text{ m}^3/\text{s.}$$

(iii) $\dfrac{P^2}{A} = \dfrac{0.48^2}{0.008} = 28.8.$

$$\beta = 3.12\frac{P^2}{A} - 21.25 = 68.606.$$

$$H_f = \frac{\beta\mu QL}{\gamma A^2}; Q = \frac{H_f \gamma A^2}{\beta \mu L} = \frac{0.8 \times 0.94 \times 9810 \times 0.008^2}{68.606 \times 1.02 \times 3}$$

$$= 0.00225 \text{ m}^3/\text{s. (Ans.)}$$

REVIEW QUESTIONS AND PROBLEMS

13.1 Describe Reynold's experiments and explain what are upper and lower critical numbers.

13.2 Distinguish between laminar and turbulent flow. What are the mechanisms of transport of momentum between adjacent layers in both these cases?

13.3 What is intensity of turbulence?

13.4 What are the components of stress tensor?

13.5 What are the components of deformation tensor?

13.6 Explain the relationship $\sigma_{ji} + \rho\delta_{ji} = \mu D_{ji} + \lambda\theta\delta_{ji}$ between the stress tensor and the deformation tensor.

13.7 Derive the Navier–Stokes equation.

13.8 Write the Navier–Stokes equation in the three coordinate directions.

13.9 Derive the equation for a plane Poiseuille flow between parallel plates.

13.10 What is a plane Couette flow? Derive the underlying equation.

13.11 Derive the Hagen–Poiseuille equation for flow through circular pipes.

13.12 Give an equation for laminar flow through rectangular ducts.

13.13 What is eddy viscosity? Write the equation for shear stress in turbulent flow in terms of velocity gradient.

13.14 Show that in a turbulent flow, shear stresses include Reynold's stress terms like $-\rho u'v'$.

13.15 Explain Prandtl's mixing length hypothesis.

13.16 A pipe 2.5 cm in diameter has a flow of oil (sp. gr. = 0.85 and μ = 2 poise). If the discharge is 0.8 l/s, find the Reynolds number.

13.17 Two parallel plates are held 91 mm apart. Oil of dynamic viscosity 1.5 poise flows at a velocity of 8 cm/s between the plates. Assume ρ = 850 kg/m³. Considering the flow to be two-dimensional, find (i) the head loss in 1 m, (ii) the shear stress at the boundary and (iii) the shear stress 1 mm from the boundary.

13.18 A liquid of kinematic viscosity 0.8 stokes flows down a slope of 10° in a chemical process. Find the uniform depth of flow if the discharge is 9 l/s/m. [Hint: Use formula 13.15]

13.19 In a machine, a lower plate is stationary and an upper parallel plate 5 mm away (separated by lubricating oil) is moving at 0.8 m/s in a parallel direction. The pressure drop in the direction of the movement of plate is 2 kPa/m. If the viscosity of oil is 1.2 poise, find (i) shear stress on the upper plate, (ii) shear stress on the lower plate and (iii) discharge of oil/m width.

13.20 A tank 0.8 m × 0.6 m having oil of specific gravity 0.9 and viscosity of 0.15 Pa.s is emptied through a 20 cm long pipe of diameter 5 mm. If the initial head over the pipe is 2.5 m, find the time needed to collect 130 l of oil. Assume the entry to the pipe is bell-mouthed and smooth with $C_d \approx 1$. Neglect velocity head in pipe.

13.21 A rectangular pipe having a cross-section 0.3 m × 0.1 m and length 2 m is carrying fuel oil of dynamic viscosity 0.8 Pa s. If the discharge is 80 l/s, find the head loss in the pipe. Assume ρ for oil = 940 kg/m^3.

13.22 An oil of specific gravity 0.9 flows through a pipe of diameter 15 cm and length 700 m at a velocity of 2 m/s. The kinematic viscosity of oil is 9 stokes. (i) Is the flow laminar or turbulent? (ii) Find the power lost in overcoming friction.

13.23 Oil of kinematic viscosity 0.4 stokes flows through an inclined pipe of 1.25 cm diameter. If the discharge through the pipe is 80 l/hour, find the Reynolds number. At what slope should the pipe be placed so that there is no drop in pressure intensity along the length of the pipe. [Hint: Slope = h_f/L].

13.24 A flow of 60 l/s/m of glycerine of relative density 1.25 and dynamic viscosity 1.5 Pa s takes place between parallel plates having a gap of 25 mm between them. Calculate the maximum velocity and boundary shear stress.

ANSWERS

13.16. 173.19; **13.17**(i) 0.213 m; **13.17**(ii) 7.99 Pa; **13.17**(iii) 6.22 Pa; **13.18.** 0.0155 m; **13.19**(i) 14.208 Pa; **13.19**(ii) 24.192 Pa; **13.19**(iii) 21.173 $\times 10^3$ m^3/s/m; **13.20.** 12,200 s; **13.21.** 0.699; **13.22**(i) 333.33, laminar; **13.22**(ii) 57 kW; **13.23.** $\nu = 8.69°$; **13.24.** 3.6 m/s; 864 Pa.

14 Dimensional Analysis and Similitude

Dimensions of physical quantities—Concept of dimensions—Dimensional analysis— Buckingham's π theorem—Important dimensionless groups— Problems— Similitude— Reynold's criteria—Froude's criteria—Model studies—Conflicts in modelling criteria—Distorted models

14.1 Introduction

Physical problems are based on the concept of space and time. In Newtonian mechanics, these are considered as independent dimensions. For convenience, length L, time T and mass M are considered as the basic dimensions. Dimensions of force can be derived from the equation $F = ma$, (force = mass × acceleration) where acceleration is L/T^2. Hence $F = MLT^{-2}$.

14.2 Dimensions of Physical Quantities

Given below are the dimensions of some important physical quantities.

Quantity	Symbol	Dimensions
Velocity	v	LT^{-1}
Acceleration	a	LT^{-2}
Discharge	Q	L^3T^{-1}
Specific mass	ρ	ML^{-3}
Force	F	MLT^{-2}
Specific weight	γ	$ML^{-2}\ T^{-2}$
Specific gravity	S	$M^0L^0\ T^0$
Pressure	p	$ML^{-1}\ T^{-2}$
Shear stress	τ	$ML^{-1}\ T^{-2}$
Modulus of elasticity	E	$ML^{-1}\ T^{-2}$
Work	W	$ML^2\ T^{-2}$
Power	P	$ML^2\ T^{-3}$
Torque	T	$ML^2\ T^{-2}$
Dynamic viscosity	μ	$ML^{-1}\ T^{-1}$
Kinematic viscosity	ν	L^2T^{-1}

(Contd.)

Quantity	Symbol	Dimensions
Surface tension	σ	MT^{-2}
Angle (radians)	α	$M^0L^0T^0$
Frequency	f	T^{-1}
rpm	N	T^{-1}
Angular velocity	ω	T^{-1}
Stream function	ψ	L^2T^{-1}
Potential function	ϕ	L^2T^{-1}
Energy, heat, work	W	ML^2T^{-2}
Temperature	θ	θ
Coefficient of thermal conductivity	λ	$MLT^{-3}\theta^{-1}$
Gas constant, specific heats	R, C_p, C_v	$L^2T^{-2}\theta^{-1}$

14.3 Advantages of the Concept of Dimensions

The concept of dimensions is useful in checking theoretical equations, conversion of units from one system to another, obtaining dimensionless groups which affect physical phenomenon, deriving new equations and presenting experimental results in a more useful and simplified way.

14.3.1 Checking theoretical equations

Rational equations should necessarily have dimensional homogenity i.e., the terms should be dimensionally consistent. But it may be noted that this homogenity is not a sufficient condition for correctness.

Some examples are given below

(i) Consider the Stoke's equation

$$u = \frac{(\gamma_1 - \gamma_2)}{18\,\mu} d^2,$$

where u is the terminal velocity (LT^{-1}), γ_1, γ_2 are the specific weights of the solid and liquid ($ML^{-2}\ T^{-2}$) respectively, d is the diameter of the solid (L) and μ is dynamic viscosity ($ML^{-1}\ T^{-1}$).

The left-hand side has the dimensions LT^{-1}.

Right-hand side $\dfrac{(\gamma_1 - \gamma_2)}{18\mu} d^2 = \dfrac{ML^{-2}T^{-2} \times L^2}{ML^{-1}T^{-1}} = \dfrac{L}{T} = LT^{-1}$.

So, the equation is dimensionally homogenous.

(ii) Consider the boundary layer equation

$$\rho\left(u\frac{\partial u}{\partial x}+\nu\frac{\partial u}{\partial y}\right)=\mu\frac{\partial^2 u}{\partial y^2};\quad \frac{\partial^2 u}{\partial y^2} \text{ can be written as } \frac{\partial}{\partial y}\left(\frac{\partial u}{\partial y}\right).$$

Writing the dimensions,

$$\mathrm{ML}^{-3}\left[\mathrm{LT}^{-1}\times\frac{LT^{-1}}{L}+\mathrm{LT}^{-1}\times\frac{\mathrm{LT}^{-1}}{\mathrm{L}}\right]=\mathrm{ML}^{-1}\mathrm{T}^{-1}\times\frac{1}{\mathrm{L}}\times\frac{\mathrm{LT}^{-1}}{\mathrm{L}},$$

or, $\mathrm{ML}^{-2}\mathrm{T}^{-2}+\mathrm{ML}^{-2}\mathrm{T}^{-2}=\mathrm{ML}^{-2}\mathrm{T}^{-2}$.

So the equation is dimensionally homogenous.

(iii) Consider the Manning's formula

$$V=\frac{1}{n}R^{2/3}\,{S_0}^{1/2},$$

where V is the velocity, n is the rugosity coefficient, R is the hydraulic mean depth and S_0 is the slope.

$$\frac{\mathrm{L}}{\mathrm{T}}=\left(\frac{1}{n}\right)\mathrm{L}^{2/3}\,\mathrm{M}^0\mathrm{L}^0\mathrm{T}^0.$$

If n is a constant, the dimensions of RHS and LHS do not match. Hence the above equation is only an empirical equation.

14.3.2 Conversion of units

The concept of dimensions help in converting empirical formulae from one system of units to another.

Let us convert the Manning's formula

$$V=\frac{1}{n}R^{2/3}\,{S_0}^{1/2},$$

which is in SI system of units to FPS system of units, assuming that n is the same in both the systems. If n is kept the same in both the systems, the equation can be made dimensionally homogenous by changing it to

$$V = \left(\frac{k}{n}\right) R^{2/3} S_0^{1/2},$$

where k is a dimensional quantity. In metric unit $k = 1$.

$$\text{Dimensions of } k = \frac{\text{L/T}}{\text{L}^{2/3}} = \text{L}^{1/3}\text{T}^{-1};\ k_1 = (\text{m})^{1/3}/\text{s},\ k_2 = \ (3.28\ \text{ft})^{1/3}/\text{s} = 1.486\ \text{ft}^{1/3}/\text{s}.$$

Hence the formula in FPS becomes $V = \left(\dfrac{1.486}{n}\right) R^{2/3} S_0^{1/2}$.

14.3.3 Non-dimensional form of basic equations

If the equations governing a phenomenon are known, they can be transformed to a non-dimensional form. Such expressions can be very useful.

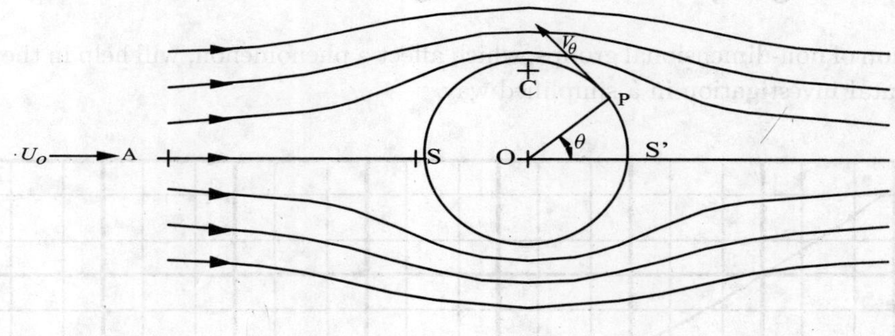

Fig. 14.1 *Irrotational flow around a cylinder*

Consider the two-dimensional irrotational flow of fluid around a circular cylinder such that its axis is perpendicular to the flow direction as in Fig. 14.1. Bernoulli's theorem can be applied to points A and P as

$$\frac{p_A}{\gamma} + \frac{U_0^2}{2g} + Z_A = \frac{p_P}{\gamma} + \frac{{V_P}^2}{2g} + Z_P$$

or, $$\frac{p_P}{\gamma} - \frac{p_A}{\gamma} = \frac{U_0^2}{2g} - \frac{V_P^2}{2g} \text{ and } (Z_A = Z_B)$$

Dividing both sides by $U_0^2/2g$,

$$\frac{\Delta p}{\rho U_0^2/2g} = 1 - \left(\frac{V_P}{U_0}\right)^2.$$

The above equation is in the non-dimensional form and has greater scope for application.

14.3.4 Obtaining non-dimensional groups which affect phenomenon

Consider the drag force F_D on a sphere moving through a fluid. F_D can be expressed as dependent on the four parameters F_D $(d,\ v,\ \mu,\ \rho)$, where μ is the dynamic viscosity, ρ the density of the fluid, d is the diameter of the sphere and v its velocity. By dimensional considerations, the relationship can be simplified (explained in Section 14.5.2) as

$$\frac{F_D}{\rho \nu^2 d^2} = f\left(\frac{\nu d \rho}{\mu}\right), \text{ where } \frac{F_D}{\rho \nu^2 d^2} \text{ and } \frac{\nu d \rho}{\mu} \text{ are dimensionless parameters.}$$

The derivation of non-dimensional parameters can be assisted using the technique of dimensional analysis. Theoretical and experimental investigations can establish relationships between the various non-dimensional parameters.

14.3.5 Planning experimental investigations

The derivation of non-dimensional groups, which affect a phenomenon, will help in the planning of experimental investigation in a simplified way.

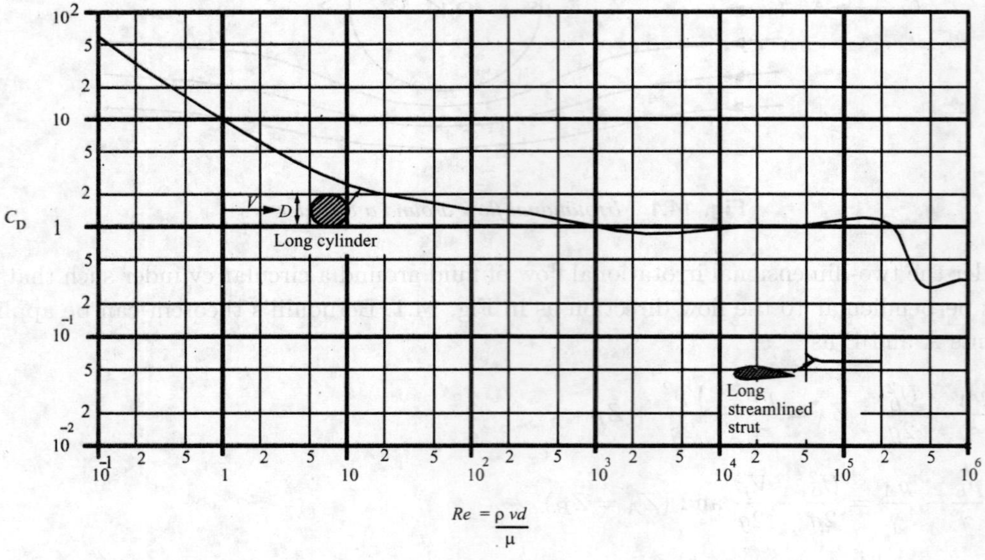

Fig. 14.2 *Graph of* $C_D = \dfrac{F_D}{\rho v^2 d^2}$ *vs* $\dfrac{\rho v d}{\mu}$ *for a cylinder*

As an example, consider drag force F_D on a smooth sphere moving through a fluid. Suppose one proceeds with an experimental investigation, varying values of the parameters, μ, ρ, d and v. The procedure will be too elaborate and lengthy, and it may also not be feasible to change the parameters as desired. The analysis of the data will be difficult and depiction of the relationship between the variables F_D, μ, ρ, d and v will require many sets of curves. However, an easier scheme of experimental investigation can proceed by lumping together the parameters, in two dimensionless groups $\frac{F_D}{\rho v^2 d^2}$ and $\frac{\rho v d}{\mu}$. The second non-dimensional group is the Reynolds number and the experiment can be performed with various Reynolds numbers and the value of $\frac{F_D}{\rho v^2 d^2}$ can be determined. The analysis will show a simple relationship as shown in Fig. 14.2.

14.4 Buckingham's π Theorem

The theorem helps in finding out the number of independent non-dimensional groups affecting a phenomenon.

It states that the number of independent non-dimensional groups called π terms which can be formed from n number of unknown physical variables affecting a phenomenon is equal to $(n - r)$, where r is the number of fundamental dimensions required to express the variables. r is more exactly equal to the rank of dimensional matrix formed with the physical variables. Buckingham referred to the dimensionless groups as π terms.

14.5 Dimensional Analysis

14.5.1 Procedure

The method for finding out the dimensionless groups involves selection of some repeating variables. These are selected using the following criteria.

(i) The repeating variables should include all the relevant fundamental dimensions.

(ii) It is desirable to select a geometrical characteristic, fluid property and a flow characteristic as the repeating variables.

(iii) No dimensionless parameter should result from the combination of the repeating variables alone.

The other variables, one at a time are combined with the powers of the repeating variables to result in non-dimensional groups. These groups or terms are independent of each other in the sense that any combination of two or more of them or their powers will not result in any other term. But these groups are not unique in the sense that many other combinations are also possible.

14.5.2 Drag force on a sphere

The drag force F_D on a sphere moving through a fluid of dynamic viscosity μ and density ρ depends on the diameter of sphere d and the velocity v. We can derive an expression for the drag force.

$$F_D = f(\mu, d, \rho, v).$$

Select d, ρ and v as the repeating variables.

The dimensional matrix is

	F_D	μ	d	ρ	v
M	1	1	0	1	0
L	1	−1	1	−3	1
T	−2	−1	0	0	−1

The 3 × 3 sub-matrices which can be formed are

$$\text{(I)} \begin{matrix} 1 & 1 & 0 \\ 1 & -1 & 1 \\ -2 & -1 & 0 \end{matrix} \qquad \text{(II)} \begin{matrix} 1 & 0 & 1 \\ 1 & 1 & -3 \\ -2 & 0 & 0 \end{matrix} \quad \text{etc.,}$$

Let us check the value of the determinants. The first matrix has a determinant −(1 + 2) = −3, which is non-zero. (Hence there is no need to check more determinants. If all such 3 × 3 matrices give zero determinants, we will have to form 2 × 2 matrices and check.). Therefore, rank $r = 3$ (r is normally the same as the number of dimensions used). Hence the number of π terms $= n - r = 5 - 3 = 2$.

$$\pi_1 = F_D\, d^{x_1} \rho^{y_1} v^{z_1}.$$

$$M^0L^0T^0 = MLT^{-2}L^{x_1}(ML^{-3})^{y_1}(LT^{-1})^{z_1}.$$

Equating the powers of M, L and T,

$$0 = 1 + y_1; 0 = 1 + x_1 - 3y_1 + z_1; \quad 0 = -2 - z_1.$$

Solving the above equations,

$$x_1 = -2, \quad y_1 = -1, \quad z = -2; \quad \text{i.e., } \pi_1 = \frac{F_D}{\rho v^2 d^2}.$$

$$\pi_2 = \mu d^{x_2} \rho^{y_2} v^{z_2}.$$

$$M^0L^0T^0 = ML^{-1}T^{-1}L^{x_2}(ML^{-3})^{y_2}(LT^{-1})^{z_2}.$$

Equating powers of M, L and T,

$$0 = 1 + y_2;\ 0 = -1 + x_2 - 3y_2 + 3z_2;\ 0 = -1 - z_2.$$

Solving the above equations,

$$x_2 = -1,\ \ y_2 = -1,\ \ z_2 = -1; \quad \text{i.e., } \pi_2 = \frac{\mu}{\rho v d}.$$

$$\pi_1 = f(\pi_2) \text{ i.e., } \frac{F_D}{\rho v^2 d^2} = f\left(\frac{\mu}{\rho v d}\right) \text{ or, } F_D = \rho v^2 d^2 f\left(\frac{\mu}{\rho v d}\right).$$

It can also be expressed as

$$F_D = \rho v^2 d^2 \phi\left(\frac{\rho v\, d}{\mu}\right).$$

A simpler procedure can be used with advantage after determining the number of π terms in the example and selecting the repeating variables.

We express M, L and T in terms of the repeating variables first [||].

Then the quantities F_D and μ are divided by their respective dimensions expressed in terms of the repeating variables to form π terms.

$$\text{M} = \rho d^3;\ \ \text{L} = d;\ \ \text{T} = d/v.$$

$$\pi_1 = F_D/\text{MLT}^{-2} = (F_D/\rho d^3 d)\ (d^2/v^2)\ = F_D/\rho v^2 d^2.$$

$$\pi_2 = \mu/\text{ML}^{-1}\ \text{T}^{-1} = (\mu/\rho d^3)\ (dd/v) = \mu/\rho v d.$$

14.6 Some Important Dimensionless Groups in Fluid Mechanics

Problems in fluid mechanics in general are governed by many variables and they may be expressed as $\Delta p(\ \rho,\ \mu,\ E,\ \sigma,\ l,\ v,\ g)$, where Δp is the change in pressure, ρ is the density of the fluid, μ the dynamic viscosity of the fluid, E the modulus of compressibility, σ is the surface tension, l the characteristic length of the body, v is the velocity and g is the acceleration due to gravity.

[||] In case it cannot be done by mere inspection, it can be obtained by equating the powers as follows. $\text{M} = \rho^{x_1} d^{y_1} v^{z_1}.\ \text{M}^1\text{L}^0\text{T}^0 = (\text{ML}^{-3})^{x_1}\text{L}^{y_1}(\text{LT}^{-1})^{z_1}$. Hence equating the powers on both sides of the equation, $x_1 = 1, y_1 = +3, z_1 = 0$. i.e. $\text{M} = \rho d^3$.

Taking l, ρ and v as the repeating variables

	Δp	μ	E	σ	g	l	ρ	v
M	1	1	1	1	0	0	1	0
L	−1	−1	−1	0	1	1	−3	1
T	−2	−1	−2	−2	−2	0	0	−1

$n = 8; r = 3$. Therefore, number of terms $= (n - r) = 8 - 3 = 5$.

$\mathrm{M} = \rho l^3; \mathrm{L} = l;$ and $\mathrm{T} = \dfrac{l}{v}$.

$$\text{Therefore, } \pi_1 = \frac{\Delta p}{\mathrm{ML^{-1}T^{-2}}} = \frac{\Delta p l l^2}{\rho l^3 v^2} = \frac{\Delta p}{\rho v^2},$$

which is a pressure parameter closely connected with the Euler number.

$$E_N = \frac{v}{\Delta p/\rho}. \tag{14.1}$$

$$\pi_2 = \frac{\mu}{\mathrm{ML^{-1}T^{-1}}} = \frac{\mu l}{\rho l^3} \times \frac{l}{v} = \frac{\mu}{\rho v l},$$

which is closely connected with the Reynolds number

$$\mathrm{Re} = \frac{\rho v l}{\mu}. \tag{14.2}$$

$$\pi_3 = \frac{E}{\mathrm{ML^{-1}T^{-2}}} = \frac{E l l^2}{\rho l^3 v^2} = \frac{E}{\rho v^2},$$

which is the equation for $1/M$, where M is the

$$\text{Mach number } \frac{v}{\sqrt{E/\rho}}. \tag{14.3}$$

$$\pi_4 = \frac{\sigma}{\mathrm{MT^{-2}}} = \frac{\sigma l^2}{\rho l^3 v^2} = \frac{\sigma}{\rho l v^2},$$

which is equal to $1/W$, where W is the

$$\text{Weber number } \frac{\rho v^2 l}{\sigma}. \tag{14.4}$$

$$\pi_5 = \frac{g}{\mathrm{LT^{-2}}} = \frac{g l^2}{l v^2} = \frac{g l}{v^2}$$

which is $1/F^2$ and F is the,

$$\text{Froude's number } \frac{v}{\sqrt{gl}}. \tag{14.5}$$

E, R, M, W and F form the most common non-dimensional parameters used in fluid mechanics.

Example 14.1 The efficiency η of a pump depends on density ρ, dynamic viscosity μ of the fluid, angular velocity ω, diameter d of the impeller, and the discharge Q. Express η in terms of the dimensionless parameters.

η is dimensionless and is a function of ρ, μ, ω, d and Q. ρ, ω and d can be taken as the repeated variables.

	μ	Q	ρ	ω	d
M	1	0	1	0	0
L	−1	3	−3	0	1
T	−1	−1	0	−1	0

$n = 3; r = 3$. Since the rank of the matrix is 3, the number of terms $m = n - r = 5 - 3 = 2$.

$$\pi_1 = \mu\rho^{x_1}\omega^{y_1}d^{z_1}.$$

Equating the dimensions,

$$\mathrm{M^0L^0T^0 = ML^{-1}T^{-1}(ML^{-3})^{x_1}(T^{-1})^{y_1}(L)^{z_1}}.$$

Equating powers of M, L, T on both sides,

$$0 = 1 + x_1;\ 0 = -1 - 3x_1 + z_1;\ 0 = -1 - y_1.$$

Solving the equations,

$$x_1 = -1; y_1 = -1; \text{ and } z_1 = -2.$$

So, $\pi_1 = \mu\rho^{-1}\omega^{-1}d^{-2} = \dfrac{\mu}{\rho\omega d^2}$.

$$\pi_2 = Q\rho^{x_2}\omega^{y_2}d^{z_2}.$$

Equating the dimensions on both sides,

$$\mathrm{M^0L^0T^0 = L^3T^{-1}(ML^{-3})^{x_2}(T^{-1})^{y_2}(L)^{z_2}}.$$

Equating powers of M, L,T on both sides,

$$0 = x_2;\ 0 = 3 - 3y_2 + z_2;\ 0 = -1 - y_2.$$

Solving,

$$x_2 = 0;\ y_2 = -1;\ z_2 = -3.$$

$$\pi_2 = Q\rho^0\omega^{-1}d^{-3} = \frac{Q}{\omega d^3}.$$

Hence, $\eta(\pi_1, \pi_2)$ or $\eta\left(\frac{\mu}{\rho d^2\omega}, \frac{Q}{\omega d^3}\right)$.

Example 14.2 The drag of a ship depends on the length of the ship l, its velocity v, density and dynamic viscosity ρ and μ respectively and the acceleration due to gravity g. Show that drag F can be expressed as $F = \rho v^2 l^2 \phi(F_N, R_N)$, where $F_N = \frac{v}{\sqrt{gl}}, R_N = \frac{\rho v l}{\mu}$.

F is a function of l, v, ρ, μ and g. In the final expression given, the non-dimensional terms required are $\frac{F}{\rho v^2 l^2}, \frac{v}{\sqrt{gl}}$ and $\frac{\rho v l}{\mu}$. By inspection, we know that the parameters ρ, l, v are repeated among these terms. Select ρ, l, v as repeated variables.

	F	μ	g	ρ	l	v
M	1	1	0	1	0	0
L	1	−1	1	−3	1	1
T	−2	−1	−2	0	0	−1

$n = 6; r = 3$. So $m = n - r = 6 - 3 = 3$. Expressing M, L, T in terms of ρ, l, v, $\text{M} = \rho l^3; \text{L} = l; \text{T} = \frac{l}{v}$.

$$\pi_1 = \frac{F}{\text{MLT}^{-2}} = \frac{Fl^2}{\rho l^3 l v^2} = \frac{F}{\rho v^2 l^2},$$

$$\pi_2 = \frac{\mu}{\text{ML}^{-1}\text{T}^{-1}} = \frac{\mu l l}{\rho l^3 v} = \frac{\mu}{\rho v l} \text{ and}$$

$$\pi_3 = \frac{g}{\text{LT}^{-2}} = \frac{gl^2}{lv^2} = \frac{gl}{v^2}.$$

Hence $\frac{F}{\rho v^2 l^2} = \phi_1(\frac{\mu}{\rho v l}, \frac{gl}{v^2})$ i.e., $F = \rho v^2 l^2 \phi(\frac{v}{\sqrt{gl}}, \frac{\mu}{\rho v l})$.

Example 14.3 The thrust F of a propeller for a boat depends on the torque τ_q, diameter d, velocity of the boat V, speed of rotation of the propeller N, density ρ and viscosity μ of the water. Find an expression for F.

$F(\tau_q, \mu, N, \rho, V, d)$

	F	τ_q	μ	N	ρ	V	d
M	1	1	0	1	0	0	0
L	1	2	−1	0	−3	1	1
T	−2	−2	−1	−1	0	−1	0

$n = 7; r = 3$; So number of π terms $m = n - r = 4$

Expressing M, L and T in terms of ρ, V and d

$\mathrm{M} = \rho d^3$; $\mathrm{L} = d$; and $\mathrm{T} = d/V$

$$\text{Hence } \pi_1 = \frac{F\mathrm{T}^2}{\mathrm{ML}} = \frac{F \times d^2}{V^2 \times \rho d^3 \times d} = \frac{F}{\rho V^2 d^2}$$

$$\pi_2 = \frac{\tau_q \times \mathrm{T}^2}{\mathrm{ML}^2} = \frac{\tau_q \times d^2}{V^2 \rho d^3 \times d^2} = \frac{\tau_q}{\rho V^2 d^3}$$

$$\pi_3 = \frac{\mu \mathrm{LT}}{\mathrm{M}} = \frac{\mu d \times d}{\rho d^3 \times V} = \frac{\mu}{\rho V d}$$

$$\pi_4 = N \times \mathrm{T} = \frac{Nd}{V}$$

$$\text{Hence } F = \rho V^2 d^2 \times \phi\left(\frac{\tau_q}{\rho V^2 d^2}, \frac{\mu}{\rho V d}, \frac{Nd}{V}\right)$$

Example 14.4 The rise of a liquid having specific weight γ and surface tension σ in a capillary tube of diameter d is h. Find an expression for h given that h is inversely proportional to γ.

h is a function of γ, σ and d.

	h	γ	σ	d
M	0	1	1	0
L	1	−2	0	1
T	0	−2	−2	0

None of the 3 × 3 matrices from above will give a non-zero determinant value. But a 2 × 2 matrix can be non-zero. So rank = 2 and the number of repeated variables = 2. Select σ and d as repeated variables. $n = 4; r = 2$; So $m = n - r = 4 - 2 = 2$. Expressing M, L and T in terms of repeated variables σ and d,

$\sigma = \mathrm{MT}^{-2}; \mathrm{L} = d.$

$$\pi_1 = \frac{h}{\mathrm{L}} = \frac{h}{d};\ \pi_2 = \frac{\gamma}{\mathrm{ML}^{-2}\,\mathrm{T}^{-2}} = \frac{\gamma d^2}{\sigma};\ \frac{h}{d} = \phi(\frac{\gamma d^2}{\sigma});\ \text{but } h \propto \frac{1}{\gamma},$$

hence $\frac{h}{d} = k\frac{\sigma}{\gamma d^2}$ or, $h = \frac{k\sigma}{\gamma d}$, where k is a constant.

Example 14.5 The velocity of flow V in a prismatic channel of wetted perimeter P and hydraulic radius R depends on the driving force per unit length ($A\rho gS$) and the fluid properties ρ and μ, where A is the area of cross-section and S is the bed slope. Show that $\frac{vR}{\nu} = \phi\left(\frac{ARgS}{\nu^2}, \frac{P}{R}\right)$.

By inspecting the final result, the repeated variables can be ν and R. i.e., μ, ρ and R

	V	$A\rho gS$	P	μ	ρ	R
M	0	1	0	1	1	0
L	1	0	1	−1	−3	1
T	−1	−2	0	−1	0	0

$n = 6; r = 3$; So, $m = n - r = 6 - 3 = 3$. Writing M, L and T in terms of repeated variables μ, ρ and R,

$$\mathrm{M} = \rho R^3; \mathrm{L} = R; \text{ and } \mathrm{T} = \frac{\rho R^2}{\mu}.$$

$$\pi_1 = \frac{V}{\mathrm{LT}^{-1}} = \frac{V\rho R^2}{R\mu} = \frac{\rho VR}{\mu} = \frac{VR}{\nu}.$$

$$\pi_2 = \frac{A\rho gS}{\mathrm{MT}^{-2}} = \frac{A\rho gS\ \rho^2 R^4}{\rho R^3\ \mu^2} = \frac{ARgS}{\nu^2}.$$

$$\pi_3 = \frac{P}{\mathrm{L}} = \frac{P}{R}, \text{ hence } \frac{VR}{\nu} = \phi\left(\frac{ARgS}{\nu^2}, \frac{P}{R}\right).$$

Example 14.6 The discharge Q through a pump depends on the brake horse power P, the diameter d, speed in rpm N, the energy to be imparted per unit mass gH, the dynamic viscosity μ and specific mass ρ. Find the dimensionless parameters affecting the phenomenon.

$$Q = Q\ (P, gH, \mu, d, \rho, N)$$

Taking d, ρ and N as the repeated variables

	Q	P	gH	μ	d	ρ	N
M	0	1	0	1	0	1	0
L	3	2	2	−1	1	−3	0
T	−1	−3	−2	−1	0	0	−1

$m = 7; r = 3$; Number of π terms $= m - r = 7 - 3 = 4$.

Expressing M, L and T in terms of repeated variables d, ρ and N,

$$\mathrm{M} = \rho d^3; \qquad \mathrm{L} = d;\ \mathrm{T} = 1/N.$$

$$\pi_1 = \frac{Q}{\mathrm{L}^3/\mathrm{T}} = \frac{Q}{Nd^3}.$$

$$\pi_2 = \frac{\mathrm{g}H}{\mathrm{L}^2/\mathrm{T}^2} = \frac{\mathrm{g}H}{d^2N^2}$$

$$\pi_3 = \frac{P}{\mathrm{ML}^2/\mathrm{T}^2} = \frac{P}{\rho d^3 d^2 N^3} = \frac{P}{\rho d^5 N^3}$$

$$\pi_4 = \frac{\mu}{\mathrm{M/LT}} = \frac{\mu \times d}{d^3 \times N} = \frac{\mu}{\rho d^2 N}$$

$$\text{Hence } f\left(\frac{Q}{Nd^3}, \frac{\mathrm{g}H}{d^2N^2}, \frac{P}{\rho d^5N^3}, \frac{\mu}{\rho d^2 N}\right) = 0.$$

Note A combination of π_1, π_2 in such a way that d is eliminated can be derived as

$$\frac{\pi_1^{1/2}}{\pi_2^{3/4}} = \frac{Q^{1/2}}{N^{1/2}d^{3/2}} \times \frac{d^{3/2}N^{3/2}}{\mathrm{g}^{3/4}H^{3/4}} = \frac{NQ^{1/2}}{\mathrm{g}^{3/4}H^{3/4}}.$$

If g is taken as a constant, the expression $\frac{N\sqrt{Q}}{H^{3/4}}$ is termed as the specific speed of a pump. Similarly $\frac{\pi_3^{1/2}}{\pi_2^{5/4}}$ will result in $\frac{N\sqrt{P}}{\rho^{1/2}\mathrm{g}^{5/4}H^{5/4}}$ which is closely connected with $N_5 = \frac{N\sqrt{P}}{H^{5/4}}$, the specific speed of a turbine.

Example 14.7 The rate of heat transfer across unit area to a boundary at a distance of x from the leading edge from hot gases dq/dt with a difference in temperature of Φ flowing past it, depends on the velocity of flow of the gas V, the length of the boundary l, the specific mass ρ, the dynamic viscosity μ, and the specific heat at constant pressure C_p and thermal conductivity λ of the gas. Find the non-dimensional parameters governing the problem.

$$dq/dt(\mu, c_p, \lambda, \rho, V, l, \Phi)$$

Taking ρ, V, l, and $\Delta\theta$ as the repeated variables

	dq/dt	μ	c_p	λ	x	ρ	V	l	Φ
M	1	1	0	1	0	1	0	0	0
L	0	−1	2	1	1	−3	1	1	0
T	−3	−1	−2	−3	0	0	−1	0	0
θ	0	0	−1	−1	0	0	0	0	1

$n = 9 : r = 4; n - r = 9 - 4 = 5$. Writing M, L T and θ in terms of the repeated variables

ρ, V, l and Φ

$\mathrm{M} = \rho l^3; \mathrm{L} = l; \mathrm{T} = l/V$ and $\theta = \Phi$

Hence $\pi_1 = \dfrac{dq/dt}{\mathrm{M/T^3}} = \dfrac{(dq/dt)l^3}{\rho l^3 V^3} = \dfrac{dq/dt}{\rho V^3}; \pi_2 = \dfrac{\mu}{\mathrm{M/LT}} = \dfrac{\mu}{\rho V l}$

$$\pi_3 = \frac{c_p}{\mathrm{L^2/T^2}\Phi} = \frac{c_p \Phi}{V^2}; \pi_4 = \frac{\lambda}{\mathrm{ML/T^3}\Phi} = \frac{\lambda\Phi}{\rho l V^3}; \pi_5 = \frac{x}{l}$$

Hence $\pi_1(\pi_2, \pi_3, \pi_4, \pi_5)$. Some combinations of the π terms are more commonly used in analysis.

$\Pi_1 = \dfrac{\pi_2\pi_3}{\pi_4} = \dfrac{\mu c_p}{\lambda}$, Pr *the Prandtl number* which represents ratio of momentum diffusivity to thermal diffusivity

$\Pi_2 = \dfrac{\pi_1\pi_3}{\pi_4} = \dfrac{(dq/dt)x}{\lambda\Phi}$, Nu *the Nusselt number* which represents heat transfer

$\Pi_3 = \dfrac{1}{\pi_3} = \dfrac{V^2}{c_p\Phi}$, Ec *the Eckert number* which represents the ratio of kinetic energy to enthalpy

14.7 Similitude

14.7.1 Models and model testing

Many engineering structures like dams, barrages, river training works etc., are very large, require many years for their completion and involve huge costs. There are many aspects of design of these structures, which can only be approximately designed analytically. Any error in the design can prove to be too expensive and in some cases result in failure. It would be more optimal to design a small model of the system. Studies on small models of the structures lead to

(i) understanding the flow problem,
(ii) observing any peculiar flow pattern,
(iii) detecting any defects in the design and possible damage to the structure,
(iv) studying alternate designs or remedial measures to ensure safety and
(v) studying the depths, velocities, forces etc., in the model and forecasting the quantities in the prototype by application of laws of similitude.

Model testing is being used successfully in various fields of hydraulic engineering, turbo machines, river engineering, harbour engineering, aeronautical engineering and marine engineering.

14.7.2 Types of similitude

The actual structure is called the prototype and the models are made to have some model–prototype conformity. Models are usually made geometrically similar. The model and the prototype are said to have geometric similarity if the ratios of lengths in the model to the homologous (geometrically corresponding) lengths in the prototype remain a constant. The angles between the lines will also be preserved.

In Fig. 14.3, $\dfrac{l_m}{l_p} = \dfrac{b}{B} = l_r =$ the length ratio.

In the operation of a geometrically similar model, the velocities of flow can be selected so that kinematic similarity is obtained. The model and prototype are said to have kinematic similarity if the ratio of velocity and acceleration of the fluid at any point in the model to the velocity and acceleration at the homologous point in the prototype is constant. The relative direction of velocities and accelerations will also be preserved. $\dfrac{\vec{V}_m}{\vec{V}_p} = \dfrac{\vec{v}_m}{\vec{v}_p}$ and $\vec{v}_m$ and $\vec{v}_p$ will have the same inclination as $\vec{V}_m$ and $\vec{V}_p$ respectively.

There are many forces that can affect fluid flow. The main forces are the gravitational and viscous forces, the resultant of which can affect changes in the inertial characteristics of the fluid elements i.e., impart an acceleration. If m is the mass of an element of the fluid and a is the acceleration produced, $m\vec{a} = \vec{F}_i = \vec{F}_p + \vec{F}_g + \vec{F}_\nu + \vec{F}_s + \vec{F}_e$, where $\vec{F}_i, \vec{F}_p, \vec{F}_g, \vec{F}_\nu, \vec{F}_s$ and $\vec{F}_e$, are the inertial, pressure, gravitational, viscous forces and forces connected with surface tension and elasticity.

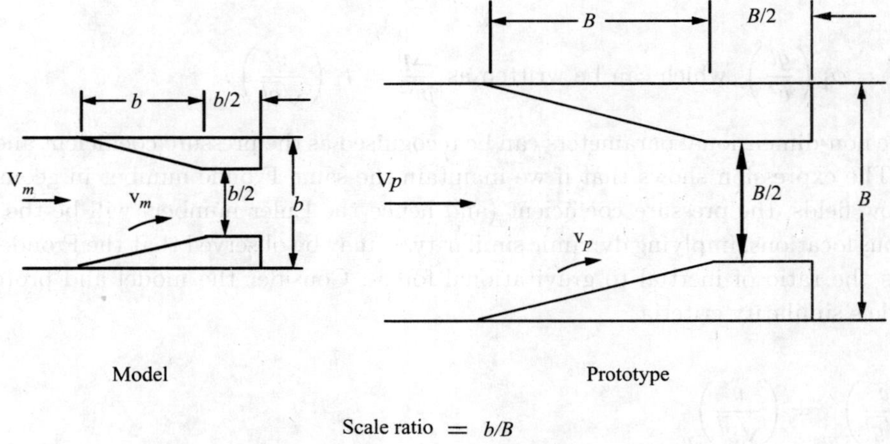

Fig. 14.3 *Illustration of linear scale ratio*

The model and prototype are said to have dynamic similitude when the forces acting on an area in the model bear a constant ratio to the forces acting on the homologous area in the prototype. If F_{im}, F_{pm}, F_{gm}, $F_{\nu m}$, F_{sm} and F_{em} are the forces on an area in the model and F_{ip}, F_{pp}, F_{gp}, $F_{\nu p}$, F_{sp} and F_{ep} are those on a corresponding area in the prototype, for dynamic similarity to exist

$$\frac{F_{im}}{F_{ip}} = \frac{F_{pm}}{F_{pp}} = \frac{F_{gm}}{F_{gp}} = \frac{F_{\nu m}}{F_{\nu p}} = \frac{F_{sm}}{F_{sp}} = \frac{F_{em}}{F_{ep}}.$$

Dynamic similarity involves geometrical and kinematic similarities. It is not possible to have perfect dynamic similarity as regards to all the forces in the models. But in many cases, the similitude of some predominant forces is attempted and found to give useful results.

14.8 Froude's Criteria for Similitude

In many problems of flow of fluid with a free surface as flow in open channels, it is necessary to find the pressure distribution or total pressure on the surfaces. The other predominant forces are F_g, the force due to gravity and F_i, the inertial force. Let the other forces be negligible. Then

$$\vec{F}_p = \vec{F}_g + \vec{F}_i. \tag{14.6}$$

i.e., $\Delta p l^2 = k_1 \rho l^3 g + k_2 \rho v^2 l^2$, where k_1 and k_2 are constants.
Dividing throughout by $\rho v^2 l^2$ representing inertial forces,

$$\frac{\Delta p}{\rho v^2} = \phi_1\left(\frac{gl}{v^2}\right), \text{which can be written as } \frac{\Delta p}{\rho v^2} = f_1\left(\frac{v}{\sqrt{gl}}\right). \tag{14.7}$$

The above non-dimensional parameters can be recognised as the pressure coefficient and Froude number. The expression shows that if we maintain the same Froude number in geometrically similar flow fields, the pressure coefficient (and hence the Euler number) will be the same at homologous locations, implying dynamic similarity. It may be observed that the Froude number represents the ratio of inertial to gravitational forces. Consider the model and prototype as per Froude's similarity criteria,

$$\left(\frac{v}{\sqrt{gl}}\right)_m = \left(\frac{v}{\sqrt{gl}}\right)_p. \tag{14.8}$$

$$\text{Let the ratio } \left(\frac{l_m}{l_p}\right) \text{ be } l_r. \tag{14.9}$$

From (14.8),

$$v_r = \frac{v_m}{v_p} = \sqrt{\frac{g_m l_m}{g_p l_p}} = g_r^{1/2}\; l_r^{1/2}.$$

If g_r is assumed to be 1, the following ratios can be worked out.
From (14.8),

(i) Velocity ratio $v_r = {l_r}^{1/2}$. (14.10)

(ii) Time scale ratio $t_r = \dfrac{l_r}{v_r} = \dfrac{l_r}{{l_r}^{1/2}} = {l_r}^{1/2}$. (14.11)

(iii) Acceleration scale ratio $a_r = \dfrac{v_r}{t_r} = \dfrac{{l_r}^{1/2}}{{l_r}^{1/2}} = 1$, because g_r is assumed to be 1. (14.12)

(iv) Force ratio $F_r = m_r a_r = \rho_r {l_r}^3 \times 1 = \rho_r {l_r}^3$. (14.13)

(v) Discharge ratio $Q_r = \dfrac{{l_r}^3}{t_r} = {l_r}^{5/2}$. (14.14)

(vi) Power ratio P_r = force ratio $\times \dfrac{l_r}{t_r} = \rho_r {l_r}^{7/2}$. (14.15)

The ratios of quantities derived above are useful in conducting experiments and interpreting results when Froude's criteria is used for modelling.

14.9 Reynolds' Criteria for Similitude

In many problems like pipe flow and flow around submerged bodies, the role of gravitational forces are negligible and viscous and inertial forces are the dominant forces which influence the pressure distribution.

$$\vec{F_p} = \vec{F_V} + \vec{F_i}.$$

$$\text{i.e., } \Delta p l^2 = k_3 l^2 \mu \frac{V}{l} + k_4 \rho v^2 l^2.$$

Dividing by $\rho v^2 l^2$, we get

$$\frac{\Delta p}{\rho v^2} = \phi_2\left(\frac{\mu}{\rho v l}\right), \text{ or, } \frac{\Delta p}{\rho v^2} = F_2\left(\frac{\rho v l}{\mu}\right). \tag{14.16}$$

The above non-dimensional numbers can be recognised as the pressure parameter and the Reynolds number. If one maintains the same Reynolds number in such cases, the pressure parameter (and hence the Euler number) will also be the same at homologous locations, implying dynamic similarity.

It may be noted that the Reynolds number represents the ratio of inertial to viscous forces. For dynamic similarity between the model and the prototype,

$$\left(\frac{\rho vl}{\mu}\right)_m = \left(\frac{\rho vl}{\mu}\right)_p. \tag{14.17}$$

Let the length ratio $\frac{l_m}{l_p} = l_r$. From (14.17), ratios of following quantities can be obtained.

(i) Velocity scale ratio $v_r = \frac{v_m}{v_p} = \frac{\mu_m/\rho_m l_m}{\mu_p/\rho_P l_P} = \frac{\mu_r}{\rho_r l_r}$. (14.18)

(ii) Time scale ratio $t_r = \frac{l_r}{V_r} = \frac{\rho_r l_r^2}{\mu_r}$. (14.19)

(iii) Acceleration ratio $a_r = \frac{v_r}{t_r} = \frac{\mu_r}{\rho_r l_r} \times \frac{\mu_r}{\rho_r l_r{}^2} = \frac{\mu_r{}^2}{\rho_r{}^2 l_r{}^3}$. (14.20)

(iv) Force ratio $F_r = m_r a_r = \rho_r l_r{}^3 \times \frac{\mu_r{}^2}{\rho_r{}^2 l_r{}^3} = \frac{\mu_r{}^2}{\rho_r}$. (14.21)

(v) Power ratio $P_r =$ Force ratio $\times\ v_r = \frac{\mu_r{}^2}{\rho_r} \times \frac{\mu_r}{\rho_r l_r} = \frac{\mu_r{}^3}{\rho_r{}^2 l_r}$. (14.22)

The ratios of quantities derived above are useful in conducting experiments and interpreting results when Reynold's criteria is used for modelling.

14.10 Conflicts in Modelling Criteria

In some cases, we may find that in addition to pressure and inertial forces, two or more forces play a dominant role. For example, such a situation arises while studying drag on a ship, where both gravitational and the viscous forces are important. If we construct a model with scale ratio l_r, the Froude criteria specifies that the velocity ratio should be $l_r{}^{1/2}$. But the Reynold's criteria specifies that the velocity ratio should be $\frac{\mu_r}{\rho_r l_r}$. If we want to maintain dynamic similarity

$$l_r{}^{1/2} = \frac{\mu_r}{\rho_r l_r} \quad \text{or,} \quad \frac{\mu_r}{\rho_r} = v_r = l_r{}^{3/2}. \tag{14.23}$$

So unless we can use fluids satisfying the above criteria in the model and the prototype, dynamic similarity cannot be obtained.

14.11 Modelling of Ships

When a ship moves in water, surface waves are formed which affect the drag or resistance of the ship. In addition, the shear forces on the boundary due to viscous action offers resistance. The total drag is thus the sum of drag forces due to waves and friction,

$$D_t = D_w + D_f.$$

Let the scale ratio for the ship model be $l_m/l_p = l_r$. The procedure in ship model testing is to find the total drag D_{tm} when towed in special towing tanks at a velocity $v_m = v_p l_r^{1/2}$, where v_p is the velocity of the ship. The frictional drag D_{fm} of the model is evaluated using the boundary layer theory. Then

$$D_{wm} = D_{tm} - D_{fm}. \tag{14.24}$$

The wave drag on the prototype can be found by Froude's law,

$$D_{wp} = \frac{D_{wm}}{\text{force ratio}} = \frac{D_{wm}}{\rho_r {l_r}^3}. \tag{14.25}$$

The frictional drag for the prototype ship D_{fp} is also evaluated by using the boundary layer theory. Then the total drag of the ship can be estimated as

$$D_{tp} = D_{wp} + D_{fp}. \tag{14.26}$$

14.12 Distorted Models

The depths of flow in rivers, reservoirs and harbours are usually small compared to the horizontal dimensions. If a geometrically similar model is constructed, the depth of flow will be too small. In such cases, the effect of surface tension and viscous forces in the model become unduly increased as compared to that in the prototype.

For such cases of modelling, the scale ratio for depths y_r, is made many times more than the scale ratio for horizontal dimensions, b_r. Such models are called distorted models. It has the following advantages.

(i) the effects of surface tension in models is reduced.
(ii) the effects of viscous forces in the model is reduced by obtaining turbulent flow in the model.
(iii) the depths and slopes can be measured easily and more accurately.
(iv) movement of sediment in the model can be obtained.

Froude's criteria is used in the model testing. Hence the following ratios can be derived.

$$v_r = {l_r}^{1/2} = {y_r}^{1/2}; \quad A_r = b_r y_r \quad \text{and } Q_r = A_r v_r = b_r {y_r}^{3/2}; \quad t_r = \frac{b_r}{{y_r}^{1/2}}. \tag{14.27}$$

The Manning's formula $v = \frac{1}{N} R^{2/3} S^{1/2}$, where v is the velocity of the flow, N is coefficient of rugosity, R is the hydraulic depth and S is the slope, is commonly used in open channel flow. The value of N depends on the roughness of the boundary. Applying the Manning's formula,

$$v_r = y_r{}^{1/2} = \frac{1}{N_r} y_r{}^{2/3} \left(\frac{y_r}{b_r}\right)^{1/2}, \text{ from which}$$

$$N_r = \frac{y_r{}^{2/3}}{b_r{}^{1/2}}. \tag{14.28}$$

The bed material should be so selected as to give the required value of N_m.

In case the slope is given an exaggeration to facilitate greater movement of sediment in the model, the above ratios are to be modified.

Due to distortion, the dynamic similarity is adversely affected so that model laws cannot be exact. Verification tests need to be done on the model to check the time scale, discharge scale etc., with known events. If there is any difference, adjustments are made to qualitatively simulate the conditions in the prototype. Very valuable qualitative results can be obtained by such testing.

Example 14.8 Model tests are to be conducted for designing a stilling basin for a spillway discharging 6 m^3/s/m. The depth of flow at the toe is estimated to be 0.4 m. What should be the discharge intensity for a 1/25 model? If in the model the force on the baffle blocks is 24 N, find the force on the baffle blocks in the prototype?

Froude's criteria is used for modelling.

$$l_r = 1/25; \text{Hence } v_r = l_r{}^{1/2}; q_m = \frac{Q_r}{l_r} = \frac{v_r a_r}{l_r} = l_r{}^{3/2}, \text{ where } a_r \text{ is the area ratio.}$$

Hence discharge intensity,

$$q_m = 6 \times \left(\frac{1}{25}\right)^{3/2} = 0.048 \text{ m}^3/\text{s/m. (Ans.)}$$

$$F_r = \frac{\mu_r l_r}{t_r{}^2} = \frac{\rho_r l_r{}^3 l_r}{l_r} = l_r{}^3. \; (\rho_r = 1)$$

Hence force on the baffle piers in the prototype $= 24 \times 25^3$

$= 3.750 \times 10^5$ N $= 375$ kN. (Ans.)

Example 14.9 A tank filled with water is drained through a bottom hole 2 cm in diameter in 32 seconds. Find the time required for kerosene to drain from a geometrically similar tank (2 1/2 times its size) having a 5 cm diameter hole at the bottom. Neglect viscous effects.

Since gravity effects are predominant, Froude's criteria is used. The second tank is considered as the prototype.

$$l_r = \frac{l_m}{l_p} = \frac{2}{5}; \; t_r = l_r{}^{1/2} = 0.6325; \; \frac{t_m}{t_p} = 0.6325; t_p = \frac{t_m}{0.6325} = \frac{32}{0.6325} = 50.59 \text{ s. (Ans.)}$$

Example 14.10 It is desired to find the head loss through a group of vanes when air flows with a velocity of 30 m/s. If tests are done with water and the scale ratio is 1/5, find the velocity of water for a dynamic similitude? $\nu_{\text{air}} = 15 \times 10^{-6}\,\text{m}^2/\text{s}$; $\nu_{\text{water}} = 10^{-6}\,\text{m}^2/\text{s}$

Reynold's criteria is to be used in modelling since viscous effects are predominant.

$$l_r = 1/5;\ \frac{v_r l_r}{\nu_r} = 1;\ \text{i.e., } v_r = \frac{\nu_r}{l_r} = \frac{10^{-6}}{15 \times 10^{-6}} \times 5 = \frac{1}{3}.$$

$$\text{Hence } v_m = \frac{30}{3} = 10\ \text{m/s. (Ans.)}$$

Example 14.11 A naval ship 400 m long has to move at a velocity of 12 m/s in sea water of specific gravity 1.025. A 1/50 model is towed through fresh water at the required velocity for similitude and the drag was found to be 90 N. The wetted area of the model is 16 m^2. The surface drag coefficient C_f for the model and the prototype in the formula $D_f = C_f \frac{1}{2}\rho V^2 \times \text{area}$ was 2.5×10^{-3} and 1.2×10^{-3} respectively. Find the drag on the ship.

Modelling is done as per Froude's criteria. Let the equivalent fresh water velocity of ship be v_e.

$$D = C_D \times \left(\frac{1}{2}\right) \times 1.025 \times 1000 \times 12^2 = C_D \times \left(\frac{1}{2}\right) \times 1000 \times V_e^2.$$

$$V_e = 12.15\ \text{m/s}.$$

$$L_r = \frac{1}{50};\ \frac{V_r}{\sqrt{g_r L_r}} = 1;\ \text{hence } V_r = L_r^{1/2};\ V_m = \frac{12.15}{\sqrt{50}} = 1.718\ \text{m/s}.$$

$$D_{fm} = C_f \times \frac{1}{2} \times \rho V_m^2 \times \text{area} = 2.5 \times 10^{-3} \times \frac{1}{2} \times 1000 \times 1.718^2 \times 16 = 59.03\ \text{N}$$

$$D_{wm} = D_m - D_{fm} = 90 - 59.03 = 30.97\ \text{N}.$$

$$F_r = \frac{\mu_r L_r}{T_r^2} = \frac{\rho L_r^3 L_r}{L_r} = \rho_r L_r^3$$

$$\text{hence, } D_{wp} = \frac{D_{wm}}{\rho_r L_r^3} = 30.97 \times 1.025 \times 50^3 = 3968\ \text{kN (Ans.)}$$

$$A_p = \frac{A_m}{L_r^2} = 16 \times 50^2 = 40000\ \text{m}^2$$

$$D_{fp} = C_f \times \frac{1}{2} \times \rho V_p^2 \times \text{area} = 1.2 \times 10^{-3} \times \frac{1}{2} \times 1.025 \times 1000 \times 12^2 \times 40000\text{N} = 3542.4\ \text{kN}$$

Total drag on the ship $= d_{fp} + D_{fm} = 3968 + 3542.4 = 7510.4$ kN (Ans.)

14.13 Similarity Relations for Turbo Machines

It may be desirable to test a model of a pump or turbine to study how a prototype will perform. The model is required to be made geometrically similar to the prototype. The velocity diagrams at the entry and exit from the impellers should also be similar.

The tests are conducted on the model, and the performance of the prototype are interpreted guided by the non-dimensional coefficients arrived at by means of the dimensional analysis. The non-dimensional groups which affect the design are

$$\pi_1 = \frac{Q}{\mathrm{L^3T^{-1}}} = \frac{Q}{Nd^3} \text{ termed as the discharge coefficient } k_d. \tag{14.29}$$

$$\pi_2 = \frac{P}{\rho d^5 N^3} \text{ termed as the power coefficient } k_p. \tag{14.30}$$

$$\pi_3 = \frac{\mathrm{g}H}{N^2 d^2} \text{ termed as the head coefficient } k_h. \tag{14.31}$$

$$\pi_4 = \frac{\mu}{\rho d^2 N} \text{ termed as the friction coefficient } k_f. \tag{14.32}$$

Among the above coefficients, the friction coefficient will manifest only as a scale effect. In most cases, it may be neglected. The bigger machines will generally perform better.

Example 14.12 A pump delivers a discharge of 0.048 $\mathrm{m^3/s}$ at a head of 30 m. The speed is 1450 rpm. Find the discharge, head and power required at 1200 rpm, if the efficiency remains at 75%.

$Q_1 = 0.048\ \mathrm{m^3/s}$; $H_1 = 30$ m; $N_1 = 1450$ rpm; $D_1 = D_2$; $N_2 = 1200$ rpm.

Q/ND^3 is a constant.

$$\text{Hence, } Q_2 = \frac{Q_1}{N_1 D_1^3} \times N_2 D_2^3 = \frac{0.048 \times 1200}{1450} = 0.04\ \mathrm{m^3/s}. \text{ (Ans.)}$$

$$\frac{gH}{N^2 D^2} \text{ is constant. Hence, } H_2 = \frac{H_1}{N_1^2} \times N_2^2 = \frac{30 \times 1200^2}{1450^2} = 20.55 \text{ m. (Ans.)}$$

$$P_2 = \frac{\gamma QH}{\eta} = \frac{9810 \times 0.04 \times 20.55}{0.75} = 10.75 \text{ kW. (Ans.)}$$

Example 14.13 Model studies are done on a 1/5 scale model at 1200 rpm. The head developed and power input were found to be 10 m and 4.5 kW respectively. The discharge was found to be 35 l/s. Find the efficiency. If the prototype runs at 360 rpm, find the head developed, discharge and power required for the prototype.

$$P = \frac{\gamma QH}{\eta}; \ \eta = \frac{\gamma QH}{P} = \frac{9810 \times 0.035 \times 10}{4.5 \times 1000} = 0.763 \text{ (Ans.)}$$

For model and prototype, gH/N^2D^2 is constant.

$$\text{Hence } H_P = \frac{H_m \times N_P^2 D_P^2}{N_m^2 D_m^2} = \frac{10 \times 360^2 \times 5^2}{1200^2 \times 1^2} = 22.5 \text{ m (Ans.)}$$

Q/ND^3 is constant.

$$\text{Hence } Q_P = \frac{Q_m}{N_m D_m^3} \times N_P D_P^3 = \frac{0.035 \times 360 \times 5^3}{1200} = 1.3125 \text{ m}^3\text{/s. (Ans.)}$$

P/N^3D^5 is constant.

$$\text{Hence } P_P = \frac{P_1}{N_m^3 D_m^5} \times N_P^3 D_P^5 = \frac{4.5 \times 360^3 \times 5^5}{1200^3} = 379.69 \text{ kW. (Ans.)}$$

REVIEW QUESTIONS AND PROBLEMS

14.1 Write the dimensions of the following quantities.

(i)	Coefficient of dynamic viscosity	(ii)	Coefficient of discharge
(iii)	Darcy–Weisbach coefficient	(iv)	Efficiency
(v)	Specific gravity	(vi)	Specific volume

14.2 Examine the following equations for dimensional homogeneity

(i) $H_f = \dfrac{flQ^2}{12.1d^5}$

(ii) $\beta = 3.12\dfrac{P^2}{A} - 21.25$, where P is the perimeter and A is the area

(iii) $f = \dfrac{0.316}{\text{Re}^{0.25}}$

(iv) $d_n = d\left(\dfrac{d}{2fl}\right)^{0.25}$

(v) $\text{Re}\sqrt{f} = \dfrac{(2gd^3S)^{1/2}}{\nu}$

(vi) $\dfrac{\partial u}{\partial t} + u\dfrac{\partial u}{\partial x} + v\dfrac{\partial u}{\partial y} + w\dfrac{\partial u}{\partial z} = -\dfrac{1}{\rho}\dfrac{\partial p}{\partial x} + \dfrac{\mu}{\rho}\left(\dfrac{\partial^2 u}{\partial x^2} + \dfrac{\partial^2 u}{\partial y^2} + \dfrac{\partial^2 u}{\partial z^2}\right) + g_x$

(vii) $v = (\frac{1}{N})R^{2/3}S^{1/2}$

(viii) $v = C\sqrt{RS}$

14.3 Explain the applications of dimensional analysis.

14.4 State Buckingham's π theorem and explain the usual criteria for selection of repeated variables. If the repeated variables are changed, will the analysis be valid?

14.5 Explain the method of determining non-dimensional numbers affecting a phenomenon.

14.6 Explain what are geometrical, kinematic and dynamic similitudes.

14.7 Explain Froude's criteria for similitude and derive the expressions for velocity, time and force ratios.

14.8 Explain Reynold's criteria for similitude and derive the expression for ratios of velocity, time and force.

14.9 Find the condition for a model to satisfy both Froude's and Reynold's criteria at the same time.

14.10 What are distorted models? What are their advantages and disadvantages?

14.11 Enumerate the advantages of model studies.

14.12 Show that the Reynolds number represents the ratio of inertial forces to viscous forces. What does the Froude number represent?

14.13 The pressure drop Δp in a laminar flow in a pipe of diameter d and length l depends on the dynamic viscosity μ of the fluid with density ρ and average velocity v. Derive the relationship between the variables on the basis of dimensional analysis.

14.14 The pressure loss through an orifice in a pipe of diameter D having flow velocity U depends on the specific mass ρ, dynamic viscosity μ and orifice diameter d. Find an equation for pressure loss using dimensional analysis.

14.15 The resistance force R of a supersonic plane during flight can be considered dependent upon the length of the aircraft l, velocity v, viscosity of air μ, specific mass ρ and bulk modulus K. Prove that $R = \rho l^2 V^2 f\left(\frac{\mu}{\rho v L}, \frac{K}{\rho v^2}\right)$.

14.16 The coefficient of discharge of a circular orifice depends on its diameter d, head H of the tank, dynamic viscosity μ and acceleration due to gravity g, specific mass ρ. Show that $C_d\left(\frac{d}{H}, \frac{\mu}{\rho\sqrt{gH^3}}\right)$.

14.17 The power developed by a hydraulic turbine of head H, depends on the acceleration due to gravity g, ρ the specific mass of water, N the speed of the turbine and D the diameter of the turbine. Show that $P = \rho N^3 D^5 \phi\left(\frac{N^2 D^2}{gH}\right)$.

14.18 The capillary rise h in a tube of diameter d depends on the specific weight γ and surface tension σ of the fluid. Show that $\frac{h}{d} = \phi\left(\frac{\sigma}{\gamma d^2}\right)$.

14.19 The head loss H_L in a pipe due to friction depends on the height of the roughness k, the velocity v, the length of the pipe l, the dynamic viscosity of the fluid μ, density ρ and diameter d of the pipe. Find the expression for the head loss.

14.20 Studies on a stilling basin is made in a 1/20 scale model. If the discharge intensity of the prototype is 20 $m^3/s/m$. What will be the discharge intensity required for the model. [Hint: Find $q_r = Q_r/l_r$].

14.21 The force on the baffle piers in a model stilling basin was found to be 12 N/m. Find the force on the prototype stilling basin if the model scale is 1/15. [Hint: Find F_r/l_r]

14.22 Model studies on a sea wall is conducted and the force measured on the model wall is 250 N/m. Find the force from the sea wall if the model scale is 1/20.

14.23 Oil is discharged through a small orifice 5 mm in diameter from a model tank and the time taken to empty half the tank was found to be 230 s. Neglecting the effect of friction, find the time required to empty half of a tank having four times the linear dimensions of the model tank by an orifice of diameter 20 mm.

14.24 A study is to be made regarding the wave resistance of a ship when moving at 40 km/hr. What should be the velocity at which a 1/36 model is to be moved in a towing tank for model studies?

14.25 A pipe 30 cm in diameter has to convey oil ($\nu = 1.1 \times 10^{-5}$ m^2/s) at a rate of 120 l/s. At what discharge of water through a 5 cm diameter pipe, will the condition of flow be similar? Assume ν for water as 1 centi-stoke.

14.26 It is decided to find the drag of a streamlined body moving at 100 m/s through air ($\nu = 1.5 \times 10^{-5}$ m^2/s). At what velocity is the model of the body ($l_r = 1/6$) to be towed in water to have the same flow conditions. ($\nu_{\text{water}} = 10^{-6}$ m^2/s)

14.27 A missile 2 m long is to move at a speed of 4000 m/s in air. ($\nu = 1.5 \times 10^{-5}$ m^2/s) At what speed is a full size model to be tested in water to have similar flow characteristics. (Assume $\nu = 10^{-6}$ m^2/s)

14.28 A centrifugal pump discharges 0.045 m^3/s of water at a head of 40 m. The speed is 1500 rpm. Find the flow rate, head and power required when the speed is reduced to 1200 rpm. Assume the same efficiency of 75% in both the cases.

14.29 The power P required to rotate a given impeller at a given speed, depends on the diameter of the impeller D_a, the specific mass of the liquid ρ, the speed of rotation of the impeller n, the dynamic viscosity of the liquid μ, the acceleration due to gravity g and a large number of factors like the number of blades of the impeller, number of baffles, the shape of the impeller and baffles and a number of ratios of the dimension of the tank, liquid depth, the height of the impeller etc. with the impeller diameter. Conduct dimensional analysis and show the relationship,

$$\text{Power number } P_N = \frac{P}{\rho n^3 D_a^5} = \left[\frac{nD_a^2}{v}, \frac{n^2 D_a}{g}, N_1, N_2, \ldots, S_1, S_2 \ldots\right]$$

where $\frac{nD_a^2}{v}$ is a form of Reynolds number, $\frac{n^2 D_a}{g}$ is a form of Froude's number, $N_1, N_2 \ldots$ are numbers and $S_1, S_2 \ldots$ are some shape factors.

ANSWERS

14.1(i) $ML^{-1}T^{-1}$; (ii) $M^0L^0T^0$; (iii) $M^0L^0T^0$; (iv) $M^0L^0T^0$; (v) $M^0L^0T^0$; (vi) $M^{-1}L^3T^0$; (vii) $M\,L^{-1}T^{-2}$; (viii) M^0LT^{-2}; **14.2** (i) No; (ii) Yes; (iii) Yes; (iv) Yes; (v) Yes; (vi) Yes; (vii) No; (vii) No; 14.13. $\dfrac{\Delta p}{\rho v^2}\left(\dfrac{l}{d}, \dfrac{\rho v d}{\mu}\right)$; **14.14.** $\dfrac{\Delta p}{\rho U^2}\left(\dfrac{d}{D}, \dfrac{\rho U d}{\mu}\right)$; **14.19.** $\dfrac{h_l}{l} = \phi\left(\dfrac{k}{d}, \dfrac{\rho v d}{\mu}\right)$; **14.20.** 0.223 $m^3/s/m$; **14.21.** 2700 N/m; **14.22.** 100 kN/m; **14.23.** 460 s; **14.24.** 6.67 m/s; **14.25.** 1.818 l/s; **14.26.** 40 m/s; **14.27.** 266.7 m/s; **14.28.** 0.036 m^3/s; 25.6 m; 12.055 kW.

15 Boundary Layer Theory

Laminar and turbulent boundary layers — Blasius solution — boundary layer thickness — Displacement thickness — Karman's integral equation — Momentum thickness — Boundary layer separation — Control of boundary layer

15.1 Introduction

So far, in our discussion, we considered problems involving the flow of non-viscous fluids or on the other extreme, flow problems where the viscosity is very high. Even in cases where the viscosity of fluid is very small, there cannot be any slip of fluid at rigid boundaries.

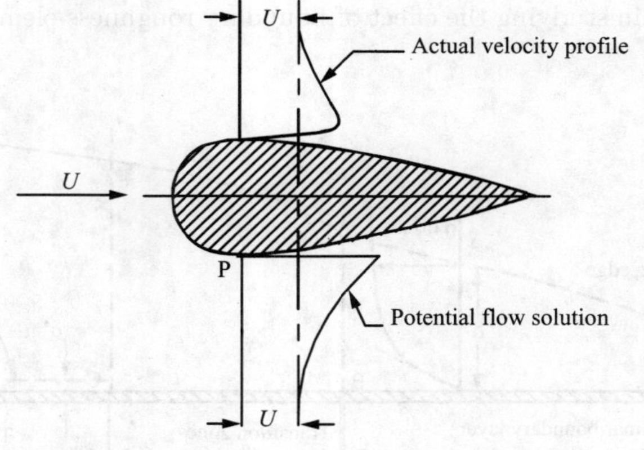

Fig. 15.1 *Velocity profile around a strut*

The potential flow solution and the actual flow around a strut are shown schematically in Fig. 15.1. The potential flow solution gives the maximum velocity at point P, whereas by virtue of the property of viscosity, the actual velocity at P should be equal to zero. For fluids of low viscosity, the velocity changes from zero at the boundary to a velocity as given by the potential flow solutions in a very thin layer called the boundary layer. Boundary layer problems occur in all flows along curved and complex boundaries. Prandtl made simplifying assumptions of the governing equations and obtained the solution for the flow along a thin flat plate held parallel to the flow. Where Blasius has given theoretical solutions for the thickness of a boundary layer, shear stress, drag etc.

15.2 Boundary Layer Development along a Flat Plate held Parallel to the Flow[28,30]

The flow over a thin smooth two-dimensional plate is considered. The ambient velocity is U. At the boundary of the plate, the velocity will be zero as there cannot be any slip. The velocity increases from zero at the boundary to nearly, say 0.99 U at a thickness δ (called boundary layer) from the boundary. Prandtl assumed that the flow can be considered practically non-viscous except in this thin boundary layer where forces due to viscosity were of the same order as those due to inertial forces. For some length AB of the plate, the thickness of the boundary layer remains small and viscous forces are very predominant so that laminar flow prevails in the boundary layer. The Reynolds number Ux/ν, where x is the distance from the leading edge may be equal to or greater than 50,000 before the inertial forces create disturbances in the flow. However, some of the disturbances may get damped by the viscous forces and a zone of flow may occur where the flow is transitional. The boundary layer can become fully turbulent after a little more distance BC. However, near the boundary, even in a turbulent boundary layer, a small thickness of fluid may have laminar flow. This layer is called the laminar sub-layer which is of great importance in studying the effect of boundary roughness elements on the main flow.

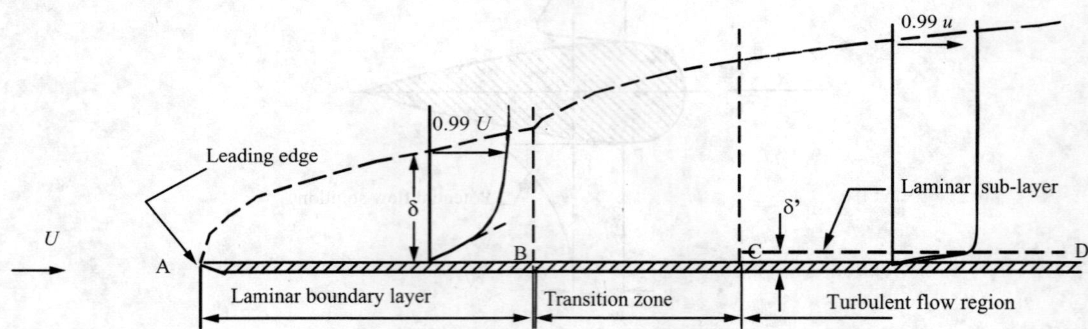

Fig. 15.2 *Development of boundary layer along a flat plate*

In the Navier–Stoke's equation in the X direction,

$$\frac{\partial u}{\partial t}+u\frac{\partial u}{\partial x}+v\frac{\partial u}{\partial y}+w\frac{\partial u}{\partial z}=-\frac{1}{\rho}\frac{\partial p}{\partial x}+\frac{\mu}{\rho}\left(\frac{\partial^2 u}{\partial x^2}+\frac{\partial^2 u}{\partial y^2}+\frac{\partial^2 u}{\partial z^2}\right)+X_i$$

and continuity equation

$$\frac{\partial u}{\partial x}+\frac{\partial v}{\partial y}+\frac{\partial w}{\partial z}=0,$$

for incompressible fluids. Introducing the simplifying assumptions:

(1) the flow is steady i.e., $\dfrac{\partial u}{\partial t} = 0$,
(2) the flow is two-dimensional, $w = 0$; $\dfrac{\partial u}{\partial z} = 0$; $\dfrac{\partial v}{\partial z} = 0$,
(3) the pressure gradient in the X direction is neglected,
(4) the body force is neglected, $X_i = 0$,
(5) the thickness of the boundary layer is very small,
(6) the Reynold's number UL/ν is very large, at least of the order of magnitude of L^2/δ^2,
(7) the velocity changes in the Y direction is of higher order than that in the X direction,

$$\frac{\partial^2 u}{\partial y^2} >> \frac{\partial^2 u}{\partial x^2}$$

The equations are simplified as

$$u\frac{\partial u}{\partial x} + v\frac{\partial u}{\partial y} = \frac{\mu}{\rho}\frac{\partial^2 u}{\partial y^2}. \tag{15.1}$$

and

$$\frac{\partial u}{\partial x} + \frac{\partial v}{\partial y} = 0, \tag{15.2}$$

with the boundary conditions $y = 0; u = 0;$ (15.3)

and $y = \infty$; $u = U$ or, when $y = \delta, u = 0.99\,U$, (15.4)

where δ is known as the boundary layer thickness.

15.2.1 Blasius' Solution of the differential equation**

L. Prandtl gave the boundary layer equations as follows:

$$u\frac{\partial u}{\partial x} + v\frac{\partial u}{\partial y} = v\frac{\partial^2 u}{\partial y^2} \quad \text{and} \quad \frac{\partial u}{\partial x} + \frac{\partial v}{\partial y} = 0$$

subject to the conditions that $u = v = 0$, at $y = 0$ and $x > 0$ and $y \to \delta, u \to U$
Prandtl proposed that when $y = \delta, u \sim 0.99U$, where δ is the thickness of the boundary layer. Blasius, a student of Prandtl assumed the velocity distribution in the boundary layer to have self-similarity, i.e.

$$\frac{u}{U} = g(\eta) \tag{15.5}$$

where

$$\eta = \frac{y}{\delta(x)} \tag{15.6}$$

**for advanced study

Introducing the stream function

$$\psi, u = -\frac{\partial \psi}{\partial y} \quad \text{and} \quad v = \frac{\delta \psi}{\delta x} \quad \text{and since}\, u = Ug(\eta)$$

$$\psi = -\int_0^y u dy = -\delta \int_0^\eta u d\eta = -\delta \int_0^\eta Ug(\eta) d\eta = -U\delta f(\eta) \tag{15.7}$$

where

$$g(\eta) = \frac{df}{d\eta} \tag{15.8}$$

Equation (15.9) shows that the similarity form for the stream function is $\psi/U\delta = f(\eta)$, signifying that the scale for the stream function is proportional to the local flow rate $U\delta$. In terms of the stream function, the governing boundary layer equations become

$$\frac{\partial \psi}{\partial y}\frac{\partial^2 \psi}{\partial x \partial y} - \frac{\partial \psi}{\partial x}\frac{\partial^2 \psi}{\partial y^2} = -v\frac{\partial^3 \psi}{\partial y^3} \tag{15.9}$$

subject to $\frac{\partial \psi}{\partial y} = \psi = 0$ at $y = 0, x > 0,$ (15.10a)

$$-\frac{\partial \psi}{\partial y} \to U \quad \text{as} \quad \frac{y}{\delta} \to \eta \tag{15.10b}$$

To express sets (15.9) and (15.10) in terms of the similarity stream function $f(\eta)$, we find the following derivatives from (15.7):

$$\frac{\partial \psi}{\partial x} = -U\left[f\frac{d\delta}{dx} + \delta\frac{\partial f}{\partial x}\right] = -U\frac{d\delta}{dx}[f - nf'] \tag{15.11}$$

$$\frac{\partial^2 \psi}{\partial x \partial y} = -U\frac{d\delta}{dx}\frac{\partial}{\partial y}[f - \eta f'] = \frac{U\eta f''}{\delta}\frac{d\delta}{dx} \tag{15.12}$$

$$\frac{\partial \psi}{\partial y} = -Uf' \tag{15.13}$$

$$\frac{\partial^2 \psi}{\partial y^2} = -\frac{Uf''}{\delta} \tag{15.14}$$

$$\frac{\partial^3 \psi}{\partial y^3} = -\frac{Uf'''}{\delta^2} \tag{15.15}$$

where primes on f denote derivatives with respect to η. Substituting these derivatives in (15.5) and cancelling terms, we obtain

$$-\left(\frac{U\delta d\delta}{v dx}\right) ff'' = f''' \tag{15.16}$$

In (15.15), f and its derivatives are independent of the value of x. The equation can be valid only if $\frac{U\delta}{v}\frac{d\delta}{dx} =$ constant. Choosing the constant to be $\frac{1}{2}$ for eventual algebraic simplicity, an integration gives

$$\delta = \sqrt{\frac{vx}{U}} \tag{15.17}$$

Then (15.12) becomes

$$\frac{1}{2}ff'' + f''' = 0 \tag{15.18}$$

and the boundary conditions become

$$f'(\infty) = 1 \text{ and } f(0) = f'(0) = 0 \tag{15.19}$$

A series solution of the non-linear equation (15.14) is given by Blasius. It is easier to solve by the Runge–Kutta technique. The solution makes the profile at various downstream distances collapse into a single curve of $\frac{u}{U}$ vs. $y\sqrt{\frac{U}{vx}}$, and is in excellent agreement with experimental data for laminar flows at high Reynolds numbers (Nikuradse's experiments).

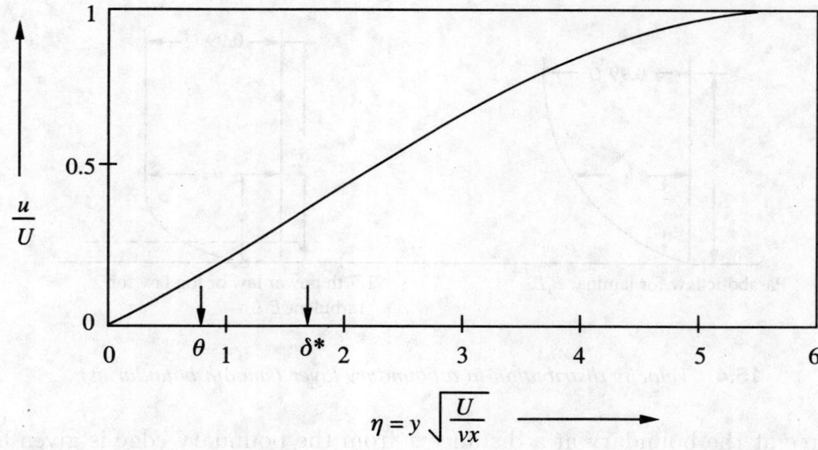

Fig. 15.3 *Variation of velocity with non-dimensional parameter* η

The solution showed that $0.99U$ is attained when $\eta \approx 5$ defining the boundary layer thickness δ by the equation

$$\delta = 5\sqrt{\frac{vx}{U}} \text{ or } \frac{\delta}{x} = \frac{5}{\sqrt{R_x}} \tag{15.20}$$

where R_x the Reynolds number $= \frac{Ux}{v}$

15.2.2 Blasius solution

Blasius has found a solution for the Prandtl's boundary layer equations and they are supported by Nikuradse's experiments.

In the laminar boundary layer, the thickness δ has been found to be given by

$$\frac{\delta}{x} = \frac{5}{\sqrt{Ux/\nu}}, \tag{15.21}$$

where x is the distance from the leading edge.

The velocity distribution within the laminar boundary layer (Fig. 15.3) is of the form $u/U = f(\eta)$, where $\eta = y/\delta$ and $f(\eta)$ is a polynomial. This may be approximated by the parabolic equation of the type

$$\frac{u}{U} = 2\frac{y}{\delta} - \left(\frac{y}{\delta}\right)^2, \quad \text{or} \quad \frac{u}{U} = \frac{3}{2}\frac{y}{\delta} - \frac{1}{2}\left(\frac{y}{\delta}\right)^3, \tag{15.22}$$

as done by many investigators.

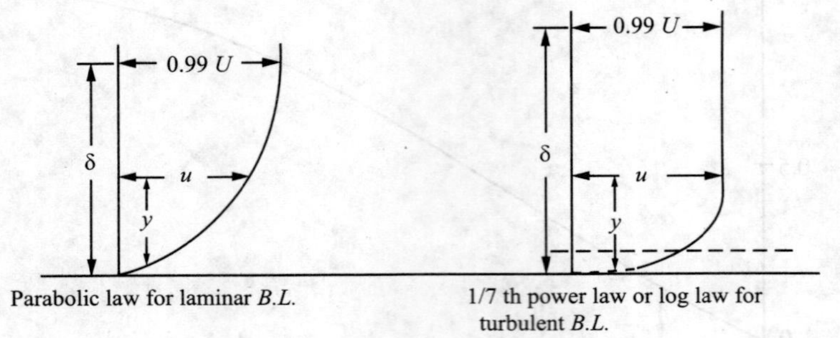

15.4 *Velocity distribution in a boundary layer (smooth boundaries)*

The shear force at the boundary at a distance x from the boundary edge is given by

$$\tau_0 = c_f \frac{\rho U^2}{2}, \tag{15.23}$$

where c_f is the local drag coefficient.

$$c_f = \frac{0.664}{R_x^{1/2}}, \tag{15.24}$$

where $R_x = \dfrac{Ux}{\nu}$. The total drag on the plate of length L if the boundary layer is laminar throughout will be

$$D_f = c_f \frac{\rho U^2}{2}(2 \times B \times L), \tag{15.25}$$

where c_f is the total drag coefficient, B is the breadth of the plate and L is the length.

$$c_f = \frac{1.328}{\sqrt{R_L}}. \tag{15.26}$$

and $R_L = \dfrac{UL}{\nu}$.

15.2.3 Turbulent boundary layer

Due to the extreme complexity of the equations governing turbulent flow, the solution of the turbulent boundary layer equation proceeds from observed experimental results. The thickness of the boundary layer is given by

$$\frac{\delta}{x} = \frac{0.377}{{R_x}^{1/5}}. \tag{15.27}$$

$$\text{Shear stress } \tau_0 = c_f \frac{\rho U^2}{2}, \tag{15.28}$$

where the local drag coefficient

$$c_f = \frac{0.059}{{R_x}^{1/5}}. \tag{15.29}$$

The total drag is given by

$$D_f = c_f \frac{\rho U^2}{2}(2 \times B \times L). \tag{15.30}$$

The value of c_f, the total drag coefficient, can be obtained by the formula

$$c_f = \frac{0.074}{{R_L}^{1/5}}, \tag{15.31}$$

where $R_L > 2 \times 10^7$.

More accurate results for total drag coefficient are obtained using the Karman–Schoenherr equation

$$\frac{1}{c_f} = 4.13 \log_{10}(R_L c_f).$$

In the above equation, it is assumed that the turbulent boundary layer starts from the very beginning of the plate and the laminar boundary layer is neglected.

The transition from laminar to turbulent boundary layer may usually occur at the Reynolds number of 5×10^5 depending on the free stream flow characteristics and the roughness of the plate. But in some cases, it may start at a Reynolds number of 2×10^5 or even be delayed until the Reynolds number is well above 4×10^6. If the length of plate is in the transition region, the drag coefficient will be smaller and can be calculated by the formula

$$c_f = \frac{0.074}{{R_L}^{1/5}} - \frac{A}{R_L}. \tag{15.32}$$

If R_L exceeds 10^7, a better estimation for c_f is given by the formula

$$c_f = \frac{0.455}{(\log_{10} R_L)^{2.58}} - \frac{A}{R_L}. \tag{15.33}$$

In the above equation, A depends on the Reynolds number R_L at which transition takes place. A is usually taken as 1700, the value corresponds to $\text{Re} = 5 \times 10^5$.
With smooth boundaries, the velocity distribution in the turbulent boundary layer above the laminar sub-layer is found to confirm closely to the equation,

$$\frac{u}{u_*} = 5.75 \log_{10} \frac{u_* y}{\nu} + 5.5, \tag{15.34}$$

where

$$u_* = \sqrt{\frac{\tau_0}{\rho}}, \tag{15.35}$$

and τ_0 is shear stress at the boundary. The term u_* is known as the shear velocity. There is a thin laminar layer at the boundary in a turbulent flow known as the laminar sub-layer. The velocity distribution in the laminar sub-layer is given by the equation

$$\frac{u}{u_*} = \frac{u_* y}{\nu}. \tag{15.36}$$

The velocity distribution in the turbulent boundary layer outside the sub-layer can be approximated by the equation

$$\frac{u}{U} = \left(\frac{y}{\delta}\right)^{1/7}, \tag{15.37}$$

or by the logarithmic velocity defect law,

$$\frac{u - U}{u_*} = 5.75 \log_{10} \left(\frac{y}{\delta}\right). \tag{15.38}$$

Example 15.1 A flat thin plate 4.5 m long and 0.8 m wide is held parallel to an air flow 6 m/s. $\nu_{\text{air}} = 1.44 \times 10^{-5}\ \text{m}^2/\text{s}$ and $\rho = 1.21\ \text{kg/m}^3$. Assume the boundary layer to be laminar up to a Reynolds number of 5×10^5. Find (i) the maximum thickness of the laminar boundary layer, (ii) shear stress 0.6 m from the leading edge and (iii) drag on the first 1 m length of the plate (iv) total drag on the plate.

$l = 4.5$ m; $b = 0.8$ m; $U = 6$ m/s; $\nu_{\text{air}} = 1.44 \times 10^{-5}\ \text{m}^2/\text{s}$.

(i) $R_x = R_c = 5 \times 10^5 = \dfrac{Ux}{\nu} = \dfrac{6 \times x}{1.44 \times 10^{-5}} \rightarrow x = 1.2$ m.

$$\delta_l = \frac{5}{{R_x}^{1/2}} \times x = \frac{5 \times 1.2}{(5 \times 10^5)^{1/2}} = 8.485 \times 10^{-3} \text{ m } = 8.485 \text{ mm. (Ans.)}$$

(ii) $R_{0.6} = \dfrac{6 \times 0.6}{1.44 \times 10^{-5}} = 2.5 \times 10^5$.

$$\tau_{0.6} = c_f \times \rho \frac{U^2}{2} = \frac{0.664}{{R_{0.6}}^{1/2}} \times 1.21 \times \frac{6^2}{2} = 0.0289 \text{ N/m}^2. \text{ (Ans.)}$$

(iii) $R_1 = \dfrac{6 \times 1}{1.44 \times 10^{-5}} = 4.1667 \times 10^5$ which is less than 5×10^5. Hence the boundary layer is laminar.

$$\text{Drag on 1 m length} = c_f \times \rho \frac{U^2}{2} \times 2 \times b \times 1$$

$$= \frac{1.328}{(4.1667 \times 10^5)^{1/2}} \times 1.21 \times \frac{6^2}{2} \times 2 \times 0.8 \times 1$$

$$= 0.0717 \text{ N. (Ans.)}$$

(iv) $R_L = \dfrac{6 \times 4.5}{1.44 \times 10^{-5}} = 1.875 \times 10^6$. Hence the boundary layer is turbulent.

$$\text{Total drag on plate} = c_f \times \rho \frac{U^2}{2} \times 2 \times b \times l$$

$$= \left(\frac{0.074}{{R_L}^{1/5}} - \frac{1700}{R_L} \right) \times \frac{1.21}{2} \times 6^2 \times 2 \times 0.8 \times 4.5$$

$$= 3.2108 \times 10^{-3} \times 156.82 = 0.5035 \text{ N. (Ans.)}$$

Example 15.2 Assuming the velocity distribution in a laminar boundary layer is given by the equation $\dfrac{u}{U} = 2\left(\dfrac{y}{\delta}\right) - \left(\dfrac{y}{\delta}\right)^2$, find the velocity at half the thickness of the boundary layer from the plate.

$$\frac{u_{0.5\delta}}{U} = 2 \times 0.5 - 0.5^2 = 0.75; u_{0.5\delta} = 0.75\, U. \text{ (Ans.)}$$

Example 15.3 A flat plate 12 m long and 0.6 m wide is held in an air stream of velocity 8 m/s. Assume $\nu = 1.44 \times 10^{-5}$ m^2/s and $\rho = 1.21$ kg/m^3. Find at the end of the plate (i) thickness of the boundary layer, (ii) the shear stress at the boundary, (iii) velocity in the boundary layer at half the thickness of the boundary layer by the power law and (iv) velocity in the boundary layer at half the thickness of the boundary layer as per the log law.

$L = 12$ m ; $b = 0.8$ m ; $U = 8$ m/s; $\nu = 1.44 \times 10^{-5}$m^2/s.

$$R_L = \frac{UL}{\nu} = \frac{8 \times 12}{1.44 \times 10^{-5}} = 6.667 \times 10^6.$$

It is a turbulent boundary layer.

(i) $$\delta = \frac{0.377 \times x}{{R_L}^{1/5}} = \frac{0.377 \times 12}{(6.667 \times 10^6)^{1/5}} = 0.1953 \text{ m. (Ans.)}$$

(ii) $$\tau_0 = c_f \times \rho \frac{U^2}{2} = \frac{0.059}{{R_L}^{1/5}} \times 1.21 \times \frac{8^2}{2} = 0.0986 \text{ N/m}^2\text{. (Ans.)}$$

(iii) $$\frac{u}{U} = \left(\frac{y}{\delta}\right)^{1/7}; \frac{y}{\delta} = 0.5; \text{ and } U = 8 \text{ m/s.}$$

$$u = U\left(\frac{y}{\delta}\right)^{1/7} = 8 \times (0.5)^{1/7} = 7.246 \text{ m/s. (Ans.)}$$

(iv) $$\frac{u - U}{u_*} = 5.75 \log_{10}\left(\frac{y}{\delta}\right); U = 8 \text{ m/s.}; \frac{y}{\delta} = 0.5.$$

$$u_* = \sqrt{\frac{\tau_0}{\rho}} = \sqrt{\frac{0.0986}{1.21}} = 0.2855 \text{ m/s.}$$

$$u = u_* \left(5.75 \log_{10} \frac{y}{\delta}\right) + U = 0.2855\, [5.75 \log_{10} (0.5)] + 8 = 7.506 \text{ m/s. (Ans.)}$$

Example 15.4 Assuming that a laminar boundary layer is developed on a long flat plate, find the ratios of the first half length of the plate to the drag on the full length of the plate.

$$\text{The drag on half length} = D_1 = C_{f_1} \times \rho \frac{U^2}{2} \times 2b \times \frac{L}{2}$$

$$= \frac{1.328}{(UL/2\nu)^{1/2}} \times \frac{\rho U^2}{2} \times b \times L = \frac{1.328}{(UL/\nu)^{1/2}} \times 2^{1/2} \times \rho U^2 bL.$$

$$\text{The drag on full length} = D_2 = C_{f_2} \frac{\rho U^2}{2} \times 2bL$$

$$= \frac{1.328}{(UL/\nu)^{1/2}} \times \frac{\rho U^2}{2} \times 2bL = \frac{1.328}{(UL/\nu)^{1/2}} \times \rho U^2 bL.$$

$$\frac{D_1}{D_2} = \frac{2^{1/2} \times 1/2}{1} = 0.707. \text{ (Ans.)}$$

15.3 The Laminar Sub-layer and Boundary Roughness

Even when the boundary layer is turbulent, the flow in the immediate vicinity of the boundary will be laminar. This region is known as the laminar sub-layer and has a thickness of δ'. Experimentally, δ' has been found to be given by the equation

$$\delta' = \frac{11.6\ \nu}{u_*}. \tag{15.39}$$

The surface may have roughness elements of height k_s. The relative value of k_s with δ' governs the effectiveness of the roughness in creating disturbances in the main flow.
When

$$\frac{u_* k_s}{\nu} \leq 5, \tag{15.40}$$

the plate will act as a hydrodynamically smooth boundary.
When

$$\frac{u_* k_s}{\nu} \geq 70, \tag{15.41}$$

the plate will act as a hydrodynamically rough boundary.
The condition $5 \leq \dfrac{u_* k_s}{\nu} \leq 70$ indicates a transition condition.
When the plate is rough, the local drag coefficient for the turbulent layer will be more than that for smooth plates and is dependent on $\dfrac{x}{k_s}$ in addition to the Reynolds number $\dfrac{u_* x}{\nu}$, where x is the distance from the leading edge. Also $c_f = f\left(\dfrac{L}{k_s}, \dfrac{u_* L}{\nu}\right)$.

Example 15.5 A long plate having roughness $k_s = 0.01$mm is moving through water ($\nu = 10^{-2}$ stokes). At a point in the turbulent boundary layer, the boundary shear stress is 90 N/m^2. Find (i) the thickness of the laminar sub-layer and (ii) whether the boundary is hydrodynamically smooth or rough.

(i) $\tau_0 = 90$ N/m^2; $\rho = 1000$ kg/m^2.

$$u_* = \sqrt{\frac{\tau_0}{\rho}} = \left(\frac{90}{1000}\right)^{1/2} = 0.3 \text{ m/s}.$$

$$\delta' = \frac{11.6\ \nu}{u_*} = \frac{11.6 \times 10^{-6}}{0.3} = 3.87 \times 10^{-5} \text{ m/s. (Ans.)}$$

(ii) $\dfrac{u_* k_s}{\nu} = \dfrac{0.3}{10^{-6}} \times \dfrac{0.01}{1000} = 3$ which is less than 5.

Hence the boundary is hydrodynamically smooth.

15.4 Displacement and Momentum Thickness

Consider a central volume ABCD of unit width (Fig. 15.4).

The mass rate of flow across AD = $\rho U\delta$.

The mass rate of flow across BC = $\int_0^\delta \rho u dy$.

To maintain continuity, a flow of $\rho \int_0^\delta (U - u)dy$ will leave across DC. *A displacement thickness δ^* is defined as the equivalent thickness by which the external stream lines are displaced because of the plate.*

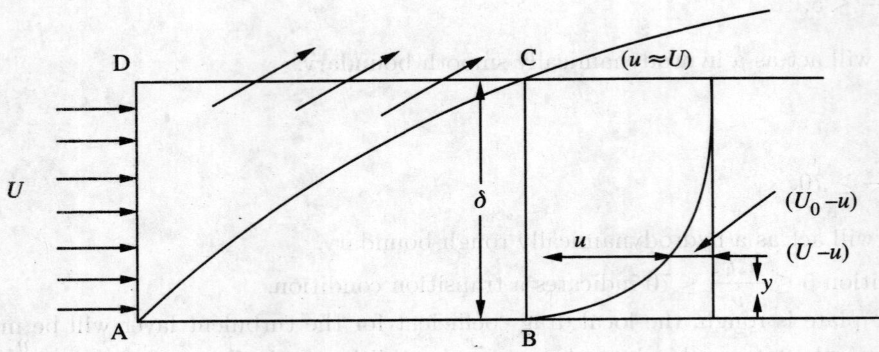

Fig. 15.5 *Definition sketch for the boundary layer*

$$\rho U\delta^* = \int_0^\delta \rho U\, dy - \int_0^\delta \rho u dy.$$

$$\delta^* = \frac{1}{U}\int_0^\delta (U - u)\, dy. \tag{15.42}$$

When we apply the force momentum transport equation to volume ABCD, the drag force on the plate D_f, is also taken into account.

i.e., Drag = (M.T. through AD) – (M.T. through DC) – (M.T. through BC)

$$D_f = \rho U^2\delta - \rho\int_0^\delta U\,(U-u)\,dy - \rho\int_0^\delta u^2 dy.$$

$$= \rho\int_0^\delta u(U-u)\,dy.$$

This can be equated to the momentum transport rate through a thickness θ,

$$D_f = \rho U^2 \theta = \rho \int_0^\delta u(U - u)\, dy,$$

or, the momentum thickness $\theta = \dfrac{1}{U^2} \displaystyle\int_0^\delta u(U - u)\, dy.$ (15.43)

15.5 Von Karman's Integral Equation

Von Karman a student of L.Prandtl made a gross analysis of the boundary layer formed on a flat plate. A control volume is selected with a thickness Y greater than δ, between the distance x and $x + dx$ from the leading edge. The plate was kept parallel to the flow and the ambient velocity was U. The boundary layer could be laminar or turbulent. A unit width of the plate for the control volume ABCD in Fig. 15.6 is considered. The pressure gradient $\dfrac{dp}{dx}$ is considered equal to $-\rho U \dfrac{dU}{dx}$.

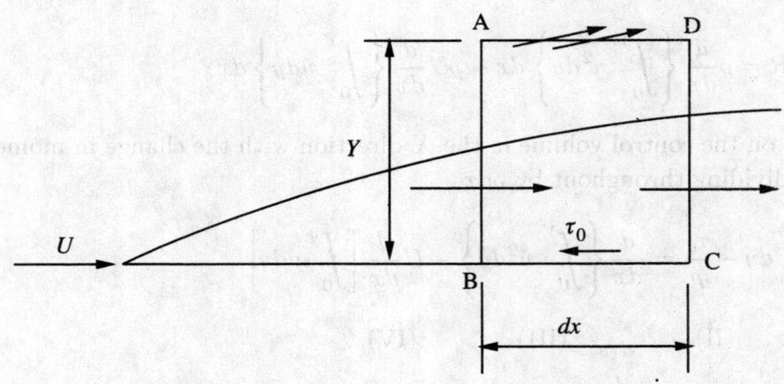

Fig. 15.6 *Boundary layer with control volume*

Referring to Fig. 15.6, the mass flow rate across AB = $\dot{m}_{AB} = -\rho \displaystyle\int_0^Y udy$

$$\dot{m}_{BC} = 0; \quad \dot{m}_{CD} = \rho \int_0^1 udy + \rho \frac{d}{dx} \left\{ \int_0^Y udy \right\} dx$$

By applying continuity equation for the control volume,

$$\dot{m}_{AD} = -\rho \frac{d}{dx} \left\{ \int_0^Y udy \right\} dx \qquad \text{(A)}$$

Force due to pressure:

$$p \times AB - (p + \frac{dp}{dx}dx) \times CD = -\frac{dp}{dx}dx \times Y = \rho U \frac{dU}{dx} dx \times \int_0^Y dy \qquad \text{(B)}$$

The shear force on the boundary

The average shear stress is assumed to be equal to τ_0 at a distance x from the boundary. Hence the shear force $= -\tau_0 dx$ (C)

Considering the momentum transport rates

$$MTR_{AB} = -\rho \int_0^Y u^2 dy \qquad \text{(D1)}$$

$$MTR_{CD} = -\rho \int_0^Y u^2 dy + \rho \frac{d}{dx}\left\{ \int_0^Y u^2 dy \right\} dx \qquad \text{(D2)}$$

$$MTR_{AD} = \rho U \frac{d}{dx}\left\{ \int_0^Y u dy \right\} dx \qquad \text{(D3)}$$

$$\text{Net } MTR = \rho \frac{d}{dx}\left\{ \int_0^Y u^2 dy \right\} dx - \rho U \frac{d}{dx}\left\{ \int_0^Y u dy \right\} dx$$

Equating force on the control volume in the X direction with the change in momentum transport rate and dividing throughout by ρdx,

$$U\frac{dU}{dx}\int_0^Y dy - \frac{\tau_0}{\rho} = \frac{d}{dx}\left\{ \int_0^Y u^2 dy \right\} - U\frac{d}{dx}\left[\int_0^y u dy \right]$$

(I) (II) (III) (IV)

Observing that U is a function of x and not y and re-arranging

$$\frac{\tau_0}{\rho} = \frac{dU}{dx}\int_0^Y U dy - \frac{d}{dx}\left\{ \int_0^Y u^2 dy \right\} + \frac{d}{dx}\left\{ U \int_\theta^Y u dy \right\} - \frac{dU}{dx}\int_0^Y u dy$$

(II) (I) (III) (IVa) (IVb)

which can be written as $\frac{\tau_0}{\rho} = U\frac{dU}{dx}\int_0^Y \left(1 - \frac{u}{U}\right) dy + \frac{d}{dx}\left\{ U^2 \int \frac{u}{U}\left(1 - \frac{u}{U}\right) dy \right\} dx$

(I–IVb) (VIa–III)

Hence

$$\frac{\tau_0}{\rho} = U\frac{dU}{dx}\delta^* + \frac{d}{dx}(U^2\theta) \tag{15.44}$$

where δ^* the displacement thickness and θ is the momentum thickness. This equation is known as the Von Karman integral equation.

When the pressure gradient $\frac{dp}{dx}$ can be neglected,

$$\frac{\tau_0}{\rho} = U^2\frac{d\theta}{dx} \tag{15.45}$$

Example 15.6 Assuming that the velocity distribution in the laminar boundary layer along a plate is given by $\frac{u}{U} = 2\frac{y}{\delta} - \left\{\frac{y}{\delta}\right\}^2$. (i) What are the displacement and momentum thicknesses? (ii) Find the expression for τ_0. (iii) Find the expression for the total drag on the plate for a length L.

(i) $\delta^* = \frac{1}{U}\int_0^\delta (U-u)dy = \int_0^\delta \left\{1 - \frac{u}{U}\right\} dy$. Substituting $\frac{u}{U} = 2\frac{y}{\delta} - \left\{\frac{y}{\delta}\right\}^2$

δ^* can be obtained as $\frac{1}{3}\delta$. [Ans.]

$\theta = \frac{1}{U^2}\int u(U-u)dy = \int \left[\frac{u}{U} - \left\{\frac{u}{U}\right\}^2\right] dy$. Substituting $\frac{u}{U} = 2\frac{y}{\delta} - \left\{\frac{y}{\delta}\right\}^2$

θ can be obtained as $\frac{2}{15}\delta$ [Ans.]

$$\text{(ii)}\ \frac{u}{U} = 2\frac{y}{\delta} - \left\{\frac{y}{\delta}\right\}^2; \tau_0 = \left\{u\frac{du}{dy}\right\}_{y=0} = 2\mu\frac{U}{\delta} \tag{A}$$

From the Karman integral theorem for zero pressure gradient (15.45),

$$\tau_0 = \rho U^2\frac{d\theta}{dx} = \frac{2}{15}\rho U^2\frac{d\delta}{dx} \tag{B}$$

Equating the two expressions for τ_0 (A) and (B) and rearranging,

$$\delta d\delta = \frac{15\mu}{\rho U}dx;$$

Integrating and simplifying $\delta = \frac{\sqrt{30\mu x}}{\sqrt{\rho U}}$

Or $\frac{\delta}{x} = \frac{\sqrt{30}}{\sqrt{R_x}} = \frac{5.48}{\sqrt{R_x}}$ where $R_x = \frac{\rho U x}{\mu}$

$$\tau_0 = \left\{\mu\frac{du}{dy}\right\}_{y=0} = 2\mu\frac{U}{\delta} = \frac{2\mu U\sqrt{\rho U}}{\sqrt{30\mu x}} = \frac{4}{5.48} \times \frac{\rho U^2}{2} \times \frac{\sqrt{\mu}}{\sqrt{\rho U x}}$$

Comparing with the equation $\tau_0 = c_f \times \dfrac{\rho U^2}{2}$

$$c_f = \frac{4}{5.48\sqrt{R_x}} = \frac{0.73}{\sqrt{R_x}} \text{ and } \tau_0 = \frac{0.73}{\sqrt{R_x}} \times \frac{\rho U^2}{2} \text{ (Ans).}$$

Total drag on a plate of length L and width $B = D_f = 2B \times \int_0^L \tau_0 dx$

Substituting the expression for τ_0 and simplifying,

$$D_f = \frac{2B \times 0.73 \times \rho U^2 \sqrt{\mu}}{2 \times \sqrt{\rho U}} \times \int_0^L \frac{1}{\sqrt{x}} dx = \frac{1.46 \times \rho U^2 \times \sqrt{\mu B}}{2 \times \sqrt{\rho U}} \times \frac{\sqrt{L}}{1/2} = \frac{1.46}{\sqrt{R_L}} \times \frac{\rho U^2}{2} \times 2BL.$$

Comparing with the equation $D_f = C_f \times \dfrac{\rho U^2}{2} \times 2BL$, we get $C_f = \dfrac{1.46}{\sqrt{R_x}}$.

It may be noted that the expression for τ_0 and D_f calculated are different from more exact values derived from the Blasius solution because the velocity profile assumed is less accurate.

15.6 Boundary Layer Separation

The flow in the boundary layer is retarded by the viscous shear at the boundary. When there is an accelerating main flow outside the boundary layer, transfer of momentum from the main flow to the boundary layer will sustain the flow in the boundary layer. But in a decelerating flow with an adverse pressure gradient (pressure increasing in the direction of flow), the velocity pattern can be reversed or back flow can set in.

Consider the flow along a curved boundary as in Fig. 15.7.

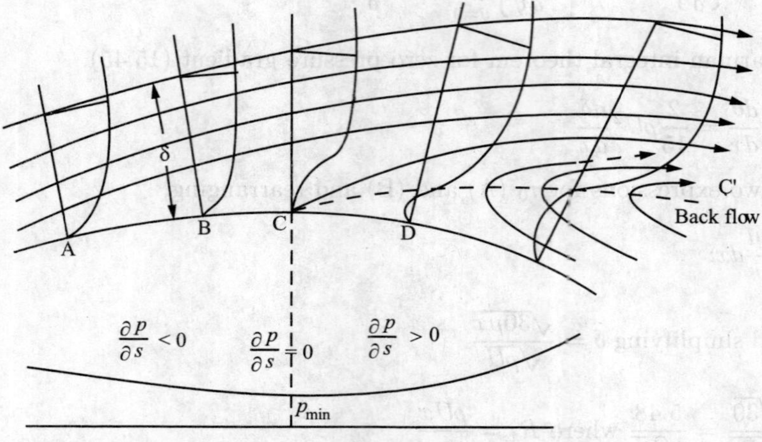

Fig. 15.7 *Boundary layer separation*

As the boundary layer develops from A to C, the skin friction on the boundary will retard the motion. But the boundary layer gets additional momentum from the main flow since $\partial p/\partial s$ is negative. But at point C, the boundary layer encounters an adverse pressure gradient. The fluid in the boundary layer at C cannot overcome the pressure hill and hence it separates from the boundary. A back flow sets in and the separated flow is established starting from a point near C.

Note As the back flow sets in, the separating point may move upstream of C if the boundary layer is laminar. If the boundary layer is turbulent, the point of separation may move quite downstream because additional momentum is transferred from the turbulent flow to the lower layers in the turbulent flow.

15.7 Boundary Layer Control

The phenomenon of separation of boundary layer and the consequent energy loss in the separated region is of great importance in the design of bodies moving in a fluid. The resistance of the body in motion, the drag, consists of the skin·friction drag (due to viscous shear at the boundary) and the form drag or pressure drag. The latter portion of the drag could be the main portion of the total drag known also as the profile drag. It can be reduced by avoiding or delaying the separation of the boundary layer and the formation of large wakes. The effect is more pronounced in the case of airplane wings and propeller blades.

The usual methods of controlling the boundary layer are

(i) Moving the boundary Boundary layer separation on a cylinder can be effectively avoided by rotating the cylinder as in Fig. 15.7(a).

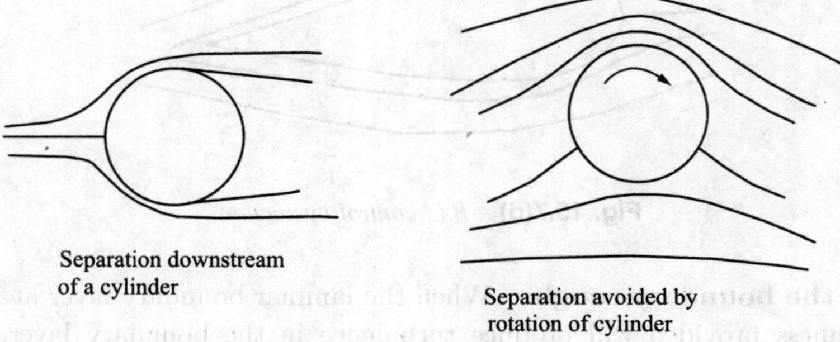

Fig. 15.7(a) *B.L. control by moving boundary*

(ii) Accelerating the boundary layer by blowing out Before the point B, where the boundary layer is likely to separate, the fluid is blown tangentially so that the boundary layer gets more momentum (Fig. 15.7(b)).

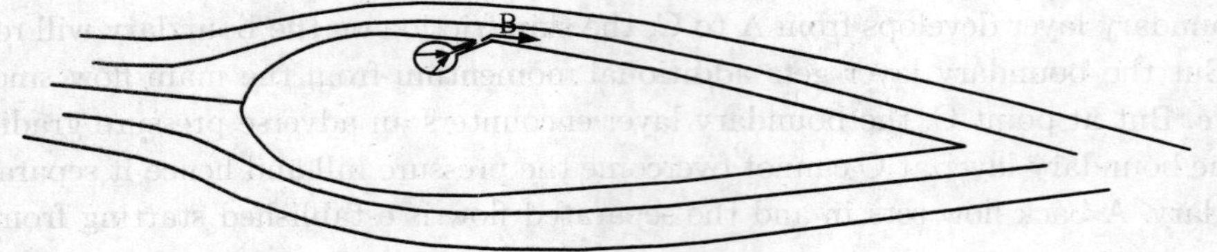

Fig. 15.7(b) *B.L. control by blowing out*

(iii) Accelerating the boundary layer by providing slotted wings The fluid moving in the slot transfers momentum to the boundary layer fluid at B (Fig. 15.7(c)).

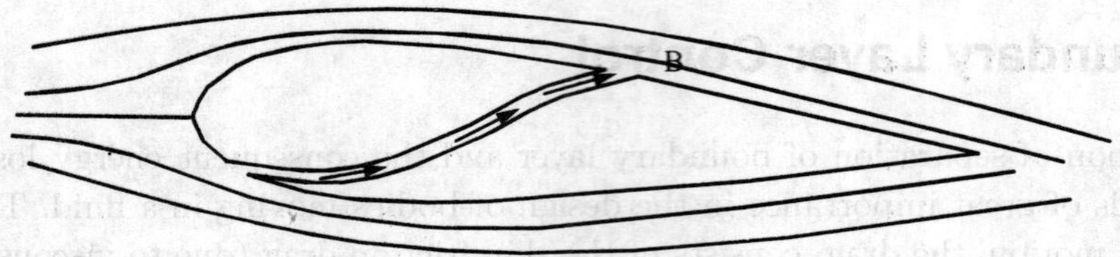

Fig. 15.7(c) *B.L. control by slotted wings*

(iv) Suction At point B where the boundary layer flow is retarded, the flow in the boundary is sucked into a cavity. This allows a fresh boundary layer to develop past B which can resist separation (Fig. 15.7(d)).

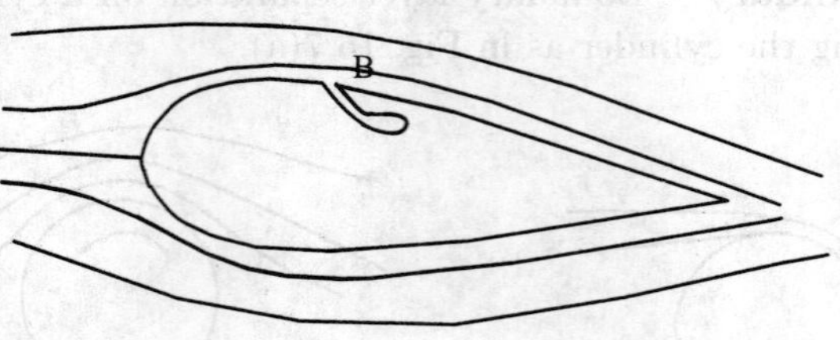

Fig. 15.7(d) *B.L. control by suction*

(v) Making the boundary rough When the laminar boundary layer at B is retarded, the roughness provided will produce turbulence in the boundary layer. Since in the turbulent boundary layer, more momentum is transferred from the main flow to the boundary layer, it can move further without separation (Fig. 15.7(e)).

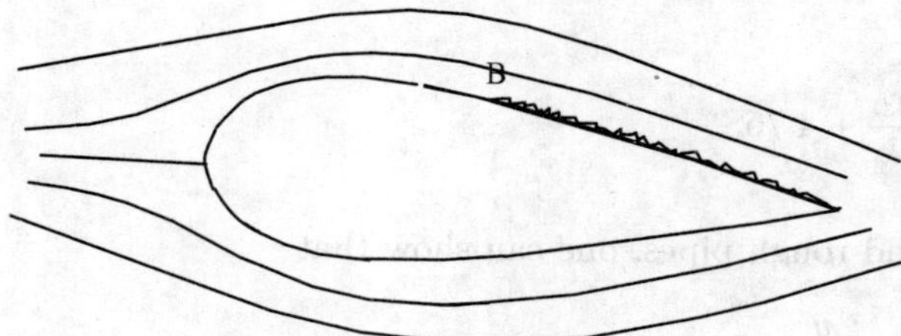

Fig. 15.7(e) *B.L. control by roughening the surface*

15.8 Velocity Distribution in a Turbulent Flow

The condition of flow near the boundary could be steady or unsteady, uniform or non-uniform. Only in steady uniform conditions of flow, can general results for velocity distribution be obtained. When the flow is laminar, experimental results show that the velocity distribution is parabolic as in the case of laminar boundary layers. But in turbulent flow, a logarithmic velocity distribution is found to fit experimental data more closely. However, as an approximation for Reynolds number below 70,000, the 1/7th power law has been found to simplify analysis.

15.9 Velocity Distribution in a Pipe

The velocity distribution in a turbulent flow away from the smooth wall,

$$\frac{v}{v_*} = 5.75 \log_{10} \frac{v_* y}{\nu} + 5.5$$

can be assumed to hold good along the radius of the pipe. The discharge can be found by integrating (neglecting the boundary sub-layer).

$$Q = \int_0^{r_0} 2\pi r v \, dr = 2\pi v \int_0^{r_0} r \left[5.75 \log_{10} \frac{v_*(r_0 - r)}{\nu} + 5.5 \right] dr$$

$$= \pi r^2 v_* \left(5.75 \log_{10} \frac{v_* r_0}{\nu} + 1.75 \right).$$

Average velocity $V = \dfrac{Q}{A} = \dfrac{Q}{\pi r^2}$.

For smooth pipes

$$\frac{V}{v_*} = 5.75 \log_{10} \frac{v_* r_0}{\nu} + 1.75. \tag{15.46}$$

In the same way, for rough pipes starting from equation

$$\frac{v}{v_*} = 5.75 \log_{10} \frac{y}{k} + 8.5,$$

one can show that

$$\frac{V}{v_*} = 5.75 \log_{10} \frac{r_0}{k} + 4.75. \tag{15.47}$$

In both the smooth and rough pipes, one can show that

$$\frac{v - V}{v_*} = 5.75 \log_{10} \frac{y}{r_0} + 3.75, \tag{15.48}$$

where y is the distance from the boundary.

Substituting $v_* = \sqrt{\tau_0/\rho} = V\sqrt{f/8}$ and $v = v_{\max}$ when $y = r_0$,

the following equation for maximum velocity can also be derived,

$$\frac{v_{\max}}{V} = 1.0 + 1.33\sqrt{f}. \tag{15.49}$$

Example 15.6 A smooth pipe 15 cm in diameter has a discharge of 0.03 m^3/s. (i) Find the shear stress at the boundary, (ii) find the velocity at a radius of 0.03 m. Assume $\nu = 10^{-6}$ m^2/s and (iii) find the maximum velocity.

$D = 0.15$ m; $\quad A = 0.0177$ m^2;

$Q = 0.03$ m^3/s; $\quad V = Q/A = 0.03/0.0177 = 1.698$ m/s;

$\text{Re} = 1.698 \times 0.15/10^{-6} = 2.547 \times 10^5$.

For a smooth pipe, $\dfrac{1}{\sqrt{f}} = 1.8 \log \text{Re} - 1.5$; $f = 0.0148$,

$v_* = V\sqrt{f/8} = 0.073 = \sqrt{\tau_0/\rho}$.

(i) $\tau_0 = \rho v_*^2 = 1000 \times 0.073^2 = 5.329$ Pa.

(ii) $r = 0.03$; $y = (r_0/2) - 0.03; = 0.045$ m.

$$\frac{v}{v_*} = 5.75 \log_{10} \frac{v_* y}{\nu} + 5.5.$$

$$\frac{v}{0.073} 5.75 \log_{10} \frac{0.073 \times 0.045}{10^{-6}} + 5.5.$$

$v = 1.877$ m/s. (Ans.)

(iii) $\dfrac{v_{\max}}{V} = 1.0 + 1.33\sqrt{f} = 1.0 + 1.33\sqrt{0.0148} = 1.1618$ m/s. Hence $v_{\max} = 1.1618\, V = 1.1618 \times 1.698 = 1.973$ m/s. (Ans.)

REVIEW QUESTIONS AND PROBLEMS

15.1 Explain what is a boundary layer.

15.2 Explain with sketches how an ideal fluid flow differs from a real fluid flow.

15.3 Explain the development of a boundary layer.

15.4 What are Prandtl's boundary layer equations? In a two-dimensional flow along a flat plate, show how the Navier–Stokes equation and the continuity equation are reduced to boundary layer equations, stating the assumptions made.

15.5 What are the approximate equations for velocity distribution in the laminar and turbulent boundary layer?

15.6 Explain the principle of self-similarity used in boundary layer velocity profiles at various distances along a flat plate.

15.7 What are the equations to find the thickness of (i) a laminar boundary layer and (ii) a turbulent boundary layer at a distance x from the leading edge of a flat plate?

15.8 Explain what are local and total drag coefficients on a flat plate. Give the expression to calculate the above coefficients (i) in a laminar boundary layer and (ii) in a turbulent boundary layer.

15.9 Why is the transition formula required for finding the total drag coefficient in the turbulent range.

15.10 What are hydrodynamically smooth and rough boundaries?

15.11 Explain the terms displacement thickness and momentum thickness and explain their significance.

15.12 Explain the phenomenon of separation of boundary layer.

15.13 What are the different methods of boundary layer control?

15.14 What is the common logarithmic equation for turbulent flow in smooth and rough pipes?

15.15 What is the equation connecting the maximum velocity, average velocity and Darcy–Weisbach coefficient for flow through a pipe?

15.16 Calculate approximately the maximum length of a flat plate over which a boundary layer will remain laminar for an air speed of 5 m/s and $\rho = 1.22$ kg/m^3. Assume $\nu_{\text{air}} = 15 \times 10^{-6}$ m^2/s. If the plate is 0.2 m wide, what is the total drag on the plate?

15.17 A smooth flat plate with a sharp leading edge is placed along a free stream of water flowing at 1 m/s. Calculate the distance from the leading edge and the thickness of the boundary layer where the transition from the laminar to turbulent boundary layer may commence.

15.18 A flat plate 0.5 m wide and 3 m long is placed in an air stream of 12 m/s, with the 3 m side parallel to the flow. Find (i) what is the maximum thickness of a laminar boundary layer? (ii) What is the thickness of the boundary layer at 0.04 m from the leading edge? (iii) What is the shear stress at the boundary layer at 0.04 m from the leading edge? $\nu = 15 \times 10^{-6}$ m^2/s and $\rho = 1.2$ kg/m^3.

15.19 A flat plate 0.3 m wide and 1 m long is towed through water at 3 m/s. Find (i) the thickness of the boundary layer at the end of the plate, (ii) the shear stress at the end of the plate and (iii) total drag on the two sides of the plate. Assume $\nu = 1 \times 10^{-6}$ m²/s.

$\left[\text{Hint : use the transition formula. } C_f = \dfrac{0.074}{\text{Re}^{1/5}} - \dfrac{1700}{\text{Re}}\right]$

15.20 Oil with a stream velocity of 6 m/s flows over a thin plate 2.5 m wide and 2.5 m long. Calculate the boundary layer thickness and shear stress at the trailing edge. Determine the total drag on the plate. Assume $S = 0.84$ and $\nu = 10^{-5}$ m^2/s.

15.21 A model airplane wing with a 15 cm chord length and a 50 cm span is tested in a wind tunnel under atmospheric pressure with a wind velocity of 2.5 m/s. Treating the wing as a flat plate at zero angle of incidence, find (i) thickness of the boundary layer at the end of the plate and (ii) the drag on the model wing. $\nu = 15 \times 10^{-6}$ m^2/s; $\rho = 1.22$ kg/m^3.

15.22 A flat plate 2 m long and 0.5 m wide is kept in an air flow of 3 m/s. Find (i) the shear stress at 0.2 m from the leading edge. (ii) What is the thickness of the boundary layer? $\nu = 15 \times 10^{-6}$ m^2/s; $\rho = 1.22$ kg/m^3.

15.23 A flat plate 1 m long is being towed in water at a velocity of 1 m/s. (i) Find the thickness of the boundary layer at the end of the plate. (ii) What is the shear velocity? (iii) Assuming that the velocity distribution on the turbulent boundary layer is given by $\dfrac{v}{v_*} = 5.25 \log_{10} \dfrac{v_* y}{\nu} + 5.5$, find the velocity at half the boundary layer thickness at the end of the plate.

15.24 A plate 0.3 m long and 0.2 m wide is towed along its length with a velocity of 0.8 m/s in an oil of specific gravity 0.9 and dynamic viscosity 1.5 poise. (i) Find the drag. (ii) If the plate is towed parallel to the 0.2 m side, what will the drag be? (iii) Explain why there is a difference.

15.25 A plate 1.5 m long is being towed along its length in water at 2 m/s. If the height of roughness elements on the plate is 1.2 mm, (i) find what is the thickness of the laminar sub-layer and (ii) find whether the plate is hydrodynamically smooth or rough.

15.26 Find the displacement thickness and the momentum thickness for the velocity distribution in the boundary layer given by $\dfrac{u}{v} = 2\left(\dfrac{y}{\delta}\right) - \left(\dfrac{y}{\delta}\right)^2$.

15.27 A smooth pipe 15 cm in diameter conveying water, has an average velocity of 1.5 m/s. (i) At what radius will the velocity be 1.5 m/s? (ii) What is the maximum velocity?

ANSWERS

15.16. 1.5 m, 0.01719 N; **15.17.** 0.5 m; **15.18.**(i) 4.419×10^{-3} m; **15.18**(ii) 1.118×10^{-3} m; **15.18.**(iii) 0.321 N/m^2; **15.19.**(i) 0.0191 m; **15.19.**(ii) 13.446 N/m^2; **15.19.**(iii) 8.586 N; **15.20.** 0.0548; 51.9 Pa; 599.5 N. **15.21.**(i) 0.0047 m; **15.21.**(ii) 4.803×10^{-3}N; **15.22.**(i) 0.0182 Pa; **15.22.**(ii) 0.005 m; **15.23.**(i) 0.0238 m; **15.23.**(ii) 0.0431 m/s; **15.23.**(iii) 0.909 m/s; **15.24.** (i) 0.2869 N; **15.24.**(ii) 0.4057 N; **15.25.**(i) 1.5×10^{-4} m; **15.25.**(ii) hydrodynamically rough; **15.26.** Displacement thickness = $\delta/3$; Momentum thickness = $(2/15)\delta$; **15.27.** (i) 0.0416 m; **15.27.**(ii) 1.745 m/s.

16 Drag and Lift on Immersed Bodies

Drag and lift — Types of drag — Drag of spheres, cylinder and other bodies — Drag coefficient — Airfoil shapes — Development of lift — Induced drag

16.1 Introduction

Bodies moving in fluids encounter drag due to pressure and viscous forces acting on the surface. In many cases like airplanes, vehicle bodies and projectiles, there is a need to reduce the drag to a minimum. Streamlining reduces the drag considerably. Shapes which give high lift/drag ratios are selected for airfoils.

16.2 Forces Acting on Moving Bodies

When a body moves relative to a fluid surface, forces of pressure and shear act on the body.

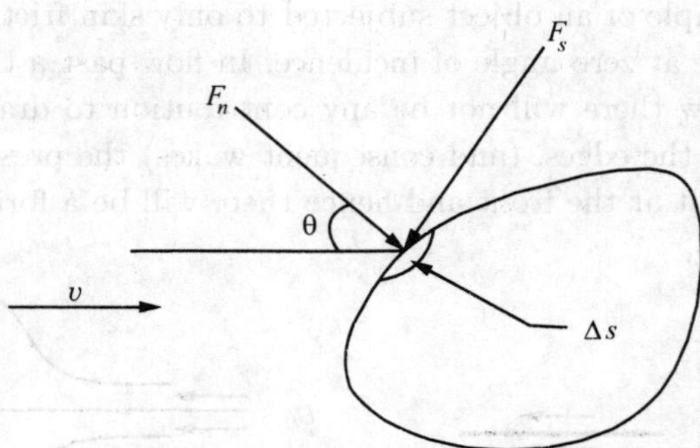

Fig. 16.1 *Normal and tangential forces acting on an elementary area*

Let an elementary surface on the body have an area Δs and let its normal be at an angle θ with the direction of motion (Fig. 16.1). Let F_n and F_s be the normal and tangential forces acted upon by the fluid on the surface,

$$p = \frac{F_n}{\Delta s} \text{ and } \tau = \frac{F_s}{\Delta s}.$$

Total pressure drag or form drag,

$$D_p = \iint_s p \cos\theta \, ds. \tag{16.1}$$

Total skin friction drag,

$$D_s = \iint_s \tau \sin\theta \, ds. \tag{16.2}$$

$$\text{Total drag} \;= D_p + D_s. \tag{16.3}$$

Drag is the sum of the components of the surface forces exerted by the fluid on the body in the direction opposite to the motion of the body.

Lift is the sum of the components of the surface forces acted upon by the fluid on the body in the direction perpendicular to the motion of the body.

$$\text{Lift} = \iint_s p \sin\theta \, ds + \iint_s \tau \cos\theta \, ds. \tag{16.4}$$

16.3 Drag on Bodies

We will consider an example of an object subjected to only skin friction drag in the case of a flow past a thin flat plate at zero angle of incidence. In flow past a thin flat plate (Fig. 16.2) held perpendicular to flow there will not be any contribution to drag from the shear forces. But due to separation at the edges, (and consequent wakes) the pressures on the back of the plate will be less than that at the front and hence there will be a form drag.

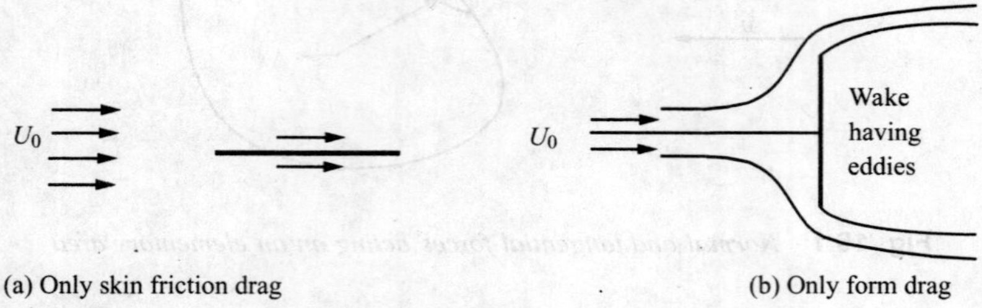

Fig. 16.2 *Flow past a flat plate*

Let us consider the flow of an ideal fluid past a circular cylinder as shown in Fig. 16.3. At any point P, the velocity is given by the expression $v = -2U_0 \sin\theta$, S and S′ being stagnation points where velocity is zero. Applying Bernoulli's equation between A and P at the same elevation,

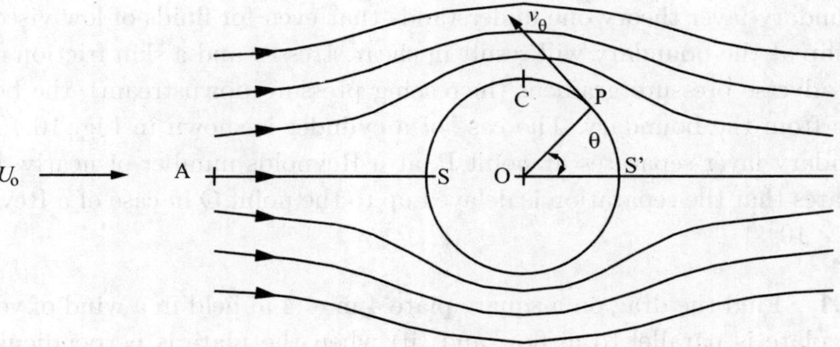

Fig. 16.3 *Ideal fluid flow around a cylinder*

$$\frac{p_A}{\gamma} + \frac{{U_0}^2}{2g} = \frac{p}{\gamma} + \frac{v^2}{2g},$$

where p is the pressure at P.

$$\frac{p - p_A}{\rho U^2/2} = 1 - 4\sin^2\theta.$$

The pressure distribution around the cylinder is symmetric about the Y axis. Hence the pressure forces on the front and the back of the cylinder are equal and opposite. Theoretically in this case, the form drag should be zero. Further, since it is a non-viscous fluid, the shear force is zero and skin friction drag should be zero. Thus, we should get the result that the total drag is zero.

But it is common knowledge that bodies moving relative to fluids of even negligible viscosities experience drag. The above result is known as the D'Alembert's paradox.

16.4 Effect of Viscosity on Drag

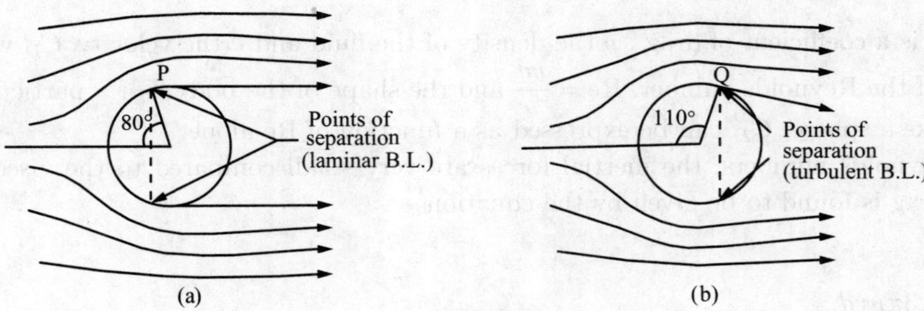

Fig. 16.4 *Separation for laminar and turbulent boundary layer*

From the boundary layer theory one understands that even for fluids of low viscosity, the condition of no slip at the boundary will result in shear stresses and a skin friction drag. Further, in regions of adverse pressure gradient (increasing pressure downstream), the boundary layer may separate from the boundary. The case of a cylinder is shown in Fig. 16.4(a), where the laminar boundary layer separates at point P, at a Reynolds number of nearly 40,000. Figure 16.4(b) indicates that the separation is delayed up to the point Q in case of a Reynolds number of nearly 2.1×10^5.

Example 16.1 Find the drag on a square plate 4 m × 4 m held in a wind of velocity 20 m/s (i) when the plate is parallel to airflow and (ii) when the plate is perpendicular to airflow. Assume $\nu = 15 \times 10^{-6}\,\text{m}^2/\text{s}$: $\rho = 1.22\,\text{kg/m}^3$: C_D for the square plate held normal to the flow = 1.10.

$v = 20\,\text{m/s}; \rho = 1.22\,\text{kg/m}^3; \nu = 15 \times 10^{-6}\ \text{m}^2/\text{s}.$

$$\text{(i) Re} = \frac{vL}{\nu} = \frac{20 \times 4}{15 \times 10^{-6}} = 5.33 \times 10^6.$$

$$C_f = \frac{0.074}{\text{Re}^{1/5}} - \frac{1700}{\text{Re}} = 3.022 \times 10^{-3}.$$

$$\text{Drag} = C_f \times \frac{\rho v^2}{2} \times 2 \times 4 \times 4 = 11.798.\ \text{(Ans.)}$$

$$\text{(ii) Drag} = C_D \times \frac{\rho v^2}{2} \times \text{area} = 1.1 \times 1.22 \times \frac{20^2}{2} \times 4 \times 4 = 4.295\ \text{kN. (Ans.)}$$

16.5 Variation of Drag on a Sphere Moving in a Fluid

The general expression for total drag on a body can be

$$D = C_D \rho \frac{v^2}{2}, \tag{16.5}$$

where C_D is a coefficient of drag , ρ the density of the fluid and v the velocity. C_D will be the function of the Reynolds number, $\text{Re} = \frac{vd}{\nu}$ and the shape of the body. For a particular shape of body like a sphere, C_D can be expressed as a function of Re alone.
At low Reynolds numbers, the inertial forces are very small compared to the viscous forces and the drag is found to be given by the equation

$$D = 3\pi\mu v d. \tag{16.6}$$

The result is known as Stokes law. Stokes law can also be expressed as

$$C_D = \frac{24}{\text{Re}}. \tag{16.7}$$

It also applies to spherical particles settling under gravity in viscous fluids. The terminal velocity U is given by the formula

$$U = \frac{(\gamma_d - \gamma_f)\, d^2}{18\, \mu}, \tag{16.8}$$

where γ_d and γ_f are the specific weights of the particle and the fluid respectively. Stokes law has been found to be applicable up to a Reynolds number of 0.2. At higher Reynolds numbers—nearly 0.2 to 2, the value of C_D has been given by Oseen's approximation

$$C_D = \frac{24}{\text{Re}}\left(1 + \frac{3}{16}\text{Re}\right). \tag{16.9}$$

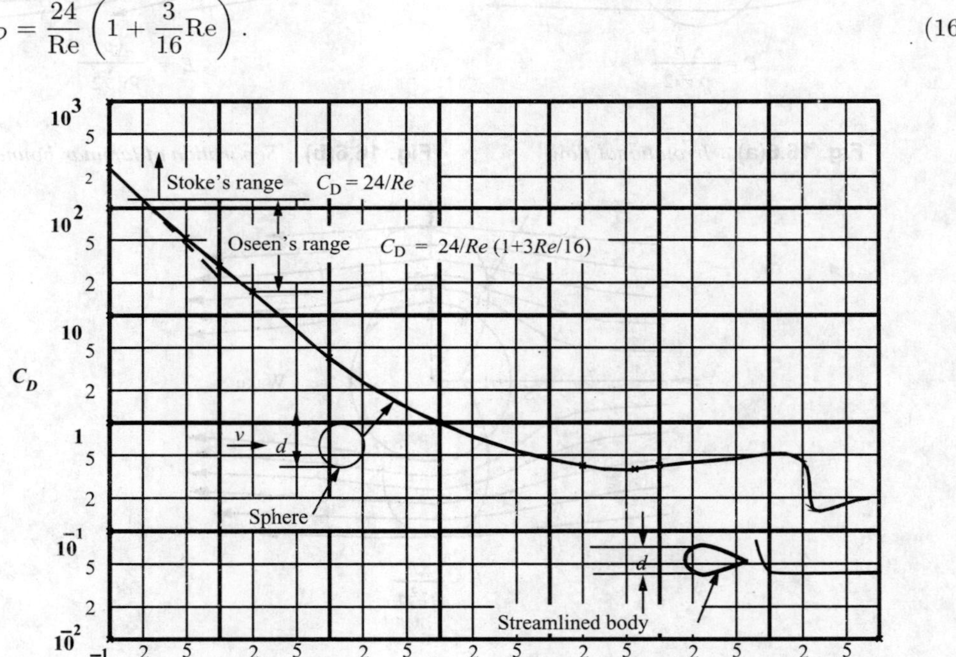

Fig. 16.5 *Variation of C_D with Reynolds number for spheres*

Experiments have shown that the variation of C_D for a smooth sphere moving through a fluid is depicted by the curve in Fig. 16.5. The value of C_D reduces to a value of nearly 0.4 at a Reynolds number of 3×10^3 and increases slightly above 0.5 at a Reynolds number of 10^5. This shows the condition of separation of a laminar boundary layer. When turbulence sets in, where the Reynolds number exceeds 2×10^5, the separation is delayed and C_D drops suddenly to a value of nearly 0.16. The pressure distribution around the sphere is depicted in Fig. 16.6 (a)–(c). Figure 16.6(a) shows the case of irrotational flow. Figure 16.6(b) shows the condition when the laminar boundary layer has separated. Figure 16.6(c) depicts the condition of turbulent boundary layer separation.

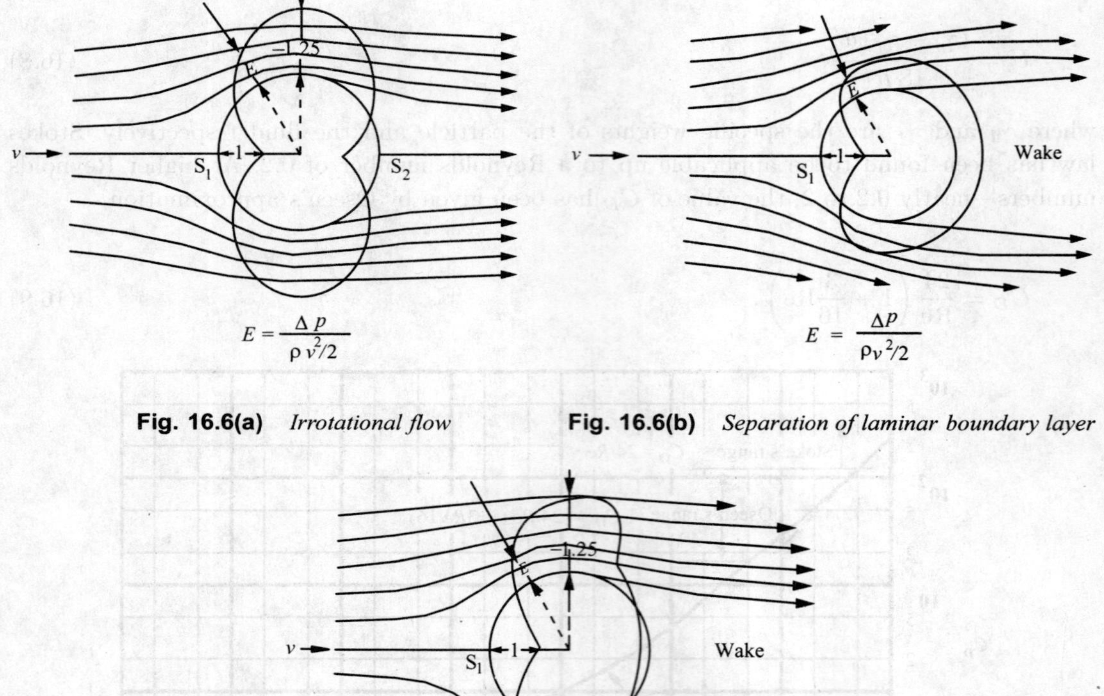

Fig. 16.6(a) *Irrotational flow*

Fig. 16.6(b) *Separation of laminar boundary layer*

Fig. 16.6(c) *Separation of turbulent boundary layer*

Example 16.2 Water drops 3 mm in diameter are falling through oil of specific gravity 0.94. (i) If the viscosity of oil is 0.08 Pa s, what is the terminal velocity? (ii) If they are falling in air, find the terminal velocity, assuming that the drops maintain a spherical shape, given $\nu_{\text{air}} = 15 \times 10^{-6} \text{m}^2/\text{s}$ and $\rho_{\text{air}} = 1.22 \text{ kg/m}^3$.

(i) $\nu = \mu/\rho = 0.08/940 = 8.51 \times 10^{-5}\ \text{m}^2/\text{s}$.

Assuming Stokes law,

$$U = \frac{(\gamma_w - \gamma_o)\, d^2}{18\,\mu} = \frac{(9810 - 0.94 \times 9810) \times 0.003^2}{18 \times 0.08} = 3.679 \times 10^{-3} \text{ m/s. (Ans.)}$$

Check:

$$\text{Re} = \frac{Ud}{\nu} = \frac{3.679 \times 10^{-3} \times 0.003 \times 940}{0.08} = 0.1279,$$

i.e. less than 0.2. Hence Stokes law is valid.

(ii) Assume $C_D = 0.5$.

At terminal velocity, W = drag. (neglecting weight of displaced air)

$$\gamma_w \frac{\pi d^3}{6} = C_D \frac{\rho_a V^2}{2} \times \frac{\pi d^2}{4}\ ; V^2 = \frac{4\gamma_w d}{3\rho_a C_D} = 64.33$$

Hence $V = 8.02$ m/s

$$\text{Re} = \frac{Vd}{v} = \frac{8.02 \times 0.003}{15 \times 10^{-6}} = 1604 \text{ from the graph is } 0.4$$

Assuming $C_D = 0.4$; $V = 8.97$ m/s and Re = 1794

For Re = 1794, C_D from the graph is nearly = 0.4 Hence $V = 8.97$ m/s (Ans)

16.6 Drag on Other Bodies Moving through a Fluid

Bodies having sharp edges like flat plates and discs (held perpendicular to the flow) have defined edges where separation occurs and hence the variation of C_D is not much when Reynolds number is higher than 1000. But in case of bodies having smooth boundaries, the point of separation will shift when the boundary layer becomes turbulent and hence there will be a sudden drop of the coefficient of drag. The table which follows gives the coefficients of drag for some forms of bodies[28].

It can be observed that the drag of a body can be reduced considerably by having a rounded upstream face as part of the streamlining.

The comparison of C_D for cylinders shows that when the flow conditions around the body becomes more two-dimensional in nature, the drag coefficient increases.

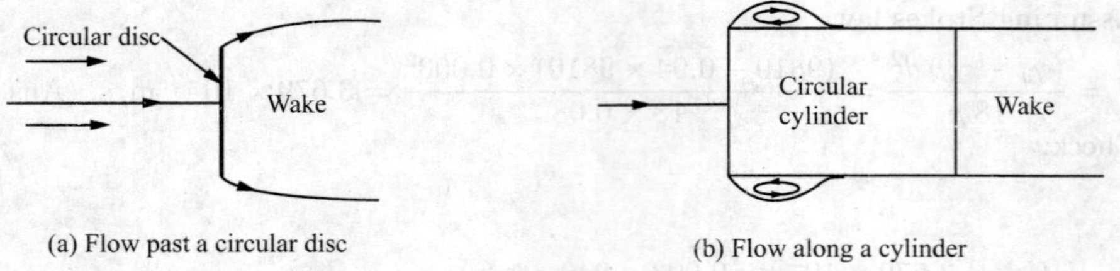

(a) Flow past a circular disc

(b) Flow along a cylinder

Fig. 16.7 *Reattachment of separated streamline*

When the flow is parallel to the axis of a circular disc (Fig. 16.7(a)), the coefficient of drag is nearly 1.12. The flow separates out at the edges and a wake is formed. As the thickness of the disc increases to some level (a cylinder), the separated streamline may get re-attached (Fig. 16.7(b)) to the surface of the cylinder reducing the size of the wake and the drag. The phenomenon of re-attachment of jet is called the Coanda effect. When the length of the cylinder is further increased, the friction on the surface may become more pronounced, resulting in an increase in the drag coefficient.

Form of body	L/D	Re	C_D
Circular cylinder with axis perpendicular to flow	1	$> 10^3$	0.63
	5		0.74
	20		0.90
	∞		1.20
	5	$> 5 \times 10^5$	0.35
	∞		0.33
Circular cylinder with axis parallel to flow	0(disc)	$> 10^3$	1.12
	1		0.91
	2		0.85
	4		0.87
Rectangular plate (L width, D width)	1	$> 10^3$	1.10
	5		1.20
	20		1.50
	∞		1.90
Hemisphere			
Hollow upstream		$> 10^3$	1.33
Hollow downstream			0.34
Sphere		10^5	0.5
		$> 3 \times 10^5$	0.2
Ellipsoid (1 & 2 major axis parallel to flow)		$> 2 \times 10^5$	0.07
Streamlined foil (1–3 airship structure)	∞	4×10^4	0.07
Model airship hull		$> 2 \times 10^5$	0.05

16.7 Drag on Cylinders having Axis Normal to the Flow

Figure 16.8 shows the variation of C_D with the Reynolds number for long cylinders placed in an uniform flow when the axis of the cylinder is normal to the flow. When the cylinder is of a small length, the flow past the cylinder will be three-dimensional. Consequently, the coefficient of drag will be smaller.

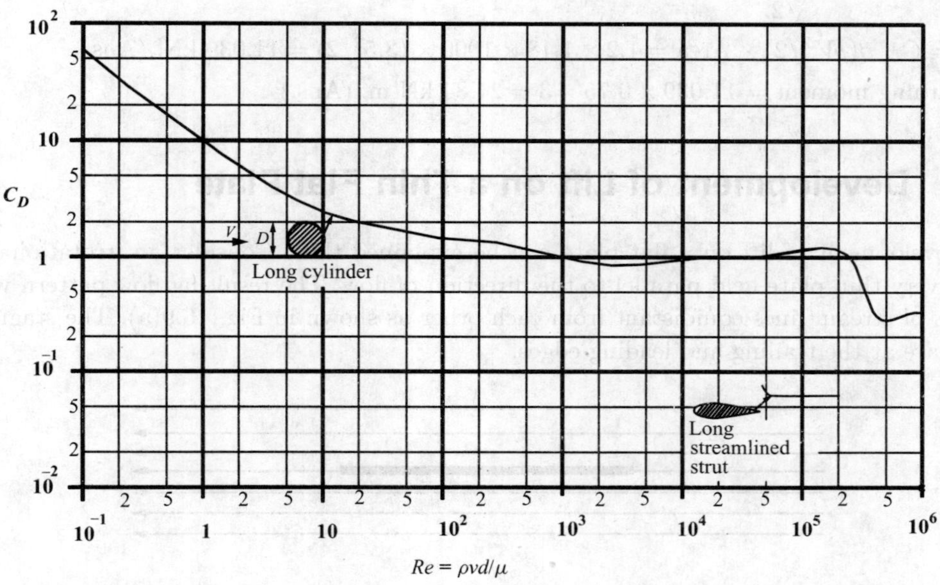

Fig. 16.8 *Variation of C_D with the Reynolds number for a cylinder*

The wake behind a cylinder at Reynolds numbers 20 or more has a distinct pair of vortices, which are unsymmetrical and move downstream. They are known as Karman's vortex trail. As the vortices move downstream, new vortices are shed at some frequency given by the formula

$$f = 0.2\frac{U_0}{d}\left(1 - \frac{20}{\text{Re}}\right). \tag{16.10}$$

The non-dimensional number

$$\frac{fd}{U_0}, \tag{16.11}$$

is known as the Strouhal number and is related to C_D. The frequency of vortex shedding is important when it nears the natural frequency of the cylindrical members of the structures subjected to fluid flow.

Example 16.3 A concrete pile 30 cm × 30 cm square is driven on the bed of the river with the faces making a 45 angle with the flow. The depth of the water in the river is 3 m and the average velocity is 3.5 m/s. Assuming that the momentum correction factor is 1.18, find the drag on the piles. If the resultant force is acting at 0.75 times the depth of flow from the bed, what is the overturning moment. Assuming $C_D = 1.2$.

$$\text{Projected area} = \frac{0.3}{\sqrt{2}} \times 2 \times 3 = 1.2728 \text{ m}^2.$$

$$\text{Drag} = C_D\ \beta(\rho V^2/2) \times \text{Area} = 1.2 \times 1.18 \times 1000 \times (3.5^2/2) = 11.039 \text{ kN. (Ans.)}$$

$$\text{Overturning moment} = 11.039 \times 0.75 \times 3 = 24.84 \text{ kN m. (Ans.)}$$

16.8 Development of Lift on a Thin Flat Plate

The development of lift on a flat plate can be explained thus. Consider an irrotational flow past a very thin plate held parallel to the direction of flow. The resulting flow pattern will be a series of stream lines equidistant from each other as shown in Fig. 16.9(a). The stagnation points are at the trailing and leading edges.

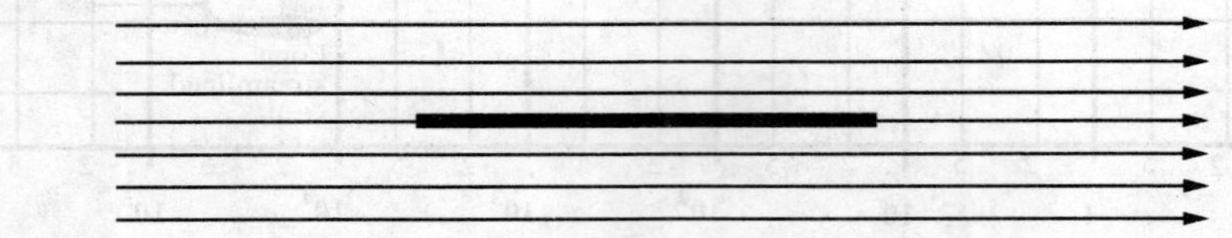

Fig. 16.9(a) *Irrotational flow past a parallel plate*

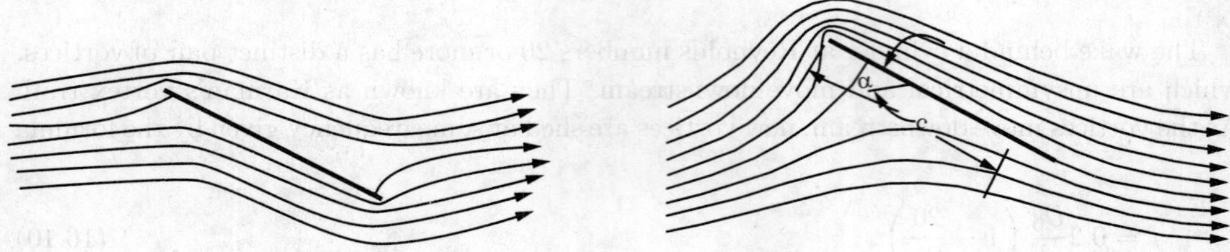

Fig. 16.9(b) *Irrotational flow past inclined plate* **Fig. 16.9(c)** *Real fluid flow past inclined plate*

Let the plate be held at an angle α to the direction of motion. The ideal flow solution gives two asymmetric stagnation points as shown in Fig. 16.9(b). The pressure on the plate produces a couple which tends to rotate the plate about its mid-point. But the sharp reversal of flow at the trailing edge is impossible for real fluids even when the viscosity is very low. The stream lines will leave the plate at the trailing edge only tangentially as in Fig. 16.9(c). The resulting flow pattern is equivalent to a superposition of a proper degree of circulation (clockwise), which will shift the stagnation point downstream to the trailing edge. The circulation required is given by the relationship

$$-\Gamma = \pi\, c\, U \sin\alpha, \tag{16.12}$$

where c is the length of the plate and α is the angle of attack. Since the total circulation is maintained at zero as in the initial conditions (Thomson's theorem), the wing in its wake will leave behind trailing vortices of circulation Γ.
The pressure at the bottom of the plate for condition of flow as shown in Fig. 16.9(c) is much higher than at the top, resulting in a lift force.

16.9 Airfoil Shapes

16.9.1 Development of airfoil shapes

Airfoil shapes should offer high lift and low drag. Even though a plate held at a very small angle to the flow direction will develop lift, separation will occur on the leading edge. Rounding the leading edge, and tapering the profile gradually towards the rear, are done to avoid separation. The profile is given a camber to reduce the tendency for separation even at greater angles of incidence. The mathematical method for obtaining the shape and flow patterns past such airfoils was developed by Joukowski.

As explained earlier, a body in motion submerged in a fluid is subjected to drag, which is the sum of the pressure drag and the skin friction drag. The total drag can be reduced considerably by avoiding or minimizing the form drag. This is achieved by making the body streamlined.

An airfoil is a streamlined body which is shaped in such a manner that there is no separation of the fluid from the body, or the region of separation is confined to a small portion near the trailing edge. The airfoil should develop high lift and have only a low drag. The airplane moving at some velocity has to overcome the drag on the wings as well as the body. Lift is developed on the wings depending on the angle of attack of the wings and the velocity. When the lift is greater than the weight of the plane, the plane ascends and at steady flight, the lift becomes equal to the weight of the airplane.

16.9.2 Definitions

Chord line It is a straight line joining the centres of curvature at the leading and trailing edges in the cross-section of the airfoil. The length of the chord line is usually designated by c. (Fig. 16.10).

Camber line It is the centreline of the airfoil cross-section. Camber is the maximum distance between the camber line and the chord line.

Span It is the length of the airfoil in the direction perpendicular to the airfoil cross-section.

Plan area It is the projected area of the airfoil on a plane perpendicular to the airfoil cross-section and containing the chord line.

Mean chord It is defined as the ratio of the plan area to the span.

Aspect ratio It is defined as the ratio of the span to the mean chord. This is also equal to the span divided by the plan area.

Angle of attack Angle of attack α is the angle between the direction of the oncoming fluid and the chord line. It is also known as the angle of incidence.

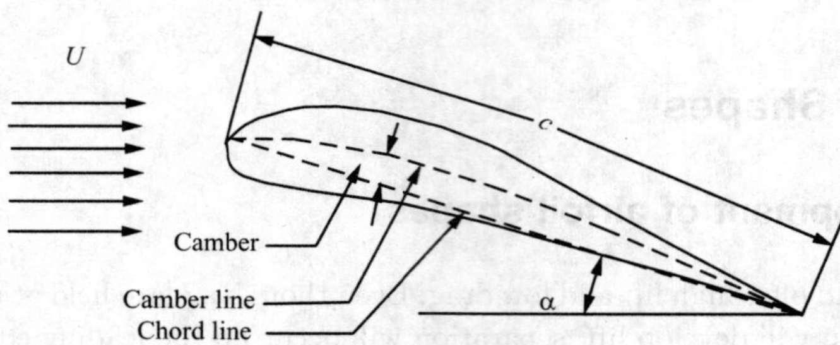

Fig. 16.10 *Details of a cambered airfoil*

16.10 Lift and Drag on an Airfoil

The development of lift and drag on an airfoil can be explained by comparing it with a flat plate held at an angle α to the direction of the free stream velocity. In both cases, as the airfoil is assumed to be of infinite length, the flow condition can be assumed to be two-dimensional.

In the case of an airfoil held at an angle, the necessary circulation is produced by vortices generated at the trailing edge because of velocity difference on the upper and lower surfaces at the trailing edge. These trailing vortices are shed off and washed downstream. Since the airfoil is held at an angle with the direction of flow, the pressure at the lower surface will be more. It will be less on the upper surface. This pressure difference causes a lift force and can be expressed in terms of the circulation. Kutta–Joukowski has shown that the lift force is given by $F_L = b\ \rho\ U\ \Gamma$ and circulation $\Gamma = \pi\ c\ U\ \sin\alpha$. Theoretically, the coefficient of lift $C_L = 2\ \pi\ \sin\alpha$. The actual values of C_D and C_L are found experimentally.

Lift and drag are generally expressed as

$$F_L = C_L \frac{\rho U^2}{2} A. \tag{16.13}$$

$$F_D = C_D \frac{\rho U^2}{2} A. \tag{16.14}$$

It may be noted that in the above formulae, the area is the plan area of the aerofoil.

16.11 Stall of an Airfoil

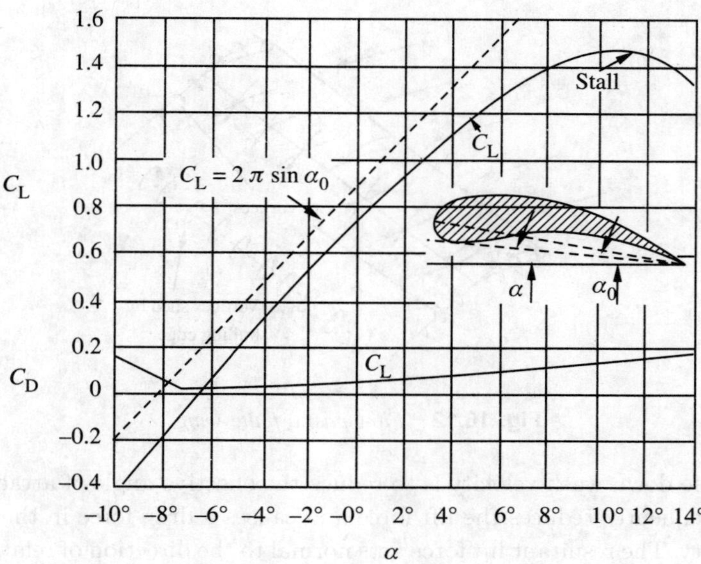

Fig. 16.11 *Variation of C_L and C_D with α*

The lift of an airfoil as can be seen from the equation $C_L = 2\pi \sin\alpha$, will increase as the angle of attack is increased. In practical situations, the coefficient of lift C_L increases up to a certain angle of attack, beyond which it comes down drastically. This point is known as the stalling point.

It can also be observed that there is an increase in the value of C_D. This can be explained by the fact that beyond a certain angle of attack, the separation of flow starts taking place much before the trailing edge, causing an increase in the drag. The experimental and theoretical values of C_L and C_D for various values of α are shown in Fig. 16.11.

16.12 Wing Spans of Finite Length: Induced Drag

The coefficients of lift C_L and drag C_D presented in the previous section was calculated on the assumption that the flow was truly two-dimensional. An airfoil of infinite length was considered and the effect of sides ignored. However, in practice, because the aerofoil is of finite length, the flow approaches three-dimensional rather than two-dimensional conditions. In the case of a two-dimensional flow, vortices are produced only at the trailing edge. But, when the length of the wing is finite, the pressure difference between the upper and lower regions causes the flow to also take place from the centre to the sides, as shown in Fig. 16.12. This results in the generation of circulation around the wing tips, causing tip vortices. The tip vortices combined with trailing vortices produce a down wash velocity v_1, which makes the absolute velocity of the wing different from the velocity of the air stream.

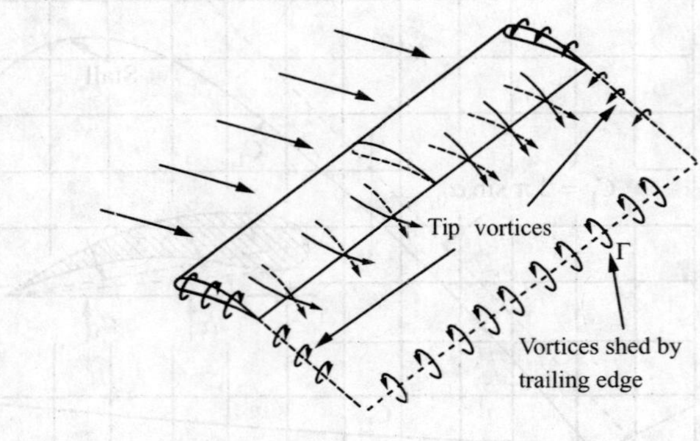

Fig. 16.12 *Flow past a finite wing*

The effect of the down wash velocity is to reduce the effective angle of attack by an amount say δ, which consequently reduces the lift force and causes a drag force in the direction of the free stream velocity. The resultant lift force acts normal to the direction of relative velocity. The true lift is defined as the force component at right angles to the mean velocity, $F_L \cong F \cos \delta$. The horizontal component of the true lift $F_D = F \sin \alpha$, will not be negligible and this component is commonly known as the induced drag (Fig. 16.13). This causes an increase in the actual drag.

Prandtl has shown that for an aerofoil having an elliptical distribution of lift, the down wash velocity v_1 is constant along the span and equal to $\dfrac{\Gamma}{2b}$.

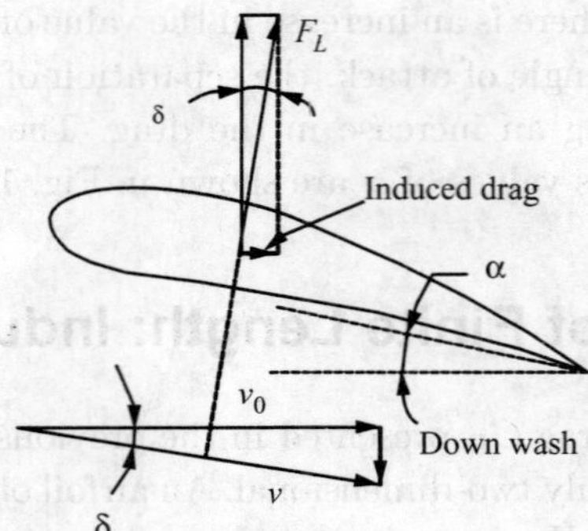

Fig. 16.13 *Induced drag*

It can be shown that the coefficient of induced drag

$$C_{D_i} = \frac{C_L^2}{\pi l/c} \tag{16.15}$$

and

$$\delta = \frac{F_{D_i}}{F_L} = \frac{C_L}{\pi l/c}. \tag{16.16}$$

Example 16.4 A model of a wing of area 2 m^2 is tested at an angle of attack of 3 in a wind tunnel at a velocity of 15 m/s. If the lift and drag are measured to be 90 N and 13.5 N respectively, find the coefficient of lift and drag. Assume $\rho = 1.2$ kg/m^3.

$A = 2$ m^2; $V = 15$ m/s; $\rho = 1.2$ kg/m^3.

$L = C_L \times (pV^2/2) \times$ area; $90 = C_L \times 1.2 \times (15^2/2) \times 2$; Hence $C_L = 0.33$. (Ans.).

$D = C_D \times (\rho V^2/2) \times$ area; $13.5 = C_D \times 1.2 \times (15^2/2) \times 2$; Hence $C_D = 0.05$. (Ans.).

Example 16.5 An airplane weighs 2100 kg and has a wing area of 20 m^2. If it is moving at 360 km/hr, find the lift coefficient. Assume $\rho = 1.22$ kg/m^3

$V = 360$ km/hr $= 100$ m/s; $W = 2100 \times 9.81$ N $= 20601$ N;

Lift $= W = 20601 = C_L \times (\rho V^2/2) \times$ area $= C_L \times 1.22 \times (100^2/2) \times 20$.

$C_L = 0.1689$. (Ans.)

Example 16.6 A kite of size 0.9 m × 0.6 m weighs 300 g$_f$. It is flying in a wind of velocity 25 km/hr and the string attached to it makes an angle of 35 with the horizontal. The tension in the string is 14 N. Find the lift and drag coefficients.

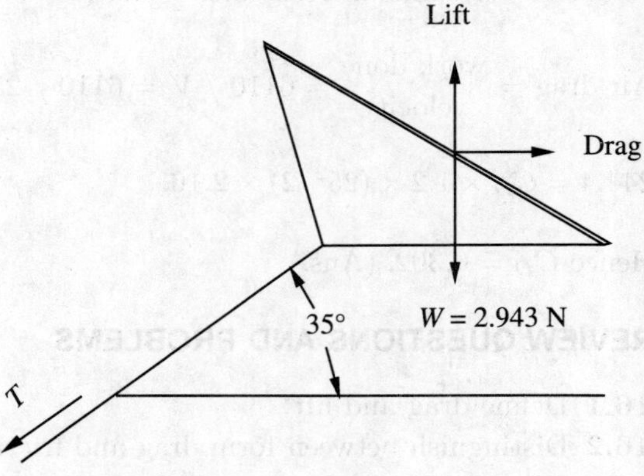

Example 16.6

$W = 300$ g$_f$ $= 2.943$ N;

Lift $= 14 \times \sin 35° + 2.943 = 10.973$ N.

Drag $= 14 \times \cos 35° = 11.47$ N.

Area $= 0.9 \times 0.6 = 0.54$ m^2; $V = 25$ km/hr $= 6.944$ m/s;

Lift $= 10.973 = C_L \times (\rho V^2/2) \times$ area $= C_L \times 1.22 \times (6.944^2/2) \times 0.54.$

$C_L = 0.690$. (Ans.)

Drag $= C_D \times (\rho V^2/2) \times$ area; $11.47 = C_D \times 1.22 \times (6.944^2/2) \times 0.54.$

Hence $C_D = 0.722$. (Ans.)

Example 16.7 A parachute of diameter 5.6 m and weighing 6 kg is used for air dropping food packets. If the velocity when reaching the ground should not exceed 5.5 m/s, find the maximum weight of the food packet. Assume $\rho = 1.2\ \text{kg/m}^3$ and $C_D = 1.33$.

$W = 6\ \text{kg}_f = 58.86$ N; $d = 5.6$ m; $A = 24.63\ \text{m}^2$.

Let the weight of the packet be P newton.

Total weight $= P + 58.86 = C_D \times (\rho V^2/2) \times \text{area} = 1.33 \times 1.2 \times (5.5^2/2) \times 24.63$
$= 594.56$ N.

Hence $P = 594.56 - 58.86 = 535.70$ N. (Ans.)

Example 16.8 The car Mercedes 500 SEL has a projected area of 2.16 m^2 and is moving at a speed of 90 km/hr. The drag due to rolling resistance is 35% of the total drag. Find the value of C_D if the total power required is 9.4 kW. Assume $\rho = 1.2\ \text{kg/m}^3$ for air.

$V = 90\ \text{km/hr} = 25\ \text{m/s};$

Power to overcome air resistance $= 9.4\ (1 - 0.35) = 6.11\ \text{kW} = 6110$ W.

$$\text{Air drag} = \frac{\text{work done}}{\text{velocity}} = 6110 / V = 6110 / 25 = 244.4\ \text{N}.$$

$244.4 = C_D \times 1.2 \times (25^2/2) \times 2.16.$

Hence $C_D = 0.302$. (Ans.)

REVIEW QUESTIONS AND PROBLEMS

16.1 Define drag and lift.
16.2 Distinguish between form drag and friction drag.
16.3 What is D'Alembert's paradox? Illustrate the paradox with reference to flow past a cylinder.
16.4 What are the effects of viscosity on the drag of a body?

16.5 Show in a diagram, the variation of the coefficient of drag C_D for a sphere with the Reynolds number.

16.6 What is Stokes law? Express it in terms of (i) the coefficient of drag, (ii) drag and (iii) the terminal velocity of a falling sphere. Show that these formulae are essentially the same.

16.7 Explain why there is a sudden drop of C_D for spheres when the Reynolds number is near 2×10^5.

16.8 Show the flow patterns around a sphere (i) for an irrotational flow, (ii) at a Reynolds number of nearly 50,000 and (iii) at a Reynolds number of 2.1×10^5. In the diagram, show the pressure distribution around the sphere. Explain the change in drag.

16.9 What is a wake? How does the wake affect the drag on a body?

16.10 A two-dimensional body like a long cylinder (axis normal to flow) has a higher coefficient of drag than that for a short cylinder. Give the reason.

16.11 Explain why for a cylinder with axis parallel to the flow, the coefficient of drag initially, suddenly decreases with length and then increases.

16.12 Explain the purpose of streamlining. Can it eliminate drag?

16.13 How is the flow condition for a finite wing different from that of a two-dimensional wing.

16.14 What is down wash velocity?

16.15 What is induced drag?

16.16 Explain the development of lift for an aerofoil held at an angle of incidence to an air flow.

16.17 A bill board 4 m × 2 m is subjected to a wind of velocity 100 km/hr normal to it. If $C_D = 1.15$, find the force on the bill board. Assume $\rho = 1.2$ kg/m^3 for air.

16.18 A chimney 12 m high has a diameter of 3 m at base and 2 m at top. Assuming that a wind of 120 km/hr is acting on the chimney, find the drag on the chimney. Assume uniform velocity, $\rho = 1.2$ kg/m^3 for air and $C_D = 0.8$.

16.19 A steel ball 2 mm in diameter is dropped in a column of glycerin. ($S = 1.26$ and $\mu = 10.5$ poise) Find the terminal velocity. Assume specific gravity of steel is 7.85.

16.20 Find the terminal velocity of a pebble (assume spherical shape) of mass 10 g falling freely in water. Assume that the specific gravity of the pebble is 2.67 and $\mu = 1$ centipoise for water. [Hint: Turbulent flow and assume $C_D = 0.4$ for trial]

16.21 A particle of silt (assumed spherical) is settling in water with a terminal velocity of 15 cm/min. If the specific gravity of the silt particle is 2.67 and the kinematic viscosity for water is 0.95 centistokes, find the size of the silt particle.

16.22 A sphere 0.5 mm in diameter is moving in a liquid of dynamic viscosity 1 poise at a velocity of 1cm/sec. What is the drag? What is the coefficient of the drag? Assume $S = 0.90$ for the liquid.

16.23 A sphere of diameter 10 cm and weighing 1.27 N is hung from the top plate in a test section of a wind tunnel by a string. When the velocity in the test section is 12 m/s, the string makes an angle of 15° with the vertical. Find the coefficient of drag. Assume the free stream velocity is constant near the sphere and $\rho = 1.2$ kg/m^3 for air.

16.24 A kite 0.8 m × 0.6 m weighs 0.6 kg and is pulled by a string making an angle θ with the horizontal. The wind speed is 40 km/hr. If the coefficient of lift and drag are 0.6 and

0.3 respectively, find the tension in the string and the angle the string makes with the horizontal.

16.25 A man descends by a parachute 5 m in diameter and weighing 5 kg. The man weighs 65 kg. At what velocity would he reach the ground? Assume $C_D = 1.33$ and $\rho = 1.22\ \text{kg/m}^3$ for air.

16.26 A small monoplane has a wing area of 12 m^2 and a weight of 900 kg. Forty percentage of the total drag is due to the wing. If its speed is 200 km/hr and the power consumed in 270 kW, find (i) the coefficient of drag of the wing and (ii) coefficient lift for the wing. (iii) Find the parasite drag. Assume $\rho = 1.05\ \text{kg/m}^3$. [Hint: Parasite drag is the drag of the body of the airplane except for the wing.]

16.27 An airplane weighing 40 kN is flying in a horizontal direction at 360 km/hr. The wing surface area is 35 m^2. Determine the lift coefficient and the power required to overcome the drag. Assume $\rho = 1.2\ \text{kg/m}^3$ for air and $C_D = 0.03$.

16.28 An inclined flat plate of length 2 m and width 1 m is immersed in water flowing with a velocity of 5 m/s. Assuming $C_D = 0.05$ and $C_L = 0.2$, find the lift and the drag.

ANSWERS

16.17. 4.26 kN; **16.18.** 16 kN; **16.19.** 0.0137 m/s; **16.20.** 1 m/s; **16.21.** 0.05 mm; **16.22.** 4.71×10^{-6} N; 532.8; **16.23.** 0.5; **16.24.** 19.16 N; 55.540°; **16.25.** 6.57 m/s; **16.26(i)** $C_D =$ 0.454; **16.26(ii)** $C_L = 0.1$; **16.26(iii)** Parasite drag = 37.065 kN; **16.27.** 0.190; 630kW; **16.28.** lift = 5000 N; drag = 1250 N.

17 Flow in Open Channels

Introduction — Types of flow — Uniform flow — Characteristics — Uniform flow equations — Most efficient section — Standard sections — Specific energy — Critical depth -- Hydraulic jump — Gradually varied flow — Surges in channels

17.1 Introduction

Open channels are liquid conveyance systems with a free surface, generally open to the atmosphere. Streams and rivers, overland flow, canals and sewers flowing partially are examples of open channels. The resistance to flow that is offered by the free surface is usually very small.

Natural open channels have varying cross-sections and their plan forms are complex. The beds of the channels as in rivers can be of loose material like silt, sand and gravel and flow may cause movement of the bed materials. Many man-made channels can have rigid boundaries, smooth or rough, and prismatic in shape, maintaining the same cross-section. The flow in open channels is mostly turbulent. Even in the case of a uniform flow in prismatic open channels, a condition which will occur when the bed is at a constant slope and the cross-section of the flow remains unchanged, the velocity distribution in the channel and equations describing the flow are not clearly defined. A typical velocity distribution is shown in Fig. 17.1 by means of isovels, i.e., equal velocity lines.

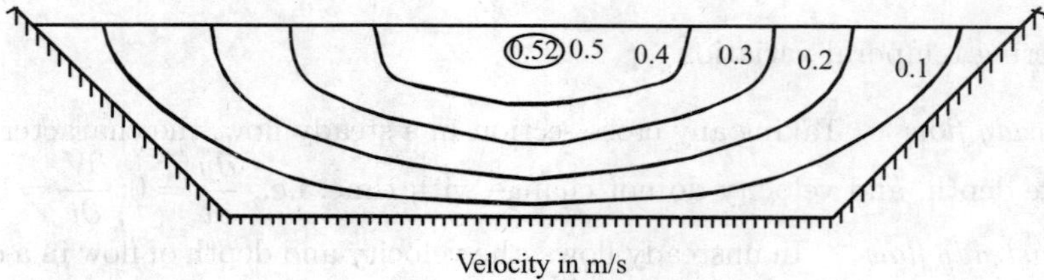

Fig. 17.1 *Velocity distribution in a channel cross-section*

The velocity at the boundary in rigid bed channels will be zero; and the maximum velocity will be near the centre of the channel, a little below the surface. The patterns of isovels are very rarely symmetric. Away from the boundary, along the normal to the boundary, a theoretical approximation of velocity distribution is logarithmic.

Keeping in view the complex nature of the open channel flow, it is not strange that only empirical working equations (supported by vast observational data) are available for resistance in open channels.

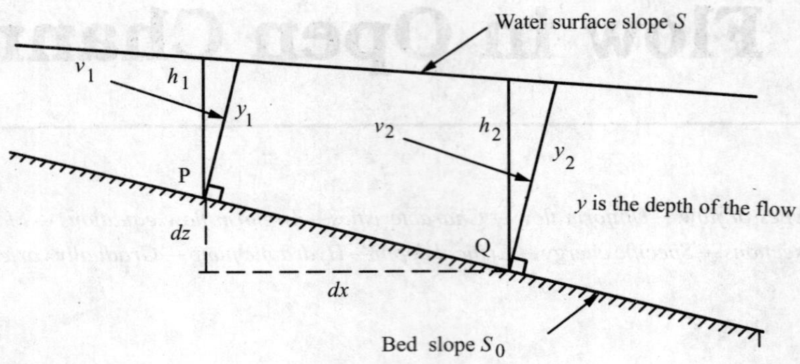

Fig. 17.2 *Flow through a channel*

In prismatic channels, the bed slope S_0 is the fall of the bed for a unit horizontal distance along the channel. In Fig. 17.2, bed slope $S_0 = \dfrac{dz}{dx}$. The depths of flow y_1 and y_2 at P and Q are the depths measured normal to the bed. But when the slope is small, the depths y_1 and y_2 can be approximated by the vertical depths h_1 and h_2 respectively. The average velocity V in the channel at any section will be the discharge across the section divided by the cross-sectional area.

17.2 Types of Flow

The flow in open channels can be classified as follows:

(a) Considering temporal variation

(i) *Steady flow* Taking any cross-section in a steady flow, the characteristics of flow like depth, and velocity do not change with time. i.e., $\dfrac{\partial y}{\partial t} = 0; \dfrac{\partial V}{\partial t} = 0.$

(ii) *Unsteady flow* In unsteady flows, the velocity and depth of flow in a cross-section change with time. i.e., $\dfrac{\partial y}{\partial t} \neq 0; \dfrac{\partial V}{\partial t} \neq 0.$

(b) Considering spatial variation

(i) *Uniform flow* In uniform flow, the flow characteristics at various cross-sections of flow along the channel are the same. i.e., $\dfrac{\partial y}{\partial s} = 0; \dfrac{\partial V}{\partial s} = 0.$

(ii) *Non-uniform flow* In non-uniform flows, the depth and velocity vary in different cross-sections along the channel. i.e., $\dfrac{\partial y}{\partial s} \neq 0; \dfrac{\partial V}{\partial s} \neq 0.$

(c) Considering the specific energy of flow i.e., total energy above the bed

(i) *Critical flow* The depth of flow at which the specific energy is minimum is the critical depth of flow. The corresponding velocity of flow is known as the critical velocity.

(ii) *Sub-critical flow* Flow at velocities lower than the critical velocity.

(iii) *Super-critical flow* Flow at velocities higher than the critical velocity.

(d) Considering the variation in depth of flow along the channel

(i) *Gradually varied flow* In non-uniform flow, if the variation of the depth of flow is gradual, it is a gradually varied flow.

(ii) *Rapidly varied flow* The flow occurring near a fall or a hydraulic jump is a rapidly varied flow.

(e) Considering the variation of discharge along the channel

(i) *Spatially varied flow* In a spatially varied flow, the discharge through the channel varies from one section to another due to lateral inflow or outflow.

17.3 Uniform Flow

Uniform flow can occur in prismatic channels having uniform slope when the water surface slope is the same as the bed slope.

Consider a prismatic channel of cross-sectional area A as shown in Fig. 17.3. Let S_0 be the bed slope. The length of the wetted boundary (wetted perimeter), $P = \text{AB} + \text{BC} + \text{CD}$. Let us consider the volume of water in a small length L of the channel.. The component of the weight of water along the channel = Volume × specific weight $\times S_0 = AL\gamma S_0$.

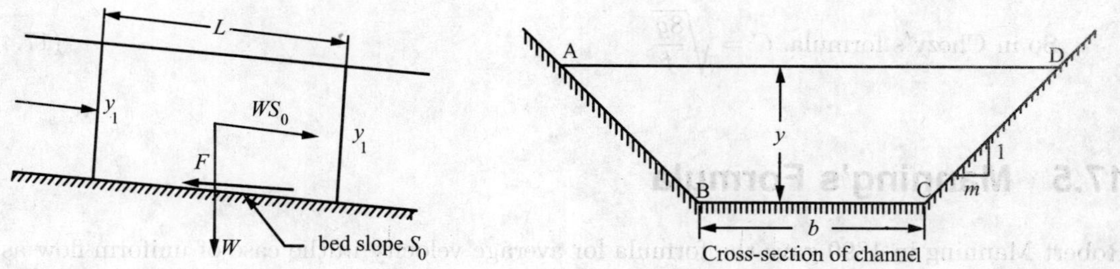

Fig. 17.3 *Forces acting on an elementary prism of liquid*

If τ_0 is the average shear stress on the bed, the resisting force $= \tau_0 PL$. In uniform flow, water does not accelerate along the direction of flow and hence the resultant force = 0. Therefore, $AL\gamma S_0 = \tau_0 PL$, or

$$\tau_0 = \gamma \frac{A}{P} S_0. \tag{17.1}$$

Thus A/P becomes an important parameter in the formulae for open channel flow. It is known as the hydraulic mean depth or hydraulic mean radius, R

$$R = \frac{A}{P}. \tag{17.2}$$

17.4 Chezy's Formula

An empirical formula for velocity in uniform flow is Chezy's formula

$$V = C\sqrt{RS_0} \tag{17.3}$$

where, C is a constant. C is estimated by applying empirical formulae, either the one developed by Ganguillet–Kutter or the other developed by Bazin. It is to be noted that the value of C in the above empirical formulae is dependent on R, which varies with depth of flow. The structure of Chezy's formula can be obtained on more theoretical grounds.

The average shear stress at the boundary

$$\tau_0 = \gamma RS_0 = \frac{f}{8}\rho V^2,$$

where f is the Darcy–Weisbach resistance coefficient.

$$\text{Hence } V = \sqrt{\frac{8\gamma}{f\rho}}\sqrt{RS_0} = \sqrt{\frac{8g}{f}}\sqrt{RS_0}.$$

$$\text{So in Chezy's formula, } C = \sqrt{\frac{8g}{f}}. \tag{17.4}$$

17.5 Manning's Formula

Robert Manning in 1899 gave the formula for average velocity in the case of uniform flow as

$$V = \frac{1}{n}R^{2/3}S_0^{1/2}, \tag{17.5}$$

where R is the hydraulic mean depth, S_0 the bed slope and n the Manning's coefficient of rugosity. In most cases, the variation of n with the depth and shape of the channel can be neglected and it is assumed to be dependent only on the surface characteristics of the bed. The values of n for some commonly used surfaces are given below.

Surface	value of n
Smooth concrete	0.012
Brick surface lined with cement mortar	0.015
Cement	0.015
Earthen canals in fair condition	0.020
Earthen canals in good upkeep	0.025
Earthen canals with weeds	0.035

Chezy's and Manning's formula are connected by the relationship

$$C = \frac{1}{n} R^{1/6}. \tag{17.6}$$

Manning's formula is most commonly used because of the ease with which value n can be assumed to get practically significant results.

17.6 Calculation of Discharge in Channels

In case of uniform flow in channels, the discharge can be calculated using Manning's formula,

$$Q = AV = A\frac{1}{n}R^{2/3}{S_0}^{1/2}, \tag{17.7}$$

where S_0 is the bed slope which will be equal to the water surface slope S_w and the energy slope S_f.

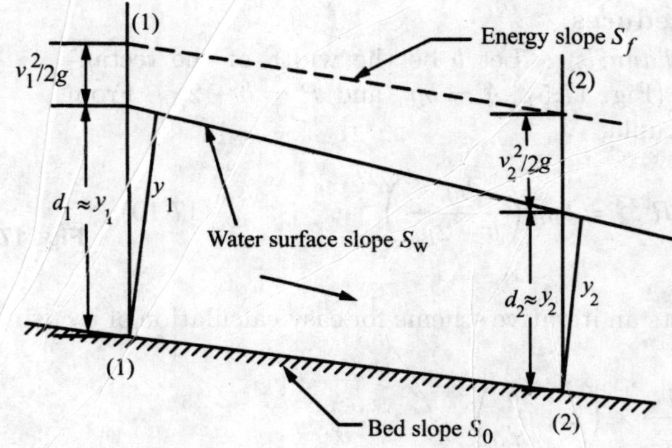

Fig. 17.4 *Non-uniform flow in an open channel*

When the flow is non-uniform, S_0, S_w and S_f are different and hence S_0 is replaced by the energy slope S_f in (17.7) resulting in

$$Q = \frac{A_m}{n} {R_m}^{\frac{2}{3}} {S_f}^{\frac{1}{2}} \tag{17.8}$$

as an approximation. A_m and R_m represent average values of the area of cross-section and the hydraulic mean radius at sections (1) and (2) in Fig. 17.4.

17.7 Calculation of Normal Depth or Uniform Flow Depth

Given a prismatic channel of specified geometry and bed slope, one can find a depth of flow at which uniform flow is possible for a given discharge Q. It is known as the normal depth y_n. For uniform flow, by Manning's formula,

$$Q = \frac{A}{n} R^{2/3} {S_0}^{1/2}; \text{ hence } \frac{Qn}{{S_0}^{1/2}} = AR^{2/3}.$$

In a given problem $\frac{Qn}{{S_0}^{1/2}}$ reduces to a constant, and a value of y is found which gives the value of

$$AR^{2/3} = \frac{Qn}{{S_0}^{1/2}}. \tag{17.9}$$

It can be done by a trial and error procedure. A value of y_n can be assumed initially and $AR^{2/3}$ can be worked out. y_n is modified until the corrected value of $AR^{2/3}$ is equal to $\frac{Qn}{{S_0}^{1/2}}$.

Easy iterative procedures

(i) *Rectangular channels* Let b be the width of the rectangular channel (Fig. 17.5). $A = by_n$ and $P = b + 2y_n$. From Manning's formula,

$$\frac{Qn}{{S_0}^{1/2}} = AR^{2/3} = by_n \left(\frac{by_n}{b + 2y_n}\right)^{2/3}. \tag{17.10}$$

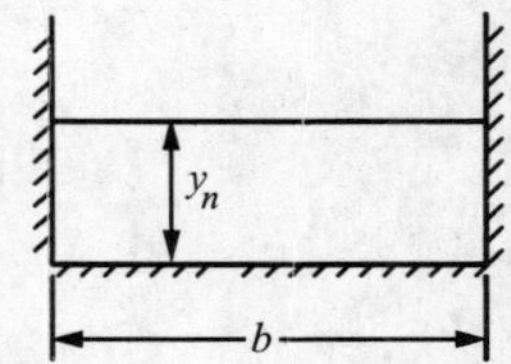

Fig. 17.5 *Cross-section of a rectangular channel*

Pillai[20] suggests an iterative scheme for easy calculation of y_n using a hand calculator.

$$y_n = \frac{Qn}{b^{\frac{5}{3}} {S_0}^{\frac{1}{2}}} \times \left(2 + \frac{b}{y_n'}\right)^{\frac{2}{3}}, \tag{17.11}$$

where y_n' is an assumed approximate solution and y_n, a better solution.

(ii) *Trapezoidal channels* Most man-made channels are trapezoidal. A typical section is shown in Fig. 17.6. A side slope m:1 (m horizontal to 1 vertical) is provided. The value of m can vary, usually between 1 to 2. Let Q be the discharge, S_0 the bed slope, n the coefficient of rugosity and y_n the normal depth of flow.

$A = (b + my_n)y_n$.

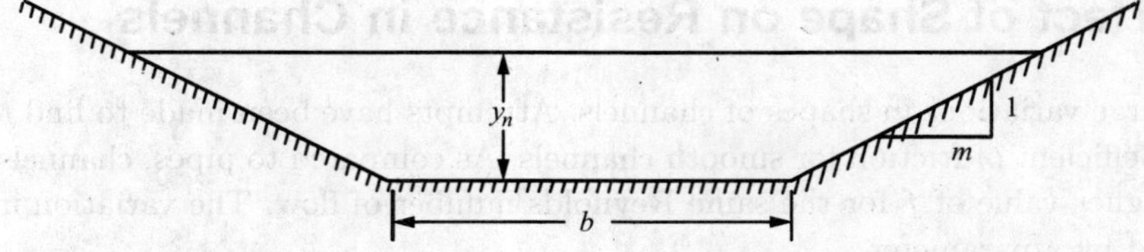

Fig. 17.6 *Cross-section of a trapezoidal channel*

$P = b + 2\sqrt{1+m^2}y_n.$

$$\begin{aligned} Q &= AV = A\frac{1}{n}R^{2/3}S_0{}^{1/2} = \frac{A}{n}\left(\frac{A}{P}\right)^{2/3} S_0{}^{1/2} \\ &= y_n(b+my_n)\frac{[y_n(b+my_n)]^{2/3}}{(b+2\sqrt{1+m^2}y_n)^{2/3}}S_0{}^{1/2}. \end{aligned}$$

$$\text{Hence, } \frac{Qn}{S_0{}^{1/2}} = y_n{}^{5/3}\frac{(b+my_n)^{5/3}}{(b+2\sqrt{1+m^2}y_n)^{2/3}}. \tag{17.12}$$

An iteration solution is given by Pillai[20] as

$$y_n \approx \left(\frac{Qn}{S_0{}^{1/2}}\right)^{0.6}\frac{(b+2\sqrt{1+m^2}y_n')^{0.4}}{(b+my_n')}, \tag{17.13}$$

where y_n' is an assumed solution and y_n a better approximation.

(iii) *Normal depth in very wide channels* In very wide rectangular channels, the depth of flow is very small compared to the width, and hence

$R = \frac{A}{P} = \frac{by_n}{b+2y_n}$

will be nearly equal to y_n. Hence,

$$Q = AV = \frac{A}{n}R^{2/3}S_0{}^{1/2} = \frac{by_n}{n}y_n{}^{2/3}S_0{}^{1/2}.$$

$$\text{Hence, } y_n{}^{5/3} = \frac{Qn}{S_0{}^{1/2}}; y_n = \left[\frac{Qn}{bS_0{}^{1/2}}\right]^{3/5} = \left[\frac{qn}{S_0{}^{1/2}}\right]^{3/5}, \tag{17.14}$$

where q is the discharge per unit width.

17.8 Effect of Shape on Resistance in Channels

There are large variations in shapes of channels. Attempts have been made to find the Darcy–Weisbach coefficient of friction for smooth channels. As compared to pipes, channels are found to have a higher value of f for the same Reynolds number of flow. The variation in shapes is well-depicted by a parameter

$$\psi = \frac{P^2}{A}, \tag{17.15}$$

introduced by Pillai[18,23]. In case of rough channels, the effect of shape is less but the parameter $\psi = \dfrac{P^2}{A}$ has been found to be very useful.

In Manning's formula,

$$V = \frac{1}{n} R^{2/3} S_0{}^{1/2} = \frac{1}{n}\left(\frac{A}{P}\right)^{2/3} S_0{}^{1/2} = \frac{A^{1/3} S_0{}^{12}/n}{(P^2/A)^{1/3}}.$$

$$V = \frac{A^{1/3} S_0{}^{1/2}}{n\psi^{1/3}}, \tag{17.16}$$

where $\psi = \dfrac{P^2}{A}$ is a non-dimensional number representing the effect of shape.

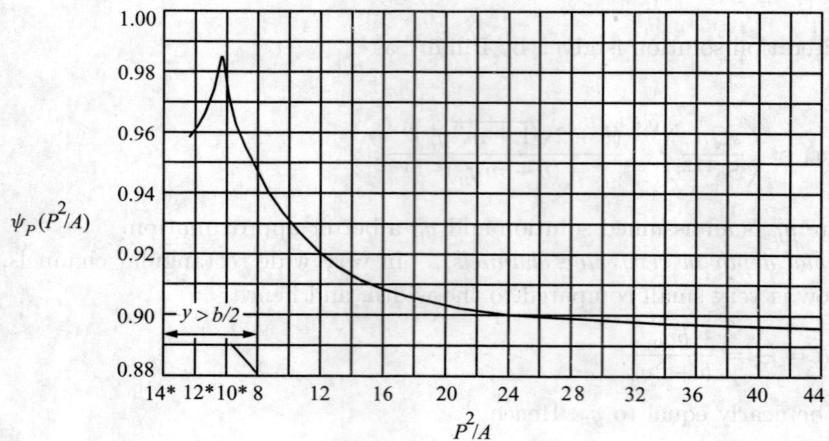

Fig. 17.7 *Effect of shape in smooth rectangular channels (Pillai[18,23])*

Pillai[18,23] has found that the resistance in smooth rectangular channels can be studied by modifying the smooth pipe formula as

$$\frac{1}{\sqrt{f'}} = 2 \log \mathrm{Re}\sqrt{f'} - 0.8, \tag{17.17}$$

where $\text{Re} = \dfrac{4vR}{\nu}$ and $f' = \psi_P\left(\dfrac{P^2}{A}\right)$ for channels and $f' = f$ for pipes. The variation of ψ_P with P^2/A is shown in Fig. 17.7. When $y > b/2$, the values of P^2/A are denoted with an asterisk.

Example 17.1 A trapezoidal channel of bed width 6 m and side slopes 1:1 is laid to a slope of 1 in 2000. If a uniform flow of 50 m^3/s occurs at a depth of 3 m, find (i) average bed shear, (ii) Manning's n and (iii) Chezy's C .

$\gamma = 9810$ N/m^3; $A = y(b + my) = 3(6 + 1 \times 3) = 27$ m^2.

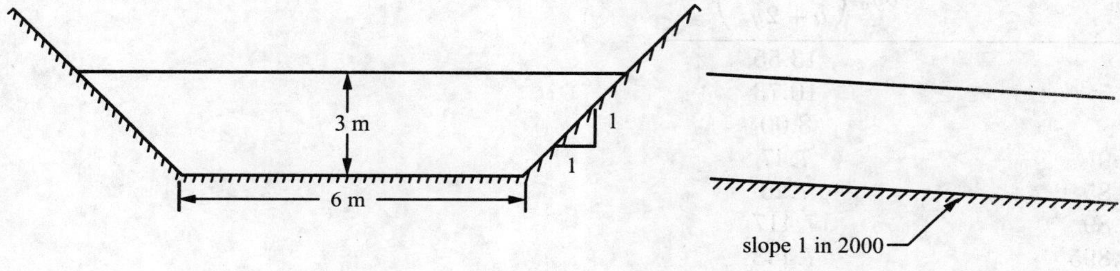

Example 17.1

$$P = b + 2y\sqrt{(m^2 + 1)} = 6 + 2 \times 3\sqrt{(1 + 1)} = 14.485 \text{ m}.$$

$$R = \frac{A}{P} = \frac{27}{14.485} = 1.864 \text{ m}; \tau_0 = \gamma R S_0 = 9810 \times 1.864 \times \frac{1}{2000} = 9.143 \text{ N/m}^2. \text{ (Ans.)}$$

$$V = \frac{Q}{A} = \frac{50}{27} = 1.852 \text{ m/s. } V = \frac{1}{n}R^{2/3}{S_0}^{1/2};$$

$$\text{Hence } n = \frac{R^{2/3}{S_0}^{1/2}}{V} = 0.01828. \text{ (Ans.)}$$

$$C = \frac{1}{n}R^{1/6} = 60.69. \text{ (Ans.)}$$

Example 17.2 A rectangular concrete channel of bed width 4 m is laid to a slope of 1 in 1500. If the discharge is of 12 m^3/s, find the normal depth of flow. Assume $n = 0.016$.

$S_0 = 1/1500; Q = 12$ m^3/s.

When uniform flow occurs,

$$AR^{2/3} = \frac{Qn}{{S_0}^{1/2}}; \quad \text{i.e., } by_n\left(\frac{by_n}{b + 2y_n}\right)^{2/3} = \frac{12 \times 0.016}{(1/1500)^{1/2}} = 7.436.$$

y_n is found by trial and error.

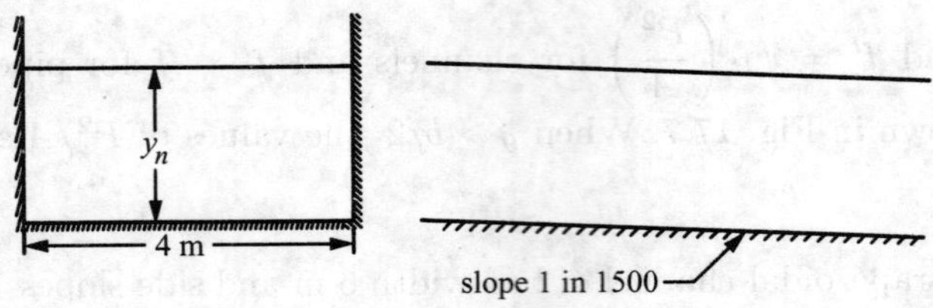

Example 17.2

y_n	$by_n\left(\dfrac{by_n}{b+2y_n}\right)^{2/3}$
3	13.55
2.5	10.73
2	8.00
1.9	7.47
1.85	7.20
1.89	7.417
1.895	7.443

Desired value is 7.436. Hence $y_n \approx 1.894$ m. (Ans.)

Alternate solution

Alternatively, the iterative formula by Pillai, (17.11) can be used as follows.

$$y_n = \frac{Qn}{b^{5/3}{S_0}^{1/2}} \times \left(2 + \frac{b}{y_n'}\right)^{2/3}.$$

$$\text{Substituting } Q = 12; b = 4 \text{ and } S_0 = \frac{1}{1500},$$

$$y_n = 0.738 \times \left(2 + \frac{4}{y_n'}\right)^{2/3}.$$

$$y_n' = 3, \quad \text{gives } y_n = 1.646.$$

$$y_n' = 2, \quad \text{gives } y_n = 1.857.$$

$$y_n' = 1.89, \quad \text{gives } y_n = 1.895.$$

$$y_n' = 1.894, \quad \text{gives } y_n = 1.894.$$

Hence $y_n \approx 1.894$ m. (Ans.)

Example 17.3 A trapezoidal channel 5.0 m wide and side slopes of 1.25:1 is laid on a slope of 1 in 3000. If $n = 0.014$, find the normal depth when discharge is 25 m^3/s.

$b = 5$ m; $m = 1.25$; $S_0 = 1/3000$; $n = 0.014$; $Q = 25\ m^3/s$.

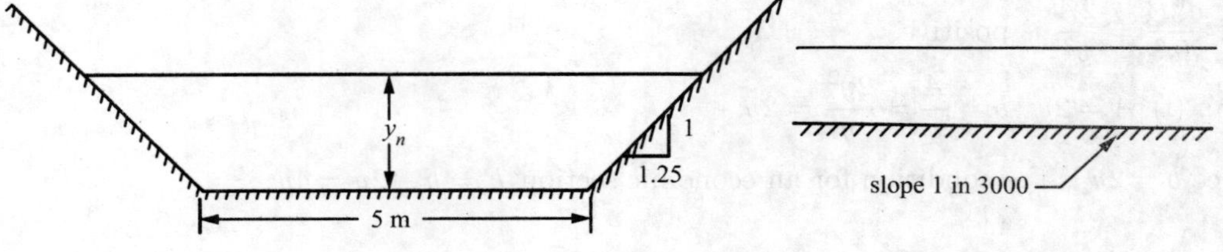

Example 17.3

Using the iterative scheme (17.13) by Pillai,

$$y_n = \left(\frac{Qn}{S_0{}^{1/2}}\right)^{0.6} \times \frac{(b + 2\sqrt{m^2+1}y_n')^{0.4}}{(b + my_n')} = 5.883 \times \frac{(5 + 3.2y_n')^{0.4}}{(5 + 1.25y_n')}.$$

$$\text{Assume } y_n' = 2, \quad y_n = 5.883 \times 2.647/7.5 = 2.076.$$

$$y_n' = 2.06, \quad y_n = 5.883 \times 2.665/7.575 = 2.07.$$

$$y_n' = 2.068, \quad y_n = 5.883 \times 2.667/7.585 = 2.0\dot{6}85.$$

Hence $y_n = 2.068$ m. (Ans.)

17.9 Hydraulically Most Efficient Section of Channels

A channel section is hydraulically the most efficient section, when for given values of side slope m and bed slope S_0, it conveys a given discharge through a minimum area of cross-section. It can also be the cross-sectional shape which will convey maximum discharge for a given area of cross-section and bed slope S_0.

17.9.1 Rectangular channels

Consider a rectangular channel of base width b as shown in Fig. 17.5. Let the rugosity coefficient be n and slope S_0 for the channel. Let A be the given area of cross-section. The condition for maximum discharge through a channel with width b and depth y is to be found out.

$A = by; P = b + 2y = A/y + 2y; Q = \dfrac{A}{n} \times R^{\frac{2}{3}} S_0{}^{\frac{1}{2}} = \dfrac{A}{n}\left(\dfrac{A}{P}\right)^{\frac{2}{3}} S_0{}^{\frac{1}{2}}$. Since A, n and S_0 have given values, when Q is maximum, $P = A/y + 2y$ should be minimum.

Hence,

$$\frac{dP}{dy} = -\frac{A}{y^2} + 2 = 0 \qquad \text{(i)}$$

and $\dfrac{d^2P}{dy^2} = \dfrac{2A}{y^3}$ is positive.

From (i), $A = 2y^2; b = \dfrac{A}{y} = \dfrac{2y^2}{y} = 2y;$

hence $b = 2y$ is the condition for an economic section $P = b + 2y = 4y;$

$$R = \frac{A}{P} = \frac{2y^2}{4y} = \frac{y}{2} \tag{17.18}$$

for an economic section.

Also

$$\psi = \frac{P^2}{A} = \frac{(4y)^2}{2y^2} = 8 \tag{17.19}$$

for an economic section

17.9.2 Trapezoidal section

(i) *When side slope is given as m*:1 Refer to Fig. 17.6. Let A be the given cross-sectional area. Let the bed width be b and depth y.

$$A = y\,(b + my) \tag{i}$$

or

$$b = A/y - my. \tag{ii}$$

Assume a given area of cross-section of A.

$$P = b + 2\sqrt{(m^2+1)}y = \frac{A}{y} - my + 2\sqrt{(m^2+1)}y. \tag{iii}$$

When $Q = \dfrac{A}{n} R^{2/3} {S_0}^{1/2} = \dfrac{A}{n}\left(\dfrac{A}{P}\right)^2 {S_0}^{1/2}$ is maximum, P is minimum.

$$\text{i.e., } \frac{dP}{dy} = 0 \text{ or } \frac{-A}{y^2} - m + \sqrt{m^2+1} = 0 \tag{iv}$$

and $\dfrac{d^2P}{dy^2} = \dfrac{2A}{y^3}$ is positive.

From (iv), $\dfrac{-y(b+my)}{y^2} - m + 2\sqrt{m^2+1} = 0.$

Multiplying by y and rearranging,

$$b + 2my = 2\sqrt{(m^2+1)}y \tag{17.20}$$

$$\text{or,}\quad b = 2y(\sqrt{(m^2+1)} - m) \tag{17.21}$$

is the condition for maximum discharge.

Adding $b + 2my$ to both sides,

$2(b + my) = b + 2\sqrt{(m^2+1)}y$ which is equal to P. Hence $P = 2(b + my)$.

$$R = \frac{A}{P} = \frac{y(b+my)}{2(b+my)} = \frac{y}{2}.$$

$R = \dfrac{y}{2}$ is the same equation (17.18) as in rectangular channels for maximum discharge.

Equation (17.19) also indicates that

$$\frac{b+2my}{2} = \sqrt{(m^2+1)}y. \tag{17.22}$$

i.e., half water line width = length of sloping side.

(ii) *When side slope is a variable* In this case, y and m are considered as variables.

$$P = \frac{A}{y} - my + 2\sqrt{m^2+1}y; \quad \frac{dP}{dm} = 0 \text{ i.e., } -y + \frac{2\times 1/2}{\sqrt{m^2+1}} \times 2my = 0.$$

$$\text{i.e., } \frac{2m}{\sqrt{m^2+1}} = 1.$$

$$\text{Squaring, } \frac{4m^2}{m^2+1} = 1 \quad\text{or}\quad 3m^2 = 1 \quad\text{or}\quad m = \frac{1}{\sqrt{3}}.$$

Hence for maximum discharge (Fig. 17.8),

$$m = 1/\sqrt{3}. \tag{17.23}$$

In addition to the above, the channel section has to satisfy conditions (17.20) to (17.21).

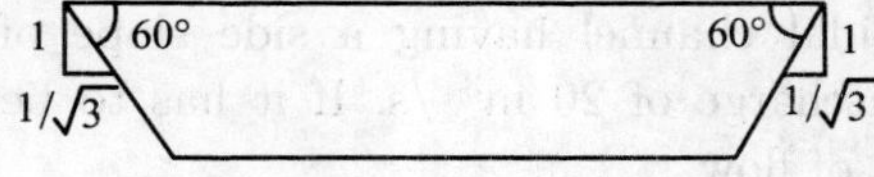

Fig. 17.8 *Economic section of a trapezoidal channel*

17.10 Additional Relationships

$$Q = \frac{A}{n} R^{2/3} S_0^{1/2} = \frac{A}{n}\left(\frac{A}{P}\right)^{2/3} S_0^{1/2} = \frac{A^{4/3}}{n}\frac{S_0^{1/2}}{\psi^{1/3}}, \quad \text{where} \quad \psi = \frac{P^2}{A}.$$

Q is maximum where ψ is minimum or P is minimum.

Hence the condition derived in the earlier section for trapezoidal channels, $b + 2my = 2\sqrt{(m^2+1)}y$, holds good or $b = 2\sqrt{(m^2+1)}y - 2my = 2y(\sqrt{(m^2+1)} - m)$.

$$\psi = \frac{P^2}{A} = \frac{(b + 2\sqrt{(m^2+1)}y)^2}{y(b+my)} = \frac{(2b+2my)^2}{y(b+my)}$$

$$= \frac{4(b+my)^2}{y(b+my)} = \frac{4(b+my)}{y}$$

$$= \frac{4\left(2y\sqrt{m^2+1} - 2my + my\right)}{y} = 4\left(2\sqrt{m^2+1} - m\right).$$

For an economical section,

$$A = y(b+my) = y(2\sqrt{m^2+1}y - my) = y^2(2\sqrt{m^2+1} - m) = \frac{\psi}{4}y^2.$$

$$P = b + 2\sqrt{m^2+1}y = 2\sqrt{m^2+1}y - 2my + 2\sqrt{m^2+1} = 2y(2\sqrt{m^2+1} - m) = \frac{\psi}{2}y.$$

So the relationships for an economic section are,

$$Q = \frac{A^{4/3}S^{1/2}}{n\psi^{1/3}}. \qquad (17.16)$$

$$\psi_E = 4(2\sqrt{m^2+1} - m). \qquad (17.24)$$

$$A = \psi_E\frac{y^2}{4}. \qquad (17.25)$$

$$P = \psi_E\frac{y}{2}. \qquad (17.26)$$

$R = \dfrac{A}{P} = \dfrac{y}{2}$ is the same equation as (17.18).

Example 17.4 A trapezoidal channel having a side slope of 1.5:1, $S_0 = 1/3600$ and $n = 0.012$, has to pass a discharge of 20 m^3 /s. If it has to be an economic section, find the bed width and the depth of flow.

$Q = 20$ m^3/s; $m = 1.5$; $S_0 = 1/3600$; $n = 0.012$.

For an economic section,

$$b + 2my = 2\sqrt{m^2+1}\,y.$$

i.e., $b = 2y(\sqrt{m^2+1} - m) = 0.605y.$

So, $A = y(b + my) = y(0.605y + 1.5y) = 2.105y^2.$

For an economic section, $R = \dfrac{y}{2}.$

Hence, $Q = 20\text{ m}^3/\text{s} = \dfrac{A}{n}R^{2/3}S_0^{1/2} = \dfrac{2.105y^2}{0.012} \times \left(\dfrac{y}{2}\right)^{3/2} \times \left(\dfrac{1}{3600}\right)^{1/2} = 1.842y^{8/3}.$

So, $y = \left(\dfrac{20}{1.842}\right)^{3/8} = 2.446\text{ m. (Ans.)}; \; b = 0.605y = 1.48\text{ m. (Ans.)}$

Alternate solution

For the economic section of trapezoidal channels,

$$\psi_E = 4(2\sqrt{m^2+1} - m) = 8.422.$$

$$Q = AV = \frac{A^{4/3}S^{1/2}}{n{\psi_E}^{1/3}};$$

$$20 = \frac{A^{4/3} \times 1}{0.012 \times 8.422^{1/3} \times 3600^{1/2}}, \text{ from which } A = 12.593\text{ m}^2.$$

$$A = \frac{\psi_E y^2}{4}; \quad y = \sqrt{\frac{4A}{\psi_E}} = \sqrt{\frac{4 \times 12.593}{8.422}} = 2.446\text{ m. (Ans.)}$$

$$b = \frac{A}{y} - my = 1.48\text{ m. (Ans.)}.$$

17.11 Standard Lined Canal Sections

17.11.1 General

Two standard canal sections are recommended in IS 4745–1968. Sharp corners of the cross-sections are avoided to reduce the resistance to flow. The sections are shown in Fig. 17.9 and Fig. 17.10. The triangle section is used for small discharges below 85 m^3/s. The simplified formulae developed by Pillai[22] can be used for designing canals,

$$\text{a parameter, } X = m + \tan^{-1}\left(\frac{1}{m}\right) \tag{17.27}$$

is used.

17.11.2 Triangular channels

Referring to Fig. 17.9, for triangular channels,

$$\tan\theta = 1/m; l = my$$

and hence

$$A = my^2 + y^2\theta = y^2[m + \tan^{-1}(1/m)] = Xy^2 \tag{17.28a}$$

and $P = 2l + 2r\theta = 2y[m + \tan^{-1}(1/m)] = 2Xy$ (17.28b)

Hence

$$\psi = \frac{P^2}{A} = 4X. \tag{17.29}$$

$Q = \dfrac{A^{4/3}{S_0}^{1/2}}{n\psi^{1/3}}$ can also be used.

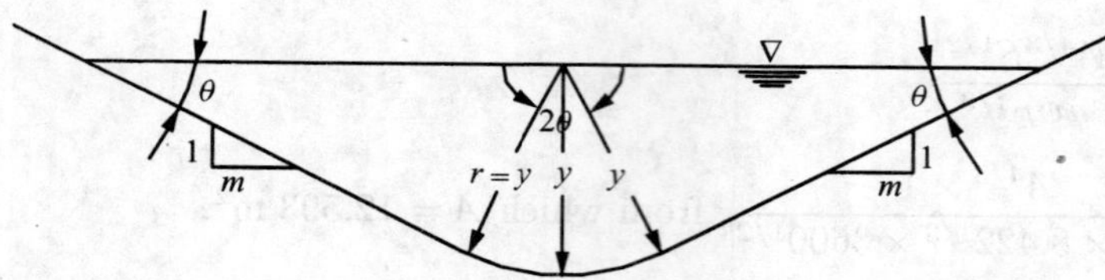

Fig. 17.9 *Standard triangular section*

Example 17.5 Design a lined canal section for discharge of 50 m^3/s at 1 in 10000 bed slope. Assume $n = 0.018$ and side slope 1.25:1.

$$Q = 50\ \text{m}^3/\text{s}; S_0 = 1/10000; n = 0.018; m = 1.25.$$

Hence, $X = m + \tan^{-1}(1/m) = 1.925$.

Since the discharge is less than 85 m^3/s, a triangular channel with a circular arc may be used.

ie., $\alpha = 0; \psi = P^2/A = 4X = 7.7$.

$$Q = \frac{A^{4/3}S_0^{1/2}}{n\psi^{1/3}}.$$

Hence $A^{4/3} = \dfrac{Qn\psi^{1/3}}{{S_0}^{1/2}} = \dfrac{50 \times 0.018 \times 7.7^{1/3}}{(1/10000)^{1/2}} = 177.71.$

So $A = 48.67\ \text{m}^2$.

$$A = Xy^2$$

Hence $y = \sqrt{(48.675/1.925)} = 5.03$ m. (Ans.)

$$V = Q/A = 1.027 \text{ m/s. (Ans.)}$$

17.11.3 Trapezoidal channels

For trapezoidal channels, it can be shown that

$$A = y^2(\alpha + X), \tag{17.30}$$

where $\alpha = b/y$.

$$P = y(\alpha + 2X). \tag{17.31}$$

$$\psi = \frac{P^2}{A} = \alpha + 3X + \frac{X^2}{(\alpha + X)} \tag{17.32}$$

and $\quad Q = \dfrac{A^{4/3}{S_0}^{1/2}}{n\psi^{1/3}}$ is the formula to find discharge.

When ψ is given in a problem and α is to be found out, at first an overestimated value of α can be found out,

$$\alpha_1 = (\psi - 3X). \tag{17.33}$$

The better value of α can be obtained by using an iterative scheme,

$$\alpha_{i+1} = \alpha_1 - X^2(\alpha_i + X). \tag{17.34}$$

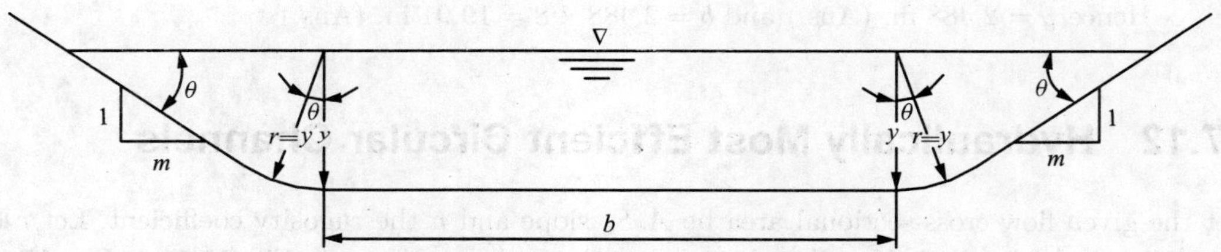

Fig. 17.10 *Standard trapezoidal section*

Example: 17.6. (i) Design a trapezoidal shaped concrete lined canal to carry a discharge of 100 m^3/s at a slope of 25 cm/km. The side slope of the canal is 1.5:1. The value of n may be taken as 0.016. Assume velocity as 1.5 m/s. (ii) Design the same canal, if instead of giving the limiting velocity, the b/y ratio is given as 8.

(i) $Q = 100\ \text{m}^3/\text{s}$; $S = 25/100000$; $n = 0.016$; $v = 1.5$ m/s ; $m = 1.5$;
$X = m + \tan^{-1}(1/m) = 2.088$.

$$A = Q/V = 100/1.5 = 66.667\ \text{m}^2.$$

$$\psi = \frac{P^2}{A} = \frac{(A^4S^{3/2})}{Q^3n^3} = 19.063.$$

$$\alpha_1 = (\psi - 3X) = 19.063 - 3X = 19.063 - 3 \times 2.088 = 12.799.$$

$$\alpha_2 = \frac{12.799 - (2.088)^2}{12.799 + 2.088} = 12.506.$$

$$\alpha_{i+1} = \frac{12.799 - (2.088)^2}{12.506 + 2.088} = 12.500.$$

Hence $\alpha = 12.5$.

$$A = 66.667 = y^2(\alpha + X);$$

Hence $y = \left(\dfrac{66.667}{14.588}\right)^{1/2} = 2.138$ m. (Ans.)

$b = 12.5 \times 2.138 = 26.725$ m. (Ans.)

(ii) $\alpha = 8$, hence $\psi = \alpha + 3X + \left(\dfrac{X^2}{\alpha + X}\right)$.

$$\psi = 14.696 = \left(\frac{A^4S^{3/2}}{Q^3n^3}\right).$$

Hence $A = 14.696 \times \dfrac{Q^3n^3}{S^{3/2}} = 62.47\ \text{m}^2$.

$$A = 62.47 = y^2(\alpha + X) = y^2(8 + 2.088).$$

Hence $y = 2.488$ m, (Ans.) and $b = 2.488 \times 8 = 19.91$ m. (Ans.)

17.12 Hydraulically Most Effcient Circular Channels

Let the given flow cross-sectional area be A, S_0 slope and n the rugosity coefficient. Let r be the radius and θ be the half angle subtended at the centre as shown in Fig. 17.11 or Fig. 17.12.

$$A = r^2\left(\theta - \frac{1}{2}\sin 2\theta\right). \tag{i}$$

$$P = 2r\theta. \tag{ii}$$

From (i), $r = \dfrac{A^{1/2}}{(\theta - \frac{1}{2}\sin 2\theta)^{1/2}}$; $P = 2r\theta = \dfrac{2A^{1/2}\theta}{(\theta - \frac{1}{2}\sin 2\theta)^{1/2}}$.

When θ is to be maximum for a given value of A, P is to be minimum; i.e., $\dfrac{\theta}{(\theta - \frac{1}{2}\sin 2\theta)^{1/2}}$ is minimum.

$$\text{i.e., } \frac{dP}{d\theta} = 0, \text{ i.e., } \frac{(\theta - \frac{1}{2}\sin 2\theta)^{1/2} - \frac{1}{2}\theta(\theta - \frac{1}{2}\sin 2\theta)^{-1/2}(1 - \cos 2\theta)}{(\theta - \frac{1}{2}\sin 2\theta)} = 0.$$

Multiplying the numerator by $(\theta - \frac{1}{2}\sin 2\theta)^{1/2}$ and equating to zero,

$$(\theta - \frac{1}{2}\sin 2\theta) - \frac{\theta}{2}(1 - \cos 2\theta) = 0.$$

Here $\theta = \pi/2$ is the acceptable solution. The channel will be seen to be of a semi-circular shape.

Area of cross-section $A = \dfrac{\pi d^2/4}{2} = \dfrac{\pi d^2}{8}$; Wetted perimeter $P = \dfrac{\pi d}{2}$;

$$R = \frac{A}{P} = \frac{d}{4};\quad Q = \frac{A}{n}R^{2/3}S_0^{1/2} = \frac{\pi d^2/8}{n}\left(\frac{d}{4}\right)^{2/3} S_0^{1/2} = \frac{0.1559}{n}d^{8/3}S_0^{1/2}.$$

$$\text{Hence, } d = 2.008\left(\frac{Qn}{S_0^{1/2}}\right)^{3/8} \tag{17.35}$$

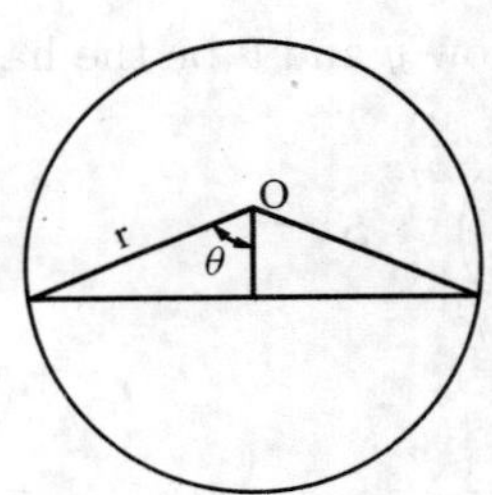

Fig. 17.11 *Cross-section of a circular channel*

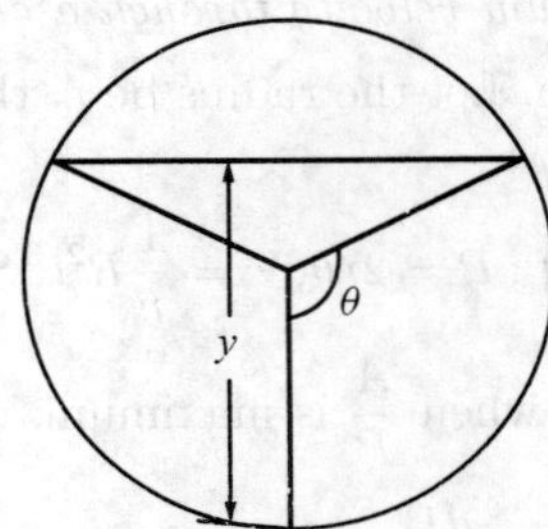

Fig. 17.12 *Cross-section of a circular channel*

17.13 Special Problems in Circular Channels

(i) *Condition for maximum discharge through a given pipe flowing partially full*

Let r be the radius of the pipe and let S and n be given. Let y be the depth of the flow and θ be the half angle subtended at the centre.

$$A = r^2\left(\theta - \frac{1}{2}\sin 2\theta\right);\quad P = 2r\theta.$$

$Q = \frac{A}{n}\left(\frac{A}{P}\right)^{2/3} S^{1/2}$ is maximum when $\frac{A^{5/3}}{P^{2/3}}$ is maximum or $\frac{A^5}{P^2}$ is maximum.

$$\frac{d\left(\frac{A^5}{P^2}\right)}{d\theta} = \frac{P^2 \times 5A^4 \times \frac{dA}{d\theta} - A^5 \times 2P \times \frac{dP}{d\theta}}{P^4} = 0.$$

i.e., $5P\frac{dA}{d\theta} - 2A\frac{dP}{d\theta} = 0.$

i.e., $5 \times 2r\theta \times r^2\left(1 - \frac{1}{2}2\cos\theta\right) - 2r^2\left(\theta - \frac{1}{2}\sin 2\theta\right) \times 2r = 0.$

Simplifying, $5\theta(1 - \cos 2\theta) = 2\left(\theta - \frac{1}{2}\sin 2\theta\right); 5\theta - 5\theta\cos 2\theta = 2\theta - \sin 2\theta.$

$3\theta + \sin 2\theta - 5\theta \cos 2\theta = 0.$

Solving by trial and error, $\theta = 2.639$ radians or $\theta = 151.2$.

$$y = r - r\cos\theta = 1.876r \approx 0.94d, \tag{17.36}$$

where d is the diameter.

So maximum discharge in the circular channel will occur when the depth of flow is 0.94 d.

(ii) *Condition for maximum velocity through a circular pipe flowing partially full*

Let n and S_0 be given. Let the radius be r, the depth of flow y and θ be the half angle subtended at the centre.

$A = r^2\left(\theta - \frac{1}{2}\sin 2\theta\right); P = 2r\theta; V = \frac{1}{n}R^{2/3}S^{1/2} = \frac{1}{n}\left(\frac{A}{P}\right)^{2/3} S^{1/2}.$

Velocity is maximum when $\frac{A}{P}$ is maximum.

i.e., $\frac{d\left(\frac{A}{P}\right)}{d\theta} = \frac{P\frac{dA}{d\theta} - A\frac{dP}{d\theta}}{P^2} = 0$ or $2r\theta \times r^2(1 - \cos 2\theta) - r^2\left(\theta - \frac{1}{2}\sin 2\theta\right) \times 2r = 0.$

Simplifying, $\theta - \theta\cos 2\theta = \theta - \frac{1}{2}\sin 2\theta; \quad \frac{1}{2}\sin 2\theta - \theta\cos 2\theta = 0.$

By trial, $\theta = 2.247$ radians $= 128.74$.

$$y = r - r\cos\theta = 1.626r = 0.813d, \tag{17.37}$$

where d is the diameter of the pipe.

So the maximum velocity in a circular channel occurs when the depth of flow is 0.813 d.

17.14 Total Energy and Specific Energy

Referring to Fig. 17.13 which shows the condition of a non-uniform flow in a channel with large slope, total head above a datum at Section (1) and (2) are

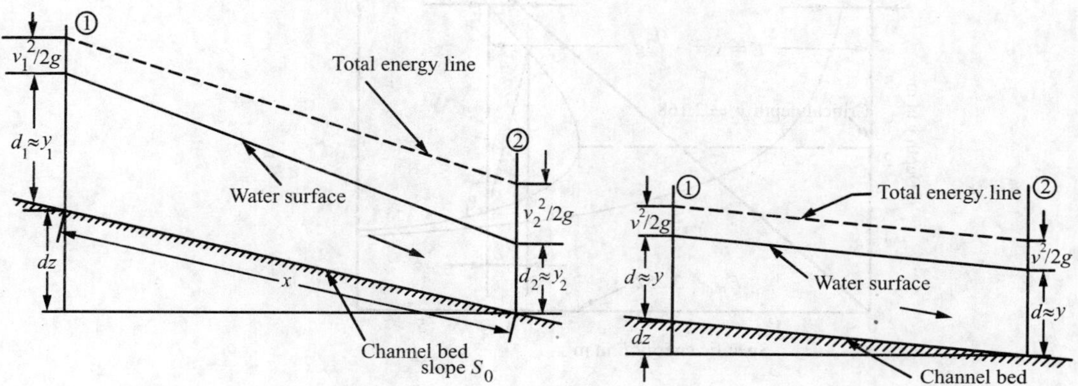

Fig. 17.13 *Non-uniform flow* **Fig. 17.14** *Uniform flow*

$$H_1 = dz + d_1 + \frac{v_1^2}{2g} \text{ and } H_2 = d_2 + \frac{v_2^2}{2g}.$$

But when there is uniform flow in a channel with a small slope, as in Fig. 17.14, $d_1 \approx y_1$, and $y_2 = y_1$ the total energy head at Section (1) and (2) are

$$H_1 = dz + y_1 + \frac{v_1^2}{2g} \text{ and } H_2 = y_2 + \frac{v_2^2}{2g} = y_1 + \frac{v_1^2}{2g}.$$

The total energy at Section (1) is higher than that at Section (2) by dz.

The flow conditions at Sections (1) and (2) in Fig. 17.14 are the same. In order to have the same energy head parameter for both the sections, the energy head E is measured above the respective bed levels. Thus,

$$E = y + \frac{v^2}{2g}, \text{ for both Sections (1) and (2).} \tag{17.38}$$

$$E = y + \frac{v^2}{2g}, \text{ is termed as the specific energy head.}$$

17.14.1 Specific energy curve and critical depth of flow

The variation of specific energy head can be studied in a rectangular channel keeping the discharge per unit width q as a constant.

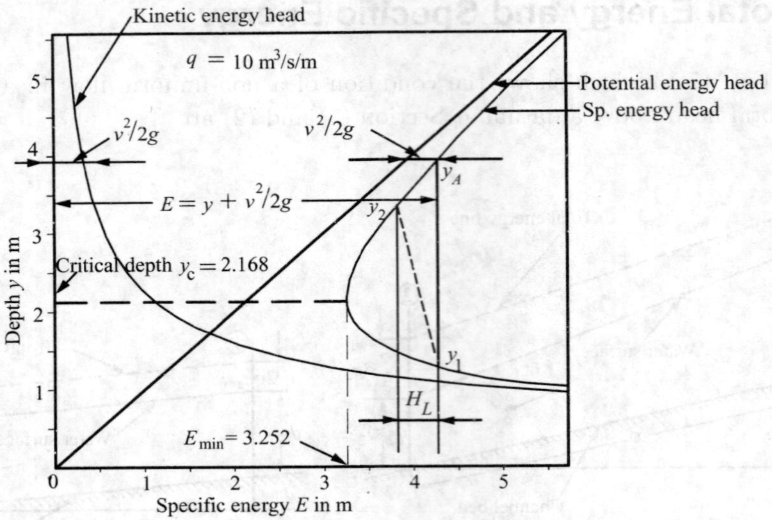

Fig. 17.15 *Specific energy curve*

$$E = y + \frac{v^2}{2g} = y + \frac{q^2}{2gy^2}.$$

It is convenient to consider the specific energy in two parts, the potential energy E_p and the kinetic energy head $E_k = v^2/2_g$ or $q^2/2gy^2$.

Figure 17.15 shows the variation of specific energy in a rectangular channel with depth of flow y when the discharge per unit width $q = 10\ \mathrm{m^3/s/m}$. The specific energy is plotted along the X axis and the depth y along the Y axis. For a given depth of flow, the potential energy head y, and kinetic energy head $q^2/2gy^2$ can be added to get the specific energy head E.

From the curve, it can be observed that the specific energy head is minimum at some depth y_c, known as the critical depth. The corresponding velocity in the channel $V_c = q/y_c$. For depths of flow less than the critical depth, the velocities are greater than the critical velocity and the flow is called the super-critical flow. For depths above the critical depth, the flow is sub-critical.

17.14.2 Formulae for critical depth of flow in a rectangular channel

The specific energy head is minimum at a critical depth y_c.

$$E = y + \frac{q^2}{2gy^2} \text{ is minimum, when } \frac{dE}{dy} = 0.$$

$$\text{i.e., } 1 - \frac{2q^2}{2gy_c^3} = 0; \quad q^2 = gy_c^3 \text{ or } y_c = \sqrt[3]{q^2/g}. \tag{17.39}$$

$$\frac{d^2E}{dy^2} = +\frac{3q^2}{gy^4}$$

which is positive. Hence the minima is confirmed. Corresponding to a specific energy E_1, alternate depths y_1 and y_A can be found by solving the equation,

$$E_1 = y + \frac{q^2}{2gy^2}$$

by a trial and error procedure.

17.15 Specific Discharge Curve

Let us consider discharges possible through a rectangular channel of width b with the specific energy E as a constant and Q as a variable. Discharge per unit width $= Q/b = q$.

$$E = y + \frac{v^2}{2g} = y + \frac{q^2}{2gy^2}.$$

Since $q = by$,

$$q = \sqrt{2gy^2(E - y)}. \tag{17.40}$$

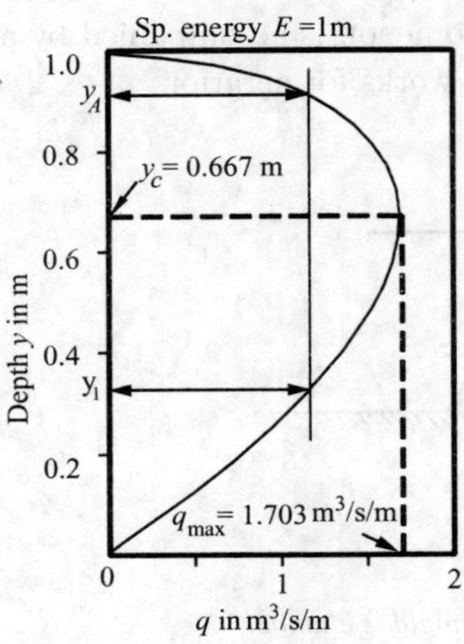

Fig. 17.16 *The specific discharge curve*

The graph between y and q for a constant value of E is known as the specific discharge curve. In Fig. 17.16, a specific discharge curve is plotted for $E = 1$ m. When $y = 0, q = 0$ and when $y = E, q = 0$. At some depth y between 0 and E, the discharge is maximum. The depth y_c is called the critical depth. Figure 17.16 shows that the same discharge q can occur at two alternate depths y_1 and y_A. They are known as alternate depths of flow and solutions of the equation

$$E = y + \frac{q^2}{2gy^2};$$

q is maximum when

$$y_c = 2/3E. \tag{17.41}$$

and

$$\frac{{q_{\max}}^2}{2g{y_c}^2} = \frac{1}{3}E \text{ so that } {q_{\max}}^2 = 2g{y_c}^2 \times \frac{1}{3}E = 2g \times \frac{4}{9}E^2 \times \frac{1}{3}E \text{ or}$$

$$q_{\max} = \sqrt{2g} \times \frac{\sqrt{4}}{\sqrt{27}}E^{3/2} = 1.705\ E^{3/2}. \tag{17.42}$$

This equation applies to the flow over a broad crested weir as shown in Fig. 17.17.

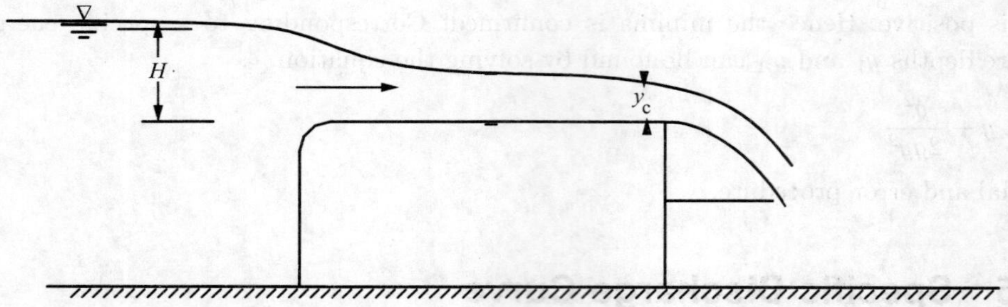

Fig. 17.17 *Flow over a broad crested weir*

17.16 The Hydraulic Jump and Sequent Depths

When a super-critical flow meets a flow with a higher depth, a surge is formed which may move upstream, be stationary or move downstream. When it is stationary, it is called a standing wave or a hydraulic jump.

In the initial part of the hydraulic jump, a roller is formed above the high velocity sheet of flow (Fig. 17.18). Intense shear exists in the layer between the high velocity stream and the roller, causing a high level of turbulence and energy loss. But the turbulence is reduced and the flow becomes uniform in a short length. This phenomenon is accompanied by a large quantity of air entrainment and is used in water treatment works for aeration.

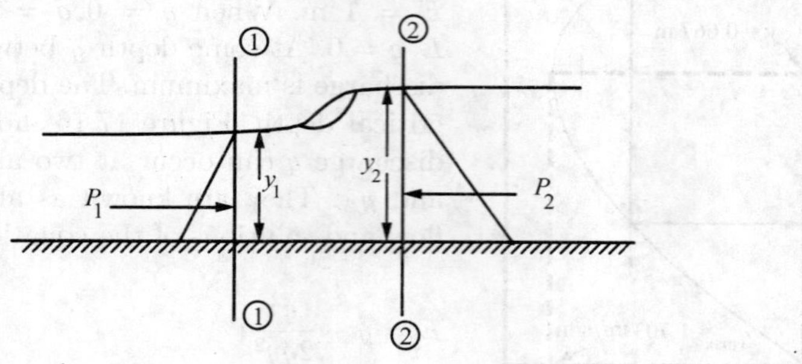

Fig. 17.18 *Plain hydraulic jump in a rectangular channel*

Since a hydraulic jump is accompanied by considerable energy loss, the downstream energy is less and the depth attained is called a sequent depth or conjugate depth y_2. The sequent depth is less than the alternate depth y_A as shown in Fig. 17.16.

17.17 Specific Force Diagram and Sequent Depth

As the hydraulic jump is accompanied by a considerable loss of energy, the relationship between its parameters can be obtained only by taking recourse to the force – momentum change equation as per Newton's second law .

In a rectangular channel of width b, let the discharge be Q. Hence $q = Q/b$. Let the depth of the flow before the jump be y_1 and after the jump be y_2 respectively as in Fig. 17.18. Considering a unit width of channel,

Net force of pressure acting in the X direction,

$$\frac{1}{2}\gamma {y_1}^2 - \frac{1}{2}\gamma {y_2}^2. \tag{i}$$

$$\text{Change of momentum transport rate } = \rho q v_2 - \rho q v_1 = \frac{\rho q^2}{y_2} - \frac{\rho q^2}{y_1}. \tag{ii}$$

Equating (i) and (ii),

$$\frac{1}{2}\gamma {y_1}^2 - \frac{1}{2}\gamma {y_2}^2 = \frac{\rho q^2}{y_2} - \frac{\rho q^2}{y_1}$$

$$\text{or } \frac{1}{2}\gamma {y_1}^2 + \frac{\rho q^2}{y_1} = \frac{1}{2}\gamma {y_2}^2 + \frac{\rho q^2}{y_2}. \tag{17.43}$$

The quantity $\frac{1}{2}\gamma y^2 + \frac{\rho q^2}{y}$ is termed as the specific force F. Figure 17.19 shows a specific force diagram for a discharge intensity of 10 m^3/s/m.

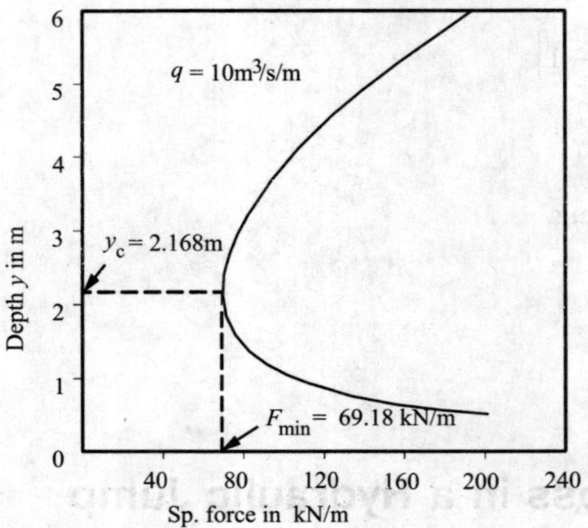

Fig. 17.19 *Specific force diagram*

Minimum specific force can be shown to occur at the critical depth,

$$\frac{1}{2}\gamma {y_1}^2 - \frac{1}{2}\gamma {y_2}^2 = \frac{\rho q^2}{y_2} - \frac{\rho q^2}{y_1}.$$

$${y_1}^2 - {y_2}^2 = \frac{q^2}{2g}\left[\frac{1}{y_2} - \frac{1}{y_1}\right] = \frac{2q^2}{g}\left[\frac{y_1 - y_2}{y_1 y_2}\right].$$

Rearranging,

$$y_1 y_2 (y_1 + y_2) = \frac{2q^2}{g}. \tag{17.44}$$

$$y_1 {y_2}^2 + {y_1}^2 y_2 - \frac{2q^2}{g} = 0.$$

$$\text{Solving, } y_2 = -\frac{y_1}{2} \pm \frac{1}{2}\sqrt{\left({y_1}^2 + \frac{8q^2}{gy_1}\right)}. \tag{17.45}$$

If n is the depth ratio,

$$n = \frac{y_2}{y_1} = -\frac{1}{2} + \frac{1}{2}\sqrt{\left(1 + \frac{8q^2}{g{y_1}^3}\right)};$$

$$\text{Since } {F_1}^2 = \left(\frac{v_1}{\sqrt{gy_1}}\right)^2 = \frac{q^2}{gy^3}, n = -\frac{1}{2} + \frac{1}{2}\sqrt{1 + 8{F_1}^2}.$$

$$n = \frac{1}{2}\left[\sqrt{(1 + 8{F_1}^2} - 1\right]. \tag{17.46}$$

$$(2n+1)^2 = 1 + 8{F_1}^2.$$

Rearranging and simplifying,

$${F_1}^2 = \frac{n(n+1)}{2}. \tag{17.47}$$

17.18 Energy Loss in a Hydraulic Jump

Total energy of flow $H = z + y + \dfrac{q^2}{2gy^2}$.

Referring to Fig. (17.18),

$$H_L = H_1 - H_2 = \left(z_1 + y_1 + \frac{q^2}{2g}\right) - \left(z_2 + y_2 + \frac{q^2}{2g}\right).$$

Assuming $z_1 - z_2 = 0$ in the short length of the channel,

$$H_L = y_1 - y_2 + \frac{q^2}{2g}\left(\frac{1}{{y_1}^2} - \frac{1}{{y_2}^2}\right).$$

substituting for $\frac{q^2}{2g}$ from (17.44),

$$\text{i.e., } y_1 - y_2 + y_1 y_2 \left(\frac{y_1 + y_2}{4}\right) \times \frac{{y_2}^2 - {y_1}^2}{{y_1}^2 {y_2}^2}.$$

$$y_1 - y_2 + \frac{(y_2 + y_1)^2}{4y_1y_2}(y_2 - y_1) = \frac{y_2 - y_1}{4y_1y_2}\left[(y_2 + y_1)^2 - 4y_1y_2\right].$$

Hence $H_L = \dfrac{(y_2 - y_1)^3}{4y_1y_2}$. (17.48)

Example 17.7. Water issues out of a sluice gate at a velocity of 12 m/s and depth 0.8 m. What is the Froude number of flow? Find the sequent depth. If a jump is formed, calculate the head lost in the jump.

$V_1 = 12$ m/s; $y_1 = 0.8$ m.

$$F_1 = \frac{V_1}{\sqrt{gy_1}} = \frac{12}{\sqrt{9.81 \times 0.8}} = 4.2854. \text{ (Ans.)}$$

$$n = \frac{1}{2}\left(-1 + \sqrt{1 + 8F_1^2}\right) = 5.579.$$

$y_2 = ny_1 = 4.463$ m. (Ans.)

$$H_L = \frac{(y_2 - y_1)^3}{4y_1y_2} = 3.44 \text{ m. (Ans.)}$$

Example 17.8 A hydraulic jump occurs with tail-water depth of 2.35 m and velocity of 1.2 m/s. What is the depth and velocity of the flow before the jump?

$y_2 = 2.35$ m; $V_2 = 1.2$ m/s.

$q = y_2 \times V_2 = 2.82$ m^3/s/m.

$${y_1 y_2}^2 + {y_1}^2 y_2 - \frac{2q^2}{g} = 0. \text{ (From (17.44))}$$

$$y_1 = \frac{-y_2}{2} + \frac{1}{2}\sqrt{y_2{}^2 + \frac{8q^2}{gy_2}} = 0.264 \text{ m. (Ans.)}$$

$$V_1 = \frac{q}{y_1} = 10.682 \text{ m/s. (Ans.)}$$

17.19 Finding the Sequent Depths of Flow given H_L and q

In barrage designs, problems often arise when we need to find y_1 and y_2, given H_L and q, as the flow takes place on a slope where a hydraulic jump is formed. The slope being 1 in 4 or less as in Fig. 17.20, its effect is often neglected in the analysis.

The problem can be solved by the trial and error method. Assuming a value of y_1, one can find

$$F_1{}^2 = \frac{V^2}{gy_1} = \frac{q^2}{gy_1{}^3} \text{ and } n = \frac{y_2}{y_1} = \frac{1}{2}\left(-1 + \sqrt{1 + 8F_1{}^2}\right).$$

y_2 can be estimated and one can check whether $\frac{(y_2 - y_1)^3}{4y_1y_2}$ is equal to the given value of H_L. Otherwise, another value of y_1 is assumed and the trial repeated.

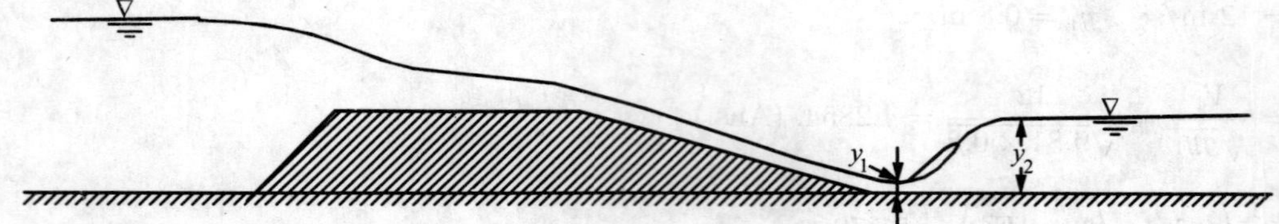

Fig. 17.20 *Cross-section of a weir*

Empirical formula

The following empirical formula given by Pillai[24] gives accurate results.

$$N = \left(3.175\frac{H_L}{y_c}\right)^{0.75} + 2.5, \tag{17.49}$$

where $y_c = \sqrt[3]{\frac{q^2}{g}}$.

$$n = 1 + 1.5(N - 2.5)^{1/2}; \quad 2.5 \leq N < 2.6. \tag{17.50a}$$

$$n = N - \frac{2.125}{N - 12/N^3}; \quad 2.6 \leq N < 5. \tag{17.50b}$$

$$n = N - \frac{2.125}{N}; \quad N \geq 5. \tag{17.50c}$$

$$y_1 = \left(\frac{2}{n(n+1)}\right)^{1/3} y_c \quad \text{and} \quad y_2 = ny_1.$$

Example 17.9 The depth and velocity of a high velocity flow at the base of a spillway is 0.85 m and 18 m/s. A stilling basin operates with a tail-water of 6.8 m. Find the force per unit width on the appurtenances in the stilling basin (see Section 17.22).

$V_1 = 18$ m/s; $\quad y_1 = 0.85$ m.

$q = y_1 \times V_1 = 15.3\ \text{m}^3/\text{s/m}.$

$$F_1 = \frac{V_1}{\sqrt{gy_1}} = 6.233; \quad n = \frac{1}{2}\left(-1 + \sqrt{1 + 8F_1^2}\right) = 8.33.$$

$y_2 = ny_1 = 7.08$ m; but $y_2' = 6.8$ m, hence a forced hydraulic jump is formed.
$V_2 = q/y_2' = 15.3/6.8 = 2.25$ m/s.

$$\frac{1}{2}\gamma {y_2}^2 - \frac{1}{2}\gamma {y_1}^2 + F = \rho q V_1 - \rho q V_2.$$

$$1/2 \times 9810 \times 6.8^2 - 1/2 \times 9810 \times 0.85^2 + F = 1000 \times 15.3 \times (18 - 2.25).$$

$$2.233 \times 10^5 + F = 2.410 \times 10^5; F = 17.7 \text{ kN. (Ans.)}$$

Example 17.10 The head loss in a hydraulic jump occurring on a mild slope is found to be 1.25 m. If the discharge intensity is 18 m³/s, find the depth of flow before and after the jump.

$$H_L = 1.25 \text{ m}; y_c = \sqrt[3]{\frac{q^2}{g}} = \sqrt[3]{\frac{18^2}{9.81}} = 3.208 \text{ m}.$$

$$\frac{H_L}{y_c} = \frac{1.25}{3.208} = 0.3897.$$

$$N = \left(3.175\frac{H_L}{y_c}\right)^{0.75} + 2.5 = 3.673; \quad n = N - \frac{2.125}{N - 12/N^3} = 3.054.$$

$$y_1 = \left(\frac{2}{n(n+1)}\right)^{1/3} y_c; \quad y_1 = 1.747 \text{ m}; y_2 = ny_1 = 5.335 \text{ m. (Ans.)}$$

$$\text{Check } H_L = \frac{(y_2 - y_1)^3}{4y_1y_2} = 1.24 \text{ m} \approx 1.25 \text{ m}.$$

17.20 Critical Depth in Irregular Channels

Consider an irregular channel as in Fig. 17.21

Specific energy $E = y + \dfrac{Q^2}{2gA^2}$.

Critical depth occurs when E is minimum.

$$\frac{dE}{dy} = 0; \quad \frac{dE}{dy} = 1 - \frac{2Q^2}{2gA^3}\frac{dA}{dy} = 0;$$

but $\dfrac{dA}{dy} = T$. (see Fig. 17.21)

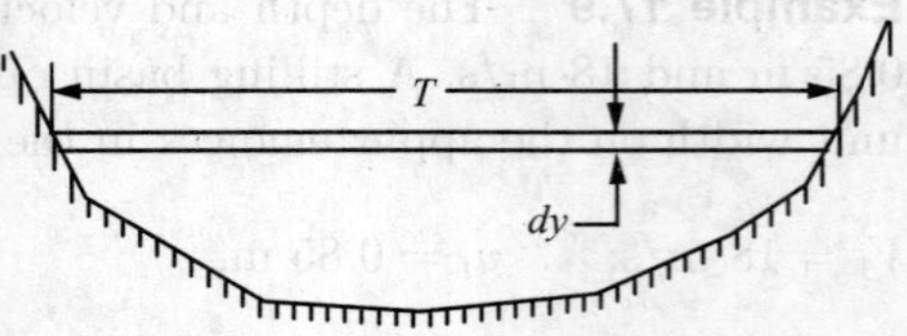

Fig. 17.21 *Channel of irregular shape*

$$\text{i.e.,} \quad \frac{Q^2T}{gA^3} = 1, \text{ i.e.,} \quad \frac{A^3}{T} = \frac{Q^2}{g}. \tag{17.51}$$

This equation can be solved by a trial and error procedure. Assuming a value of y, A^3/T can be worked out. When it equals Q^2/g, the value of $y = y_c$.

17.21 Critical Depth in Trapezoidal Channels

Critical depth can be found out by trial and error, assuming various values of y. Another iterative procedure by Pillai[20] is illustrated in the following example.

Example 17.11 Compute the critical depth for a trapezoidal channel with a 10 m bed width and a side slope of 1.5 :1 to carry a discharge of 30 m^3/s.

(i) *By trial and error procedure*

$$\frac{Q^2}{g} = \frac{30^2}{9.81} = 91.743; \quad A = y(b + my); \; T = b + 2my.$$

When $y = y_c$, $\dfrac{A^3}{T} = \dfrac{{y_c}^3(b + my_c)^3}{b + 2my_c} = 91.743.$

By adopting trial and error method,

y_c	A^3/T
1.0	162.96
0.8	58.0
0.9	83.92
0.92	89.94
0.93	93.05
0.926	91.29

Desired value = 91.743.

Therefore $y_n = 0.926$ m. (Ans.)

(ii) *By iterative procedure used by Pillai*[20]

Assuming

$$K_1 = \frac{b}{2m}. \tag{17.52}$$

and

$$K_2 = \left(\frac{2Q^2}{gm^2}\right)^{1/3}, \tag{17.53}$$

an iterative procedure for finding y_c is

$$y_{c_{1+1}} = \sqrt{K_1^2 + K_2(y_{c(i)} + K_1)^{1/3}} - K_1. \tag{17.54}$$

Alternate solution

$b = 10$ m ; $\quad Q = 30$ m^3/s $\quad m = 1.5$.

$$K_1 = \frac{b}{2\ m} = 3.333; \quad K_2 = \left(\frac{2Q^2}{gm^2}\right)^{\frac{1}{3}} = 4.3365.$$

$$\begin{aligned} y_{c(i+1)} &= \sqrt{K_1{}^2 + K_2(y_{c(i)} + K_1)^{1/3}} - K_1 \\ &= \sqrt{11.1109 + 4.3365(y_{c(i)} + 3.333)^{1/3}} - 3.33. \end{aligned}$$

Solving,

$y_1 = 1$; $y_2 = 0.931$; $y_3 = 0.926$; $y_4 = 0.926$,

hence $y_c = 0.926$ m. (Ans.)

17.22 Hydraulic Jump as an Energy Dissipater

In a hydraulic jump, very intense turbulence is developed at the discontinuity layers between the high velocity flow and the roller above, causing high energy dissipation. At higher Froude numbers of inflow—greater than 5—the jump is strong and entrains a lot of air. The length of the jump is nearly 5 times the downstream depth of flow and in this length, the disturbance in the flow is very much reduced.

Hydraulic jumps are used in stilling basins below spillways and sluice gates. To increase the stability of the jump and increase the energy dissipation, some appurtenances like chute blocks, baffle piers and end sills are used. By the use of these appurtenances, the length required for the 'forced jump' is considerably reduced.

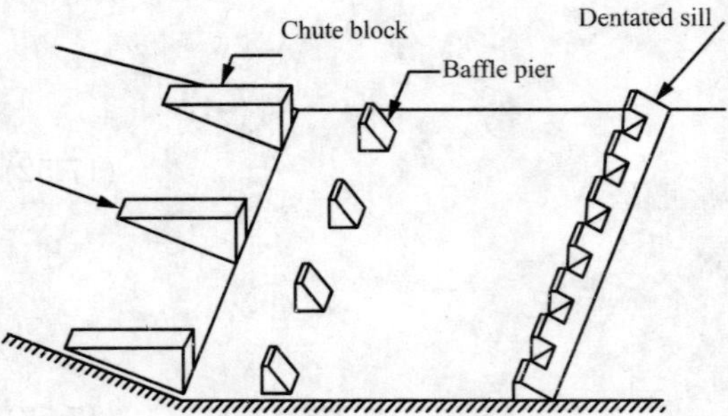

Fig. 17.22 *I.S. Stilling basin*

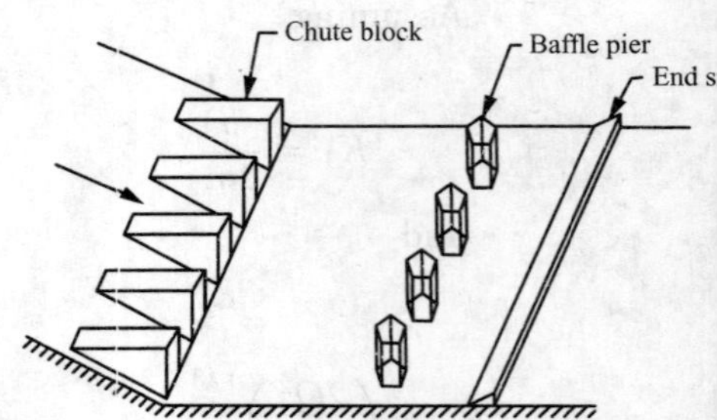

Fig. 17.23 *Stilling basin (Pillai)*

The floor of the stilling basin may be lowered to get the required depth of flow to form the hydraulic jump, depending on the available tail-water depth. Figures 17.22 and 17.23 show two designs of a hydraulic jump type stilling basin where the Froude number of inflow is nearly three.

Figure 17.22 shows the design of an I.S. stilling basin. It has a length of 4 y_2 and uses appurtenances like chute blocks, rectangular baffle piers and a dentated end sill. Investigations by Pillai[19,24,25,26] have shown that the baffle piers can be modified to give more drag by making them wedge-shaped with an front-angle of 150°. It is found that by providing such baffle piers, a short and efficient stilling basin as shown in Fig. 17.23 can be designed.

17.23 Change in Specific Energy along the Channel

In a channel, the specific energy may change due to fall in the level of the bed or increase in the level in a short length. The energy loss in the short length may be negligible in many cases. Depending upon the fall or rise in the bed level, the specific energy will increase or decrease. The specific energy diagram in Fig. 17.24 can be useful to determine whether the depth of flow will increase or decrease after the change in level.

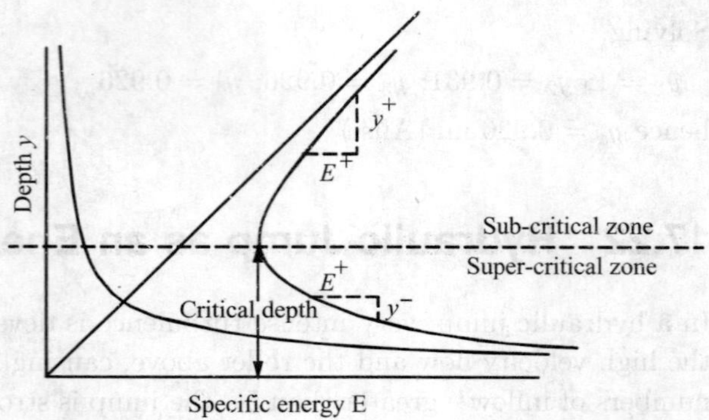

Fig. 17.24 *Zones of flow*

In the specific energy diagram, two zones of flow are indicated. Above the critical depth it is sub-critical flow wherein any increase in specific energy will result in an increase in the depth of flow. A decrease in specific energy results in decrease in depth of flow. It is indicated by the symbols $E^+ \longrightarrow y^+$ and $E^- \longrightarrow y^-$

On the other hand, if the flow is super-critical, the resulting change will be indicated by $E^+ \longrightarrow y^-$ and $E^- \longrightarrow y^+$.

17.23.1 Small fall in the bed of the channel

When there is small fall in the bed of the channel for a short distance as shown in Fig. 17.25, the specific energy will be increased by ΔF after the fall. In case the flow is sub-critical, $E_2 = E_1 + \Delta F$, i.e., E^+ condition which will result in y^+ indicating that the depth will increase downstream.

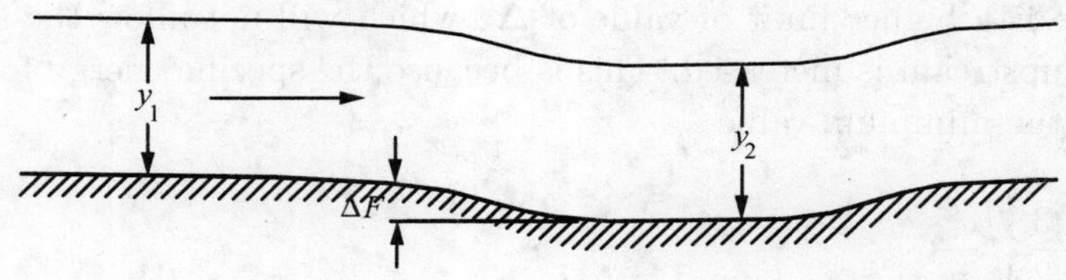

Fig. 17.25 *Flow with fall in bed level ($y_2 > y_1$ for sub-critical flow)*

But if the downstream water level is not sufficient, it may result either in a hydraulic drop as in Fig. 17.26 or in a super-critical flow condition as in Fig. 17.27.

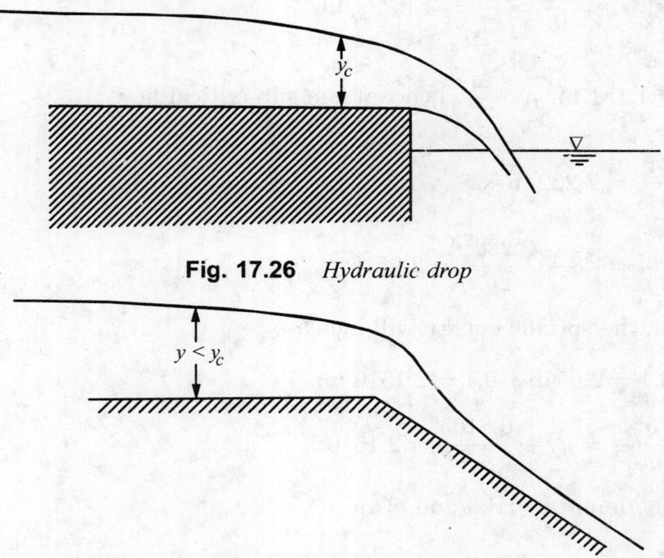

Fig. 17.26 *Hydraulic drop*

Fig. 17.27 *Super-critical flow after a fall*

17.23.2 Rise in the bed of the channel

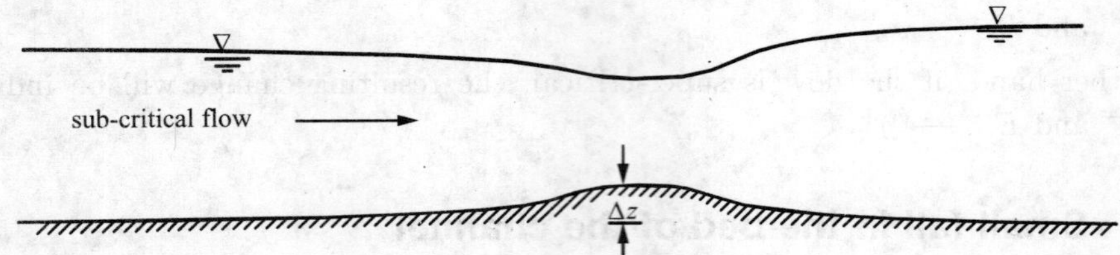

Fig. 17.28 *Channel with rise in bed*

If the bed of the channel rises by Δz as shown in Fig. 17.28, it will result in a decrease of specific energy at the hump. In case the flow is sub-critical, the E^- condition will result in y^-.

However, there is a higher limit of value of Δz which will not allow the same flow over it unless the depth upstream is increased. This is because the specific energy for the flow rate q, cannot be below the minimum value

$$E_{\min} = \frac{3}{2} y_c = \frac{3}{2} \sqrt[3]{\frac{q^2}{g}}.$$

Example 17.12 A rectangular channel 3 m wide discharges at the rate of 12 m^3/s at a depth of 1.8 m. If the bed level falls by 0.1 m in a short distance and energy loss can be neglected, find the depth of flow after the fall (refer to Fig. 17.25).

$$Q = 12 \text{ m}^3/\text{s}; \quad q = \frac{Q}{b} = \frac{12}{3} = 4 \text{ m}^3/\text{s/m}.$$

$$y_c = \sqrt[3]{\frac{q^2}{g}} = 1.181 \text{ m}; y_1 > y_c, \text{ hence it is a sub-critical flow.}$$

$$V_1 = \frac{q}{y_1} = \frac{4}{1.8} = 2.222 \text{ m/s}.$$

$$E_1 = y_1 + \frac{V_1^2}{2g} = 1.8 + \frac{2.222^2}{2g} = 2.0516.$$

Because of the fall, the specific energy will increase,

$$E_2 = E_1 + 0.1 = 2.0516 + 0.1 = 2.1516 \text{ m}.$$

$$E_2 = y_2 + \frac{q^2}{2g{y_2}^2} = y_2 + \frac{0.8155}{{y_2}^2} = 2.1516.$$

y_2 at the fall can be found by trial and error.

y_2	E_2
1.9	2.2159
1.95	2.1645
1.94	2.1566
1.935	2.1528
1.933	2.1513

Desired value of $E_2 = 2.1516$. y_2 is equal to 1.933 m. (Ans.)

17.23.3 Fluming of channels

Let us assume a rectangular channel of width b_1. Let the width of channel be reduced to b_2 in the flumed portion as in Fig. 17.29. Let the bed be raised by Δz in the flumed portion.

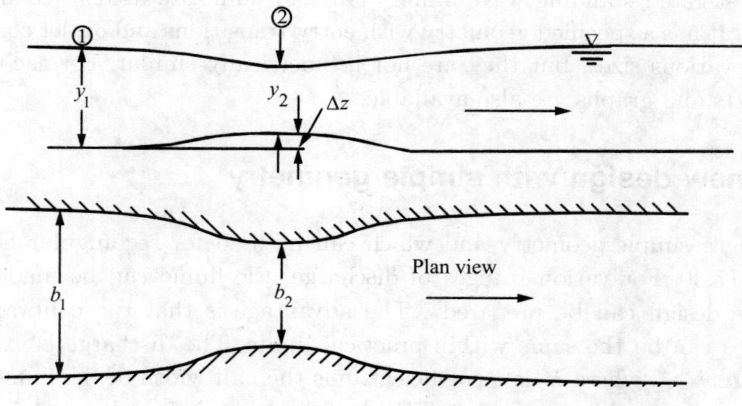

Fig. 17.29 *Flumed channel*

Let the cross-sectional area of the channel be A_1, depth y_1 and discharge Q. The discharge per unit width does not remain the same in the channel and in the flumed section,

$$q_1 = \frac{Q}{b_1};\ q_2 = \frac{Q_2}{b_2}.$$

Specific energy at Section (1),

$$E_1 = y_1 + \frac{{v_1}^2}{2g} = y_1 + \frac{Q^2}{2g{b_1}^2{y_1}^2}$$

Specific energy at Section (2) will be

$$E_2 = E_1 - \Delta z = y_1 + \frac{Q^2}{2g{b_1}^2{y_1}^2} - \Delta z.$$

From this expression E_2 can be calculated. But $E_2 = y_2 + \frac{Q^2}{2gb_2{}^2y_2{}^2}$, from which y_2 can be calculated by trial and error procedure.

17.24 Measurement of discharge in channels by standing wave flumes

17.24.1 Standing wave flumes

Many types of standing wave flumes—with raised sill or reduced width (or both)—are available for measuring the discharge in a channel. The flow is made to pass through a critical section and a hydraulic jump or standing wave may form downstream. In contrast to broad crested weirs, the silt in the channel can easily pass through the device.

A much investigated standing wave flume, 'Parshall flume', is used in channels for irrigational purposes. It has a specified geometry with entry transitions and outlet conditions. There are designs for various sizes, but they are not geometrically similar. For each size, separate calibration charts and graphs are also available.

17.24.2 A new design with simple geometry[8]

A device having a simple geometry and which can be used for rectangular field channels is shown in Fig. 17.30. For various ranges of discharge, the flume can be made geometrically similar and the design can be prepared[8]. The advantage is that the calibration curves for the various sizes can be the same within practical limits. The discharge is expressed by the equation, $Q = Kbh_u^{3/2}$, where K is a coefficient, b is the half width of the flume and h_u is the head over the crest of the flume. The coefficient of discharge is found to be given by

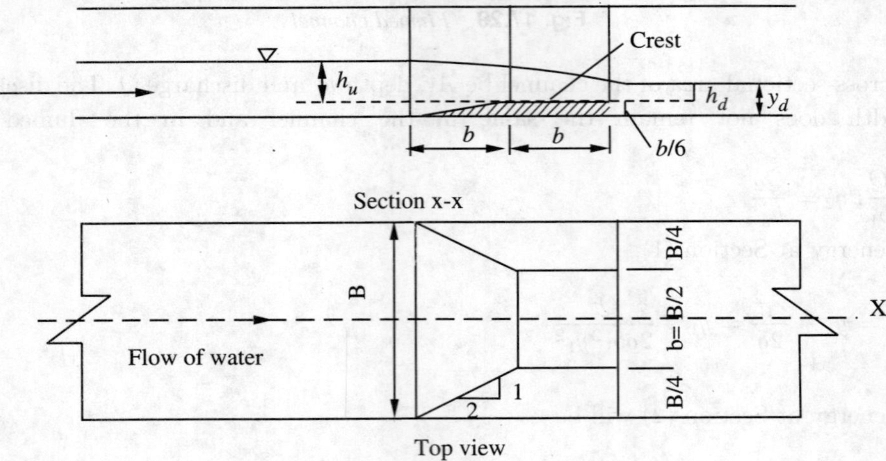

Fig. 17.30 *Details of flow meter*

$K = 1.781 - 0.154(b/h_u)$ for the range $0.6 < b/h_u < 2.5$ as shown in Fig.17. 31. In case of submergence, the coefficient can be found by using Fig.17.31, where the effect of submergence is also considered by using the parameter S.

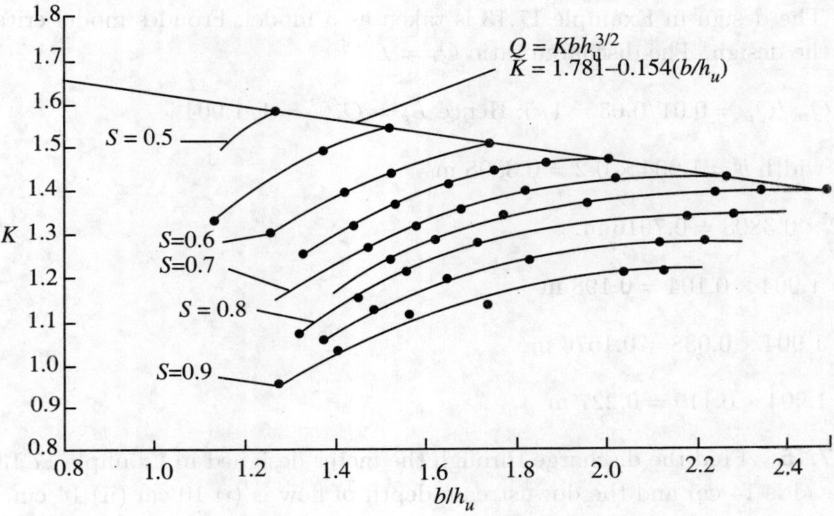

Fig. 17.31 *Variation of* K *with* b/h_u *and* $S = h_d/h_u$

Example 17.13 Design a flow meter for a rectangular field channel to measure a normal design discharge of $Q_n = 0.01$ m^3/s. The flow meter should be able to measure a discharge of 75% of the normal discharge, Q_s as well as 125% of the normal discharge.

Solution Assume free flow conditions. For the design discharge of 0.01 m^3/s, assume a value of b/h_u as 1.9. Hence $K = 1.781 - 0.154\, b/h_u = 1.488$.

$$Q_d = Kbh^{3/2} = K(b/h_u) \times h_u^{5/2}$$

$$h_u = \left[\frac{Q_d}{K(b/h_u)}\right]^{2/5} = \left[\frac{0.01}{1.488 \times 1.9}\right]^{2/5} = 0.1046$$

$$b = 0.1046 \times 1.9 = 0.1987 \text{ m.}$$

Adopt a flume of contracted width 0.20 m and total width 0.40 m. Normal discharge of Q_n will be attained when $h_{un} = 0.104$ m. Similarly it can be seen that 75% of the normal discharge $Q_s = 0.075$ m^3/s, can be obtained when $h_{us} = 0.088$ m and 125% normal discharge $Q_l = 0.0125$ m^3/s can be obtained when $h_{ul} = 0.119$ m.

Discussion The above design can be taken as a model for designing other channels of different sizes.

Example 17.14 Design a flow meter for a rectangular field channel to measure a normal discharge of 0.05 m^3/s. The flow meter should be able to measure discharges in the range of 0.0375 m^3/s and 0.0625 m^3/s.

Solution The design in Example 17.13 is taken as a model. Froudes model criteria can be applied for the design. The discharge ratio $Q_r = L_r^{5/2}$.

$$Q_r = Q_m/Q_p = 0.01/0.05 = 1/5; \text{ Hence } L_r = Q_r^{2/5} = 1/1.904 .$$

Contracted width $b = 1.904 \times 0.2 = 0.3808$ m

$$B = 2 \times 0.3808 = 0.7616 \text{ m.}$$

$$h_{un} = 1.904 \times 0.104 = 0.198 \text{ m}$$

$$h_{us} = 1.904 \times 0.088 = 0.1676 \text{ m}$$

$$h_{ul} = 1.904 \times 0.119 = 0.227 \text{ m}$$

Example 17.15 Find the discharge through the meter designed in Example 17.13, when the upstream head is 14 cm and the downstream depth of flow is (i) 10 cm (ii) 14 cm.

Solution The meter has $b = 0.20$ m.

(i) $h_u = 0.14$ m; $b/h_u = 0.20/0.14 = 1.429$; $Y_d = 0.10$ m.

$$h_d = Y_d - b/6 = 0.1 - 0.20/6 = 0.0667.$$

$$S = h_d/h_u = 0.0667/0.14 = 0.476$$

From Fig.17.31, for $b/h_u = 1.429, S = 0.429$, it can be seen that it will be free flow. Hence $K = 1.781 - 0.154 \times 1.429 = 1.56$.

$$Q = 1.56 \times 0.2 \times 0.14^{3/2} = 0.0163 \text{ m}^3/\text{s (Ans.)}$$

(ii) $h_u = 0.14$ m; $b/h_u = 0.20/0.14 = 1.429$; $Y_d = 0.14$ m

$$h_d = Y_d - b/6 = 0.14 - 0.20/6 = 0.1067 \text{ m.}$$

$$S = h_d/h_u = 0.1067/0.14 = 0.762$$

From Fig. 17.31, for $b/h_u = 1.429$ and $S = 0.762$, it is submerged flow and $K = 1.19$ Hence $Q = 1.19 \times 0.20 \times 0.14^{3/2} = 0.0125$ m^3/s (Ans.)

17.25 Steady, Gradually Varied Flow through Channels

A common example of a gradually varied flow occurs upstream of a weir in a river having a gentle slope. Weirs are constructed to raise the level of water in the river so that water can be diverted to canals. The high water level upstream of the weir will be sufficient for the required discharge to occur over the weir. However, far away, upstream of the weir, sometimes extending to many kilometers, the depth of flow will be near the normal depth of flow. The depth then gradually increases towards the weir through a very long distance. This is known as the backwater curve and is shown in Fig. 17.32. It was later recognized as a M_1 curve.

Another type of gradually varied flow known as the drawdown curve occurs when a gently sloping channel has a sudden fall. A hydraulic drop will occur and the decrease in depth of flow will occur through a long distance upstream as shown in Fig. 17.33. It was later termed as a M_2 curve.

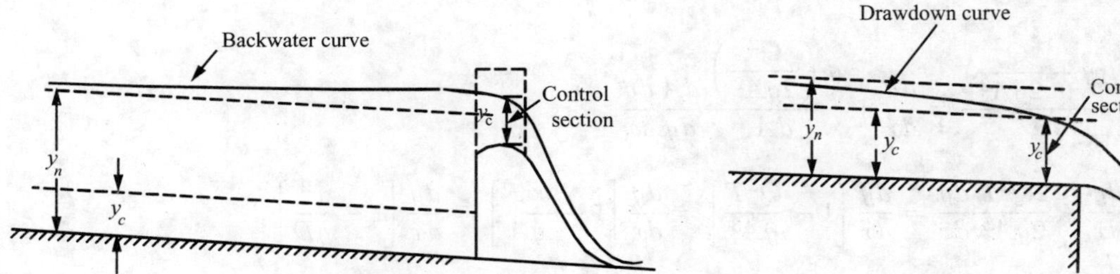

Fig. 17.32 *The backwater curve upstream of a weir* **Fig. 17.33** *The drawdown upstream of a fall*

17.26 Analysis of Gradually Varied Flow

Figure 17.34 shows a gradually varied flow in a rectangular channel. Let the bed slope be S_0 and let the depth of flow change from y_1 at Section 1 to y_2 at Section 2, at a distance Δx. Let S_f be the friction slope i.e., the rate at which total energy is lost due to friction.
From the figure,

$$S_0 \Delta x + y_1 + \frac{{v_1}^2}{2g} = y_2 + \frac{{v_2}^2}{2g} + S_f \Delta x. \tag{i}$$

Change in specific energy between Section 1 and 2 = $E_2 - E_1 = \Delta E$.

$$\Delta E = (y_2 + \frac{{v_2}^2}{2g}) - (y_1 + \frac{{v_1}^2}{2g}).$$

So from (i),

$$\Delta E = (S_0 - S_f)\Delta x.$$

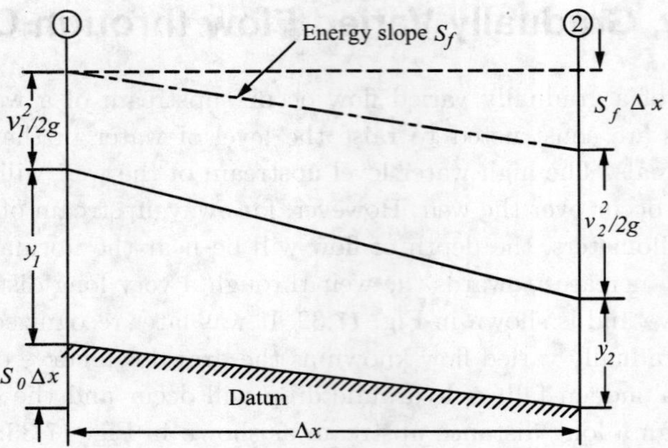

Fig. 17.34 *Gradually varied flow*

$$\frac{dE}{dx} = \frac{d\left(y + \dfrac{Q^2}{2gA^2}\right)}{dx} = \frac{dy}{dx} + \frac{d\left(\dfrac{Q^2}{2gA^2}\right)}{dA}\,\frac{dA}{dy}\,\frac{dy}{dx}$$

$$= \frac{dy}{dx} - \frac{2Q^2T}{2gA^3}\,\frac{dy}{dx} = \frac{dy}{dx}\left[1 - \frac{Q^2T}{gA^3}\right] = \frac{dy}{dx}\left[1 - \frac{v^2T}{gA}\right] = \frac{dy}{dx}\left[1 - \frac{v^2}{gD}\right],$$

where D is the average depth $\dfrac{A}{T}$.

$$\text{Hence } \frac{dy}{dx} = \frac{dE}{dx\left(1 - \dfrac{v^2}{gD}\right)} = \frac{S_0 - S_f}{1 - \dfrac{v^2}{gD}} = \frac{S_0 - S_f}{1 - F^2}. \tag{17.55}$$

In case of rectangular channels, $D = y$, the depth of flow.

17.27 Control Sections

In Fig. 17.32 and 17.33, the positions at which critical depth occur are well-defined and they act as control points for the formation of gradually varied flow profiles. Another case where a control section is formed is at the outlet from a sluice gate as shown in Fig. 17.35.

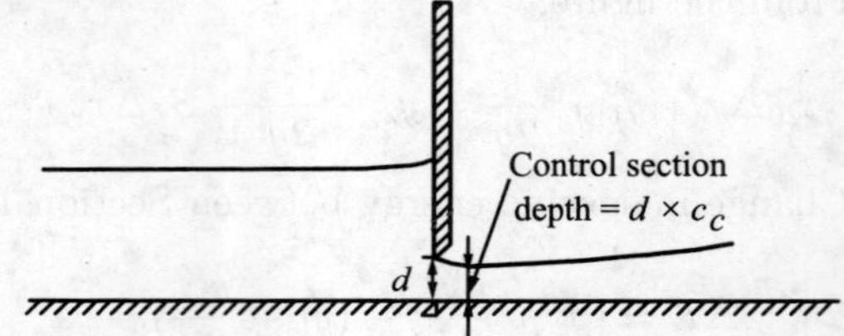

Fig. 17.35 *Outflow from a sluice gate*

17.28 Types and Shapes of Gradually Varied Flow Profiles

In order to determine the type and shape of the gradually varied flow profile, the following criteria are developed.

(a) Zones of flow

The space above the channel is divided into three zones.

y ¿ y_c and y ¿ y_n Zone I

y between y_c and y_n Zone II

y ¡ y_c and y ¡ y_n Zone III

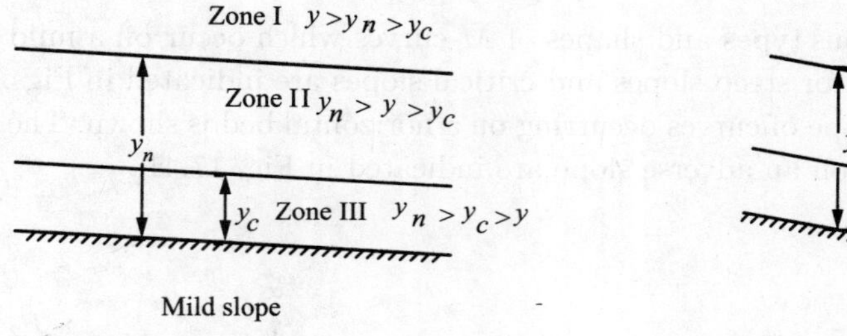

Fig. 17.36 *Zones of flow*

(b) Types of curve also depends on the slope

Condition	Type of slope	Type of curve
$y_n > y_c$	mild slope	M
$y_n = y_c$	critical slope	C
$y_n < y_c$	steep slope	S
$y_n = \alpha$	$S_0 = 0$ or horizontal	H
S_0 −ve	adverse slope	A

(c) When the profiles approach normal depth and critical depth

(i) *When the depth of flow is nearing normal depth*

$$\frac{dy}{dx} = \frac{S_0 - S_f}{1 - F^2} \text{ and } S_f \to S_0$$

and hence from (17.45), $dy/dx = 0$ i.e., the curve is asymptotic to the normal depth line.

(ii) *When the depth of flow is nearing critical depth*

$$\frac{dy}{dx} = \frac{S_0 - S_f}{1 - F^2} \text{ and } F^2 = \frac{v^2}{gy} \text{ tends to be equal to 1 i.e., } \frac{dy}{dx} \to \infty.$$

i.e., the curve will pass critical depth nearly normal to it.

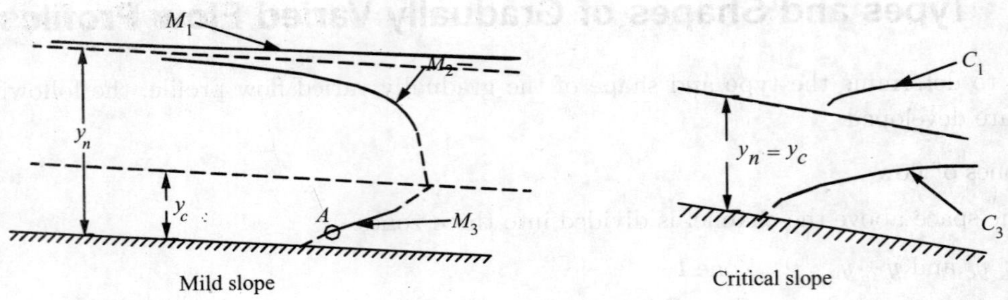

Fig. 17.37 *Flow profile in a mild slope*

Fig. 17.38 *Profile in a critical slope*

Figure 17.37 indicates the various types and shapes of M curves which occur on a mild slope. The shape of profiles occurring for steep slopes and critical slopes are indicated in Figs. 17.38 and 17.39. In Fig. 17.40, the shape of curves occurring on a horizontal bed is shown. The shape of curves A_2 and A_3 occurring on an adverse slope are indicated in Fig. 17.41.

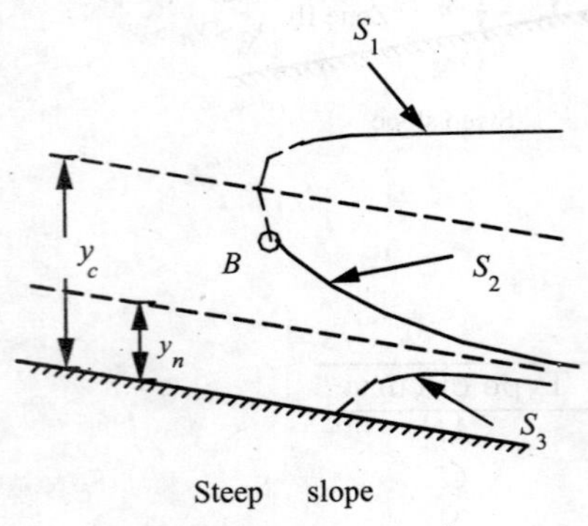

Fig. 17.39 *Profile in a steep slope*

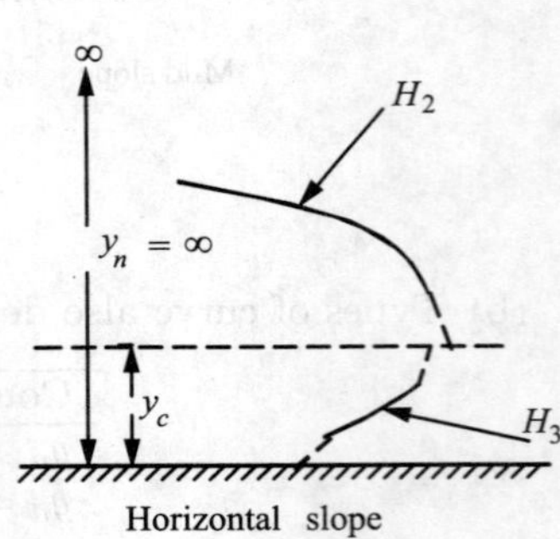

Fig. 17.40 *Profile in a horizontal slope*

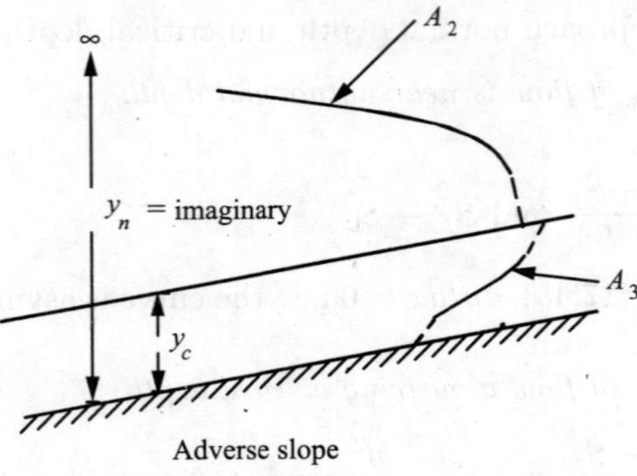

Fig. 17.41 *Profile in a adverse slope*

17.29 Procedure to Find the Type and Shape of Profiles

The procedure for finding out the type and shape of the gradually varied flow profiles will be illustrated in two situations prevailing at point A in Fig. 17.37 and point B in Fig. 17.39,

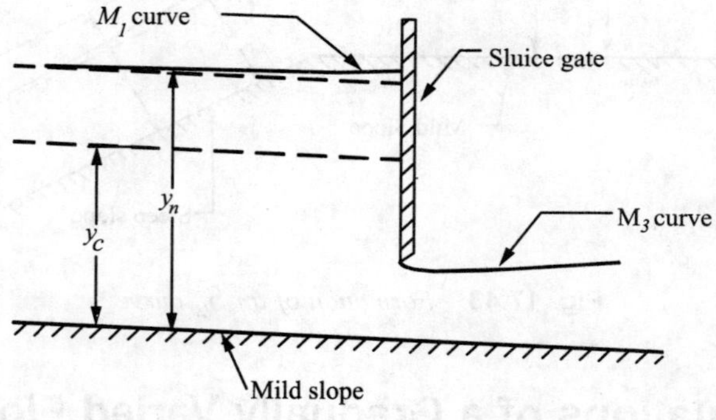

Fig. 17.42 *Flow under a sluice gate*

(a) Point A in Fig. 17.37.
In the figure,

(i) $y_n > y_c$. So it is a mild slope.
(ii) $y < y_n$. Therefore, $S_0 - S_f$ is negative,
(iii) $y < y_c$. i.e. $F > 1$. So $1 - F^2$ is negative.
(iv) $y < y_n$ and $y < y_c$. So y is in zone III.

$$\text{Hence } \frac{dy}{dx} = \frac{S_0 - S_f}{1 - F^2} = \frac{-\text{ ve}}{-\text{ ve}} = +\text{ve.}$$

So y increases downstream when nearing the critical depth. It becomes nearly vertical. The curve will be an M_3 curve as shown in Fig. 17.42

(b) Point B in Fig. 17.39.
In the figure,

(i) $y_c > y_n$. So it is a steep slope.
(ii) $y > y_n$. Therefore, $S_0 - S_f$ is positive.
(iii) $y < y_c$. i.e. $F > 1$. So $1 - F^2$ is negative.
(iv) $y_n < y < y_c$. So y is in zone II.

$$\text{Hence } \frac{dy}{dx} = \frac{S_0 - S_f}{1 - F^2} = \frac{+\text{ ve}}{-\text{ ve}} = -\text{ ve.}$$

So y decreases downstream. The curve is an S_2 curve and will approach the normal depth line asymptotically downstream as shown in Fig. 17.43.

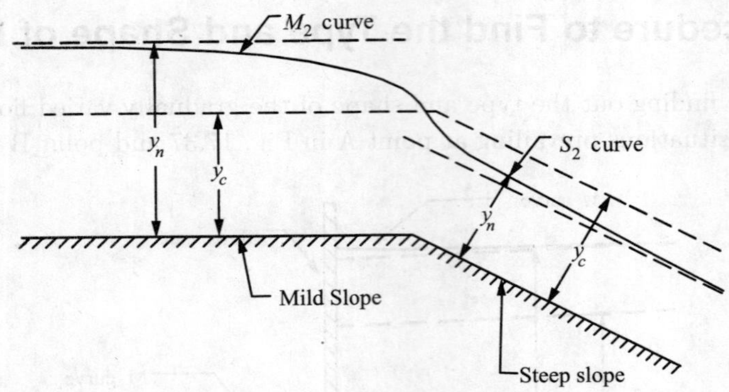

Fig. 17.43 *Formation of an S_2 curve*

17.30 Computations of a Gradually Varied Flow Profile

One simple method of computation is to use (17.55)

$$\frac{dE}{dx} = S_0 - S_f \quad \text{or} \; ; \Delta x = \frac{\Delta E}{S_0 - S_f}.$$

After finding the shape of the profile, the problem is to find out the distance between the known Section 1-1 and another Section 2-2 where a small change of depth is assumed. The slope of the energy lines S_{f1} and S_{f2} at these sections are found out. By applying the formula, average value of $S_f = \dfrac{(S_{f_1} + S_{f_2})}{2}$ may be worked out, where $S_{f1} = \dfrac{{v_1}^2 n^2}{{R_1}^{4/3}}$ and $S_{f2} = \dfrac{{v_2}^2 n^2}{{R_2}^{4/3}}$. Further computation of another reach of Δx from Section (2) to Section (3) etc., may be made progressively.

Example 17.16 A rectangular channel 4 m wide and bed slope 1/4000, conveys a discharge of 4.4 m^3/s. The depth of flow at a section is 0.9 m. How far upstream will the depth of flow be 0.95 m. Assume $n = 0.012$.

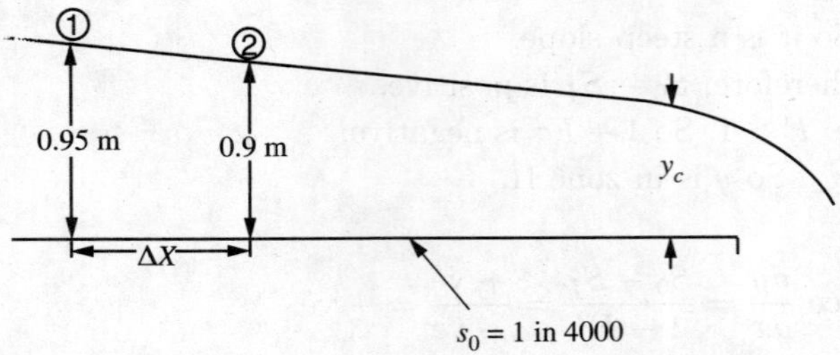

Example 17.16

$$\Delta x = \frac{\Delta E}{S_0 - S_f}.$$

$$q = \frac{4.4}{4} = 1.1 \text{ m}^3/\text{s/m};\ y_1 = 0.95 \text{ m};\ y_2 = 0.9 \text{ m};\ v_1 = 1.1579 \text{ m/s};\ v_2 = 1.2222 \text{ m/s}.$$

$$E_1 = 0.95 + \frac{{v_1}^2}{2g} = 0.95 + \frac{1.1579^2}{2g} = 1.01833 \text{ m}.$$

$$E_2 = 0.9 + \frac{v_2^2}{2g} = 0.9 + \frac{1.2222^2}{2g} = 0.97614 \text{ m}.$$

$$\Delta E = E_2 - E_1 = 0.97614 - 1.01833 = -0.04219 \text{ m}.$$

$$R_1 = \frac{4\times 0.95}{4 + 2\times 0.95} = 0.644 \text{ m};\ R_2 = \frac{4\times 0.9}{4 + 2\times 0.9} = 0.621 \text{ m};\ R_m = 0.6325;\ v_m = 1.19 \text{ m/s}.$$

$$S_f = \frac{{v_m}^2 n^2}{{R_m}^{4/3}} = 3.756 \times 10^{-4}.$$

$$S_0 = \frac{1}{4000} = 2.5 \times 10^{-4};\ S_0 - S_f = -1.256 \times 10^{-4}.$$

$$\Delta x = \frac{\Delta E}{S_0 - S_f} = \frac{-0.04219}{-1.256 \times 10^{-4}} = 335.90 \text{ m. (Ans.)}$$

17.31 Surges in Channels

Surges are unsteady flows in a channel due to change in the rate of flow and hence change in velocity and depth. If the depth of flow is increased suddenly from the initial condition of flow, it is a positive surge. If it causes depletion, it is a negative surge.

Positive surges are encountered in power channels due to rejection of load and hence reduction of flow. Also in case of a sudden increase in discharge in a canal, a positive surge with celerity V_w in the positive direction can occur. Positive surges are moving hydraulic jumps with the wave front moving upstream or downstream. The wave front formed between the river and the sea called a tidal bore, during high tide is an example of a positive surge.

Negative surges are formed downstream of a dam break or when the discharge in a canal is suddenly reduced.

17.32 Positive Surges in Rectangular Channels

Let the initial flow condition have depth y_1 and velocity V_1 as in Fig. 17.42(a). Let the condition of flow be changed to have depth y_2 and velocity V_2 after a sudden change. Let V_w be the wave velocity. It can be transformed to a steady motion by applying a velocity V_w in the same direction as V_1 as in Fig. 17.42(b).

The equation of continuity gives

$$y_1(V_1 - V_w) = y_2(V_2 - V_w). \tag{17.56}$$

The force-momentum equation is

$$\rho g\frac{y_2{}^2}{2} - \rho g\frac{y_1{}^2}{2} = \rho y_1(V_1 - V_w)(V_1 - V_2). \tag{17.57}$$

The above equations are simplified by Pillai[21] as follows

$$\text{Assuming } r = \frac{y_2}{y_1}, \tag{17.58}$$

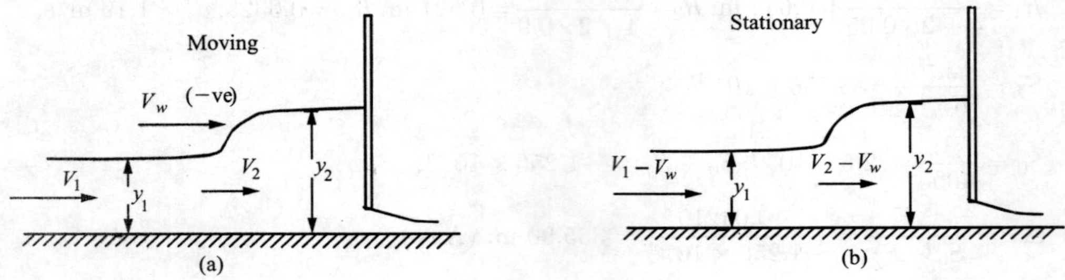

Fig. 17.42 *Positive surge due to gate closure*

$$\pm\frac{V_1 - V_w}{\sqrt{gy_1}} = \left(\frac{r(r+1)}{2}\right)^{1/2} \tag{17.59}$$

and

$$\pm\frac{V_1 - V_2}{\sqrt{gy_1}} = (r-1)\left(\frac{r+1}{2r}\right)^{1/2}. \tag{17.60}$$

Example 17.17 A power channel having a velocity of 1.5 m/s and a depth of flow of 0.8 m is suddenly closed. What is the height and velocity of the resulting surge?

$V_1 = 1.5$ m/s; $y_1 = 0.8$; $V_2 = 0$.

$$\left(\frac{V_1 - V_2}{\sqrt{gy_1}}\right) = 0.5354 = (r-1)\left(\frac{r+1}{2r}\right)^{1/2} = f(r).$$

The value of r can be found by trial and error method

r	$f(r)$
1.7	0.623
1.6	0.5410
1.59	0.5324
1.594	0.5358

Desired value of $f(r) = 0.5358$.

Hence $r \approx 1.594, y_2 = 1.594 \times 0.8 = 1.2752$ m.

Height of surge $= 1.2752 - 0.8 = 0.4752$ m. (Ans.)

By continuity equation,

$$y_1(V_1 - V_w) = y_2(V_2 - V_w).$$

So, $\quad 0.8(1.5 - V_w) = 1.2752(0 - V_w)$.

Solving,

$$V_w = \frac{-1.2}{0.4752} = -2.5225 \text{ m/s. (Ans.)}$$

Example 17.18 A rectangular channel 3 m wide conveys a discharge of 3.6 m^3/s at a depth of 1.2 m. If by partially closing a gate abruptly, the depth is increased to 1.5 m, what is the velocity of the resulting surge? What is the reduction in discharge?

$Q_1 = 3.6 \text{ m}^3/\text{s};\ y_1 = 1.2 \text{ m};\ b = 3 \text{ m}.$

$$V_1 = \frac{Q}{by_1} = \frac{3.6}{3 \times 1.2} = 1 \text{ m/s}.$$

$$y_2 = 1.5 \text{ m. Hence } r = 1.5/1.2 = 1.25.$$

$$\pm\frac{V_1 - V_w}{\sqrt{gy_1}} = \left(\frac{r(r+1)}{2}\right)^{1/2} = 1.186.$$

$$\pm\,(V_1 - V_w) = 1.186(\sqrt{gy_1}) = 4.069 \text{ m/s}.$$

V_w is $-$ve and hence $V_w = 3.069$ m/s. (Ans.)

$$\pm\frac{V_1 - V_2}{\sqrt{gy_1}} = (r-1)\left(\frac{r+1}{2r}\right)^{1/2} = 0.237.$$

Hence $V_1 - V_2 = 0.237\sqrt{gy_1} = 0.813$ m/s.

$V_2 = V_1 - 0.813 = 1 - 0.813 = 0.187$ m/s.

Hence discharge $= bV_2y_2 = 3 \times 0.187 \times 1.5 = 0.842$ m^3/s. (Ans.)

Reduction in discharge $= 3.6 - 0.842 = 2.758$m^3/s. (Ans.)

Example 17.19 Discharge in a rectangular canal with depth of flow 0.8 m and velocity 1m/s is doubled suddenly creating a surge. Find the depth of flow and velocity of surge.

$q_2 = 0.8 \times 1 = 0.8$ m^3/s/m; $q_1 = 0.8 \times 2 = 1.6$ m^3/s/m;

$y_2 = 0.8$; $V_2 = 1$ m/s.

$$\pm\frac{V_1 - V_w}{\sqrt{gy_1}} = \left[\frac{r(r+1)}{2}\right]^{1/2}.$$

$$\pm\frac{V_1 - V_2}{\sqrt{gy_1}} = (r-1)\left(\frac{r+1}{2r}\right)^{1/2}.$$

A trial and error procedure is required to solve the problem. Assume some value of r. Then calculate $y_1 = y_2/r$. Then $V_1 = q_1/y_1$.

$$\text{Let } k = (r-1)\left(\frac{r+1}{2r}\right)^{1/2}.$$

Evaluate k from the assumed value of r. Calculate $V_1 = k\sqrt{(gy_1)} + V_2$ and enter in column 5. If V_1 in column 3 and 5 match, then the assumed value of r is correct. Otherwise another value of r is to be tried.

r	y_1	V_1	k	V_1
0.800	1.0000	1.600	−0.2120	1.664
0.810	0.9877	1.620	−0.2008	1.625
0.812	0.9864	1.622	−0.1997	1.621

Hence $r \approx 0.811$and $y = 0.9864$ and $V_1 = 1.622$ m/s

$$\left|\frac{V_1 - V_w}{\sqrt{gy_1}}\right| = \left[\frac{r(r+1)}{2}\right]^{1/2} = 0.857$$

and V_w has the same sign as V_1.

$$|V_1 - V_w| = 0.857 \times \sqrt{9.81 \times 0.9864} = 2.666 \text{ m/s};$$

Hence $V_w = 2.666 + 1.622 = 4.288$ m/s. (Ans.)

REVIEW QUESTIONS AND PROBLEMS

17.1 Draw a typical isovel pattern of flow in a river cross-section and indicate the possible position of the maximum velocity.

17.2 Distingush between the flow conditions indicated and give examples.
- (i) Steady flow and unsteady flow.
- (ii) Uniform and non-uniform flow.
- (iii) Critical flow, sub-critical flow and super-critical flow.
- (iv) Gradually varied flow and rapidly varied flow.

17.3 What is a spatially varied flow? Give an example.

17.4 Show that in an uniform flow through a channel, the average shear stress at the bed $\tau = \gamma RS$.

17.5 Give Chezy's and Manning's formula and explain their relationships.

17.6 What is the normal depth in a channel? How is it calculated for a given slope and type of bed?

17.7 What is meant by hydraulically efficient rectangular and trapezoidal channels?

17.8 Show that for a rectangular or trapezoidal channel to be hydraulically efficient, the hydraulic mean radius should be half the depth of flow.

17.9 Show that the side slope of $1/\sqrt{3} : 1$ for a trapezoidal channel can give the maximum hydraulic efficiency.

17.10 Show that if the cross-section of a channel is to be part of a circle, the semi-circular section is hydraulically most efficient.

17.11 Define specific energy. Explain how the concept is useful.

17.12 Find the uniform depth of flow for maximum discharge through a open channel of circular section (diameter d) laid to a slope.

17.13 Find the uniform depth of flow for maximum velocity through an open channel of circular cross-section (diameter d) laid to a slope S.

17.14 Draw the specific energy diagram for a discharge intensity $q = 3$ m^3/s/m through a rectangular channel. Show the critical depth of flow. Schematically show the alternate depths of flow and sequent depths of flow.

17.15 Draw the specific discharge diagram for a specific energy of 2 m and show the position of critical depth of flow. Schematically show alternate depths of flow.

17.16 What is critical depth? Derive the formula for critical depth in a rectangular channel.

17.17 Explain the method for calculating critical depth for a channel of any shape.

17.18 What is a hydraulic jump? Derive a relationship between the depths of flow before and after a jump in a rectangular channel.

17.19 Derive the formula to calculate the head loss in a hydraulic jump with sequent depths of flow y_1 and y_2.

17.20 What is the purpose of a stilling basin? How is the hydraulic jump used as an energy dissipater? Give an example.

17.21 Explain how slopes are classified as mild and steep.

17.22 Give examples with sketches of gradually varied flow profiles of mild and steep slopes. Justify the classification of curves.

17.23 Derive an equation for gradually varied flow $\frac{dy}{dx} = \frac{S_0 - S_t}{1 - F^2}$.

17.24 Derive the varied flow equation $\Delta x = \frac{\Delta E}{S_0 - S_f}$.

17.25 Give examples of surges in channels.

17.26 What are the equations governing the positive surges in rectangular channels.

17.27 A rectangular channel 4 m wide has a uniform flow with a depth of 1.2 m. If the bed slope is 1 in 2000, find the average shear stress.

17.28 A long concrete rectangular channel 4 m wide has to pass a discharge of 5.5 m^3/s at a depth of 1.35 m . If $n = 0.012$, find the bed slope required.

17.29 A trapezoidal channel has a bed width of 4 m and side slope of 1.5 : 1. The channel has a bed slope of 1 in 1500 and a uniform flow depth of 0.8 m. What is the discharge if $n = 0.012$. What is the value of Chezy's C for the channel.

17.30 A long rectangular channel of bed slope 1 in 3000 has a width of 8 m. If $n = 0.012$, find the uniform flow depth when passing a discharge of 15 m^3/s.

17.31 A long trapezoidal channel conveys a discharge of 30 m^3/s. The bed width is 10 m and side slope is 1 : 1. If $S = 1/2500$ and $n = 0.014$, find the uniform flow depth.

17.32 A wide rectangular channel passes a discharge of 2.5 $m^3/s/m$. The channel has a bed slope of 1 in 4000 and $n = 0.02$. Find the uniform flow depth.

17.33 A long channel of semi-circular cross-section passes a discharge of 3 m^3/s. It is laid to a slope of 1 in 600 and $n = 0.015$. Find the diameter of the channel.

17.34 A long trapezoidal channel is to be made in an excavation to pass a discharge of 16 m^3/s. If the bed slope is 1 in 2000 and $n = 0.012$, find the cross-section of the channel so that the excavation is minimum. [Hint: $m = 1/\sqrt{3}$].

17.35 A trapezoidal channel of side slope 1 :1 is to be designed to have a most economical cross-section to pass a discharge of 7.5 m^3/s. If the velocity is 1.5 m/s, what are the dimensions of the channel? If $C = 50$, find the slope of the channel.

17.36 A trapezoidal channel of side slope 1.5:1 is designed to carry discharge of 18 m^3/s with a slope of 1 in 4000. Assuming $n = 0.012$, find the dimensions of an economical channel.

17.37 Design the bed slope of a most efficient trapezoidal channel to convey 12 m^3/s at a depth of 2 m . Assume $n = 0.016$. [Hint: $m = 1/\sqrt{3}$]

17.38 Design a section of a standard triangular canal to carry a discharge of 12 m^3/s. Given $S = 1/3000$; $n = 0.014$; and $m = 1$.

17.39 Design a standard section of a trapezoidal channel to carry 120 m^3/s at a slope of 1 in 3000. Given side slope 1.25:1; $n = 0.014$; $b/y = 10$.

17.40 A long circular sewer 1.2 m in diameter is laid to a slope of 1 in 1000. If $n = 0.013$, find (i) the maximum discharge under open channel conditions and (ii) the maximum velocity under open channel conditions.

17.41 A rectangular channel 4 m wide conveys a discharge of 16 m^3/s. What is the minimum specific energy?

17.42 A rectangular channel 8 m wide carries 60 m^3/s. If the flow depth is 1.2 m, what is the specific energy? Is the flow sub-critical or super-critical?

17.43 The depth before and after a jump was observed to be 0.2 m and 1.8 m respectively. Find the Froude number of flow and discharge/m width.

17.44 A discharge of 18 m^3/s is passing under a sluice gate 3 m wide. If the depth of flow before a jump is 0.4 m, what is the Froude number? What is the tail-water depth required? How much energy is spent in the jump/m width.

17.45 In a jump, the loss of head was observed as 2 m and the discharge intensity as 20 $m^3/s/m$. Find the depths of flow before and after the jump.

17.46 The tail-water after a jump below a spillway has a depth of 1.6 m and velocity 0.8 m/s. What is the inflow Froude number?

17.47 A trapezoidal channel of bed width 8 m has a side slope of 1.25 : 1 and discharges 25 m^3/s. Find the critical depth of flow.

17.48 The critical depth in a rectangular channel is 0.9 m. If the depth of flow is 0.5 m, find (i) the alternate depth and (ii) the sequent depth.

17.49 A rectangular channel has a discharge intensity of 1.2 m^3/s and the depth of flow is 1.4 m, what is the specific energy. If a smooth hump 0.2 m high is in the channel, what will be the depth of flow over the hump.

17.50 A rectangular channel 6 m wide discharges 18 m^3/s at a depth of 2.8 m. If the bed is raised in a small reach by 0.3 m, find the depth of flow in the reach.

17.51 A rectangular channel is 4 m wide and discharges 10 m^3/s at a depth of 1.5 m. What is the Froude number? The bed in some portion of the channel is to be raised by a smooth hump. What is the maximum height of the hump without affecting the upstream depth of flow?

17.52 Measurement of discharge is to be made in a rectangular channel 4 m wide with a depth of flow of 1.5 m. The bed width is reduced to 2.5 m, and the bed is raised by a smooth hump 0.15 m high. Neglecting energy losses, what is the discharge when the fall in level in the flumed portion is 0.12 m.

17.53 A lined rectangular channel 3 m wide has a bed slope of 1 in 1000 and conveys a discharge of 15 m^3/s. If $n = 0.014$, find whether the channel is steep or mild. What is the critical slope for the channel? [Hint: At critical slope $y_n = y_c$]

17.54 A river 30 m wide and 1.5 m deep has a slope of 1 in 10,000 and $n = 0.025$. A weir produces an afflux of 0.6 m, how much upstream of the weir will the afflux be 0.3 m?

17.55 A rectangular channel of 4 m wide discharges 6 m^3/s at a depth of 1.2 m. If a gate at the tail-end is suddenly closed, what will be the height of the surge and its velocity?

17.56 A power canal, rectangular in shape, discharging 15 m^3/s has a width of 3 m and depth of flow 1.5 m. If a gate at the tail-end reduces the discharge by 25%, what is the height and velocity of the resulting surge?

17.57 A river having an average depth of 2.5 m joins the sea at a velocity of 1.2 m/s. If a sea bore travelling upstream increases the depth to 4 m, what is the velocity of the bore and river velocity downstream of the bore?

ANSWERS

17.27. 3.68 Pa ; **17.28.** 1 in 5021.5; **17.29.** 6.394 m^3/s; $C = 76.6$; **17.30.** 1.2665 m; **17.31.** 1.5625 m; **17.32.** 1.995 m; **17.33.** 2.083 m; **17.34.** $b = 2.503$ m; $y = 2.1675$ m; $m = 0.577$; **17.35.** $b = 1.370$ m; $y = 1.654$ m; $m = 1$; **17.36.** $b = 1.452$ m; $y = 2.397$; $m = 1.5$; **17.37.** 1 in 1302; **17.38.** $y = 2.2$ m; $m = 1$; **17.39.** $b = 22.34$ m; $y = 2.234$ m; $m = 1.25$; **17.40.** 1.326 m^3/s; 1.242 m/s; **17.41.** 1.766 m; **17.42.** 3.190 m; supercritical **17.43.** 6.708; 1.879 $m^3/s/m$; **17.44.** 7.57; 4.088 m; 451.46 kW/m; **17.45.** 1.718 m; 6.082 m; **17.46.** 9.67; **17.47.** 0.948 m; **17.48.** 1.852 m; 1.474 m; **17.49.** 1.185 m; **17.50.** 2.484m; **17.51.** 0.351 m; **17.52.** 5.495 m^3/s; **17.53.** mild; 1 in 243.4; **17.54.** 4517 m; **17.55.** 0.4716 m; -3.181 m/s; **17.56.** 0.6915 m; - 1.81 m/s; **17.57.** -5.941 m/s; -1.479 m/s.

18 Water Hammer in Pipes

Phenomenon of water hammer—Gradual closure of valves—Rapid closure of valves—Effect of elasticity of pipe and compressibility of liquid.

18.1 General

When valves located downstream of pipes conveying liquids are closed suddenly, the sudden increase in pressure can be very high, causing the pipes to burst. The pressure rise can be observed in domestic water lines accompanied by noises which sound like hammering and vibration. This phenomenon is known as water hammer. The local increase in pressure at the valve and hence the compression of water cannot affect a region at a distance away from the valve until a compression wave produced by the forces travel that distance. Water hammer problems involve the compressibility of liquid, which was found to have no significant role in earlier discussions of fluid flow problems. In hydro-electric projects, the penstocks leading water to turbines from the reservoir will be subjected to pressures due to water hammer when the gates or valves leading to the turbine are closed rapidly. Measures have to be taken to reduce the effect of water hammer, for the safety of penstocks.

18.2 Phenomenon of Water Hammer

The high pressure difference created by water hammer is transmitted through the medium by elastic wave propagation.

18.2.1 Rapid closure of valves

Figure 18.1 shows a reservoir and a long pipe connected to it. Imagine that the valve at the end is initially open allowing water to flow out. When the valve is suddenly closed (it can be rapid when a solenoid valve is used), the water hammer head can be worked out. At first it may be assumed that the pipe is inelastic and the loss of head due to friction is neglected.

Let the velocity of water in the pipe be V_0 and the velocity of propagation of elastic wave through the liquid (celerity) be equal to C. In a time Δt, the wave will proceed from the valve to the reservoir by a distance $C\Delta t$. The volume of water which has come to rest $= AC\Delta t$, where A is the area of cross-section of pipe. Let Δp be the pressure rise due to water hammer. Applying Newton's second law,

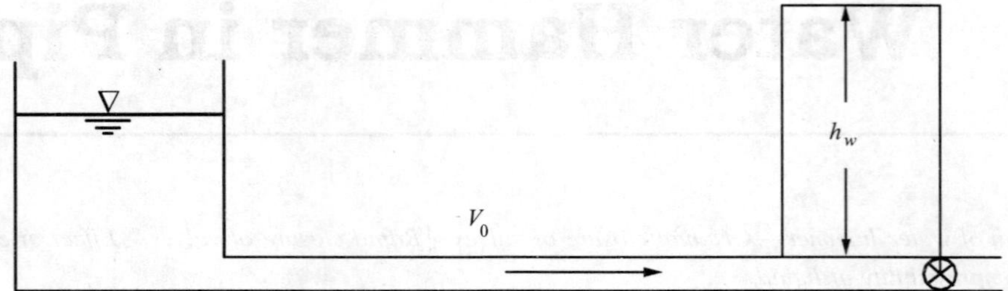

Fig. 18.1 *Phenomenon of water hammer*

Force = Rate of change in momentum (in the same direction).

$$\Delta pA = \frac{(\rho AC\Delta t)V_0}{\Delta t}.$$

$$\Delta p = pCV_0.$$

$$\text{Or } h_w = \frac{\Delta p}{\gamma} = \frac{CV_0}{g}. \tag{18.1}$$

The pressure wave will reach the reservoir in time L/C. The water in the whole pipe will come to rest and the pressure will be high. But the boundary condition at the reservoir will not permit a pressure head greater than the head in the reservoir. Hence, flow will be induced in the pipe in the opposite direction. i.e., towards the reservoir. This effect will be transmitted as an expansion wave (release of compression) downstream at a velocity C and will reach the valve in time $2L/C$.

The velocity of flow towards the reservoir will be sustained by the release of compressed water in the pipe. But when the wave reaches the valve, it is positively reflected. i.e., a further reduction in pressure will take place at the valve and an expansion wave will move upstream. In time $3L/C$, the whole pipe will be at low pressure. When this expansion wave reaches the reservoir, it is negatively reflected inducing flow towards the valve and the condition will return to the original one in time $4L/C$. The cycle of events will repeat but the intensity of pressure will be damped by the action of viscosity.

When the pipe is elastic, the pipe will expand when subjected to the compression pressure wave and contract when subjected to the expansion pressure wave. The celerity of the wave will be affected by this as will be shown later.

18.2.2 Gradual closure of valves

Let the valve be closed in time T, greater than $2L/C$. Let it be assumed that the initial velocity in the pipe is V_0 and the discharge through it varied linearly during time T. The operation can be assumed to consist of reduction of velocity in stages of ΔV. Pressure waves at increments of head equal to $C\Delta V/g$ will be propagated from the valve and go upstream. The effect will go on until the expansion waves from the reservoir reaches the valve in time greater than $2L/C$.

Velocity change in time, $\dfrac{2L}{C} = \dfrac{V_0}{T}\dfrac{2L}{C} = \dfrac{2LV_0}{TC}$.

Hence the total maximum pressure head developed

$$= \frac{C}{g} \times \frac{2LV_0}{TC} = \frac{2LV_0}{gT}. \qquad (18.2)$$

18.3 Celerity of Propagation of an Elastic Wave through Water in an Elastic Pipe

Let the velocity in a pipe be V, pressure p, density ρ and let the area of cross-section of pipe be A. Let d be the diameter of the pipe and t the thickness of the material of the pipe.

Let water have a bulk modulus of elasticity E_w and pipe an elastic modulus of E_p. Due to the sudden closure of the valve, let the velocity near the valve be zero, the increase in pressure be dp as shown in Fig. 18.2. Let the density of water be $\rho + d\rho$ and the area be increased to $A + dA$. Let the pressure at the assumed area be taken as p.

The unsteady flow depicted in Fig. 18.2(a) is transformed to the steady condition by the application of a velocity C towards the right side. The steady condition is shown in Fig. 18.2(b).

By applying the pressure–momentum transport balance equation for mass of fluid, $\rho A(V + C)$

$$pA + (p + dp)dA - (p + dp)(A + dA)$$
$$= \rho A(V + C)[C - (V + C)] \approx \rho AC(-V). \ (C \gg V)$$

The above expression can be simplified as

$$-dpA = -\rho ACV.$$

So

$$C = \frac{dp}{(\rho V)}. \qquad (18.3)$$

By applying the continuity principle,

$$\rho A(V + C) = (\rho + d\rho)(A + dA)C.$$

$$\rho\ A\ V + \rho\ A\ C = \rho\ A\ C + \rho\ dA\ C + d\rho\ A\ C + d\rho\ dA\ C.$$

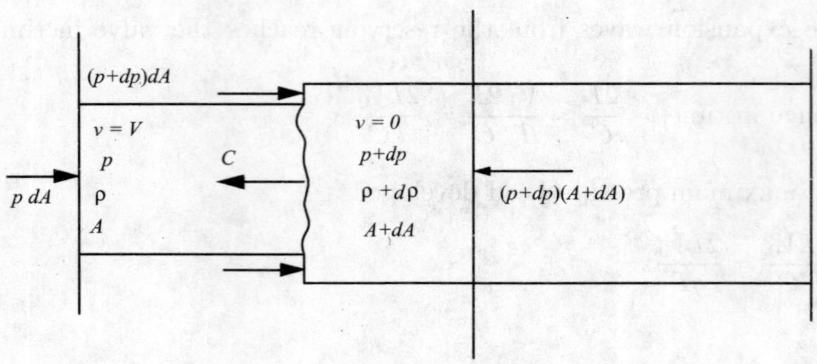

Fig. 18.2(a) *Unsteady state*

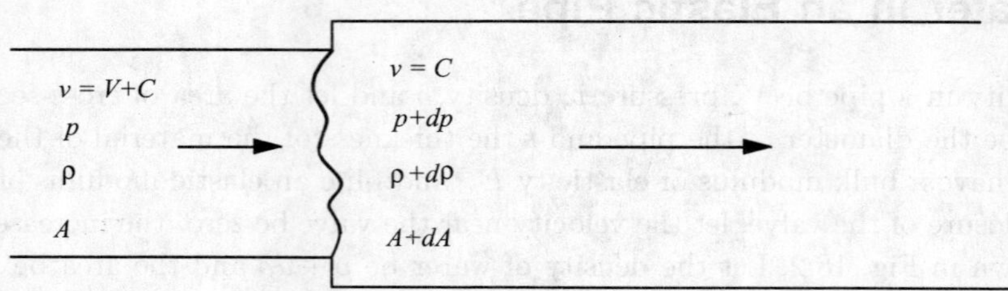

Fig. 18.2(b) *Steady state*

Neglecting the term $d\rho\ dA\ C$,

$$\rho\ A\ V = C(\rho\ dA + d\rho\ A).$$

$$C = \frac{V}{\left(\frac{d\rho}{\rho} + \frac{dA}{A}\right)}. \tag{18.4}$$

Multiplying (18.3) and (18.4) and finding the square root,

$$C = \sqrt{\frac{\frac{dp}{\rho}}{\left(\frac{d\rho}{\rho} + \frac{dA}{A}\right)}}. \tag{18.5}$$

In case of a rigid pipe $E_m >>> E_w$, the expansion of pipe $dA = 0$ and hence

$$C = \sqrt{\frac{\frac{dp}{\rho}}{\frac{d\rho}{\rho}}} = \sqrt{\frac{E}{\rho}}. \tag{18.6}$$

When the pipe is elastic,

$$\text{linear strain} = \frac{\text{linear stress}}{E_m} = \frac{dp\,d}{2tE_m},$$

$$\frac{dA}{A} \text{ is the areal strain} = 2 \text{ times the linear strain} = \frac{dpd}{tE_m}. \tag{18.7}$$

$$\text{Also, } \frac{d\rho}{\rho} = -\frac{dV}{V} = \frac{dp}{E_w}. \tag{18.8}$$

Substituting (18.7) and (18.8),

$$C = \sqrt{\frac{\dfrac{dp}{\rho}}{\left(\dfrac{dp}{E_w} + \dfrac{dp\,d}{tE_m}\right)}} = \sqrt{\frac{\dfrac{E_w}{\rho}}{\left(1 + \dfrac{E_w d}{tE_m}\right)}}. \tag{18.9}$$

Hence the velocity of propagation of the elastic wave will be slower in an elastic pipe as compared to a rigid pipe.

18.4 Role of the Expansion Wave

During the expansion wave $(L/C) < t < (2L/C)$, the pressure in the pipe is restored to that in the reservoir. But when it is reflected positively at the valve i.e., when $(2L/C) < t < (3L/C)$, the pressure head gets reduced to less than the reservoir head and the pipe may collapse due to low pressure. Such expansion waves can also result due to sudden opening of valves. The establishment of flow will take some time during which there will be alternatively negative and positive pressure surges in the pipe.

18.5 Role of Friction in Pipes

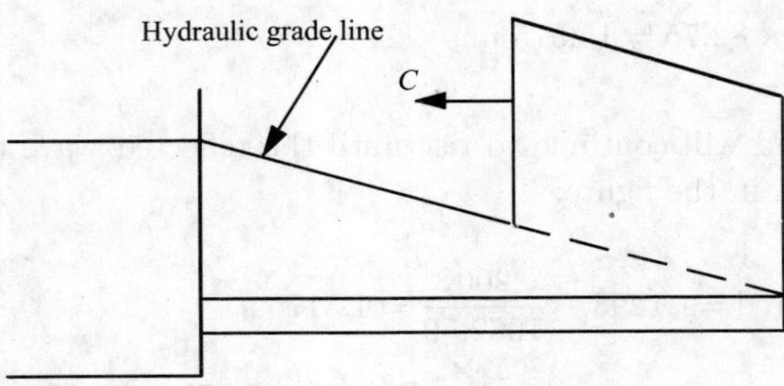

Fig. 18.3 *Role of friction*

The periodic pressure fluctuations will be damped due to the action of viscosity after many oscillations. When there is flow in the pipe and a hydraulic gradient is established, the pressure rise due to water hammer will be above the hydraulic gradient line as shown in Fig. 18.3.

Example 18.1 A steel pipe 1 m in diameter and 1200 m long has a wall thickness of 1.2 cm and is connected to a reservoir. The discharge is 0.6 m^3/s. Find (i) the celerity of the elastic wave. (ii) What will be the maximum water hammer pressure head, if the valve is closed in 1s? (iii) What will be the maximum water hammer pressure head 200 m from the reservoir? (iv) What will be the maximum water hammer pressure head if the valve is closed in 4s? Assume $E_w = 2.07 \times 10^6$ kN/m² and $E_s = 207 \times 10^6$ kN/m².

$$\text{(i) } C = \sqrt{\frac{\dfrac{E_w}{\rho}}{\left(1 + \dfrac{E_w d}{t E_m}\right)}} = \frac{1438.75}{1.354} = 1062.59 \text{ m/s. (Ans.)}$$

$$\text{(ii) } \frac{2L}{C} = \frac{2 \times 1200}{1062.59} = 2.259 \text{ s.}$$

Hence closure in 1 second is a case of rapid closure.

$$V_0 = \frac{Q}{\pi d^2/4} = \frac{0.6}{\pi/4} = 0.764 \text{ m/s;}$$

$$h_w = \frac{C V_0}{g} = \frac{1062.59 \times 0.764}{9.81} = 82.75 \text{ m. (Ans.)}$$

(iii) The time for pressure wave to reach reservoir $= \dfrac{1200}{1062.59} = 1.1293$ s.

The pressure head diagram after 1.1293 s of start of closure is shown in the figure. Distance traveled by wave in 1 s $= C \times 1 = 1062.59$ m.

Pressure head developed 200 m from the reservoir after 1.1293 s.

$$= \frac{200}{1062.59} \times 82.75 = 15.575 \text{ m.}$$

The pressure head will continue to rise until the reflected wave from reservoir reaches point D as shown in the figure.

$$\text{Time required} = 1.1293 + \frac{200}{1062.59} = 1.3175 \text{ s.}$$

Hence the maximum pressure head at B $= 2 \times 15.575 = 31.15$ m. (Ans.)

(iv) $t = 4$ s.

$$\text{The maximum pressure head} = \frac{2LV_0}{gT} = \frac{2 \times 1200 \times 0.764}{9.81 \times 4} = 46.73\text{m. (Ans.)}$$

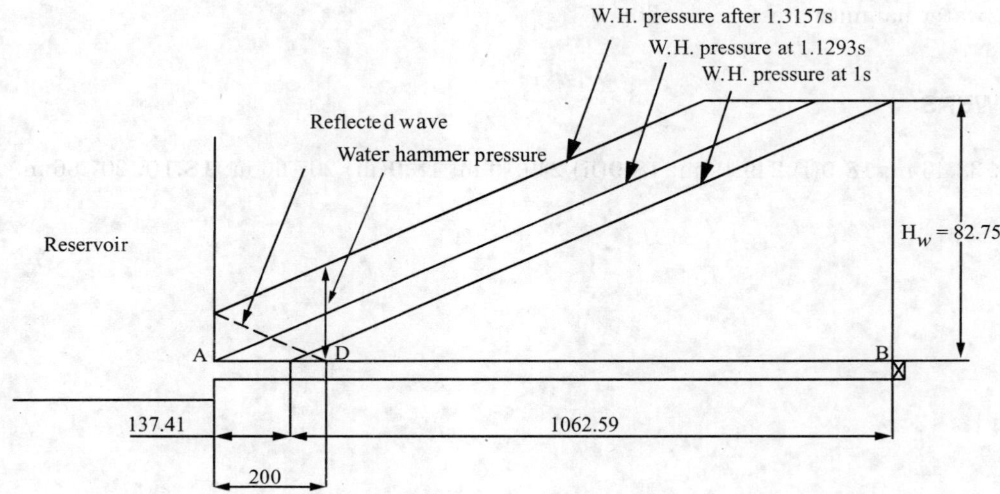

Example. 18.1

REVIEW QUESTIONS AND PROBLEMS

18.1 Explain the phenomenon of water hammer.

18.2 Describe the cycle of changes in pressure that occur in a long pipe conveying water as a valve at the end is suddenly closed.

18.3 What is meant by sudden closure of valve?

18.4 What is the pressure rise due to sudden closure of valve at the end of a long pipe connected to a reservoir.

18.5 Derive an expression for the maximum water hammer pressure head developed in a pipe, in case of a gradual closure of valve in time T.

18.6 What is the expression for the celerity of the pressure wave if the pipe is rigid?

18.7 How is low pressure caused in pipes conveying water when a valve at the end of a pipe is suddenly closed? [Hint: Expansion waves by reflection at the valve].

18.8 A 2000 m long penstock , 0.6 m in diameter, conveys 0.4 m^3/s of water. A valve at the end of the penstock is closed in 15 s. Assume $K = 2.07 \times 10^9$ Pa. Find the maximum water hammer pressure developed.

18.9 A pipe 1200 m long and 0.3 m in diameter conveys a discharge of 0.12 m^3/s. Find the maximum water hammer pressure if (i) a valve at the end is closed in 0.5 s,

(ii) the valve is closed in 1 s and (iii) the valve is closed in 2 s. Assume C = 1440 m/s.

18.10 A steel penstock 1.2 m in diameter and 1500 long conveys water at the rate of 1.2 m^3/s. A valve at the end is closed in 2.5 s. Assume E for steel as 2.07×10^8 kN/m^2, $K = 2.07 \times 10^6$ kN/m^2 and the thickness of the pipe wall as 2 cm. Find the maximum water hammer pressure developed.

ANSWERS

18.8. 38.46 m; **18.9**(i) 249.19 m; **18.9**(ii) 249.19 m; **18.9**(iii) 207.66 m; **18.10.** 207.66 m.

19 Turbo-machines

Introduction—Types of turbo-machines—Non-dimensional terms—Centrifugal pumps—Velocity triangles—Head developed—Cavitation—Diffuser pumps—Specific speed—Characteristics— Multistage pumps— Pumps connected parallel—Selection of pumps—Turbine—Specific speed—Francis turbine—Kaplan turbine—Tubular turbine—Pelton turbine—Characteristics

19.1 Introduction

Turbo-machines are of different types like pumps, turbines, compressors and fans. A common feature is that they have a rotating part called an impeller or runner consisting of vanes or blades mounted on a shaft or cone. They are also called roto-dynamic machines. Some of them like pumps, compressors and fans derive their power from a motor and pass on energy to a fluid. But in turbines, the energy of the fluid is transferred to the runner which rotates a generator. The path followed by the fluid from entry to exit in the machine decides whether it is a radial flow, axial flow or mixed flow. In a Pelton wheel, the flow is tangential to the rotating runner.

The principle on which the turbo-machines work is that the torque on the runner is equal to the rate of change of moment of momentum of the fluid during its passage through the runner. This is known as the Euler's principle and can also be derived from Newton's second law:

Newton's second law can be expressed as

$$\frac{d}{dt}(m\vec{v}) = \vec{F},$$

where $\vec{F}$ is the force on the vane (in this specific case). Finding the cross product with $\vec{R}$, the radius vector

$$\vec{R} \times \frac{d}{dt}(m\vec{v}) = \vec{R} \times \vec{F}.$$

$$\text{But } \vec{R} \times \frac{d}{dt}(m\vec{v}) = \frac{d}{dt}\left(\vec{R} \times m\vec{v}\right) - \frac{d\vec{R}}{dt} \times m\vec{v} = \frac{d}{dt}\left(\vec{R} \times m\vec{v}\right) \text{ since } \frac{d\vec{R}}{dt} = 0.$$

$$\text{Hence } \frac{d}{dt}\left(\vec{R} \times m\vec{v}\right) = \vec{R} \times \vec{F}. \tag{19.1}$$

Thus, the time rate of change of angular momentum of a mass equals the moment of the force acting on the mass, which is equal to the torque.

In this chapter, we will confine our discussion to pumps and water turbines.

19.2 Types of Turbo-machines

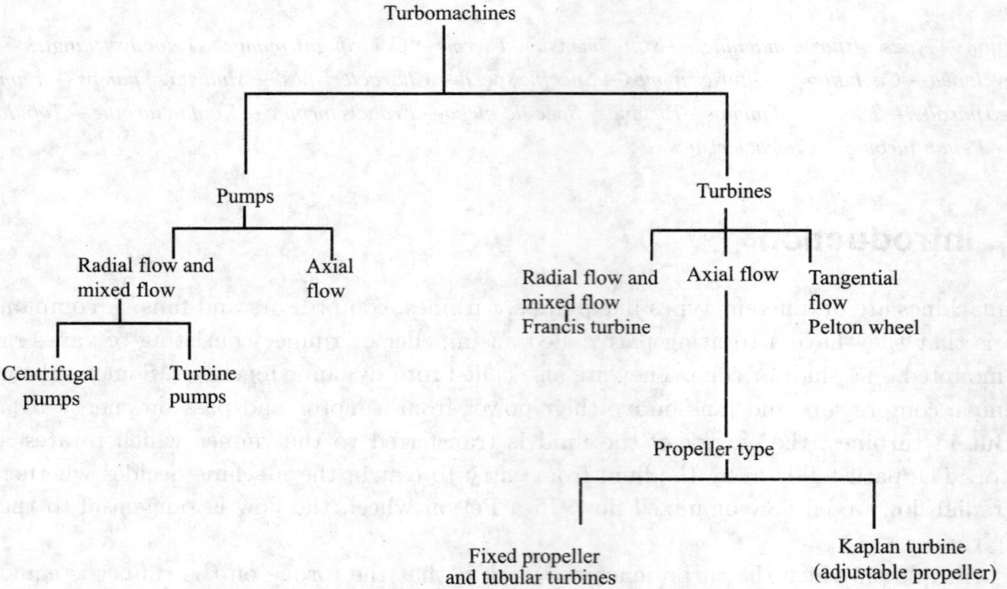

Fig. 19.1 *Types of turbo-machines*

19.3 Non-Dimensional Terms Governing Turbo-machines

In Example 14.6 (Chapter 14), non-dimensional numbers governing Turbo-machines are derived.

$$\pi_1 = \frac{Q}{Nd^3} \text{ termed as the discharge coefficient } k_d, \tag{19.2}$$

$$\pi_2 = \frac{P}{\rho d^5 N^3} \text{ termed as the power coefficient } k_p, \tag{19.3}$$

$$\pi_3 = \frac{gH}{N^2 d^2} \text{ termed as the head coefficient } k_h, \tag{19.4}$$

and when the viscosity is considered, we get a term

$$\pi_4 = \frac{\mu}{\rho d^2 N} \text{ termed as the friction coefficient } k_f. \tag{19.5}$$

Among the above coefficients, the friction coefficient k_f will manifest itself only as a scale effect. In most cases it may be neglected unless the sizes of the units are widely different.

A parameter used in the design of pumps and turbines is the non-dimensional specific speed.

In case of pumps, by elimination of terms in d,

$$\frac{\pi_1^{1/2}}{\pi_3^{3/4}} = \frac{Q^{1/2}}{N^{1/2}d^{3/2}} \times \frac{d^{3/2}N^{3/2}}{g^{3/4}H^{3/4}} = \frac{NQ^{1/2}}{g^{3/4}H^{3/4}}$$

can be termed as the specific speed which is non-dimensional. But in SI units, specific speed for pump is Ω_{sp}

$$\Omega_{sp} = \frac{\omega Q^{1/2}}{g^{3/4}H^{3/4}}, \tag{19.6}$$

where ω is the angular velocity.

In case of turbines by elimination of term in d,

$$\frac{\pi_2^{1/2}}{\pi_3^{5/4}} = \frac{NP^{1/2}}{\rho^{1/2}g^{5/4}H^{5/4}}$$

is the specific speed, which is non-dimensional.

In SI units specific speed for turbines Ω_{st} is given by

$$\Omega_{st} = \frac{\omega\sqrt{P/\rho}}{g^{5/4}H^{5/4}}, \tag{19.7}$$

However, at present non-dimensional specific speeds are not used as a design parameter for classification and selection of turbo-machines.

19.4 The Concept of Flow through Cascade

To study the actual condition of flow over the blades/vanes of rotor of turbo-machines, it is usual to make models of blades/vanes and study the flow through it in a wind tunnel. Blades of given geometry arranged in rectilinear, cylindrical or any other pattern is called cascade or lattice or grid. The pattern of flow in the cascade is studied keeping the Reynolds number of flow same in the model and the prototype.

19.5 Centrifugal Pumps

19.5.1 Introduction

Centrifugal pumps find wide applications in the field of industry, agriculture, water supply etc.,. They are available in various sizes (very small to large) to suit the particular discharge and head. The power of the pump can be as small as 0.25 HP and as high as 20 HP or more.

19.5.2 The principle of a centrifugal pump

The centrifugal pump has an impeller or vanes mounted on a shaft rotated by a motor. The impeller is enclosed in a volute chamber. It has a spiral shape terminating in a delivery pipe. Liquid can enter the pump from a suction pipe connected on the opposite side of the shaft. The end of the suction pipe is immersed in liquid of the source. The centrifugal pump has to deliver liquid to the delivery pipe at the desired pressure and discharge.

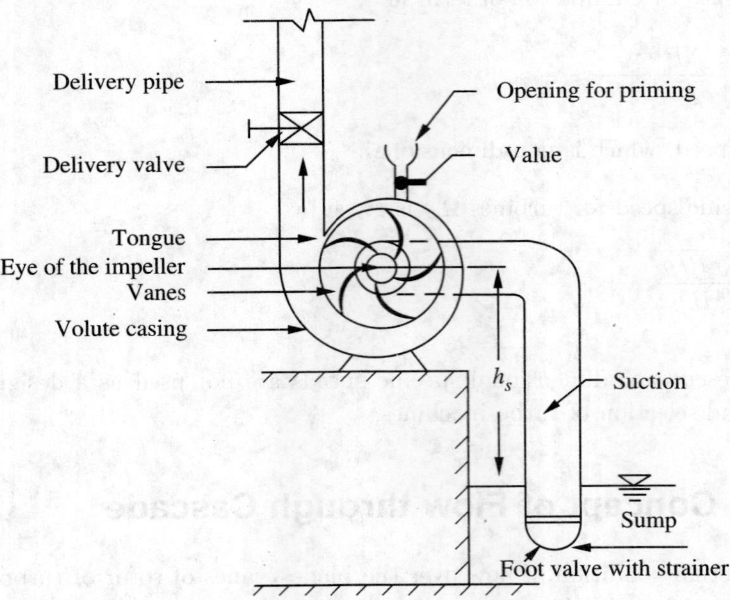

Fig. 19.2 *Principle components of a centrifugal pump*

When the pump is filled with liquid and the impeller is rotated, low pressure at the center of the runner will cause the rise of liquid from the source (by the higher atmospheric pressure) and liquid is delivered at a high head.

It is important that the centrifugal pump is initially filled with the liquid for its working *(priming)*. Usually an opening on the top of the volute with a valve is provided to pour water inside the volute chamber (priming) if it is drained. A foot valve at the bottom of the suction pipe can ensure that it is not drained after it is operated and the delivery valve is closed. It is better to start with the valve on the delivery end closed so as to reduce the load on the motor.

19.5.3 The forced vortex and head developed

The flow condition created by the impeller in a centrifugal pump and the pressure head developed is closely connected with the forced vortex. If the radius at the outlet is r_2 and ω is the angular velocity, the tangential velocity is $U_2 = \omega r_2$ and

$$\text{the head due to a forced vortex} = \frac{\mathrm{U}_2^2}{2g} = \frac{\omega^2 r_2^2}{2g}.$$

When the delivery valve is closed and the impeller rotates, the liquid in the impeller circulates and forms a forced vortex. When the pump has to develop a head H when the valve is opened, the minimum angular velocity required for the pump will be ω_s such that

$$\frac{U_2^2 - U_1^2}{2g} = \frac{\omega_s^2(r_2^2 - r_1^2)}{2g} = H, \tag{19.8}$$

where r_2 and r_1 are the radii of the impeller at the outlet and inlet respectively. At higher speeds when the delivery valve is opened, the pump will begin discharging liquid through the delivery pipe. As liquid is discharged, the flow conditions inside the pump becomes a spiral-forced vortex and the power requirement will increase to maintain the additional radial flow.

Example 19.1 A centrifugal pump working against a static head of 8 m has outlet to inlet diameter ratio as 3. If the outer diameter is 0.8 m, find the minimum starting speed required.

$d_2/d_1 = 3; d_2 = 0.8$ m

$d_1 = 0.8/3 = 0.267$ m; $H = 8$ m

$U_1 = \pi d_1 N/60 = 0.014$ N; $\quad U_2 = \pi d_2 N/60 = 0.0419$ N

At the minimum starting speed $\dfrac{U_2^2}{2g} - \dfrac{U_1^2}{2g} = H$

i.e. $(0.0419^2 - 0.014^2)N^2 = 2 \times 9.81 \times 8$

Solving $N = 317.24$ rpm (Ans)

19.5.4 The velocity triangles for flow in a centrifugal pump

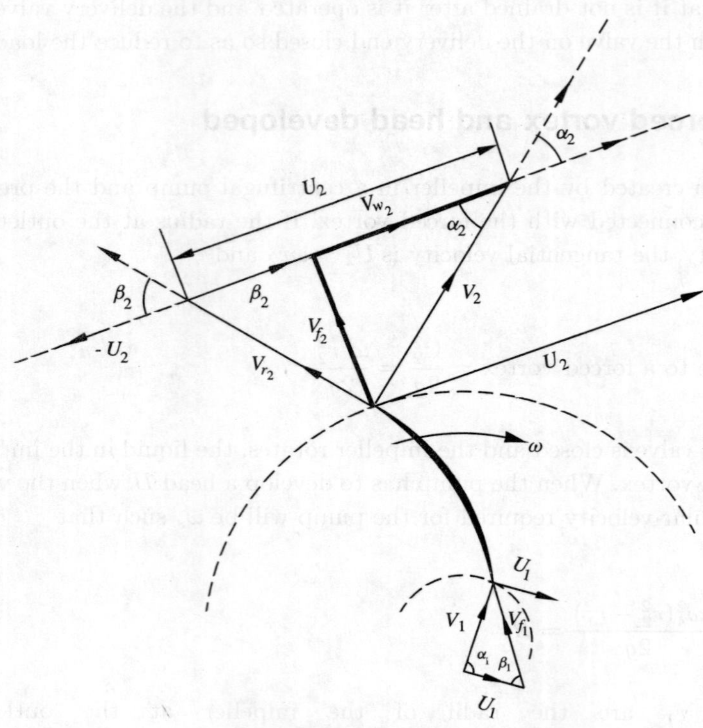

Fig. 19.3 *Velocity diagrams for entry and outlet of a centrifugal pump*

Convention: The following conventional symbols are used in the analysis.

The inflow radius r_1
Inflow velocity V_1
Tangential velocity at inlet $U_1 = \omega\ r_1$
Inlet angle of flow = α_1,
i.e., angle between V_1 and U_1
Radial velocity of inflow = $V_{f_1} = V_1 \sin \alpha_1$

Tangential velocity at inflow
$V_{w_1} = V_1 \cos \alpha_1$
(positive in direction of U_1)
Relative velocity at inlet
$\vec{V}_{r_1} = \vec{V}_1 - \vec{U}_1$
Blade angle at inlet β_1 to avoid shock at entry. β_1 is angle between V_{r_1} and $-U_1$

The outflow radius r_2
Outflow velocity V_2
Tangential velocity at outlet $U_2 = \omega\ r_2$
Outlet angle of flow = α_2,
i.e., angle between V_2 and U_2
Radial velocity of outflow = $V_{f_2} =$
$V_2 \sin \alpha_2$
Tangential velocity at outflow
$V_{w_2} = V_2 \cos \alpha_2$
(positive in direction of U_2)
Relative velocity
$\vec{V}_{r_2} = \vec{V}_2 - \vec{U}_2$
Blade angle at outlet β_2 to avoid shock at exit. β_2 is the angle between V_{r_2} and $-U_2$

In Fig. 19.3, the velocity triangles are drawn for inflow and outflow. For higher efficiency, V_1 should be normal to U_1 and hence $V_{w_1} = 0$ and $V_{f_1} = V_1$. β_2 is usually kept less than 90°. (Blades curved backwards). It may be noted that

$$\vec{V}_{r_1} = \vec{V}_1 - \vec{U}_1 \tag{19.9}$$

and

$$\vec{V}_{r_2} = \vec{V}_2 - \vec{U}_2. \tag{19.10}$$

Also the inlet angle β_1 and outlet angle β_2 of the blade are made such that V_{r1} and V_{r2} are tangential to the blade to avoid shock.

19.5.5 Head developed in the pump

The head developed can be found out using the Euler's principle of moment of momentum. "If a body in steady motion undergoes a change in moment of momentum (angular momentum), the resultant of external forces acting on the body will produce a torque equal to the rate of change of moment of momentum".

$$T = \text{Torque} \ = \rho Q \left(V_1 \cos \alpha_1 r_1 - V_2 \cos \alpha_2 r_2\right). \tag{19.11}$$

$$\text{Power } P = T \times \omega = \rho Q \omega \left(V_1 \cos \alpha_1 r_1 - V_2 \cos \alpha_2 r_2\right). \tag{19.12}$$

hence $P = \rho Q(\omega V_1 \cos \alpha_1 r_1 - \omega V_2 \cos \alpha_2 r_2)$

Assuming $V_{w_1} = V_1 \cos \alpha_1$ and $V_{w_2} = V_2 \cos \alpha_2$,

$$P = \rho Q(U_1 V_{w_1} - U_2 V_{w_2}). \tag{19.13}$$

For a centrifugal pump, the power is negative indicating that the power is to be supplied by a motor. (In the case of a turbine Eq. 19.13 holds good.)
Therefore, the required theoretical power for pump

$$P = \gamma Q H = \rho Q(U_2 \, V_{w_2} - U_1 V_{w_1}). \tag{19.14}$$

$$\text{Head developed } H = \frac{P}{\rho g Q} = \frac{U_2 V_{w_2} - U_1 V_{w_1}}{g}. \tag{19.15}$$

If the entry to the pump is radial $P = \rho Q U_2 V_{w_2}$.

Note: Since $\omega = 2\pi n$, where n is revolutions/s,

$$P = \rho Q \, 2\pi n(V_1 \cos \alpha_1 r_1 - V_2 \cos \alpha_2 r_2) = \rho Q n(V_1 \cos \alpha_1 \, 2\pi r_1 - V_2 \cos \alpha_2 \, 2\pi r_2)$$

$= \rho Qn\,(\Gamma_1 - \Gamma_2)$, where Γ_1, Γ_2 are the circulations at inlet and outlet. Hence the tangential components of the velocities of inflow and outflow, V_{w_1} and V_{w_2} are called the velocities of whirl.

Referring to Fig. 19.3 it can be shown that

$$H = \rho Q U_2 V_{w_2} / \rho g Q = U_2 V_{w_2}/g = \frac{U_2}{g}\left[U_2 - V_{f_2}\cot\beta_2\right].$$

$$H = \frac{U_2^2}{g} - \frac{U_2 Q \cot\beta_2}{2\pi r_2 b_2 g} = a - bQ. \tag{19.16}$$

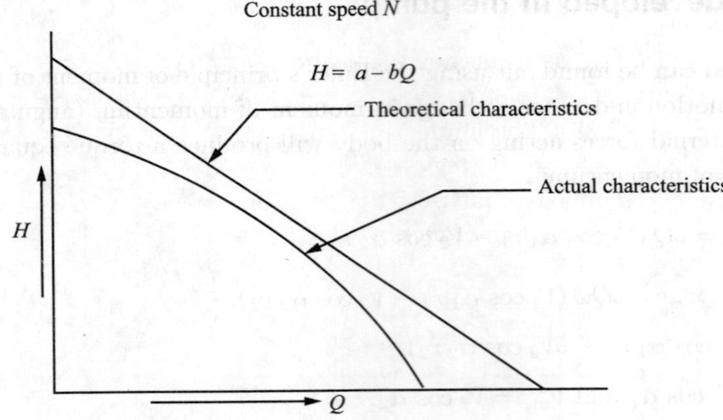

Fig. 19.4 *Head characteristic curve of a centrifugal pump*

Fig. 19.4 shows the theoretical and actual head characteristics of a centrifugal pump. The head developed in a centrifugal pump is less because of the energy losses in the runner.

19.5.6 Head developed in centrifugal pumps in terms of velocity heads

In terms of velocity heads, the expression for head developed in the centrifugal pump can be derived.

Referring to Fig. 19.3

$$V_{f_2}^2 = V_{r_2}^2 - \left(U_2 - V_{w_2}\right)^2 = V_{r_2}^2 - U_2^2 - V_{w_2}^2 + 2U_2 V_{w_2}. \tag{A}$$

When the inflow is not radial (general case, but usually the inflow is kept normal with $V_{w1} = 0$)

$$V_{f_1}^2 = V_{r_1}^2 - \left(U_1 - V_{w_1}\right)^2 = V_{r_1}^2 - U_1^2 - V_{w_1}^2 + 2U_1 V_{w_1}. \tag{B}$$

From (A), $U_2V_{w_2} = \frac{1}{2}\left(V_{f_2}^2 + V_{w_2}^2 - V_{r_2}^2 + U_2^2\right) = \frac{1}{2}\left(V_2^2 - V_{r_2}^2 + U_2^2\right).$

From (B), $U_1V_{w_1} = \frac{1}{2}\left(V_{f_1}^2 + V_{w_1}^2 - V_{r_1}^2 + U_1^2\right) = \frac{1}{2}\left(V_1^2 - V_{r_1}^2 + U_2^2\right).$

$$H = \frac{U_2V_{w_2} - U_1V_{w_1}}{g} = \frac{V_2^2 - V_1^2}{2g} + \frac{V_{r_1}^2 - V_{r_2}^2}{2g} + \frac{U_2^2 - U_1^2}{2g}. \tag{19.17}$$

The first term represents the change in kinetic energy of the fluid, the second term is the head developed due to reduction of relative velocity from inlet to outlet and the third term is the pressure head developed in the forced vortex.

The above equation with proper signs, known as the energy equation is applicable for all turbo-machines.

19.5.7 Cavitation in centrifugal pumps

The phenomenon of cavitation has been explained in Section 2.3. In centrifugal pumps, zones of lowest pressure occur at the inlet to the impeller at the eye of the vortex. If the pressure is below the vapour pressure of the liquid at the prevailing temperature, vapour cavities are formed. They are transported to the regions of higher pressure where they implode near the boundaries causing cavitation. The pitting of the boundaries generally occurs at the backside of the impeller very near to the zone of inception of cavitation. The flow may be accompanied by noise, vibration and low efficiencies.

If h_a is the atmospheric pressure head, V_i the velocity at the inlet of impeller, p_i the pressure at inlet, h_s the suction head and h_{Ls} the head loss in the suction pipe, at the inlet

$$\frac{p_i}{\gamma} + \frac{V_i^2}{2g} = h_a - h_s - h_{Ls}$$

To avoid cavitation, the minimum value of p_i can be p_v, the vapour pressure of the liquid at the prevailing temperature.

At the limit,

$$\frac{V_i^2}{2g} = h_a - h_s - h_{Ls} - h_v$$

where $h_v = \dfrac{p_v}{\gamma}$.

A term

$$NPSH = h_a - h_s - h_{Ls} - h_v \tag{19.18}$$

indicating the net positive suction head (NPSH) is defined. It should be sufficiently high so that the velocity head will be obtained without reducing the pressure head below the vapour pressure head.

A non-dimensional cavitation number, Thomas' number is defined as

$$\sigma = \frac{h_a - h_s - h_{Ls} - h_v}{H_m} \tag{19.19}$$

The value of σ for any operating conditions for the pump can be determined. If the $NPSH > \sigma H_m$, pressure at the inlet will be greater than p_v.

But in turbo-machines, the maximum velocity may prevail not at the inlet but inside the pumps, a higher value of σ, σ_{cr} is required to prevent cavitation.

$$\sigma > \sigma_{cr} \tag{19.20}$$

Many manufacturers recommend the value of σ_{cr} as a function of the specific speed. Additionally the performance curves for pumps may be supplied with the recommended values of NPSH as a function of discharge.

19.5.8 Diffuser pumps or turbine pumps

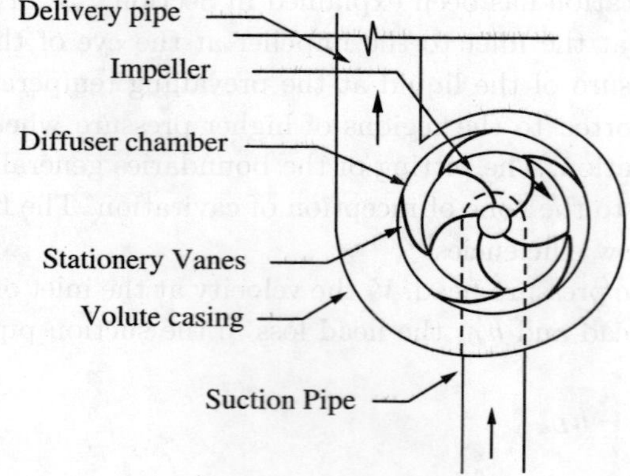

Fig. 19.5 *Diffuser pump*

The efflux velocities from the impeller have a considerable radial component of velocity, and most of its energy gets lost in the volute chamber. A part of this energy can be recovered if a flow condition like an irrotational spiral vortex is created around the impeller. A vortex chamber or a system of stationary vanes is provided to recover some pressure head. The arrangement is shown in Fig. 19.5. In some designs of the diffuser or turbine pumps, the vanes in the diffusion chamber are given special shapes and the outlet angles are adjusted so that the outlet from the pump can be at the centre.

19.5.9 Definition of head and efficiencies

Suction head (h_s) is the difference in the level of pump and the level of liquid in the reservoir from which the liquid is pumped.

Delivery head (h_d) is the head to which the liquid is to be pumped above the center of the pump when the delivery valve is open.

$$\text{Static head is the sum of suction head and delivery head} = h_s + h_d. \tag{19.21}$$

Manometric head is the net head developed by the impeller. ie.,

$$H_m = \frac{V_{w_2}U_2}{g} - H_L, \tag{19.22}$$

where H_L is the head loss in the impeller and the casing. Another useful expression is

$$H_m = \left(\frac{p_2}{\gamma} + z_2 + \frac{V_2^2}{2g}\right) - \left(\frac{p_1}{\gamma} + z_1 + \frac{V_1^2}{2g}\right), \tag{19.23}$$

where 1 and 2 refer to the sections in the suction pipe and the delivery pipe very near the pump.

It can also be written as

$$H_m = h_s + h_d + h_{fs} + h_{fd} + (V_d^2/2g). \tag{19.24}$$

Manometric efficiency is given by

$$\eta_{\text{mano}} = \frac{H_m}{V_{w_2}U_2/g}. \tag{19.25}$$

Mechanical efficiency is given by

$$\eta_{\text{mech}} = \frac{\text{power transmitted to motor}}{\text{shaft horse power}} = \frac{\gamma Q V_{w_2} U_2/g}{\text{shaft power}} \tag{19.26}$$

$$= \frac{\rho Q V_{w_2} U_2}{\text{shaft power}}. \tag{19.27}$$

$$\text{Overall efficiency } \eta = \eta_{\text{mano}} \times \eta_{\text{mech}} = \gamma Q H_m/\text{shaft power} \tag{19.28}$$

Example 19.2 A centrifugal pump delivers 0.04 m^3/s of water to a height of 18 m. If the overall efficiency of the pump is 80%, find the power required.

$Q = 0.04$ m^3/s; $H = 18$ m; $\eta = 80\% = 0.8$.

$$P = \frac{\gamma QH}{\eta} = \frac{9810 \times 0.04 \times 18}{0.8} \text{ W} = 8.83 \text{ kW. (Ans.)}$$

Example 19.3 A centrifugal pump works against a head of 20 m. The pump runs at 800 rpm and the velocity of flow at the outlet is 3 m/s. The outlet vane angle is 35°. If the discharge is 0.3 m^3/s, find (i) the diameter of the impeller and (ii) the width of the impeller at the outlet. Assume manometric efficiency = 0.75.

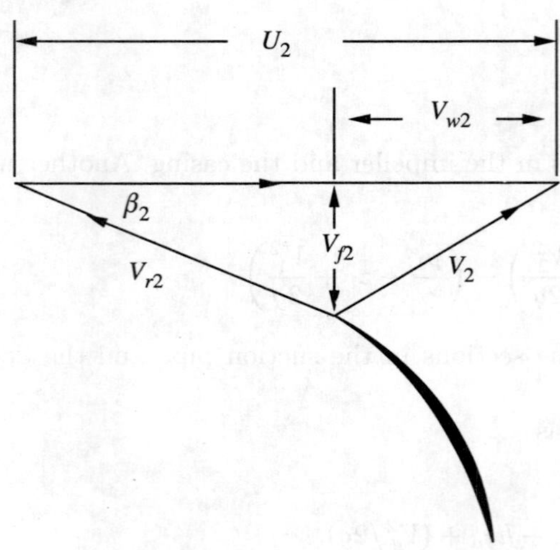

Example 19.3 *Outlet velocity diagram*

$$H = 20 \text{ m}; V_{f_2} = 3 \text{ m/s} ; \beta_2 = 35° ; Q = 0.3 \text{ m}^3\text{/s}.$$

$$\tan \beta_2 = \frac{V_{f_2}}{U_2 - V_{w_2}}; \text{ i.e. } \tan 35° = \frac{3}{U_2 - V_{w_2}};$$

$$U_2 - V_{w_2} = \frac{3}{\tan 35°} = 4.28 \text{ m/s.} \qquad (1)$$

$$\eta = \frac{gH}{U_2 V_{w_2}} = 0.75 = \frac{9.81 \times 20}{U_2 V_{w_2}}; U_2 V_{w_2} = \frac{9.81 \times 20}{0.75} = 261.6. \qquad (2)$$

From (1) and (2), $(U_2 + V_{w_2})^2 = (U_2 - V_{w_2})^2 + 4U_2 V_{w_2} = 1064.72.$

$$U_2 + V_{w_2} = 32.63. \qquad (3)$$

From (1) and (3), $U_2 = 18.46$ m/s.

$$U_2 = \frac{\pi D_2 N}{60}; D_2 = \frac{60 \times U_2}{\pi N} = \frac{60 \times 18.46}{\pi \times 800} = 0.44 \text{ m. (Ans.)}$$

$$b_2 = \frac{Q}{\pi D_2 V_{f_2}} = \frac{0.3}{\pi \times 0.44 \times 3} = 0.072 \text{ m} = 72 \text{ mm. (Ans.)}$$

Example 19.4 A centrifugal pump has a 300 mm diameter impeller and an outlet width of 45 mm. The pump is running at 1200 rpm. The manometric head is 12 m and the vanes are curved backwards at 30° at the outlet. If the manometric efficiency is 90%, calculate the discharge.

$D_2 = 300$ mm $= 0.3$ m; $b_2 = 45$ mm $= 0.045$ m; $N = 1200$ rpm; $H = 12$ m; $\beta_2 = 30°$;

$\eta_m = 90\% = 0.9$.

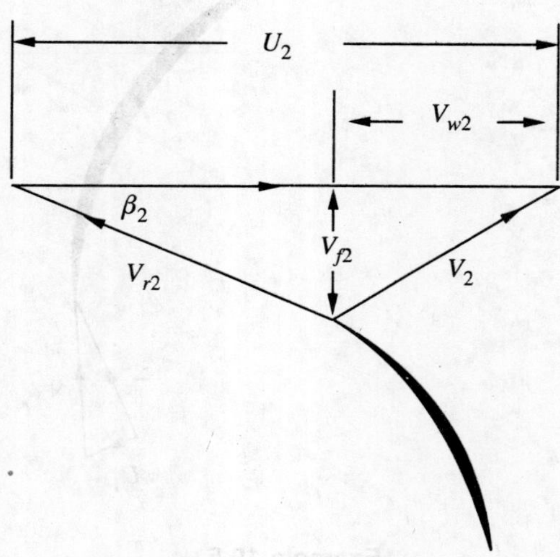

Example 19.4 *Outlet velocity diagram*

$$U_2 = \frac{\pi D_2 N}{60} = \frac{\pi \times 0.3 \times 1200}{60} = 18.85 \text{ m/s.}$$

$$\eta_m = \frac{gH}{U_2 V_{w_2}}; V_{w_2} = \frac{9.81 \times 12}{18.85 \times 0.9} = 6.94 \text{ m/s.}$$

$$\tan \beta_2 = \frac{V_{f_2}}{U_2 - V_{w_2}}; V_{f_2} = (U_2 - V_{w_2}) \tan \beta_2 = (18.85 - 6.94) \times \tan 30° = 6.88 \text{ m/s.}$$

$$Q = \pi D_2 b_2 V_{f_2} = \pi \times 0.3 \times 0.045 \times 6.88 = 0.292 \text{ m}^3\text{/s. (Ans.)}$$

Example 19.5 A centrifugal pump having a speed of 1440 rpm has an impeller diameter of 0.8 m. The blades are curved backwards making an angle of 30° to the tangent at periphery.

The velocity of flow at the outlet is 15 m/s. Find the pressure head developed. If a diffuser causes reduction of outlet velocity by 60%, find the additional head developed because of the diffuser.

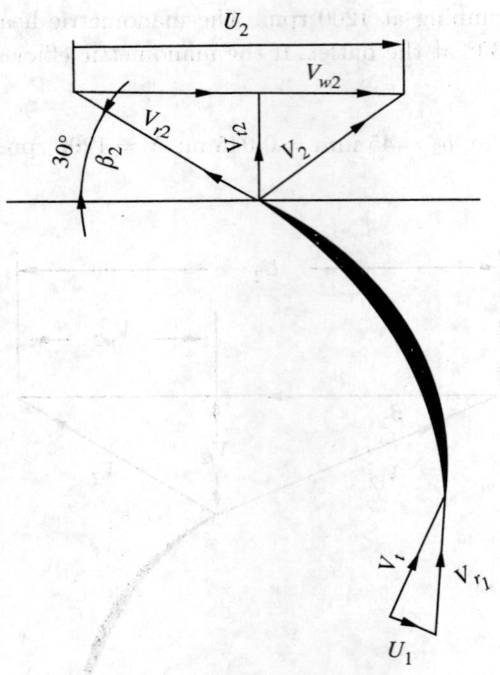

Example 19.5

$D = 0.8$ m; N = 1440 rpm; $V_{f2} = 15$ m/s; $\beta_2 = 30°$

$$U_2 = \frac{\pi d N}{60} = 60.3 \text{ m/s}; \qquad V_{w2} = U_2 - V_{f2} \cot 30° = 34.32 \text{ m/s}$$

$$V_2 = \sqrt{V_{f2}^2 + V_{w2}^2} = 40.35 \text{ m/s}$$

$$\text{Velocity head} = \frac{V_2^2}{2g} = \frac{40.35^2}{2 \times 9.81} = 82.98 \text{ m}$$

$$\text{Total head developed} = \frac{V_{w2} \times U_2}{g} = \frac{34.32 \times 60.3}{9.81} = 210.96 \text{ m}$$

Pressure head developed $= 210.96 - 82.98 = 127.98$ m.

Reduced velocity at outlet due to the diffuser. $= 0.4V_2 = 0.4 \times 40.35 = 16.14$ m/s

Velocity head after diffuser $= (16.14)^2/2 \times 9.81 = 13.28$ m.

Pressure head = 210.96 – 13.28 = 197.68 m.

Additional pressure head developed due to diffuser = 197.68 – 127.98 = 70.7 m. (Ans.)

19.5.10 Specific speed of a centrifugal pump

Specific speed N_{sp} of a centrifugal pump is defined as the speed of a homologous pump which will deliver one unit of discharge at unit head and is given by the expression

$$N_{sp} = \frac{N\sqrt{Q}}{H^{3/4}},$$

where N is the speed, Q the discharge, H the head and N_{sp} is the specific speed of the pump. It can be obtained as follows. If d is the diameter of the impeller and U is the tangential speed of the pump,

$$U \propto H^{1/2}$$

$$Q \propto \text{Area} \times \text{velocity} \propto d^2 H^{1/2} \quad \text{or} \quad Q^{1/2} = k_1 d H^{1/4} \qquad \text{(A)}$$

$$N \propto U/d \text{ or } N \propto k_2 H^{1/2}/d \qquad \text{(B)}$$

Eliminating D from equations (A) and (B), $NQ^{1/2} = k_3 H^{3/4}$

$$\text{Hence } N_{sp} = \frac{N\sqrt{Q}}{H^{3/4}} \qquad (19.29)$$

N is in rpm, Q is in m^3/s and H is in m.

where N is in rpm, Q is in m^3/s and H is in m.

This definition of N_{sp} is commonly used. It has the dimension of $L^{3/4}/T^{3/2}$. The specific speed is immensely useful in pump design, the type of runner and their characteristics is reflected by the value of N_{sp}.

The following are the usual range of specific speeds for the roto-dynamic pumps.

Type of runner	Specific speed
Radial	10–50
Mixed flow	50–160
Axial flow	160–500

Figure 19.6, shows the type of runners for different specific speeds.

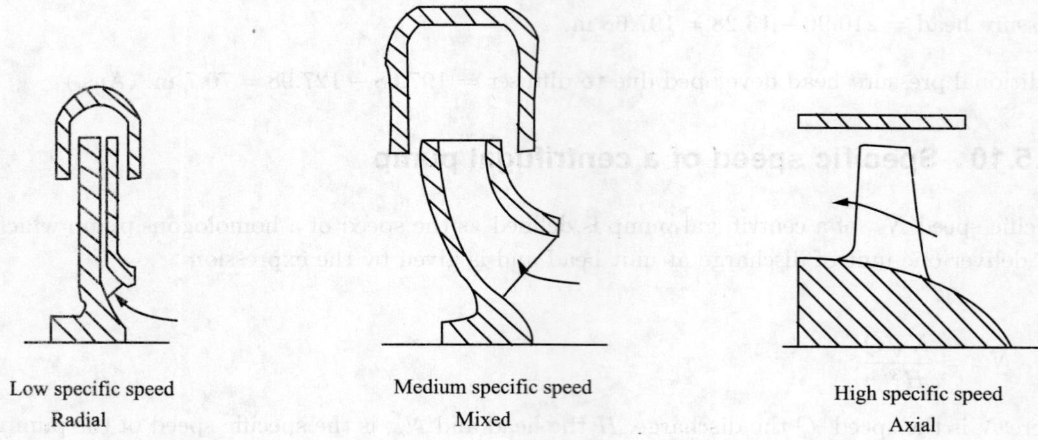

Fig. 19.6 *Different types of runners*

Example 19.6 A centrifugal pump delivers 0.3 m^3/s of water to a height of 18 m. If the pump runs at 1200 rpm, find the specific speed.

$$Q = 0.3 \text{ m}^3/\text{s};\ H = 18 \text{ m};\ N = 1200 \text{ rpm};$$

$$N_{sp} = \frac{NQ^{1/2}}{H^{3/4}} = \frac{1200 \times 0.3^{1/2}}{18^{3/4}} = 13.73. \text{ (Ans.)}$$

19.5.11 Characteristics of a centrifugal pump

The centrifugal pump when tested at constant speed will give variations of head, shaft power and efficiency for varying discharges, and the resulting curves are the characteristics of the centrifugal pump.

For a particular speed, the following curves are plotted

(i) Q vs head

(ii) Q vs shaft power

(iii) Q vs efficiency

These curves help to obtain best efficiency point design discharge and head corresponding to maximum efficiency. They are depicted in Fig. 19.7.The best efficiency head H^* and discharge Q^* are indicated in the figure.

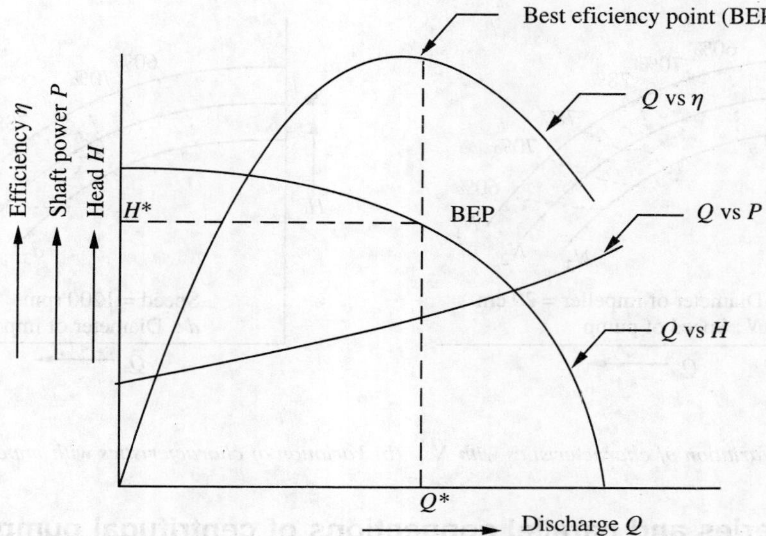

Fig. 19.7 *Characteristic curves*

19.5.12 Effect of change of speed and diameter of impeller on the characteristics

The head vs. discharge characteristics for a pump can be altered by changing the speed of the motor as indicated in Fig. 19.8(a). The speed can be varied by using a variable frequency speed controller. A four pole electric motor usually has a speed of 1450 rpm. It can also be changed to nearly 950 rpm by using a six pole electrical induction motor. The new value of discharge and head can be calculated by using the non-dimensional numbers

$$k_d = \pi_1 = \frac{Q}{Nd^3}$$

and $k_h = \pi_3 = \dfrac{gH}{N^2d^2}$ i.e. $Q \propto N$ and $H \propto N^2$. In the diagram, the equal efficiency lines known as Muschel curves can also be drawn as in Fig. 19.8(a).

Many manufacturers supply impellers of different sizes to be used with the same volute allowing a change in the characteristics of the pump to suit the pumping requirement. The impellers may be trimmed in small amounts by grinding, at the same time assuring smooth outlets. Model laws using the non-dimensional numbers $k_d = \pi_1 = \frac{Q}{Nd^3}$ and $k_h = \pi_3 = \frac{gH}{N^2d^2}$ i.e. $Q \propto d^3$ and $H \propto d^2$ can be used to get the new characteristics. The equal efficiency lines are shown in Fig. 19.8(b) when applying model laws for pumps of different sizes, the effect of viscosity as indicated by the number $\pi_4 = \frac{\mu}{\rho d^2 N}$ may be kept in view. For bigger pumps, the effect of friction can be less and the efficiency higher.

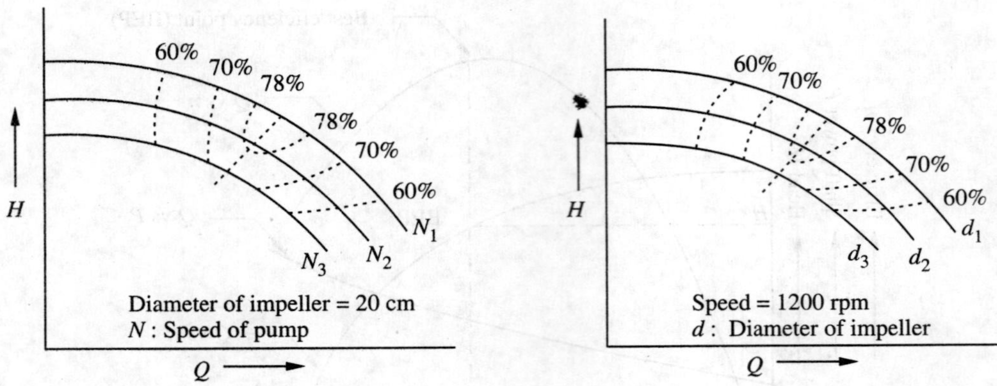

Fig 19.8 *(a) Variation of characteristics with N* *(b) Variation of characteristics with impeller diameter.*

19.5.13 Series and parallel connections of centrifugal pumps

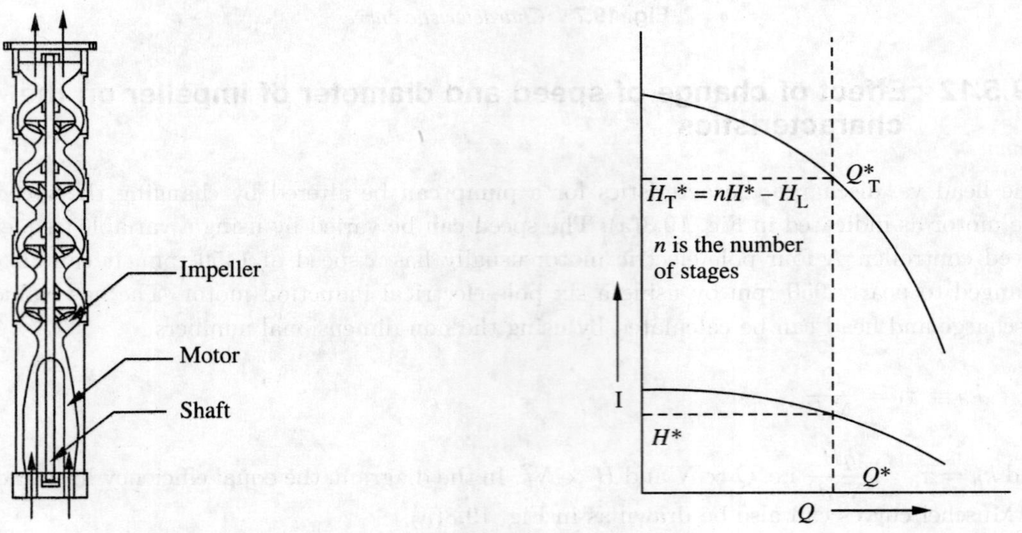

Fig 19.9(a) *Multistage submersible pump for tube wells*

Fig 19.9(b) *Characteristics curve for multistage pump*

The combinations are best done with identical pumps. A serial connection aims at adding the heads developed by the pumps as in multistage pumps used for deep tube wells. Figure 19.9(a) shows schematically such an arrangement. The discharge from the impeller in one stage is led to the suction inlet for the next stage. The resulting characteristics are shown in Fig. 19.9(b).

Combinations of centrifugal pumps can also be used in pipe lines as booster pumps to increase the head when it falls below satisfactory levels.

Two or more centrifugal pumps can be connected parallel to increase the discharge as in Fig. 19.10(a). The resulting characteristics when two pumps are connected parallel is shown in Fig. 19.10(b).

Centrifugal pumps are connected in series for adding up the discharges from the pumps. It may be noted that in all combinations, the characteristics of the pumps should match to give better performance.

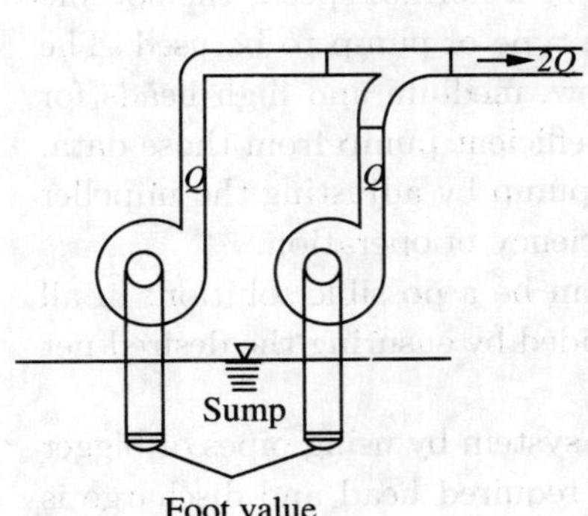

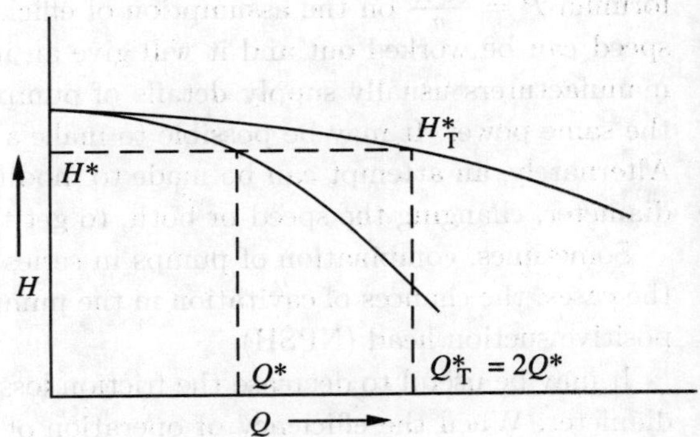

Fig. 19.10(a) *Centrifugal pumps connected parallel connected parallel*

Fig. 19.10(b) *Characteristics curve for pumps*

19.5.14 Requirements for the pumping system

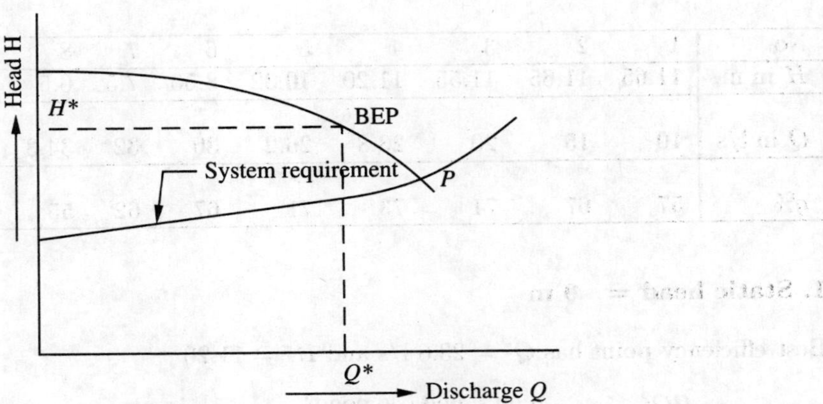

Fig. 19.11 *Requirements for the pumping system*

The requirement may be to pump a particular discharge against a static head ΔZ. The total head required will be $H_T = \Delta Z + H_L + V^2/2g$. As shown in Fig. 19.11, the point P may be far removed from BEP and the efficiency may be too low. In that case alternative arrangements may be explored.

19.5.15 Selection of centrifugal pumps

The requirement of power for the pump can be estimated for the required discharge Q by formula $P = \frac{\gamma Q H}{\eta}$ on the assumption of efficiency, say 65%. For a normal speed, the specific speed can be worked out and it will give an indication of the type of pump to be used. The manufacturers usually supply details of pumps suitable for low, medium and high heads for the same power. It may be possible to make a selection of an efficient pump from those data. Alternately, an attempt can be made to modify working of a pump by adjusting the impeller diameter, changing the speed or both, to get the required efficiency of operation.

Sometimes, combination of pumps in series or in parallel can be a possible solution. In all the cases, the chances of cavitation in the pump should be avoided by ensuring the desired net positive suction head (NPSH).

It may be useful to decrease the friction losses in the piping system by using pipes of bigger diameter. When the efficiency of operation of a pump at the required head and discharge is very low it may even be advantageous to throttle the pipe or use a pipe of smaller diameter so that operation is done close to the BEP.

Example 19.7 A 3.7 kW centrifugal pump is used to pump water from a sump to a reservoir. The quantity of water to be pumped is 10^6 l/day. The characteristics of the pump are given in table below. The static head varies from 4 m to 9 m. The pipe line is 15 cm in diameter and 200 m long. ($f = 0.02$). Find the pumping schedule so that the power consumed is minimum.

No.	1	2	3	4	5	6	7	8	9
H in m.	11.65	11.65	11.55	11.20	10.32	8.50	7.5	6.5	5.40
Q in l/s	10	15	20	23.8	26.2	30	32	34.3	36.6
η%	57	67	71	73	71	67	62	55	46

1. Static head = 9 m

Best efficiency point has $Q^* = 23.8$ l/s and $H^* = 11.20$.

$$H_T = 9 + \frac{flQ^2}{12.1d^5} = 9 + \frac{0.02 \times 200 \times 0.0238^2}{12.1 \times 0.15^5} = 11.466 \text{ m.}$$ The head at BEP is not sufficient.

Hence we may have to operate with $Q = 20$ l/s

Power required $= \gamma QH/\eta = 9810 \times 0.020 \times 11.55/0.71W = 3.192$ kW, which is safe

Time required for pumping, $t = \dfrac{1 \times 10^6}{20 \times 3600} = 13.9$ h.

Total energy required. $= 13.9 \times 3.192 = 44.37$ kW.h.(Ans.).

2. Static head = 4

Alternative 1 Assuming a discharge of 36.6 l/s, head from the characteristics = 5.4 m and $\eta = 0.476$

$$\text{Head required} = 4 + \frac{flQ^2}{12.ld^5} = \frac{4 + 0.02 \times 200 \times 0.0366^2}{12.1 \times 0.15^5} = 4 + 5.83 = 9.83\,\text{m} > 5.4$$

Hence the discharge is to be reduced. Assuming a discharge of 30 l/s, the head from the characteristics = 8.5 m and $\eta = 0.67$.

$$\text{Head required} = 4 + \frac{flQ^2}{12.1d^5} = 4 + \frac{0.02 \times 200 \times 0.030^2}{12.1 \times 0.15^5} = 7.92\text{ m} < 8.5\text{ m. Hence OK.}$$

Power required $= (\gamma QH/\eta) = 9810 \times 0.030 \times 8.5/0.67$ W $= 3.73$ kW. Hence OK.

$$\text{Time of pumping required} = \frac{1 \times 10^6}{30 \times 3600} = 9.26\text{ hrs.}$$

Total energy required $= 3.73 \times 9.26 = 34.54$ kW.h. (Ans.)

Alternative 2 A variable frequency speed controller may be used with the motor and the speed may be reduced to 70%. The motor efficiency will nearly be the same.

By model law $Q \propto N$ and $H \propto N^2$; Hence at the best efficiency point discharge $= 23.8 \times 0.7 = 16.66$ l/s

The head $= 0.7^2 \times 11.2 = 5.488$ m.; and $\eta = 0.73$.

$$\text{Head required} = 4 + \frac{flQ^2}{12.1d^5} = 4 + \frac{0.02 \times 200 \times 0.01666^2}{12.1 \times 0.15^5} = 5.2\text{ m. Hence OK}$$

Power required $= (\gamma QH/\eta) = 9810 \times 0.01666 \times 5.488/0.73\text{W} = 1.224$ kW

$$\text{Time of pumping required} = \frac{1 \times 10^6}{16.66 \times 3600} = 16.67\text{ hrs.}$$

Total energy requirement $= 1.224 \times 16.67 = 20.4$ kW.h Ans.

Discussion

When the static head is 9 m, the delivery valve may be adjusted to give the discharge of 20 l/s and the energy requirement will be 44.37 kW/day.

When the static head is 4 m, the same pump can be used and the delivery valve should be adjusted to give a discharge of 30 l/s. The energy requirement will be 34.54 kW.h

If a speed regulation is done for the motor and 70% of the speed is maintained, the delivery valve should be adjusted to give a discharge of 16.6 l/s and the energy requirement will only be 20.4 kW.h

19.5.16 Application of model laws for centrifugal pumps

Centrifugal pumps have been made in very large sizes. To ensure its efficient performance, it is advantageous to conduct tests on smaller models, and if required make alterations in the design. The non-dimensional numbers,

$$\pi_1 = k_d = \frac{Q}{Nd^3};\ \pi_2 = k_h = \frac{gH}{N^2d^2};\ \pi_3 = k_p = \frac{P}{\rho N^3 d^5} \text{ and } \pi_4 = k_f = \frac{\mu}{\rho d^3 N}$$

govern the modelling. The last number k_f is the scale factor, the effect of viscous friction and energy loss. This can be assumed the same for the model ratio $L_r = \dfrac{L_m}{L_p} \approx 1$. But when $L_r << 1$, a correction for efficiency η_p can be made by a formula similar to that given by Moody for turbines[39].

$$(1-\eta_p) \cong (1-\eta_m) \times L_r^{1/5} \tag{19.30}$$

Pumps of the same type are characterised by the same design-specific speed. In addition, velocities like the tangential velocity, relative velocity etc. are proportional to Nd and also $H^{1/2}$. If two pumps are similar, the velocity diagrams in both the cases are also to be similar.

Example 19.8 A single stage centrifugal pump with impeller diameter of 30 cm rotates at 2000 rpm and discharges 3 m³/s at a head of 30 m with an efficiency of 75%. Find the number of stages and diameter of each impeller of a similar multistage pump to lift 5 m³ /s of water to a height of 200 m when rotating at 1500 rpm.

$$d_m = 0.3 \text{ m};\quad N_m = 2000 \text{ rpm};\quad Q_m = 3 \text{ m}^3/\text{s};\quad H_m = 30 \text{ m};\quad \eta_m = 75\%$$

$$Q_p = 5 \text{ m}^3/\text{s};\ H_p = 200 \text{ m};\ N_p = 1500 \text{ rpm}.$$

$$\text{specific speed} = N_{sp} = N_{sm} = \frac{N_m Q_m^{1/2}}{H_m^{3/4}} = \frac{2000 \times 3^{1/2}}{30^{3/4}} = 270.24.$$

Let head for one stage be H_{1p}

$$N_{sp} = 270.24 = \frac{N_P Q_P^{1/2}}{H_{1P}^{3/4}} = \frac{1500 \times 5^{1/2}}{H_{1p}^{3/4}};\ H_{1p} = 28.74 \text{ m}$$

$$\text{Number of stages required } n \approx \frac{200}{28.74};\ n = 7. \text{ (Ans.)}$$

$$\frac{H_m^{1/2}}{N_m d_{mx}} = \frac{H_p^{1/2}}{N_p d_p};$$

Hence $\quad d_p = \dfrac{d_m N_m H_p^{1/2}}{N_p H_m^{1/2}} = \dfrac{0.30 \times 2000 \times 28.57^{1/2}}{1500 \times 20^{1/2}} = 0.3904 \text{ m (Ans.)}$

Example 19.9 Two geometrically similar pumps are running at the same speed of 1000 rpm. One pump has an impeller diameter of 0.3 m and lifts water at the rate of 20 l/s against a head of 15 m. Determine the head and impeller diameter of the other pump to deliver half the discharge.

$N_m = 1000$ rpm; $d_m = 0.3$ m; $Q_m = 0.020 \text{ m}^3/\text{sw}$; $H_m = 15$ m.

$N_p = 1000$ rpm; $Q_p = 0.010 \text{ m}^3/\text{s}$

$$N_{sp} = \frac{N_m Q_m^{1/2}}{H_m^{3/4}} = \frac{1000 \times 0.02^{1/2}}{15^{3/4}} = 18.15$$

$N_{sp} = 18.15 = \dfrac{1000 \times 0.01^{1/2}}{15^{3/4}} = 18.15$; Hence $H_p = 9.45$ m. (Ans.)

Because N is the same $\dfrac{H_m^{1/2}}{d_m} = \dfrac{H_p^{1/2}}{d_p}$ i.e. $d_p = \dfrac{0.3 \times 9.45^{1/2}}{15^{1/2}} = 0.238$ m. (Ans.)

Example 19.10 A 1/5 scale model of a a pump was tested in a laboratory at 1000 rpm. The head developed and the power input at the best efficiency poi of 75% was found to be 8 m and 30 kW respectively. If the prototype pump has to work against a head of 25 m, determine its working speed and the power required

$L_r = 1/5$; $N_m = 1000$ rpm; $H_m = 8$ m; $P_m = 30$ kW; $H_p = 25$ m.

$$\frac{H_m^{1/2}}{N_m d_m} = \frac{H_p^{1/2}}{N_p d_p}; N_P = \frac{d_m}{d_p} \times \frac{H_p^{1/2}}{H_m^{1/2}} \times N_m = \frac{1}{5} \times \frac{25^{1/2}}{8^{1/2}} \times 1000 = 353.55 \text{ rpm. (Ans.)}$$

$$Q_r = N_r . d_r^3 = \frac{1000}{353.55} \times \left(\frac{1}{5}\right)^2 = 0.0226$$

$Q_p/Q_m = 1/Q_r = 1/0.0226 = 44.19$ (Ans.)

$$P_r = N_r^3 \times d_r^5 = \left[\frac{1000}{353.55}\right]^3 \times \left[\frac{1}{5}\right]^5 = 0.0724$$

$P_p = P_m/P_r = 30/0.0724 = 4143.6$ kW. (Ans.)

Let the efficiency of the prototype be η_p; $\eta_m = 0.75$; $L_r = 1/5$

$$(1 - \eta_p) \cong (1 - \eta_m) \times L_r^{1/5} = 0.181$$

$$\eta_P \cong 1 - 0.181 = 0.819$$

The power required $= 4143.6 \times 0.75/0.819 = 3794.5$ kW. (Ans.)

19.6 Turbines

19.6.1 General

Turbines are fluid machines which convert the energy of fluid due to pressure and velocity into mechanical energy to rotate a generator. In a reaction turbine, like the Francis type or the Kaplan type, the water is led under pressure through a scroll case to the runner. The components of the velocity of inflow to the runner blades and outflow from the runner blades, the V_{w1} and V_{w2} is used to calculate the power developed by (19.13)

$$P = \rho Q(U_1 V_{w1} - U_2 V_{w2}).$$

In impulse turbines like the Pelton wheel, the energy of flow is converted to kinetic energy of flow through a nozzle and the jet is made to impinge on a series of buckets which deflect the jet. Work done by the jet can be calculated by using (19.13).

An example of a lawn sprinkler will illustrate the moment of momentum principle as applied to the reaction turbines.

Example 19.11 A lawn sprinkler as shown in the figure has three arms ending in 1 cm diameter nozzles. It receives water at a rate of 5 l/s from a central pipe. The sprinkler is free to rotate without friction. Find (i) the speed at which the sprinkler will rotate when $\theta = 30°$. (ii) If a small generator of speed 420 rpm is attached to the rotating head, find the power developed (neglecting all losses) when $\theta = 30°$. (iii) If the water leaves tangentially, what is the power developed? (iv) If the sprinkler is held stationary, what torque will be developed when the water leaves tangentially?

$$Q_T = 5 \text{ l/s} = 5 \times 10^{-3} \text{ m}^3/\text{s}; \; d = 1 \text{ cm} = 0.01 \text{ m.}; \; A = 7.854 \times 10^{-5} \text{m}^2$$

$$V_{r2} = \frac{Q_T}{3 \times A} = \frac{5 \times 10^{-3}}{3 \times 7.8543 \times 10^{-5}} = 21.22 \text{ m/s}$$

$$R = 0.2 \text{ m}; \; d = 0.4 \text{ m}$$

Case (i) when the sprinkler is rotating freely, the torque will be zero. (Total angular momentum will be zero) i.e. $V_{w2} = 0$

$$U = V_{r2} \cos 30° = 21.22 \cos 30° = 18.377 \text{ m/s}.$$

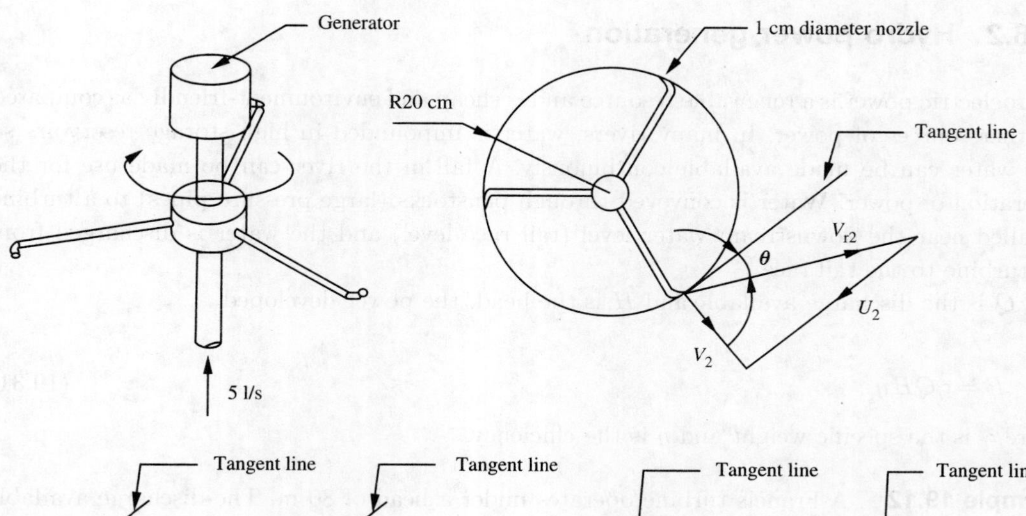

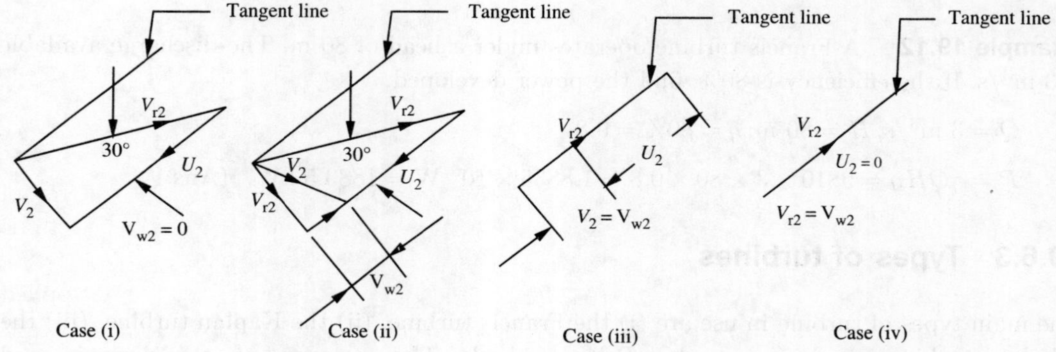

Example 19.11

$$U = \frac{\pi d N}{N}; \quad N = \frac{60U}{\pi d} = \frac{60 \times 18.377}{\pi \times 0.4} = 877.44 \text{ rpm. (Ans.)}$$

Case (ii) $N = 450$ rpm; $U = \dfrac{\pi d N}{60} = \dfrac{\pi \times 0.4 \times 450}{60} = 9.425$ m/s

$V_{w2} = V_{r2} \cos 30° - U = 18.377 - 9.425 = 8.952$ m/s.

$P = \rho Q V_{w2} U W = 1000 \times 5 \times 10^{-3} \times 8.952 \times 9.425\text{W} = 421.86\text{W} = 0.422$ kW. (Ans)

Case (iii) In this case $\theta = 0°$ and $V_{w2} = V_{r2} - U = 21.22 - 9.425 = 11.795$ m/s.

$P = 1000 \times 5 \times 10^{-3} \times 11.795 \times 9.425 = 555.84\text{W} = 0.556$ kW. (Ans)

Case (iv) $U = 0; V_{w2} = V_{r2} - U = 21.22 - 0 = 21.22$ m/s.

Torque $T = \rho Q V_{w2} \times r = 1000 \times 5 \times 10^{-3} \times 21.22 \times 0.2 = 21.22$ N m. (Ans)

19.6.2 Hydro power generation

Hydroelectric power is a renewable resource and is cheap and environment-friendly as compared to other sources of power. In many rivers, water is impounded in high storage reservoirs so that water can be made available continuously. A fall in the river can be made use for the generation of power. Water is conveyed through penstocks (large pressure pipes) to a turbine installed near the downstream water level (tail race level) and the water is discharged from the turbine to the tail race.

If Q is the discharge available and H is the head, the power developed

$$P = \gamma Q H \eta \tag{19.31}$$

where γ is the specific weight and η is the efficiency.

Example 19.12 A Francis turbine operates under a head of 80 m. The discharge available is 3 m^3/s. If the efficiency is 80%, find the power developed.

$$Q = 3 \text{ m}^3/\text{s}; H = 80 \text{ m}; \eta = 80\% = 0.8.$$

$$P = \gamma Q H \eta = 9810 \times 3 \times 80 \times 0.8 = 1.8835 \times 10^6 \text{ W} = 1883.5 \text{ kW}. \text{ (Ans.)}$$

19.6.3 Types of turbines

The main types of turbine in use are (i) the Francis turbine, (ii) the Kaplan turbine, (iii) the tubular turbines and (iv) the Pelton wheel. The runners of the Francis and Kaplan turbines are enclosed in scroll cases (counterpart of volute chambers in pumps) ensuring flow under pressure whereas in a Pelton turbine, the inflow to the runner is in the form of a jet impinging on buckets at atmospheric pressure. In the case of tubular turbines, the runner works inside the tube or penstock and the flow takes place axially through the runner blades.

19.6.4 Specific speed of turbines

The specific speed of a turbine is the speed of a geometrically similar turbine that would develop one kilowatt power under a head of one meter.
This is usually expressed as

$$N_{st} = \frac{N\sqrt{P}}{H^{5/4}}. \tag{19.32}$$

The expression for specific speed is derived as follows: If U is the tangential velocity

$$U = \pi DN/60 \text{ and } U \propto \sqrt{H}; \text{ Hence } N = k_1\sqrt{H}/D. \tag{A}$$

$$P = \gamma Q H \text{ and } Q \propto D^2 H. \text{ Hence } \sqrt{P} = k_2 D H^{3/4} \tag{B}$$

Eliminating D from equations (A) and (B), $N\sqrt{P} = k_3 H^{5/4}$ or $N_{st} = \dfrac{N\sqrt{P}}{H^{3/4}}$

19.6.5 The Francis turbine

One of the most common turbines, the Francis turbine is used when medium heads are available. The flow in the Francis turbine is a reversal of that in a diffuser or turbine pump. The runner of the Francis turbine is made to flow full by enclosing it in a scroll case (counterpart of the volute chamber in a diffuser pump) and providing a draft tube , the end of which is submerged in the tail race. The arrangement is shown in Fig. 19.12.

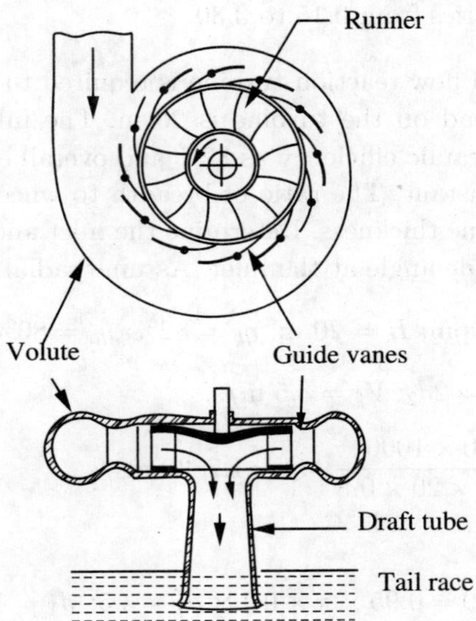

Figure 19.12 *The Francis turbine*

The discharge through the penstock enters the scroll case and gets distributed nearly equally around and passes through the adjustable guide vanes before entering the runner. The setting of the guide vane governs the angle α_1 at which the flow enters the runner blades. The runner can be low speed ($U_1 < V_{w1}$ and $\beta_1 > 90°$) or fast speed ($U_1 > V_{w1}$ and $\beta_1 < 90°$).

By application of the principle of conservation of moment of momentum, the power developed is equal to

$$P = \rho Q \left(U_1 V_{w_1} - U_2 V_{w_2}\right). \tag{19.33}$$

The discharge Q through the turbine at the inlet will be through an area $\pi d_1 b_1$, where b_1 is the width of runner and d_1 is the radius at inlet.

Hence the velocity of flow $V_{f_1} = \dfrac{Q}{\pi d_1 b_1}$. (19.34)

Similarly, the velocity of flow at exit will be

$$V_{f_2} = \frac{Q}{\pi d_2 b_2}, \tag{19.35}$$

where b_2 is the width of the runner at the exit. In case the vane thickness is considered, the flow area will be reduced and the velocity of flow will increase due to blockage.

Hence flow area will be $= b(\pi d - nt) = k \times \pi db$
where n is the number of blades, t is the thickness of each blade and k is the area factor. In the case of the Francis turbine, the speed ratio C_U (which is the ratio of tangential velocity to $\sqrt{2gH}$) usually ranges between 0.58 to 1.0 and the flow ratio C_f (which is the ratio of flow velocity to $\sqrt{2gH}$) usually varies from 0.15 to 0.30.

Example 19.13 An inward flow reaction turbine is required to produce a power of 280 kW at 200 rpm. The effective head on the turbine is 20 m. The inlet diameter is twice as the outlet diameter. Assume hydraulic efficiency as 82% and overall efficiency as 80%. The radial velocity is 3.5 m/s and is constant. The ratio of breadth to wheel diameter is 0.1 and 5% of the flow area is blocked by vane thickness. Determine the inlet and outlet diameters, inlet and exit vane angle and guide blade angle at the inlet. Assume radial discharge.

$P = 280$ kW; $N = 200$ rpm; $H = 20$ m; $\eta_h = 82\%$; $\eta_o = 80\%$; $b = 0.1\ D_1$;

Area blocked $= 5\%$; $d_1 = 2d_2$; $V_f = 3.5$ m/s.

$$P = \gamma Q H \eta_o;\ Q = \frac{280 \times 1000}{9810 \times 20 \times 0.8};\ Q = 1.7839 \text{ m}^3/\text{s}.$$

We know that,

$$Q = 0.95\pi d_1 b V_{f_1};\ 1.7839 = 0.95 \times \pi \times 0.1 \times d_1^2 \times 3.5;\ d_1 = 1.3068 \text{ m. (Ans.)}$$

$$d_2 = d_1/2 = 0.6534 \text{ m (Ans.)};\quad b = 0.1 d_1 = 0.13068 \text{ m.}$$

$$\text{Now, } U_1 = \frac{\pi d_1 N}{60} = \frac{\pi \times 1.3068 \times 200}{60} = 13.685 \text{ m/s.}$$

$$\text{Given } \eta_h = \frac{V_{w_1} U_1}{gH} = 0.82; 0.82 = \frac{V_{w_1} \times 13.685}{9.81 \times 20}; V_{w_1} = 11.756 \text{ m.}$$

From the inlet velocity triangle,

$$\tan \alpha_1 = \frac{3.5}{11.756} = 0.298;\ \alpha_1 = 16.58°. \text{ (Ans.)}$$

$$\tan \beta_1 = \frac{V_{f_1}}{U_1 - V_{w_1}};\ \tan \beta_1 = \frac{3.5}{13.685 - 11.756} = 1.8144;\ \beta_1 = 61.14°. \text{ (Ans.)}$$

$$\text{Also, } U_2 = \frac{\pi D_2 N}{60} = 6.8425 \text{ m/s.}$$

From the outlet velocity triangle,

$$\tan \beta_2 = \frac{V_{f_2}}{U_2}; \ \tan \beta_2 = \frac{3.5}{6.8425} = 0.5115; \ \beta_2 = 27.09°. \text{ (Ans.)}$$

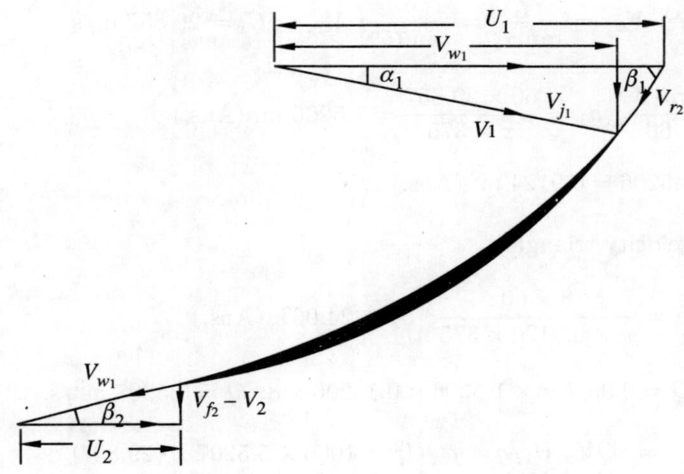

Example 19.13 *Inlet and outlet velocity triangles*

Example 19.14 In a Francis turbine, the guide blade angle is 15° and the flow enters in a radial direction. The flow velocity is constant and is equal to 8 m/s. The outlet diameter is 0.6 times the inlet diameter and the runner rotates at 375 rpm. The width of the wheel is 0.1 times the diameter at the inlet and 5% of the flow passage is blocked by blade thickness. Assume radial flow at the outlet. Calculate (a) diameters at the inlet and outlet, (b) blade angle at the outlet and (c) the head and power developed.

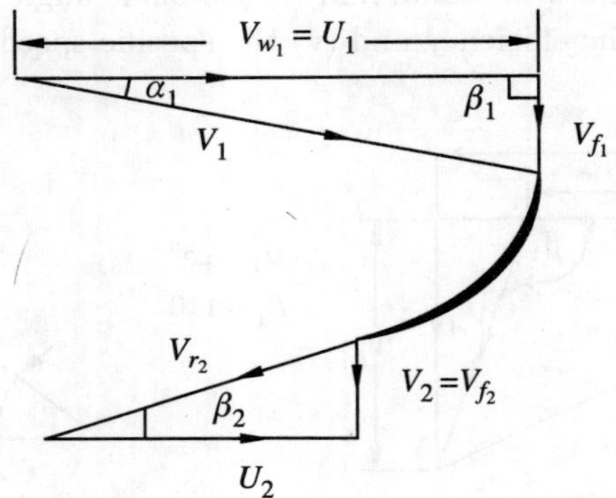

Example 19.14 *Inlet and outlet velocity triangles*

$\alpha_1 = 15°$; $V_f = 8$ m/s; $d_2 = 0.6\ d_1$; $N = 375$; $b = 0.1\ d_1$; $k = 0.95$; k is the coefficient representing the percentage of discharge actually flowing through the machine.
From the inlet velocity triangle,

$$\tan\alpha_1 = \frac{V_{f_1}}{V_{w_1}};\ V_{w_1} = \frac{V_{f_1}}{\tan\alpha_1} = \frac{8}{\tan 15°};\ V_{w_1} = U_1 = 29.857 \text{ m/s.}$$

$$\text{Now } U_1 = \frac{\pi d_1 N}{60};\ d_1 = \frac{60 \times 29.857}{\pi \times 375} = 1.5206 \text{ m. (Ans.)}$$

$$d_2 = 0.6 \times 1.5206 = 0.9124 \text{ m. (Ans.)}$$

From the outlet velocity triangle,

$$\tan\beta_2 = \frac{V_{f_2}}{U_2} = \frac{8 \times 60}{\pi \times 0.9124 \times 375};\ \beta_2 = 24.06°. \text{ (Ans.)}$$

$$\text{Discharge, } Q = 0.95 \times \pi \times 1.5206 \times 0.15206 \times 8;\ Q = 5.5207 \text{ m}^3\text{/s.}$$

$$\text{Power, } P = \gamma Q V_{w_1} U_1/g = \rho Q U_1^2 = 1000 \times 5.5207 \times (29.857)^2.$$

$$\text{W} = 4921.4 \text{ kW. (Ans.)}$$

Head utilised is given by,

$$H = \frac{V_{w_1}U_1}{g} + \frac{V_2^2}{2g};\ H = \frac{(29.857)^2}{9.81} + \frac{8^2}{2 \times 9.81} = 94.133 \text{ m. (Ans.)}$$

Example 19.15 A slow speed Francis turbine has an outer diameter of 0.8 m and inner diameter of 0.4 m. The flow area is constant, equal to 0.25 m^2. The head is 60 m and the turbine runs at 500 rpm. The guide vane angle at the inlet is 25° and the inlet blade angle 110° respectively. If the outflow is radial, find (i) the blade angle at the outlet, (ii) discharge, (iii) power, (iv) the hydraulic efficiency and (v) the specific speed.

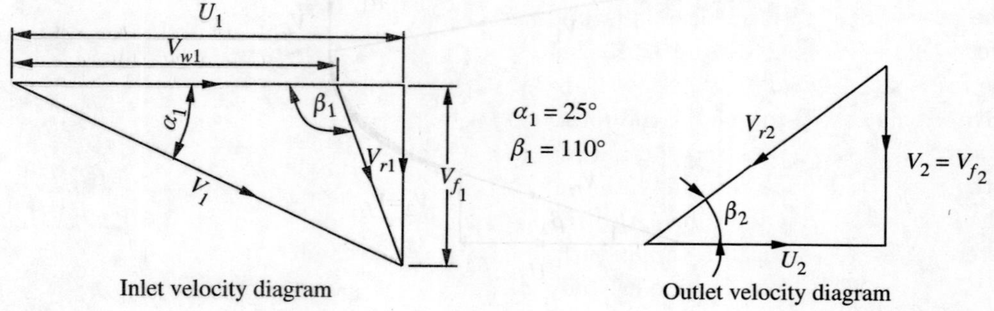

Example 19.15 *Velocity diagram for the turbine*

$d_1 = 0.8$ m; $d_2 = 0.4$ m; $N = 500$ rpm; $H = 60$ m: $\alpha_1 = 25°$; $\beta_1 = 110°$

$$U_1 = \frac{\pi d_1 N}{60} = 20.94 \text{ m/s};$$

From the inlet velocity diagram, $V_{w1} \tan 25° = (U_{w1} - U_1) \tan 70°$

$$V_{w1} = \frac{U_1 \tan 70°}{\tan 70° - \tan 25°} = \frac{20.94 \tan 70°}{2.747 - 0.466} = 25.22 \text{ m/s}$$

$$V_{f1} = V_{w1} \times \tan 25° = 25.22 \times \tan 25° = 11.76 \text{ m/s}$$

$$Q = A_f \times V_{f1} = 0.25 \times 11.76 = 2.94 \text{ m}^3\text{/s (Ans)}$$

$$U_2 = \frac{\pi d_2 N}{60} = 10.47 \text{ m/s}; \; V_{w2} = 0 \text{ (radial outflow)}$$

From outlet velocity diagram, $\tan \beta_2 = \dfrac{V_{f2}}{U_2} = \dfrac{11.76}{10.47}$; $\beta_2 = 48.32°$ (Ans.)

Power developed $= \rho Q V_{w1} U_1 = 1000 \times 2.94 \times 25.22 \times 20.94$ W $= 1552.6$ kW (Ans)

Theoretical power $= \gamma Q H = 9810 \times 2.94 \times 60$ W $= 1730.5$ kW

Hydraulic efficiency $= \dfrac{1552.6}{1730.5} = 0.897$ (Ans)

Specific speed $= \dfrac{N\sqrt{P}}{H^{5/4}} = \dfrac{500 \times \sqrt{1552.6}}{60^{5/4}} = 118$ (Ans)

19.6.6 The Kaplan turbine

Kaplan turbines are used when low to medium heads are available. It is a propeller type of turbine. The turbine has the flow entering the scroll case distributed fairly equally to the adjustable guide vanes. The flow is made axially at the inlet of the runner. The Kaplan turbine has the runner blades (propeller blades) adjustable so that at varying discharges also it can give very high efficiencies. Figure 19.10 shows the sketch of a Kaplan turbine.

The force and hence momentum is transferred to the blades by the flow and the moment will give the necessary torque for the rotation. The equation governing the torque developed is the same as in all the other turbo-machines.

In the case of the Kaplan turbine, the value of the speed ratio C_U varies between 1.0 to 2.0 and the flow ratio C_f is about 0.7. Also the hub or the boss diameter is about 0.35 to 0.60 of diameter of outer diameter. In Kaplan turbines, $U_1 = U_2$; $V_{f_1} = V_{f_2}$; and it is usual to assume $V_{r_1} = V_{r_2}$ also. The Kaplan turbine has only four to six vanes normally and is designed so that the outlet flow is axial causing no velocity of whirl at the outlet.

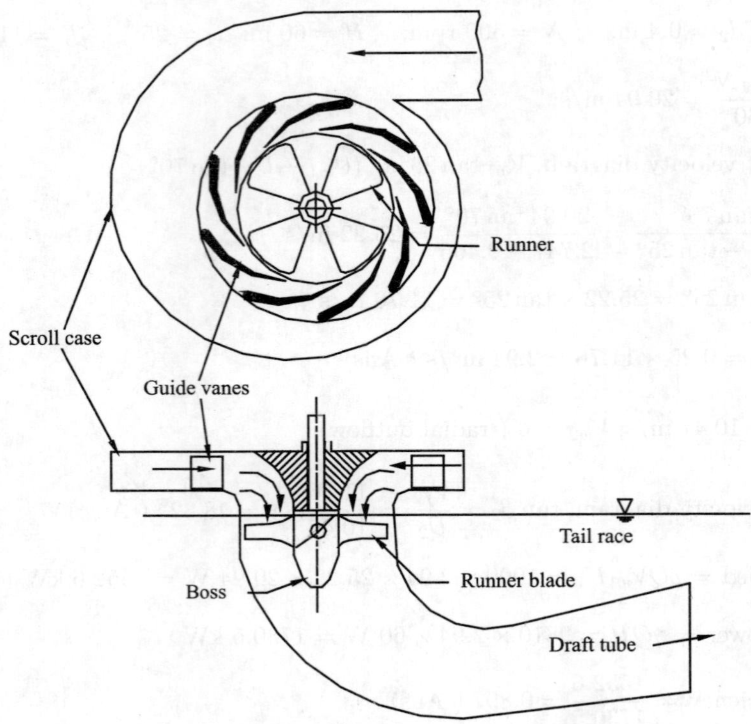

Fig. 19.13 *The Kaplan turbine*

Example 19.16 A Kaplan turbine develops 13500 kW at a head of 25 m. The diameter of the boss is 0.35 times the diameter of the runner. Assume a speed ratio of 2 and flow ratio of 0.65. If the overall efficiency is 92%, calculate (i) diameter of runner, (ii) rotational speed, (iii) specific speed.

$$P = 13500 \text{ kW}; C_u = 2; C_f = 0.65; d_b = 0.35d; \eta = 0.92.$$

$$U = C_u\sqrt{2gH} = 2 \times \sqrt{2 \times 9.81 \times 25} = 44.295 \text{ m/s}.$$

$$V_f = C_f\sqrt{2gH} = 0.65 \times \sqrt{2 \times g \times H} = 14.396 \text{ m/s}.$$

$$\text{Power developed, } P = \gamma QH\eta_0; Q = \frac{P}{\gamma H\eta_0} = \frac{13500}{9810 \times 25 \times 0.92}; Q = 59.833 \text{ m}^3/\text{s}.$$

$$Q = \frac{\pi\left(d^2 - {d_b}^2\right)V_f}{4}; \; d = 2.456 \text{ m. (Ans.)}$$

Now, $U = \frac{\pi dN}{60}$; $N = \frac{60U}{\pi d}$; $N = \frac{60 \times 44.295}{\pi \times 2.456}$; $N = 344.4$ rpm. (Ans.)

Specific speed, $N_{st} = \frac{N\sqrt{P}}{H^{5/4}}$, $N_{st} = 715.8$. (Ans.)

Example 19.17 A Kaplan turbine develops 12000 kW at a head of 20 m, when the speed is 250 rpm. The outer diameter of the runner is 3.0 m and hub diameter is 1.2 m. The hydraulic and overall efficiencies of the turbine are 88% and 85% respectively. Find the discharge, the inlet flow angle and the blade angles at the inlet and outlet.

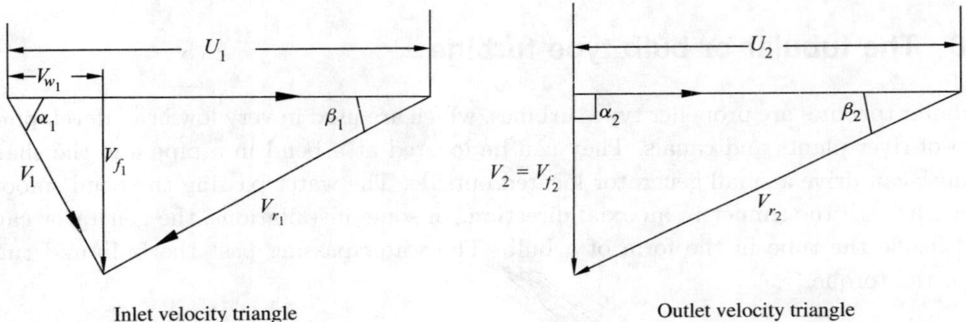

Example 19.17

$H = 20$ m; $P = 12000$ kW; $\eta_o = 85\%$; $\eta_h = 88\%$; $N = 250$ rpm; $D = 3$ m; $D_b = 1.2$ m.

Power $P = \gamma Q H \eta_o$; $Q = \frac{12000 \times 1000}{9810 \times 20 \times 0.85} = 71.9553 \text{ m}^3/\text{s}$. (Ans.)

$$Q = \frac{\pi\left(d^2 - d_b^2\right)}{4} \times V_{f_1};\ V_{f_1} = \frac{71.9553 \times 4}{\pi\left(3^2 - 1.2^2\right)} = 12.19 \text{ m/s.}$$

Now, $U = \frac{\pi dN}{60} = \frac{\pi \times 3 \times 250}{60} = 39.27$ m/s.

Also, $\eta_h = \frac{V_{w_1} U_1}{gH} = 0.88$; $V_{w_1} = 4.397$ m/s.

From the inlet velocity triangle, $\tan \alpha_1 = \frac{V_{f_1}}{V_{w_1}}$; $\tan \alpha_1 = \frac{12.19}{4.397}$; $\alpha_1 = 70.165°$. (Ans.)

$\tan \beta_1 = \frac{V_{f_1}}{U_1 - V_{w_1}} = \frac{12.19}{39.27 - 4.397}$; $\beta_1 = 19.27°$. (Ans.)

From the outlet velocity triangle, $\tan\beta_2 = \dfrac{V_{f_2}}{U_2} = \dfrac{12.19}{39.27}$; $\beta_2 = 17.25°$. (Ans.)

19.6.7 The draft tube for reaction turbines

The flow leaving the runner of a Francis or Kaplan turbine may have high exit velocities. Part of the head can be recovered by giving a gradual expansion to the outlet pipe at the exit. This pipe called the draft tube connects the runner to the tail race and makes the runner flow full. The draft tube can be in the shape of a cone. When the turbine is located very low compared to the tail water level, as is the case in many Kaplan turbines, the draft tube can be of elbow shape. By provision of the draft tube, the gross difference of head from the tail race to the fore bay is made use of in the turbine.

19.6.8 The tubular or bulb type turbine

The tubular turbines are propeller type turbines, which are used in very low head developments like run-of-river plants and canals. They can be located at a bend in a pipe and the shaft of the runner can drive a small generator located outside. The water passing the bend smoothly will flow through the runner in an axial direction. In some installations, the generator can be located inside the tube in the form of a bulb. The water passing past the bulb and runner develops the torque.

19.6.9 The Pelton turbine

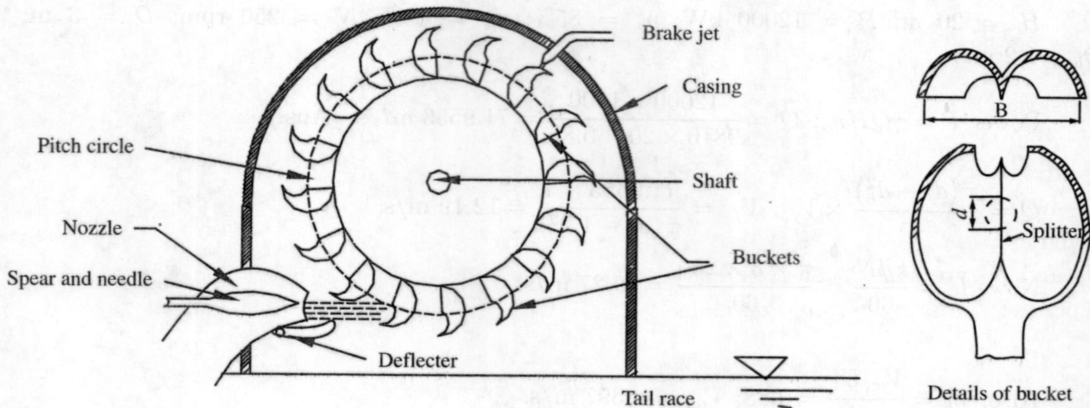

Fig. 19.14 *A Pelton turbine*

A Pelton wheel or Pelton turbine is an impulse turbine in which all the available potential energy of water is converted into kinetic energy as the water jet strikes the vanes or buckets through a nozzle. The Pelton turbine essentially consists of a series of split hemispherical cups or buckets attached to the periphery of a wheel. The jet of water issuing from a nozzle strikes the buckets causing the wheel to rotate as shown in Fig. 19.14. The buckets are even in number, generally ranging from 16 to 30, symmetrically placed on the wheel. Though theoretically the cups are hemispherical, the deflection angle of the jet is kept nearly 165° to avoid splashing back of water on to the incoming bucket which may cause a braking action. The nozzle is provided with a spear and needle arrangement to control the rate of flow.

As the vanes are at atmospheric pressure from inlet to outlet, the casing or hood has no special function to perform except in preventing splashing of water and to prevent accidents . Large turbines are provided with a braking jet to bring the wheel to a stop in a short time to carry out repairs etc.

19.6.9.1 Work done and efficiency

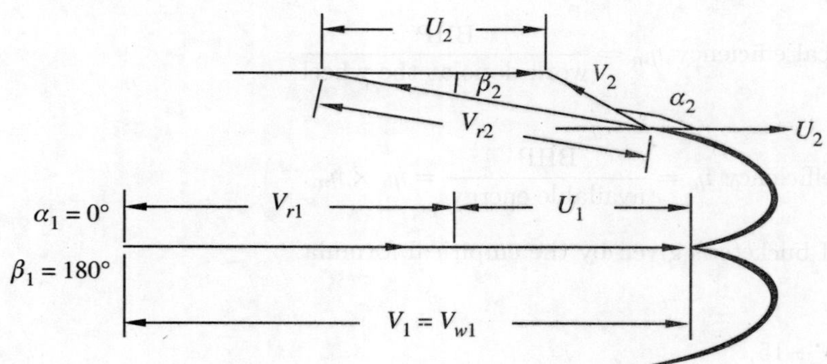

Fig. 19.15 *Inlet and outlet velocity triangles*

$H-$ available head
$D-$ diameter of the pitch circle
$d-$ diameter of the nozzle
$V-$ velocity of jet at the inlet $= C_V\sqrt{2gH}$, where C_V is the coefficient of velocity, usually taken as 0.98.
U_1 and U_2 are tangential velocities at the inlet and outlet. Since the inlet and outlet vane types are at the same radial distance

$$U_1 = U_2 = U = C_U\sqrt{2gH},$$

where C_U is the speed ratio, usually assumed to be 0.46
Let V_r be the relative velocity, which is assumed to be unchanged. Since the jet and the tangential velocity are in the same direction, the relative velocity V_r at the inlet is equal to $V - U$ and it is the same as the relative velocity at the outlet. Referring to Fig. 19.12,

Rate at which work is done $= F \times U = \rho Q(V - U)(1 + \cos\beta_2) \times U$.

$$\text{Hydraulic efficiency } \eta_h = \frac{\text{rate at which work is done}}{\text{rate of energy input}} = \frac{\rho QU(V-U)(1+\cos\beta_2)}{\rho QV^2/2}$$

$$= \frac{2U(V-U)(1+\cos\beta_2)}{V^2}. \qquad (19.36)$$

It can be shown that the efficiency is maximum when

$$U = V/2. \qquad (19.37)$$

Hence $\eta_{h\max} = 0.5(1 + \cos\beta_2)$.

The efficiency can be made 100% by making $\beta_2 = 0$. i.e., by making the cups hemispherical. As pointed out earlier the outlet vane angle is kept about 15° to avoid splashing back.

$$\text{Mechanical efficiency } \eta_m = \frac{\text{BHP}}{\text{work done at the wheel}}. \qquad (19.38)$$

$$\text{Overall efficiency } \eta_o = \frac{\text{BHP}}{\text{available energy}} = \eta_h \times \eta_m. \qquad (19.39)$$

The number of buckets is given by the empirical formula

$$z = 0.5m + 15, \qquad (19.40)$$

where $m = D/d$, D is the diameter of pitch circle for buckets and d is the diameter of the jet.

19.6.10 Efficiency curves

The curves showing the efficiency versus part load/full load for different turbines are shown in Fig. 19.16.

Example 19.18 A Pelton wheel works under a head of 250 m. The output is 2500 kW. The overall efficiency is 80%. If $C_V = 0.98$, find the diameter of the nozzle.

$P = 2500$ kW $= 2500 \times 1000$ W; $H = 250$ m; $\eta_o = 0.80$.

$2500 \times 1000 = \gamma QH \times \eta_o = 9810 \times Q \times 250 \times 0.8$.

$$Q = \frac{2500 \times 10^3}{9810 \times 250 \times 0.8} = 1.274 \text{ m}^3/\text{s}.$$

$$V = C_V\sqrt{2gH} = 0.98 \times 4.43 \times \sqrt{250} = 68.6 \text{ m/s}; \; Q = \frac{\pi d^2}{4}V.$$

$$1.274 = \frac{\pi d^2}{4} \times 68.6.$$

$$d^2 = \frac{1.274 \times 4}{\pi \times 68.6} = 0.0236 \text{ m}^2.$$

$$d = 0.1538 \text{ m} = 15.38 \text{ cm say } 16 \text{ cm. (Ans.)}$$

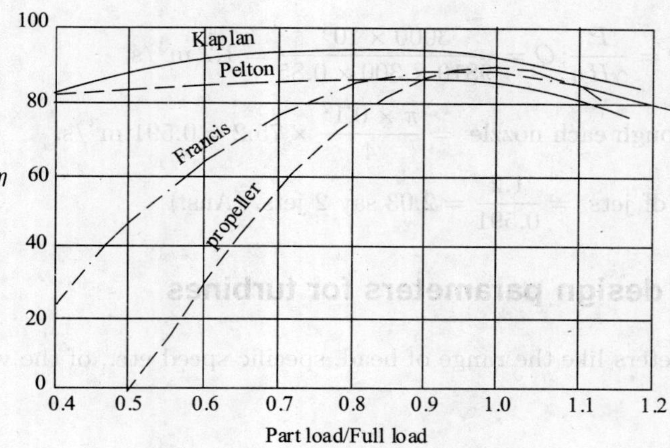

Fig. 19.16 *Efficiency vs Part load/Full load*

Example 19.19 A Pelton wheel running at 1000 rpm generates 2500 kW. The head available is 300 m and the overall efficiency is 85%. If $C_U = 0.45$, find the diameter of the pitch circle. If $C_V = 0.98$, find the diameter of the jet. Find also the number of buckets.

$$P = 2500 \times 1000 \text{ W};\ H = 300 \text{ m};\ \eta = 0.85.$$

$$2500 \times 10^3 = \gamma QH \times 0.85; \quad Q = \frac{2500 \times 10^3}{9810 \times 300 \times 0.85} = 1.0 \text{ m}^3/\text{s}.$$

$$V = C_V\sqrt{2gH} = 0.98 \times 4.43 \times \sqrt{300} = 75.2 \text{ m/s}.$$

$$Q = \frac{\pi d^2}{4} \times V;\ d^2 = \frac{4Q}{\pi V};\ d^2 = \frac{4 \times 1.0}{\pi \times 75.2} = 0.017 \text{ m}^2;\ d = 0.13 \text{ m} = 13 \text{ cm. (Ans.)}$$

$$U = C_U\sqrt{2gH} = 34.53 \text{ m/s}.$$

$$D = \frac{60U}{\pi N} = \frac{60 \times 34.53}{\pi \times 1000} = 0.659 \text{ m} = 65.9 \text{ cm.(Ans.)}$$

$$m = \frac{D}{d} = \frac{65.9}{13} = 5.07$$

$$Z = 0.5m + 15 = 0.5 \times 5.07 + 15$$

$$= 17.53 \text{ say } 18. \text{ (Ans.)}$$

Example 19.20 A Pelton wheel generates 3000 kW, when working under a head of 300 m. The overall efficiency is 85% and $C_V = 0.98$. If diameter of the nozzle is 100 mm, find the number of jets.

$P = 3000$ kW; efficiency = 85% = 0.85; $C_V = 0.98$; $H = 300$ m; $d = 100$ mm = 0.1 m.

$$V = C_V\sqrt{2gH} = 0.98 \times 4.43 \times \sqrt{300} = 75.2 \text{ m/s}.$$

$$P = \gamma Q H \eta; Q = \frac{P}{\gamma H \eta}; Q = \frac{3000 \times 10^3}{9810 \times 300 \times 0.85} = 1.2 \text{ m}^3/\text{s}.$$

$$\text{Discharge through each nozzle} = \frac{\pi \times 0.1^2}{4} \times 75.2 = 0.591 \text{ m}^3/\text{s}.$$

$$\text{Therefore no. of jets} = \frac{1.2}{0.591} = 2.03 \text{ say 2 jets. (Ans.)}$$

19.6.11 Some design parameters for turbines

Some design parameters like the range of head, specific speed etc., of the various turbines are given below:

Table 19.1 **Types of turbines and ranges of important parameters**

Type of turbine design parameter	Pelton wheel	Francis turbine	Kaplan turbine	Tubular turbine
Head in m	1500–300	500–30	70–10	10–3
Specific speed	8.5–60*	50–300	250–850	850–1000
Efficiency %	89	93	93	91
Speed ratio	0.43–0.48	0.58–1.0	1.0–2.0	1.0–2.0
Flow ratio	–	0.15–0.30	About 0.70	About 0.70

* For higher specific speeds multi-jets are used.

19.6.12 Cavitation in turbines

In Pelton turbines, there is possibility of cavitation occurring at the jet nozzle. In reaction turbines the region where cavitation commences is at the top portion of the draft tubes. The Thomas' cavitation number

$$\sigma = \frac{H_a - h_v - h_s}{H}. \tag{19.41}$$

has been found to be a very useful parameter to study cavitation. To avoid cavitation,

$$\sigma > \sigma_{cr}. \tag{19.42}$$

σ_{cr} is found to be a function of the specific speed of the turbine.

19.6.13 Unit quantities to study turbine performance

The non-dimensional numbers associated with turbines,

$$\pi_1 = \frac{Q}{ND^3}, \pi_2 = \frac{gH}{N^2D^2}; \pi_3 = \frac{P}{\rho D^5 N^3}; \text{ and } \pi_4 = \frac{\mu}{\rho D^2 N}$$

are sufficient to study the performance of a turbine under varying parameters. However simplified quantities can be used for a given turbine to study its performance under varying heads, discharge, and speed.

Combinations of the π terms can also be used for studying the characteristics.

$$\pi_5 = \frac{1}{\sqrt{\pi_2}} = \frac{D}{g} \times \frac{N}{\sqrt{H}}$$

$$\pi_6 = \frac{\pi_1}{\pi_2^{1/2}} = \frac{Q}{ND^3} \times \frac{ND}{\sqrt{gH}} = \frac{1}{D^3 g} \times \frac{Q}{\sqrt{H}}$$

Instead of using π_5 and π_6, it is conventional to use the terms N_u and Q_u known as unit speed and unit discharge. It is defined as the speed and discharge of the turbine when (theoretically only) working under unit head.

$$N \propto \sqrt{H};\ N = k_1 \times \sqrt{H}$$

When $H = 1, N = N_u = k_1 \times \sqrt{1} = k_1$

Hence $N_u = N/\sqrt{H}$ known as the unit speed.

Similarly it can be shown that $Q_u = Q/\sqrt{H}$ known as the unit discharge.

The unit power is also derived as $P_u = P/H^{3/2}$

The quantity N_u can be used to find the speed of the turbine for any head H_2 using the formula $N_2 = N_u \times \sqrt{H_2}$. Similarly, the values of Q_2 and P_2 can also be worked out.

Example 19.21 A turbine operates at 200 rpm under a head of 30 m when the discharge is 8 m^3/s. If the efficiency is 90%, find the speed, discharge and power when operating under a head of 25 m.

$$N_1 = 200 \text{ rpm};\quad Q_1 = 8 \text{ m}^3/\text{s};\ H_1 = 25 \text{ m};\ \eta = 0.9$$

$$P = \gamma Q_1 H_1 \eta = 9810 \times 8 \times 25 \times 0.9 \text{ W} = 2118.96 \text{ kW}.$$

$$N_u = \frac{N_1}{\sqrt{H_1}} = \frac{200}{\sqrt{30}} = 36.51;\ N_2 = N_u \times \sqrt{H_2} = 36.51 \times \sqrt{25} = 182.57 \text{ rpm. (Ans)}$$

$$Q_u = \frac{Q_1}{\sqrt{H_1}} = \frac{8}{\sqrt{30}} = 1.46 \quad Q_2 = Q_u \times \sqrt{H_2} = 1.46 \times \sqrt{25} = 7.3 \text{ m}^3/\text{s (Ans)}$$

$$P_n = \frac{P}{H_1^{3/2}} = \frac{2118.96}{30^{3/2}} = 12.896;\ P_2 = P_u \times H_2^{3/2} = 12.896 \times 25^{3/2} = 1612 \text{ kW. (Ans)}$$

In the derivation of the equations, apart from the similarity of the turbine, the similarity of the velocity diagrams at inlet and outlet of the turbine is assumed. Hence care should be taken that the value of H_2 should not be too much different from the value of H for which the unit speed is derived so that the range of applicability holds good.

The concept of unit quantities is used to experimentally study the performance of a turbine. The turbine with a particular gate opening and a head of H, increases its speed when the load on the turbine is decreased. In such a condition, the discharge, power and efficiency also will change. Figure 19.17(a) depicts the variation of unit discharge with unit speed for a Pelton turbine, a Kaplan turbine and a Francis turbine.

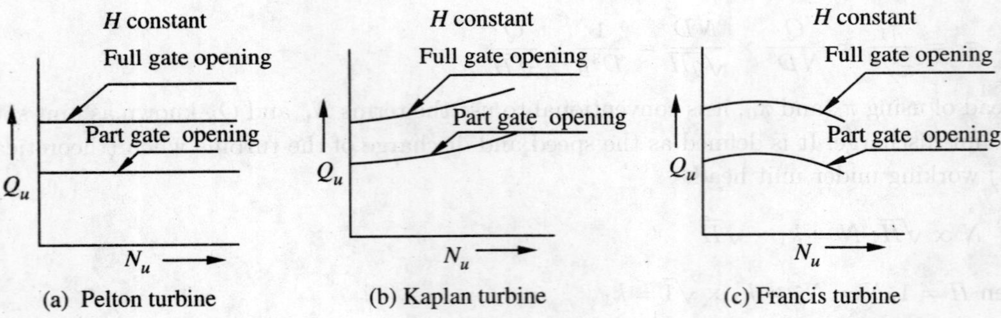

Fig. 19.17 *Change of unit discharge with unit speed for turbines.*

It may be noted that in the case of a Pelton turbine, the unit discharge is constant. This is because the jet flow is not affected by the speed of the turbine.

In case of the Kaplan turbine, for a given head, the discharge increases with the speed in certain ranges. This is because w hen the velocity triangles are assumed to be similar, the velocity of flow through the turbine increases with speed. The variation of Q_u with N_u is schematically shown in Fig. 19.17(b). The curve start from a particular value of unit discharge because there will be flow through the turbine even when the turbine does not rotate. Q_u increases with N_u.

The Francis turbine can have some tendency for increase in discharge with speed in some range. But the Francis turbine is an inward flow turbine. Hence as the speed is increased, the angular velocity will create a centrifugal head opposing the motion and the effective head will be reduced. The combined effect of the two is reflected in the variation of Q_u with N_u in Fig.19.17(c). The figures also schematically show the variation due to change in gate opening.

19.6.14 Some aspects of operation of hydro-power plants

19.6.14.1 Synchronous speed

Turbines are directly coupled to generators. The frequency of power generation f is to be kept a constant. In India it is 50 cycles per second. If p is the number of poles in the generator (p should be an even number, preferably exactly divisible by four), the speed of the generator and the turbine should be $N_s = \dfrac{120f}{p}$, known as the synchronous speed.

19.6.14.2 The load and speed

The electrical load varies from time to time and when there is breakdown in supply, the load can even be zero. At lower loads, the speed of the generator and turbine can increase (when load is zero, it can run at high speed termed as the runaway speed). When the load is increased, the speed is reduced. Maintaining a constant frequency needs constant speed of the turbine. The mechanism for maintaining a speed close to the normal speed is called governing.

19.6.14.3 Governing of turbines

When the load is rejected, the discharge reaching the turbine blades (or buckets) can be reduced either by operation of the gates or valves, or by deflecting the flow. The mechanism can be a centrifugal governor with servo-motor and links. When the load is increased, more flow is to be allowed to reach the turbine. Decrease or increase in discharge in the penstock can lead to high water hammer pressures which can endanger the penstock. (Please see Chapter 18 for a discussion on water hammers). Details about the mechanism of governing is not discussed in this book.

19.6.14.4 Water hammer and surge tanks

When the discharge in the penstock is suddenly changed, pressure waves as explained in Chapter 18 will be transmitted in the penstock. It is costly to design the penstocks for high water hammer pressures. An economical and safe method is to provide a surge tank at the end of the penstock near the turbine. Surge tanks are of different designs, the simplest being a vertical shaft and a tank above. A higher pressure in the penstock is released as it is allowed to flow into the surge tank. When there is a high demand of water for the turbine to take up high load, the surge tank can supply water to the turbine until flow is established in the penstock. A more detailed design of this surge tank is beyond the scope of this book.

REVIEW QUESTIONS AND PROBLEMS

19.1 Define the term turbo-machines.
19.2 How are turbo-machines classified?
19.3 Differentiate between turbines and pumps.
19.4 Name different parts of a centrifugal pump
19.5 Explain the principles of the working of a turbine
19.6 What is the function of volute casing?
19.7 What is priming? Why is priming needed in centrifugal pumps and not in reciprocating pumps.
19.8 Explain free and forced vortex flow.
19.9 Obtain an expression for the minimum starting speed of a centrifugal pump?
19.10 Draw a typical inlet and outlet velocity triangle of a centrifugal pump.
19.11 Define velocity of whirl and velocity of flow, clearly specifying their importance.
19.12 Obtain an expression for the work done by the impeller of a centrifugal pump per second per unit weight of water.
19.13 Define manometric head in centrifugal pumps.
19.14 What is the principle of a diffuser pump?
19.15 What are the causes of cavitation in centrifugal pumps?
19.16 What is net positive suction head?
19.17 Define specific speed of a centrifugal pump, giving its importance.
19.18 Derive the expression for specific speed.
19.19 Draw the characteristic curves of a centrifugal pump
19.20 Explain the classification of pumps.
19.21 Show that the rise of pressure head in the impeller of a centrifugal pump is given by $\frac{1}{2g}\left(V_{f_1}^2 + V_2^2 - V_{f_2}^2 \text{ cosec}^2\phi\right)$, where subscript 1 refers to inlet and 2 refers to outlet.
19.21b What are the model laws for interpreting model test results on a centrifugal pump?
19.21c Show how the characteristics of a centrifugal pump gets modified by changing the speed.
19.21d Explain how the characteristics of a centrifugal pump change when the diameter of the impeller is reduced.
19.21e Show the change in characteristics of a centrifugal pump combination (i) when identical pumps are connected in series; (ii) when they are connected parallel.
19.21f What are the important considerations for selection of a pump to meet the requirements of a system.
19.22 Define a turbine. Explain Eulers momemt of momentum principle.
19.23 Distinguish between impulse turbines and reaction turbines.
19.24 Explain the terms hydraulic efficiency; mechanical efficiency; overall efficiency of a turbine.
19.25 How is a Kaplan turbine different from a Francis turbine?
19.26 Give the range of specific speed values for a Kaplan turbine.
19.27 Why is the Kaplan turbine best suited for variable loads?

19.28 What type of hydraulic turbine will you select when the head is (i) 200 m, (ii) 60 m, (iii) 20 m and (iv) 5 m.

19.29 Explain with sketches the working of a Francis turbine. What are the purposes of a draft tube?

19.31 Explain with a sketch the principle of operation of a Kaplan turbine. Give its characteristics details.

19.32 Describe the Pelton wheel bucket and justify its shape.

19.33 State the condition for maximum hydraulic efficiency of a Pelton wheel.

19.34 According to hydraulic action and direction of flow, how will you classify a Pelton wheel?

19.35 Sketch the velocity triangles for a Pelton wheel blade.

19.36 How will you decide the number of jets for a Pelton wheel?

19.37 What is cavitation? How does it occur in turbines?

19.38 Describe methods to avoid cavitation in water turbines.

19.39 What are the factors which affect the overall efficiency of a hydraulic turbine?

19.40 Define unit speed, unit discharge and unit power for a turbine. Explain the use of the concept of unit quantities.

19.41 A centrifugal pump has an inner diameter of 0.4 m and an outer diameter of 0.9 m. What is the minimum starting speed required so that it develops a head of 12 m.

19.42 A centrifugal pump has a 25 cm diameter impeller, an outlet width of 5 cm and runs at 1100 rpm delivering water against a head of 11 m. The vanes are curved backwards 30° with the periphery at the outlet. The manometric efficiency of the pump is 90%. Calculate the discharge

19.43 A centrifugal pump is used to pump a liquid of sp.gravity 1.25 at the rate of 3000 l/minute against a pressure of 3 kg/cm^2. Find the head of the liquid and power required if the overall efficiency is 65%.

19.44 A centrifugal pump has an impeller diameter of 30 cm and an outlet width of 5 cm. The vanes are curved back to an angle of 30° with the periphery. Find the discharge if it develops a head of 15 m when rotating at a speed of 1200 rpm. Assume manometric efficiency of 0.95.

19.45 The following observations were made in laboratory test on a centrifugal pump. The diameter of the suction pipe was 15 cm. Diameter of the delivery pipe was 10 cm. Discharge = 0.026 m^3/s. The gauge on the delivery side is kept 0.6 m above the gauge on the suction side. The pressure on the suction gauge was −3.1 m of water. The delivery gauge indicated a pressure of 138 kPa. If the output of the motor indicated 6.4 kW, what is the overall efficiency? [Hint: Add the height between the gauges also to get H_m].

19.46 A centrifugal pump has an impeller of 60 cm diameter. It delivers 0.75 m^3/s against a head of 75 m. The speed is 1200 rpm and the width of the outlet is 7.5 cm. If the mechanical efficiency is 95% and hydraulic efficiency 80%, find the power required, blade angle at outlet and overall efficiency.

19.47 A centrifugal pump works against a head of 8 m and pumps 1500 litres/s, while running at a speed of 200 rpm. Diameter of the impeller at the outlet is 1.3 m and the area at the outer periphery is 0.6 m^2. Assuming the ratio of the external to the internal diameter to be 3 and the blade angle at the outlet to be 30°, find (i) the hydraulic efficiency, (ii) the power required and (iii) the minimum starting speed.

19.48 A single stage centrifugal pump with impeller diameter of 30 cm rotates at 200 rpm. It delivers 3 m^3/s of water at a head of 30 m with an efficiency of 70%. Find the number of stages and diameter of each impeller of a similar multistage pump to deliver 5 m^3/s of water at a head of 200 m when rotating at 1500 rpm

19.49 Find the number of stages of pumps required to take water from a deep well under a total head of 89 m. All pumps are identical and are running at 800 rpm. The specific speed of each pump is given as 25 while the capacity of each pump is 0.16 m^3/s.

19.50 The impeller of a centrifugal pump is 300 mm in diameter, 50 mm wide at the periphery and has blades whose tip angles are inclined backwards 30°. Calculate the speed of water leaving the impeller. The pump delivers 0.4 m^3/s and the impeller rotates at 1440 rpm. Assuming the pump is designed to admit radically, calculate the shaft power required and the total lift of the pump, taking mechanical efficiency as 95% and hydraulic efficiency as 75%.

19.51 Two geometrically similar pumps are running at the same speed of 1000 rpm. One pump has impeller diameter of 0.3 m and lifts water at the rate of 20 l/s against a head of 15 m. Determine the head and impeller diameter of the other pump to deliver half the discharge

19.52 A centrifugal pump running at 1800 rpm delivers 4530 l/minute against a total head of 24 m and requires 14.92 kW. Determine the discharge, head and power for the pump when it runs at 2000 rpm for a homologous operation.

19.53 A 1/5 model of a pump was tested in a laboratory at 1000 rpm. The head developed and the power input at the best efficiency point was found to be 8 m and 30 kW respectively. The efficiency was found to be 75%. If the prototype pump has to work against a head of 25 m, determine its working speed, the power required to drive it and the ratio of the flow rates handled by the two pumps. If we take into account the scale effect what will be power requirement for the pump.

19.54 Water approaches a rotor in a turbomachine with an absolute velocity of 10 m/s in the radial direction. At this point, the rotational speed of the rotor is 20 m/s. Define the magnitude and direction of the relative velocity at this point.

19.55 The external diameter of an inward flow reaction turbine is 45 cms. The width of the wheel at the inlet is 12 cms, and the velocity of flow at the inlet is 1.2 m/s, find the rate of flow passing through the turbine.

19.56 A Francis turbine develops 130 kW of power operating under a head of 15 m. The overall efficiency is 80%. The radial velocity is $0.25\ H\ (2gH)^{1/2}$ and the tangential velocity is $0.75\ (2gH)^{1/2}$. The runner speed is 120 rpm. If the hydraulic efficiency is 85%, determine (i) the diameter of the runner, (ii) guide vane angle, (iii) the runner blade angle and (iv) the discharge through the turbine

19.57 The following data were obtained from a Kaplan turbine operating under a head of 25 m. Power = 60000 kW; overall efficiency = 90%; speed ratio = 1.6; flow ratio = 0.5; hub diameter = 0.35 times the outer diameter. Find the diameter and the speed of the turbine.

19.58 A Kaplan turbine develops 60,000 kW at an overall efficiency of 68% under a head of 25 metres. If the speed ratio is 1.60, the flow ratio is 0.5 and the boss diameter is 0.35 times the runner diameter, find the diameter of the runner and the speed of the turbine.

19.59 A Kaplan turbine runner is to be designed to develop 9000 kW. The net available head is 40 m. Assume a speed ratio of 1.1, flow ratio of 0.65 and total efficiency of 89%. The diameter of boss is half the diameter of the runner. Find the diameter of the runner, its speed and the specific speed of the turbine.

19.60 A Pelton wheel is to develop 13250 kW under a net head of 800 m while running at a speed of 600 rpm. If the coefficient of jet = 0.97, speed ratio 0.46 and the ratio of jet diameter is 1/15 of wheel diameter, calculate (i) number of jets, (ii) diameter of jets, (iii) diameter of pitch circle and (iv) quantity of water supplied to wheels. Assume overall efficiency as 85%.

19.61 A Pelton wheel runs under a head of 400 m at a speed of 1000 rpm. It develops 5000 kW. Find the least diameter of the jet and the pitch circle diameter of the wheel. Assume overall efficiency of turbine as 85%. $C_V = 0.99$ and speed ratio as 0.45. Also find the number of buckets. Assume any other data required.

19.62 A Pelton wheel working under a head of 500 m produces 13 MW at 430 rpm. If the efficiency of the wheel is 85%, determine (i) discharge of turbine (ii) the diameter of the wheel. Assume $C_V = 0.98$ and speed ratio as 0.45.

19.63 A twin jet Pelton wheel is required to generate 7500 kW when the available head at the nozzle is 400 m. Assuming coefficient of velocity as 0.98, overall wheel efficiency as 80%, speed ratio as 0.46, reduction in relative velocity as 15% and that the jet is deflected through 165° by the bucket, find the diameter of each jet, total flow in litres and the force exerted by a single jet on buckets in the tangential direction.

ANSWERS

19.41. 363.95 rpm; **19.42.** 0.138 m^3/s;**19.43.** 24 m; 22.638 kW. **19.44.** 0.289 m^3/s; **19.45.** 0.69. **19.46.** 703.7 kW; 21.47°; 0.784 **19.47.** 62.1%; 189.57 kW; 195.23 rpm; **19.48.** 7; 0.39 m. **19.49.** 3. **19.50.** 11.61 m/s; 100.54 kW; 13.7 m; **19.51.** 9.45m; 0.238 m; **19.52.** 5034 l/minute; 29.63 m; 20.47 kW; **19.54.** 353.55 rpm; 4143.6 kW; 1/44.19; 3794.5 kW; **19.54.** 22.36 m/s; 26.57°; **19.55.** 0.204 m^3/s; **19.56.** 2.048 m; 23.8°; 126.27°; 1.104 m^3/s; **19.57.** 5.967 m; 113.4 rpm; **19.58.** 6.867 m; 98.46 rpm; **19.59.** 1.544 m; 381.7 rpm; 359.47; **19.60.** 2; 12.2 cm; 1.834 m; 1.986 m^3/s; **19.61.** 15 cm; 76 cm; 18; **19.62.** 3.118 m^3/s; 1.976 m; **19.63.** 13.24 cm; 2390 l/s; 104 kN.

20 Positive Displacement Pumps

Introduction—Reciprocating pumps—Single acting—Double acting-Slip velocity and acceleration head—Theoretical indicator diagram—Effect of acceleration head and friction head on the indicator diagram—Air vessels—Work saved in overcoming friction—Characteristic curves—Rotary pumps—Gear pumps—Vane pumps—Comparison with centrifugal pumps

20.1 Introduction

Positive displacement pumps are pumps in which the necessary energy or head to raise the fluid to the required height is transferred by the displacement of the fluid caused by the to and fro motion of the plunger in a cylinder or by the rotating movement of the displacer in a closely fitting chamber. Hence depending upon the manner in which the energy is transferred to the fluid, the positive displacement pumps are classified into

1. Reciprocating pumps
2. Rotary pumps

20.2 Reciprocating Pumps

Reciprocating pumps impart energy to the fluid by the reciprocating (back and forth) action of the plunger or a piston in a cylinder, which gets alternately filled and emptied.

20.2.1 Main components

The main components of a reciprocating pump are:

1) Plunger or a piston
2) Cylinder
3) Connecting rod and crank connected to a motor
4) Suction pipe with inlet valve
5) Delivery pipe with outlet valve

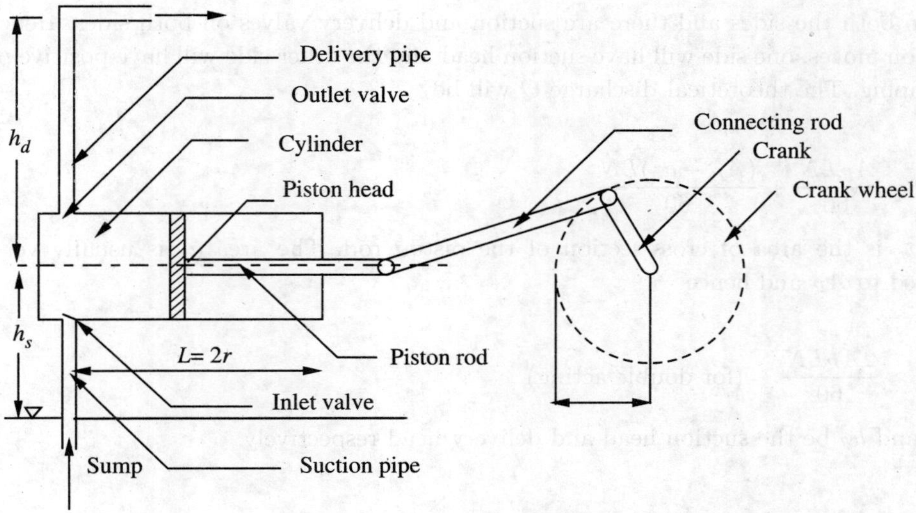

Fig. 20.1 *Reciprocating pump*

20.2.2 Working principle

When the motor is switched on, the crank rotates causing the piston or plunger to move inside the cylinder from the initial extreme position (suction stroke). This causes the inlet valve to open and the fluid to enter into the cylinder closely following the piston head till the end of the suction stroke. The outlet valve remains closed during the suction stroke. Now the direction of the movement of the piston is changed and the fluid inside the cylinder is pushed into the delivery side (delivery stroke). During the delivery stroke the outlet valve or the delivery valve remains opened and the suction valve gets closed. This process is repeated till the motor is switched off.

In the case of single acting reciprocating pumps, for each revolution of the crank wheel there is one delivery stroke and one suction stroke. Hence the average volume of fluid swept is calculated thus.

Let r be the radius of the crank wheel.
Length of the cylinder $L = 2r$.
Let N be the speed in rpm.
Let D_P be the diameter of the piston head or the plunger.
Let A_P be the area of the piston head or the plunger.
Volume swept per revolution $= A_P L$.

$$\text{Average discharge per second } Q = \frac{A_P L N}{60}. \tag{20.1}$$

In double acting reciprocating pumps, the cylinder is connected to the suction and delivery pipes on both the sides and there are suction and delivery valves on both sides. Hence when the piston moves, one side will have suction head and the other side will have positive pressure for pumping. The theoretical discharge Q will be

$$Q = \frac{A_P L N}{60} + \frac{(A_P - a_r) L N}{60}, \tag{20.2}$$

where a_r is the area of cross-section of the piston rod. The area a_r is usually very small compared to A_P and hence

$$Q \approx \frac{2 A_P L N}{60} \quad \text{(for double acting)} \tag{20.3}$$

Let h_s and h_d be the suction head and delivery head respectively.

$$\text{In both cases theoretical power required to drive the pump} = \gamma Q\,(h_d + h_s) \tag{20.4}$$

20.2.3 Slip

The actual discharge may be smaller than the theoretical discharge if some water escapes through the suction valve or by the side of the piston during a delivery stroke. Then the difference is called the slip and will be positive.

$$\text{Slip} = Q_{th} - Q_a. \tag{20.5}$$

$$\text{Percentage slip} = \frac{Q_{th} - Q_a}{Q_{th}} \times 100\%. \tag{20.6}$$

If the delivery pipe length is small, it may so happen that more water is delivered through the delivery valve because of the late closing of the suction valve. In such a case, the slip can be negative.

$$\text{Coefficient of discharge } C_d = Q_a / Q_{th}. \tag{20.7}$$

Example 20.1 A single acting reciprocating pump has a piston diameter 40 cm and a stroke of 30 cm. The pump lifts water to a height of 12 m. The speed of the pump is 50 rpm. Actual average discharge of the pump is 0.030 m^3/s. Find the slip and percentage slip. Calculate the theoretical power required to drive the pump.

Diameter D_P of the piston = 40 cm = 0.4 m; length of the stroke $L = 2r$ = 30 cm = 0.3 m; H = 12 m.

Speed $N = 50$ rpm; $Q_a = 0.03$ m^3/s.

$$Q_{th} = AL(N/60) = \frac{\pi \times 0.4^2 \times 0.3 \times 50}{4 \quad 60} = 0.0314 \text{ m}^3/\text{s}.$$

$$\text{Slip} = 0.03142 - 0.03 = 0.00142 \text{ m}^3/\text{s}.$$

$$\% \text{ slip} = \frac{0.00142}{0.03142} \times 100 = 4.5\%. \text{ (Ans.)}$$

Theoretical power required $= \gamma\, Q\, H = 9810 \times 0.03142 \times 12$ W $= 3.699$ kW. (Ans.)

20.3 Velocity and Acceleration of the Piston and the Fluid

The piston rod is assumed to execute simple harmonic motion (SHM) (this is justified if the length of the connecting rod is large compared to the radius of the crank). The distance moved by the piston,

$$x = r - r\cos\theta = r - \cos\omega t, \tag{20.8}$$

where ω is the angular velocity and is equal to $\frac{\theta}{t}$. When $t = 0$, the piston is at the beginning of the suction stroke.

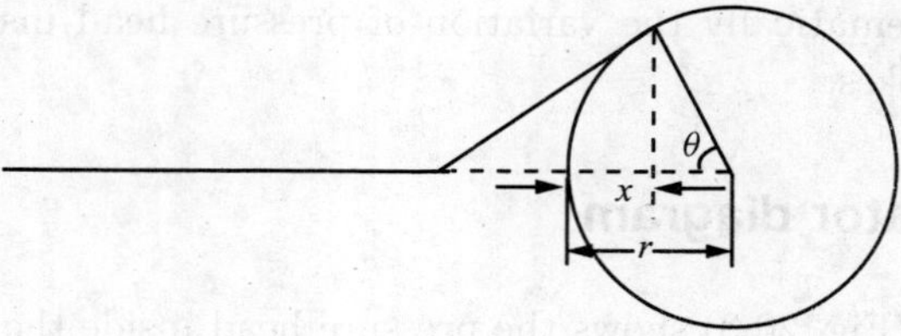

Fig. 20.2 *Motion of piston (SHM)*

$$\text{Velocity of the piston, } v_p = \frac{dx}{dt} = r\sin\omega t \times \omega = r\omega\sin\omega t. \tag{20.9}$$

$$\text{Velocity of the fluid on the suction side } v_s = \frac{v_p A_p}{a_s} = \frac{A_p}{a_s}.r\omega\sin\omega t, \tag{20.10}$$

where a_s is the area of cross-section of the suction pipe.

$$\text{Acceleration of the piston, } f_p = \frac{d^2x}{dt^2} = r\omega^2\cos\omega t. \tag{20.11}$$

$$\text{Acceleration of the fluid on the suction side } f_s = \frac{f_p A_p}{a_s} = \frac{A_p}{a_s}.r\omega^2\cos\omega t. \tag{20.12}$$

$$\text{Force} = \frac{l_s a_s \gamma}{g}.f_s = \frac{l_s a_s \gamma}{g}.\frac{A_p}{a_s}\ r\omega^2 \cos \omega t. \tag{20.13}$$

$$\text{Pressure} = \text{force}/a_s = \frac{l_s \gamma}{g}.\frac{A_p}{a_s}.r\omega^2 \cos \omega t. \tag{20.14}$$

$$\text{Acceleration head on the suction side} = \text{pressure}/\gamma = \frac{l_s}{g} \cdot \frac{A_p}{a_s}.r\omega^2 \cos \omega t. \tag{20.15}$$

$$\text{Velocity of the fluid on the delivery side} = \frac{A_p}{a_d}.r\omega \sin \omega t, \tag{20.16}$$

where a_d is the area of cross-section of the delivery pipe.

$$\text{Acceleration of the fluid on the delivery side} = \frac{A_p}{a_d}.r\omega^2 \cos \omega t. \tag{20.17}$$

$$\text{Acceleration head on the delivery side} = \frac{l_d}{g}\frac{A_p}{a_d}.r\omega^2 \cos \omega t. \tag{20.18}$$

20.4 Indicator Diagram

This diagram shows schematically the variation of pressure head inside the cylinder during suction and delivery strokes.

20.4.1 Ideal indicator diagram

Ideal indicator diagram (Fig. 20.3) shows the pressure head inside the cylinder due to suction and delivery heads only with reference to the atmospheric pressure head H_a

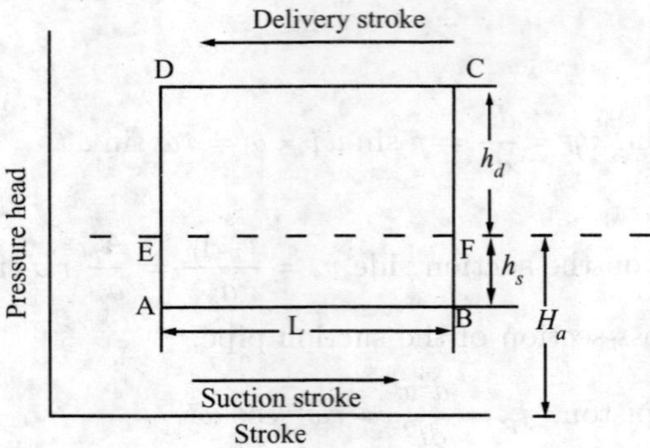

Fig. 20.3 *Ideal indicator diagram*

Work done per revolution = C × area of the rectangle ABCDA = $CL\ (h_s + h_d)$, where $C = \gamma A_P$

Theoretical power required $P_s = \dfrac{\gamma A_P L N(h_s + h_d)}{60}$ for a single acting pump. (20.19a)

$$P_d = \frac{2\gamma A_P L N(h_s + h_d)}{60} \text{ for double acting pump.} \quad (20.19b)$$

20.4.2 Effect of acceleration head on the indicator diagram

The acceleration head varies linearly from the beginning of the suction or delivery stroke to the end of the suction or delivery stroke, the maximum magnitude being $\frac{l}{g}\frac{A_P}{a}\omega^2 r$ (i.e., when $t = n\ \pi$ and $n = 0, 1, 2.$ etc.,). Here l and a refer to length and area of the suction pipe or the delivery pipe respectively and hence the corresponding acceleration head on the suction or delivery pipe can be obtained. The effect of acceleration head is to increase the suction head at the beginning of the suction stroke and reduce the suction head at the end of the suction stroke by the same magnitude. During delivery stroke, the acceleration head increases the pressure head at the beginning and reduces the pressure head at the end of the delivery stroke. Figure 20.4 gives the modified indicator diagram.

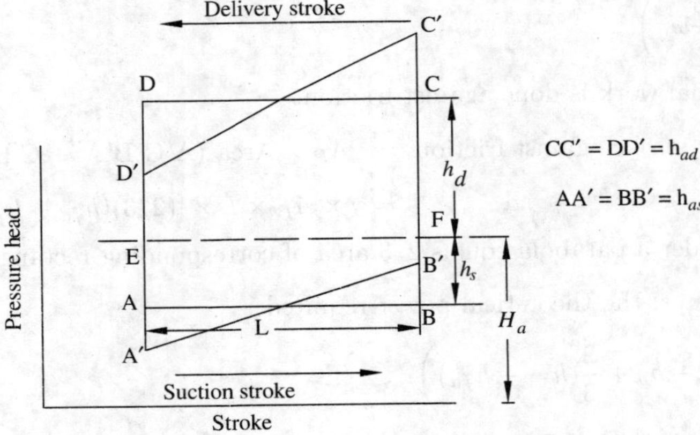

Fig. 20.4 *Effect of acceleration head on indicator diagram*

Work done per revolution = $\gamma A_P \times$ area A′B′C′D′ = $\gamma A_P \times$ area ABCD = $\gamma A_P \times L(h_a + h$
Theoretical power required is the same as in the case without acceleration.

20.4.3 Effect of friction on the indicator diagram

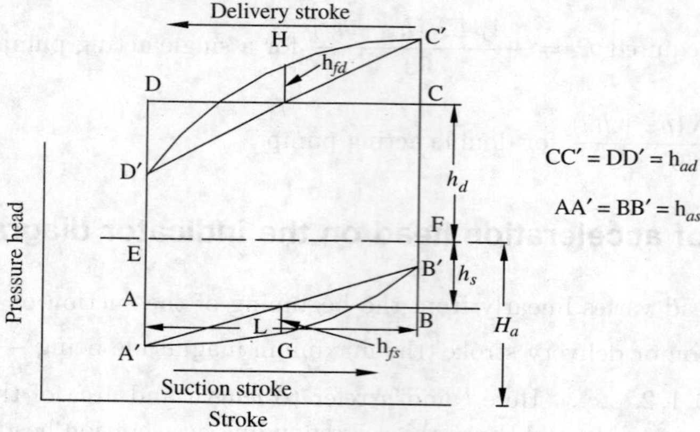

Fig. 20.5 *Effect of friction head on indicator diagram*

The velocity at a given time t is given by $\frac{A_P}{a}\omega r \sin\theta$. The velocity is zero at the beginning and end of the strokes and maximum at the middle, and the maximum friction head is given by

$$h_f = \frac{fl}{2gd}\left(\frac{A_P}{a}\omega r\right)^2, \tag{20.20}$$

In this case, additional work is done against friction.

$$\begin{aligned}\text{Work done per stroke against friction } &= \gamma A_P \times \text{Area (A}'\text{G B}'\text{A}' + \text{C}'\text{H D}'\text{C}') \\ &= \gamma \times A_P \times L \times [(2/3)(h_{fd} + h_{fs})].\end{aligned} \tag{20.21}$$

Note The area under a parabola equals 2/3 area of corresponding rectangle.

For single stroke pumps, the theoretical power required

$$P_s = \frac{\gamma A_P LN}{60}\left(h_s + h_d + \frac{2}{3}(h_{fs} + h_{fd})\right). \tag{20.22a}$$

and for double stroke pumps

$$P_d = \frac{\gamma 2 A_P LN}{60}\left(h_s + h_d + \frac{2}{3}(h_{fs} + h_{fd})\right). \tag{20.22b}$$

20.5 Separation and Cavitation in Reciprocating Pumps

When the pressure inside the cylinder during any time falls below the vapour pressure of the fluid at the prevailing temperature, vapour cavities will start forming and the flow will no longer be continuous (refer to Section 2.3). These cavities will later collapse resulting in very high local pressure, vibration and pitting causing damage to the pump. To prevent cavitation, it should be ensured that the pressure inside the cylinder does not fall below vapour pressure.

20.6 Maximum Permissible Speed

On the suction side, it can be observed that the atmosphere has to provide the necessary suction head, acceleration head, friction head, loss of head due to various valve fittings and head loss due to entry. Also it is essential that the pressure inside should not fall below vapour pressure. From the indicator diagram, it is clear that usually the critical point is the beginning of the suction stroke. Once the suction lift is fixed, it is the acceleration head which decides the speed, since vapour pressure at a given location is fixed and the other losses like friction losses are zero.

Atmospheric head = suction lift + acceleration head + vapour pressure, from which maximum permissible speed can be calculated.

Note In case the suction pipe is of short length and delivery pipe is long, the acceleration head for delivery stroke can be very large and maximum permissible speed may be governed by the condition at the end of delivery stroke. Also the separation on the delivery side depends upon the arrangement of the pipe (Fig. 20.6).

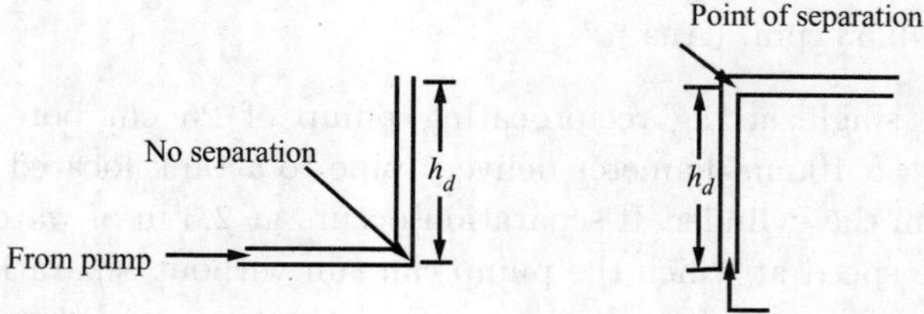

Fig. 20.6 *Position of bend in delivery pipe*

(i) *The delivery pipe runs first horizontally and then vertically*
In this case, considerable delivery head h_d is available at the end of the delivery stroke and there is no chance of separation at the bend. Hence the maximum permissible speed is calculated using the relation

$$H_a + h_d - h_{ad} = h_v. \tag{20.23}$$

(ii) *The pipe runs vertically first and then horizontal*
In this case, the delivery head at the end of the delivery stroke becomes zero and separation can occur at the bend which is at a height of h_d above the pump. The critical head at the bend is $H_a + h_d - h_{ad} - h_d = h_v$ The maximum permissible speed is calculated from the relation

$$H_a - h_{ad} = h_v. \tag{20.24}$$

Example 20.2 A single acting reciprocating pump has a cylinder of bore 9 cm and a stroke of 18 cm. Water is to be drawn from a sump 3 m below the axis of the cylinder through a 5 cm diameter and a 6 m long pipe. The pump delivers water to a tank at a height of 8 m through a 10 m long and 5 cm diameter pipe. If separation occurs at a pressure head of 2.5 m, find the maximum speed at which the pump can run. Take $\mathrm{H_m}$ = 10.3 m of water.

$D_P = 9$ cm $= 0$ .09 m; $L = 2r = 18$ cm $= 0.18$ m; $h_s = 3$m; $d_s = 5$ cm $= 0.05$ m; $l_s = 6$ m; $h_d = 8$ m; $l_d = 25$ cm; $d_d = 5$ cm $= 0.05$ m; $h_v = 2.5$ m; $H_a = 10.3$ m.

The acceleration head at the beginning of the suction stroke decides the maximum permissible speed.

$$H_a = h_s + h_{as} + h_v.$$

$$10.3 = 3 + h_{\mathrm{as}} + 2.5;\ h_{\mathrm{as}} = 10.3 - 5.5 = 4.8 \text{ m}.$$

$$h_{as} = 4.8 = \frac{l_s}{g}\frac{A_P}{a_s}\omega^2 r = \frac{6}{9.81} \times \frac{\pi \times .09^2 \times 4}{4 \times \pi \times 0.05^2} \times \omega^2 \times \frac{0.18}{2}.$$

$$\omega^2 = 26.91;\ \omega = 5.187 \text{ rad/s}.$$

$$N = \frac{\omega \times 60}{2\pi} = 49.53 \text{ rpm. (Ans.)}$$

Example 20.3 A single acting reciprocating pump of 25 cm bore and 40 cm stroke delivers water through a 10 cm diameter delivery pipe to a tank located at 15 m above and 20 m horizontally from the cylinder. If separation occurs at 2.3 m of water absolute, find the maximum permissible speed at which the pump can run without separation for the following two conditions. (i) The delivery pipe is horizontal from the pump and then vertical.(ii) The delivery pipe is vertical from the pump and then horizontal. Take atmospheric pressure as 10.3 m water.

$D_p = 0.25$ m; $d_d = 0.1$ m; $L = 0.4$ m; $h_v = 2.34$ m

In the first case, the critical point is at the start of the delivery pipe because the length of delivery pipe is maximum. In the second case, the bend is located high, but length of the delivery pipe is smaller.

Case (i) $l_{d_1} = 35$ m; $A_p = 0.0491$ m^2; $a_d = 7.85 \times 10^{-3}$ m^2; $r = L/2 = 0.2$.

$$h_{ad_1} = \frac{l_{d_1} A_p}{g a_d}\,\omega^2 r = \frac{35 \times 0.0491}{9.81 \times 7.85 \times 10^{-3}} \times 0.2\omega^2 = 4.463\,\omega^2.$$

$$H_a + h_d - h_{ad} = h_v$$

$$10.3 + 15 - 4.463\,\omega^2 = 2.3.$$

$$4.463\,\omega^2 = 23\ ;\quad \omega^2 = 5.153\ ;\ \omega = 2.27.$$

$$N = \frac{60 \times \omega}{2\pi} = \frac{60 \times 2.27}{2\pi} = 21.68 \text{ rpm. (Ans).}$$

Case (ii) $l_{d_2} = 20$ m; (after the critical point)

$$h_{ad_2} = \frac{l_{d_2} A_p}{g a_d}\omega^2 r = \frac{20 \times 0.0491}{9.81 \times 7.85 \times 10^{-3}} \times 0.2\,\omega^2 = 2.55\omega^2.$$

$$H_a - h_{ad} = h_v.$$

$$10.3 - 2.55\omega^2 = 2.3.$$

$$2.55\,\omega^2 = 8;\quad \omega^2 = 3.137;\ \omega = 1.771.$$

$$N = \frac{60 \times \omega}{2\pi} = \frac{60 \times 1.771}{2\pi} = 16.91 \text{ rpm. (Ans.)}$$

20.7 Air Vessels — Their Purpose and Principle of Working

Air vessels are closed pressure chambers, connected to the delivery and suction pipes very near the pump cylinder as shown in Fig 20.7. The vessels as the name implies have some air at the top portion and liquid on the bottom portion. As the pressure increases in the delivery pipe, liquid flows into the air vessel compressing the air inside and when the pressure is reduced, liquid from the air vessel flow into the pipe making the flow uniform. Thus the air vessel will act as a balancing mechanism for high pressure variations in the pipe.

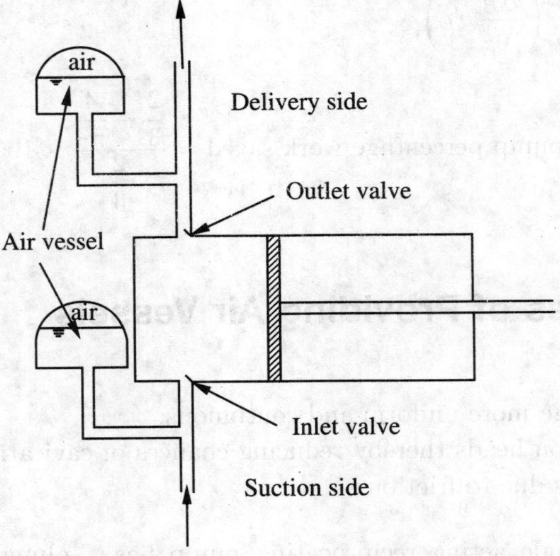

Fig. 20.7 *Pump fitted with air vessels*

20.7.1 Work saved against friction by fitting an air vessel

Without air vessel maximum velocity $V_{\max} = \dfrac{A_P}{a}\omega r$

$$H_{\text{fav}} = \frac{2}{3}\frac{fl}{2gd}\left(\frac{A_P}{a}\omega r\right)^2 \qquad (20.25)$$

(assuming parabolic variation)
With air vessel, the flow is uniform.

$$V = \frac{Q}{a} = \frac{A_P \times 2r \times N}{a \times 60}.$$

$$\text{Substituting } \omega = \frac{2\pi r \times N}{60}$$

$$h_f = \frac{fl}{2gd} \times V^2 = \frac{fl}{2gd}\left(\frac{A_P}{a}\frac{\omega r}{\pi}\right)^2 \qquad (20.26)$$

(for single acting pump)

The power required will be proportional to head loss due to friction.

Therefore percentage work saved

$$= \frac{\dfrac{2}{3}\dfrac{f\,l}{2g\,d}\left(\dfrac{A_P}{a}\omega\,r\right)^2 - \dfrac{f\,l}{2g\,d}\left(\dfrac{A_P}{a}\dfrac{\omega}{2\pi}2r\right)^2}{\dfrac{2}{3}\dfrac{f\,l}{2g\,d}\left(\dfrac{A_P}{a}\omega\,r\right)^2} \times 100\% = \frac{\dfrac{2}{3} - \dfrac{1}{\pi^2}}{\dfrac{2}{3}} \times 100\% = 84.8\%.$$

For double acting pump percentage work saved $= \dfrac{\dfrac{2}{3} - \dfrac{4}{\pi^2}}{\dfrac{2}{3}} \times 100\% = 39.2\%.$ (20.27)

20.8 Advantages of Providing Air Vessels

(a) Makes the discharge more uniform and continuous.
(b) Reduces acceleration heads thereby reducing chances of cavitation even at high speeds.
(c) Reduces power loss due to friction.

Example 20.4 A single acting reciprocating pump has a plunger 200 mm and stroke 400 mm. The diameter of the delivery pipe is 100 mm and length 40 m. Find the power saved by fitting an air vessel on the delivery side of the pump. The speed of the pump is 60 rpm and $f = 0.02$. Assume SHM.

$D_P = 200$ mm $= 0.2$ m; $L = 2r = 400$ mm $= 0.4$ m; $r = 0.2$ m.
$d_d = 100$ mm $= 0.1$ m; $N = 60$ rpm; $f = 0.02$.
$A_p = 0.0314\ \text{m}^2$; $a_d = 7.854 \times 10^{-3}\ \text{m}^2$; $\omega = \dfrac{2\pi N}{60} = 6.283$ c/s

(i) Without air vessel

$$V_{d\max} = \frac{A_P}{a_d}\omega r = \frac{0.0314}{7.854 \times 10^{-3}} \times 6.283 \times 0.2 = 5.0264\ \text{m/s}.$$

$$Q = \frac{A_P L N}{60} = \frac{0.0314 \times 0.4 \times 60}{60} = 0.0126\ \text{m}^3/\text{s}.$$

$$h_{fd\max} = \frac{fl}{2gd_d}V_{d\max}^2 = \frac{0.02 \times 40}{2g \times 0.10} \times 5.0264^2 = 10.302\ \text{m}$$

$$h_{fd\text{av}} = \frac{2}{3} \times h_{fd\max} = \frac{2}{3} \times 10.302 = 6.868\ \text{m}$$

Work done against friction $= \gamma Q \times h_{fd_{av}} = 9810 \times 0.0126 \times 6.868 = 848.93$ W

(ii) With air vessel

$$\text{uniform velocity } V_d = \frac{Q}{a_d} = \frac{0.0126 \times 4}{\pi \times 0.1^2} = 1.604\ \text{m/s}.$$

$$\text{head loss } h_d = \frac{flV_d^2}{2gd_d} = \frac{0.02 \times 40 \times 1.604^2}{2 \times 9.81 \times 0.1} = 1.0491\ \text{m}.$$

work done against friction $\gamma Q h_d = 9810 \times 0.0126 \times 1.0491 = 129.68$ W.

Therefore work saved $= 848.93 - 129.68 = 719.25$ W. (Ans.)

20.9 Characteristic Curves of Reciprocating Pumps

(a) Operating characteristic curves (speed N constant)

(i) Discharge versus head
(ii) Power input versus head
(iii) Overall efficiency versus head

Typical variation of the above curves are shown in Fig. 20.8

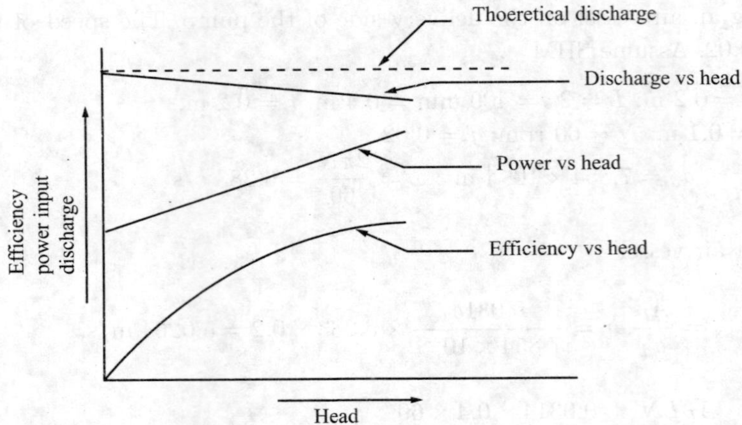

Fig. 20.8 *Characteristic curves (speed N constant)*

It can be seen that the variation of discharge with head is small.

20.10 Rotary Displacement Pumps

There are many types of rotary displacement pumps, out of which only the external gear pump and the vane pump are discussed here.

20.10.1 External gear pump

In the simplest form, these pumps consist of two identical spur gear wheels intermeshed together, which move inside a cylinder having a very fine clearance as shown in the Fig. 20.9. Shafts of one of the wheels is connected to the motor whereas the other will have idle motion. As the wheel rotates, the volume of liquid trapped between two consecutive teeth is displaced towards the delivery side.

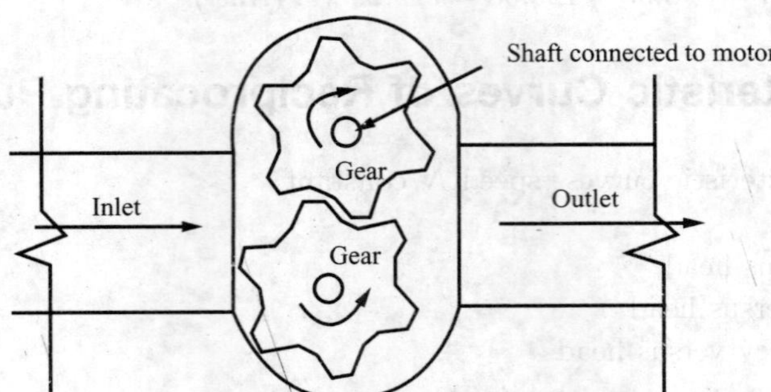

Fig. 20.9 *External gear pump*

If n is the number of teeth in each gear, b is the breadth, a is the area between the teeth and N is the number of revolutions per second,

$$\text{the volume swept per second} = (2abn) \times N60. \tag{20.28}$$

20.10.2 Vane pump

The vane pump (Fig. 20.10) consists of a number of vanes, which move inside the slots provided in a wheel which has eccentric motion with respect to the cylinder. These vanes touch the wall of the chamber due to centrifugal action when in motion. As the vanes move, the liquid between the vanes is pushed to the delivery side. In some cases, the vanes are spring loaded.

There are other types of rotary pumps like internal gear pump, lob type, swinging vane type, screw type etc., which will not be discussed here.

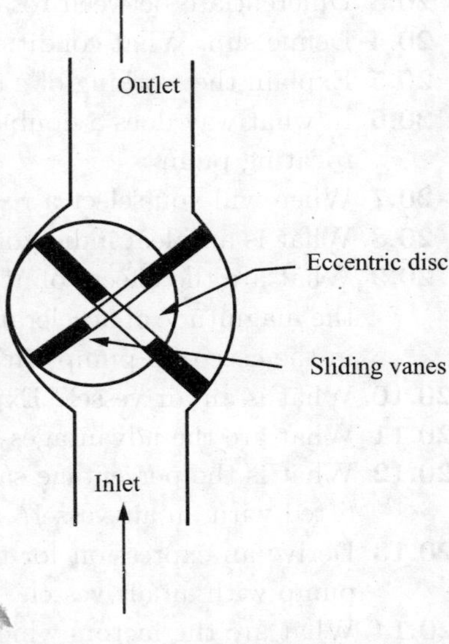

Fig. 20.10 *Sliding vane pump*

20.11 Comparison of Reciprocating Pumps and Centrifugal Pumps

Centrifugal pumps	Reciprocating pumps
(i) These pumps can run at higher speeds and hence the discharge is high	(i) The speed is less and hence the discharge is low. Has only little variation of discharge head.
(ii) The wear and tear is less because of less moving parts.	(ii) The wear and tear is more because of more moving parts.
(iii) As there are no valves, these pumps can handle grit, slurry etc.,	(iii) These pumps can handle only cleaner liquids.
(iv) They occupy less space and the maintenance cost is less even though they have slightly costlier initial expenses.	(iv) They occupy larger space but the installation costs are less.
(v) The flow is uniform.	(v) The flow is not uniform unless it is fitted with air vessels.
(vi) The efficiency is generally more.	(vi) The efficiency is generally less.
(vii) Requires priming.	(vii) Priming not required.
(viii) The delivery valve should be closed before switching on the pump.	(viii) The delivery valve should not be closed while working.

REVIEW QUESTIONS AND PROBLEMS

20.1 Explain the working of positive displacement pumps.

20.2 Explain classification of positive displacement pumps.

20.3 Differentiate between rotary pumps and rotodynamic pumps.

20.4 Define slip. What condition leads to a negative slip?

20.5 Explain the working of a single acting reciprocating pump.

20.6 In what way does a double acting reciprocating pump differ from a single acting reciprocating pump

20.7 When will you select a reciprocating pump for your use?

20.8 What is an ideal indicator diagram? Explain its features.

20.9 What are the effects of acceleration and friction on the ideal indicator diagram? Write the magnitude of acceleration head at the beginning, middle and end of a suction stroke in the case of a pump without an air vessel.

20.10 What is an air vessel? Explain the need for air vessels in reciprocating pumps.

20.11 What are the advantages of air vessel?

20.12 What is the percentage saving in friction heads of a double acting reciprocating pump fitted with an air vessel?

20.13 Derive an expression for the work saved against friction in the case of a single acting pump with an air vessel.

20.14 What are the factors which influence the speed of a reciprocating pump?

20.15 Define separation in a reciprocating pump.

20.16 Explain characteristic curves of a reciprocating pump?

20.17 Explain with neat sketches the working of an external gear pump.

20.18 Explain with neat sketches a vane pump.

20.19 A double acting reciprocating pump, with a cylinder of diameter 20 cm and a stroke of 30 cm is running at 40 rpm. It raises water through a height of 30 m. If the pump efficiency is 75%, find the power required to drive the pump. If the actual discharge is 0.012 m^3/s, find the slip and percentage slip.

20.20 A single acting reciprocating pump has a plunger of diameter 200 mm and a stroke length of 300 mm. It has to be driven at 60 rpm and with SHM. It draws water from a sump 3.6 m below the pump center line. Find the least diameter of the suction pipe, which is 4.5 m long in order to prevent separation at this speed. Separation occurs at a pressure of 2.6 m of water absolute? Take atmospheric pressure as 10.3 m of water.

20.21 A single acting reciprocating pump running at 60 rpm has a plunger diameter of 0.25 m and a stroke length of 0.5 m. The delivery pipe is 0.1 m in diameter and 50 m in length. Find the power required to overcome friction of the delivery pipe (i) with air vessel and (ii) without air vessel. ($f = 0.04$)

20.22 A single acting reciprocating pump, having a plunger diameter 200 mm and 300 mm stroke, is placed 4 m above the water level of a sump. The suction pipe is 75 mm in diameter and 5 m long. If the separation takes place at a pressure head of 2.4 m of water, find the maximum speed of the pump, in order to avoid separation. Take barometer reading as 10.4 m of water.

ANSWERS

20.19 4.93 kW; 4.52%; **20.20** 163 mm; **20.21** 15.77 kW; 2.398 kW; **20.22** 25.9 rpm.

21 Elements of Compressible Flow

Speed of sound — Mach number — Enthalpy — Isothermal, adiabatic and isentropic flow — Entropy, Euler's, energy and momentum equations — Stagnation quantities — Pitot tube — Isentropic one-dimensional flow — Convergent–divergent nozzle — Venturimeter — Normal shock waves — Fanno and Rayleigh lines — Characteristic Mach numbers — Prandtl's equation — Oblique shock waves — Oblique compressive and expansion wave in two dimensions — Isothermal flow through pipes with friction — Adiabatic flow through pipes with friction — Analogy of open channel flow.

21.1 Introduction

Gases are highly compressible and in many cases the analysis of their flow is complicated due to thermodynamic effects. When the change in specific mass of a gas is within 2%, the effect of compressibility is normally neglected. The design of pipes to transport gas; airplanes and rockets to ensure flight poses a lot of problems since calculating the pressure and temperature of the gas is difficult. The shock waves generated by high speed moving bodies and gas flow systems are of special interest. In the present book only elements of a one-dimensional steady compressible flow is attempted.

21.2 The Propagation of Small Disturbances in One-dimensional Steady Flow

Figure 21.1(a) shows a disturbance in the one-dimensional flow of gas on the left side which moves at a velocity of c towards the undisturbed still gas on the right. The pressure, velocities and the density of gases on both sides are indicated in the figure. Let us analyse 1 m^2 area of the flow.

The unsteady pattern of flow can be transformed to a steady condition by adding a velocity c towards the left making the wave front stationary. Figure 21.1(b) shows the transformed velocities and other parameters.

Applying the continuity equation,

$$\rho c = (\rho + d\rho)(c - dV)$$

Neglecting higher powers of infinitesimal quantities

$$c d\rho = \rho dV \text{ or } c = \frac{\rho dV}{d\rho} \tag{A}$$

Applying force momentum transport equation,

$$p - (p + dp) = \rho c(c - dV) - \rho c^2 \quad \text{or} \quad -dp = -\rho c dV \text{ or } c = \frac{dp}{\rho dV} \tag{B}$$

Multiplying (A) and (B)

$$c^2 = \frac{dp}{d\rho};$$

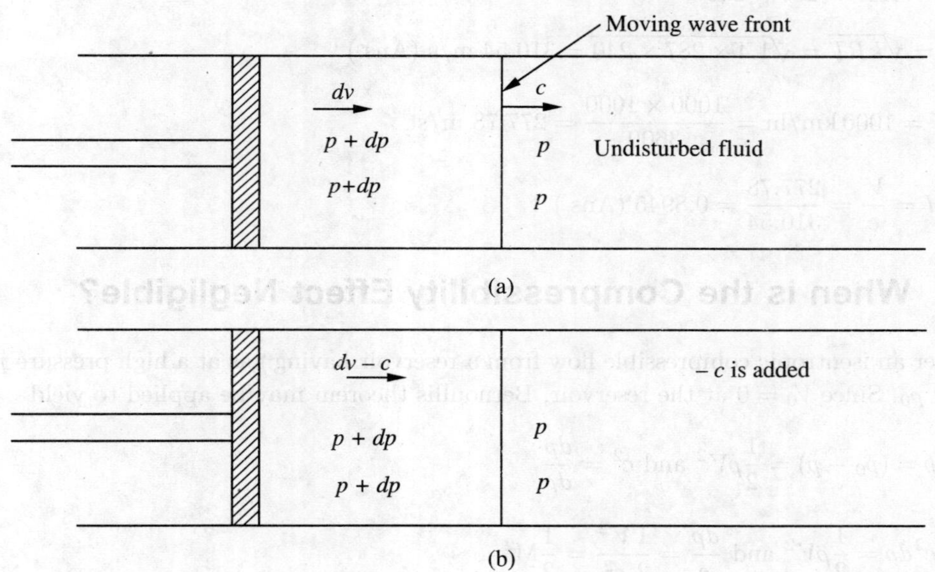

Fig. 21.1 *(a) Propagation of disturbance (b) Wave front made stationary*

The change in the wave can be assumed to be adiabatic, governed by the equation,

$$\frac{p}{\rho^k} = \text{constant}$$

Differentiating with respect to ρ,

$$\frac{dp}{d\rho} \times \rho^{-k} - kp\rho^{-k-1} = 0 \quad \text{or} \quad \frac{dp}{d\rho} = \frac{kp}{\rho} = kRT$$

Hence

$$c = \sqrt{\frac{dp}{d\rho}} = \sqrt{kRT} \tag{21.1}$$

where c is the velocity of propagation of the elastic wave in gas, identified to be the speed of sound. When the speed of the gas is V, the ratio of V to c is known as the Mach number M.

Example 21.1 The temperature and pressure at an altitude of 7 km is −33° C and 40 kPa respectively. Find (i) the density of air, (ii) the speed of sound, (iii) the Mach number when a plane is flying at a speed of 1000 km/hr at that altitude.

$$T = 273 - 33 = 240 \text{ K};\ p = 40 \text{ kPa} = 40 \times 10^3 \text{ Pa};\quad R = 287 \text{ J/ kg K}$$

$$\rho = \frac{p}{RT} = \frac{40 \times 10^3}{287 \times 240} = 0.581\,\text{kg/m}^3 \text{ (Ans.)}$$

$$c = \sqrt{kRT} = \sqrt{1.4 \times 287 \times 240} = 310.54 \text{ m/s (Ans.)}$$

$$V = 1000\,\text{km/hr} = \frac{1000 \times 1000}{3600} = 277.78 \text{ m/s}$$

$$M = \frac{V}{c} = \frac{277.78}{310.54} = 0.8945 \text{ (Ans.)}$$

21.3 When is the Compressibility Effect Negligible?

Consider an isentropic compressible flow from a reservoir having gas at a high pressure p_0 and density ρ_0. Since $V_0 = 0$ at the reservoir, Bernoullis theorem may be applied to yield

$$dp = (p_0 - p) = \frac{1}{2}\rho V^2 \text{ and } c^2 = \frac{dp}{d\rho}$$

$$\text{Hence } c^2 d\rho = \frac{1}{2}\rho V^2 \text{ and } \frac{d\rho}{\rho} = \frac{1}{2}\frac{V^2}{c^2} = \frac{1}{2}\text{M}^2$$

If $\dfrac{d\rho}{\rho}$ is limited to 2%, M will be limited to 0.2.

21.4 Flow Characterisation

Compressible flow is characterised according to the Mach number. When the Mach number is less than one, the disturbances created by a body in the flow will travel upstream also. But when it is equal to one or greater than one, the disturbance cannot travel upstream. In such cases shock waves can be formed. In general, the flow is subsonic when $M < 1$; transonic when M is between 0.8 to 1.2; supersonic when $M > 1$; and hypersonic when $M > 5$.

21.5 Some Thermodynamic Principles

21.5.1 The specific heats and their relationships

When heat is supplied to 1 kg of a gas kept under constant volume causing an increase in the temperature of the gas,

$$dq_1 = c_v \times dT,$$

where c_v is the specific heat at constant volume, dq_1 is the quantity of heat supplied and dT is the increase in temperature. The heat dq_1 will cause an increase in the internal energy of the gas by dU resulting in the temperature rise of dT. On the other hand, when heat is supplied to a kg of gas maintaining constant pressure, the amount of heat supplied is

$$dq_2 = c_p \times dT$$

where c_p is the specific heat at constant pressure. It causes work to be done equal to $d(pv) = RdT$ in addition to raising the internal energy of the gas by dU, by increasing the temperature by dT.

Hence

$$dq_2 = dq_1 + d(pv) \quad \text{or} \quad c_2 dT = c_v dT + RdT \quad \text{or} \quad c_p = c_v + R.$$

The quantity $c_p/c_v = k$ and value of R are constants, important in the study of compressible flows. The value of R for air is 287 J/kg K and $k = 1.4$.

$c_p = Rk/(k-1)$ and $c_v = R/(k-1)$.

So c_p for air is 1004.5 J/kg K and c_v = 717.5 J/kg K

21.5.2 The Enthalpy

Enthalpy is the measure of the energy per unit mass of the gas, given by the expression

$$h = c_p T = U + pv = c_v T + RT.$$

It is the total energy when the potential energy due to elevation and kinetic energy of the gas are neglected. U denotes the internal energy of the gas due to the energy of the motion in the gas at molecular level. If the kinetic energy is also included,

$$h_0 = h + V^2/2$$

and h_0 is called the stagnation enthalpy.

21.5.3 Isothermal, adiabatic and isentropic processes

Gases are governed by the process equation

$$p\nu^n = a \text{ constant}$$

where ν is the specific volume.. In an *isothermal process* the temperature remains constant and $n = 1$. In an *adiabatic process*, no exchange of heat takes place between the system and the environment, and any work done will be at the expense of the internal energy. A frictionless and reversible adiabatic process is called an *isentropic process* and the value of $k = c_p/c_\nu$. The value of k for air and usual diatomic gases is 1.4. In case of frictional loss of energy, in a process of expansion, $n < k$, and in a compression process, $n > k$ (polytropic process).

Example 21.2 5 kg of air at 80°C and pressure 4 bar is expanded isothermally to a pressure of 1 bar. Find the volume of air after expansion, density and the heat absorbed.

$$T = 273 + 80 = 353 \text{ K}; \; p_1 = 4 \times 10^5 \text{ Pa}; \; p_2 = 1 \times 10^5 \text{ Pa}.$$

$$\frac{p_1}{\rho_1} = RT; \; \rho_1 = \frac{4 \times 10^3}{287 \times 353} = 3.948 \,\text{kg/m}^3$$

$$T \text{ being constant, } \frac{p_1}{\rho_1} = \frac{p_2}{\rho_2}; \; \rho_2 = \frac{p_2\rho_1}{p_1} = 0.987 \,\text{kg/m}^3 \text{ (Ans.)}$$

$$\nu_2 = \frac{1}{\rho_2} = \frac{1}{0.987} = 1.013 \,\text{m}^3/\text{kg}; \text{ Final volume of air} = 5 \times \nu_2 = 5.065\text{m}^3 \text{ (Ans.)}$$

Heat absorbed = work done

$$= \int_1^2 pdv = \int_1^2 p\nu \frac{d\nu}{\nu} = RT \ln\frac{\nu_2}{\nu_1} = RT\ln\frac{p_1}{p_2}$$

$$= 287 \times 353 \times \ln 4 = 140.45 \text{ kJ/kg}$$

Total heat absorbed = 140.45 × 5 = 702.25 kJ. (Ans.)

Example 21.3 5 kg of air at 80°C and a pressure of 4 bar is allowed to expand adiabatically so that the pressure is 1 bar. Find the temperature of air and volume of air after the expansion.

$$T_1 = 273 + 80 = 353 \text{ K}; \; p_1 = 4 \times 10^5 \text{ Pa}; \; p_2 = 10^5 \text{ Pa}.$$

$$\rho_1 = \frac{p_1}{287 \times 353} = 3.948 \,\text{kg/m}^3$$

Taking the adiabatic equation $\dfrac{p}{\rho^k}$ = constant

$$\frac{p_1}{\rho_1^{1.4}} = \frac{p_2}{\rho_2^{1.4}};\ \rho_2 = \left(\frac{p_2\rho_1^{1.4}}{p_1}\right)^{1/1.4} = 1.467\,\text{kg/m}^3$$

$$\nu_2 = \frac{1}{\rho_2} = 0.682;\ \text{Volume} = 5 \times 0.682 = 3.409\,\text{m}^3\ \text{(Ans.)}$$

$$\frac{p_2}{\rho_2} = RT;\ T_2 = \frac{p_2}{\rho_2 R} = 237.5\ \text{K (Ans.)}$$

21.5.4 Entropy, a state variable

The $p - \nu$ diagram is used to study the different states of the unit mass of gas. The variables are p, ν and T. The isotherms $p\nu = RT$ and adiabatic lines $p\nu^k$ = constant are used to study many processes and cycles.

Enthalpy is a state variable. The constant enthalpy $h = c_pT$ depicts the isotherms. If p and h are given, we can find the specific volume and T.

A process where there is no exchange of heat with the environment is called adiabatic. In an adiabatic condition, the energy spent in expansion is at the expense of heat energy by reduction of temperature. If the gas is compressed to the original volume, the temperature will again rise to the original level. In these cases, the role of viscous energy dissipation and friction is negligible and the process can be assumed to be reversible.

We have the equation for work

$$dW = pd\nu \tag{21.2}$$

and

$$W = \int pd\nu \tag{21.3}$$

Similar to work per unit mass, another parameter of importance in thermodynamics is dq the heat exchange per unit mass. Using the work equation as an analogy, in the case of an isentropic process, we can introduce a parameter s called entropy such that

$$dq = Tds \tag{21.4}$$

and $$q = \int Tds \tag{21.5}$$

Figure 21.2(a) and 21.2(b) show schematically the two diagrams, a $p - \nu$ diagram and a $T - s$ diagram.

In case of thermally ideal gases, the workenergy equation reads

$$dq = dU + dW$$

$$dq = Tds,\ dU = c_v dT;\ \text{ and }\ dW = pd\nu;$$

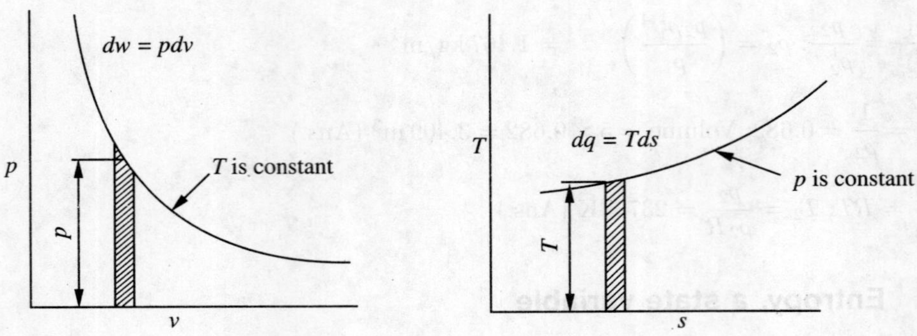

Fig. 21.2 *(a.) The p–ν diagram. (b.) The T–s diagram.*

Hence

$$Tds = dU + pd\nu$$

$$= dU + RT\frac{d\nu}{\nu}$$

$$ds = \frac{c_v dT}{t} + \frac{Rd\nu}{\nu};$$

Integrating between limits of state 1 to state 2,

$$s_2 - s_1 = c_\nu \ln\frac{T_2}{T_1} + R\ln\frac{\nu_2}{\nu_1} \tag{21.6}$$

It can be expressed alternatively as,

$$s_2 - s_1 = c_\nu \ln\frac{T_2}{T_1} - R\ln\frac{p_2 T_1}{p_1 T_2} = c_v \ln\frac{T_2}{T_1} - R\ln\frac{p_2}{p_1} \tag{21.7}$$

and

$$s_2 - s_1 = c_\nu \ln\frac{T_2}{T_1} - R\ln\frac{\rho_2}{\rho_1} \tag{21.8}$$

When $s_2 - s_1 = 0$, the process is called isentropic.

It may be noted that when there is viscous energy dissipation and friction contributing to the production of heat, the heat will always add to the mass of fluid and hence the entropy is bound to increase. Only in cases where the role of viscosity in the process is negligible, can the system be assumed to be reversible. In general, $ds \geq 0$. ($ds = 0$ for isentropic process and $ds > 0$ for all non-reversible cases.)

There are cases in compressible flow like flow through nozzles or in short distances, where the frictional losses can be neglected. It is found that along with the enthalpy h, the entropy s can be used to indicate the state of the gas.

It has been established that since under no condition, does the total entropy decrease, the entropy in the universe is increasing. Entropy is found to be a measure of disorder and energy dispersion.

Example 21.4 1 kg of air at 27°C is expanded isothermally to double the volume by reducing the pressure. What is the change in entropy? If 1 kg of air at 27°C is expanded adiabatically, what will be the temperature of air? Verify about the change in entropy.

Isothermal case

$T = 273 + 27 = 300$ K;. $\nu_2/\nu_1 = 2$

Since in the process T is kept constant,

$s_2 - s_1 = R\ln(\nu_2/\nu_1) = 287 \times \ln 2 = 198.93$ J/kgK (Ans.)

Adiabatic case

$p_1\nu_1^k = p_2\nu_2^k$; Hence $p_2/p_1 = (\nu_1/\nu_2)^{1.4} = 0.5^{1.4} = 0.37893$

$T_2/T_1 = p_2\nu_2/p_1\nu_1 = 0.37893 \times 2 = 0.75786$; $T_2 = 0.75786 \times 300 = 227.36$ K (Ans.)

$s_2 - s_1 = c_\nu \ln(T_2/T_1) + R\ln(\nu_2/\nu_1) = 717.5 \times \ln 0.75786 + 287 \times \ln 2$

$= -198.93 + 198.93 = 0$; i.e. there is no change in entropy. (Ans.)

21.6 Basic Equations in One-dimensional Compressible Flow

(i) The equation of continuity.

The mass transport rate $= \dot{m} = \rho AV$ is constant (21.9)

(ii) The Eulers equation:

$$dp/\rho + VdV = 0 \quad (21.10)$$

(iii) The energy equation.

In compressible flow of gases, the body force (weight) is negligible and energy in the form of heat and kinetic energy is accounted for.

Energy per unit mass,

$$h_1 + \frac{V_1^2}{2} + q = h_2 + \frac{V_2^2}{2} \quad (21.11)$$

where h refers to the enthalpy equal to c_pT, V the velocity and q the heat transferred per unit mass. In case we express

$$h_0 = h + \frac{V^2}{2} = c_pT + \frac{V^2}{2} \tag{21.12}$$

as the stagnation enthalpy,

$$h_{02} = h_{01} + q \tag{21.13}$$

Eulers equation can be integrated to obtain Bernoullis equation for application in isothermal flow: since $\rho = p/RT$,

$$\frac{dp}{\rho} = RT\frac{dp}{p}. \text{ Hence } \int \frac{dp}{\rho} = RT \ln p$$

$$RT \ln p_1 + \frac{V_1^2}{2} = RT \ln p_2 + \frac{V_2^2}{2} \tag{21.14}$$

In the adiabatic case, Bernoullis equation becomes

$$\frac{k}{k-1}\left(\frac{p_1}{\rho_1}\right) + \frac{V_1^2}{2} = \frac{k}{k-1}\left(\frac{p_2}{\rho_2}\right) + \frac{V_2^2}{2} \tag{21.15}$$

(iv) Force momentum transport equation

It can also be called the impulse momentum equation and be written as

$$\sum F = p_1A_1 - p_2A_2 = \rho_2A_2V_2^2 - \rho_1A_1V_1^2 \tag{21.16}$$

Example 21.5 Carbon dioxide at 15°C is flowing through a horizontal tapering pipe. The area of cross-section at inlet and outlet are 50 cm² and 20 cm² respectively. If the inlet pressure is 400 k Pa and outlet pressure is 300 kPa , find the mass flow rate assuming isothermal conditions. Given that $R = 188.8$ J/kg K and $k = 1.289$.

$$p_1 = 400 \text{ k Pa}; \; p_2 = 300 \text{ k Pa}; \; T = 273 + 15 = 288 \text{ K}$$

$$A_1 = 5 \times 10^{-3}\text{m}^2 \; ; \; A_2 = 2 \times 10^{-3}\text{m}^2$$

$$\rho_1 = \frac{p_1}{RT} = 7.35\,\text{kg/m}^3; \; \rho_2 = \frac{p_2}{RT} = 5.514\,\text{kg/m}^3;$$

By the equation of continuity,

$$V_2 = \frac{\rho_1A_1V_1}{\rho_2A_2} = \frac{7.35 \times 5 \times 10^{-3}V_1}{5.514 \times 2 \times 10^{-3}} = 3.333V_1$$

For isothermal flow,

$$RT\ln(p_1/p_2) = 0.5(V_2^2 - V_1^2).$$

$$188.9 \times 288 \times 0.288 = 0.5V_1^2(3.33^2 - 1);\ V_1 = 55.73 \text{ m/s};$$

Mass flow rate $= \dot{m} = \rho_1 A_1 V_1 = 7.35 \times 5 \times 10^{-3} \times 55.73 = 2.048$ kg/s.(Ans.)

21.7 One-dimensional Isentropic Flow

Let the parameters of flow at a section (1) be V_1, T_1, $p_1 1$, ν_1 and ρ_1 and at section (2) be V_2, T_2, p_2, ν_2 and ρ_2. Let $T_r = T_2/T_1$; $p_r = p_2/p_1$ and $\rho_r = \rho_2/\rho_1$. In (21.7), $s_2 - s_1 = 0$ and substitute $c_p/R = k/(k-1)$, one can prove that

$$p_r = (T_r)^{k/(k-1)} \tag{21.17}$$

From (21.8), it can be proved that

$$\rho_r = (T_r)^{1/(k-1)} \tag{21.18}$$

Combining (21.17) and (21.18)

$$\rho_r = (p_r)^{1/k} \tag{21.19}$$

Example 21.6 Air flows through an expanding pipe with an inlet pressure of 60 kPa and outlet pressure of 80 kPa. If the inlet velocity is 250 m/s and temperature 30°C, find the outlet velocity. Assume isentropic flow.

$$T_1 = 273 + 30 = 303 \text{ K};\ p_1 = 60 \text{ kPa};\ p_2 = 80 \text{ kPa};\ V_1 = 250 \text{ m/s}.$$

$$R = 287 \text{ J/ kg K and } k = 1.4$$

$$\rho_1 = \frac{p_1}{RT_1} = 0.69\,\text{kg/m}^3;$$

Due to adiabatic change

$$\frac{p_1}{\rho_1^k} = \frac{p_2}{\rho_2^k};\ \rho_2 = \left(\frac{p_2}{p_1}\right)^{1/k};\ \rho_1 = 0.8474$$

Applying Bernoulli's theorem

$$\frac{k}{k-1}\left(\frac{p_2}{\rho_2} - \frac{p_1}{\rho_1}\right) = 0.5(V_1^2 - V_2^2)$$

i.e. $26075 \times 2 = 62500 - V_2^2;\ V_2 = 101.74$ m/s. (Ans.)

Alternate method

$$h_0 = c_p T_1 + V_1^2/2 = 1004.5 \times 303 + 250^2/2 = 335613.5 \text{ J/kg}.$$

$p_r = 8/6 = 1.333$; $T_r = (p_r)^{(k-1)/k} = (p_r)^{1/3.5} = 1.0856$.

$T_2 = T_r \times T_1 = 1.0856 \times 303 = 328.94$ K.

$h_0 = 335613.5 = c_p T_2 + V_2^2/2 = 1004.5 \times 328.94 \times V_2^2/2$

from which $V_2 = 101.9$ m/s (Ans)

21. 8 Stagnation Quantities in Isentropic Flow

In compressible flow, if we can imagine a stagnation point where the velocity is zero,

$h_0 = c_p T + V^2/2 = c_p T_s$

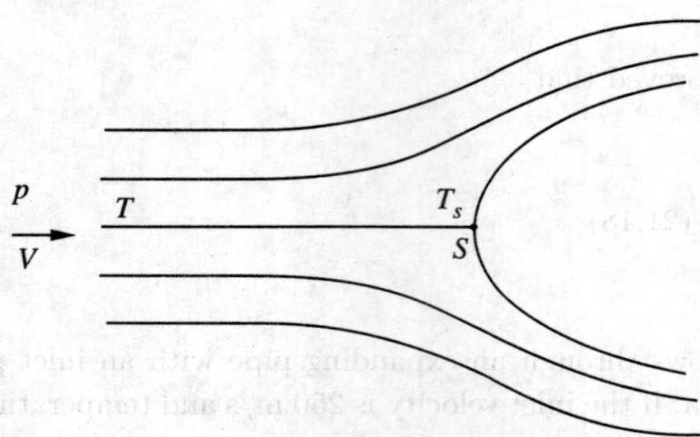

Fig. 21.3 *Temperature at stagnation point*

or $T_s = T + V^2/(2c_p) = T(1 + V^2/(2c_p T))$.

Let $T_{sr} = \dfrac{T_s}{T}$

$$T_{sr} = 1 + \frac{V^2}{2c_p T} = 1 + \frac{V^2(k-1)}{2kRT} = \frac{k-1}{2}\text{M}^2 \tag{21.20}$$

where M is the Mach number for the flow.

It may be noted that (21.20) requires only the flow to be adiabatic.

Let us denote $p_{sr} = \dfrac{p_s}{p}$ and $\rho_{sr} = \dfrac{\rho_s}{\rho}$. From (21.7) for isentropic case $ds = 0$ and

$$p_{sr} = T_{sr}^{k/k-1} \tag{21.21}$$

and $\rho_{sr} = T_{sr}^{1/k-1} = \ldots (p_{sr})^{1/k}$ (21.22)

When relating the temperature at a section (2) to that at a section (1) in isentropic flow, one can use the equation

$$T_r = \frac{T_2}{T_1} = \frac{T_s/T_1}{T_s/T_2} = \frac{T_{sr1}}{T_{sr2}} = \frac{1 + \dfrac{k-1}{2}\mathrm{M}_1^2}{1 + \dfrac{k-1}{2}\mathrm{M}_2^2} = \frac{2 + (k-1)\mathrm{M}_1^2}{2 + (k-1)\mathrm{M}_2^2} \tag{21.23}$$

p_r and ρ_r can be calculated using (21.17) and (21.18).

The results for M = 1 is of special interest in designs of nozzles and are marked with an asterisk. For a value of $k = 1.4$,

$$T_{sr^*} = \frac{T_s}{T^*} = \frac{k+1}{2} = 1.2 \tag{21.24a}$$

$$\text{Therefore } \frac{T^*}{T_s} = 0.833 \tag{21.24b}$$

$$p_{sr^*} = \frac{p_s}{p^*} = (T_{sr})^{k/(k-1)} = 1.894 \tag{21.25a}$$

$$\text{Therefore } \frac{p^*}{p_s} = 0.528 \tag{21.25b}$$

$$\rho_{sr^*} = \frac{\rho_s}{\rho^*} = (T_{sr})^{1/(k-1)} = 1.579 \tag{21.26a}$$

$$\text{Therefore } \frac{\rho^*}{\rho_s} = 0.634 \tag{21.26b}$$

Example 21.7 Find the Mach number and stagnation quantities for methane flowing at 250 m/s if the pressure and temperature of the undisturbed flow are 200 kPa and 20 °C respectively. For methane, $R = 520$ J/kg K and $k = 1.3$

$$T = 273 + 20 = 293 \text{ K};\ p = 200 \text{ kPa};\ V = 250 \text{ m/s.};\ \rho = \frac{p}{RT} = 1.313.$$

$$c = \sqrt{kRT} = \sqrt{1.3 \times 520 \times 293} = 445.05 \text{ m/s};\ \mathrm{M} = \frac{V}{c} = \frac{250}{445.05} = 0.562 \text{ (Ans.)}$$

$$T_{sr} = \frac{T_s}{T} = 1 + \frac{k-1}{2}\mathrm{M}^2 = 1.0474;\ T_s = T \times T_{sr} = 293 \times 1.0474 = 306.88 \text{ K (Ans.)}$$

$$p_{sr} = p_s/p = T_{sr}^{k/(k-1)} = 1.0474^{4.333} = 1.222;\ p_s = 200 \times 1.222 = 244.4 \text{ kPa (Ans.)}$$

$$\rho_{sr} = \rho_s/\rho = T_{sr}^{1/(k-1)} = 1.0474^{3.333} = 1.167;\ \rho_s = 1.313 \times 1.167 = 1.532\,\text{kg/m}^3 \text{ (Ans.)}$$

21.9 The Differential Pressure for a Pitot tube at Stagnation Point

A Pitot tube can be placed at the stagnation point to measure the velocity of flow in air having a Mach number less than one. But the differential head indicated will be higher and the velocity calculated will be higher than the actual velocity due to the compressibility of air.

From the relations $kp/\rho = c^2$ and $M^2 = V^2/c^2$,

$$p = \frac{2}{kM^2} \times \frac{\rho V^2}{2} \tag{21.27}$$

Differential pressure indicated by the Pitot tube,

$$\Delta p = p_s - p = p(p_{sr} - 1)$$

$$= \frac{2}{kM^2} \times \frac{\rho V^2}{2}(p_{sr} - 1) = \frac{2}{kM^2} \times \frac{\rho V^2}{2}(T_{sr}^{k/k-1} - 1)$$

$$\text{Hence } \Delta p = \frac{2}{kM^2}(T_{sr}^{k/k-1} - 1) \times \frac{\rho V^2}{2} \tag{21.28}$$

The factor, $\frac{2}{kM^2}(T_{sr}^{k/k-1} - 1)$ known as compressibility correction factor is greater than 1 and gives an overestimation of the differential pressures for calculating the velocity using a Pitot tube. The differential pressure Δp has to be divided by the factor indicated before calculating the velocity. When the Mach number is less than 0.2, the correction factor to be applied is nearly about 0.5%.

Example 21.8 Calculate the compressibility correction factor for a Pitot tube when the Mach number is 0.85. What is the change in actual velocity from that indicated by the differential pressure. $M = 0.85$; $k = 1.4$

$$T_{sr} = \frac{T_s}{T} = 1 + \frac{k-1}{2}M^2 = 1.1445$$

$$\text{The correction factor} = \frac{2}{kM^2}(T_{sr}^{k/k-1} - 1) = 1.193 \text{ (Ans.)}$$

correction for velocity $=$ (correction factor) $^{1/2} = 1.193^{1/2} = 1.092$. Actual velocity will be $1/1.092 = 0.916$ times that is indicated by the Pitot tube.

21.10 Isentropic One-dimensional Flow through a Tube with Gradual Change in Area

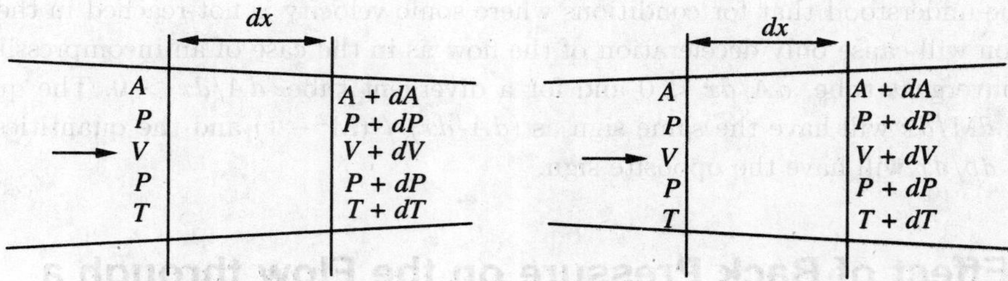

Fig. 21.4 *Pipe with gradual change in area*

The one-dimensional flow in a pipe changing area gradually is shown in Fig. 21.4. By the continuity equation, the mass flow rate $\dot{m} = \rho AV$ is a constant in a tube. Differentiating after taking logarithms

$$\frac{d\rho}{\rho} + \frac{dA}{A} + \frac{dV}{V} = 0 \tag{21.29}$$

From Euler's equation,

$$\frac{dp}{\rho} = -VdV = -\frac{V^2 dV}{V}$$

Because the length considered is short, friction is neglected.

$$\frac{d\rho}{\rho} = \frac{d\rho}{dp} \times \frac{dp}{\rho} = \frac{-1}{c^2} \times \frac{V^2 dV}{V} = \frac{-dV}{V} \times \mathrm{M}^2$$

From (21.26),

$$\frac{dA}{A} = -\frac{d\rho}{\rho} - \frac{dV}{V} = \frac{dV}{V}(\mathrm{M}^2 - 1) \tag{21.30}$$

The above equation is of great importance in the design of convergent and divergent nozzles in compressible flow.

Let us imagine the flow of gas occurring through a converging nozzle from a reservoir of air, kept at high pressure. The velocity of flow accelerates from zero in the reservoir, as the gas flows in the convergent tube. For the subsonic flow $(\mathrm{M}^2 - 1) < 0$, implies that the behavior is similar to the condition of incompressible flow i.e., the increase in area will reduce the velocity of flow. If the area is sufficiently reduced, the velocity can reach the sonic velocity. If the tube is longer and the area is further reduced, the velocity will not increase above the sonic velocity. There will be reduction of the mass flow rate maintaining the sonic velocity at the outlet.

Further increase in velocity can be attained only by attaching a divergent tube at the end of the converging section (throat). The device is called a Laval nozzle. The flow can continue to accelerate in the supersonic range with increasing Mach numbers until a shock wave is formed depending on the downstream conditions of the tube.

It may be understood that for conditions where sonic velocity is not reached in the throat, an expansion will cause only deceleration of the flow as in the case of an incompressible flow.

For a convergent tube, $dA/dx < 0$ and for a divergent tube, $dA/dx > 0$. The quantities dV/dx and dM/dx will have the same sign as (dA/dx) / $(M^2 - 1)$ and the quantities dp/dx, dT/dx and $d\rho/dx$ will have the opposite sign.

21.11 Effect of Back Pressure on the Flow through a Converging–Diverging Nozzle

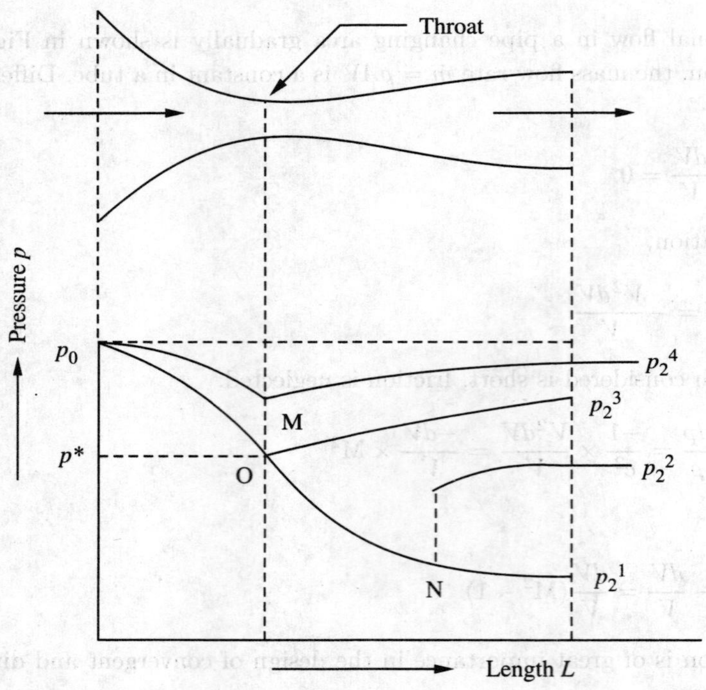

Fig. 21.5 *Effect of back pressure on flow in a converging–diverging nozzle*

If a converging–diverging nozzle is connected to a reservoir at high pressure ($p_0 = p_s$) with gas at some known temperature T_s, it is possible to have sonic conditions obtained at the throat. The pressure p^* at the throat can be worked out by applying the formula (21.25b), $\frac{p^*}{p_s} = 0.528$. If the back pressure is low, p_2^1 or lower as indicated in Fig. 21.5, supersonic flow will exist after the flow becomes sonic at the throat. If the back pressure is increased to p_2^2 at some point N, a normal shock wave will form. Still further increase of pressure will advance the shock wave towards the throat. When the back pressure is p_2^3, the pressure will increase from the throat from p^*. A higher pressure $p_2^4 > p_2^3$, the pressure at the throat will be higher as indicated by point M and the pressure will increase in the diverging section.

Example 21.9 Air enters a Laval nozzle at a pressure of 1200 kPa and temperature of 120 °C from a reservoir and expands to a pressure of 200 kPa. If the mass flow rate is 2 kg/s, find (i) the pressure, density and area of cross-section of the Laval nozzle at the throat, (ii) the area and the Mach number of flow when the pressure is 75% of the inlet pressure and (iii) the area and Mach number of flow when the pressure is 20% of the inlet pressure.

$$p_0 = 1200 \text{ kPa}; \; T_s = 273 + 120 = 393 \text{ K}; \; \dot{m} = \rho A V = 2 \text{ kg/s}; \; k = 1.4$$

$$\rho_s = \frac{p_s}{RT} = \frac{1200}{287 \times 393} = 10.64 \, \text{kg/m}^3$$

(i) M =1 at the throat.

Hence

$$\frac{T^*}{T_s} = \frac{2}{k+1} = \frac{2}{2.4} = 0.833; \; T^* = 0.833 \times 393 = 327.37 \text{ K}$$

$$\frac{p^*}{p_s} = \left(\frac{2}{k+1}\right)^{k/k-1} = 0.528; \; p^* = 0.528 \times 1200 = 633.6 \text{ kPa (Ans.)}$$

$$V = \sqrt{2c_p(T_0 - T)} = 363.2 \text{ m/s}$$

$$\frac{\rho^*}{\rho_s} = \left(\frac{2}{k+1}\right)^{1/k-1} = 0.634; \; \rho^* = 0.634 \times 10.64 = 6.746 \, \text{kg/m}^3 \text{ (Ans.)}$$

$$A = \frac{\dot{m}}{\rho V} = \frac{2}{6.746 \times 363.2} = 8.16 \times 10^{-4} \, \text{m}^2 \text{ (Ans.)}$$

(ii) $p = 0.75 \times 1200 = 900$ kPa.

$$p_{sr} = (T_{sr})^{k/k-1} = (T_{sr})^{3.5}; \text{ hence } T_{sr} = (p_{sr})^{1/3.5} = (1200/900)^{1/3.5} = 1.086$$

$$T = T_s/1.086 = 361.87 \text{ K} \; ; \; T_s - T = 31.13 \text{ K}$$

$$V = \sqrt{2c_p(T_s - T} = \sqrt{2 \times 1005 \times 31.13} = 250.14 \text{ m/s}$$

$$\rho = \frac{p}{RT} = \frac{900 \times 1000}{287 \times 361.87} = 8.666 \, \text{kg/m}^3$$

$$A = \frac{\dot{m}}{\rho V} = \frac{2}{8.666 \times 361.87} = 9.22 \times 10^{-4} \, \text{m}^2 \text{ (Ans.)}$$

$$c = \sqrt{kRT} = \sqrt{1.4 \times 287 \times 361.87} = 381.31$$

$$\mathrm{M} = V/c = 250.14/381.31 = 0.656 \text{ (Ans.)}$$

(iii) $p = 0.2 \times 1200 = 240$ kPa; $p_{sr} = 1200/240 = 5.0$

$$T_{sr} = (p_{sr})^{k-1/k} = 5.0^{1/3.5} = 1.584;\ T = T_{sr}/1.584 = 393/1.584 = 248.11 \text{ K.}$$

$$V = \sqrt{2c_v(T_s - T)} = \sqrt{2 \times 1005 \times 144.89} = 539.66 \text{ m/s}$$

$$\rho = \frac{p}{RT} = \frac{240 \times 1000}{287 \times 248.11} = 3.37 \,\text{kg/m}^3$$

$$A = \frac{\dot{m}}{\rho V} = \frac{2}{3.37 \times 539.66} = 11 \times 10^{-4}\,\text{m}^2 \text{ (Ans.)}$$

$$c = \sqrt{kRT} = \sqrt{1.4 \times 287 \times 248.11} = 315.74 \text{ m/s}$$

$$\mathrm{M} = \frac{V}{c} = \frac{539.66}{315.74} = 1.709 \text{ Ans.}$$

21.12 Area Ratio to get a Desired Mach Number

The area at the throat for a Laval nozzle is designed to get sonic velocity and the Mach number 1. The area in the divergent portion is increased to get the desired Mach number. Let the area at the throat be A^* and at a section downstream, the area is A, where the Mach number desired is M. Let the mass flow rate be $\dot{m}$.

Let $V_r = \dfrac{V^*}{V};\ T_r = \dfrac{T^*}{T};\ \rho_r = \dfrac{\rho^*}{\rho};$

Being an adiabatic flow

$$T_r = \frac{T^*}{T} = \frac{T_s/T}{T_s/T^*} = \frac{T_{sr}}{T_{sr^*}} = \frac{1 + \dfrac{k-1}{2}\mathrm{M}^2}{\dfrac{k+1}{2}} = \frac{2 + (k-1)\mathrm{M}^2}{k+1} \qquad \text{(A)}$$

$$V_r = \frac{V^*}{V} = \frac{\sqrt{kRT^*}}{\mathrm{M} \times \sqrt{kRT}} = \frac{1}{\mathrm{M}} \times \left(\frac{T^*}{T}\right)^{0.5} \qquad \text{(B)}$$

Being an isentropic flow by (21.8),

$$\rho_r = T_r^{1/(k-1)} \qquad \text{(C)}$$

$$\dot{m} = \rho A V = \rho^* A^* V^*;$$

Substituting the relationships (A), (B) and (C)

$$\frac{A}{A^*} = \frac{\rho^* V^*}{\rho V} = \rho_r \times V_r = T_r^{1/(k-1)} \times \frac{1}{\text{M}} T_r^{0.5} = \frac{1}{\text{M}} \times T_r^{k+1/2(k-1)}$$

$$\frac{A}{A^*} = \frac{1}{\text{M}} \left[\frac{2 + (k-1)\text{M}^2}{k+1} \right]^{k+1/2(k-1)} \tag{21.31}$$

Example 21.10 In a Laval nozzle, for air flow, the throat has an area of 8 cm^2. Find the area where the Mach number is (i) 0.6 and (ii) 1.5. When $k = 1.4$, the formula for $\dfrac{A}{A^*} = \dfrac{1}{\text{M}} \times \left[\dfrac{1 + 0.2\text{M}^2}{1.2}\right]^3$

(i) $\text{M} = 0.6$; $A/A^* = 1.188$; $A = 8 \times 1.188 = 9.504$ cm^2 (Ans.)

(ii) $\text{M} = 1.5$; $A/A^* = 1.176$; $A = 8 \times 1.176 = 9.41$cm^2 (Ans.)

21.13 Measurement of Mass Flow Rate using a Venturimeter

A venturimeter can be used for the measurement of the mass flow rate of gas, if measurements of pressure and temperature are taken at the inlet and throat of the venturimeter. The pressure and temperature at a point will help in calculating the density of the gas at that point. The values of c_p and c_v for the gas is considered to be known. By considering the flow to be adiabatic, stagnation enthalpy will be the same at inlet and throat and

$$(V_2^2 - V_1^2) = 2c_p(T_1 - T_2) = 2c_pT_1(1 - T_2/T_1) = 2c_pT_1(1 - T_r) \tag{A}$$

By equation of continuity,

$$\rho_1 A_1 V_1 = \rho_2 A_2 V_2;\ V_2 = \frac{\rho_1 A_1 V_1}{\rho_2 A_2} = \frac{1}{\rho_r^2 A_r^2} V_1 \text{ and}$$

$T_r = p_r^{(k-1)/k}$. Also $T_1 = p_1/(\rho_1 R)$

From (A),

$$V_1^2 \left(\frac{1}{\rho_r^2 A_r^2} - 1 \right) = \left(2R\frac{k}{k-1} \times \frac{p_1}{\rho_1 R} \times (1 - p_r^{(k-1)/k}) \right)$$

$$\text{Hence } V_1 = \sqrt{\frac{\dfrac{2k}{k-1}\dfrac{p_1}{\rho_1}(1 - p_r^{(k-1)/k})}{\dfrac{1}{(\rho_r^2 A_r^2)} - 1}}$$

Substituting the values $\rho_r = p_r^{1/k}$ and hence $\dfrac{1}{\rho_r^2} = p_r^{-2/k} = \dfrac{1}{p_r^{2/k}}$

The mass flow rate

$$\rho_1 A_1 V_1 = A_1 \sqrt{\frac{\frac{2k}{k-1} p_1 \rho_1 (1 - p_r^{(k-1)/k})}{\frac{1}{A_r^2 p_r^{2/k}} - 1}} \tag{21.32}$$

Example 21.11 A venturimeter is used for measuring the flow of nitrogen (R = 297 J/kg K; and k = 1.4). The inlet diameter is 8 cm and the outlet diameter is 5 cm. The inlet pressure is 150 kPa and temperature is 330 K. If the throat pressure is 125 kPa and C_d = 0.97, find the flow rate.

$d_1 = 0.08$ m; $d_2 = 0.05$ m; $p_1 = 150$ kPa; $p_2 = 125$ kPa ; $T_1 = 300$ K

$A_1 = 5.03 \times 10^{-3} \text{m}^2$; $A_2 = 1.963 \times 10^{-3} \text{m}^2$; $A_r = A_2/A_1 = 0.39$

$p_r = p_2/p_1 = 125/150 = 0.833$;

$$\rho_1 = \frac{p_1}{RT_1} = \frac{150 \times 1000}{297 \times 300} = 1.684 \, \text{kg/m}^3$$

$$\text{The mass flow rate} = \rho_1 A_1 V_1 = C_d A_1 \sqrt{\frac{\frac{2k}{k-1} p_1 \rho_1 (1 - p_r^{(k-1)/k})}{\frac{1}{A_r^2 p_r^{2/k}} - 1}}$$

$$= 0.97 \times 5.03 \times 10^{-3} \left[\frac{\frac{2 \times 1.4}{0.4} \times 150 \times 10^3 \times 1.684 (1 - 0.833^{1/3.5})}{\frac{1}{0.39^2 \times 0.833^{2/1.4}} - 1} \right]^{0.5} = 0.533 \text{ kg/s. (Ans.)}$$

21.14 Mass Flow Rate from a Reservoir through a Converging Nozzle

Consider flow from a reservoir through a convergent–divergent nozzle as shown in Fig. 21.6. V_0 can be assumed to be zero. Let the temperature, density and pressure in the reservoir be T_0, ρ_0 and p_0 respectively. Let the velocity, temperature , density, and pressure at the throat be V, T, ρ and p respectively. From the stagnant enthalpy considerations,

$$V^2 = 2c_p(T_0 - T) = 2c_p \times T_0(1 - T/T_0)$$

Assuming $T_r = T/T_0$ and $p_r = p/p_0$

$$= 2c_p \times \frac{p_0}{\rho_0 R}(1 - T_r) = \frac{2k}{k-1} \times \frac{p_0}{\rho_0}(1 - p_r^{(k-1)/k})$$

Mass flow rate

$$= \rho AV = A\left[\frac{2k}{k-1} \times \frac{p_0 \rho_0 \rho^2}{\rho_0^2} \times (1 - p_r^{(k-1)/k})\right]^{0.5}$$

$$= A\rho_0\left[\frac{2k}{k-1} \times \frac{p_0}{\rho_0} \times p_r^{2/k}(1 - p_r^{(k-1)/k})\right]^{0.5} \quad (21.33)$$

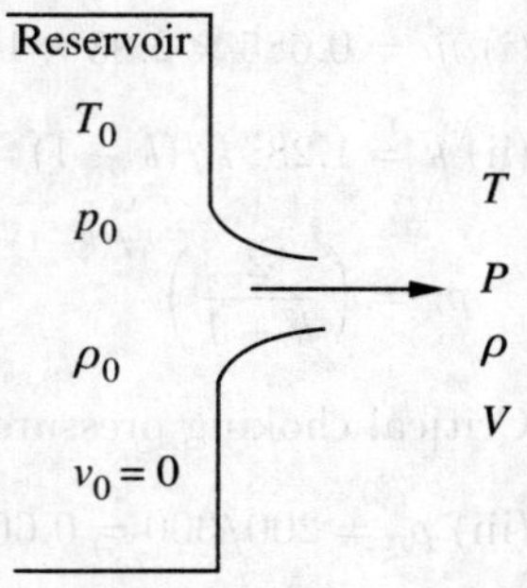

Fig. 21.6 *Flow through a converging nozzle from a reservoir*

When the pressure at the throat is equal to the inlet pressure there will not be any flow. The flow increases as the pressure difference increases. The maximum mass flow rate that can be obtained by reducing the throat pressure can be found.

$F(p_r) = p_r^{2/k}(1 - p_r^{(k-1)/k})$ should be maximum. It can be found that the condition is

$p_r = \left(\frac{2}{k+1}\right)^{k/(k-1)}$, which is the same as (21.25b) for sonic conditions. So at a Mach number of one the mass flow rate will attain a maximum. A further decrease in pressure at the throat will not create any disturbance upstream and the mass flow rate will not get affected. The nozzle is said to have choked. Looking at it in another way, the nozzle will give a constant discharge when the back pressure is low and as the back pressure increases above a critical value, the mass flow rate will be decreased.

Assuming $k = 1.4$, $p_r = \left(\frac{2}{k+1}\right)^{k/(k-1)} = 0.528$, and the mass flow rate can be proved to be

$$\dot{m} = 0.685 A\sqrt{p_0 \rho_0} \quad (21.34)$$

Example 21.12 A reservoir contains carbon dioxide at a pressure of 300 kPa and a temperature of 298 K. For carbon dioxide, $R = 188$ and $k = 1.28$. A converging nozzle has a diameter of 6 cm at the exit. (i) What is the maximum mass flow rate possible? (ii) Find the maximum pressure at the exit, for which the above flow can be maintained? (iii) If the pressure at the exit is 200 kPa, find the mass flow rate.

$p_1 = p_0 = 300$ kPa; $d_e = 0.06$ m ; $A_e = 2.83 \times 10^{-3}\,\text{m}^2$; $T = 298$ K.

$$\rho_0 = \frac{p_0}{RT_0} = \frac{300 \times 1000}{188 \times 298} = 5.355 \text{ kg/m}^3$$

(i) $\dot{m} = 0.685 \times 2.83 \times 10^{-3} \times \sqrt{300 \times 1000 \times 5.355} = 2.457$ kg/s (Ans.)

(ii) $k = 1.28$; $k/(k-1) = 4.571$

$$p_r = \left(\frac{2}{k+1}\right)^{k/(k-1)} = 0.877^{4.571} = 0.5488$$

Critical choking pressure $= 0.5488 \times 300 = 164.64$ kPa (Ans.)

(iii) $p_r = 200/300 = 0.667$; $k = 1.28$; $2/k = 1.5625$; $(k-1)/k = 0.21785$.

$2k/(k-1) = 9.143$; $p_0/\rho_0 = 300 \times 1000/5.355 = 56020$;

Mass flow rate

$$= A\rho_0 \left[\frac{2k}{k-1} \times \frac{p_0}{\rho_0} \times p_r^{2/k}(1 - p_r^{(k-1)/k})\right]^{0.5}$$

$$= 2.83 \times 10^{-3} \times 5.355[9.143 \times 56020 \times 0.677^{1.5625} \times (1 - 0.667^{0.21785})]^{0.5} = 2.3 \text{ kg/s (Ans.)}$$

21.15 Shock Waves

21.15.1 General

When a supersonic flow encounters a subsonic flow the pressure change may occur suddenly in a thin layer. This layer becomes a region of intense shear and energy loss. It is called a shock wave. Since the change occurs quite suddenly, there is no heat exchange with the surroundings and the process can be considered adiabatic. However there will be entropy change. The shock waves in compressible flow are analogous to the formation of a hydraulic jump in open channels. The Mach number is analogous to the Froudes number.

Shock waves occur in supersonic flight of bodies like bullets and planes. It can also occur in a Laval nozzle in the divergent portion if the back pressure is increased. The shock waves may be of different forms, plane attached, unattached and oblique. Also it may be moving or stationary. .

Even when the Mach number of a movement of a body is 0.7, near some local points in the body, the velocity may be supersonic. For bodies moving at subsonic velocities, drag can be reduced by providing a rounded nose. But in supersonic velocities the drag can be reduced by providing a sharp nose. Shock waves dissipates considerable amount of energy and affect the boundary layer flow. It may cause separation and increase in drag..

21.15.2 The Normal Shock Wave

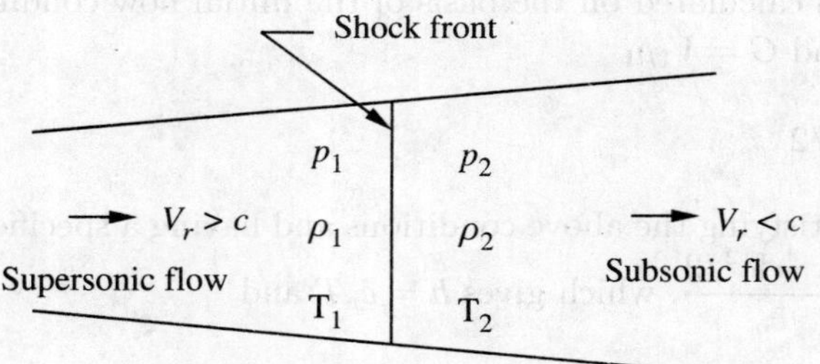

Fig. 21.7 *Shock wave in divergent pipe*

21.15.2.1 The governing equation

Figure 21.7 shows the parameters of flow when a one-dimensional shock wave occurs in a diffuser.

The mass flow rate across the shock wave

$$= \dot{m} = \rho_1 A V_1 = \rho_2 A V_2 \tag{21.35}$$

Since an adiabatic flow can be assumed in the shock, the stagnation enthalpy before and after the shock will be the same.

i.e. $$h_{01} = c_p T_1 + V_1^2/2 = h_{02} = c_p T_2 + V_2^2/2 \tag{21.36a}$$

It can also be written as the energy equation,

$$V_2^2 - V_1^2 = 2c_p(T_2 - T_1) \tag{21.36b}$$

which can be written as

$$V_2^2 - V_1^2 = \frac{2k}{k-1} \times (p_1 \nu_1 - p_2 \nu_2) \tag{21.36c}$$

In addition, the force momentum transport equation will be

$$A(p_1 - p_2) = \dot{m}(V_2 - V_1) \tag{21.37}$$

21.15.2.2 The Fanno and Rayleigh lines

In order to understand the phenomenon of shock wave better, the following two conditions of flow are studied in plots between the enthalpy and the entropy.

A. Condition 1: The Fanno line

(i) The mass flow rate/unit area $G = \dot{m}/A$ remain the same before and after the shock wave.

(ii) The stagnation enthalpy before and after the shock wave remain the same. The stagnation enthalpy is calculated on the basis of the initial flow conditions, V_1, p_1 and ρ_1 and $T_1 = p_1/R\rho_1$ and $G = V_1\rho_1$

So $\quad h_0 = c_p T_1 + V_1^2/2$

Assuming any flow satisfying the above conditions and having a specific mass of ρ for the fluid, $V = G/\rho$ and $T = \dfrac{h_0 - V^2/2}{c_p}$, which gives $h = c_p T$ and

$$s = s_1 + c_v \ln \frac{T}{T_1} - R \ln \frac{\rho}{\rho_1}$$

where s_1 can be arbitrary constant. The pairs of values of h and s for various assumed values of ρ can be calculated and a graph can be drawn between them as in Fig. 21.8. This is known as the Fanno line.

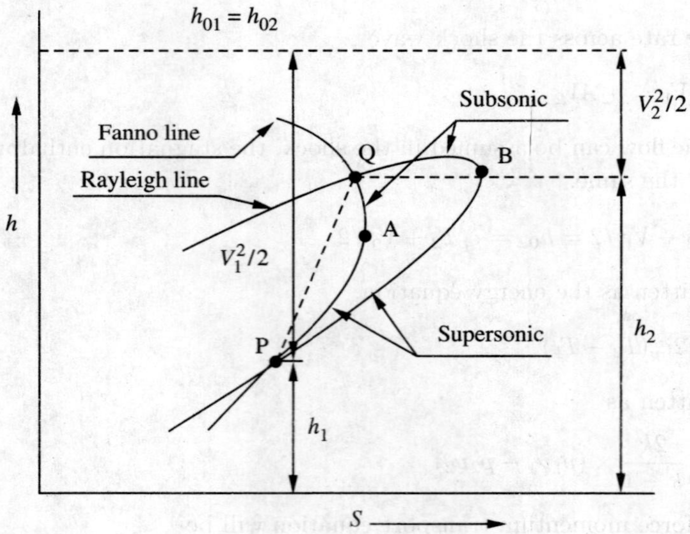

Fig. 21.8 *The Fanno and Rayleigh lines*

B. Condition 2: The Rayleigh line

(i) The mass flow rate/unit area $G = \dot{m}/A$ remain the same before and after the shock wave

(ii) The pressure + the momentum transport rate before and after the shock wave will remain the same.

i.e. $\quad A \times (p + \rho V^2) = A \times (p_1 + \rho_1 V_1^2) = A \times B$, where B is a constant.

$$T_1 = p_1/R\rho_1$$

Assuming any flow satisfying the above conditions and having a specific mass of $\rho$for the fluid

$$V = G/\rho;\ p = B - \rho V^2 \text{ and } T = \frac{p}{\rho R}$$

$$h = c_p T \text{ and}$$

$$s = s_1 + c_v \ln\frac{T}{T_1} - R\ln\frac{\rho}{\rho_1}$$

The pairs of values of h and s for various values of ρ can be calculated and a graph can be drawn between them as shown in Fig. 21.8. This is termed as the Rayleigh line.

C. Discussion

In the figure, the Fanno line and the Rayleigh line intersect at two points, P and Q, the lower point depicting the condition before the shock wave and the other representing the condition after the shock wave. At these points, the stagnation enthalpy will be the same. The change from P to Q involves a change in entropy. The points where the value of s is maximum in both curves, A and B will represent a Mach number of 1. The upper part of both the curves will represent conditions of subsonic flow and the lower part, the supersonic flow conditions.

21.15.2.3 The characteristic Mach numbers

The concept of characteristic Mach numbers is useful for analysing flow in a shock wave. For a state of flow before the shock, the parameters of flow are

$$\rho_1, p_1, V_1, \text{ and } T_1;$$

$$T_s = T_1 + \frac{V_1^2}{c_p} \text{ and } \frac{T^*}{T_s} = 0.833.$$

T^* is the temperature when the flow is sonic and Mach number is 1 and

$$C^* = \sqrt{kRT^*} \qquad (21.38)$$

The characteristic Mach numbers are defined as

$$M^* = V/c^* \qquad (21.39)$$

$$M_1 = V_1/c^* \qquad (21.40a)$$

$$M_2 = V_2/c^* \qquad (21.40b)$$

21.15.2.4 The Prandtl's equation

Considering the pressure momentum equation along with the continuity equation,

$$p_1 + \rho_1 V_1^2 = p_2 + \rho V_2^2 \tag{1}$$

and $\rho_1 V_1 = \rho_2 V_2$ (2)

From (1) and (2)

$$p_1 + \rho_1 V_1^2 = \rho_1 V_1 V_2$$

$$\frac{\rho_1 c_1^2}{k} + \rho V_1^2 = \frac{\rho_2 c_2^2}{k} + \rho_2 V_1 V_2$$

Dividing by $\rho_1 V_1$ and re-arranging,

$$\frac{c_1^2}{kV_1} - \frac{c_2^2}{kV_2} = V_1 - V_2 \tag{3}$$

From energy equation,

$$c_p T_1 + \frac{V_1^2}{2} = c_p T_2 + \frac{V_2^2}{2} = c_p T^* + \frac{V^{*2}}{2} \text{ (since } V^* = c^*) \tag{4}$$

From (4)

$$\frac{kRT_1}{k-1} + \frac{V_1^2}{2} = \frac{kRT_2}{k-1} + \frac{V_2^2}{2} = \frac{kRT^*}{k-1} + \frac{c^{*2}}{2} = c^{*2}\frac{k+1}{k-1} \tag{5}$$

Simplifying,

$$2c_1^2 = (k+1)c^{*2} - (k-1)V_1^2 \tag{6}$$

and $2c_2^2 = (k+1)c^{*2} - (k-1)V_2^2$ (7)

Equation (3) can be re-written as

$$2V_2 c_1^2 - 2V_1 c_2^2 = 2kV_1 V_2 (V_2 - V_1) \tag{8}$$

Substituting (6) and (7) in (8) it can be shown that

$$c^{*2} = V_1 V_2 \tag{21.41}$$

This is known as Prandtl's equation[2]. This equation can help to analyse shock waves as illustrated in the following example.

Example 21.13 In the expanding portion of a Laval nozzle, the velocity of air is 700 m/s and the pressure and temperature are 95 kPa and 20 °C respectively. A shock wave is formed.

Find the pressure, temperature, density, and Mach number after the shock. Find the strength of the shock. What is the change in entropy?

$$T_1 = 293 \text{ K}; \; c_1 = \sqrt{kRT_1} = 343.1 \text{ m/s};$$

$$\text{M}_1 = \frac{700}{343.1} = 2.04$$

$$p = 95 \text{ kPa}; \; \rho_1 = \frac{p_1}{RT_1} = 1.13\,\text{kg/m}^3$$

$$T_s = T_1\left(1 + \tfrac{k-1}{2}\text{M}_1^2\right) = 1.832 \times 293 = 536.78 \text{ K}$$

$$T^* = 0.833 T_s = 0.833 \times 536.78 = 447.14 \text{ K}$$

$$c^* = \sqrt{kRT^*} = 423.4 \text{ m/s}; \; V_2 = \frac{c^{*2}}{V_1} = 256.653$$

$$\rho_1 V_1 = \rho_2 V_2; \; \rho_2 = \frac{\rho_1 V_1}{V_2} = 3.08\,\text{kg/m}^3 \text{(Ans.)}$$

$$p_1 + \rho_1 V_1^2 = p_2 + \rho_2 V_2^2$$

By the momentum equation

$$\text{i.e. } 95 \times 10^3 + 1.13 \times 700^2 = p_2 + 3.08 \times 256.653^2; \; p_2 = 445.8 \text{ kPa (Ans.)}$$

$$T_1 = \frac{p_2}{\rho_2 R} = \frac{445.8 \times 10^3}{3.08 \times 287} = 504.7 \text{ K (Ans.)}$$

$$c_2 = \sqrt{kRT_2} = 449.25; \; \text{M}_2 = \frac{256.653}{449.25} = 0.571\text{(Ans.)}$$

$$\text{Strength of shock} = \frac{p_2 - p_1}{p_1} = \frac{445.8 - 95}{95} = 3.693 \text{ (Ans.)}$$

$$ds = s_2 - s_1 = c_p \ln\frac{T_2}{T_1} - R\ln\frac{p_2}{p_1} = 1004.5 \times \ln\frac{504.7}{293} - 287 \times \ln\frac{445.8}{95} = 1286.58\,\text{J/kg K (Ans.)}$$

Discussion

In a Laval nozzle, if the inlet pressure and the contraction is sufficient, sonic velocities can be reached at the throat provided the back pressure is not high. After the throat, the flow is accelerated to give supersonic velocities. If we consider that the back pressure is slowly increased, subsonic flow will occur at the end of the divergent pipe (the flow will be in the same direction as the inlet). The subsonic flow downstream will prevail further upstream to a section where the ratio $\frac{p_2}{p_1} = \frac{2k\text{M}_1^2 - (k-1)}{k+1}$ is attained and a shock wave will be formed.

21.15.2.5 Relation between parameters in a shock wave

The independent parameters before the shock wave can be considered to be p_1, V_1 and T_1 and the parameters after the shock wave p_2, V_2 and T_2.

$$\frac{T_1}{T^*} = \frac{T_s/T^*}{T_s/T_1} = \frac{k+1}{2+(k-1)\mathrm{M}_1^2}$$

$$\mathrm{M}_1^{*2} = \mathrm{M}_1^2 \times \frac{c^2}{c^{*2}} = \mathrm{M}_1^2 \times \frac{T_1}{T^*} = \frac{\mathrm{M}_1^2(k+1)}{2+(k-1)\mathrm{M}_1^2};$$

$$\text{Similarly } \mathrm{M}_2^{*2} = \frac{\mathrm{M}_2^2(k+1)}{2+(k-1)\mathrm{M}_2^2}$$

By applying the relationship $\mathrm{M}_2^{*2} = \dfrac{1}{\mathrm{M}_1^{*2}}$

$$\left[\frac{\mathrm{M}_2^2(k+1)}{2+(k-1)\mathrm{M}_2^2}\right] = \left[\frac{\mathrm{M}_1^2(k+1)}{2+(k-1)\mathrm{M}_1^2}\right]^{-1}$$

Expanding, simplifying and solving for M_2^2,

$$\mathrm{M}_2^2 = \frac{2+(k-1)\mathrm{M}_1^2}{2k\mathrm{M}_1^2-(k-1)} \tag{21.42}$$

$$\frac{\rho_2}{\rho_1} = \frac{V_1}{V_2} = \frac{V_1V_2}{V_2^2} = \frac{c^{*2}}{V_2^2} = \frac{1}{\mathrm{M}_2^{*2}} = \mathrm{M}_1^{*2} = \frac{(k+1)\mathrm{M}_1^2}{2+(k-1)\mathrm{M}_1^2} \tag{21.43}$$

and

$$\frac{V_2}{V_1} = \frac{2+(k-1)\mathrm{M}_1^2}{(k+1)\mathrm{M}_1^2} \tag{21.44}$$

$$p_2 - p_1 = \rho_1V_1^2 - \rho_2V_2^2 = \rho_1V_1^2 - \rho_1V_1V_2 = \rho_1V_1^2\left(1-\frac{V_2}{V_1}\right)$$

$$\frac{p_2-p_1}{p_1} = \frac{\rho_1V_1^2\left(1-\dfrac{V_2}{V_1}\right)}{\rho_1RT_1} = k\mathrm{M}_1^2\left(1-\frac{2+(k-1)\mathrm{M}_1^2}{(k+1)\mathrm{M}_1^2}\right)$$

and hence it can be proved that

$$\frac{p_2}{p_1} = \frac{2k\mathrm{M}_1^2-(k-1)}{k+1} \tag{21.45}$$

$$\frac{T_2}{T_1} = \frac{p_2}{p_1} \times \frac{\rho_1}{\rho_2} = \frac{2k\mathrm{M}_1^2-(k-1)\times(2+(k-1)\mathrm{M}_1^2)}{(k+1)^2)\mathrm{M}_1^2} \tag{21.46}$$

21.15.2.6 Simplified relationships for shock wave

The relationship derived above can be simplified by making the following substitutions:

$$F_1 = 2kM_1^2 - (k-1);\ F_2 = 2 + (k-1)M_1^2;\ \text{and}\ F_3 = (k+1)M_1^2;$$

$$\frac{p_2}{p_1} = \frac{F_1}{k+1} \tag{21.47}$$

$$\frac{T_2}{T_1} = \frac{F_1 F_2}{(k+1)F_3} \tag{21.48}$$

$$\frac{\rho_2}{\rho_1} = \frac{F_3}{F_2} \tag{21.49}$$

$$M_2 = \sqrt{\frac{F_2}{F_1}} \tag{21.50}$$

21.15.2.7 A convenient graphical relationship

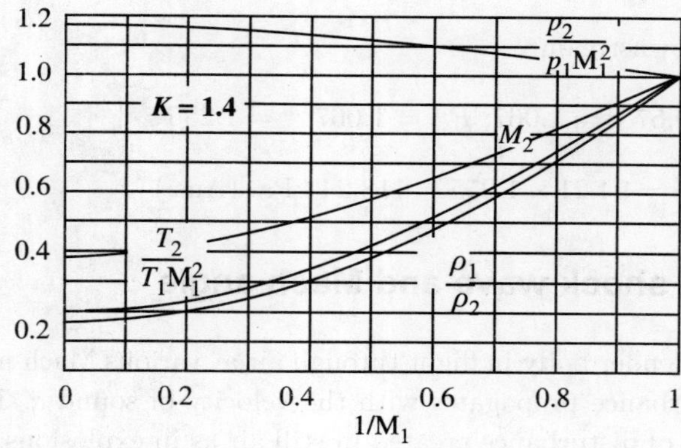

Fig. 21.9 *Relationships for normal shock wave*

A convenient way of graphically depicting the relationship between the parameters in the formation of normal shock waves is given in Fig. 21.9.

Example 21.14 A normal shock wave occurs in a flow of air where the pressure is 21 kPa, temperature 210 K and the velocity of air is 580 m/s. Calculate the stagnation pressure and Mach number upstream of the shock as well as pressure, temperature, velocity, Mach number and stagnation pressure downstream of the shock.

$p_1 = 21$ kPa; $T_1 = 210$ K; $V_1 = 580$ m/s; $c_1 = \sqrt{kRT_1} = \sqrt{1.4 \times 287 \times 210} = 290.48$ m/s.

$M_1 = V_1/c_1 = 1.997$ (Ans.)

$$T_{sr} = T_s/T_1 = \left(1 + \frac{k-1}{2}\text{M}_1^2\right) = (1 + 0.2 \times \text{M}_1^2) = 1.798;\ T_s = 210 \times 1.798 = 377.5 \text{ K}$$

$$p_{s1} = p_1 \times (T_{sr})^{k/(k-1)} = 21 \times (T_{sr})^{3.5} = 163.67 \text{ kPa. (Ans.)}$$

$$F_1 = 2k\text{M}_1^2 - (k-1) = 10.766;\ F_2 = 2 + (k-1)\text{M}_1^2 = 3.595;\ F_3 = (k+1)\text{M}_1^2 = 9.571;$$

$$\frac{p_2}{p_1} = \frac{F_1}{k+1} = \frac{10.776}{2.4} = 4.486;$$

$$p_2 = 21 \times 4.486 = 94.21 \text{ kPa. (Ans.)}$$

$$\frac{T_2}{T_1} = \frac{F_1 F_2}{(k+1)F_3} = \frac{10.766 \times 3.595}{2.4 \times 9.571} = 1.685;\ T_2 = 210 \times 1.685 = 353.85 \text{ K (Ans.)}$$

$$c_2 = \sqrt{kRT_2} = \sqrt{1.4 \times 287 \times 353.85} = 377.06 \text{ m/s}$$

$$\text{M}^2 = \sqrt{\frac{F_2}{F_1}} = \sqrt{\frac{3.595}{10.766}} = 0.578 \text{ (Ans.)};\ V_2 = 0.578 \times 377.06 = 217.94 \text{ m/s. (Ans.)}$$

Stagnation pressure downstream:

$$T_{sr} = 1 + 0.2 \times 0.578^2 = 1.067;\ P_{sr} = 1.067^{3.5} = 1.255$$

Hence, $p_s = p_2 \times 1.255 = 94.21 \times 1.255 = 118.24$ kPa. (Ans.)

21.15.3 Oblique shock wave and Mach angle

Figure 21.10 shows a slender body in flight through air at various Mach numbers. The pressure wave due to the disturbance propagates with the velocity of sound c. The figures are drawn to illustrate the limits of disturbance created in still air as in explosions, and when bodies are moving at the subsonic velocities, sonic velocity and supersonic velocities.

Figure 21.10(a) shows the body at rest and a disturbance propagating. In other cases, the velocity of the body is assumed and its present position and positions 1, 2, 3 and 4 seconds earlier are shown. The limits of the travel of the pressure wave as circles are also indicated. They travel at the velocity c whereas the body moves at the velocity V. Figure 21.10 (b) and Fig. 21.10(c) show no formation of the shock wave. Figure 21.10(d) shows that the shock wave formed may be attached to the body and make an angle β with the direction of movement so that

$$\sin\beta = \frac{1}{M} \tag{21.51}$$

The wave front is called the Mach wave. Such waves can be formed as weak waves in a supersonic flow. In case of greater disturbances, it may form an oblique shock wave. In three-dimensional bodies like a cone of small angles, the angle β at which the shock wave is formed can be approximated by μ whereas for two-dimensional cases, the angle β can be much more as discussed in Section. The supersonic flow past a cone and the shock wave is schematically shown in Figure 21.11(a). When a blunt body is held in supersonic flow it will produce a bow shaped detached shock wave (Fig. 21.11b).

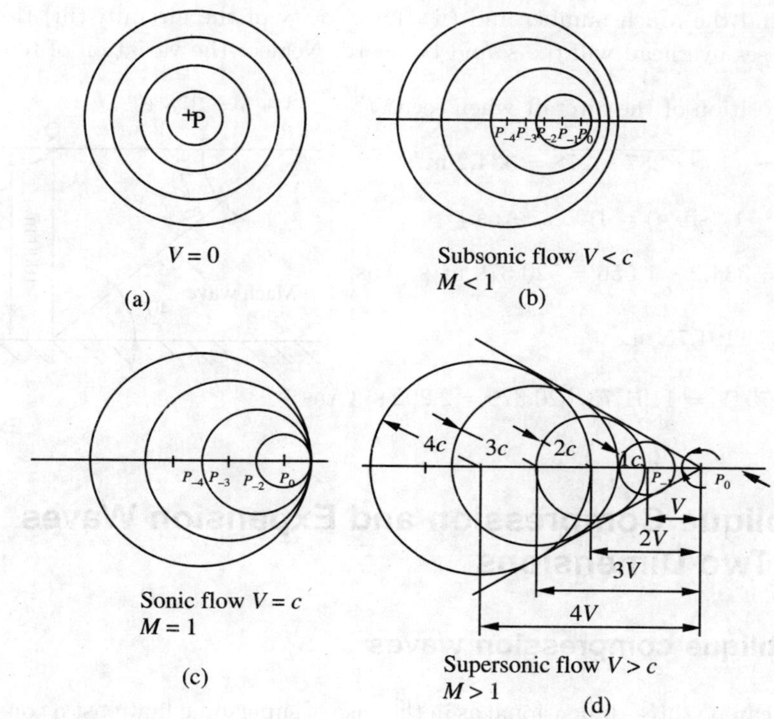

Fig. 21.10 *Propagation of disturbance*

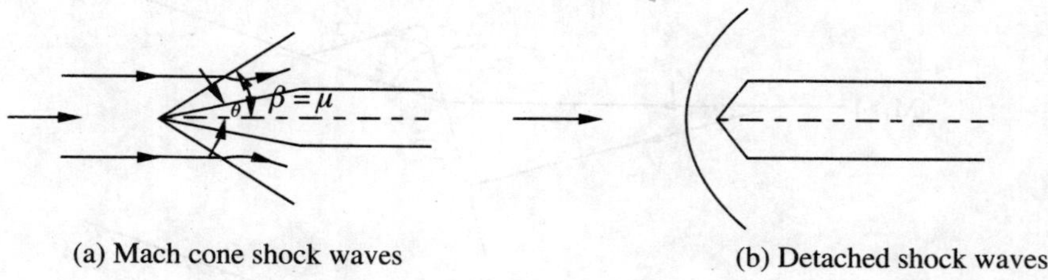

Fig. 21.11 *Supersonic flow past a three-dimensional body*

Example 21.15 A bullet fired shows a Mach angle of 35°C. If the pressure is 0.8 bar and temperature 255 K, find the velocity of the bullet.

$\beta = 35°\text{C}; \ \dfrac{1}{\text{M}} = \sin\beta$; hence $\text{M} = 1.743; c = \sqrt{kRT} = \sqrt{1.4 \times 287 \times 255} = 320.09$ m/s

$\text{M} = V/C; \ V = \text{M} \times C = 1.743 \times 320.09 = 559.92$ m/s. (Ans.)

Example 21.16 A supersonic aircraft was seen at an elevation of 40°C when the sonic boom was heard. If the aircraft was flying overhead at an altitude of 1000 m and the temperature was 5 °C, (i) find the Mach number and (ii) the velocity of the aircraft. (iii) How long after the aircraft passes overhead will the sound be heard. Neglect the variation of temperature.

Let R be the position of the aircraft when seen. $T = 273 + 5 = 278$ K;

$$c = \sqrt{kRT} = \sqrt{1.4 \times 287 \times 278} = 334.2 \text{ m/s}$$

$$\beta = 45°; \ \text{M} = 1/(\sin\beta) = 1.556. \text{ (Ans.)}$$

$$V = c \times \text{M} = 334.2 \times 1.556 = 520.379 \text{ m/s (Ans.)}$$

$$\text{QR} = \frac{1000}{\tan 40°} = 1191.75 \text{ m.}$$

$$t = 1191.75/V = 1191.75/520.379 = 2.292 \text{ s. (Ans.)}$$

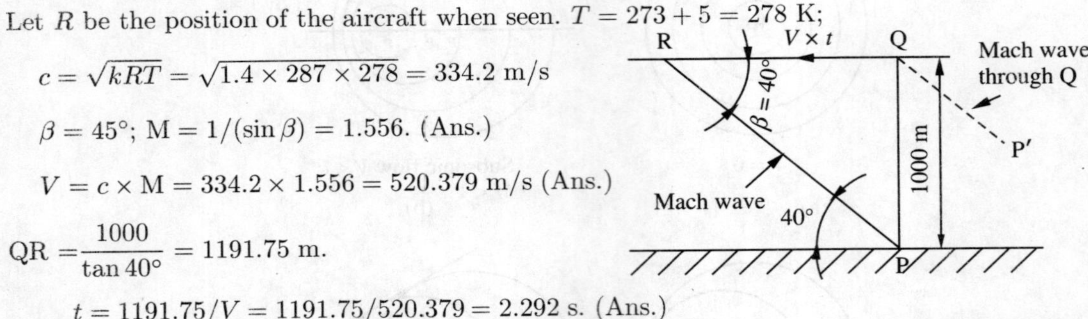

Example 21.16

21.16 Oblique Compression and Expansion Waves in Two Dimensions

21.16.1 Oblique compression waves

Oblique waves can be three-dimensional as in the case of supersonic flow past a cone (Fig. 21.11a) or two-dimensional as the flow takes place past a wedge or around a corner (Fig. 21.12). They are compression waves.

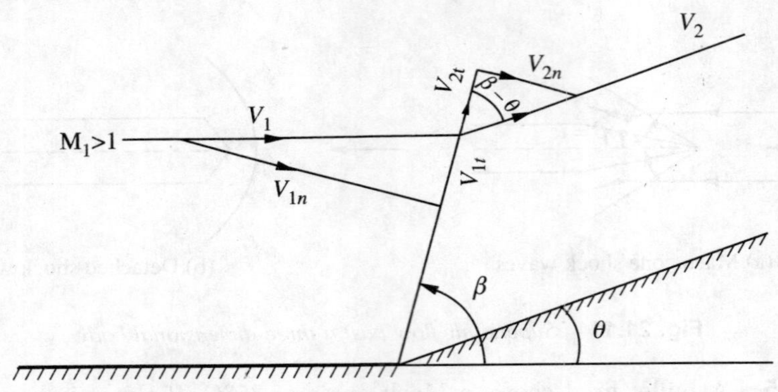

Fig. 21.12 *Supersonic flow past a concave corner*

Consider a supersonic flow parallel to the boundary with $M = M_1$ and the boundary is deflected by a small angle θ as shown in Fig. 21.12. A shock front will form making an angle β with the boundary. The flow will be parallel to the deflected boundary making an angle $\beta - \theta$ with the shock front as shown in the figure. Let the velocities before and after the shock front be V_1 and V_2 parallel to the respective boundaries. They can be resolved into components normal and tangential to the shock front. Since there is no change in momentum transport in the tangential direction of the shock, the tangential component $V_{1t} = V_{2t}$.

$$V_{2n} = V_{2t} \tan(\beta - \theta) = V_{1t} \tan(\beta - \theta) = \frac{V_{1n}}{\tan \beta} \times \tan(\beta - \theta)$$

Considering the mass flow rate across the shock wave, the equation of continuity ensures

$\rho_1 V_{1n} = \rho_2 V_{2n}$. Hence

$$\frac{\rho_1}{\rho_2} = \frac{V_{1n}}{V_{2n}} = \frac{\tan \beta}{\tan(\beta - \theta)}$$

$$M_{1n} = M_1 \sin \beta;$$

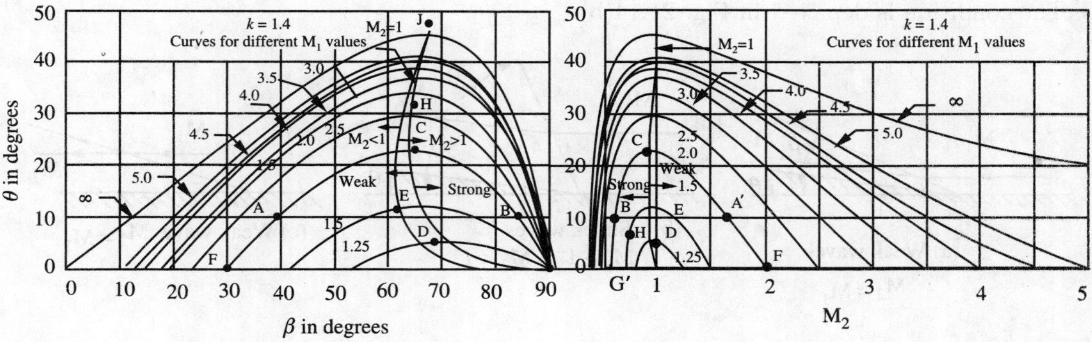

Fig. 21.13 *Relationship between β, M_1, θ, M_2*

Hence by using the relationship for a shock wave for $\dfrac{\rho_1}{\rho_2}$ across the oblique shock,

$$\frac{\rho_2}{\rho_1} = \frac{(k+1)M_1^2 \sin^2 \beta}{2 + (k-1)M_1^2 \sin^2 \beta} = \frac{\tan \beta}{\tan(\beta - \theta)}$$

After some trigonometric simplifications, the relationship between θ, β, M_1 and k can be obtained as

$$\tan \theta = 2 \cot \beta \left[\frac{M_1^2 \sin^2 \beta - 1}{M_1^2 (k + \cos 2\beta) + 2} \right] \tag{21.52}$$

By applying the relationships $M_{2n} = M_2 \sin(\beta - \theta)$ and the relationship for the shock wave

$$M_{2n}^2 = \frac{(k-1)M_{1n}^2 + 2}{2kM_1^2 - (k-1)},$$

$$M_2 \sin(\beta - \theta) = \sqrt{\frac{(k-1)M_1^2 \sin^2 \beta}{2kM_1^2 \sin^2 \beta - (k-1)}} \qquad (21.53)$$

Figure 21.13 shows two sets of curves: (i) for obtaining β when M_1 and θ are given in the case of air; and (ii) for obtaining M_2 when M_1 and θ are given. Using the curves, we can study the various possibilities of occurrence of the oblique Mach waves or the oblique shock waves.

21.16.2 Explanation for Fig. 21.13

Referring to Fig. 21.13, the following points can be observed.

Point A $M_1 = 2.0$; $\theta = 10°$; $\beta = 39.35°$; weak wave and $M_2 = 1.638$ as indicated at point A′. The condition is depicted in Fig. 21.14(a).

Point B $M_1 = 2.0$; $\theta = 10°$; $\beta = 83.8°$; shock wave and $M_2 = 0.603$ as indicated at point B′.The condition is depicted in Fig. 21.14(b).

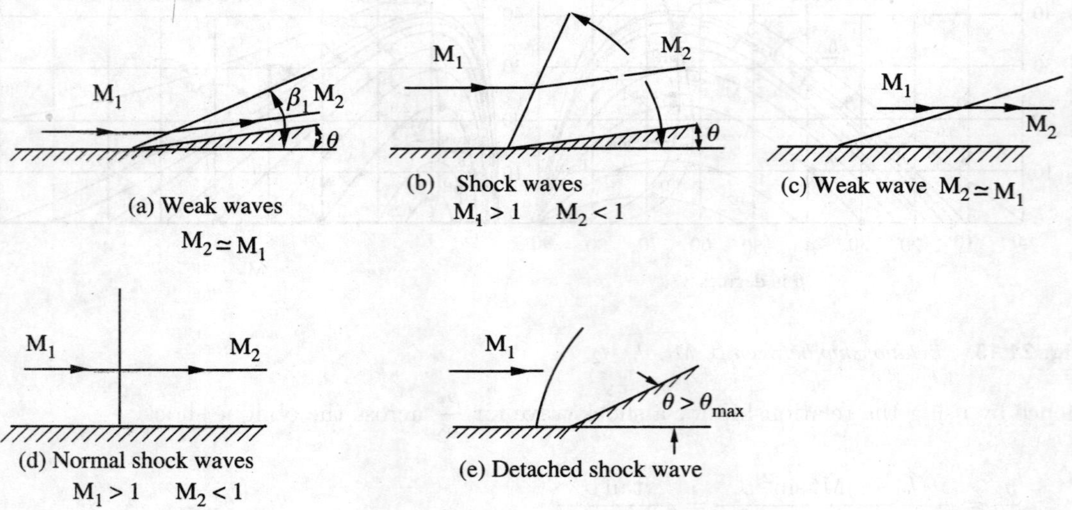

Fig. 21.14 *Some cases of supersonic flow past convex boundaries*

Point C $M_1 = 2.0$; $\theta = \theta_{max} = 23°$; $\beta = 65°$; shock wave and $M_2 = 0.603$ as indicated at point C′.

Point D $M_1 = 1.25$; $\theta = 5.2° < \theta_{max}$; $\beta = 69°$; weak wave with $M_2 < 1$ as indicated at point D′.

Point E $M_1 = 1.5$; $\theta = 11.1° < \theta_{max}$; $\beta = 62°$; weak wave with $M_2 = 1$ as indicated at point E′.

Point F $M_1 = 2$; $\theta = 0°$; $\beta = 30°$; weak wave with $M_2 = 2$ as indicated by point F′. The condition is depicted in Fig. 21.14(c).

Point G $M_1 = 2$; $\theta = 0°$; $\beta = 90°$ strong normal shock wave and $M_2 = 0.577$ as indicated by point G′. The condition is depicted in Fig. 21.14(d).

Point H $M_1 = 2.5$; $\theta = 32° > \theta_{max}$; oblique wave cannot form and detached shock wave is formed.The condition is depicted in Fig. 21.14(e).

Point J $\theta = 47° > \theta_{max}$ of 45.6° for infinite value of M_1 and only detached shock weave can form.

21.16.3 Relationship for oblique expansion waves

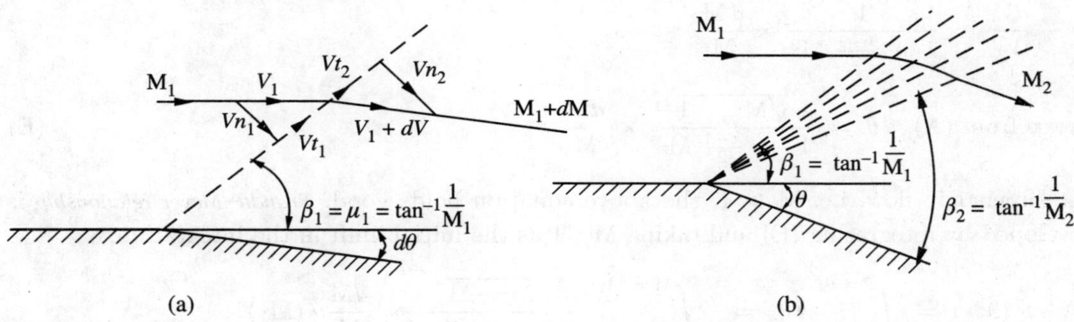

Fig. 21.15 *Oblique expansion waves*

When there is an expansion in a supersonic flow, no sudden change like a shock can occur. The velocity will increase downstream. The increase in the velocity is accompanied by a reduction in density, pressure and temperature. In the expansion as shown in Fig. 21.15(a), Mach waves which are practically isentropic can form. The direction of change θ can be assumed in infinitesimal incremental steps of $d\theta$, the consequence of which is studied and the total effect is found by integration.

In Fig. 21.15(b), a Mach wave is shown to occur making an angle $\beta = \mu_1$ with the boundary. The angle μ_1 will be equal to $\sin^{-1}\frac{1}{M_1}$. Let the velocity before the wave be V and after the wave, $V + dV$. Since the momentum transport in the tangential direction of the wave front is constant, $V_{1t} = V_{2t}$

i.e. $V \cos \mu = (V + dV) \cos (\mu + d\theta) = (V + dV) \times (\cos \mu \cos d\theta - \sin \mu \sin d\theta)$ (A)

Since $d\theta$ is very small $\cos d\theta = 1; \sin d\theta = d\theta$; and $dv \sin d\theta$ can be neglected. Hence (A) can be simplified as $V \sin \mu \, d\theta = \cos \mu \times dV$. Substituting $\sin \mu = \frac{1}{M}$

$$d\theta = \frac{dV}{V}\sqrt{M^2 - 1} \tag{B}$$

$$V = \sqrt{kRT}; \text{ Differentiating, } \frac{dV}{V} = \frac{dM}{M} + \frac{1}{2} \times \frac{dT}{T} \tag{C}$$

The stagnation temperature in an isentropic flow is given by $T\left\{1 + \frac{k-1}{2}M^2\right\} = T_s$

Differentiating and rearranging,

$$\frac{dT}{T} = \frac{-(k-1)\,M\,dM}{1 + \frac{k-1}{2}M^2} \tag{D}$$

Substituting (D) in (C) and simplifying,

$$\frac{dV}{V} = \frac{1}{1 + \frac{k-1}{2}M^2} \times \frac{dM}{M}$$

Hence from (A), $$d\theta = \frac{\sqrt{M^2 - 1}}{1 + \frac{k-1}{2}M^2} \times \frac{dM}{M} \tag{E}$$

For supersonic flow, i.e. M > 1, the above equation holds good. *Prandtl–Meyer relationship* is developed by integrating (E) and taking M =1 as the initial limit in the integration.

$$\nu(M_1) = \int_{\theta=\theta_i}^{\theta=\theta_1} d\theta = \int_{M=1}^{M=M_1} \frac{\sqrt{M^2-1}}{1 + \frac{k-1}{2}M^2} \times \frac{dM}{M} \nu(M_1)$$

The integral has been evaluated as

$$\nu(M_1) = \sqrt{\frac{k+1}{k-1}} \tan^{-1}\sqrt{\frac{k-1}{k+1}(M_1^2 - 1)} - \tan^{-1}\sqrt{M_1^2 - 1} \tag{21.54}$$

When M =1, $\nu(M) = 0$.

When the initial Mach number of flow before the expansion is M_1, $\theta_i = \nu(M_1)$is worked out. After an expansion if the Mach number is M_2, the angle of expansion required, θ, can be calculated as

$\theta = \nu(M_2) - \theta_i$. In case the expansion angle is given and the Mach number after the expansion is to be calculated, a trail and error procedure will be required. The calculations are made easy using Fig. 21.16, where ν (M)is given as a function of $\frac{1}{M}$.

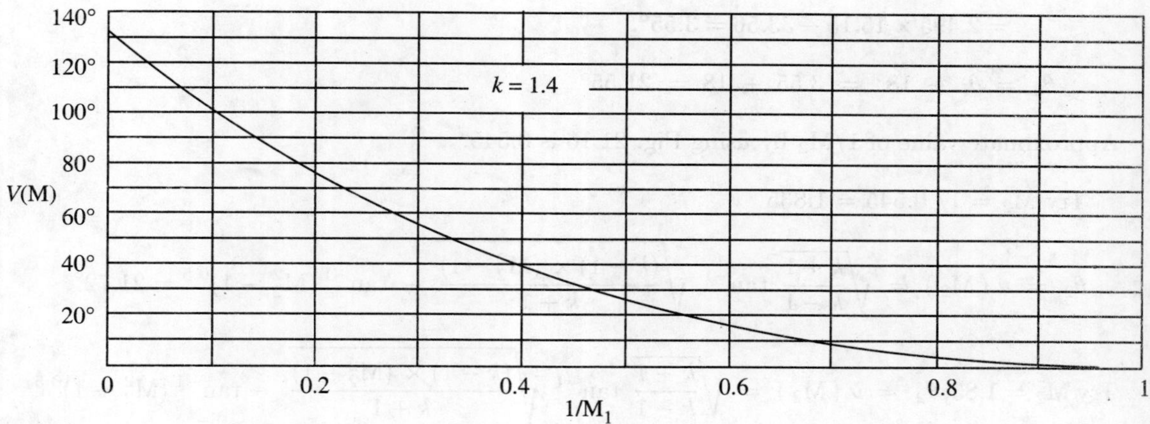

Fig. 21.16 *Relationship between* ν (M) *and 1/M*

Example 21.17 Air at a temperature of 40°C is flowing at a velocity of 500 m/s along a straight boundary. If the Mach number after a convex deflection should be 2.2, what will be the angle of deflection? Find the temperature of air after the deflection.

$$T_1 = 273 + 40 = 313 \text{ K};\ k = 1.4;\ c = \sqrt{k\,R T_1} = 354.63 \text{ m/s}$$

$$\mathrm{M}_1 = 500/354.63 = 1.414$$

$$\theta_i = \nu\,(M_1) = \sqrt{\frac{k+1}{k-1}}\tan^{-1}\sqrt{\frac{(k-1)\times(\mathrm{M}_1^2-1)}{k+1}} - \tan^{-1}(\mathrm{M}_1^2-1)$$

$$= 2.4495 \times 22.2 - 44.99 = 9.389°.$$

$$\mathrm{M}_2 = 2.2\,;\ \text{Hence } \theta_2 = \nu\,(\mathrm{M}_2) = \sqrt{\frac{k+1}{k-1}}\tan^{-1}\sqrt{\frac{(k-1)\times(\mathrm{M}_2^2-1)}{k+1}} - \tan^{-1}(\mathrm{M}_2^2-1)^{0.5}$$

$$= 2.4495 \times 38.69 - 62.96 = 31.73°.$$

$$\text{Hence } \theta = \theta_2 - \theta_i = 31.73 - 9.389 = 22.34°. \text{ (Ans.)}$$

$$T_2 = T_1 \times \frac{2 + (k-1)\,\mathrm{M}_1^2}{2 + (k-1)\,\mathrm{M}_2^2} = 313 \times \frac{1.4}{1.968} = 22.66°. \text{ (Ans)}$$

Example 21.18. A channel makes a convex deviation of 18°. If the initial Mach number is 1.2, find the Mach number after the deviation.

$$\mathrm{M}_1 = 1.2\,;\ \theta_i = \nu\,(\mathrm{M}_1) = \sqrt{\frac{k+1}{k-1}}\tan^{-1}\sqrt{\frac{(k-1)\times(\mathrm{M}_1^2-1)}{k+1}} - \tan^{-1}(\mathrm{M}_1^2-1)^{0.5}$$

$= 2.495 \times 15.15 - 33.56 = 3.55°.$

$$\theta_2 = \theta_i + 18° = 3.55 + 18 = 21.55°$$

Approximate value of $1/M_2$ by using Fig. 21.16 is 0.545.

Try $M_2 = 1/\ 0.545 = 1.835$

$$\theta_2 = \nu\,(M_2) = \sqrt{\frac{k+1}{k-1}}\ \tan^{-1}\sqrt{\frac{(k-1)\times(M_2^2-1)}{k+1}} - \tan^{-1}(M_2^2-1)^{0.5} = 21.72°.$$

$$\text{Try } M_2 = 1.83;\ \theta_2 = \nu\,(M_2) = \sqrt{\frac{k+1}{k-1}}\ \tan^{-1}\sqrt{\frac{(k-1)\times(M_2^2-1)}{k+1}} - \tan^{-1}(M_2^2-1)^{0.5}$$

$= 21.57° \approx 21.55°$

Hence $M_2 = 1.83$ (Ans.)

21.17 Isothermal Flow through Pipes with Friction

21.17.1 Equation governing flow

Long un-insulated pipe lines which are laid to convey gas can exchange heat with the surroundings and have the same temperature along the pipe. It is important to consider this case while transporting petroleum gases across long distances. The value of Darcy–Weisbach's coefficient of friction f as given by Moody's diagram is used even though some investigators have found that it may be an overestimate for supersonic flow.

Let the flow be maintained in the pipe from a reservoir through a convergent nozzle giving subsonic flow or through a converging–diverging nozzle designed to give supersonic flow in the pipe. A steady mass flow rate $\dot{m}$, diameter d of the pipe and temperature T of the surroundings are constants. Since T is constant p/ρ is constant. Also since the mass flow rate , $\dot{m} = \rho A V$ and A are constants, ρV is constant. Since $p \propto \rho$ and ρV is constant, pV is constant and $p_1/p_2 = V_2/V_1$; and $dp/p = -dV/V$. The velocity of sound given by the formula $c = \sqrt{kRT}$ is also a constant.

Since ρV , D and μ are constants, the Reynolds number and hence the value of the Darcy–Weisbach coefficient of friction f is the same for flow throughout the length of the pipe. In summary, T, A, $\dot{m}$, ρ; V; pV; Re; f and c are constants for the flow. The following relationships are also useful in the analysis. $V = cM$ and pV being constant, $p \propto \dfrac{1}{M}$.

The pressure head due to gas column $\rho g dz$ being negligible, the Euler's equation for flow to include the friction loss in the pipe can be written as

$$\frac{dp}{\rho} = -V\,dV - \frac{f\,dx\,V^2}{2D} \tag{21.55}$$

where dx is the increment in the length of pipe. Multiplying by $p\,\rho$, (21.55) can be written as

$$-p\,dp = p\,\rho\,V^2\left(\frac{dV}{V} + \frac{f\,dx}{2\,D}\right) = \rho^2\,R\,T\,V^2\left(\frac{dV}{V} + \frac{f\,dx}{2\,D}\right).$$

$$-p\,dp = \frac{\dot{m}^2\,R\,T}{2\,A^2}\left(\frac{2\,dV}{V} + \frac{f\,dx}{D}\right)$$

Integrating the above equation and setting the limits for parameters in section (1) to (2),

$$p_1^2 - p_2^2 = \frac{\dot{m}^2\,R\,T}{A^2}\left(2\,\ln\frac{V_2}{V_1} + \frac{f\,L}{D}\right)$$

which after division by p_1^2 can be reduced to

$$\frac{p_2^2}{p_1^2} = 1 - \frac{R\,T \times \rho_1^2\,V_1^2\,A^2}{p_1^2\,A^2}\left(2\,\ln\frac{p_1}{p_2} + \frac{f\,L}{D}\right)$$

$$\text{or } \frac{p_2^2}{p_1^2} = 1 - k\,\mathrm{M}_1^2\left(2\,\ln\frac{p_1}{p_2} + \frac{f\,L}{D}\right). \tag{21.56a}$$

Equating $\dfrac{p_2}{p_1} = \dfrac{\mathrm{M}_1}{\mathrm{M}_2}$,

$$\frac{\mathrm{M}_1^2}{\mathrm{M}_2^2} = 1 - k\,\mathrm{M}_1^2\left(2\,\ln\frac{\mathrm{M}_2}{\mathrm{M}_1} + \frac{f\,L}{D}\right)$$

$$\text{or} \quad 1 - \frac{\mathrm{M}_1^2}{\mathrm{M}_2^2} = k\mathrm{M}_1^2\left(\frac{fL}{D} - 2\,\ln\frac{\mathrm{M}_1}{\mathrm{M}_2}\right) \tag{21.56b}$$

Equations (21.56a) or (21.56b) can be used to calculate the parameters of flow in the pipe .

21.17.2 Limiting value of M_2

Equation (21.55) can be written as

$$\frac{dp}{p} \times RT + \frac{V^2\,dV}{V} = -\frac{f\,dx\,V^2}{2\,D}.$$

Substituting $\dfrac{dp}{p} = -\dfrac{dV}{V}$,

$$\frac{dp}{p} - \frac{V^2}{RT} \times \frac{dp}{p} = -\frac{f\,dx}{2\,D} \times \frac{V^2}{R\,T}.$$

Since $\dfrac{V^2}{RT} = k\mathrm{M}^2$,

$$\frac{dp}{p} \times \left(1 - k\,\mathrm{M}^2\right) = -\,k\,\mathrm{M}^2 \times \frac{f\,dx}{2\,D}$$

So, $$\frac{dp}{p} = -\,\frac{k\,\mathrm{M}^2}{1 - k\,\mathrm{M}^2} \times \frac{f\,dx}{2\,D} \qquad (21.57)$$

In (21.57), $\dfrac{dp}{p}$ becomes infinite when $1 - k\mathrm{M}^2$ becomes zero. There is a Mach number $\mathrm{M}_{cr} = 1/\sqrt{k}$ nearing which the flow becomes choked. This is the case when the initial flow in the pipe has $\mathrm{M} < 1/\sqrt{k}$ or the initial flow in the pipe has $\mathrm{M} > 1/\sqrt{k}$. From (21.56b) one can see that the restriction comes because of the length of the pipe, i.e., a limiting length can be found out.

It can be shown that the quantities $\frac{dV}{dx}$ *and* $\frac{d\mathrm{M}}{dx}$ *will have the same sign as* $(1 - k\mathrm{M}^2)$ *and* $\frac{dp}{dx}$ *will have the opposite sign to that of* $(1 - k\mathrm{M}^2)$.

21.17.3 Limiting length

Substitution of $\dfrac{dp}{p} = -\dfrac{dV}{V} = -\dfrac{d\mathrm{M}}{\mathrm{M}}$, in (21.57)will give

$$\frac{d\mathrm{M}}{\mathrm{M}} = \frac{k\mathrm{M}}{1 - k\,\mathrm{M}^2} \times \frac{f\,dx}{D}.$$

This will lead to the equation

$$\int_0^{L_{\max}} \frac{f}{D}\,dx = \int_{\mathrm{M}}^{1/\sqrt{k}} \frac{2\,(1 - k\,\mathrm{M}^2)\,d\mathrm{M}}{k\,\mathrm{M}^2\,\mathrm{M}}.$$

This integral when evaluated will lead to the result

$$L_{\max} = \frac{D}{f} \times \left(\frac{1 - k\,\mathrm{M}^2}{k\,\mathrm{M}^2} + \ln\left(k\,\mathrm{M}^2\right)\right). \qquad (21.58a)$$

Or $$\frac{L_{\max} f}{D} + 1 = (z - \ln z), \text{ where } z = \frac{1}{k\mathrm{M}^2} \qquad (21.58b)$$

The flow will be choked if the length of the pipe exceeds $L_{\max}$.

Example 21.19 Air is to be conveyed through a 30 cm diameter 150 m long smooth pipe at the rate of 40 kg/s at 20 °C. The pressure at the inlet is 450 kPa. (i) What is the maximum length of pipe for which the flow rate can be maintained. (ii) Find the pressure at the outlet. (iii) What is the maximum rate at which air can be supplied if the length is 150 m?. (iv) What will be the choking pressure for increased discharge?.

$$\dot{m} = 40 \text{ kg/s} = \rho\,V\,A;\ D = 0.3\text{ m};\ A = 0.0707\text{ m}^2;\ T = 20 + 273 = 293\text{ K}$$

$\rho V = 40/0.0707 = 565.77$; $\rho = p/RT = 450 \times 1000/(287 \times 293) = 5.351$ kg /m^3.

$V = \rho V/\rho = 105.73$ m/s; $C = \sqrt{kRT} = 343.1$ m/s; M $= 105.73/343.1 = 0.3082$.

$k\text{M}^2 = 1.4 \times 0.3082^2 = 0.133$

$\mu_{20} = 18 \times 10^{-6}$ Pa s ; $\text{Re} = \dfrac{\rho V D}{\mu} = 9.375 \times 10^6$.

Using A.K. Jain's explicit equation,

$1/\sqrt{f} = 1.8 \log \text{Re} - 1.5$; $f = 0.0082$

$z = 1/k\text{M}^2 = 7.5188$; $\dfrac{f L_{max}}{D} + 1 = z - \ln z = 5.5014$;

(i) $L_{max} = (5.5014 - 1) \times D/f = 16468$ m. (Ans.)

$L_{max} > 150$ m. Hence the flow can be maintained.

(ii) $1 - \dfrac{p_2^2}{p_1^2} = k\text{M}^2 \left(\dfrac{f L}{D} - 2 \ln \dfrac{p_2}{p_1} \right)$

This is to be solved by trial and error method.

Assumed value of p_2/p_1	LHS	RHS
0.6	0.64	0.681
0.5	0.75	0.729
0.55	0.697	0.704
0.536	0.712	0.711

Hence the outlet pressure is nearly $0.536 \times 450 = 242.1$ kPa. (Ans.).

(iii) $\dfrac{f L_{max}}{D} + 1 = \dfrac{0.0082 \times 150}{0.3} + 1 = 5.1 = z - \ln z$;

$z - lnz - 5.1 = 0$

z can be found out by the Newton–Raphson method to be 7.054.

$z = 1/(k\text{M}_2)$; M $= 0.3182$:

$V_1 = C \times \text{M} = 343.1 \times 0.3182 = 109.17$ m/s.

Max mass flow rate $= \rho_1 A_1 V_1 = 5.351 \times 0.0707 \times 109.17 = 41.7$ kg/s (Ans.)

(iv) Choking pressure $= p_1 \times \text{M} \times \sqrt{k} = 450 \times 0.3182 \times \sqrt{1.4} = 169.32$ kPa. (Ans)

21.18 Adiabatic Flow through Pipes with Friction (Fanno Flow)

21.18.1 Introduction

The adiabatic flow through pipes with friction finds application in conveying refrigerants and steam. Heat is generated due to friction on the boundaries and the process is not reversible. So the flow will not be isentropic and entropy will increase downstream. It can be shown that the maximum entropy will be reached at a limiting value of Mach number one as evident from the Fanno line in Fig. 21.8. There will also be a limiting value of the distance where the Mach number will be equal to 1.

Due to viscosity of gas, the boundary layer developed in the pipe will reduce the area of cross-section and the result will be similar to that of an isentropic flow in converging pipes. Just as in the case of a converging portion of the Laval nozzle, in subsonic flow the values of M and V will increase downstream and p, T and ρ will decrease, whereas in supersonic flow, the reverse will be the case.

21.18.2 The Fanno flow function

The analysis of flow is made under the gross assumption that the value of f, the Darcy–Weisbach coefficient of friction remains the same along the pipe. The shear force at the pipe boundary $\tau = \frac{f}{8} \times \rho V^2$ varies along the pipe since the velocity varies. Hence for taking into account the friction, a differential approach in length dx will be necessary.

Since the flow is adiabatic, the stagnation temperature is constant.

$$\text{i.e. } T_s = T\left(1 + \frac{k-1}{2}\text{M}^2\right) = \text{constant}$$

$$\text{or } \ln T + \ln\left(1 + \frac{k-1}{2}\text{M}^2\right) \text{ is constant.}$$

$$\text{So } \frac{dT}{T} = \frac{k-1}{1 + \frac{k-1}{2}\text{M}^2} \times \text{M}\,d\text{M} \text{ or } \frac{dT}{T} = \frac{-2(k-1)}{2+(k-1)\text{M}^2} \times \frac{\text{M}^2\,d\text{M}}{\text{M}} \quad \text{(A)}$$

$$V^2 = \text{M}^2c^2 = \text{M}^2kRT \text{ where } R \text{ and } k \text{ are constants}$$

$$\text{Hence } \frac{2dV}{V} = \frac{2d\text{M}}{\text{M}} + \frac{dT}{T}$$

Substituting (A) in the equation

$$\frac{dV}{V} = \frac{2}{2+(k-1)\text{M}^2}\,\frac{d\text{M}}{\text{M}} \quad \text{(B)}$$

$$p = \rho RT;\ \frac{dp}{p} = \frac{d\rho}{\rho} + \frac{dT}{T} = \frac{dT}{T} - \frac{dV}{V}.$$

Substituting values of $\frac{dT}{T}$ and $\frac{dV}{V}$ from (A) and (B),

$$\frac{dp}{p} = -\frac{2+2(k-1)\mathrm{M}^2}{2+(k-1)\mathrm{M}^2} \times \frac{d\mathrm{M}}{\mathrm{M}} \tag{C}$$

$$\frac{dp}{\rho V^2} = \frac{dp}{p} \times \frac{p}{\rho} \times \frac{c^2}{kRT} \times \frac{1}{V^2} = \frac{dp}{p} \times \frac{1}{M^2} \tag{D}$$

The resistance to flow by the boundary can be included in the force–momentum balance equation. If τ is shear stress at the boundary, A is the area of cross-section of the pipe, P is the wetted perimeter,

$$\tau = \frac{f}{8} \times \rho V^2 \text{ and } \frac{A}{P} = \frac{D_H}{4},$$

where D_H is the hydraulic diameter (4 times the hydraulic mean radius, for a circular pipe. $D_H = d$ the diameter of the pipe.)

$$-\tau \times P\,dx - A\,dp = \rho\,A\,V\,dV\,.$$

Substituting for values of τ and $\frac{A}{P}$ and simplifying

$$\frac{f\,dx}{2D_H} + \frac{dp}{\rho V^2} + \frac{dV}{V} = 0 \tag{E}$$

Substituting (D) in (E),

$$\frac{f\,dx}{2D_H} = -\frac{1}{k\mathrm{M}^2} \times \frac{dp}{p} - \frac{dV}{V} \tag{F}$$

Substituting (B) and (C) for $\frac{dV}{V}$ and $\frac{dp}{p}$, in (F) and simplifying,

$$\frac{f\,dx}{D_H} = \frac{4\,(1-\mathrm{M}^2)}{k\mathrm{M}^2\,\{2+(k-1)\mathrm{M}^2\}}\frac{d\mathrm{M}}{}.$$

Integrating between the limits M = M and M = 1 and noting that the length will be L^* to the section where the Mach number is one,

$$\frac{f\,L^*}{D_H} = \frac{1-\mathrm{M}^2}{k\mathrm{M}^2} + \frac{k+1}{2k}\ln\frac{(k+1)\,\mathrm{M}^2}{2+(k-1)\,\mathrm{M}^2} \text{ which can be written as}$$

$$\frac{f\,L^*}{D_H} = \frac{1-\mathrm{M}^2}{k\mathrm{M}^2} + \frac{k+1}{2k}\ln\frac{M^2}{T_{*r}} \tag{21.59}$$

$$\text{where } T_{*r} = \frac{T^*}{T} = \frac{2+(k-1)\,\mathrm{M}^2}{k+1} \tag{21.60}$$

The procedure for finding the length in which the Mach number will change from M_1 to M_2 is to find out

$$\left[\frac{f\,L^*}{D_H}\right]_{M=M_1} - \left[\frac{f\,L^*}{D_H}\right]_{M=M_2} \tag{21.61}$$

21.18.3 The other parameters of flow

Since the flow is adiabatic,

$$T_{*r} = \frac{T^*}{T} = \frac{2 + (k-1)\,M^2}{k+1} \tag{21.62}$$

$$V_{*r} = \frac{V^*}{V} = \frac{\sqrt{kRT^*}}{M\sqrt{kRT}} = \frac{\sqrt{T_{*r}}}{M} \tag{21.63}$$

$$\rho_{*r} = \frac{\rho^*}{\rho} = \frac{V}{V^*} = \frac{M}{\sqrt{T_{*r}}} \tag{21.64}$$

$$p_{*r} = \frac{p^*}{p} = \frac{p^*}{\rho^*} \times \frac{\rho^*}{\rho} \times \frac{\rho}{p} = \frac{RT^*}{RT} \times \frac{\rho^*}{\rho} = M\sqrt{T_{*r}} \tag{21.65}$$

Example 21.20 A smooth duct 10 cm diameter conveys air adiabatically The inlet conditions are $T_1 = 310$ K ; $p_1 = 150$ kPa; and M = 0.2. Find the duct length required to accelerate the flow to a Mach number of one. Find the flow rate and exit pressure. Assume $f = 0.0267$.

$T_1 = 310$ K; $p_1 = 150$ kPa; $M_1 = 0.2$; $D = 0.1$ m; $A = 0.007854$ m^2;

$$c = \sqrt{k\,R\,T_1} = \sqrt{1.4 \times 287 \times 310} = 352.93 \text{ m/s}$$

$$V = cM = 352.93 \times 0.2 = 70.586 \text{ m/s}$$

$$\rho_1 = \frac{p_1}{R\,T} = \frac{150 \times 1000}{287 \times 310} = 1.686 \text{ kg/m}^3 .$$

$$\frac{T}{T^*} = \frac{k+1}{2 + (k-1) \times M^2} = \frac{2.4}{2.016} = 1.1905$$

$$\frac{f\,L^*}{D} = \frac{1 - M^2}{kM^2} + \frac{k+1}{2\,k} \times \ln\left(\frac{T_1}{T^*} \times M^2\right) = 17.14 - 2.6096 = 14.53.$$

$$L^* = \frac{14.53 \times 0.1}{0.0267} = 14.53 \text{ (Ans.)}$$

Flow rate $= \rho_1\,A\,V = 1.686 \times 7.8 \times 10^{-3} \times 70.588 = 0.935$ kg/s (Ans.)

$$\frac{p_1}{p^*} = \frac{1}{M} \times \left(\frac{T_1}{T^*}\right)^{0.5} = \frac{1}{0.2} \times 1.1905 = 5.456$$

$$p^* = \frac{p}{5.456} = \frac{150}{5.456} = 27.49 \text{ kPa (Ans.)}$$

21.19 Analogy between Flow in Open Channels and of Compressible Fluids

Many equations in open channel flow are similar to equations in compressible flow—an analogy exists in some ranges Any small disturbance in open channel flow travels at a velocity of $V_{cr} = \sqrt{g\,y}$, where V_{cr} is the critical velocity and y is the depth of flow. At the critical velocity, the Froude's number F, representing the ratio of inertial forces to gravitational forces is equal to one. In compressible flow, the Mach number M represents the ratio of the inertial forces to the elastic forces and will be equal to one at the sonic speed of $\sqrt{k\,R\,T} = \sqrt{k\,p/\rho}$. When the Froude's number is greater than one, it is a supercritical flow and any disturbance created at a source will not be able to travel upstream. In a similar way, when the Mach number exceeds one, it is supersonic speed and no disturbance by any source can travel upstream

The analogy is very close for values of F and M within 1.5 . Formation of oblique hydraulic jumps on thin sheet flow over table models had been used for studies on the formation of oblique shock waves and Mach interactions between them. Both the cases of hydraulic jump and shock waves are accompanied by high energy losses and both the processes are irreversible. In expansions, both the cases have similar oblique ripples and oblique rarefaction waves.

Some of the similarities of the two phenomena are clear by studying the equations governing them.

	Open channel flow (on horizontal channels)	Compressible flow
Equation of continuity	Vy is constant (per unit width)	$V\,\rho$ is constant (per unit area)
Eulers equation	$VdV + gdy$ is constant	$VdV + dp/\rho$ constant
	$= VdV + V_{cr}^2 dy/y$	$= VdV + c^2 d\rho/\rho$
Energy equation	$p/\rho + V^2/2$ is constant	$h + V^2/2$ is constant
Momentum equation	$\sum F = \rho\,A_2 V_2^2 - \rho\,A_1 V_1^2$	$\sum F = \rho_2\,A_2 V_2^2 - \rho_1\,A_1 V_1^2$

The difference in the phenomena is observed mainly due to comparatively high compressibility and thermodynamic effects for gases.

REVIEW QUESTIONS AND PROBLEMS

21.1 Show that the velocity of propagation of a pressure wave in a compressible fluid is given by $c = \sqrt{k/\rho}$, where k is the bulk modulus of fluid and ρ is the density of the fluid.

21.2 Derive an expression for the velocity of sound wave for compressible fluids when the process is (i) isothermal (ii) adiabatic.

21.3 Show that the speed of sound in a gas is $\sqrt{kRT}$.

21.4 For small velocities of flow, the analysis in compressible flow can be done similar to the incompressible flow. Find the limit of velocity so that the error is limited to 2 %.

21.5 What is enthalpy? Differentiate it from stagnation enthalpy.

21.6 Distinguish between isothermal, adiabatic and polytropic processes.

21.7 Explain what is entropy . Distinguish between adiabatic and isentropic processes.

21.8 Show that in a $p-v$ diagram every point can have specific values of enthalpy. Also show that if a point is given a value of entropy, the values of other points can be calculated.

21.9 Write down the Bernoulli's equation neglecting the losses for (i) isothermal flow and (ii) for adiabatic flow.

21.10 Write the force–momentum transport equation incompressible flow.

21.11 Show how the stagnation temperature T_s is related to the temperature at a point in the ambient flow assuming adiabatic conditions..

21.12 Derive the relation between the pressure ratio and temperature ratio between two sections in an isentropic flow.

21.13 Express the stagnation pressure as a function of the pressure at a point and the temperature ratio.

21.14 Prove that in a one-dimensional compressible flow through a pipe of varying area $dA/A = (dV/V)(\mathrm{M}^2 - 1)$.

21.15 Explain the nature of change of p, T, ρ, V and M when the flow of a compressible fluid is (i)) subsonic in a convergent tube; (ii) supersonic in a convergent tube.

21.16 Explain the nature of change of p, T, ρ, V and M when the flow of compressible flow is (i) subsonic in a divergent tube; (ii) supersonic in a divergent tube.

21.17 What is a Laval nozzle? Show that in a Laval nozzle, the formation of a supersonic flow downstream depends on the flow rate in the tube and the exit pressure..

21.18 Explain when the Laval nozzle will be choked.

21.19 Explain the effect of back pressure on the flow conditions in the diverging portion of a converging–diverging nozzle, when the nozzle discharges from a high pressure reservoir.

21.20 Does the mass flow rate of compressible fluid calculated by using the formula for a venturi meter get affected by the downstream pressure? Why?

21.21 How can one increase the flow in a converging mouthpiece from a reservoir of gas under pressure?

21.22 What decides the formation of a shock wave in the expansion region of a Laval nozzle?

21.23 How does the temperature on the nose of an aircraft differ from that of air at some distance from the aircraft?.

21.24 How does the value of c compare at 20°C for pressures of 1 bar and 3 bar?

21.25 In a Fanno flow, M reduces from 1.8 to 1.2 downstream. What happens to the stagnation temperature, temperature, pressure and entropy.

21.26 In an isothermal flow of air through a pipe, find how the pressure and velocity will change along the pipe (i) if the Mach number is 0.7; (ii) 0.9 and (ii) 1.5.

21.27 A test plane attained Mach number of 1.8 at an altitude of 2 km when the temperature was −45°C. Determine the speed of the plane. Assume $k = 1.4$ and $R = 287$ J/ kg.K.

21.28 A test on an aircraft is to be conducted in a supersonic wind tunnel. The temperature is 20°C. If the model size is 1/80 and the aircraft has to fly at a velocity of 500 m/s at a temperature of −35°C, find the velocity at which the model is to be tested.

21.29 Determine the Mach number when a bullet moves at 2400 km/hr. in still air at −5°C.

21.30 Find the temperature of air at which a velocity of 1500 m/s will have a Mach number of 5.

21.31 3 kg of air at 60°C and a pressure of 2 bar is allowed to expand adiabatically so that the pressure is 1 bar. Find the temperature and volume of air after the expansion.

21.32 1 kg of air at 100°C and pressure of 1 bar and 1 kg of air at 40°C at pressure of 1 bar are mixed in an insulated chamber (total volume remaining the same). What is the resulting temperature of air? What is the change in entropy of the system?

21.33 A pressure vessel contains 4 m^3 of air at 20 bar and temperature of 288 K. The temperature of gas is increased to 300 K. Calculate the change in entropy and change in total entropy.

21.34 Air flows through a long converging pipe of inlet diameter 20 cm and outlet diameter 15 cm. If the inlet pressure is 120 kPa and outlet pressure is 107.2 kPa, find the mass flow rate in the pipe. Assume isothermal flow at a temperature of 20°C.

21.35 Air is released adiabatically from an inflated tyre. The temperature of the air released was less than the temperature in the tyre by 30°C. Find the speed of the jet of air.

21.36 The stagnation pressure and temperature for a flowing air through a device are 0.75 kPa and 605 K respectively. If the velocity of air is 540 m/s, find (i) the static temperature; (ii) the static pressure and (iii) the Mach number of flow.

21.37 A stream of air has a pressure of 20 kPa (vacuum) and velocity of 250 m/s. The temperature is 30° C. If the atmospheric pressure is 101 kPa, find the stagnation properties.

21.38 Calculate the compressibility correction factor when a Pitot tube is used to measure the velocity of an aircraft when the Mach number is 0.9. By what factor is the velocity indicated to be multiplied to get the actual velocity.

21.39 Find whether the Mach number and density of fluid increases or decreases in an isentropic compressible flow for a pipe of gradually varying cross-section given below:
(i) diverging pipe $M_1 = 0.8$; (ii) converging pipe $M_1 = 0.8$; (iii) diverging pipe $M_1 = 1.2$; (iv) diverging pipe $M_1 = 1.0$

21.40 A converging duct from a reservoir containing carbon dioxide conveys the gas at the rate of 2 kg/s. The pressure and temperature of the gas are 1000 kPa and 180°C respectively. Find the sonic velocity reached. Find the area of cross-section of the duct and pressure where the sonic velocity is reached. Assume for carbon dioxide $R = 188.9$ J/kg K, and $k = 1.289$.

21.41 In a Laval nozzle, the velocity of air in a section is 200 m/s, temperature 60°C and pressure 280 kPa. Find the pressure and temperature at the throat. If the throat area is 8.6 cm^2, find the area where the Mach number will be 1.4.

21.42 A Laval nozzle in an air duct has a sonic velocity at the throat section having an area of 16 cm^2. If the stagnation pressure and temperature at the throat are 1200 kPa and 600 K respectively, find the area, temperature, pressure and velocity at a section where the Mach number is 2.5.

21.43 Air flow is to be measured by using a venturimeter having an area ratio of 0.39. Find out the increase in mass flow rate if the throat pressure is decreased from 0.833 to 0.7 of the inlet pressure.

21.44 In a flow of carbon dioxide in a pipe, the velocity is 250 m/s, the pressure is 200 kPa and temperature is 35°C. Assuming isentropic condition, find the pressure and temperature where the velocity is 450 m/s in a downstream section. Assume $R = 188.9$ J/kg K and $k = 1.289$.

21.45 A reservoir contains carbon dioxide at a pressure of 400 kPa at a temperature of 35°C. A converging nozzle has a diameter of 6 cm. What is the maximum rate of flow. What is the maximum exit pressure to have at that flow. Assume $k = 1.28$ and $R = 188$ J/kg.K for carbon dioxide.

21.46 A normal shock wave is formed in air. The velocity before the shock wave is 520 m/s and the temperature is 40°C. If the area of cross-section is 20 cm^2 and the mass flow rate is 0.8 kg/s, find the pressure and temperature after the shock wave.

21.47 A shock wave occurs at the exit of a converging –diverging nozzle when the Mach number of air flow is 2.5. If the stagnation pressure and temperature are 500 kPa and 550 K respectively, find (i) the temperature, pressure, and velocity before the shock and (ii) the pressure, temperature, density and velocity after the shock. (iii) What is the change in entropy?

21.48 Before a normal shock wave in air, the velocity was 500 m/s with a Mach number of 1.4. Find the velocity after the shock wave.

21.49 A bullet was fired at a velocity of 500 m/s at an altitude where the temperature was −40°C. Find the Mach angle.

21.50 A sonic boom of a supersonic plane flying at an altitude of 2500 m was heard 6.5 s after it passed overhead. If the temperature of air was - 10 °C, find the Mach number.

21.51 Using the graph for oblique shock waves, find the condition of flow when initial flow details are as given below: Make suitable sketches.

(i) $M_1 = 2.5$; $\theta = 35°$
(ii) $M_1 = 2.5$; $\theta = 10°$ $\beta = 32°$
(iii) $M_1 = 5$; $\theta = 20°$ $\beta = 84.5°$
(iv) $M_1 = 2$; $\theta = 23°$ $\beta = 67°$

21.52 A channel deflects air flow convexly by 20°. If the initial Mach number is 1.2, find the Mach number after the deflection. Use the formula

$$\nu\,(\mathrm{M}) = \sqrt{\frac{k+1}{k-1}}\tan^{-1}\sqrt{\frac{(k-1)\,(\mathrm{M}^2-1)}{k+1}} - \tan^{-1}\sqrt{\mathrm{M}^2-1}$$

21.53 Oxygen at 20 °C ($R = 260$ J/kg K; $k = 1.4$) flows through a 2 cm diameter tube. The entrance velocity is 60 m/s. If the exit velocity is 100 m/s, find the length of the tube. If pressure at the entrance is 120 kPa, find the pressure at the exit and the mass flow rate. Assume $f = 0.012$ and isothermal flow.

21.54 Nitrogen at 20 °C is to be conveyed through a 1 cm diameter smooth tube. The entrance velocity is 100 m/s. If $f = 0.016$, find the maximum length of the tube. Assume isothermal flow. Gas constant for nitrogen = 297 J/kg K and $k = 1.4$.

21.55 Air is to be supplied through a 20 cm diameter pipe adiabatically. The inlet conditions are $T_1 = 290$ K; $p_1 = 200$ kPa and $V_1 = 90$ m/s. What is the mass flow rate? What can be the maximum length of the pipe? Assume $f = 0.02$.

Answers

21.26. (i) p decreases, V increases (ii) p increases, V decreases (iii) p increases, V decreases; **21.27.** $T_s = 334.12$ K; $p_s = 114.05$ kPa; $\rho_s = 1.1894$ kg/m^3; **21.28.** 554.77 m/s; **21.29** 2.03; **21.30.** −49°C; **21.31.** 273.07 K; 2.351 m^3; **21.32.** 343 K; 1 bar, 3.857 J/kg K; **21.33.** 29.2755 J/kg..K ; 2833.5 J/K; **21.34.** 3.595 kg/s; **21.35.** 245.5 m/s; **21.36.** (i) 459.85 K; (ii) 0.287 kPa. (iii) 1.256; **21.37.** $T_s = 334.12$ K; $p_s = 114.05$ kPa; $\rho_s = 1.1894$ kg/m^3; **21.38.** 1.219; 0.0906;; **21.39.** (i) M decrease s, ρ increases (ii) M increases, ρ decreases (iii) M increases, ρ decreases (iv) M increases, ρ decreases; **21.40** 332.1 m/s; 5.15×10^{-4} m^2; 500 kPa; **21.41.** $P^* = 147.91$ kPa; $T^* = 293.99$ K; $A = 9.889$ cm^2; **21. 42**. 42.188 cm^2; 266.7 K; 70.23 kPa; 818.38 m/s; **21.43.** 20.19 %; **21.44.** $p = 83.11$ kpa; $T = 322.1$ K **21.45.** 3.242 kg/s; 219.52 kPa; **21.46.** $p = 161.86$ kPa: $T = 402.28$ K; **21.47.**(i) 244.4 K; 29.264 kPa; 783.42 m/s. (ii) 522.3 K; 208.506 kPa; 1.5846 kg/m^3; 235 m/s. (iii) 199.5 J/kg K; **21.48.** 255.1m/s ; **21.49..** 37.73°; **21.50.** 1.871; **21.51.** (i) detached shock wave (ii) $M_2 = 2.2$; weak wave; (iii) $M_2 = 0.45$; shock wave (iv) $M_2 = 0.95$, shock wave; **21.52.** M = 1.9; 1.871; **21.53.** 20.9 m; 71.99 kPa; 0.0297 kg/s; **21.54.** 3.346 m; **21.55.** 6.791 kg/s; 74.18 m.

References

1. Aggarwal, S.K. *Fluid Mechanics and Machinery*. 1997: Tata McGraw Hill Publishing Co.Ltd, New Delhi.
2. Anderson, John, D. *Modern Compressible Flow with Historical Perspective*, Third Edition. 2003: McGraw Hill, New York, 2003.
3. Bensal, R. K. *Fluid Mechanics and Hydraulic Machines*. 1998: Lakshmi Publications (P) Ltd..
4. Chow, V.T. Open Channel Hydraulics. 1959: McGraw Hill Book Company, New York.
5. Daugherty, R.L., Joseph B Franzini and John Finnermore. Fluid Mechanics with Engineering Applications. 1989: McGraw Hill Book Company.
6. Fay James, A. Introduction to Fluid Mechanics. 1996: Prentice Hall of India.
7. Garde, R. J. and A.G Mirajgoaker. Engineering Fluid Mechanics. 1977: Nem Chand & Bros, Roorkeee.
8. Goel, A. and N. Narayana Pillai. A flowmeter for irrigation field channels. *Water Management* 161(WM3): 135–139. 2008.
9. Hinze, J.O. *Turbulence*. 1959: McGraw Hill Book Company, New York.
10. Houghton, E.L and P.W Carpenter. *Aerodynamics for Engineering Students*, Fourth Edition. 2005: CBS Publishers and Distributors, New Delhi.
11. Jain, A.K. *Fluid Mechanics*. Khanna Publishers. 1998: New Delhi.
12. Douglas, Janus M. Gasiorek and John A. Swaffield. *Fluid Mechanics*, Fourth Edition. 2006: Pearson Education, published in India by Dorling Kinderley (India) Pvt. Ltd.
13. Joseph B. Franzini, and E. John Finnemore. *Fluid Mechanics with Engineering Applications*, Ninth Edition. 1997: The McGraw-Hill Companies, Inc.
14. Liggett, James A. *Fluid Mechanics*. 1994: McGraw Hill International Edition.
15. Milne-Thomson, L. M. *Theoretical Hydrodynamics*, Fifth Edition. 1996: Denver Publishers, Inc., New York.
16. Modi, P.N. and Seth, S.M. *Hydraulics and Fluid Mechanics*. 1991: Standard Book House, Delhi.
17. Nagarathnam, S. *Fluid Mechanics*. 1995: Khanna Publishers, Delhi.
18. Pillai, N. N. On uniform flow through smooth rectangular channels. J. *f Hyd. Research, Intl. Association for Hydraulic Research*. 4. 1970.
19. Pillai, N. N., Goel, Arun and Dubey, A. K. Hydraulic jump type stilling basins for low Froude numbers. *J. of Hyd. Engg*. ASCE 115(7). 1989.
20. Pillai, N. N., Gupta, S. S. and Subodh Ranjan. Simple iterative solutions for problems of flow through trapezoidal channels. *IE (I) Journal- CV* 30, Nov. 1989.
21. Pillai, N. N. and D.V.S. Verma. Moving hydraulic jump in rectangular channels. *J. of Inst. of Engineers*, Civil Engineering Divison, India,. 57, March 1977.

22. Pillai, N. N. Simple design procedure for lined irrigation canals. *J. of Inst. Of Engineers*, Civil Engineering Divison, India. 77, Nov. 1996.
23. Pillai, N. N. Effect of shape for uniform flow through smooth rectangular Open channels. *J. of Hyd. Engg.* ASCE, 23(7). 1997.
24. Pillai, N. N. and T. E. Unny. Shapes for appurtenances in stilling basins. *J. of Hyd.* Div. Proc. American Society of Civil Engineers, May 1964.
25. Pillai, N. N. Stilling basins using wedge shapes baffle blocks. *J. of Water and Water Engg.* Dec. London. 1969
26. Pillai, N. N. On stability and economy of stilling basins for barrages. *Intl. Symposium on New Technology in Model Testing in Hydraulic Research*. Pune. Sept. 1987.
27. Rangaraju, K.G. *Flow through Open Channels*. 1981: Tata McGraw-Hill Publishing Co. Ltd. New Delhi.
28. Rathakrishnan, E. *Gas Dynamics.* 1995: Prentice Hall Intl. Eastern Economy Edition, New Delhi.
29. Robert W. Fox and Alan T. McDonald. Introduction to *Fluid Mechanics*. Fifth Edition. Reprint, Students Edition. John Wiley & Sons Inc. 2008: New Delhi.
30. Rouse, H. (ed). *Engineering Hydraulics*. 1950: John Wiley & Sons.
31. Rouse, H. *Elementary Mechanics of Fluids*. 1946: John Wiley & Sons.
32. Rouse, H. *Advanced Mechanics of fluids*. 1959: John Wiley & Sons.
33. Schlichting, H. *Boundary Layer Theory. 1955*: McGraw-Hill Series in Mechanical Engineering.
34. Shames, Irwin H. *Mechanics of Fluid.* 1992: McGraw Hill International Edition, 1992.
35. Streeter, V. L. and Benjamin Wylie. *Fluid Mechanics*. 1981: McGraw Hill Book Company.
36. Streeter,V.L. *Handbook of Fluid Mechanics*. 1961: McGraw-Hill.
37. Subramanya, K. *Flow in Open Channels*. 1986: Tata McGraw-Hill, New Delhi.
38. Subramanya, K. *Theory and Application of Fluid Mechanics*. 1997: Tata McHill Publishing company Ltd., Delhi.
39. Tasos C Tapanastasiou, et. al. *Viscous fluid flow*. 2000: CRC Press, Boca Roton, London.
40. Vallentine, H.R. *Applied Hydrodynamics*. 1959: Butterworth and Co, Ltd.
41. Vasandani, V. P. *Hydraulic Machines – Theory and Design*. Tenth Edition. 1992: Khanna Publishers, New Delhi.
42. White, Frank M. *Fluid Mechanics*. 1986: McGraw Hill International Editions 1986.
43. Yahya, S.M. *Fundamentals of Compressive Flow*. Second Edition. 1997: New Age Intl. (P) Ltd. New Delhi.
44. Yuan, S.Y. *Foundations of Fluid Mechanics*. 1976: Prentice Hall of India Pvt. Ltd., Delhi.
45. Yunus A. Cengel and John M. Cimbala. *Fluid Mechanics*. 2006: Tata McGraw-Hill Company Ltd., New Delhi.

Index